THE BIRDWATCHER'S YEARBOOK 2015

Designed and published by
Hilary Cromack

Edited by
David Cromack

BUCKINGHAM PRESS LTD

In association with

SWAROVSKI
OPTIK

Published in 2014 by
Buckingham Press Ltd
55 Thorpe Park Road, Peterborough
Cambridgeshire PE3 6LJ
United Kingdom

01733 561 739
e-mail: admin@buckinghampress.com
www.buckinghampress.co.uk

© Buckingham Press Ltd 2014

ISBN 978-0-9569876-8-6
ISSN 0144-364 X

Cover image: Black Grouse by Michael Demain.
Michael Demain can be reached at 175 Richmond Road, Accrington, BB5 0JB; 01254 237 378; e-mail: mdemainwildart@aol.com; www.michaeldemainwildlifeart.co.uk

Black and white images: by Dan and Rosie Powell.
Dan and Rosie Powell can be contacted on 01329 668 465;
e-mail: dan.powell@care4free.net
www.powellwildlifeart.com

Printed and bound in Great Britain by
Ashford Colour Press Ltd,
Gosport, Hampshire.

CONTENTS

PREFACE   **5**

FEATURES   **7**
New Hope for the Future of British Birding   8
Key News from the World of Birds   12
Hen Harriers' Last Stand   18
Best Bird Books of the Year   21

BIRDWATCHER'S DIARY   **27**
Events guide for 2015 includes bird fairs, conferences and
other key UK events, plus some international conferences   28
Day-by-day diary, plus blank sheets for recording your birding outings   30
Year planner for 2016   54

LOG CHARTS   **55**
Guide to using the log charts   56
Full log charts for BOU-approved British List   58
Log charts for British butterflies   86
Log chart for British dragonflies   88

BIRD RESERVES AND OBSERVATORIES   **89**
With county maps in colour and an updated listing of sites

ENGLAND
Central England   90
Eastern England   112
Northern England   130
South East England   151
South West England   168

SCOTLAND
Border Counties   180
Central Scotland   182
Eastern Scotland   187
Highlands & Islands   190

WALES
Eastern Wales   195
Northern Wales   197
Southern Wales   200
Western Wales   202

ART, PHOTOGRAPHY AND LECTURERS   **205**
Art galleries   206
Artists, birds and wildlife   206
Photographers, birds and wildlife   209
Lecturers, a nationwide guide and BTO talks listing   210

CONTENTS

TRADE DIRECTORY 219
Bird garden suppliers 220
Bird and wildlife publications 220
Book publishers 221
Book sellers 221
Clothing suppliers 222
Equipment suppliers 222
Holiday companies 222
Optical dealers 225
Optical manufacturers and importers 226
Optical repairs and servicing 227
Technology products 228

COUNTY DIRECTORY 229
Under each county heading you will find:
Bird atlases/avifaunas; bird recorders; bird reports; BTO
regional representatives; clubs and societies; ringing groups;
RSPB local groups; wildlife hospitals and county Wildlife Trusts.

England 230
Isle of Man 270
Scotland 271
Wales 279
Channel Islands 284
Northern Ireland 285
Republic of Ireland 286

NATIONAL DIRECTORY 287
National organisations 288
National projects 301

INTERNATIONAL DIRECTORY 305
International organisations 306
Special interest organisations 312

QUICK REFERENCE SECTION 313
Tide tables 2015-16 314
Sunrise and sunset times 2015 320
Sea Areas 322
Schedule 1 species 323
Birdwatchers and twitchers take note!
— the dangers of ticks (the insect variety) when out birdwatching 323
National and regional birdlines 325
Other bird information services 325

INDEX TO RESERVES 326

PREFACE

FOR THOSE of us who pick up binoculars to go in search of wild birds these are troubling times. The pollution and habitat loss that stems from our ever-growing human population is having a devastating effect on birdlife around the globe.

Though we might have some sympathy for third world governments which prioritise their citizens' welfare concerns above those of wildlife, surely there can be no excuse for the UK's rulers to turn a blind eye to the impending extinction of a bird species in England. I must admit that raising the plight of Hen Harriers is a cause very close to my heart, so I was glad to commission Michael Demain, the wellknown wildlife artist to write about his experiences with a group trying to protect the raptor in Lancashire.

A campaign headed by Chris Packham and Mark Avery kicked off on Hen Harrier Day in August 2014 and all concerned birdwatchers should do their best to support this initiative (see page 18 for details).

While endorsing the RSPB's Skydancer project to provide more protection for Hen Harriers, I'd welcome the organisation going one step further and using membership funds to buy an English grouse moor and manage it to benefit all forms of birdlife. Waiting for commercial grouse estates to do 'the right thing' I fear will come too late to save the Hen Harrier as a breeding species in England.

After the 'doom and gloom' of the situation facing Hen Harriers, and sadly up to 10% of other native species headed towards extinction (according to the Conference For Nature in September 2014), it is very pleasing to tell our readers about a great new initiative within the birdwatching community – Next Generation Birders. Having met some of these under-25-year-old enthusiasts, I am greatly reassured that birdwatching in this country has a bright future. See page 8 for their story.

Elsewhere in this edition Richard Facey presents his annual survey of bird-related news stories that have caught his eye and Gordon Hamlett sifts through huge numbers of wildlife titles to select his Best Books of the Year.

With retirement now on the horizon, Hilary and I are looking for a 'safe pair of hands' to take on ownership of the *Birdwatcher's Yearbook*. Thanks to the continuing support of our regular buyers and the many people who supply information each year, it is clear that the birding community wants the *Yearbook* to continue for many years to come.

David Cromack (Editor)

A MESSAGE FROM THE SPONSORS
OF THIS BOOK

1981 WAS a momentus year in the UK because the Wildlife and Countryside Act came into force, making it an offence to kill, injure or take birds from the wild, to possess wild bird eggs or to disturb Schedule 1 species on or near the nest. Those found guilty faced fines of up to £5,000 or a six month prison sentence.

Also making its debut that year, though with a lot less fanfare, was the first ever edition of *The Birdwatcher's Yearbook*, the brainchild of John E Pemberton, librarian at The University College of Buckingham. In his Preface, John stated that the *Yearbook* had been launched to provide 'a comprehensive and convenient work of reference for all sections of the birdwatching community…' and 35 years on, the *Yearbook* continues to provide this invaluable service for a community that has grown phenomenally since its inception.

In the mid to late 1980s many younger people caught the twitching bug and helped to change the image of birdwatching in Britain. Since that time there has been a steady growth in interest and the many developments in our hobby have been charted in succeeding volumes of the *Yearbook*. It is certainly interesting to hear about Next Generation Birders, a new wave of young people using social media to foster a deeper interest in wild birds (see pages 8 to 11).

Today, a first-time visitor to the British Birdwatching Fair at Rutland Water each August, will be non-plussed by the staggering number of companies offering products and services to those interested in watching and photographing birds and other forms of wildlife. Exhibitors from all corners of the globe vie for attention alongside domestic companies, and the optics marquee is a three-day frenzy of activity as birders try all the latest binoculars, telescopes and cameras.

My colleagues and I have found that visitors to the Swarovski stand at Birdfair and other events are both discerning and highly informed when it comes to discussing binoculars and telescopes and the feedback they give us is extremely valuable when it comes to the development of new products.

To them and all the other readers of *The Birdwatcher's Yearbook*, I'd like to wish them another year full of wonderful sightings and continued enjoyment of the natural world.

Peter Antoniou
Country Manager, UK and Republic of Ireland
Swarovski Optik UK

SWAROVSKI
OPTIK

FEATURES

Keith Offord

The plight of Hen Harriers in England has now reached a critical point...... can a new campaign be the beginning of a recovery?

New Hope for the Future of British Birding   8

Key News from the World of Birds   12

Hen Harriers' Last Stand   18

Best Bird Books of the Year   21

NEW HOPE FOR THE FUTURE OF BRITISH BIRDING

If you are concerned that not enough youngsters are coming into birdwatching, then relax. Committee member Liam Curson (aged 18) tells the story of Next Generation Birders, an internet-savvy organisation dedicated to encouraging under-25s to deepen their interest in birds.

WE KNOW MOST bird clubs and RSPB member groups are struggling with the challenge of attracting young people to their meetings. With grey hair and spectacles the norm at any UK gathering of people with an interest in wild birds, is it any surprise that under-25s find the prospect of joining such a group so unappealing?

Yet young birders do exist. Aged four years old, I can remember seeing an Eleonora's Falcon in Ibiza, but the thing that really got me hooked on birds was a picture of a Scarlet Ibis in a book about a year earlier. Throughout my childhood, birding was quite a lonely pastime, even though I'm sure it was better for me than many, as I had the support of a veritable birding encyclopaedia of a father, plus all his friends and two brothers, who had grown up birding together around south-east London.

Viewed from my youthful perspective, the gathering of birders that had formed the Croydon Young Ornithologists Club branch of the 1970s surely could never exist again... could it? How wrong I was! At 6.35pm on November 20, 2005 a user of a still quite young website called Birdforum, started a thread called 'Young Birder'. The writer , who was aged 13, was interested in gathering tips from 'someone their age' to keep his birding passion alive and held the ambition of one day having a world bird list larger than Phoebe Snetsinger *[Ed: This American heiress had set a world record of seeing 8,398 bird species by the time of her death, aged 68 in 1999].*

The Birdforum poster's username was "The Barn Owl", but the true identity is still something of a mystery (rumour suggests it was a boy called Sam Coppard from the Midlands, and that he's no longer a birder), but one thing is for certain, this individual made one of the biggest contributions of all to modern young birder folklore.

Over the coming years, this Birdforum

The RSPB strives to inspire youngsters of all ages to take a greater interest in nature and the environment and its Wildlife Explorers marquee at Birdfair is always busy with games and other activities.

NEW HOPE FOR THE FUTURE OF BRITISH BIRDING

Clearly impressed by the potential of Next Generation Birders, the RSPB provided display stands for the group at the 2014 British Birdfair. One pleasing result was that membership increased from 376 to 392 by the end of the event. From left to right: Liam Curson (Youth Engagement Officer), Jonathan Scragg, Matthew Bruce (Chairperson) and Espen Quinto-Ashman.

thread was to prove a focal point for many of the young people who would later form Next Generation Birders. By the time I joined Birdforum in 2010, it was one of the most popular threads on the whole site, with daily posts from members all over Britain and the world. At this point, we were all starting to add one another's names on another strange new social media platform called Facebook: I first joined purely for easy communication with like-minded birders, who I'd found so hard to come by locally.

Eventually two friends, Jonathan Scragg and Andrew Kinghorn, took it upon themselves to create a group where young birders could communicate. By making our group private, we avoided the unimaginable embarassment of having our passion outed on public Facebook profiles, and thus were free to discuss birds to our hearts' content! We started out with something like 15 members in November 2011. At the time, I'd never met any of them in person.

Slowly and surely more people joined; whenever someone met a new YB (young birder) in the field, or found them in another Facebook group, we'd covertly whisper the name of this secret haven. Normally, when we asked "Do you want in?", they'd respond joyously and resoundingly, and a new NGB would be born.

We didn't actually adopt the name 'Next Generation Birders' until 2012, when it occurred to us that quite a few of our ranks were already into their 20s, and it would perhaps be inaccurate to describe them as 'young' any longer! We plodded along in our everyday lives, going to school, frantically revising and then bitterly regretting not frantically revising enough once exam results came in: the normal teenage story.

Secretly we all longed to clock off from school for two things; birding, and logging onto Facebook to talk about birding! It may seem bizarre, or even lacking in dedication to some older birders, but I think we all need that social factor to keep us interested. At times it was so addictive that we'd be online past midnight, then up at the crack of dawn for the real birding!

NGB reached 100 members in 2013: quite an achievement considering three years before, I couldn't have named a single other young birder! With such a rapidly expanding user base, we began thinking about some rather big questions, such as how could we, a ragtag bunch of

NEW HOPE FOR THE FUTURE OF BRITISH BIRDING

teenagers and twenty-somethings, be a positive force in the British birding scene? How could we encourage enough new birders to take up the hobby to give birding, and conservation as a whole, a hope of surviving in the 21st Century?

More particularly, could we create in Britain a replacement for the YOC that had died out so many years beforehand? We weren't thinking of usurping Phoenix, a great RSPB-run organisation for teenage general wildlife enthusiasts, but creating a place where tomorrow's authors, artists, guides, patchers, twitchers and folk dedicated enough to birding to discuss primary-projections and crossbill sonograms, could cut their teeth. Hence we went public, altering our identification from a private little community to an official organisation.

Our philosophy is simple, but I think it's effective. We're for young birders, so we're run by young birders. Eight are elected each September by our members, and form the committee that takes on the responsibilities of our organisation. So far, my fellow members have done a majestic job, securing NGB discounts on birding equipment, organising trips, staffing an NGB stall at Birdfair and a myriad of other great things, all of which are designed to:

a: increase awarenesss among young birders and
b: give them a helping hand in developing this wonderful passion.

Most of what we do is on a shoestring budget, with members funding their own travel and costs of accommodation whenever we stage a 'meet-up'. But we're also completely free to be a part of, and the collective knowledge, experience and friendship of 300+ birders in exchange for absolutely nothing is a pretty good deal!

This makes me sound a bit like a promoter, but I can't really resist giving my glowing opinion on all things NGB whenever I can. And really, all I'm trying to do is persuade readers to encourage any under-25 birder they know to make contact! The 'not-as-covert-as-I'd-like' advert is now over, so I'll resume telling you about our philosophy, which I still hadn't finished explaining.

Basically, we want to encourage young enthusiasts to develop the birdwatching hobby, and become great birders. We think that if there isn't help for young birders to develop their passion, the lifeblood of our hobby might start running dangerously thin. And we try to help the best we can, offering advice

NGB member Jonnie Fisk (left) is an 18-year-old Yorkshire-based birder, invertebrate enthusiast and talented artist who produced this distinctive poster for NGB featuring the key birds seen in 2013.

NEW HOPE FOR THE FUTURE OF BRITISH BIRDING

and experience, the contacts we've accumulated over a collective period of several centuries of birdwatching, and the opportunity for trips and meet-ups across the UK.

I imagine that plenty of alumni from YOC groups will be reading this and may be wondering how NGB compares to their organisation. How does an online group replace those monthly meet-ups at local bird sites for instance? Well, it can't. Health and Safety regulations and tighter policing of would-be leaders make it a lot more difficult to lead organised walks for young people these days, even if we could find a large enough concentration of members in one area to create a viable group for an age-range where lifts with a parent, trains and buses are your only hope of making it to the meeting point.

So, the YOC glory days can probably never be truly reached again, but I for one am hopeful that NGB will offer something different. Different, but no less valuable. And perhaps a bit more informal, because we're independent of any established organisations.

For a group less than a year old, I'm delighted that we've already organised two official meet-ups in the spring of 2014, with several more in the pipeline. We've also recruited a lot of new members, organised stands at Birdfair and provided the medium for a lot of young birders to find others in their local area.

In seven and a bit years time, when I eventually hit the age limit of 25 (and move onto becoming a 'Nearly Geriatric Birder' (I personally want to create a group with this name for NGB alumnis to keep in contact), I hope I can look back on helping create a wonderful contribution to the future of birding.

Thanks for reading: I can't tell you how much of an honour it's been to write for *The Birdwatchers Yearbook*!

Liam Curson (member of the NGB Committee, 2013-14).

The Next Generation Birders' Mission Statement

"...... in an attempt to address the age imbalance in British birding, Next Generation Birders is an active and growing group of 13-25-year-olds who have taken it upon themselves to encourage other young people to join in their obsession and passion.

"NGB plans to create a network of young people to increase the interest in serious birding among the younger generation of wildlife enthusiasts. It will encourage various bird-related activities from patching, twitching, and involvement in local and national birding, to recording, surveying, identification discussion and anything else that will stimulate interest in birding among young people, with a massive focus on networking and making friends. NGB believes that there is great potential within the younger generations that no other organisation or group is yet tapping into and thus have decided to tap into it ourselves!"

Matt Bruce (NGB chairman)

To contact Next Generation Birders: E-mail: ngbirders@gmail.com or visit: http://nextgenerationbirders.blogspot. co.uk/

KEY NEWS FROM THE WORLD OF BIRDS

Richard Facey presents a selection of interesting stories about wild birds from Britain and further afield.

Happy homecoming for ultra-rare wader

SPOON-BILLED SANDPIPER is among the most endangered bird species in the world with fewer than 100 pairs left and continuing to decline by nearly a quarter, year on year. Rearing birds on the breeding grounds, to increase the annual number of fledglings by 25%, is just part of a multi-faceted conservation programme involving Wildfowl & Wetlands Trust, Birds Russia, Moscow Zoo and the RSPB, working alongside staff from the BTO, BirdLife International, ArcCona and the Spoon-billed Sandpiper Task Force.

Even a single chick raised successfully could make a difference to the long-term survival prospects of Spoonbilled Sandpipers.

For the last two summers, WWT aviculturalist Ronald Digby has reared 24 Spoon-billed Sandpipers on the species' breeding grounds. Faced with a 5,000 mile migration to south Asia there was no guarantee that any would survive, so it must have been a moment filled with relief when he received the news that one of his charges, 'Green 8' from 2012 had been re-sighted in Russia. Not only that but the bird was in good condition and ready to breed; it appears she made two attempts to breed and on July 17 she was observed with one healthy chick… the first success for hand-reared parents.

Originally hatched towards the end of June, she:- was released on August 10, 2012. After staying on the breeding grounds for seven days she then migrated; facing threats such as starvation, habitat loss and illegal hunting on the way. Her next sighting was not until early April 2014 at Kinmen Island, Taiwan, before being seen on the breeding grounds.

Breeding success for uk rarities

BETTER-THAN AVERAGE summer weather coincided with some rare UK breeders making the headlines in 2014. Two of the Great Crane Project's star pupils, Monty and Chris, hatched two chicks at the WWT's Slimbridge reserve, the first to hatch in western Britain in 400 years. Sadly, neither chick survived to fledge.

KEY NEWS FROM THE WORLD OF BIRDS

A second pair of Cranes made overtures but decided not to breed this year. A few months later, the final release of Cranes chicks on to the Somerset Levels took place as part of the Great Crane Project.

At least three pairs of Black-winged Stilts made attempts to breed in Britain in 2014.

While the Cranes failed to fledge chicks, two pairs of another long-legged species managed just that. RSPB Medmerry (West Sussex) and RSPB Cliffe Pools (Kent) each played host to pairs of Black-winged Stilts in 2014. Sadly only the Medmerry pair beat the odds, managing to fledge their brood, though news of a family at Cavenham Pits, Suffolk, indicated that a third pair had successfully bred. This species was last confirmed breeding in the UK at a site in Norfolk in 1987.

The Isle of Wight boasted a pair of successful Bee eaters; a species which last bred in the UK in 2002. After setting up home on the National Trust's Wydacome estate, the pair was under 24 hour guard and went on to fledge four young, making them only the third of their species succeed in the UK.

Meanwhile, at RSPB Frampton Marsh in Lincolnshire a pair of Glossy Ibis displayed to each other and even went as far as building a nest but failed to breed. This is believed to be the first nesting attempt by the species in modern history – could Glossy Ibis be the next species to colonise the UK?

Osprey and Bewick's Swan landmarks

TWO BIRD STUDY projects reached milestones in 2014. Loch Garten celebrated the 60th anniversary of the return of the Osprey to Scotland. Having been driven to extinction the species returned to Scotland in 1954. The site also celebrated another milestone in 2014 when the current pair in residence, Odin and EJ, produced the Loch's 100th chick!

Further south the Wildfowl & Wetlands Trust celebrated the 50th anniversary of the initiation of its Bewick's Swan study; a project started by the late Sir Peter Scott in 1964 while painting Bewick's Swans outside his window in Slimbridge.

Bewick's Swans breed in the Arctic before migrating to NW Europe, and Central and

East Asia to take advantage of milder climates in winter. After reaching a peak population of nearly 30,000, the species has declined markedly from the mid-1990s and is now listed 'of conservation concern'. While painting Bewick's Swans, Scott noticed that each had a unique bill pattern. His daughter Dafila, who trained as a zoologist before making her name as an accomplished wildlife artist, helped identify more individual swans before turning it into a full blown scientific study.

Fifty years on more than 9,000 individuals have been recorded based on their bill pattern – a matchless performance for a study that does not rely on ringing to identify individuals.

Technology reveals a remarkable trans-atlantic migration

THE SECRET journeys of more and more species are now being revealed by technology. For instance, in 2014 one of the UK's Red-necked Phalaropes, of which only 15-50 males nest annually, returned to its nesting grounds on Fetlar, Shetland Isles, having clocked up an amazing 22,000 mile migration round trip.

The RSPB, in conjunction with the Swiss Ornithological Society and Shetland Ringing, fitted geolocators to 10 phalaropes nesting on Fetlar, Shetland, in 2012.

It was previously believed that Scottish birds joined Scandinavian phalaropes in their wintering grounds, believed to be in or near the Arabian Sea. The tag

Phalarope species in North America are known to make long distance migration flights, but who would have expected a Red-necked Phalarope from Scotland to end up off the coast of Peru?

however, revealed a different story. After leaving Fetlar, the bird flew across the Atlantic, before heading south following the USA's eastern seaboard, then crossed the Caribbean, Mexico before finally taking up winter residence along South America's Pacific coast.

This made the bird's journey 60% longer than had been assumed and is the first example of a Eurprean breeding bird overwintering in the Pacific. Tracking of Red-necked Phalaropes will continue to confirm that this is where all the Scottish population over winters. If it does, scientists hope to study how and if the species is affected by 'El Niño' events which affect plankton populations in the Pacific.

KEY NEWS FROM THE WORLD OF BIRDS

Climate change provides a breeding boost

CLIMATE CHANGE is usually associated with detrimental effects on the environment but a study published by a team of scientists from Sheffield University and the BTO has shown that the Long-tailed Tit could be a species that will benefit as a result of higher temperatures.

Using a 19-year data set, the team was able to extrapolate from historical survival rates to predict how these might change in the future. The recent trend toward warmer springs in Britain has led to an increase in survival rate, which is likely to have contributed to the increase in Long-tailed Tit populations.

Wetter autumn conditions seemed to reduce survival, and this season was more important than winter at determining if these diminutive birds survived until the next year. Current thinking is that our autumns will become wetter but analysis showed that losses in autumn are likely to be offset by the benefits of warmer springs. By

Small birds such as Long-tailed Tits are susceptible to extreme weather conditions, but have benefited from recent mild springs.

modelling future conditions the team found that the Long-tailed Tit came out a winner, with increased survival rates, for every possible climate change scenario modelled.

Parakeets put native birds off their food

THE INTRODUCTION of non-native species of flora and fauna has been happening in Britain for centuries and remains a very contentious issue. The Rose-ringed Parakeet is one of 2,721 alien species audited in 2005 and it has become an established part of our avifauna, especially in the south east of England, particularly around London.

The potential impact from this species on our native wildlife has long been debated; especially its potential to affect native cavity-nesting species, for which it is a strong competitor. So far there appear to have been negligible impact but new research, published in 2014 by scientists from Imperial College London and the Institute of Zoology, shows that the Rose-Ringed Parakeets might be having subtle but significant impacts on the foraging behaviour of native species in urban areas.

15

As a larger, gregarious species, it can dominated bird feeders. At more than 40 sites within a 50-km radius of the centre of London, the team examined the potential of the parakeet to impact on the foraging behavior of species, such as Blue and Great Tits. To do this they compared the behavior of native species in the presence of parakeets and another feeder-dominating species – the Great Spotted Woodpecker.

Overall the presence of a parakeet did have a disruptive effect on the tit's foraging behaviour, which showed significantly reduced feeding rates. Furthermore native species using the feeding stations greatly increased their degree of vigilance in the presence of the parakeet compared to Great Spotted Woodpecker.

Native species did show a degree of habituation to the parakeets: the researchers measured feeding in the presence of a parakeet was more likely at sites within the latter's current range than outside it. However, feeding rates were still lower than when compared to the control treatments.

Noisy and aggressive, Rose-ringed Parakeets have been shown to intimidate smaller birds at British bird feeders.

Black grouse bouncing back

GOOD NEWS from Wales: numbers of Black Grouse in the north of the country are almost back to those recorded in 2011. As with the rest of the UK the Black Grouse, or Grugiar Dduas as they are known in Welsh, has undergone a serious decline in both range and population; by 2000 the species has disappeared from mid and south Wales.
The species has now begun to recover thanks to suite of management techniques from a consortium of organisations including RSPB Cyrmu, Denbighshire County Council, Wynnstay Estate, and local farmers and foresters, as well as Natural Resources Wales.
In 2011 a record breaking 328 lekking males were counted but there were lower counts in the next two years 297 in 2012 and just 249 in 2013. The number of lekking males took a major upswing in 2014 however, when 320 were counted, including a buoyant population centred on the RSPB's Lake Vyrnwy reserve. Habitat management, predator control and a more favourable summer in 2013 are believed to be behind the increase.

KEY NEWS FROM THE WORLD OF BIRDS

Bright prospects for Garganey

DURING the winter the UK plays host to internationally important numbers of waders and waterfowl and the BTO's army of Wetland Bird Survey (WeBs) volunteers are there to count them.

The wildfowl reports for winter 2012/13 makes for a mixed bag of results, with Shelduck numbers at their lowest for nearly 40 years and Mallard at their lowest ever. Pintail numbers also remain low, having halved since 2006. However, watchers along the Ouse Washes in Cambridgeshire would have been happy with their August count of 127 Garganey; the highest WeBS count ever for this species.

The situation regarding waders is equally mixed: Redshank, following a 25 year trend of minus 16%, has reached its lowest point for 30 years, while Curlew populations are at their lowest for 25 years. Both Black-tailed and Bar-tailed Godwits have continued to increase, with the former showing a 388% increase over the last 25 years. This is eclipsed by the Avocet whose rise seems to continue unabated with a 25 year trend showing an increase of more than a 1,000%. The highest count came from Alde Complex (Suffolk) where a staggering 2,039 Avocets were counted in March 2013.

A short summary such as this cannot do justice to the Wetland Bird Survey report, the full version of which can be read at: *http://www.bto.org/volunteer-surveys/webs/publications/webs-annual-report/waterbirds-in-the-uk/wituk-2012-13*

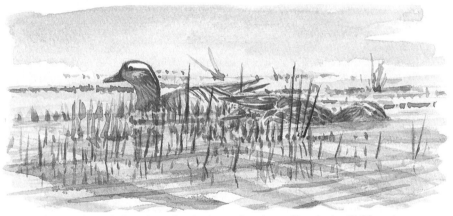

Garganey is one duck species to show increases when observed by volunteer WeBS counters.

HEN HARRIERS' LAST STAND

Wildlife artist Michael Demain, a member of the Bowland Raptor Study Group, reports on major new initiatives to save an iconic uplands species from continuing persecution.

FOLLOWING A YEAR when Hen Harriers failed to breed in England, conservationists launched a major media campaign to confront continuing illegal persecution of this beautiful bird of prey on the country's grouse moors. August 10, 2014 was chosen as the first 'Hen Harrier Day' because of its proximity to 'the Glorious 12th', the official start date of the grouse shooting season. It aims to raise awareness about the abuses being inflicted on this particular raptor species throughout the UK.

In a high profile media launch for an on-line petition to ban driven grouse shoots, naturalist Chris Packham and conservation activist Mark Avery addressed around 570 protesters gathered in pouring rain at Derwent Water in the Peak District National Park. Similar protests were staged in Northumberland, Lancashire and Dorset.

Chris Packham told the crowd that the shooting industry had let down the entire nation by failing to sort out the 'bad apples' who continued to persecute birds of prey. "The time for compromise has ended…. we must accept that we've failed and now we need new ways, such as a ban on driven grouse shoots, to protect vulnerable species."

Reinforcing the message, Mark Avery reported that in 2014 just three pairs of harriers were nesting in England, when government agencies state that there is sufficient suitable habitat to accommodate up to 300 pairs.

When launching the e-petition, Mark Avery claimed: "I'm not really very keen on banning things, so it has taken a lot of thought to launch this petition. However, after 60 years of complete legal protection the Hen Harrier is rarer than it was (in England at least) when it got that protection!

"And after at least a couple of decades of talking about solutions with the moorland community, in which I played a part for a while, the Hen Harrier is almost extinct in England. There are times when one can reach an understanding with 'the other side' but this doesn't appear to be one of them. "The systematic, illegal, wholesale removal of a protected bird from our countryside is a disgrace.

"Of course, I would be rather surprised if this e-petition led to the banning of driven grouse shooting but I hope it will highlight the issues around this land use (which are far wider than a protected bird of prey) and make it easier for some sort of sensible solution to emerge."

Referring to the issue on his blog, Avery wrote: "In the UK as a whole, the science shows that there could be around 2,500 pairs of Hen Harrier, and yet there is a third of that number. "This species isn't just rarer than it should be across the country: there are also some striking gaps in its range. Seemingly ideal areas have practically no Hen Harriers nesting in them — southern and eastern Scotland and the north of England are the main examples. What do these areas have in common? Their upland land use is dominated by intensive grouse moor management.

HEN HARRIERS' LAST STAND

"A fully protected and wonderful bird is being criminally killed because it is in conflict with a 'countryside sport' or 'countryside industry', depending on how you regard grouse shooting.

"This year we are all waking up to the fact that we can do something about it. The summer of 2014 is seeing an unprecedented backlash against grouse shooting. We have been quiet for too long, and now birders, anti-shooting groups, those worried about damage to blanket bogs, ramblers and a host of other people are pointing at intensive grouse moor management and saying that it must clean up its act or its days are numbered.

"There are several new initiatives under way that have been designed to help Hen Harriers by supporting the growing movement for change:

- **Support future Hen Harrier Days**
- **Sign the e-petition** to ban driven grouse shooting: epetitions.direct.gov.uk/petitions/65627.
- **Support the campaign** to boycott the grouse industry and hotels, restaurants and businesses associated with it — see www.bit.ly/bw266EthicalConsumer for more details," Mark concluded.

Volunteers committed to the cause

Wellknown wildlife artist Michael Demain is an active member of the Bowland Raptor Study Group and has seen the damage inflicted on Hen Harriers for himself.

"Bowland used to be the English stronghold for Hen Harriers and the upland bird of prey is even the symbol of the Forest of Bowland Area of Outstanding Natural Beauty. However, the 2014 nests represent the first breeding attempts in the area for two years. In just five years I've seen the Hen Harrier population go from 14 pairs down to none for the last two years," he said.

"In a good year we may have between ten and 20 pairs of harriers in England, with most of these in the forest of Bowland and in particular the United Utilities Bowland Estate. Here the species finds a safe haven watched over by The RSPB and Natural England as part of Skydancer, a four-year project aimed at protecting and conserving nesting Hen Harriers in the English uplands.

"Since 2007 I have been actively involved with a team of dedicated

Male Hen Harrier in Flight **(acrylic on watercolour board) by Michael Demain.**

volunteers helping the RSPB to find and monitor nests. When the birds arrive back early in the season we quickly identify the sites which are going to be used and as soon as the eggs are laid the nests are checked and contents noted. Nests are then monitored from a safe distance throughout the breeding cycle.

"The chicks are later ringed and some are wing tagged or fitted with satellite transmitters. Wing tagging helps us to identify individuals and a great deal can be learned from this. We also monitor Peregrine, Merlin and Short-eared Owl, which takes up a great deal of my time from March until the end of July, and to say that my work suffers as a result would be an understatement.

Michael explains: "The bird's plight stems from the fact that Hen Harriers sometimes eat Red Grouse, which brings them into conflict with the driven grouse shooting industry. This particular type of shooting requires large numbers of grouse, so some game managers feel they must illegally kill or disturb harriers to protect their stock.

"Some gamekeepers feel obliged to systematically take out Hen Harriers, Peregrines, Short-eared Owls, and sometimes Merlins, in an attempt to eradicate all 'vermin', so that there is an unnaturally high number of grouse for the guns to shoot when they arrive in August."

A legal method that could reduce the number of grouse chicks lost to Hen Harriers is a management technique known as diversionary feeding. This involves providing Hen Harriers with an alternative food source during the period when the adults are feeding their chicks. The RSPB and the local shooting tenant are currently using the method in Bowland, under licence from Natural England.

Jude Lane, the RSPB's Bowland Project Officer, continues: "Diversionary feeding is a simple, inexpensive and effective technique. Previous trials have shown it can reduce the number of grouse eaten by Hen Harriers by up to 86 per cent." For more information about the project, visit: www.rspb.org.uk/skydancer.

Disappearing from the skies

Michael Demain continues: "For the birdwatcher the Hen Harrier is a spectacular bird. Its aerial display, affectionately known as sky dancing, is a sight to behold and birdwatchers make the pilgrimage to Bowland year after year to witness it. "Every spring I'll see familiar faces, scopes at the ready, scanning the skies in the hope of catching a glimpse. These same people are now asking "Where have all the birds of prey gone from Bowland?"

He continued: "Sadly, this is not the only part of the UK uplands where abuse is happening. It is now a land where the balance of nature has been disrupted to such an extent that there are no longer any predators to take out the weak and infirm. Louping ill, a virus which attacks the nervous system of grouse and *Trichostrongylus tenuis,* a nematode worm that can occur in the gut lining of an adult Red Grouse and cause strongylosis, are big problems for the grouse shooting industry. The latter is made worse when you have unnaturally high numbers of grouse.

"Surely for future generations we need to make a stand now against the selfish few who would see the Hen Harrier persecuted to extinction in the name of sport," pleads Michael.

BEST BIRD BOOKS OF THE YEAR

A new wave of fieldguides head up an interesting year for those interested in wildlife books. Wellknown reviewer Gordon Hamlett picks out those titles most deserving of your attention.

ANOTHER YEAR brings another bumper crop of bird books for your delectation. In the news, Bloomsbury continues its quest for world domination, adding the New Holland back catalogue to its Helm and Poyser ranges. Equally interesting is the fact that Princeton University Press, is now including some titles which are specifically British in their content, most unusual for an American publisher.

When is a fieldguide not a fieldguide? The answer to this Alice-in-Wonderland-like conundrum is when it is only part of a fieldguide. *Birds ID Insights* (Couzens and Nurney, Bloomsbury, ISBN 978-1-4729-0983-1, hb 272pp, £16.99) and *The Helm Guide to Bird Identification* (Vinicombe et al, Helm, ISBN 978-1-4081-3035-3, pb 398pp, £24,99) assume that you know what the common birds look like, and concentrate instead on separating trickier species.

The former book is taken from the popular series in *Bird Watching* magazine and is aimed at beginners and improvers, though there are some strange inclusions such as Thekla and Crested Larks. The book concentrates on plumage only, ignoring useful behavioral tips such as Shags flying much lower than Cormorants and leaping out of the water when they dive.

These details are included in the Helm Guide, which is far more advanced and comprehensive in its scope. This book is an updated version of the much-loved MacMillan guide from 25 years ago and includes recent splits such as Eastern and Western Subalpine Warblers. While strongly recommended, there is still scope for improvement: several species are detailed without being illustrated and this really does not work in a fieldguide. Still, the next edition should be an absolute cracker and there remains the tantalising prospect of an updated guide to the companion volume to Middle Eastern species.

If you are interested in a book mentioned in this article, then I would normally say go ahead and buy it, but this is not the case with the *Crossley ID Guide: Britain and Ireland* (Crossley and Couzens, Princeton, ISBN 978-0-691-15194-6, pb, 302pp, £16.95). This is a photo ID guide, with many images of each species 'photoshopped' onto the one plate. Plates for larger birds work best, but you will either love or hate this format

21

and really need to see it in the flesh before you splash the cash.

Two American fieldguides are the pick of this year's 'foreign' crop. *The North American Bird Guide* (Sibley, Helm, ISBN 978-1-4729-0927-5, pb, 600pp, £24.99) has long been my favourite guide to the region, and the second edition boasts major revisions to some 20% of the species, as well as redesigned layouts etc.

Rare Birds of North America (Howell et al, Princeton, ISBN 978-0-691-11796-6, hb 428pp, £24.99) covers 262 vagrant species that have reached America's shores. Though the species accounts are first class, it is the exquisite plates, drawn by Ian Lewington that will draw most plaudits. Both these books are too big for the pocket, but should never be far from your car or hotel room if you are visiting the States. They complement each other perfectly.

It would be fair to say that Gerard Gorman is obsessed by woodpeckers. His latest tome, *Woodpeckers of the World – The Complete Guide* (Helm, ISBN 978-1-4081-4715-3, hb 528pp, £34.99) is a photographic guide to all 239 species. As well as 750 stunning pictures, you get distribution maps, and descriptions of plumage and vocalisations. The definitive guide for the foreseeable future.

ATLAS ABUNDANCE

If you want just one book on the current state of Britain's birds, then you must read the magisterial *Bird Atlas 2007-11: The Breeding and Wintering Birds of Britain and Ireland* (Balmer et al, BTO, ISBN 978-1-90858128-0, hb 720pp, £69.99), which charts the distribution, abundance and population change of nearly 300 species.

The wealth of data collated for the Atlas means that there is plenty for county avifaunas to get their teeth into, if you want the extra detail for your particular patch. Liverpool University Press has published three mighty volumes – *The Birds of Derbyshire* (Frost and Shaw, ISBN, 978-1-84631-956-3, £44.99), *The Birds of Gloucestershire* (Kirk and Phillips, ISBN 978-1-84631-808-5, £44.99) and *The Breeding Birds of North Wales* (Brenchley et al, ISBN 978-1-84631-858-0, £44.99).

BEST BIRD BOOKS OF THE YEAR

Slightly different, i.e. no distribution maps, is the *Birds of London*, (Helm, Self, ISBN 978-1-4081-9404-1, £49.99), which examines the status of every species found within a 20-mile radius of St Paul's Cathedral. If you thought that major metropolitan areas were environmental deserts, then prepare to have your eyes opened.

ART BOOKS TO SAVOUR

Pick of this year's art books is *Ghosts of Gone Birds* (Aldhous, Bloomsbury, ISBN 978-1-4081-8746-3, pb 256pp, £24.99). The story of the eponymous exhibition, 120 artists each depicts their vision of an extinct bird. The styles are many and varied and there are plenty of 'behind-the-scenes' illustrations too. The only downside is the lack of page numbers and an index, forcing you to flick through the whole book every time you want to find one particular piece. On reflection though, that's not necessarily a bad thing.

Norfolk Wildlife (Riley, Brambleby Books, ISBN 978-1-908241-04-7, pb 300pp, £19.99) is a combination of site guide and calendar. Profusely illustrated, it doesn't include maps to sites (directions only) but does contain plenty of information about plants, mammals, flowers, butterflies and dragonflies as well as birds.

Langford Press continue to produce art books of the highest quality, and it speaks volumes for the popularity of Solway artist John Threlfall that his work has been selected for a second volume in the Wildlife Art Series. *Drawn To The Edge* (ISBN 978-1-904078-38-8, hb 190pp, £38) features sketches, works in pastel, watercolour, acrylic and oil of the birds and landscapes of Britain's coastal areas – from Norfolk to the Outer Hebrides.

TOP TITLES FOR FANS OF RAPTORS AND OWLS

For raptor lovers, all your birthdays and Christmases have come at once. I loved *A Sparrowhawk's Lament* (Cobham, Princeton, ISBN 978-0-691-15764-1, hb 256pp, £24.99) which details how Britain's 15 species of raptor are faring, through a fine mix of history, current facts and figures, and personal observations.

Urban Peregrines (Drewitt, Pelagic Publishing, ISBN 978-1-907807-81-7, hb 208pp, £24.99) is another title that is pitched at just the right level. Charting the move

BEST BIRD BOOKS OF THE YEAR

of Peregrines into city environments, it tells you everything you need to know about this magnificent hunter.

It is never a bad day if you see an eagle, and *A Saga of Sea Eagles*, (Love, Whittles Publishing, ISBN 978-1-84995-080-0, pb 248pp, £19.99) and *The Eagle's Way* (Crumley, Saraband, ISBN 978-190864347-6, pb 214pp, £12.99) brought back many happy memories of birding in Scotland.

Even the cover suggests that many people thought that author, film-maker and raconteur Mike Tomkies was dead! His latest adventures, and details of his observations of Peregrines, Barn Owls, wild cats and eagles, as detailed in *Running Wild* (Whittles Publishing, ISBN 978-1-84995-123-4, pb 172pp, £18.99) suggest that the obituaries might be somewhat premature.

Owls (Toms, ISBN 978-0-00-742557-0, pb 420pp, £35) is the latest title from the Collins New Naturalist stable. As well as species accounts, their biology, behavior and relation with man are also considered and this is a first class one-stop source of information.

SCIENCE TITLES TO MAKE YOU THINK

When it comes to academic studies, the heavyweight crown goes to *Birds and Climate Change* (Pearce-Green, Cambridge UP, ISBN 978-0-521-13219-0, pb 468pp, £39.99), which takes a global view of the impact of climate change and examines likely responses.

Much more accessible is *Bird Populations* (Newton, Collins New Naturalist, ISBN 978-0-00-752798-4, pb 596pp, £35). Newton's books are always highly readable and you are guaranteed to come away saying 'I never knew that'.

Mixing science with history, *Ten Thousand Birds* (Birkhead et al, Princeton, ISBN 978-0-691-15197-7, hb 524pp. £29.95) looks at all the major and ground-breaking scientific studies since 1860, discussing how they have advanced our ornithological knowledge. There are also pen pictures of many of the scientists involved. I would read a shopping list written by Tim

BEST BIRD BOOKS OF THE YEAR

Birkhead, and with an awful lot of book for your money, this is one of my favourite titles of the year.

GUIDES FOR THE OUTDOORS

Fieldcraft seems to be a dying art, so here are three books that try to reverse that trend. *The Nature Tracker's Handbook* (Baker, Bloomsbury, ISBN 978-1-4081-5150-1, pb 288pp, £14.99) and *Tracks and Signs of the Animals and Birds of Britain and Europe* (Olsen, Princeton, ISBN 978-0-691-15753-5, pb 274pp, £17.95) cover more or less the same ground (no pun intended) of footprints, droppings, gnawed nuts etc. The former is more suited to a younger audience and would make an ideal present for a young relative just getting interested in wildlife.

Slightly more left-field, *The Walker's guide to Outdoor Clues and Signs* (Gooley, Sceptre, ISBN 978-1-444-78008-6, hb 438pp, £20) shows you what you can tell about your local landscape by studying everything from birds and animals to clouds, trees, plants, the sun and moon etc. It is interesting to look at folklore ditties and see how they have changed over the years. 'Seagull, seagull sit on the sand, it's never good weather when you're on the land' was certainly true when I was growing up, less so now as gulls have discovered the benefits of landfill sites.

THE HISTORICAL APPROACH

Based on a ground-breaking radio format, *A History of Birdwatching in 100 Objects* (Callahan, Bloomsbury, ISBN 978-1-4081-86183-3, hb 222pp, £19.99) attempts to plot the history of our hobby through 100 landmark items. Some are spot on, others rather too vague.

Yes, the invention of the personal computer was relevant to birding, just as it was to more or less everything else in society today. Surely the field could have been narrowed down a bit, to the first mainstream birding program or website etc?. You might as well celebrate caveman Ugg for inventing the wheel. But that's the great thing about lists. My views are going to be completely different from yours, and this book is going to provide hours of arguments over a pint or two.

Feasting, Fowling and Feathers (Shrubb, Poyser, ISBN 978-1-4081-5990-3, hb 264pp, £49.99) looks at the many ways mankind has exploited birds over the centuries, whether for

food or fashion. Something of a departure from the usual Poyser monograph, I found this historical account utterly enthralling.

If you don't know your *auratus* from your *atricilla*, then *Latin for Bird Lovers* (Lederer and Burr, Timber Press, ISBN 978-1-60469-546-5, hb 224pp, £14.99) explains the origins of some 3,000 scientific names. The book is lovingly illustrated with dozens of old paintings by the likes of Audubon and there are full page articles on some of the more interesting species.

I have a great passion for historical bird books but alas, my pocket does not run deep enough to afford antiquarian prices. So I was pleased to discover a series of facsimile reprints from Cambridge University Press. The titles that have come my way include *Studies in Bird Migration* (two volumes) by the wonderfully named William Eagle Clarke (ISBN 978-1-108-06697-6 and -06698-3, 324 and 346pp, £24.99/volume) originally published in 1912. Volume one deals with seasonal bird movements and a study of weather systems, while the second volume has a huge section on birding the likes of St Kilda and Fair Isle.

CUP has also reproduced *Genera of Birds* by Thomas Pennant, which dates back to 1781 and is an early study in bird taxonomy (ISBN 978-1-108-06778-2, 100pp, £14.99). Some 100 species from around the world are included. Much attention is paid to the size and shape of birds' nostrils, a field mark we tend to ignore today!

The History of British Birds by Thomas Bewick (two volumes) was first published in 1797 and was effectively our first practical field guide. Every species account is illustrated with one of Bewick's famous engravings (ISBN 978-1-108-06540-5 and -06507-8, 336 and 400pp, £48.99).

All the above titles are recommended, but the three books that I have enjoyed most throughout the year are:-

BIRD ATLAS 2007-11: THE BREEDING AND WINTERING BIRDS OF BRITAIN AND IRELAND

A SPARROWHAWK'S LAMENT

TEN THOUSAND BIRDS

DIARY 2015

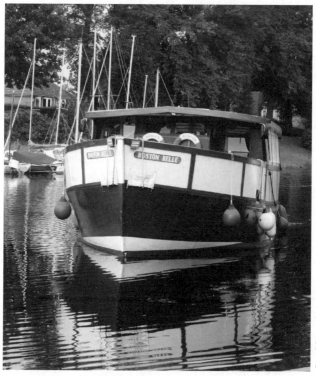

David Cromack

Birdwatchers wanting to get close to the birds of the Wash can book places on the Boston Belle on 14 dates between April and October. RSPB volunteers accompany each trip to help with identification. These trips are extremely popular so early booking is recommended.

Events guide for 2015   28

Day-by-day diary for 2015   30

Year planner for 2016   54

EVENTS DIARY 2015

While every effort has been made to check the accuracy of these entries, the publishers advise making contact with the event organisers to ensure there are no late changes. TBA = To Be Announced (for those dates not settled before the *Yearbook* went to press).

JANUARY

5-Feb 13: Big Schools Birdwatch
UK-wide event to get children interested in wild birds.
Contact: www.rspb.org./schoolswatch for events in your area.

14-15: BTO bird survey techniques course for environmental professionals
Stirling University, Scotland.
Contact: Phone 01786 466 560 or e-mail ann. cotton@bto.org for details of all BTO residentential and non-residential courses.

24-25: Big Garden Birdwatch
UK-wide survey of garden birds.
Contact: www.rspb.org.uk/birdwatch

31 to Feb 3: 5th Global Bird Watchers Conference
Dhordo, Kutch, Gujarat, India.
Contact: info@gbwc.org or www.gbwc.org

FEBRUARY

2: World Wetlands Day
Various events around the globe celebrating the importance of wetland environments.
Contact: www.ramsar.org

14-21: National Nest Box Week
A BTO initiative to encourage more people to erect nestboxes. Various events around the UK – see website for details.
Contact: www.bto.org/about-birds/nnbw

19-22: Pacific Seabird Group 42nd annual meeting
San Jose Airport Garden Hotel, California.
Contact: www.pacificseabirdgroup.org

MARCH

7: North-East Ringers Conference
Bishop Monkton Village Hall, Knaresborough Road, Bishop Monkton, North Yorkshire HG3 3QG.

21: SOC/BTO Scottish Birdwatchers' Conference
Western Infirmary Lecture Theatre, Glasgow University.
Contact: www.the-soc.org.uk

31 to April 2: BOU2015 | Birds in time and space: avian tracking and remote sensing.
Gilbert Murray Conference Suite, University of Leicester Oadby campus.
Contact: www.bou.org.uk

11: African Bird Club AGM, plus full programme of talks on research and conservation work in Africa.
Flett Theatre, Natural History Museum, Cromwell Road, London SW7 5BD. Starts 10:15am.
Contact: info@africanbirdclub.org or www.africanbirdclub.org

22: BTO introduction to bird surveys course
South Staffs College (Rodbaston campus).

27-29: RSPB Members' Weekend
University of York.
Contact: www.rspb.org.uk

29: BTO introduction to bird surveys course
Warwickshire College (Moreton Morrell campus).

MAY

1-3: BTO bird identification residential course
Rhyd-y-Creuau FSC, Snowdonia.

5-7: BTO bird identification residential course
Dale Fort FSC, Pembrokeshire.

8-10: Coll Wildlife Festival

TBA: Go Green Fair
Promoting recycling, nature conservation and energy-reduction. BTO among the stall-holders. 10am to 4pm, Mell, Square, Solihull.
Contact: www.solihullfaithsforum.org

8-10: BTO bird survey techniques and bird ID residential courses
Malham Tarn FSC, North Yorks.

10-11: Scottish Birdfair
More than 110 exhibitors and varied events programme at new venue.
Contact: stacey.maden@rspb.org.uk or visit www. scottishbirdfair.org.uk

13: BTO survey workshop
Ashtead Common, Surrey.

EVENTS DIARY 2015

16-17: Norfolk Bird Fair
For birdwatchers, photographers, wildlife enthusiasts and families. Mannington Hall, near Aylsham, Norfolk.
Contact: birdfairnorfolk@yahoo.com or 01603 219 119.

15-17: BTO bird survey techniques residential course.
The Kingcombe Centre, Dorset.

17: Hawk and Owl Trust Members, Friends and Supporters Day.
Elmley NNR, Isle of Sheppey, Kent.
Contact: David Briley, Hawk and Owl Trust Head Office, 0844 984 2824;
e-mail: enquiries@hawkandowl.org

TBA: Neotropical Bird Club general meeting
AGM, plus talks, quizzes and book sales. Venue not decided. Starts 10.30am.
Contact: d.j.fisher@ntlworld.com or secretary@neotropicalbirdclub.org.uk

29-31: BTO bird survey techniques residential course. Dale Fort FSC, Pembrokeshire.

JULY

4: AGM of OSME (Ornithological Society of the Middle East, Caucasus and Central Asia).
Doors open 10am. Non-members welcome for five talks on the region's birds.
The Nunnery, Thetford, Norfolk.
Contact: secretary@osme.org

17-Aug 2: National Exhibition of Wildlife Art
Preview evening: July 16
Gordale Nursery, Chester High Road, Burton, South Wirral CH64 8TF.
Contact: Marion Tuffrey, 07748 533 448 or visit:
www.newa-uk.com

28-31: Annual meeting of American Ornithologists Union (held jointly with Cooper OS and Society of Canadian Ornithologists)
University of Oklahoma, Norman, Oklahoma
Contact: http://www.nmnh.si.edu/BIRDNET/ornith/birdmeet.html

AUGUST

11-15: The Waterbird Society's 39th annual meeting
Bar Harbor, Maine, USA.
Contact: www.waterbirds.org

21-23: British Birdwatching Fair
Egleton Nature Reserve, Rutland Water, Rutland.

Contact: callen@birdfair.org.uk or visit www.birdfair.org.uk

24-28: 10th European Ornithologists' Union Conference
University of Extremadura, Badajoz, Spain.
Contact: Alfonzo Marzal (head of organising committee) at amarzal@unex.es

SEPTEMBER

4-6: BTO bird ID course
Castle Head FSC, Lake District.

18-20: BTO bird ID course
The Kingcombe Centre, Dorset.

25-27: BTO bird survey techniques course
How Hill Trust, Ludham, Norfolk.

OCTOBER

TBA: Society of Wildlife Artists Annual Exhibition
Mall Galleries, Pall Mall, London.
Contact: www.swla.co.uk

TBA: Hawk & Owl Trust AGM and Members Day

10: RSPB Members' Day and AGM
Queen Elizabeth II conference centre, London.
Visit www.rspb.org.uk

24: BTO bird survey workshop (Breeding Bird Survey) and waterbird ID
Leighton Moss RSPB reserve, Lancashire.

26-30: 2nd World Seabird Conference:
Topic: 'Seabirds: Global Ocean Sentinels'.
Cape Town Convention Centre, South Africa.
Contact: wsc@dearmondmanagement.com.
www.dearmondmanagement.com

TBA: 30 – Nov 1: Scottish Ornithologists Club Annual Conference (venue tbc).
Contact: www.the-soc.org.uk

NOVEMBER

7: Welsh Ornithological Society Annual Conference
Carno, Powys.
Contact: www.birdsinwales.org.uk

DECEMBER

4-6: BTO Annual Conference
Hayes Conference Centre, Swanwick, Derbyshire
Contact: info@bto.org

DIARY – JANUARY 2015

1	Thu	New Year holiday
2	Fri	Holiday (Scotland)
3	Sat	
4	Sun	
5	Mon	
6	Tue	
7	Wed	
8	Thu	
9	Fri	
10	Sat	
11	Sun	
12	Mon	
13	Tue	
14	Wed	
15	Thu	
16	Fri	
17	Sat	
18	Sun	
19	Mon	
20	Tue	
21	Wed	
22	Thu	
23	Fri	
24	Sat	
25	Sun	
26	Mon	
27	Tue	
28	Wed	
29	Thu	
30	Fri	
31	Sat	

DIARY – FEBRUARY 2015

1	Sun	
2	Mon	
3	Tue	
4	Wed	
5	Thu	
6	Fri	
7	Sat	
8	Sun	
9	Mon	
10	Tue	
11	Wed	
12	Thu	
13	Fri	
14	Sat	
15	Sun	
16	Mon	
17	Tue	
18	Wed	
19	Thu	
20	Fri	
21	Sat	
22	Sun	
23	Mon	
24	Tue	
25	Wed	
26	Thu	
27	Fri	
28	Sat	

1	Sun	St David's Day
2	Mon	
3	Tue	
4	Wed	
5	Thu	
6	Fri	
7	Sat	
8	Sun	
9	Mon	
10	Tue	
11	Wed	
12	Thu	
13	Fri	
14	Sat	
15	Sun	Mothering Sunday
16	Mon	
17	Tue	St Patrick's Day
18	Wed	
19	Thu	
20	Fri	
21	Sat	
22	Sun	
23	Mon	
24	Tue	
25	Wed	
26	Thu	
27	Fri	
28	Sat	
29	Sun	British Summertime begins –
30	Mon	
31	Tue	

DIARY – APRIL 2015

1	Wed	
2	Thu	
3	Fri	Good Friday
4	Sat	
5	Sun	Easter Day
6	Mon	Easter Monday
7	Tue	
8	Wed	
9	Thu	
10	Fri	
11	Sat	
12	Sun	
13	Mon	
14	Tue	
15	Wed	
16	Thu	
17	Fri	
18	Sat	
19	Sun	
20	Mon	
21	Tue	
22	Wed	
23	Thu	St George's Day
24	Fri	
25	Sat	
26	Sun	
27	Mon	
28	Tues	
29	Wed	
30	Thu	

DIARY – MAY 2015

1	Fri	
2	Sat	
3	Sun	
4	Mon	May Day
5	Tue	
6	Wed	
7	Thu	
8	Fri	
9	Sat	
10	Sun	
11	Mon	
12	Tue	
13	Wed	
14	Thu	
15	Fri	
16	Sat	
17	Sun	
18	Mon	
19	Tue	
20	Wed	
21	Thu	
22	Fri	
23	Sat	
24	Sun	
25	Mon	Spring Bank Holiday
26	Tue	
27	Wed	
28	Thu	
29	Fri	
30	Sat	
31	Sun	

DIARY – JUNE 2015

1	Mon	
2	Tue	
3	Wed	
4	Thu	
5	Fri	
6	Sat	
7	Sun	
8	Mon	
9	Tue	
10	Wed	
11	Thu	
12	Fri	
13	Sat	
14	Sun	
15	Mon	
16	Tue	
17	Wed	
18	Thu	
19	Fri	
20	Sat	
21	Sun	
22	Mon	
23	Tue	
24	Wed	
25	Thu	
26	Fri	
27	Sat	
28	Sun	
29	Mon	
30	Tue	

DIARY – JULY 2015

1	Wed	
2	Thu	
3	Fri	
4	Sat	
5	Sun	
6	Mon	
7	Tue	
8	Wed	
9	Thu	
10	Fri	
11	Sat	
12	Sun	
13	Mon	
14	Tue	
15	Wed	
16	Thu	
17	Fri	
18	Sat	
19	Sun	
20	Mon	
21	Tue	
22	Wed	
23	Thu	
24	Fri	
25	Sat	
26	Sun	
27	Mon	
28	Tue	
29	Wed	
30	Thu	
31	Fri	

DIARY – AUGUST 2015

1	Sat	
2	Sun	
3	Mon	
4	Tue	
5	Wed	
6	Thu	
7	Fri	
8	Sat	
9	Sun	
10	Mon	
11	Tue	
12	Wed	
13	Thu	
14	Fri	
15	Sat	
16	Sun	
17	Mon	
18	Tue	
19	Wed	
20	Thu	
21	Fri	
22	Sat	
23	Sun	
24	Mon	
25	Tue	
26	Wed	
27	Thu	
28	Fri	
29	Sat	
30	Sun	
31	Mon	Summer Bank Holiday

DIARY – SEPTEMBER 2015

1	Tue	
2	Wed	
3	Thu	
4	Fri	
5	Sat	
6	Sun	
7	Mon	
8	Tue	
9	Wed	
10	Thu	
11	Fri	
12	Sat	
13	Sun	
14	Mon	
15	Tue	
16	Wed	
17	Thu	
18	Fri	
19	Sat	
20	Sun	
21	Mon	
22	Tue	
23	Wed	
24	Thu	
25	Fri	
26	Sat	
27	Sun	
28	Mon	
29	Tue	
30	Wed	

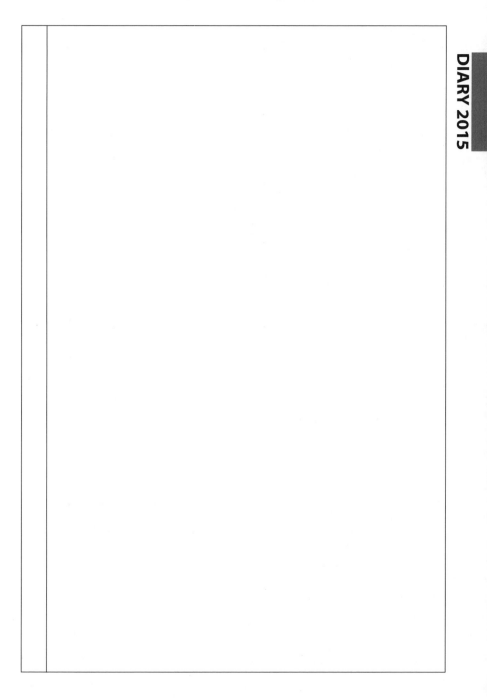

DIARY – OCTOBER 2015

1	Thu	
2	Fri	
3	Sat	
4	Sun	
5	Mon	
6	Tue	
7	Wed	
8	Thu	
9	Fri	
10	Sat	
11	Sun	
12	Mon	
13	Tue	
14	Wed	
15	Thu	
16	Fri	
17	Sat	
18	Sun	
19	Mon	
20	Tue	
21	Wed	
22	Thu	
23	Fri	
24	Sat	
25	Sun	British Summertime ends
26	Mon	
27	Tue	
28	Wed	
29	Thu	
30	Fri	
31	Sat	

DIARY – NOVEMBER 2015

1	Sun	
2	Mon	
3	Tue	
4	Wed	
5	Thu	
6	Fri	
7	Sat	
8	Sun	Remembrance Sunday
9	Mon	
10	Tue	
11	Wed	
12	Thu	
13	Fri	
14	Sat	
15	Sun	
16	Mon	
17	Tue	
18	Wed	
19	Thu	
20	Fri	
21	Sat	
22	Sun	
23	Mon	
24	Tue	
25	Wed	
26	Thu	
27	Fri	
28	Sat	
29	Sun	
30	Mon	

DIARY – DECEMBER 2015

1	Tue	
2	Wed	
3	Thu	
4	Fri	
5	Sat	
6	Sun	
7	Mon	
8	Tue	
9	Wed	
10	Thu	
11	Fri	
12	Sat	
13	Sun	
14	Mon	
15	Tue	
16	Wed	
17	Thu	
18	Fri	
19	Sat	
20	Sun	
21	Mon	
22	Tue	
23	Wed	
24	Thu	
25	Fri	Christmas Day
26	Sat	Boxing Day
27	Sun	
28	Mon	
29	Tues	
30	Wed	
31	Thu	

DIARY 2015

YEAR PLANNER 2016

January
February
March
April
May
June
July
August
September
October
November
December

LOG CHARTS

David Cromack

Spectacular numbers of Little Egrets are now being seen around the British coastline.

Guide to using the log charts   56

Full log charts for BOU-approved British List   58

Log charts for British butterflies   86

Log charts for British Dragonflies   88

A CHECKLIST OF BIRDS
Based on the British List formulated by the British Ornithologists' Union

MANY READERS have asked why our Checklist of Birds keeps changing from year to year. It is based on the official British List maintained by The British Ornithologists' Union (BOU) which sits in judgement on which birds you can count on your lists, and which you can't. They do this in two ways:

1): If someone claims to have seen a species never recorded in Britain, a panel of experts (the BOU Rarities Committee) assesses the record, making sure that the identification of the bird was proved beyond all possible doubt. Then the bird's credentials are also assessed, to determine whether it was a genuine vagrant, rather than one that had just hopped over the fence from the nearest zoo or aviary.

Only if the bird passes every single strenuous test does it get accepted onto the list....a process that may take many years. Similarly, historical records are reassessed in the light of advances in identification skills.

2): The BOU also takes advice from taxonomists on the need to split or lump together sub-species. The current trend towards splitting is usually driven by DNA evidence suggesting that a particular sub-species is sufficiently different to warrant full species status.

Since the publication of the last Birdwatcher's Yearbook, the following decisions have been reached regarding species on the list:

● Capercaillie reassigned to Category C3 because the indigenous population became extinct prior to January 1, 1800.
● Madeiran Storm Petrel removed from list.
● Scopoli's Shearwater added to the list.

As a result of these changes, the official British list now stands at 596 species, made up of 578 species in Category A, eight in Category B and ten in Category C. See below for a full description of what the different categories mean.

In addition, there have been a few minor tweaks to the order of some species such as the auks being moved forward to now sit between skuas and terns and gulls being located after terns. For a full discussion of these changes, go to the BOU's website, **www.bou.org.uk**. In this edition, species in Category C (introduced species) have been sub-divided into six separate categories (see below).

SPECIES, CATEGORIES, CODES – YOUR GUIDE TO GET THE BEST USE FROM THE CHECKLIST

Species categories (column 1)

The following categories are those assigned by the British Ornithologists' Union.

A - Species recorded in an apparently natural state at least once since January 1, 1950.

B - Species recorded in an apparently natural state at least once between January 1, 1800 and December 31,1949, but not subsequently.

C - Species that, though introduced, now derive from the resulting self-sustaining populations: **C1** (*Naturalized introduced species*) Species that have occurred only as a result of introduction, e.g. Egyptian Goose; **C2** (*Naturalized established species*) - Species resulting from introduction by Man, but which also occur in an apparently natural state, e.g. Greylag Goose; **C3** (*Naturalized re-established species*) Species successfully re-established by Man in areas of former occurrence, e.g. Red Kite; **C4** (*Naturalized feral species*) Domesticated species established in the wild, e.g. Rock Pigeon (Dove)/Feral Pigeon; **C5** (*Vagrant naturalized species*) Species from established naturalized populations abroad. There are currently no species in category C5; **C6** (*Former naturalized species*) Species formerly in C1

whose naturalized populations are either no longer self-sustaining or are considered extinct, e.g. Lady Amherst's Pheasant.

D - Species where there is reasonable doubt that they have ever occurred in a natural state. Species placed solely in Category D form no part of the British List, and are not included in the species totals.

E - Species that have been recorded as introductions, human-assisted transportees or escapees from captivity, and whose breeding populations (if any) are thought not to be self-sustaining. Species in Category E that have bred in the wild in Britain are designated as E*. Category E species form no part of the British List (unless already included within Categories A, B or C).

A species is usually placed in only one category, but some are placed in multiple categories, for example, those species occurring in Category A which now have naturalised populations (e.g. Red Kite).

The British List comprises only those species in Categories A, B and C.

LOG CHARTS

Species list (column 2)

The *Yearbook* Checklist includes all species from categories A, B and C on the British List, based on the latest BOU listing. Selected species included in categories D and E are listed separately at the end of the log chart.

Vagrants which are not on the British List, but which may have occurred in other parts of the British Isles, are not included. Readers who wish to record such species may use the extra rows provided on the last page. In this connection it should be noted that separate lists exist for Northern Ireland (kept by the Northern Ireland Birdwatchers' Association) and the Isle of Man (kept by the Manx Ornithological Society), and that Irish records are assessed by the Irish Rare Birds Committee.

The commoner species in the log charts are indicated by the * symbol to help make record-keeping easier.

The species names are those most widely used in the current fieldguides and each is followed by its scientific name, printed in italics.

Life list (column 3)

Ticks made in the 'Life List' column suffice for keeping a running personal total of species. However, added benefit can be obtained by replacing ticks with a note of the year of first occurrence. To take an example: one's first-ever Marsh Sandpiper, seen on April 14, 2013, would be logged with '13' in the Life List and '14' in the April column (as well as a tick in the 2013 column). As Life List entries are carried forward annually, in years to come it would be a simple matter to relocate this record.

First and last dates of migrants

Arrivals of migrants can be recorded by inserting dates instead of ticks in the relevant month columns. For example, a Common Sandpiper on March 11 would be recorded by inserting '11' against Common Sandpiper in the March column. The same applies to departures, though dates of last sightings can only be entered at the end of the year after checking one's field notebook.

Unheaded columns

The three unheaded columns on the right of the December column of each chart are for special (personal) use. This may be, for example, to cater for a second holiday, a particular county or a 'local patch'. Another use could be to indicate species on, for example, the Northern Ireland List or the Isle of Man List.

BTO species codes (column 23)

British Trust for Ornithology two-letter species codes are shown in brackets in the fourth column from the right. Readers should refer to the BTO if more codes are needed.

Rare breeding birds (column 24)

Species monitored by the Rare Breeding Birds Panel (see National Directory) comprise all those on Schedule 1 of the Wildlife and Countryside Act 1981 (see Quick Reference) together with all escaped or introduced species breeding in small numbers. The following annotations in the charts (third column from the right) reflect the **RBBP's categories:**

A) Rare Breeding Birds in UK (Regular Breeders); B) Rare Breeding Birds in UK (Occasional Breeders); C) Rare Breeding Birds in UK (Potential Breeders); D) Rare Non-native Breeding Birds in UK (Regular Breeders); E) Rare Non-native Breeding Birds in UK (Occasional Breeders); F) Rare Non-native Breeding Birds in UK (Potential Breeders).

Rarities (column 25)

Rarities are indicated by a capital letter 'R' in the column headed BBRC (British Birds Rarities Committee).

EURING species numbers (column 26)

EURING databanks collect copies of recovery records from ringing schemes throughout Europe and the official species numbers are given in the last column. As they are taken from the full Holarctic bird list there are many apparent gaps. It is important that these are not filled arbitrarily by observers wishing to record species not listed in the charts, as this would compromise the integrity of the scheme.

Similarly, the addition of a further digit to indicate sub-species is to be avoided, since EURING has already assigned numbers for this purpose. The numbering follows the Voous order of species so some species are now out of sequence following the re-ordering of the British List. For full details, visit: www.euring.org

BOU	SWANS, GEESE, DUCKS		Life list	2015 list	24 hr	Garden	Holiday	Jan	Feb	Mar	Apr	May	Jun	Jul	Aug	Sep	Oct	Nov	Dec			BTO	RBBP	BBRC	EU No
*AC2	Mute Swan	Cygnus olor	✓		✓			✓	✓		✓	✓	✓	✓	✓							MS			0152
*AE	Bewick's Swan	Cygnus columbianus	✓	✓	✓													✓				BS	C		0153
AE	Whooper Swan	Cygnus cygnus	✓											✓								WS	A		0154
*AE	Bean Goose	Anser fabalis																				BE	E		0157
*AE	Pink-footed Goose	Anser brachyrhynchus	93																			PG	E		0158
*AE	White-fronted Goose	Anser albifrons	93																			WG	E		0159
AE	Lesser White-fronted Goose	Anser erythropus	95																			LC	F	R	0160
AC2C4E	Greylag Goose	Anser anser	✓	✓	✓				✓		✓	✓	✓	✓	✓							GJ			0161
AC2E	Snow Goose	Anser caerulescens	✓	✓													✓					SJ	D		0163
AC2E	Canada Goose	Branta canadensis	✓	✓	✓						✓		✓	✓	✓		✓	✓				CG			0166
AC2E	Barnacle Goose	Branta leucopsis	✓	✓										✓					✓			BY	D		0167
*AE	Brent Goose	Branta bernicla	✓	✓															✓			BG			0168
AE	Red-breasted Goose	Branta ruficollis	08	✓	✓																	EB	E	R	0169
C1E	Egyptian Goose	Alopochen aegyptiaca	93					✓	✓				✓	✓	✓		✓					EG	D		0170
BDE	Ruddy Shelduck	Tadorna ferruginea	94																			UD	D		0171
*A	Shelduck	Tadorna tadorna	✓	✓				✓	✓		✓	✓					✓		✓			SU			0173
C1E	Mandarin Duck	Aix galericulata	✓																			MN			0178
AE	Wigeon	Anas penelope	✓	✓					✓								✓		✓			WN	A		0179
AE	American Wigeon	Anas americana	94																			AW			0180
*AC	Gadwall	Anas strepera	✓	✓	✓			✓	✓		✓								✓			GA			0182
*AE	Baikal Teal	Anas formosa																						R	1830
*A	Teal	Anas crecca	✓	✓	✓			✓	✓		✓			✓			✓		✓			T			0184
A	Green-winged Teal	Anas carolinensis	11																				C		1842
AC2C4E	Mallard	Anas platyrhynchos	✓	✓	✓			✓			✓			✓	✓		✓	✓	✓			MA	·		0186
	Sub total																								

DUCKS Cont

BOU	DUCKS Cont		Life list	2015 list	24 hr	Garden	Holiday	Jan	Feb	Mar	Apr	May	Jun	Jul	Aug	Sep	Oct	Nov	Dec			BTO	RBBP	BBRC	EU No
A	Black Duck	*Anas rubripes*	93																			BD	B	R	0187
*AE	Pintail	*Anas acuta*	✓	✓							✓								✓			PT	A		0189
*A	Garganey	*Anas querquedula*	96	✓																		GY	A		0191
AE	Blue-winged Teal	*Anas discors*	94	✓																		TB	E	R	0192
*A	Shoveler	*Anas clypeata*	✓						✓						✓		✓	✓				SV	A		0194
AC2E	Red-crested Pochard	*Netta rufina*	96	✓										✓			✓					RQ	D	R	0196
AE	Canvasback	*Aythya valisineria*																						R	0197
AE	Pochard	*Aythya ferina*	✓	✓					✓		✓						✓					PO	A		0198
AE	Redhead	*Aythya americana*																				AZ		R	0199
A	Ring-necked Duck	*Aythya collaris*	94																			NG	B		0200
AE	Ferruginous Duck	*Aythya nyroca*	98																			FD	B		0202
*A	Tufted Duck	*Aythya fuligula*	✓	✓					✓				✓	✓			✓					TU			0203
*A	Scaup	*Aythya marila*	73																			SP	B		0204
*A	Lesser Scaup	*Aythya affinis*	✓										✓									AY		R	0205
*A	Eider	*Somateria mollissima*	✓	✓									✓									E			0206
*A	King Eider	*Somateria spectabilis*																				KE	C	R	0207
A	Steller's Eider	*Polysticta stelleri*																				ES		R	0209
A	Harlequin Duck	*Histrionicus histrionicus*	14																			HQ		R	0211
*A	Long-tailed Duck	*Clangula hyemalis*	94																			LN	C		0212
*A	Common Scoter	*Melanitta nigra*	94																			CX	A		0213
A	White-winged Scoter	*Melanitta deglandi*																							
A	Black Scoter	*Melanitta americana*																						R	2132
*A	Surf Scoter	*Melanitta perspicillata*	73																			FS			0214
A	Velvet Scoter	*Melanitta fusca*	73																			VS	C		0215
	Sub total																								

59

DUCKS, GAMEBIRDS, DIVERS, ALBATROSS

BOU	Species	Scientific name	Life list	2015 list	24 hr	Garden	Holiday	Jan	Feb	Mar	Apr	May	Jun	Jul	Aug	Sep	Oct	Nov	Dec	BTO	RBBP	BBRC	EU No
AE	Bufflehead	*Bucephala albeola*	93																	VH		R	0216
A	Barrow's Goldeneye	*Bucephala islandica*	14					✓														R	0217
AE	Goldeneye	*Bucephala clangula*	✓	✓	✓													✓	✓	GN	A		0218
A	Hooded Merganser	*Lophodytes cucullatus*	12																				R	2190
*A	Smew	*Mergellus albellus*	96																	SY	C		0220
*A	Red-breasted Merganser	*Mergus serrator*	✓	✓	✓			✓										✓	✓	RM			0221
*A	Goosander	*Mergus merganser*	✓	✓	✓					✓										GD			0223
C1E	Ruddy Duck	*Oxyura jamaicensis*	✓	✓	✓														✓	BY	D		0225
*A	Red Grouse	*Lagopus lagopus*	14													✓				RG			0329
*A	Ptarmigan	*Lagopus muta*																		PM			0330
*AE	Black Grouse	*Tetrao tetrix*																		BK			0332
*BC3	Capercaillie	*Tetrao urogallus*																		CP	A		0335
*A	Quail	*Coturnix*	96																	Q	A		0370
C1E	Red-legged Partridge	*Alectoris rufa*	✓																	RL			0358
AC2E	Grey Partridge	*Perdix perdix*																		P			0367
C1E	Pheasant	*Phasianus colchicus*	✓	✓		✓		✓	✓			✓	✓	✓	✓	✓		✓		✓	PH			0394
C6E	Lady Amherst's Pheasant	*Chrysolophus amherstiae*																		LM	D		0397
C1E	Golden Pheasant	*Chrysolophus pictus*	✓																	GF	D		0396
*A	Red-throated Diver	*Gavia stellata*	91																	RH	A		0002
*A	Black-throated Diver	*Gavia arctica*	92																	BV	A		0003
A	Pacific Diver	*Gavia pacifica*																				R	0033
*A	Great Northern Diver	*Gavia immer*	✓																	ND	C		0004
A	White-billed Diver	*Gavia adamsii*																		IW	C		0005
A	Black-browed Albatross	*Thalassarche melanophris*																		AA	C	R	0014
	Sub total																						

FULMAR, PETRELS, SHEARWATERS, CORMORANTS, FRIGATEBIRDS, BITTERNS

BOU	Species	Scientific name	Life list	2015 list	24 hr	Garden	Holiday	Jan	Feb	Mar	Apr	May	Jun	Jul	Aug	Sep	Oct	Nov	Dec	BTO	RBBP	BBRC	EU No
A	Yellow-nosed Albatross	Thalassarche chlororhynchos																				R	0150
*A	Fulmar	Fulmarus glacialis	✓	✓									✓							F			0020
A	Fea's Petrel	Pterodroma feae																				R	0026
A	Capped Petrel	Pterodroma hasitata																				R	0029
A	Cory's Shearwater	Calonectris borealis	10																	CQ			0036
A	Scopoli's Shearwater	Calonectris diomedea																					
*A	Great Shearwater	Puffinus gravis																			GQ			0040
*A	Sooty Shearwater	Puffinus griseus																			OT			0043
A	Manx Shearwater	Puffinus puffinus	✓																		MX			0046
A	Balearic Shearwater	Puffinus mauretanicus	00																					0046
A	Macaronesian Shearwater	Puffinus baroli																				C	R	0048
*A	Wilson's Petrel	Oceanites oceanicus																						0050
B	White-faced Petrel	Pelagodroma marina																					R	0051
*A	Storm Petrel	Hydrobates pelagicus																			TM			0052
A	Leach's Petrel	Oceanodroma leucorhoa																			TL			0055
A	Swinhoe's Petrel	Oceanodroma monorhis																					R	0056
A	Red-billed Tropicbird	Phaethon aethereus																					R	0064
*A	Gannet	Morus bassanus	✓											✓							GX			0071
*A	Cormorant	Phalacrocorax carbo	93	✓				✓	✓	✓		✓	✓	✓	✓		✓			CA			0072
A	Double-crested Cormorant	Phalacrocorax auritus													✓			✓	✓			R	0078
*A	Shag	Phalacrocorax aristotelis	✓	✓									✓							SA			0080
A	Ascension Frigatebird	Fregata aquila																					R	
A	Magnificent Frigatebird	Fregata magnificens	62																	BI		R	0093
*A	Bittern	Botaurus stellaris	98																			A		0095
	Sub total																						

BITTERNS, HERONS, STORKS, SPOONBILL, GREBES, RAPTORS

BOU	Species	Scientific name	Life list	2015 list	24 hr	Garden	Holiday	Jan	Feb	Mar	Apr	May	Jun	Jul	Aug	Sep	Oct	Nov	Dec				BTO	RBBP	BBRC	EU No
A	American Bittern	Botaurus lentiginosus	01																				AM		R	0096
A	Little Bittern	Ixobrychus minutus	96																				LL	B	R	0098
AE*	Night Heron	Nycticorax nycticorax	02																				NT	E		0104
A	Green Heron	Butorides virescens	97																				HR		R	0107
A	Squacco Heron	Ardeola ralloides	95																				QH		R	0108
AE	Cattle Egret	Bubulcus ibis																					EC	B		0111
A	Snowy Egret	Egretta thula																							R	0115
*A	Little Egret	Egretta garzetta	✓	✓				✓		✓	✓		✓	✓	✓		✓	✓	✓				ET	A		0119
A	Great White Egret	Ardea alba	✓	✓							✓				✓			✓	✓				HW	C		0121
A	Grey Heron	Ardea cinerea	✓	✓							✓		✓		✓		✓		✓				H			0122
A	Great Blue Heron	Ardea herodias	93																						R	1230
A	Purple Heron	Ardea purpurea	98												✓									UR	B		0124
AE	Black Stork	Ciconia nigra	96																					OS		R	0131
AE	White Stork	Ciconia ciconia	85																					OR	C		0134
AE	Glossy Ibis	Plegadis falcinellus	78																					IB		R	0136
*AE	Spoonbill	Platalea leucorodia	90	✓							✓													NB	A		0144
A	Pied-billed Grebe	Podilymbus podiceps	94																					PJ	B	R	0006
*A	Little Grebe	Tachybaptus ruficollis	✓	✓				✓	✓		✓		(✓)		✓				✓				LG			0007
*A	Great Crested Grebe	Podiceps cristatus	✓	✓				✓	✓		✓		✓		✓		✓	✓	✓				GG			0009
*A	Red-necked Grebe	Podiceps grisegena	00																					RX	B		0010
*A	Slavonian Grebe	Podiceps auritus	✓					✓																SZ	A		0011
*A	Black-necked Grebe	Podiceps nigricollis	00																					BN	A		0012
*A	Honey-buzzard	Pernis apivorus	00																					HZ	A		0231
AE	Black Kite	Milvus migrans	92																					KB	B		0238
	Sub total																									

62

BOU	RAPTORS Cont		EU No	BBRC	RBBP	BTO	Dec	Nov	Oct	Sep	Aug	Jul	Jun	May	Apr	Mar	Feb	Jan	Holiday	Garden	24 hr	2015 list	Life list
AC3E	Red Kite	Milvus milvus	0239		A	KT			✓						✓	✓	✓					✓	96
*AC3E	White-tailed Eagle	Haliaeetus albicilla	0243		A	WE					✓		✓	✓									09
BDE	Egyptian Vulture	Neophron percnopterus	0247	R																	✓		89
A	Short-toed Eagle	Circaetus gallicus	0256	R																	✓		96
*A	Marsh Harrier	Circus aeruginosus	0260		A	MR						✓									✓		92
*A	Hen Harrier	Circus cyaneus	0261		A	HH	✓														✓		92
A	Pallid Harrier	Circus macrourus	0262	R	C																		00
*A	Montagu's Harrier	Circus pygargus	0263		A	MO									✓						✓		96
AC3E	Goshawk	Accipiter gentilis	0267		A	GI																	10
*A	Sparrowhawk	Accipiter nisus	0269			SH								✓							✓		✓
AE	Buzzard	Buteo buteo	0287			BZ					✓	✓	✓	✓	✓	✓	✓				✓		✓
*AE	Rough-legged Buzzard	Buteo lagopus	0290		C	RF	✓		✓												✓		11
B	Greater Spotted Eagle	Aquila clanga	0293	R																			98
*AE	Golden Eagle	Aquila chrysaetos	0296		A	EA						✓	✓	✓									✓
AE	Osprey	Pandion haliaetus	0301		A	OP						✓	✓	✓	✓						✓		✓
A	Lesser Kestrel	Falco naumanni	0303	R																			92
*A	Kestrel	Falco tinnunculus	0304			K	✓		✓			✓	✓			✓	✓				✓		✓
AE	American Kestrel	Falco sparverius	0305	R																			94
*A	Red-footed Falcon	Falco vespertinus	0307		A	FV		✓					✓	✓									98
A	Amur Falcon	Falco amurensis	3080	R																			
*A	Merlin	Falco columbarius	0309		A	ML																	✓
*A	Hobby	Falco subbuteo	0310		A	HY																	✓
A	Eleonora's Falcon	Falco eleonorae	0311	R																			01
*AE	Gyrfalcon	Falco rusticolus	0318	R	C	YF																	
	Sub total																						

63

CRAKES, GALLINULES, CRANES, BUSTARDS AND WADERS

BOU	Species	Scientific name	Life list	2015 list	24 hr	Garden	Holiday	Jan	Feb	Mar	Apr	May	Jun	Jul	Aug	Sep	Oct	Nov	Dec	BTO	RBBP	BBRC	EU No
*AE	Peregrine	Falco peregrinus	✓	✓										✓					✓	PE	A		0320
*A	Water Rail	Rallus aquaticus	95	95							H									WA	A		0407
*A	Spotted Crake	Porzana porzana																		AK	A		0408
A	Sora	Porzana carolina																				R	0409
A	Little Crake	Porzana parva	00																	JC		R	0410
A	Baillon's Crake	Porzana pusilla																		VC	C	R	0411
AE	Corncrake	Crex crex	98																	CE	A		0421
*A	Moorhen	Gallinula chloropus	✓	✓						✓	✓	✓	✓	✓	✓		✓	✓	✓	MH			0424
A	Allen's Gallinule	Porphyrio alleni																				R	0425
A	Purple Gallinule	Porphyrio martinica																				R	0426
*A	Coot	Fulica atra	1	1				✓		✓	✓	✓	✓	✓	✓		✓	✓		CO			0429
A	American Coot	Fulica americana	94																			R	0430
*A	Crane	Grus grus																		AN	A		0433
A	Sandhill Crane	Grus canadensis																				R	0436
A	Little Bustard	Tetrax tetrax	13																			R	0442
A	Macqueen's Bustard	Chlamydotis macqueenii																				R	0444
AE*	Great Bustard	Otis tarda	98																	US	B	R	0446
*A	Stone-curlew	Burhinus oedicnemus	75																	TN	A		0459
*A	Black-winged Stilt	Himantopus himantopus																		IT	B	R	0455
*A	Avocet	Recurvirostra avosetta	✓	✓				✓					✓	✓				✓		AV	A		0456
*A	Oystercatcher	Haematopus ostralegus	✓	✓				✓			✓		✓	✓	✓		✓		✓	OC			0450
A	American Golden Plover	Pluvialis dominica										✓								ID			0484
A	Pacific Golden Plover	Pluvialis fulva													✓					IF		R	0484
*A	Golden Plover	Pluvialis apricaria	✓	✓														✓		GP			0485
	Sub total																						

BOU	WADERS Cont		Life list	2015 list	24 hr	Garden	Holiday	Jan	Feb	Mar	Apr	May	Jun	Jul	Aug	Sep	Oct	Nov	Dec			BTO	RBBP	BBRC	EU No
*A	Grey Plover	Pluvialis squatarola	✓	✓	✓			✓						✓				✓				GV			0486
A	Sociable Plover	Vanellus gregarius	98																		IP		R	0491
A	White-tailed Plover	Vanellus leucurus	✓	✓	✓				✓					✓			✓		✓			L		R	0492
*A	Lapwing	Vanellus vanellus	✓	✓	✓						✓				✓				✓				L			0493
*A	Little Ringed Plover	Charadrius dubius	96	✓							✓			✓								LP	A		0469
*A	Ringed Plover	Charadrius hiaticula	✓	✓							✓							✓				RP			0470
A	Semipalmated Plover	Charadrius semipalmatus	02																			TV		R	0471
A	Killdeer	Charadrius vociferus	94																			KL	C	R	0474
A	Kentish Plover	Charadrius alexandrinus	95																			KP	B		0477
A	Lesser Sand Plover	Charadrius mongolus																						R	0478
A	Greater Sand Plover	Charadrius leschenaultii																						R	0479
A	Caspian Plover	Charadrius asiaticus																						R	0480
*A	Dotterel	Charadrius morinellus	88																			DO	A		0482
A	Upland Sandpiper	Bartramia longicauda		✓	✓									✓								UP	A	R	0544
A	Little Whimbrel	Numenius minutus		✓	✓									✓	✓									R	0536
B	Eskimo Curlew	Numenius borealis		✓	✓								✓		✓									R	0537
																							R	
*A	Hudsonian Whimbrel	Numenius hudsonicus	15	✓	✓									✓								WM	A		0538
*A	Whimbrel	Numenius phaeopus	✓	✓								✓		✓	✓			✓				CU			0541
*A	Curlew	Numenius arquata	✓	✓				✓				✓		✓	✓			✓	✓			BW	A		0532
*A	Black-tailed Godwit	Limosa limosa	✓	✓	✓			✓				✓	✓✓		✓				✓			HU		R	0533
A	Hudsonian Godwit	Limosa haemastica																				BA	C		0534
*A	Bar-tailed Godwit	Limosa lapponica	✓	✓	✓			✓									✓	✓				TT	C		0561
*A	Turnstone	Arenaria interpres	✓✓																			KO		R	0495
A	Great Knot	Calidris tenuirostris																							
	Sub total																								

65

BOU	WADERS Cont		Life list	2015 list	24 hr	Garden	Holiday	Jan	Feb	Mar	Apr	May	Jun	Jul	Aug	Sep	Oct	Nov	Dec		BTO	RBBP	BBRC	EU No
*A	Knot	*Calidris canutus*	✓	(✓)																		KN			0496
*A	Ruff	*Calidris pugnax*	✓	✓										✓	✓		(2)	(✓)			RU	A		0517
A	Sharp-tailed Sandpiper	*Calidris acuminata*																			VV		R	0508
A	Broad-billed Sandpiper	*Calidris falcinellus*																			OA	C	R	0514
*A	Curlew Sandpiper	*Calidris ferruginea*	91	✓										✓							CV			0509
A	Stilt Sandpiper	*Calidris himantopus*																					R	5150
A	Red-necked Stint	*Calidris ruficollis*																					R	0500
A	Long-toed Stint	*Calidris subminuta*																					R	0503
*A	Temminck's Stint	*Calidris temminckii*	95	✓										✓							TK	B		0502
*A	Sanderling	*Calidris alba*	✓	✓										✓							SS	C		0497
*A	Dunlin	*Calidris alpina*	✓	✓				✓						✓				✓			DN			0512
*A	Purple Sandpiper	*Calidris maritima*	✓	✓																	PS	A		0510
A	Baird's Sandpiper	*Calidris bairdii*																				BP		R	0506
*A	Little Stint	*Calidris minuta*	96																		LX			0501
A	White-rumped Sandpiper	*Calidris fuscicollis*	98																		WU			0505
A	Least Sandpiper	*Calidris minutilla*																			EP		R	0504
A	Buff-breasted Sandpiper	*Calidris subruficollis*	09																		BQ	C		0516
A	Pectoral Sandpiper	*Calidris melanotos*	97																		PP	C		0507
A	Western Sandpiper	*Calidris mauri*	11																		ER		R	0499
A	Semipalmated Sandpiper	*Calidris pusilla*																			PZ		R	0498
A	Wilson's Phalarope	*Phalaropus tricolor*																			WF	C	R	0563
*A	Red-necked Phalarope	*Phalaropus lobatus*																			NK	A		0564
*A	Grey Phalarope	*Phalaropus fulicarius*	10																		PL			0565
A	Terek Sandpiper	*Xenus cinereus*																			TR		R	0555
	Sub total																							

WADERS Cont, PRATINCOLES AND SKUA

BOU			Life list	2015 list	24 hr	Garden	Holiday	Jan	Feb	Mar	Apr	May	Jun	Jul	Aug	Sep	Oct	Nov	Dec		BTO	RBBP	BBRC	EU No
*A	Common Sandpiper	Actitis hypoleucos	94	✓												✓					CS			0556
A	Spotted Sandpiper	Actitis macularius	95		✓										✓						PQ	B	R	0557
*A	Green Sandpiper	Tringa ochropus	95		✓																GE	A		0553
A	Solitary Sandpiper	Tringa solitaria			✓																I		R	0552
A	Grey-tailed Tattler	Tringa brevipes																			YT		R	0558
*A	Spotted Redshank	Tringa erythropus	93	✓									✓	✓					✓		DR			0545
A	Greater Yellowlegs	Tringa melanoleuca	✓	✓																	LZ		R	0550
*A	Greenshank	Tringa nebularia	02					✓											✓		GK	A		0548
A	Lesser Yellowlegs	Tringa flavipes	95																		LY		R	0551
*A	Marsh Sandpiper	Tringa stagnatilis																			MD		R	0547
*A	Wood Sandpiper	Tringa glareola	95																		OD	A		0554
*A	Redshank	Tringa totanus	✓	✓				✓					✓	✓	✓		(✓)	✓	✓		RK			0546
*A	Jack Snipe	Lymnocryptes minimus																			JS	C		0518
A	Short-billed Dowitcher	Limnodromus griseus	62																				R	0526
A	Long-billed Dowitcher	Limnodromus scolopaceus	78																		LD		R	0527
*A	Woodcock	Scolopax rusticola	98																		WK			0529
*A	Snipe	Gallinago gallinago	✓	✓										✓							SN			0519
A	Wilson's Snipe	Gallinago delicata																					R	5192
A	Great Snipe	Gallinago media																			DS	C	R	0520
A	Collared Pratincole	Glareola pratincola	05																				R	0465
A	Oriental Pratincole	Glareola maldivarum																			GM		R	0466
A	Black-winged Pratincole	Glareola nordmanni																			KW		R	0467
A	Cream-coloured Courser	Cursorius cursor																					R	0464
*A	Pomarine Skua	Stercorarius pomarinus	10																		PK			0566
	Sub total																							

SKUAS Cont. AUKS AND TERNS

BOU	Species	Scientific name	Life list	2015 list	24 hr	Garden	Holiday	Jan	Feb	Mar	Apr	May	Jun	Jul	Aug	Sep	Oct	Nov	Dec	BTO	RBBP	BBRC	EU No
*A	Arctic Skua	Stercorarius parasiticus	96																	AC	A		0567
*A	Long-tailed Skua	Stercorarius longicaudus	10																	OG			0568
*A	Great Skua	Stercorarius skua	96																	NX			0569
A	Tufted Puffin	Fratercula cirrhata																				R	
*A	Puffin	Fratercula arctica	✓																	PU			0654
A	Long-billed Murrelet	Brachyramphus perdix																✓				R	6412
*A	Black Guillemot	Cepphus grylle	92																	TY			0638
A	Ancient Murrelet	Synthliboramphus antiquus																				R	0645
*A	Razorbill	Alca torda	✓	✓									✓							RA			0636
B	Great Auk (extinct)	Pinguinus impennis																					
*A	Little Auk	Alle alle	10																	LK			0647
*A	Guillemot	Uria aalge	✓	✓									✓							GU			0634
A	Brunnich's Guillemot	Uria lomvia	10																	TZ		R	0635
A	Aleutian Tern	Onychoprion aleuticus																				R	0617
A	Sooty Tern	Onychoprion fuscatus																				R	0623
A	Bridled Tern	Onychoprion anaethetus																				R	0622
*A	Little Tern	Sternula albifrons	94																	AF	A		0624
A	Gull-billed Tern	Gelochelidon nilotica																		TG	B	R	0605
A	Caspian Tern	Hydroprogne caspia																		CJ		R	0606
*A	Whiskered Tern	Chlidonias hybrida	98																	WD		R	0626
*A	Black Tern	Chlidonias niger	94																	BJ	C		0627
*A	White-winged Black Tern	Chlidonias leucopterus	11								✓		✓							WJ			0628
A	Cabot's Tern	Sterna acuflavida																				R	
*A	Sandwich Tern	Sterna sandvicensis	✓	✓																TE			0611
	Sub total																						

BOU	TERNS Cont, GULLS		Life list	2015 list	24 hr	Garden	Holiday	Jan	Feb	Mar	Apr	May	Jun	Jul	Aug	Sep	Oct	Nov	Dec		BTO	RBBP	BBRC	EU No
A	Royal Tern	Sterna maxima	02																		QT		R	0607
A	Lesser Crested Tern	Sterna bengalensis																			TF	B	R	0609
A	Forster's Tern	Sterna forsteri		✓																	FO		R	0618
*A	Common Tern	Sterna hirundo	✓											✓							CN			0615
*A	Roseate Tern	Sterna dougallii	01																		RS	A		0614
*A	Arctic Tern	Sterna paradisaea	✓																		AE			0616
A	Ivory Gull	Pagophila eburnea	10											✓							IV		R	0604
*A	Sabine's Gull	Xema sabini	11																		AB			0579
*A	Kittiwake	Rissa tridactyla	✓	✓									✓								KI			0602
A	Slender-billed Gull	Chroicocephalus genei																			EI	C	R	0585
A	Bonaparte's Gull	Chroicocephalus philadelphia																			ON		R	0581
*A	Black-headed Gull	Chroicocephalus ridibundus	✓	✓				✓	✓	✓	✓						✓		✓		BH			0582
*A	Little Gull	Hydrocoloeus minutus	89	✓							✓	✓	✓	✓	✓	✓	✓	✓	✓		LU	B		0578
A	Ross's Gull	Rhodostethia rosea																			QG		R	0601
*A	Laughing Gull	Larus atricilla									✓	✓	✓	✓	✓	✓	✓				LF		R	0576
A	Franklin's Gull	Larus pipixcan																			FG		R	0577
*A	Mediterranean Gull	Larus melanocephalus	95	✓																	MU	A		0575
A	Audouin's Gull	Larus audouinii	96																				R	0589
B	Great Black-headed Gull	Larus ichthyaetus																					R	0573
*A	Common Gull	Larus canus	✓	✓				✓											✓		CM			0590
*A	Ring-billed Gull	Larus delawarensis																			IN	B		0588
*A	Lesser Black-backed Gull	Larus fuscus	✓	✓				✓	✓	✓	✓	✓	✓	✓	✓	✓	✓	✓	✓		LB			0591
*A	Herring Gull	Larus argentatus	✓	✓				✓	✓	✓	✓	✓	✓	✓	✓	✓	✓	✓	✓		HG		R	0592
A	Yellow-legged Gull	Larus michahellis	✓																				A		5927
	Sub total																							

BOU	GULLS Cont. DOVES, CUCKOOS AND OWLS	Scientific name	Life list	2015 list	24 hr	Garden	Holiday	Jan	Feb	Mar	Apr	May	Jun	Jul	Aug	Sep	Oct	Nov	Dec	BTO	RBBP	BBRC	EU No
A	Caspian Gull	Larus cachinnans																					5927
A	American Herring Gull	Larus smithsonianus																				R	26632
*A	Iceland Gull	Larus glaucoides	14																	IG			0598
A	Glaucous-winged Gull	Larus glaucescens																				R	5960
*A	Glaucous Gull	Larus hyperboreus	95																	GZ	B		0599
*A	Great Black-backed Gull	Larus marinus	✓										✓							GB			0600
A	Pallas's Sandgrouse	Syrrhaptes paradoxus																				R	0663
AC4E	Rock Dove / Feral Pigeon	Columba livia	✓	✓				✓	✓	✓	✓				✓		✓	✓	✓	DV			0665
*A	Stock Dove	Columba oenas	✓	✓				✓	✓	✓										SD			0668
*A	Woodpigeon	Columba palumbus	✓	✓				✓	✓	✓		✓	✓	✓	✓		✓	✓	✓	WP			0670
*A	Collared Dove	Streptopelia decaocto	✓	✓				✓	✓	✓	✓	✓	✓	✓	✓		✓	✓	✓	CD			0684
*A	Turtle Dove	Streptopelia turtur	✓							✓	✓	✓		✓	✓		✓	✓		TD			0687
A	Rufous Turtle Dove	Streptopelia orientalis																				R	0689
A	Mourning Dove	Zenaida macroura	92																			R	0695
C1E	Ring-necked Parakeet	Psittacula krameri	08	✓				✓	✓	✓	✓		✓		✓		✓	✓	✓	RI			0712
A	Great Spotted Cuckoo	Clamator glandarius	08	✓							24									UK		R	0716
*A	Cuckoo	Cuculus canorus												✓						CK			0724
A	Black-billed Cuckoo	Coccyzus erythropthalmus																				R	0727
A	Yellow-billed Cuckoo	Coccyzus americanus																				R	0728
AE	Barn Owl	Tyto alba	✓																	BO	C		0735
A	Scops Owl	Otus scops																			C	R	0739
*A	Snowy Owl	Bubo scandiacus	92																	SO	B	R	0749
A	Hawk Owl	Surnia ulula																				R	0750
*A	Little Owl	Athene noctua	✓																	LO			0757
	Sub total																						

OWLS Cont. NIGHTJARS, SWIFTS, KINGFISHERS, BEE-EATERS AND WOODPECKERS

BOU	English name	Scientific name	Life list	2015 list	24 hr	Garden	Holiday	Jan	Feb	Mar	Apr	May	Jun	Jul	Aug	Sep	Oct	Nov	Dec		BTO	RBBP	BBRC	EU No
*A	Tawny Owl	Strix aluco	✓	✓																		TO			0761
*A	Long-eared Owl	Asio otus	96						H									H	H	√		LE	A		0767
*A	Short-eared Owl	Asio flammeus	✓															H				SE	A		0768
A	Tengmalm's Owl	Aegolius funereus	77																					R	0770
*A	Nightjar	Caprimulgus europaeus																				NJ			0778
B	Red-necked Nightjar	Caprimulgus ruficollis																						R	0779
A	Egyptian Nightjar	Caprimulgus aegyptius																						R	0781
A	Common Nighthawk	Chordeiles minor	94																					R	0786
A	Chimney Swift	Chaetura pelagica																						R	0790
A	Needle-tailed Swift	Hirundapus caudacutus	✓										√	√	√							NI		R	0792
*A	Swift	Apus apus	94											√	√							SI			0795
A	Pallid Swift	Apus pallidus																					C	R	0796
A	Pacific Swift	Apus pacificus																						R	0797
A	Alpine Swift	Apus melba	00																			AI			0798
A	Little Swift	Apus affinis																						R	0800
*A	Kingfisher	Alcedo atthis	✓	√					√							√				√		KF		R	0831
A	Belted Kingfisher	Megaceryle alcyon	93																					R	0834
A	Blue-cheeked Bee-eater	Merops persicus																						R	0839
*A	Bee-eater	Merops apiaster	✓																			MZ	B		0840
A	Roller	Coracias garrulus	14																					R	0841
*A	Hoopoe	Upupa epops	✓					H	H	H	H	H	H	H								HP	B		0846
*A	Wryneck	Jynx torquilla	01															/				WY	A		0848
*A	Green Woodpecker	Picus viridis	✓					H	H	H	H	H	H	H				H	H			G			0856
A	Yellow-bellied Sapsucker	Sphyrapicus varius	✓	√																				R	0872
	Sub total																							

71

WOODPECKERS Cont., VIREOS, SHRIKES AND CORVIDS

BOU	Name	Scientific name	Life list	2015 list	24 hr	Garden	Holiday	Jan	Feb	Mar	Apr	May	Jun	Jul	Aug	Sep	Oct	Nov	Dec		BTO	RBBP	BBRC	EU No
*A	Great Spotted Woodpecker	Dendrocopos major	✓	✓		✓		✓	✓	✓	✓	✓	✓	✓	✓		✓		✓		GS			0876
*A	Lesser Spotted Woodpecker	Dendrocopos minor	93	✓															✓			LS	A		0887
A	Eastern Phoebe	Sayornis phoebe																						R	0909
A	Yellow-throated Vireo	Vireo flavifrons																						R	1628
A	Philadelphia Vireo	Vireo philadelphicus																				EV		R	1631
A	Red-eyed Vireo	Vireo olivaceus																				OL		R	1633
*A	Golden Oriole	Oriolus oriolus	96																				A		1508
A	Brown Shrike	Lanius cristatus																						R	1513
A	Isabelline Shrike	Lanius isabellinus	95	✓																		IL		R	1514
*A	Red-backed Shrike	Lanius collurio	95	✓																		ED	A		1515
A	Long-tailed Shrike	Lanius schach	97	✓																				R	1517
*A	Lesser Grey Shrike	Lanius minor	✓	✓																				R	1519
*A	Great Grey Shrike	Lanius excubitor	92	✓				✓	✓	✓	✓	✓										SR	C		1520
A	Southern Grey Shrike	Lanius meridionalis	95	✓																✓				R	1520
A	Woodchat Shrike	Lanius senator																				OO			1523
A	Masked Shrike	Lanius nubicus																						R	1524
AE	Chough	Pyrrhocorax pyrrhocorax	✓	✓				✓	✓	✓	✓	✓	✓	✓	✓		✓			✓		CF	A		1559
*A	Magpie	Pica pica	✓	✓		✓		✓	✓		✓	✓	✓	✓	✓		✓		✓	✓		MG			1549
*A	Jay	Garrulus glandarius	✓	✓		✓		✓	✓		✓	✓	✓	✓	✓		✓		✓			J			1539
A	Nutcracker	Nucifraga caryocatactes	14	✓				✓	✓		✓	✓						✓				NC		R	1557
*A	Jackdaw	Corvus monedula	✓	✓		✓		✓	✓		✓	✓	✓	✓	✓		✓		✓	✓		JD			1560
*A	Rook	Corvus frugilegus	✓	✓		✓		✓	✓		✓	✓	✓	✓	✓		✓		✓			RO			1563
*A	Carrion Crow	Corvus corone	✓	✓		✓		✓	✓		✓	✓	✓	✓	✓		✓		✓	✓		C		R	1567
*A	Hooded Crow	Corvus cornix	✓	✓		✓		✓									✓								1567
	Sub total																							

'CRESTS' TITS, LARKS, MARTINS AND SWALLOWS

BOU	Species	Life list	2015 list	24 hr	Garden	Holiday	Jan	Feb	Mar	Apr	May	Jun	Jul	Aug	Sep	Oct	Nov	Dec	BTO	RBBP	BBRC	EU No
*A	Raven — *Corvus corax*	✓						✓					✓						RN			1572
*A	Goldcrest — *Regulus regulus*	✓	✓		✓			✓		✓	✓	✓	✓						GC			1314
*A	Firecrest — *Regulus ignicapilla*	93	✓	✓															FC	A		1315
A	Penduline Tit — *Remiz pendulinus*	03	✓	✓															DT	C	R	1490
*A	Blue Tit — *Cyanistes caeruleus*	✓	✓	✓	✓		✓	✓	✓	✓	✓	✓	✓	✓		✓	✓	✓	BT			1462
*A	Great Tit — *Parus major*	✓	✓	✓	✓		✓	✓	✓	✓	✓	✓	✓	✓		✓	✓	✓	GT			1464
*A	Crested Tit — *Lophophanes cristatus*	96	✓																CI			1454
*A	Coal Tit — *Periparus ater*	✓		✓	✓		✓		✓	✓		✓	✓	✓		✓	✓	✓	CT			1461
*A	Willow Tit — *Poecile montana*	97	✓																WT	A		1442
*A	Marsh Tit — *Poecile palustris*	✓	✓																MT			1440
*A	Bearded Tit — *Panurus biarmicus*	4	✓	✓											(2)					BR	A		1364
A	Calandra Lark — *Melanocorypha calandra*		✓	✓																		R	0961
A	Bimaculated Lark — *Melanocorypha bimaculata*																					R	0962
A	White-winged Lark — *Melanocorypha leucoptera*																					R	0965
A	Black Lark — *Melanocorypha yeltoniensis*																					R	0966
A	Short-toed Lark — *Calandrella brachydactyla*	05	✓									✓	✓		✓					VL		R	0968
A	Lesser Short-toed Lark — *Calandrella rufescens*	08	✓									✓	✓									R	0970
AE	Crested Lark — *Galerida cristata*	92	✓								✓	✓	✓	✓								R	0972
*A	Woodlark — *Lullula arborea*	91	✓	✓							✓				✓					WL	A		0974
*A	Skylark — *Alauda arvensis*	12	✓	✓										✓						S			0976
*A	Shore Lark — *Eremophila alpestris*	✓											✓	✓						SX	B		0978
*A	Sand Martin — *Riparia riparia*	94	✓																	SM			0981
A	Tree Swallow — *Tachycineta bicolor*																					R	0983
A	Purple Martin — *Progne subis*																					R	0989
	Sub total																					

73

SWALLOWS Cont, WARBLERS

BOU		Scientific name	Life list	2015 list	24 hr	Garden	Holiday	Jan	Feb	Mar	Apr	May	Jun	Jul	Aug	Sep	Oct	Nov	Dec	BTO	RBBP	BBRC	EU No
A	Crag Martin	*Ptyonoprogne rupestris*	95												✓							R	0991
*A	Swallow	*Hirundo rustica*	✓	✓							25	✓	✓	✓	✓					SL			0992
*A	House Martin	*Delichon urbicum*	✓	✓								✓	✓	✓	✓					HM			1001
A	Red-rumped Swallow	*Cecropis daurica*	72																	VR	C		0995
A	Cliff Swallow	*Petrochelidon pyrrhonota*																				R	0998
*A	Cetti's Warbler	*Cettia cetti*	94			✓		✓						✓	✓					CW	A		1220
*A	Long-tailed Tit	*Aegithalos caudatus*	✓			✓		✓	✓	✓			✓	✓						LT			1437
A	Eastern Crowned Warbler	*Phylloscopus coronatus*									✓						✓	✓	✓			R	12860
A	Green Warbler	*Phylloscopus nitidus*																		NP	C	R	12910
A	Greenish Warbler	*Phylloscopus trochiloides*																					1293
A	Arctic Warbler	*Phylloscopus borealis*																		AP		R	1295
A	Pallas's Warbler	*Phylloscopus proregulus*																		PA			1298
*A	Yellow-browed Warbler	*Phylloscopus inornatus*	09																	YB			1300
A	Hume's Warbler	*Phylloscopus humei*																				R	1300
A	Radde's Warbler	*Phylloscopus schwarzi*																					1301
A	Dusky Warbler	*Phylloscopus fuscatus*																		UY			1303
A	Western Bonelli's Warbler	*Phylloscopus bonelli*	✓												✓					IW		R	1307
A	Eastern Bonelli's Warbler	*Phylloscopus orientalis*																				R	1307
*A	Wood Warbler	*Phylloscopus sibilatrix*	95	✓								✓	✓	✓						WO			1308
*A	Chiffchaff	*Phylloscopus collybita*	✓	✓							H	✓	✓							CC			1311
A	Iberian Chiffchaff	*Phylloscopus ibericus*	03	✓								✓									C	R	1311
*A	Willow Warbler	*Phylloscopus trochilus*	✓	✓							H	✓								WW			1312
*A	Blackcap	*Sylvia atricapilla*	✓	✓							H									BC			1277
*A	Garden Warbler	*Sylvia borin*	✓	✓																GW			1276
	Sub total																						

WARBLERS Cont

BOU	Species		Life list	2015 list	24 hr	Garden	Holiday	Jan	Feb	Mar	Apr	May	Jun	Jul	Aug	Sep	Oct	Nov	Dec	BTO	RBBP	BBRC	EU No
A	Barred Warbler	Sylvia nisoria	✓																	RR			1273
*A	Lesser Whitethroat	Sylvia curruca	08																	LW			1274
A	Orphean Warbler	Sylvia hortensis																			C	R	1272
A	Desert Warbler	Sylvia nana																			C	R	1270
*A	Whitethroat	Sylvia communis	✓								23	✓								WH			1275
A	Spectacled Warbler	Sylvia conspicillata									23	✓									C	R	1264
*A	Dartford Warbler	Sylvia undata	94																	DW	A		1262
A	Marmora's Warbler	Sylvia sarda	01																	MM	C	R	1261
A	Rüppell's Warbler	Sylvia rueppelli	92																			R	1269
A	Subalpine Warbler	Sylvia cantillans	95																		C		1265
A	Sardinian Warbler	Sylvia melanocephala	95																		C	R	1267
A	Pallas's Grasshopper Warbler	Locustella certhiola																				R	1233
A	Lanceolated Warbler	Locustella lanceolata																				R	1235
*A	Grasshopper Warbler	Locustella naevia	✓																	GH			1236
A	River Warbler	Locustella fluviatilis																			VW	C	R	1237
A	Savi's Warbler	Locustella luscinioides	01																	VI	A	R	1238
A	Thick-billed Warbler	Iduna aedon																					R	1254
A	Booted Warbler	Iduna caligata																				C	R	1256
A	Sykes's Warbler	Iduna rama																					R	12562
A	Eastern Olivaceous Warbler	Iduna pallida	05																			R	1255
A	Olive-tree Warbler	Hippolais olivetorum	10																			R	12580
*A	Icterine Warbler	Hippolais icterina	97																	IC	B		1259
*A	Melodious Warbler	Hippolais polyglotta	76																	ME	C		1260
A	Aquatic Warbler	Acrocephalus paludicola																			AQ			1242
	Sub total																						

BOU	WARBLERS Cont, WAXWNGS, NUTHATCHES, TREECREEPERS AND THRUSHES		Life list	2015 list	24 hr	Garden	Holiday	Jan	Feb	Mar	Apr	May	Jun	Jul	Aug	Sep	Oct	Nov	Dec		BTO	RBBP	BBRC	EU No
*A	Sedge Warbler	*Acrocephalus schoenobaenus*	✓	✓									✓	H H	✓						SW			1243
A	Paddyfield Warbler	*Acrocephalus agricola*																			PY		R	1247
A	Blyth's Reed Warbler	*Acrocephalus dumetorum*		✓																		C	R	1248
*A	Marsh Warbler	*Acrocephalus palustris*																			MW	A		1250
*A	Reed Warbler	*Acrocephalus scirpaceus*	✓	✓									H	H ✓							RW			1251
A	Great Reed Warbler	*Acrocephalus arundinaceus*	96																		QW	C	R	1253
A	Fan-tailed Warbler	*Cisticola juncidis*	95																				R	1226
A	Cedar Waxwing	*Bombycilla cedrorum*	93																				R	1046
*AE	Waxwing	*Bombycilla garrulus*	1?			✓															WX	C		1048
A	Wallcreeper	*Tichodroma muraria*	89										✓										R	1482
A	Red-breasted Nuthatch	*Sitta canadensis*	93										✓										R	1472
*A	Nuthatch	*Sitta europaea*	✓	✓				✓	✓								H				NH			1479
*A	Treecreeper	*Certhia familiaris*	✓	✓				✓	✓				✓								TC		R	1486
A	Short-toed Treecreeper	*Certhia brachydactyla*	96										✓								TH	C	R	1487
*A	Wren	*Troglodytes troglodytes*	✓	✓		✓		✓	✓	✓✓✓	✓✓	✓	✓	✓			✓	✓	✓		WR			1066
AE	Northern Mockingbird	*Mimus polyglottos*	93																				R	1067
A	Brown Thrasher	*Toxostoma rufum*																					R	1069
A	Grey Catbird	*Dumetella carolinensis*																					R	1080
*A	Starling	*Sturnus vulgaris*	✓	✓				✓	✓	✓	✓	✓	✓	✓			✓	✓	✓		SG			1582
A	Rose-coloured Starling	*Pastor roseus*																			OE			1594
*A	Dipper	*Cinclus cinclus*	✓	✓					✓		✓		✓				✓				DI			1050
A	White's Thrush	*Zoothera dauma*																					R	1170
A	Varied Thrush	*Ixoreus naevius*	94																		VT		R	1172
A	Wood Thrush	*Hylocichla mustelina*	02																				R	1175
	Sub total																							

THRUSHES Cont, CHATS, FLYCATCHERS, ROBINS

BOU	Species	Scientific	Life list	2015 list	24 hr	Garden	Holiday	Jan	Feb	Mar	Apr	May	Jun	Jul	Aug	Sep	Oct	Nov	Dec	BTO	RBBP	BBRC	EU No
A	Hermit Thrush	Catharus guttatus	93																			R	1176
AE	Swainson's Thrush	Catharus ustulatus	94																			R	1177
A	Grey-cheeked Thrush	Catharus minimus																				R	1178
A	Veery	Catharus fuscescens	94																			R	1179
A	Siberian Thrush	Geokichla sibirica																				R	1171
*A	Ring Ouzel	Turdus torquatus	94	✓		✓		✓		✓	✓	✓	✓	✓	✓		✓	✓		RZ			1186
*A	Blackbird	Turdus merula																			B			1187
*A	Eyebrowed Thrush	Turdus obscurus	✓	✓								✓						✓	✓	✓			R	1195
A	Dusky Thrush	Turdus eunomus																					R	1196
A	Naumann's Thrush	Turdus naumanni																					R	11960
A	Black-throated Thrush	Turdus atrogularis																					R	1197
A	Red-throated Thrush	Turdus ruficollis																					R	11970
*A	Fieldfare	Turdus pilaris	✓	✓		✓		✓							✓				✓	FF	A		1198
*A	Song Thrush	Turdus philomelos	✓	✓		✓		✓	H						✓	✓			✓	ST			1200
*A	Redwing	Turdus iliacus	✓	✓		✓		✓	H	✓	✓	✓	✓	✓					✓	RE	A		1201
*A	Mistle Thrush	Turdus viscivorus	✓	✓		✓		H	H	✓	H	H	✓						✓	M			1202
AE	American Robin	Turdus migratorius	73																	AR		R	1203
A	Rufous Bush Chat	Cercotrichas galactotes	10																				R	1095
A	Brown Flycatcher	Muscicapa dauurica											✓									R	
*A	Spotted Flycatcher	Muscicapa striata	✓	✓		✓																	1335
*A	Robin	Erithacus rubecula	✓	✓		✓		✓		✓	✓	✓	✓	✓	✓	✓		✓		✓	R			1099
A	Siberian Blue Robin	Larvivora cyane																					R	1112
A	Rufous-tailed Robin	Larvivora sibilans																					R	1102
A	White-throated Robin	Irania gutturalis																					R	1117
	Sub total																						

FLYCATCHERS Cont, CHATS, WHEATEARS

BOU		Name	Scientific name	Life list	2015 list	24 hr	Garden	Holiday	Jan	Feb	Mar	Apr	May	Jun	Jul	Aug	Sep	Oct	Nov	Dec	BTO	RBBP	BBRC	EU No
A		Thrush Nightingale	Luscinia luscinia	✓	✓																FN	C	R	1103
*A		Nightingale	Luscinia megarhynchos	78										✓							N			1104
A		Bluethroat	Luscinia svecica																		BU	B		1106
A		Siberian Rubythroat	Calliope calliope																				R	1105
AE		Red-flanked Bluetail	Tarsiger cyanurus																				R	1113
*A		Red-breasted Flycatcher	Ficedula parva																		FY			1343
A		Taiga Flycatcher	Ficedula albicilla																				R	1343
A		Collared Flycatcher	Ficedula albicollis																				R	1348
*A		Pied Flycatcher	Ficedula hypoleuca																		PF			1349
*A		Black Redstart	Phoenicurus ochruros	93									✓								BX	A		1121
*A		Redstart	Phoenicurus phoenicurus	94									✓								RT			1122
A		Moussier's Redstart	Phoenicurus moussieri	94																			R	1127
A		Rock Thrush	Monticola saxatilis	✓																	OH		R	1162
AE		Blue Rock Thrush	Monticola solitarius	✓																			R	1166
*A		Whinchat	Saxicola rubetra	94																	WC			1137
A		Siberian Stonechat	Saxicola maurus																				R	
*A		Stonechat	Saxicola rubicola	✓									✓								SC			1139
A		Isabelline Wheatear	Oenanthe isabellina	12																			R	1144
*A		Wheatear	Oenanthe oenanthe	✓								✓									W			1146
A		Pied Wheatear	Oenanthe pleschanka	75																	PI		R	1147
A		Black-eared Wheatear	Oenanthe hispanica	92																			R	1148
A		Desert Wheatear	Oenanthe deserti																				R	1149
A		White-crowned Black Wheatear	Oenanthe leucopyga																✓	✓			R	1157
*A		Dunnock	Prunella modularis	✓	✓		✓		✓	✓	✓			✓							D			1084
		Sub total																						

SPARROWS, WAGTAILS, PIPITS AND FINCHES

BOU		Scientific	Life list	2015 list	24 hr	Garden	Holiday	Jan	Feb	Mar	Apr	May	Jun	Jul	Aug	Sep	Oct	Nov	Dec	BTO	RBBP	BBRC	EU No
A	Alpine Accentor	Prunella collaris	89					✓			✓	✓	✓	✓	✓			✓	✓			R	1094
*A	House Sparrow	Passer domesticus	✓					✓	✓		✓	✓	✓	✓	✓		✓	✓	✓	HS			1591
A	Spanish Sparrow	Passer hispaniolensis	93								✓						✓					R	1592
*A	Tree Sparrow	Passer montanus	95	✓					✓								✓			TS			1598
A	Rock Sparrow	Petronia petronia	96	✓																		R	1604
*A	Yellow Wagtail	Motacilla flava	✓									✓	✓	✓	✓					YW			1017
A	Citrine Wagtail	Motacilla citreola	09																		C	R	1018
*A	Grey Wagtail	Motacilla cinerea	✓	✓					✓	✓	✓	✓		✓		✓			✓	✓	GL			1019
*A	Pied Wagtail	Motacilla alba	✓	✓					✓	✓	✓	✓	✓	✓	✓	✓		✓	✓	✓	PW			1020
A	Richard's Pipit	Anthus richardi									✓	✓		✓				✓	✓		PR			1002
A	Blyth's Pipit	Anthus godlewskii																					R	1004
A	Tawny Pipit	Anthus campestris	95																		TI			1005
A	Olive-backed Pipit	Anthus hodgsoni																			OV		R	1008
*A	Tree Pipit	Anthus trivialis	✓	✓									✓								TP			1009
A	Pechora Pipit	Anthus gustavi		✓																			R	1010
*A	Meadow Pipit	Anthus pratensis		✓								✓		✓	✓	✓					MP			1011
A	Red-throated Pipit	Anthus cervinus	95	✓				✓			✓	✓						✓			VP			1012
*A	Rock Pipit	Anthus petrosus	96	✓				✓	✓	✓	✓	✓	✓	✓	✓	✓		✓	✓	✓	RC			1014
*A	Water Pipit	Anthus spinoletta	96	✓					✓		✓	✓	✓	✓	✓	✓		✓		✓	WI			1014
A	Buff-bellied Pipit	Anthus rubescens	94	✓																			R	1014
*AE	Chaffinch	Fringilla coelebs	✓	✓		✓		✓	✓	✓	✓			✓	✓		✓	✓	✓	CH			1636
*A	Brambling	Fringilla montifringilla	94	✓				✓	✓	✓										BL	B		1638
*AE	Greenfinch	Chloris chloris	96	✓				✓	✓		✓			✓			✓	✓		GR			1649
*A	Serin	Serinus serinus	96	✓							✓	✓			✓		✓	✓	✓	NS	B		1640
	Sub total																						

FINCHES AND NEW WORLD BUNTINGS

BOU	Species	Scientific name	Life list	2015 list	24 hr	Garden	Holiday	Jan	Feb	Mar	Apr	May	Jun	Jul	Aug	Sep	Oct	Nov	Dec		BTO	RBBP	BBRC	EU No
A	Citril Finch	Carduelis citrinella																					R	1653
*A	Goldfinch	Carduelis carduelis	✓	✓				✓	✓		✓		✓	✓	✓		✓	✓			GO			1654
*A	Siskin	Carduelis spinus	✓	✓									✓	✓	✓						SK			1660
*A	Linnet	Carduelis cannabina	✓	✓							✓		✓	✓							LI			1662
*A	Twite	Carduelis flavirostris	78																		TW			1663
*A	Lesser Redpoll	Carduelis cabaret	99																		LR			1663
*A	Mealy Redpoll	Carduelis flammea	✓																			A		1664
A	Arctic Redpoll	Carduelis hornemanni																			AL			1665
*A	Two-barred Crossbill	Loxia leucoptera	74																		PD		R	1666
*A	Common Crossbill	Loxia curvirostra																			CR			1667
*A	Scottish Crossbill	Loxia scotica																			CY			1668
*A	Parrot Crossbill	Loxia pytyopsittacus																			PC	A		1676
AE	Trumpeter Finch	Bucanetes githagineus																					R	1679
*A	Common Rosefinch	Carpodacus erythrinus																			SQ	B		1699
AE	Pine Grosbeak	Pinicola enucleator																					R	1710
*A	Bullfinch	Pyrrhula pyrrhula	✓	✓							✓										BF			1717
*A	Hawfinch	Coccothraustes coccothraustes	93																		HF	A	R	1718
A	Evening Grosbeak	Hesperiphona vespertina	95																				R	1850
*A	Snow Bunting	Plectrophenax nivalis																			SB	A		1847
A	Lapland Bunting	Calcarius lapponicus																			LA	B		1786
A	Summer Tanager	Piranga rubra	62																				R	1788
A	Scarlet Tanager	Piranga olivacea																					R	1887
A	Rose-breasted Grosbeak	Pheucticus ludovicianus																					R	1892
AE	Indigo Bunting	Passerina cyanea																					R	
	Sub total																							

NEW WORLD SPARROWS AND BUNTINGS

BOU	Species	Scientific name	Life list	2015 list	24 hr	Garden	Holiday	Jan	Feb	Mar	Apr	May	Jun	Jul	Aug	Sep	Oct	Nov	Dec		BTO	RBBP	BBRC	EU No
A	**Eastern Towhee**	*Pipilo erythrophthalmus*	94																				R	1798
A	**Lark Sparrow**	*Chondestes grammacus*																					R	1824
A	**Savannah Sparrow**	*Passerculus sandwichensis*	95																				R	1826
AE	**Song Sparrow**	*Melospiza melodia*	93	✓																			R	1835
AE	**White-crowned Sparrow**	*Zonotrichia leucophrys*	93																				R	1839
AE	**White-throated Sparrow**	*Zonotrichia albicollis*	93																		JU		R	1840
AE	**Dark-eyed Junco**	*Junco hyemalis*	93																				R	1842
AE	**Black-faced Bunting**	*Emberiza spodocephala*																					R	1853
A	**Pine Bunting**	*Emberiza leucocephalos*		✓															✓		EL		R	1856
*A	**Yellowhammer**	*Emberiza citrinella*									✓	✓	✓								Y			1857
*A	**Cirl Bunting**	*Emberiza cirlus*	96	✓																	CL	A		1958
A	**Rock Bunting**	*Emberiza cia*																					R	1860
A	**Ortolan Bunting**	*Emberiza hortulana*	00																		OB		R	1866
A	**Cretzschmar's Bunting**	*Emberiza caesia*	95																				R	1868
A	**Yellow-browed Bunting**	*Emberiza chrysophrys*																					R	1871
A	**Rustic Bunting**	*Emberiza rustica*																						1873
A	**Chestnut-eared Bunting**	*Emberiza fucata*																					R	1869
A	**Little Bunting**	*Emberiza pusilla*																			LJ			1874
A	**Yellow-breasted Bunting**	*Emberiza aureola*																				C	R	1876
*A	**Reed Bunting**	*Emberiza schoeniclus*	✓								✓		✓	✓							RB			1877
A	**Pallas's Reed Bunting**	*Emberiza pallasi*	92																				R	1878
AE	**Black-headed Bunting**	*Emberiza melanocephala*																					R	1881
*A	**Corn Bunting**	*Emberiza calandra*																			CB			1882
A	**Bobolink**	*Dolichonyx oryzivorus*	✓																				R	1897
	Sub total																							

81

BOU	NEW WORLD WARBLERS		Life list	2015 list	24 hr	Garden	Holiday	Jan	Feb	Mar	Apr	May	Jun	Jul	Aug	Sep	Oct	Nov	Dec				BTO	RBBP	BBRC	EU No
A	Brown-headed Cowbird	Molothrus ater																							R	1899
AE	Baltimore Oriole	Icterus galbula																							R	1918
A	Ovenbird	Seiurus aurocapilla																							R	1756
A	Northern Waterthrush	Parkesia noveboracensis																							R	1757
A	Golden-winged Warbler	Vermivora chrysoptera																							R	1722
A	Black-and-white Warbler	Mniotilta varia	02																						R	1720
A	Tennessee Warbler	Oreothlypis peregrina	02																						R	1724
A	Common Yellowthroat	Geothlypis trichas																							R	1762
A	Hooded Warbler	Setophaga citrina																							R	1771
AE	American Redstart	Setophaga ruticilla	02																					AD		R	1755
A	Cape May Warbler	Setophaga tigrina																							R	1749
AE	Northern Parula	Setophaga americana																							R	1732
A	Magnolia Warbler	Setophaga magnolia																							R	1750
A	Bay-breasted Warbler	Setophaga castanea																							R	1754
A	Blackburnian Warbler	Setophaga fusca	02																						R	1747
A	Yellow Warbler	Setophaga petechia	04 02																						R	1733
A	Chestnut-sided Warbler	Setophaga pensylvanica																							R	1734
AE	Blackpoll Warbler	Setophaga striata	93																						R	1753
A	Yellow-rumped Warbler	Setophaga coronata																							R	1751
A	Wilson's Warbler	Cardellina pusilla																							R	1772
	Sub total																									

CATEGORY D & E SPECIES, PLUS SELECTED EUROPEAN SPECIES

BOU	Species	Scientific name	Life list	2015 list	24 hr	Garden	Holiday	Jan	Feb	Mar	Apr	May	Jun	Jul	Aug	Sep	Oct	Nov	Dec	BTO	RBBP	BBRC	EU No
D	Ross's Goose	Anser rossii																		FT		R	0181
D	Falcated Duck	A. falcata																				R	0195
D	Marbled Duck	Marmaronetta angustirostris																		WQ			0226
EU	White-headed Duck	Oxyura leucocephala	96																				0357
EU	Rock Partridge	Alectoris graeca																					0359
EU	Barbary Partridge	A. barbara	94																				0082
EU	Pygmy Cormorant	P. pygmeus																					0088
D	Great White Pelican	Pelecanus onocrotalus	98																	YP		R	0089
EU	Dalmatian Pelican	P. crispus	98																				0147
D	Greater Flamingo	Phoenicopterus roseus	95																	FL			0235
EU	Black-winged Kite	Elanus caeruleus	97																				0244
D	Bald Eagle	H. leucocephalus	93																			R	0246
EU	Lammergeier	Gypaetus barbatus	92																				0255
D	Black Vulture	Aegypius monachus	96																			R	0273
EU	Levant Sparrowhawk	A. brevipes																					0288
EU	Long-legged Buzzard	B. rufinus	00																				0292
EU	Lesser Spotted Eagle	Aquila pomarina	98																				0295
EU	Imperial Eagle	A. heliaca	98																				0298
EU	Booted Eagle	Hieraaetus pennatus	96																				0299
EU	Bonelli's Eagle	H. fasciatus	98																				0314
EU	Lanner Falcon	Falco biarmicus	10																	FB			0316
D	Saker Falcon	F. cherrug																		JF		R	
E	Griffon Vulture	Gyps fulvus E																					
EU	Andalusian Hemipode	Turnix sylvatica																					0400
	Sub total																						

83

BOU	CATEGORY D & E SPECIES, PLUS SELECTED EUROPEAN SPECIES		Life list	2015 list	24 hr	Garden	Holiday	Jan	Feb	Mar	Apr	May	Jun	Jul	Aug	Sep	Oct	Nov	Dec				BTO	RBBP	BBRC	EU No
EU	Purple Gallinule	Porphyrio porphyrio	98																							0427
EL	Crested Coot	F. cristata	97																							0431
EU	Spur-winged Plover	Hoplopterus spinosus																					UW			0487
EU	Black-bellied Sandgrouse	Pterocles orientalis																								0661
EU	Pin-tailed Sandgrouse	P. alchata																								0662
EU	Eagle Owl	Bubo bubo	4																				EO	bD		0744
EU	Pygmy Owl	Glaucidium passerinum																								0751
EU	Ural Owl	S. uralensis																								0765
EU	Great Grey Owl	S. nebulosa																								0766
EL	White-rumped Swift	Apus caffer																								0799
EU	Grey-headed Woodpecker	Picus canus	09																							0855
EU	Black Woodpecker	Dryocopus martius	02																							0863
EU	Syrian Woodpecker	D. syriacus	14																							0878
EU	Middle Spotted Woodpecker	D. medius	10																							0883
EU	White-backed Woodpecker	D. leucotos																								0884
EU	Three-toed Woodpecker	Picoides tridactylus																								0898
EU	Dupont's Lark	Chersophilus duponti																								0959
EL	Thekla Lark	G. theklae	96																							0973
EU	Black Wheatear	Oenanthe leucura	96																						R	1158
EU	Cyprus Wheater	O. cypriaca	95																							
EU	Cyprus Warbler	S. melanothorax																								1268
D	Mugimaki Flycatcher	F. mugimaki																							R	1344
EU	Semi-collared Flycatcher	F. semitorquata	95																							1347
EU	Sombre Tit	P. lugubris	10																							1441
	Sub total																								

BOU	CATEGORY D & E SPECIES, PLUS SELECTED EUROPEAN SPECIES		Life list	2015 list	24 hr	Garden	Holiday	Jan	Feb	Mar	Apr	May	Jun	Jul	Aug	Sep	Oct	Nov	Dec					BTO	RBBP	BBRC	EU No
EU	Siberian Tit	*P. cinctus*																									1448
EU	Krüper's Nuthatch	*Sitta krueperi*																									1469
EU	Corsican Nuthatch	*S. whiteheadi*																									1470
EU	Rock Nuthatch	*S. neumayer*																									1481
EU	Siberian Jay	*Perisoreus infaustus*																									1543
EU	Azure-winged Magpie	*Cyanopica cyana*	00																								1547
EU	Alpine Chough	*Pyrrhocorax graculus*	✓																								1558
D	Daurian Starling	*Sturnus sturninus*																								R	1579
EU	Spotless Starling	*S. unicolor*	96																								1583
D	Snow Finch	*Montifringilla nivalis*	02																							R	1611
D	Palm Warbler	*D. palmarum*	93																							R	1752
D	Yellow-headed Blackbird	*Xanthocephalus xanthocephalus*																									1911
EU	Cinereous Bunting	*E. cinerea*	10																								1865
D	Chestnut Bunting	*E. rutila*																								R	1875
D	Red-headed Bunting	*E. bruniceps*																									1880
D	Blue Grosbeak	*Guiraca caerulea*																								R	1891
	Sub total																									

BRITISH BUTTERFLY LIST

SPECIES	2015 list	Life list
Hesperiidae - **Skippers**		
Chequered Skipper		
Dingy Skipper		
Essex Skipper		
Grizzled Skipper		
Large Skipper		
Lulworth Skipper		
Silver-spotted Skipper		
Small Skipper		
Papilionidae		
Scarce Swallowtail (Rare migrant)		
Swallowtail		
Swallowtail European Race (Rare migrant)		
Pieridae - **The Whites**		
Bath White (rare migrant)		
Berger's Clouded Yellow (rare migrant)		
Brimstone		
Clouded Yellow (migrant)		
Green-veined White		
Large White		
Orange-tip		
Pale Clouded Yellow (rare migrant)		
Real's Wood White		
Small White		
Wood White		
Lycaenidae - **Hairstreaks, Coppers and Blues**		
Adonis Blue		
Black Hairstreak		
Brown Argus		

SPECIES	2015 list	Life list
Brown Hairstreak		
Chalkhill Blue		
Common Blue		
Green Hairstreak		
Holly Blue		
Large Blue		
Long-tailed Blue (rare migrant)		
Northern Brown Argus		
Purple Hairstreak		
Short-tailed Blue (rare migrant)		
Silver-studded Blue		
Small Blue		
Small Copper		
White-letter Hairstreak		
Riodinidae - **Metalmarks**		
Duke of Burgundy		
Nymphalidae - **Vanessids, Emperors and Fritillaries**		
Camberwell Beauty (rare migrant)		
Comma		
Dark Green Fritillary		
Gatekeeper		
Glanville Fritillary		
Grayling		
Heath Fritillary		
High Brown Fritillary		
Marsh Fritillary		
Painted Lady		
Peacock		
Pearl-bordered Fritillary		

BRITISH BUTTERFLY LIST

SPECIES	2015 list	Life list
Purple Emperor		
Queen of Spain Fritillary (rare migrant)		
Red Admiral		
Silver-washed Fritillary		
Small Pearl-bordered Fritillary		
Small Tortoiseshell		
White Admiral		
Satyridae - **The Browns**		
Gate Keeper		
Grayling		

SPECIES	2015 list	Life list
Large Heath		
Marbled White		
Meadow Brown		
Mountain Ringlet		
Ringlet		
Scotch Argus		
Small Heath		
Speckled Wood		
Wall		
TOTAL		

BRITISH DRAGONFLY LIST

SPECIES	2015 list	Life list
DAMSELFLIES		
Calopterygidae (Demoiselles)		
Banded Demoiselle		
Beautiful Demoiselle		
Coenagrionidae (Blue, blue-tailed & red damselflies)		
Small Red Damselfly		
Northern Damselfly		
Irish Damselfly		
Southern Damselfly		
Azure Damselfly		
Variable Damselfly		
Dainty Damselfly		
Common Blue Damselfly		
Red-eyed Damselfly		
Small Red-eyed Damselfly		
Blue-tailed Damselfly		
Scarce Blue-tailed Damselfly		
Large Red Damselfly		
Lestidae (Emerald damselflies)		
Southern Emerald Damselfly		
Scarce Emerald Damselfly		
Emerald Damselfly		
Southern Emerald Damselfly		
Willow Emerald Damselfly		
Winter Damselfly		
Platycnemididae (White-legged damselflies)		
White-legged Damselfly		
DRAGONFLIES		
Aeshnidae (Hawkers and Emperors)		
Southern Migrant Hawker		
Azure Hawker		
Southern Hawker		
Brown Hawker		

SPECIES	2015 list	Life list
Norfolk Hawker		
Common Hawker		
Migrant Hawker		
Vagrant Emperor		
Emperor Dragonfly		
Lesser Emperor		
Hairy Dragonfly		
Cordulegastridae (Golden-ringed Dragonflies)		
Golden-ringed Dragonfly		
Corduliidae (Emerald dragonflies)		
Downy Emerald		
Orange-spotted Emerald		
Northern Emerald		
Brilliant Emerald		
Gomphidae (Club-tailed Dragonflies)		
Common Club-tail		
Libellulidae (Chasers, Skimmers and Darters)		
Scarlet Darter		
White-faced Darter		
Broad-bodied Chaser		
Scarce Chaser		
Four-spotted Chaser		
Black-tailed Skimmer		
Keeled Skimmer		
Wandering Glider		
Black Darter		
Vagrant Darter		
Yellow-winged Darter		
Red-veined Darter		
Banded Darter		
Ruddy Darter		
Common Darter		
TOTAL		

NATURE RESERVES AND OBSERVATORIES

Mike Langman

Prominent wildlife artist Mike Langman created this sand-blasted design, for a viewing platform, at Slapton Ley NNR, one of the sites featured in the Devon section of this guide to key birding areas.

ALL ENTRIES in the Reserves Directory are listed on a regional basis as it is felt that grouping counties into regions will be more helpful to our readers.

This year we have made every effort to include postcodes for sites, to aid sat-nav users. We hope this proves helpful but welcome reader feedback on any way we can improve this section of the *Yearbook*.

Please e-mail your comments to the Editor, David Cromack at: d.cromack@btinternet.com

ENGLAND		SCOTLAND		WALES	
Central England	90	Border Counties	180	Eastern Wales	195
Eastern England	112	Central Scotland	182	Northern Wales	197
Northern England	130	Eastern Scotland	187	Southern Wales	200
South East England	151	Highlands & Islands	190	Western Wales	202
South West England	168				

Central England

Derbyshire, Gloucestershire, Leicestershire & Rutland, Lincolnshire, Northamptonshire, Nottinghamshire, Oxfordshire, Shropshire, Staffordshire, Warwickshire, West Midlands, Worcestershire

Derbyshire

WITH 75% of the county's population living in towns, Derbyshire can offer birdwatchers many square miles of open countryside, including a large part of the Peak District National Park. Other attractions include Carsington Water, Willington, Ogston and Foremark Reservoirs which attract huge gull roosts in winter. Valleys, such as those in the Peak District, attract Redstarts, Pied Flycatchers and Wood Warblers.

1. CARR VALE NATURE RESERVE

Derbyshire Wildlife Trust.
Location: Sat nav: S44 6JX. SK 459 701. 1km W of Bolsover on A632 to Chesterfield. Turn L at roundabout (follow brown tourist signs) into Riverside Way. Use Stockley Trail car park at end of road.
Access: Open all year. Follow footpath (waymarked) around Peter Fidler reserve. Dogs only on leads.
Facilities: Car park, coach parking on approach road, good disabled access, paths, viewing platforms.
Public transport: Stagecoach services from Chesterfield (Stephenson Place) pass

close to the reserve: Mon to Sat - 83 serves Villas Road, 81, 82, 82A and 83 serve the roundabout on A632. Sun - 81A, 82A serve roundabout on A632.
Habitats: Lakes, wader flashes, reedbed, sewage farm, scrub, arable fields.
Key birds: Up to 150 species seen annually. *Winter:* Large numbers of wildfowl including flocks of Wigeon and Teal, also wintering flocks of finches and buntings, Water Rail. *Spring/autumn:* Migrants include pipits and thrushes. In September Swallows gather in the marsh, in a gigantic roost of between 10-12,000 birds. They usually attract Hobbies. *Early summer:* Breeding birds, including Reed and Sedge Warblers, Whitethroat, Yellowhammer, Moorhen and Gadwall, plus Skylark. Long list of rarities.
Other notable fauna: Dragonflies, hare, grass snake, harvest mouse, water shrew.
Contact: Derbyshire Wildlife Trust, 01773 881 188; e-mail: enquiries@derbyshirewt.co.uk
www.derbyshirewildlifetrust.org.uk

2. CARSINGTON WATER

Severn Trent Water
Location: Sat nav: DE6 1ST. SK 241 515 (for visitor centre and main facilities). Off B5035 Ashbourne to Wirksworth road.
Access: Open all year except Dec 25. Car parks open 7am to sunset (Apr to end Oct), 7.30am to sunset in winter. Good access for wheelchairs, which can be borrowed at Visitor Centre. Mobility scooters for hire. Pay-and-display parking at Visitor Centre with reduced rates at Millfields and Sheepwash car parks.
Facilities: Visitor centre with exhibition, restaurant, four shops (inc RSPB), play area and toilets. Four bird hides and three car parks. Cycle and boat hire.
Public transport: TM Travel operates service 411 from Matlock and Ashbourne. Call TM on 01142 633 890.
Habitats: Open water, islands, mixed woodland, scrub and grasslands, small reedbed.
Key birds: More than 220 bird species recorded. *Winter:* Wildfowl and a large gull roost plus possibility of divers and rare grebes. *Spring:* Good spring passage including Yellow and White Wagtails, Whimbrel, Black and Arctic Terns. *Summer:* Warblers and breeding waders, inc Little Ringed Plovers. *All year:* Tree Sparrows and Willow Tits. Ospreys often stop-off during migration.
Other notable flora and fauna: Species-rich hay meadows, ancient woodlands with bluebells, three species of orchid, five species of bat, 21 species of butterfly and water vole.
Contact: Carsington Water Visitor Centre, 01629 540 696; e-mail: www.carsingtonwater@severntrent.co.uk
www.carsingtonbirdclub.co.uk

3. DRAKELOW NATURE RESERVE

E-ON, leased to Derbyshire Wildlife Trust.
Location: Sat nav: DE14 3FG. SK 223 204. Drakelow Power Station on the outskirts of Branston, one mile NE of Walton-on-Trent, off A38, S of Burton-on-Trent.
Access: Dawn to dusk for Wildlife Trust permit-holders only (plus up to two guests). No dogs.
Facilities: Four main hides, car park inside former power station grounds. Nesting platforms for Ospreys erected.
Public transport: None.
Habitats: Disused flooded gravel pits with wooded islands, riverside meadows and reedbeds.
Key birds: *Summer:* Breeding Reed and Sedge Warblers. Water Rail, Hobby. *Winter:* Wildfowl (Shoveler, Goldeneye, Gadwall), Merlin, Peregrine. Rarities have included Great White Egret, Bittern, Spotted Crake, Ring-necked Duck and American Wigeon.
Other notable flora and fauna: Good for common species of dragonflies and butterflies.
Contact: Trust HQ, 01773 881 188;
e-mail: enquiries@derbyshirewt.co.uk

4. GOYT VALLEY

Forestry Commission.
Location: Sat nav: SK17 6SX (Errwood Hall car park, SK 011 748) for woodland species, Derbyshire Bridge (SK 018 716) for moorland birds. From Buxton head N on A5004 (Manchester Road), then bear left on Goyt's Lane to Errwood Hall one-way system, between Errwood car park and Derbyshire Bridge.
Access: Open all year. Footpath between Errwood Hall and Goyt's Clough Quarry. Use Old Coach Road for walk between Derbyshire Bridge and Burbage.
Facilities: Toilets at Derbyshire Bridge and Bonsal Cob. Several picnic sites.
Public transport: Bowers bus services along A5004.
Habitats: Mixed conifer/bradleaf woodland, moorland, River Goyt and two reservoirs.
Key birds: *Spring/summer:* Breeding Wood Warbler, Pied and Spotted Flycatchers, Tree Pipit, Redstart and Cuckoo, Nightjar on restock areas, plus common woodland species. Long-eared Owls and Goshawks also present. Grey Wagtail and Dipper on river and Common Sandpiper on Errwood Reservoir. Ring Ouzel, Red Grouse, Curlew, Short-eared Owl and Whinchat breed on moorland stretches.
Contact: Forestry Commission, 01623 822 4477;
e-mail: albin.smith@forestry.gsi.gov.uk

5. HILTON GRAVEL PITS

Derbyshire Wildlife Trust.
Location: Sat nav: DE65 5FN (Willowpit Lane). SK 249 315. From Derby, take A516 from Mickleover W past Etwall onto A50 junction at Hilton. Turn R at first island onto Willowpit Lane. Turn L next to a large white house and park next to the gate. Follow track along S side of the pools.
Access: Open all year. Main path and viewing screen suitable for wheelchair users. Dogs on leads only on main perimeter track.
Facilities: Tracks, boardwalks, viewing screens.
Public transport: Local Trent Barton Villager V1 & V2 bus services from Derby to Burton-on-Trent and Arriva X50 bus service from Derby to Stoke-on-Trent.
Habitats: Ponds, lakes, scrub, woodland, fen.
Key birds: *Spring/summer:* Great Crested Grebe, Common Tern, warblers. *Winter:* Wildfowl, Siskin, Goldcrest. *All year:* All three woodpeckers, Kingfisher, tits inc Willow Tit, Tawny Owl, Bullfinch.
Other notable flora and fauna: Dragonflies (14 species inc emperor and red-eyed damselfly), great crested newt, orchids, black poplar.
Contact: Trust HQ, 01773 881 188;
e-mail: enquiries@derbyshirewt.co.uk

6. OGSTON RESERVOIR

Severn Trent Water/Ogston Bird Club
Location: Sat nav: DE55 6FN. SK 371 603. From Matlock, take A615 E to B6014, just after Tansley. From A61 (Alfreton to Chesterfield road), at White Bear pub, Stretton turn onto B6014 towards Tansley, cross the railway, take left fork in the road and continue over the hill. The reservoir is on L after hill.
Access: View from roads. Three car parks on north, south and west banks. Public hide is accessed from west bank car park. Suitable for smaller coaches. Heronry in nearby Ogston Carr Wood (private property) viewable from Ogston new road, W of reservoir. Ogston Bird Club organises monthly guided walks (see website for details).
Facilities: One public hide is wheelchair-accessible, Ogston Bird Club members have access to three hides (one wheelchair-accessible) as well as the club's own two-acre Jim Mart Nature Reserve three miles north of Ogston. Information pack provided to all new bird club members. Toilets now closed.
Public transport: Hulleys 63 bus service (Chesterfield to Clay Cross) and 64 service (Clay Cross to Matlock) both serves N end of reservoir (not Sundays).
Habitats: Open water, pasture, mixed woodland.
Key birds: All three woodpeckers, Little and Tawny Owls, Kingfisher, Grey Wagtail, warblers. Passage raptors (inc. Osprey), terns and waders. *Winter:* Gull roost attracts thousands of birds, inc regular Glaucous and Iceland Gulls. Top inland site for Bonaparte's Gull and also attracts Caspian/Herring Gull complex. Good numbers of wildfowl, tit and finch flocks.
Contact: Peter Birley, Secretary, Ogston Bird Club, 35 Rosemary Drive, Alvaston, Derby DE24 0TA. 01332 753078; e-mail: peter.birley@sky.com
www.ogstonbirdclub.co.uk

7. PADLEY GORGE (LONGSHAW ESTATE)

National Trust (East Midlands).
Location: Sat nav: S11 7TZ (Longshaw visitor centre) SK 267 802. From Sheffield, head SW on A625. After eight miles, turn L on B6521 to Nether Padley. Grindleford Station is just off B6521 (NW of Nether Padley) and one mile NE of Grindleford village.
Access: All year, dawn to dusk. Rocky paths not suitable for disabled people or those unused to steep

climbs. Some of the paths are rocky. Dogs on leads only.
Facilities: Café, shop and toilets (inc disabled) at Longshaw visitor centre. RADAR key needed for Hollin Bank, Hathersage toilets. Car parks (pay-and-display for non NT members).
Public transport: Bus: from Sheffield to Bakewell stops at Grindleford/Nether Padley. Tel: 01709 566 000. Train: from Sheffield to Manchester Piccadilly stops at Grindleford Station. Tel: 0161 228 2141.
Habitats: Steep-sided valley containing largest area of sessile oak woodland in south Pennines.
Key birds: *Spring/summer:* Pied Flycatcher, Spotted Flycatcher, Redstart, Wheatear, Whinchat, Stonechat, Ring Ouzel, Wood Warbler, Tree Pipit, plus common resident woodland species.
Contact: National Trust, High Peak Estate Office, 01433 637 904; www.nationaltrust.org.uk e-mail: peakdistrict@nationaltrust.org.u

8. WILLINGTON GRAVEL PITS

Derbyshire Wildlife Trust
Location: Sat nav: DE65 6BX (Repton Road). SK 285 274. From A50 'Toyota Island' head towards Willington and Repton. Go through village towards Repton. Just before bridge over River Trent, turn R onto un-made track (Meadow Lane). Park here and walk along lane.
Access: Access only along Meadow Lane to viewing platforms all year. No access on site. Steps prevent wheelchair access to platforms.
Facilities: Viewing platforms and benches. Limited parking in lane.
Public transport: Local trains stop at Willington, local Trent Barton Villager V3 bus service from Derby to Burton-on-Trent.
Habitats: Open water, reedbed, shingle island, grassland.
Key birds: *Summer:* Lapwing, Redshank, Oystercatcher, Common Tern, Cetti's, Reed and Sedge Warblers, raptors including Peregrine, Kestrel, Hobby and Sparrowhawk. *Winter:* Bittern, waders and large flocks of wildfowl including Wigeon, Teal, Pochard and Shoveler. *Passage:* Large numbers of Curlew in spring, up to 20 species of waders in spring/autumn.
Other notable flora and fauna: Short-leaved water starwort. Several species of dragonfly, plus occasional otter signs, fox and other mammals.
Contact: Trust HQ, 01773 881 188.

Gloucestershire

STRADDLING the mighty Severn estuary, Gloucestershire can boast a world-famous wetland site in the form of Slimbridge, but on the other side of the river, the Forest of Dean is one of the best places in Britain to see good numbers of Goshawks displaying in February and March. The county Wildlife Trust manages more than 60 nature reserves.

1. CLEVELAND LAKES

Cotswold Water Park Trust.
Location: Sat nav: SN6 6QW (Waterhay Car Park). Lakes 68a/b and 74, Cotswold Water Park. From A419 Cirencester to Swindon road, take B4696 towards Cotswold Water Park West. After 2-3 km turn left on to Fridays Ham Lane. Follow road to Ashton Keynes village and turn left on to road to Cricklade/Leigh. Waterhay Car Park is on the left next to the River Thames (SU 059 933). Take bridleway north to kissing gate on the right. Permissive path follows southern edge of Lake 68a/b before turning north towards two hides.
Access: Open at all times, most paths firm and flat but subject to severe winter flooding. Dogs on short leads at all times.
Facilities: Toilets, refreshments, car parking and information available from Gateway Centre next to A419.
Public transport: Bus: from Kemble, Cheltenham, Cirencester and Swindon. 08457 090 899. Train: Kemble station four miles. 08457 484 950.
Habitats: Lakes with reedbed, scrapes, lagoons, marsh, ditches, islands and loafing areas.

Key birds: *Winter:* Large numbers of many wildfowl species, plus Bittern, Water Rail, Stonechat. *Summer:* Breeding ducks, Great Crested Grebe, warblers, Hobby, Sand Martin, Reed Bunting, Little Egret, Grey Heron. Many of the above species and plenty of passage waders viewable from "Twitchers' Gate" on lane to the north of Lake 74 (SU 065 946).
Other notable flora and fauna: Otter, water vole, several species of dragonfly, damselfly and butterflies.
Contact: Cotswold Water Park Trust, 01793 752 413.

2. HIGHNAM WOODS

RSPB (South West England Office).
Location: Sat nav: GL2 8AA. SO 778 190. Signposted on A40 three miles W of Gloucester.
Access: Open at all times, no permit required. Nature trails can be very muddy. Some limited wheelchair access. Dogs allowed on leads. Groups should book ahead.
Facilities: One nature trail (approx 1.5 miles). One open-backed hide 150m from car park. Car park, usually restricted to reserve events, can be opened for groups by arrangement. No visitor centre or toilets.
Public transport: Contact Traveline on 0871 2002 233 between 7am-10pm each day.
Habitats: Ancient woodland in the Severn Vale with areas of coppice and scrub.
Key birds: *Spring/summer:* Up to 20 pairs of breeding Nightingale, plus common migrant warblers and Spotted Flycatcher. Resident birds include all three woodpeckers, Marsh Tit, Buzzard and Sparrowhawk. Ravens are frequently seen. *Winter:* Feeding site near car park good for woodland birds.
Other notable flora and fauna: Tintern spurge in late June-early July. White-letter hairstreak and white

admiral butterflies seen annually.
Contact: Site Manager, 01594 562 852; e-mail:
highnam.woods@rspb.org.uk; www.rspb.org.uk

3.NAGSHEAD

RSPB (South West England Office).
Location: Sat nav: GL15 4JQ. SO 606 085.
In Forest of Dean, N of Lydney. Signposted
immediately W of Parkend village on
B4431 road to Coleford.
Access: Open at all times, no permit
required. Car park open 8am to dusk.
Information centre (with toilets) open
10am to 4pm at weekends between Easter
and August Bank Holiday. The reserve
is hilly but there is limited wheelchair
access. Keep dogs on leads during bird
nesting season.
Facilities: Two nature trails (one mile
and 2.25 miles). Information centre,
with toilet facilities (including disabled),
open at weekends mid-Apr to end Aug.
Two woodland hides not accessible to
wheelchair users.
Public transport: Buses from Lydney Bus
Station (circular) stop along B4431 signposted to
Coleford. Contact Traveline (0871 2002 233).
Habitats: Much of reserve is 200-year-old oak
plantations, grazed in some areas by sheep. Rest is
a mixture of open areas and conifer/mixed woodland.
Key birds: *Spring:* Pied Flycatcher, Wood Warbler
and commoner warblers, Redstart. *Summer:* Nightjar.
Winter: Siskin, Crossbill in some years. *All year:*
Buzzard, Raven, Hawfinch, Woodcock, all three
woodpeckers.
Other notable fauna: Golden-ringed dragonfly seen
annually. Silver-washed and small pearl-bordered
fritillaries and white admiral butterflies present.
Contact: The Site Manager, 01594 562 852; e-mail:
nagshead@rspb.org.uk

4. SHORNCOTE REEDBED

Thames Water / Cotswold Water Park Trust.
Location: Sat nav: GL7 5US (South Cerney car
park). Lakes 84, 85a and 85b, Cotswold Water Park
West. From A419 Cirencester to Swindon road, take
B4696 towards Cotswold Water Park West. Turn R
at crossroads (station Road) towards South Cerney.
Follow road through village and park in playing
fields car park after sharp R bend (SU 044 970).
Take footpath through playing fields, cross road and
continue on path through reedbeds to small lakes
and hides.
Access: Open at all times. Floods regularly in winter,
so wellies essential.
Facilities: Toilets, refreshments, car parking and
information available from nearby Cotswold Country
Park (entry charge may apply). Two hides. Alternative
refreshments and toilets at Gateway Centre near
A419 junction.
Public transport: Bus: from Kemble, Cheltenham,
Cirencester and Swindon. 08457 090 899. Train:

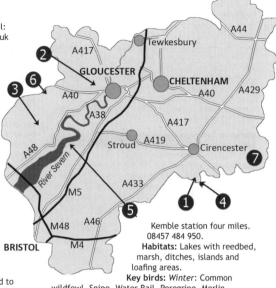

Kemble station four miles.
08457 484 950.
Habitats: Lakes with reedbed,
marsh, ditches, islands and
loafing areas.
Key birds: *Winter:* Common
wildfowl, Snipe, Water Rail, Peregrine, Merlin,
Bittern, Stonechat and Starling flocks. *Summer:*
Breeding ducks, Little Grebe, warblers, Hobby, Snipe,
Sand Martin, Reed Bunting.
Other notable flora and fauna: Otter, water vole,
several species of dragonfly and damselfly.
Contact: Cotswold Water Park Trust, 01793 752 413.

5. SLIMBRIDGE

The Wildfowl & Wetlands Trust.
Location: Sat nav: GL2 7BS. SO 723 048. On banks
of River Severn, S of Gloucester. Signposted from M5
(exit 13 or 14).
Access: Open daily (9am-5.30pm or 5pm in winter)
except Dec 25. Last entry 30 mins before closing.
Wheelchair hire (book beforehand) – all paths
wheelchair accessible. Free parking. Admission
charges for non-WWT members. Assistance dogs only.
Facilities: Restaurant, gift shop, gallery, cinema,
discovery centre. Outdoor facilities inc 15 hides,
tropical house, worldwide collection of wildfowl
species, observatory and observation tower. Plenty
of family attractions including a pond zone, wader
aviary, commentated swan feeds in the winter, Land
Rover safaris and a canoe safari trail. Binoculars for
hire.
Public transport: Request bus service – contact www.
stroud.gov.uk.
Habitats: Reedbed, saltmarsh, freshwater pools,
mudflats and wet grassland.
Key birds: More than 200 species each year. *Winter:*
Between 30,000 to 40,000 wildfowl esp. Bewick's
Swan, White-fronted Goose, Wigeon, Teal, Pintail.
Waders inc Lapwing, Golden Plover, Spotted Redshank
and Little Stint. Often there are large roosts of
Starlings and gulls. *Breeding:* Kingfisher, Lapwing,

Redshank, Oystercatcher, Common Tern, Reed Bunting and a good range of warblers. *Passage:* Waders, terns and gulls, inc Mediterranean and Yellow-legged Gulls. Yellow Wagtail and large passerine movements. Hobbies now reach double figures in summer. Good list of rarities.
Other notable flora and fauna: Brown hare, otter, polecat and water vole. Scarce chaser and hairy dragonfly among 22 recorded species.
Contact: Marketing Manager, 01453 891 900; e-mail: info.slimbridge@wwt.org.uk

6. SYMONDS YAT

RSPB/Forestry Commission England.
Location: Sat nav: HR9 6JL. SO 563 160. Hill-top site on the edge of Forest of Dean, three miles N of Coleford on B4432, signposted from Forest Enterprise car park. Also signposted from A40, S of Ross-on-Wye.
Access: Open at all times. RSPB Information Officer on site daily, April to August.
Facilities: Car park (fee payable), toilets with adapted facilities for disabled visitors, picnic area, drinks and light snacks. Environmental education programmes available.
Public transport: Very limited.
Habitats: Cliff above the River Wye and woodland.
Key birds: *Summer:* Peregrine, Buzzard, Goshawk, Raven and woodland species. Telescope is set up each day (except Tuesdays and Wednesdays) between 10am

and 4pm by RSPB volunteers to watch the Peregrines on the nest (April to August).
Contact: RSPB, 01594 562 852.

7. WHELFORD POOLS

Gloucestershire Wildlife Trust
Location: Sat nav: GL7 4EH. SU 174 995. Lakes lying in eastern section of Cotswold Water Park between Fairford and Lechlade, from minor road south of A417.
Access: Open at all times. Dogs must be on leads.
Facilities: Car park for 12 vehicles (one designated for disabled). Two bird hides.
Public transport: Cycle path from Lechlade.
Habitats: Former gravel pit workings now reverted to nature – part of SSSI. Two large lakes, plus three smaller pools for dragonflies.
Key birds: *Winter:* Wildfowl inc Wigeon, Pochard and Tufted Ducks, plus occasional Bittern sightings. *Spring/summer:* Common Tern, Kingfisher and Nightingale, plus breeding Sedge Warbler, Reed Bunting and Great Crested Grebe. Artificial nesting bank for Sand Martins. Waders on passage.
Other notable flora and fauna: County's only site for pea mussel. Emperor, migrant hawker, blacked-tailed skimmer and red-eyed damselfly all breed.
Contact: Reserve manager (GWT) 01452 383 333; e-mail: info@gloucestershirewildlifetrust.co.uk

Leicestershire and Rutland

A N INLAND COUNTY better known for fox hunting than its birding potential, Leicestershire can boast 32 Wildlife Trust reserves with a broad range of habitats. However, it is the adjoining county of Rutland that holds the jewel in the crown — Rutland Water with its breeding Ospreys, huge numbers of wildfowl, and good selection of passage waders — while nearby Eyebrook Reservoir is excellent for Smew, sizeable Golden Plover flocks and roosting gulls in winter.

1. EYEBROOK RESERVOIR

Corby & District Water Co.
Location: Sat nav: LE15 9JG. SP 853 964. Reservoir built 1940. S of Uppingham, from unclassified road W of A6003 at Stoke Dry.
Access: Access to 150 acres of private grounds granted to members of Leics and Rutland OS and Rutland NHS. All visitors should sign in at fishing lodge. Organised groups should contact Andy Miller on 01536 772 930. Otherwise view from roadside lay-bys.
Facilities: SSSI since 1956. Three bird hides. Fishing season March to Nov. Toilets and visitor centre at fishing lodge.
Public transport: None.
Habitats: Open water, plantations and pasture.
Key birds: *Summer:* Good populations of breeding birds, sightings of Ospreys and Red Kite. Passage waders and Black Tern. *Winter:* Wildfowl (inc.

Goldeneye, Goosander, Smew) and waders. Tree Sparrow and Yellowhammer at feeding station, also Barn and Short-eared Owls can be seen hunting at dusk near Great Easton village (close to recycling centre).
Other notable flora and fauna: Otter, muntjac deer, red darter, demoiselle and blue damselfly, scalloped hazel and riband wave moths.
Contact: Andy Miller, Fishery Estate Manager, 01536 772 930; e-mail: fishing.lodge@tatasteel.com www.eyebrook.com

2. HICKS LODGE

Forestry Commission.
Location : Sat nav: LE65 2UP. NGR SK 329 156. Within National Forest, approx 0.5 miles from Moira village. Follow brown tourist signs for National Forest Cycle Centre from Moira, Ashby-de-la-Zouch and from junction 12 of A42.
Access: Site open all year: 8am to 8pm. Height barrier at main site entrance is removed when site is open, so no vehicle restrictions.
Facilities: Small (approx 80 cars) pay-and display car park, with designated disabled (4) and mini-bus parking (2) bays. On-site forest centre with small café, bike hire and toilets (including disabled and baby-changing facilities). All-ability trails and cycle trails. Most birdwatching activity occurs in front of the main centre, around the Hicks Lodge Loop and on the site ponds/lakes and open fields
Public transport: None
Habitats: New native woodland, with occasional

NATURE RESERVES - CENTRAL ENGLAND

European larch, rough grassland, open seasonally-grazed fields, lakes and ponds. Largest lake has two small islands, one of which is managed for Little Ringed Plover and other ground-nesting species
Key birds: Raptors include Buzzard,Red Kite, Kestrel, Hobby, Sparrowhawk and Peregrine. Common wildfowl in winter, plus a good range of finches (inc Crossbill), buntings, tits and summer warblers. Wader records include Bar-tailed Godwit, Greenshank, Ringed and Little Ringed Plovers, Common Sandpiper, Oystercatcher, Temminck's Stint, Lapwing and Golden Plover. Migrants on passage include Cuckoo, Wheatear, Whinchat, Stonechat, Spotted Flycatcher, hirundines and Black Tern.
Contact: Forestry Commission, 01889 586 593; e-mail: info_nationalforest@forestry.gsi.gov.uk
www.forestry.gov.uk

3. NARBOROUGH BOG

Leics and Rutland Wildlife Trust.
Location: Sat nav: LE19 2DB. SP 549 979. Between River Soar and M1, 8km S of Leicester. From city, turn L off B4114 (Leicester Road) just before going under motorway, follow track to sports club. Park near club house and walk across recreation ground to reserve entrance.
Access: Open at all times, please keep to paths. Not suitable for wheelchairs. Dogs on short leads only. Site may flood after heavy rain.
Facilities: None. Small bus/coach could park in sports field car park.
Public transport: Narborough train station. Buses X5, 140 to Narborough then 1km walk. Contact Traveline for more information on 0871 200 22 33.
Habitats: Peat bog SSSI (the only substantial deposit in Leicestershire), wet woodland, reedbed, dense scrub and fen meadow.
Key birds: More than 130 species of birds recorded, including three species of woodpeckers, six species of tit, Tawny Owl, Sparrowhawk and Kingfisher.
Other notable flora and fauna: Butterflies include common blue, meadow brown, large and small skippers, small heath and gatekeeper. Banded demoiselles, also good for moths and beetles. Harvest mice and water voles recorded, also breeding grass snakes. Meadow saxifrage, common meadow-rue and marsh thistle.
Contact: Trust HQ, 0116 272 0444; e-mail: info@lrwt.org.uk

4. RUTLAND WATER

Anglian Water/Leics & Rutland Wildlife Trust
Location: Two nature reserves — 1: Egleton Reserve (Sat nav: LE15 8BT. SK 878 075: from Egleton village off A6003 or A606 S of Oakham. Hosts British Birdwatching Fair every August. 2: Lyndon Reserve SK 894 058: south shore E of Manton village off A6003 S of Oakham. Follow 'nature reserve' signs to car park.
Access: 1: Open daily 9am-5pm, (4pm Nov to Jan).

2: Open from mid-March to mid-Sept daily (9am to 5pm). Day permits available for both. Reduced admission for disabled and carers. Closed Dec 25 and 26. Book badger-watching hide from mid-April to July.
Facilities: 1: Birdwatching Centre has toilets and disabled access, mobility scooter for hire. 28 hides (disabled access possible to 12 hides). 2: Interpretive centre toilets, including disabled, paths, use of a mobility scooter. Seven hides, four accessible to wheelchairs.
Public transport: Rutland Shore Link Bus runs from Oakham at 09.35am and 12.35pm.
Habitats: Ramsar-designated reservoir, lagoons, scrapes, woods, meadows, plantations, reedbeds.
Key birds: *Spring/autumn*: Outstanding wader passage, with up to 28 species recorded. Also wide range of raptors, owls, passerine flocks, terns (Black, Arctic, breeding Common, occasional Little and Sandwich). *Winter*: Up to 28 species of wildfowl (inc internationally important numbers of Gadwall and Shoveler). Also Goldeneye, Smew, Goosander, rare grebes, all divers, Ruff. *Summer*: Ospreys among 70 breeding species.
Other notable flora and fauna: Otter, badger, fox, weasel, stoat. Up to 20 species of dragon and damselflies and 24 butterfly species.
Contact: Egleton centre 01572 770 651; www.rutlandwater.org.uk www.ospreys.org.uk

5. SENCE VALLEY FOREST PARK

Forestry Commission.
Location: Sat nav: LE67 6NW. SK 400 115. Within The National Forest. 10 miles NW of Leicester and two miles SW of Coalville, between Ibstock and Ravenstone. The car park is signposted from A447 N of Ibstock.
Access: Open all year: 8am to 7pm (April 1 to Sept 30); 9am to 4pm rest of year. (precise times on noticeboard). 2,2m height barrier at main entrance, which gives access to wheelchair-friendly surfaced paths. Week's notice required for coach or minibus.
Facilities: Two car parks, toilets (including disabled and baby-changing facilities), information and recent

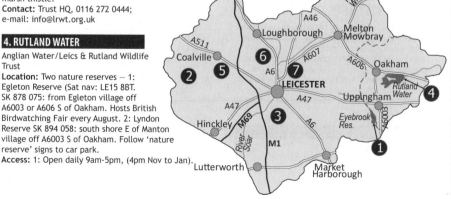

sightings boards, hide, all-abilities trails.
Public transport: None.
Habitats: New forest (native broadleaf, mixed and pine), rough grassland, wildflower meadow, pools, wader scrape, River Sence.
Key birds: *Spring/summer:* Artificial Sand Martin nesting wall, Wheatear, Whinchat, Redstart, Common and Green Sandpipers, Ringed and Little Ringed Plovers, Redshank. Dunlin and Greenshank frequent, possible Wood Sandpiper. Reed Bunting, Meadow Pipit, Skylark, Linnet, Yellow Wagtail. Possible Quail. Kestrel and Barn Owl seen occasionally. *Winter:* Stonechat, Redpoll, Short-eared Owl, Goosander and Wigeon possible.
Contact: Forestry Commission, 01889 586 593; e-mail: info_nationalforest@forestry.gsi.gov.uk www.forestry.gov.uk

6. SWITHLAND RESERVOIR

Severn Trent Water.
Location: Sat nav: LE7 7SB. SK 558 140. Lies south of Quorn, east of A6 (Leicester to Loughborough road). Use minor road between Swithland and Rothley for southern section. For northern section take Kinchley Lane along eastern shore to the dam.
Access: No access to water's edge: view from roads.
Facilities: None. **Public transport:** None.
Habitats: Large reservoir (mile long) divided by Great Central Railway line. Small area of woodland (Buddon Wood).
Key birds: Common wildfowl are regular, but site has produced seaduck such as Common Scoter, Scaup and Long-tailed Duck. Black-necked Grebe seen in late summer/autumn, while Mediterranean Gulls are annual. High water levels curb wader sightings, but Kingfishers are regular and Ravens are seen daily. All three woodpeckers are in Buddon Wood, along with a range of woodland species. It is the county's best site for wintering Peregrines. Also Buzzards, Sparrowhawks and Hobbies (summer). Good track record of rarities in recent years.
Other notable flora and fauna: Buddon Wood along Kinchley Lane is good for purple hairstreak butterflies and orange underwing moths – look for the latter around silver birch.

7. WATERMEAD COUNTRY PARK

Leics County Council
Location: LE7 1AD. SK 608 108 (car park). Located off Wanlip Road, Syston (off A46 or A607), six miles north of Leicester city centre. Watermead CP (South) is managed by Leicester City Council (parks@leicester.gov.uk).
Access: Open from 7am all year. Closing times vary from 4pm (Dec-Jan) to 8pm (May-Aug). Reedbed Nature Reserve open 9am to 4pm. Wanlip Road gives access to four car parks (fees payable). Southern entrance in Alderton Close, Thurmaston. Wheelchair access on 9km of surfaced tracks. RADAR key needed by mobility scooter riders to negotiate kissing gates on perimeter track.
Facilities: Four bird hides in nature reserve. Heronry hide now closed. Toilets, inc disabled. Sand Martin nesting wall.
Public transport: Buses on 5/5A/6 route from Leicester to Syston/East Goscote/Melton buses every few minutes in the daytime to/from Leicester and up to 3 buses an hour on Sundays. Get off at Alderton Close.
Habitats: River Soar and Grand Union Canal, plus 12 lakes and pools, wildflower meadow, woodland and reedbeds (one of largest in Midlands). Park stretches nearly two miles in length. Wanlip Meadows can be viewed from Plover Hide.
Key birds: 200 species recorded, including common wildfowl, Little Egret, Kingfisher, Water Rail, Cetti's Warbler. *Winter:* Bittern, Caspian Gull, Yellow-legged Gull and Scandinavian thrushes. *Passage:* Garganey and Black Terns. Wanlip Meadows very good for waders, including Little Ringed Plover, and is the county's best site for Temminck's Stint.
Other notable flora and fauna: Otters now regular, but elusive. Emperor and other dragonfly species.
Contact: Tel: 0116 305 5000 (8.30am to 5pm Mon - Thu, 8.30am to 4.30pm Fri); e-mail: countryparks@leics.gov.uk (week days only).
A site guide can be downloaded at: www.leics.gov.uk/watermead_country_park_leaflet.pdf

Lincolnshire

THIS large rural county sits between two major bird-friendly estuaries — the Humber and the Wash — and boasts several coastal sites such as Frieston Shore and Gibraltar Point which attract migrants and wintering wildfowl. Agriculture dominates inland, but there are reservoirs which can produce interesting birds. Lincoln Cathedral, one high point in a very flat county, has attracted breeding Peregrines.

1. ALKBOROUGH FLATS

North Lincs Council.
Location: Located on S bank of Humber where

Rivers Trent and Ouse meet to form the Humber. Follow brown tourism signs to Alkborough Flats from the A1077 near Winterton. Reach two car parks by following the duck signs through Alkborough village. Car park at the bottom of Prospect Lane (SE 879 221) is mainly for disabled visitors. Main car park (SE 887224) off Whitton Road, just north of Alkborough village. Site also accessible via a permissive footpath from Julian's Bower, Back Street, Alkborough: Sat nav: DN15 9JJ or SE 880 218.
Access: Open at all times. Limited access for disabled visitors.
Facilities: Four bird hides, including 5m tower hide at north eastern end of site. five miles of public footpaths (2 miles wheelchair-friendly). Three bird hides are accessible by wheelchair users.

NATURE RESERVES - CENTRAL ENGLAND

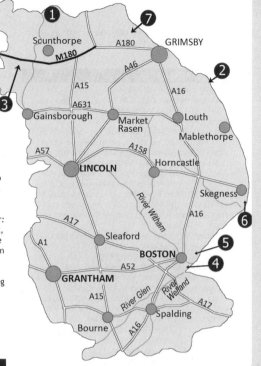

Public transport: Limited bus service to Alkborough from Scunthorpe. Traveline on 0871 200 2233.
Refreshments: The Paddocks Tea Room, Back Street, Alkborough (SE 881246). Open Thurs-Sunday and Bank Holidays.
Habitats: 440 hectare managed realignment site created by breaching the river defences to protect homes from flooding. Mixture of inter-tidal mudflats, grasslands, reedbeds and arable land.
Key birds: 200 species recorded. Lying on a key migration route, the site attracts geese and ducks in large numbers. Long-billed Dowitcher, Lesser Yellowlegs and Marsh Sandpiper brought the site's wader total to 40 species. *Winter:* Huge flocks of Lapwings (10,000 regularly) and Golden Plover (up to 14,000 but 5,000-10,000 regular), plus Marsh Harrier, Hen Harrier, Peregrine and Merlin, Teal, Wigeon, Black-tailed Godwit, while a large flock of Barnacle Geese can be seen at nearby Whitton Sands. *Summer:* Marsh Harriers have attempted to breed, Little Egret, Bearded Tit, Reed Warbler, Water Rail. Spoonbills are regular visitors. Avocets in autumn; passage waders in spring/autumn.
Other notable flora and fauna: Roe deer, badger, brown hare, water vole, otter, fox. Wall brown among a range of butterflies and black-tailed skimmer among the dragonflies.
Contact: Site manager Anna Moody 01724 721 269; e-mail: anna.moody@northlincs.gov.uk
Monthly bird reports: http://alkboroughandwalcot.co.uk/index_files/FlatsProject2.htm

2. DONNA NOOK

Lincolnshire Wildlife Trust.
Location: Sat nav: LN11 7PB. TF 422 998. Several access points off the main A1031 coastal road with parking facilities at Stonebridge (TF 422 998), Howden's Pullover (TF 449 952), Sea Lane, Saltfleet (TF 456 944) and Saltfleet Haven (TF 4679 35).
Access: Donna Nook beach is closed on weekdays as this is an active bombing range, but dunes remain open. Dogs on leads. Some disabled access.
Facilities: No toilets or visitor centre.
Habitats: Dunes, slacks and intertidal areas, seashore, mudflats, sandflats.
Key birds: *Summer:* Little Tern, Ringed Plover, Oystercatcher. *Winter:* Brent Goose, Shelduck, Twite, Lapland Bunting, Shorelark, Linnet.
Other notable flora and fauna: One of the largest and most accessible breeding colonies of grey seals in UK, plus fox, badger, stoat and weasel. Three species of shrew have been identified. Common lizard.
Contact: Lincolnshire Wildlife Trust, 01507 526 667; e-mail: info@lincstrust.co.uk; www.lincstrust.org.uk

3. EPWORTH TURBARY

Lincolnshire Wildlife Trust.
Location: Sat nav: DN9 1EA. SE 758 036. SW of Scunthorpe. Take A18 W from Scunthorpe then A161 S to Epworth. Turn R on High Street, and head towards

Wroot. The entrance is near bridge over Skyer's Drain. Park inside or on verge adjoining reserve, well away from corner.
Access: Open at all times. Keep to waymarked paths and use hides to avoid disturbing birds on the ponds.
Facilities: Car park, way-marked trail, two hides.
Habitats: One of the few relics of raised bog in Lincolnshire. Areas of active sphagnum bog still exist, plus reed swamp and mixed fen vegetation, also considerable area of birch woodland of varying ages.
Key birds: *Spring/summer:* Breeding birds include Tree Pipit, warblers, finches, Green and Great Spotted Woodpeckers and Woodcock. Greenshank, Green Sandpiper and Little Grebe are attracted to the wet area. Around Steve's Pond, occasional Hobby and Marsh Harrier, plus Teal, Little Grebe, Tree Pipit, Sparrowhawk and Buzzard. Willow Tit, Long-tailed Tit, Reed Bunting and Willow Warbler in the woodland areas. Occasionally Corn Buntings on the adjoining farmland. *Autumn/winter:* Large corvid flocks roost in reserve. At Pantry's Pond in winter occasional Hen Harrier. Other birds include Yellowhammer, Linnet, Jay and Magpie. Sometimes in winter Long-eared Owls can be observed roosting close to the path.
Other notable flora and fauna: 11 species of breeding dragonflies and damselflies recorded. Wood tiger moth is well established. Plants include sneezewort, yellow and purple loosestrife, meadow-

rue, and devil's-bit scabious.
Contact: Lincolnshire Wildlife Trust, 01507 526 667;
e-mail: info@lincstrust.co.uk
ww.lincstrust.org.uk

4. FRAMPTON MARSH

RSPB (Eastern England Office).
Location: Sat nav: PE20 1AY. TF 356 392. Four miles
SE of Boston. From A16 follow signs to Frampton then
Frampton Marsh.
Access: Visitor Centre open 10am to 4pm each day
(Oct-Mar except Dec 25); 10am to 4pm weekdays,
10am to 5pm weekends (Apr-Sept). Footpaths and
hides open at all times. **Facilities:** Visitor Centre
(including toilets), footpaths and three hides all
suitable for wheelchairs. Hot drinks and snacks at
centre, benches, viewpoints, 60-space car park (three
for disabled visitors), binocular hire, bicycle rack,
free information leaflets and events programmes.
Public transport: None.
Habitats: Saltmarsh, wet grassland, freshwater
scrapes and developing reedbed.
Key birds: *Summer:* Breeding Redshank, Avocet,
Lapwing, Skylark, Little Ringed Plover, Ringed
Plover, Sand Martin and several species of ducks plus
passage waders (inc Greenshank, Curlew Sandpiper,
Wood Sandpiper, Little and Temminck's Stints, Ruff
and Black-tailed Godwit), Marsh Harrier and Hobby.
Winter: Hen Harrier, Short-eared Owl, Merlin, dark-
bellied Brent Goose, Twite, Golden Plover, Lapland
Bunting.
Other notable flora and fauna: Water vole, stoat.
Dragonflies inc emperor, hawkers, chasers and
darters. Common butterflies plus wall brown, painted
lady and speckled wood. Scarce pug, star wort and
crescent striped moths on saltmarsh. Important
brackish water flora and fauna includes nationally
scarce spiral tassleweed and several rare beetles.
Contact: Reserve Manager, 01205 724 678; e-mail:
lincolnshirewashreserves@rspb.org.uk

5. FREISTON SHORE

RSPB (Eastern England Office).
Location: Sat nav: PE22 0LZ. TF 398 425. Four miles
E of Boston. From A52 at Haltoft End follow signs to
Freiston Shore.
Access: Open at all times, free. Keep dogs on leads
on all footpaths.
Facilities: Footpaths, two car parks, bird hide,
circular wetland trail. Free leaflets on site, guided
walks programme. Bicycle rack, benches, viewpoints,
seawatching shelter, viewing screen and viewing
platform.
Public transport: None.
Habitats: Saltmarsh, saline lagoon, mudflats, wet
grassland.
Key birds: *Summer:* Breeding waders including
Avocet, Ringed Plover and Oystercatcher, Common
Tern, Corn Bunting and Tree Sparrow. *Winter:*

Twite, dark-bellied Brent Goose, wildfowl, waders,
Short-eared Owl and Hen Harrier. *Passage:* Waders,
including Greenshank, Curlew Sandpiper and Little
Stint. *Autumn:* Occasional seabirds including Arctic
and Great Skuas.
Other notable flora and fauna: Water vole, muntjac
and roe deer, stoat. Dragonflies inc emperor, hawkers,
chasers and darters. Common butterflies plus wall
brown, painted lady and speckled wood. Scarce pug,
star wort and crescent striped moths on saltmarsh.
Important lagoon invertebrates and plants.
Contact: As Frampton Marsh

6. GIBRALTAR POINT NNR & BIRD OBSERVATORY

Lincolnshire Wildlife Trust.
Location: Sat nav: PE24 4SU. TF 556 580. Three miles
S of Skegness, signposted from town centre.
Access: Open dawn-dusk all year. Charges for
parking. Free admission to reserve, visitor centre and
toilets. Some access restrictions to sensitive sites
at S end. Dogs on leads at all times — no dogs on
beach during summer. Visitor centre and toilets, bird
observatory and four hides suitable for wheelchairs,
as well as surfaced paths. Day visit groups must be
booked in advance. Access for coaches. Contact Wash
Study Centre for residential or day visits.
Facilities: Visitor centre and café open 10am to 4pm
(Apr to end Oct), 11am to 3pm weekdays and 11am
to 4pm weekends (Nov to end Mar). Location of Wash
Study Centre and Bird Observatory. Field centre is an
ideal base for birdwatching/natural history groups in
spring, summer and autumn. Toilets open daily. Public
hides overlook freshwater and brackish lagoons. Wash
viewpoint overlooks saltmarsh and mudflats.
Public transport: Bus service from Skegness runs
occasionally but summer service only. Otherwise taxi/
car from Skegness. Cycle route from Skegness.
Habitats: Sand dune grassland and scrub, saltmarshes
and mudflats, freshwater marsh and lagoons.
Key birds: Large scale visible migration during spring
and autumn passage. Internationally important
populations of non-breeding waders between July-
Mar (peak Sep/Oct). Winter flocks of Brent Geese,
Shelduck and Wigeon on flats and marshes with Hen
Harrier, Merlin and Short-eared Owl often present.
Red-throated Divers offshore, (peak Feb). Colonies of
Little Tern and Ringed Plover in summer. More than
100 species can be seen in a day during May and Sept.
Good passage of autumn seabirds in northerly winds.
Other notable flora and fauna: Patches of pyramidal
orchids. Grey and common seal colonies, with
porpoises offshore in most months. Butterflies include
brown argus and green hairstreak.
Contact: Reserve and wildlife: Kev Wilson. Visit
bookings: Jill Hardy, Sykes Farm, Gibraltar Point
Nature Reserve, Gibraltar Road, Skegness, Lincs
PE24 4SU. 01754 898 057; e-mail: kwilson@
linwtrust.co.uk or gibadmin@lincstrust.co.uk
GibraltarPointBIrdObservatory.blogspot.com

Northamptonshire

RED KITES were re-introduced in the area north-east of Corby and they, along with Buzzards, are thriving and spreading out. Blatherwycke Lake is good for Mandarins, while Thrapston and Ditchford gravel pits, Pitsford and Hollowell reservoirs are good for a range of wildfowl, especially in winter. Harrington airfield can hold good numbers of wintering Short-eared Owls and raptors.

1. DITCHFORD LAKES AND MEADOWS

Beds, Cambs & Northants Wildlife Trust.
Location: Sat nav: NN8 1RL. SP 930 678. From Wellingborough, take A45 towards Rushden and Higham Ferrers. Take exit marked A5001 to Rushden. Turn L at roundabout onto Ditchford Road towards Irthlingborough/Ditchford. 500 m on R is small car park.
Access: Rough grass paths, flat overall. Some areas soft and muddy especially in winter. Dogs on leads.
Facilities: Car park (height restrictions).
Public transport: None.
Habitats: Part of the upper Nene valley floodplain — a complex of old gravel pits, grassland, lakes surrounded by mature scrub.
Key birds: *Winter*: Common Sandpiper, Snipe, Teal, Wigeon, Gadwall, Tufted Duck. *Spring*: Redshank, Oystercatcher, Cetti's Warbler, Little Grebe, Grey Heron. *Summer*: Reed Warbler, Sedge Warbler, Swift, House Martin. *Autumn*: Snipe, Great Crested Grebe, Moorhen, Coot, Grey Heron.
Other notable flora and fauna: Hairy dragonfly, grass snake, otter. Plants include marsh woundwort, dropwort, great burnet.
Contact: Reserves Manager, 01604 405 285; e-mail: northamptonshire@wildlifebcn.org

2. PITSFORD WATER

Anglian Water/BCN Wildlife Trust.
Location: Sat nav: NN6 9SJ. SP 786 700. Five miles N of Northampton. From A43 take turn to Holcot and Brixworth. From A508 take turn to Brixworth and Holcot.
Access: Reserve (N of causeway) open all year to permit holders. Wildlife Trust members can apply for free permit from HQ. Non-members can obtain day permits from fishing lodge, open mid-Mar to mid-Nov from 8am-dusk. Winter opening times variable, check in advance. No dogs. Disabled access from Lodge to first hide.
Facilities: Toilets available in Lodge, 15 miles of paths, nine bird hides, car parking.
Habitats: Open water (up to 120 ha), marginal vegetation and reed grasses, wet woodland, grassland and mixed woodland (40 ha).
Key birds: Typically 165-170 species per year with a total list of 253

species. *Summer*: Breeding warblers, terns, grebes, herons. *Autumn*: Waders if water levels suitable. *Winter*: Up to 10,000 wildfowl, feeding station with Tree Sparrow and occasional Corn Bunting.
Other notable flora and fauna: 32 butterfly species, 392 macro moths, 21 dragonfly species (including damselflies), 377 species of flora and 105 bryophytes, 404 fungi species.
Contact: Sarah Gibbs, Pitsford Water Lodge, Brixworth Road, Holcot, Northampton, NN6 9SJ. 01604 780 148; e-mail: pitsford@wildlifebcn.org

3. STANWICK LAKES

Rockingham Forest Trust/ East Northants Council
Location: Sat nav: NN9 6GY. SP 967 715. Entrance off the A45, eight miles N of Wellingborough.
Access: Open 7am to 9pm (March to Oct); 7am to 5pm (Nov to Feb). Visitor centre open 10am to 5pm (sometimes later in summer). Closed Dec 25. Charges for car and coach parking. Disability scooter available for hire.
Facilities: All paths, visitor centre, gift shop, toilets and bird hide are wheelchair accessible.
Habitats: 750-acre countryside park includes Ramsar-designated wetland on site of former quarry, part of Nene Valley Special Protection Area. Includes reedbeds, hedgerows and grazed areas.
Key birds: Resident Little Egret, Kingfisher, Green and Great Spotted Woodpeckers, Grey Wagtail, Cetti's Warbler and Barn Owl. *Autumn/winter*: Wildfowl inc Pintail, Goldeneye and Goosander. Bittern, Redpoll and Siskin. *Spring/summer*: Waders inc Oystercatcher (breeding), Little Ringed Plover, Greenshank and Green Sandpiper. Hobby, Yellow Wagtail, hirundines and migrant warblers.
Other notable fauna: Otter, grass snake, 150 moth species, dragonflies.

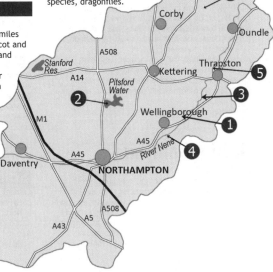

Contact: Rockingham Forest Trust. 01933 625 522; e-mail: info@rftrust.org.uk

4. SUMMER LEYS LNR

Beds, Cambs & Northants Wildlife Trust.
Location: Sat nav: NN29 7TQ. SP 885 634. Off Hardwater Road, Great Doddington, three miles from Wellingborough, accessible from A45 and A509.
Access: Open 24 hours a day, 365 days a year, no permits required. Dogs on leads. 40 space car park, small tarmaced circular route suitable for wheelchairs.
Facilities: Three hides, one feeding station. No toilets, nearest are at Irchester Country Park on A509 towards Wellingborough.
Public transport: Nearest train station is Wellingborough. Nearest bus services run regularly to Great Doddington and Wollaston, both about a mile away. Tel: 01604 670 060 (24 hrs) for copies of timetables.
Habitats: Scrape, two ponds, lake, scrub, flood meadows, hedgerow.
Key birds: *All year:* Tree Sparrow. *Spring/summer:* Common Tern, Black-headed Gull, Ringed and Little Ringed Plover, Redshank and Oystercatcher all breed. Whimbrel, Turnstone, Common Sandpiper on passage. *Winter:* Large numbers of common wildfowl, plus Lapwing, Golden Plover and Ruff.
Other notable flora and fauna: 16 species of dragonfly recorded, including hairy dragonfly (check Marigold Pond). Common blue and brown argus butterflies on grassland.
Contact: Northants office, 01604 405 285; e-mail: northamptonshire@wildlifebcn.org

5. THRAPSTON GRAVEL PITS & TITCHMARSH LNR

Natural England/BCRN Wildlife Trust.
Location: Sat nav: NN14 3EN (Lowick Road car park). TL 004 803. Seven miles E of Kettering. From A14 take A605 N. For Titchmarsh turn L at Thorpe Waterville, continue towards Aldwincle. Take first L after church (Lowick Lane) and continue to small car park on L. Take footpath to reserve.
Access: As well as the Aldwincle access point, there is a public footpath from lay-by on A605 N of Thrapston. Muddy conditions after heavy rain.
Facilities: Six hides in LNR, none on main Thrapston lake.
Public transport: Bus services to Thrapston.

Habitats: Alder/birch/willow wood; old duck decoy; series of water-filled gravel pits.
Key birds: *Summer:* Breeding Grey Heron (no access to heronry), Common Tern, Little Ringed Plover; warblers. Migrants, inc. Red-necked and Slavonian Grebes, Hobby, Bittern and Marsh Harrier recorded. *Winter:* Good range of wildfowl inc nationally important numbers of Gadwall, Wigeon and Goosander, plus gulls. Waders on passage.
Other notable flora and fauna: Banded demoiselle, red-eyed damselfly, brown, southern and migrant hawker dragonflies.
Contact: Northants office 01604 405 285; e-mail: northamptonshire@wildlifebcn.org

6. TOP LODGE-FINESHADE WOODS

Forestry Commission.
Location: Sat nav: NN17 3BB. SP 978 983. Off A43 between Stamford and Corby. Follow brown tourist signs to Top Lodge Fineshade Woods.
Access: Fully accessible visitor centre (10am to 5pm summer; closes 4pm winter weekdays 5pm on weekends between Nov and Feb). Open daily except Dec 25. Caravan Club site open Mar-Nov (please see CC website for details). Smelter's Walk is an all-ability trail leading to the hide. Electric bikes available from Fineshade Cycling shop.
Facilities: Two pay-and-display car parks. Visitor centre. Toilets, Top Lodge Café, events and activities throughout the year. Wildlife hide in wood. Orienteering course. Three way-marked walking trails (one is for all abilities, two are surfaced), 1 horse trail, 1 family cycle trail with skills loops, dedicated coach and horse box parking. Sensory garden.
Public transport: None.
Habitats: Ancient woodland, coniferous woodland, beech woodland, open areas, small pond.
Key birds: Centre of Northants' Red Kite reintroduction scheme. A wide range of birds of mixed woodlands. *All year:* Red Kite, Buzzard, Great Spotted Woodpecker, Goshawk, Nuthatch, Crossbill, Marsh Tit, Willow Tit. *Summer:* Turtle Dove, warblers. *Winter:* Hawfinch.
Other notable flora and fauna: Adder, grass snake, slow worm, common lizard. Fallow deer, badger. Orchids including greater butterfly, early purple and common spotted, other flora of ancient woodland.
Contact: Forestry Commission, Top Lodge, 01623 822447 ; e-mail: northants@forestry.gsi.gov.uk www.forestry.gov.uk/toplodge

Nottinghamshire

GRAVEL PITS dominate birding habitats in Nottinghamshire, though remnant pockets of heathland still hold iconic species such as Nightjar and Woodlark. The most recently developed gravel pit sites are the Idle Valley NR (formerly known as Lound) and the RSPB's new reserve at Langford Lowfields, near Newark. A raptor watchpoint at Welbeck can produce sightings of Honey Buzzard, Goshawk and Osprey and you can try for Hawfinches in winter in Clumber Park.

1. ATTENBOROUGH NATURE RESERVE

Cement UK/Notts Wildlife Trust
Location: Sat nav: NG9 6DY. Car park at SK 515 339. In Nottingham alongside River Trent. Signposted from A6005 between Beeston and Long Eaton.
Access: Open all year (am to 5pm (6pm on bank holidays and weekends). Dogs on leads (guide dogs

only in visitor centre). Paths suitable for disabled access. Coaches by prior appointment. Car park charge.

Facilities: Education and visitor centre with café and shop, all accessible to wheelchair users. Nature trail (leaflet from Notts WT), four bird hides including an elevated hide and new and innovative Sand Martin Hide – a sunken bird hide within an artificial Sand Martin bank.

Public transport: Railway station at Attenborough – reserve is five mins walk away, visitor centre a further 10 minutes. Trent Barton Indigo bus service between Nottingham Broadmarsh and Derby bus station runs regularly throughout day. Alight at Chilwell Retail Park and walk 500m along Barton Lane.

Habitats: Designated SSSI, composed of disused, flooded gravel workings with associated marginal and wetland vegetation.

Key birds: *Spring/summer*: Breeding Common Tern (40-plus pairs), Reed Warbler, Black Tern regular (bred once). *Winter*: Wildfowl, plus Bittern, Grey Heron colony, adjacent Cormorant roost.

Other notable flora and fauna: Smooth newt, dragonflies including four-spotted chaser and migrant hawker.

Contact: Attenborough Nature Centre, 01159 721 777;
e-mail: enquiries@attenboroughnaturecentre.co.uk
www.attenboroughnaturecentre.co.uk

2. BESTHORPE NATURE RESERVE

Nottinghamshire Wildlife Trust.

Location: Sat nav: NG23 7HL. SK 817 640 and SK 813 646 (access points north and south of Trent Lane). Take A1133 N of Newark. Turn into Trent Lane S of Besthorpe village, reserve entrances second turn on L and R turn at end of lane (at River Trent).

Access: Open access to a hide, several screens (one in south section with disabled access from car park). No access to SSSI meadows. Limited access to areas grazed with sheep. Dogs on leads.

Facilities: No toilets (pubs etc in Besthorpe village), two hides in southern section, paths, nature trail (northern part), several screens.

Public transport: Buses (numbers 22, 67, 68, 6, S7L) run by Marshalls, Lincs, Road Car and Travel Wright along A1133 to Besthorpe village (0.75 mile away). Tel: 0115 924 0000 or 01777 710 550 for information.

Habitats: Former gravel workings with islands, SSSI neutral grasslands, hedges, reedbed, etc.

Key birds: *Spring/summer*: Breeding Grey Heron, Cormorant, Little Ringed Plover, Common Tern, Kingfisher, Grasshopper Warbler. *Winter*: Large numbers of ducks (Pochard, Tufted Duck, Pintail, Wigeon) and Peregrine. Recent re-profiling of water margins has increased the numbers of visiting waders.
Other notable flora and fauna: Nationally rare plant community in meadows.

Contact: Notts Wildlife Trust, 01159 588 242;
e-mail: info@nottswt.co.uk

3. COLWICK COUNTRY PARK

Nottingham City Council.

Location: Sat nav: NG4 2DW. SK 610 395. Access from Mile End Road, off A612 two miles E of Nottingham city centre. Adjacent to park-and-ride car park.

Access: Open at all times, but no vehicle access after dusk or before 7am. Best parking is in Colwick Hall access road from the racecourse.

Facilities: Nature trails. Sightings log book in Fishing Lodge.

Public transport: Nottingham City Transport Buses: Number 44 from stop Q3 on Queens Street (outside the Post Office); Park and Ride Service: Citylink2 from stop CL2 on Lower Parliament Street (outside Victoria Centre).

Habitats: Lakes, pools, woodlands, grasslands, new plantations, River Trent.

Key birds: *Summer*: 64 breeding species recorded, inc warblers and Common Tern (15+ pairs). Good track record for rarities. *Winter*: Wildfowl (high concentrations of Goldeneye) and gulls. In nature reserve look for Lesser Spotted Woodpecker, Water Rail and Kingfisher. Passage migrants inc Stonechat and Whinchat.

Other notable flora and fauna: Pool designated a SSSI for its 14 species of breeding dragonfly. Purple and white letter hairstreak butterflies.

Contact: Head Ranger, The Fishing Lodge, Colwick, Country Park, River Road, Colwick, Nottingham NG4 2DW. 01159 870 785; www.nottinghamcity.gov.uk

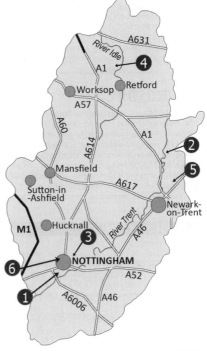

4. IDLE VALLEY (SUTTON & LOUND GRAVEL PITS)

Nottinghamshire Wildlife Trust/Tarmac/Private.
Location: Sat nav: DN22 8SG. SK 690 856. S end of
reserve is 0.5 mile N of Retford off A638 to Barnby
Moor, via entrance to Tarmac. Rural Learning Centre
is on R.
Access: Open all year. Keep to walkways and public
rights of way. Parking for reserve in first parking bay
(large car park is for Learning Centre only). Footpath
at S end is wheelchair accessible.
Facilities: Learning Centre reception and toilets
open (10am to 4pm) all year. Refreshments (vending
machine) available Mon-Sun (10am to 4pm). Idle
Valley Café open Sundays (11.30am to 3.30pm). Six
viewing screens, two overlooking Chainbridge NR
Scrape, two at Neatholme Scrape and single screens
at Neatholme Fen and Neatholme Pit. Two hides in
Chainbridge Wood.
Public transport: Buses from Doncaster,
Gainsborough and Worksop to Retford bus station,
then on Stagecoach service 27 via Lound village
crossroads (Chainbridge Lane).
Habitats: Former sand and gravel quarries, restored
gravel workings, conservation grazed areas,
woodland, reedbed, river valley, farmland, scrub,
willow plantations, open water.
Key birds: 251 species recorded. *Summer:* Gulls,
terns, wildfowl and waders. Passage waders, terns,
passerines and raptors. *Winter:* Wildfowl, gulls,
raptors. Good site for rarities, which have included
Broad-billed Sandpiper, Great White Egret, Baird's
Sandpiper and Steppe Grey Shrike in recent times.
Contacts: Lound Bird Club, Gary Hobson (chairman),
01924 384 419; e-mail: loundbirdclub@btinternet.com
James Simpson (NWT Reserve Officer), Idle Valley
Rural Learning Centre, Great North Road, Retford.
DN22 8RQ; e-mail: jsimpson@nottswt.co.uk

5. LANGFORD LOWFIELDS

RSPB Midlands Office/ Lefarge Tarmac
Location: Sat nav: NG23 7RF. SK 821 601. Lies NE of
Newark-on-Trent. From A1 take A46 (signposted to
Lincoln) and then turn onto A1133 (to Collingham).
After two miles turn left on Tarmac access road
(signposted Langford Quarry). Park in Tarmac car
park.
Access: Access to main working quarry restricted to
reserve trails at north end of site, except for working
parties and guided group walks (see RSPB website for
dates). View from public footpath around perimeter
(mostly not suitable for disabled visitors, except
for resurfaced section from new car park on NE
boundary). Cottage Lane car park open dawn to dusk.
Facilities: Viewing screen overlooking reedbed. No
toilets except for work party volunteers.
Public transport: Newark-Collingham buses will stop
near to footpath if requested.
Habitats: RSPB is working with Tarmac to create the
East Midlands' largest reedbed (currently 30 ha) at
this sand and gravel quarry site. Mature woodland,
lake and shallow pools.
Key birds: Large waterfowl numbers in winter,
plus Starling roosts, and five owl species. Bittern
also recorded. *Summer:* Ten species of warbler,
inc Cetti's, Grasshopper and regionally important
numbers of Reed and Sedge Warblers, numerous
Cuckoos, Turtle Doves, Marsh Harriers, Hobbies,
hirundines and breeding Little Ringed Plovers and
Avocets.
Other notable flora and fauna: Badgers. More than
18 species of butterflies.
Contact: Call RSPB on 01636 893 611 to book group
visits or enquire about work parties.

Oxfordshire

A LAND-LOCKED, largely agricultural county,
Oxfordshire has two outstanding birding
locations: Farmoor reservoir for passage migrants,
wintering wildfowl and rarities and Otmoor, where
wet meadows and reedbeds are being developed
by the RSPB to benefit breeding waders such as
Redshank, Snipe and Lapwing in spring and Hobbies
in summer. Wildfowl numbers increase in winter
and Hen Harriers, Merlins, Peregrines and Short-
eared Owls hunt.

1. ASTON ROWANT NNR

Natural England.
Location: Sat nav: HP14 3YL (for Beacon Hill car
park). SU 731 966. From the M40 Lewknor interchange
at J6, travel NE for a short distance and turn R onto
A40. After 1.5 miles at the top of hill, turn R and
R again into a narrow, metalled lane. Car park is
signposted from A40.
Access: Open all year. Some wheelchair access

at Cowleaze Wood (contact Reserve Manager for
details).
Facilities: On-site parking at Beacon Hill and
Cowleaze Wood, viewpoint, seats, interpretation
panels.
Public transport: Red Rose buses between High
Wycombe and Oxford stop at both Stokenchurch and
Lambert Arms, Aston Rowant. Stagecoach Oxford
Tube buses stop at Lewknor village, a short walk from
reserve.
Habitats: Chalk grassland, chalk scrub, beech
woodland.
Key birds: *Spring/summer:* Blackcap, other warblers,
Turtle Dove. Passage birds inc Ring Ouzel, Wheatear
and Stonechat. *Winter:* Brambling, Siskin, winter
thrushes. *All year:* Red Kite, Buzzard, Sparrowhawk,
Woodcock, Tawny Owl, Green and Great Spotted
Woodpeckers, Skylark, Meadow Pipit, Marsh Tit.
Other notable flora and fauna: Rich chalk grassland
flora, including Chiltern gentian clustered bellflower,
frog, bee, pyramidal and fragrant orchids. Less
common butterflies include silver-spotted, dingy and
grizzled skippers, chalkhill blue, adonis blue, green

hairstreak and green fritillary.
Contact: Natural England, Aston Rowant NNR, 01844
351 833; e-mail: enquiries@naturalengland.org.uk

2. FARMOOR RESERVOIR

Thames Water/ Environment Agency.
Location: Sat nav: OX2 9NT. SP 452 061. Lies W of
Oxford between A 40 and A420. Widely signposted by
brown tourist signs. At mini-roundabout in Farmoor
village, turn left and look for car park at Gate 3 (half
mile distance).
Access: One-day permits (£1) or year-long permits
(£10). Free car parking at Gate 3 for permit holders.
Key for Pinkhill hide can be bought at gatehouse.
No walking permitted between reservoir and Shrike
Meadows to prevent disturbance to birds.
Facilities: Car park off B4017. Bird hide at Pinkhill
Reserve, west of reservoir.
Public transport: Frequent Stagecoach 100 buses
between Oxford and Witney stop in Farmoor village
(half-mile walk to Gate 3).
Habitats: The county's largest body of fresh water
contained in two concrete basins separated by a
causeway. Shallow pools in Pinkhill Reserve. Reedbed,
wet grassland and pools in the small Shrike Meadow
and Buckthorne Meadow reserves.
Key birds: *Winter:* Wildfowl, grebes, divers and gulls.
Snipe and Water Rail at Pinkhill. *Summer:* Breeding
Little Ringed Plover, Common Tern and Black-headed
Gull. Large numbers of hirundines, Hobby, Cuckoo.
Attractive to passage migrants such as White and
Yellow Wagtails, Wheatear, Black Tern, Little Gull,
Dunlin and Little Stint, plus a long history of rarities.
Other notable fauna: Dragonflies, aquatic life-forms.
Contact: Warden's lodge: 01865 863 033.

3. FOXHOLES RESERVE

Berks, Bucks & Oxon Wildlife Trust.
Location: Sat nav: OX7 6RW. SP 254 206. Travelling
north on A424 from Burford, take right turn to
Bruern. Continue past staggered crossroads
towards Bruern for two miles then past right
turn to Shipton-under-Wychwood. Park in lay-
by after 200m and walk 600m down pot-holed
track to reserve entrance. 4x4 vehicles can
drive track to surfaced car park.
Access: Open all year. Please keep to the
paths.
Facilities: Car park. Footpaths can be very
muddy.
Public transport: None.
Habitats: Broad-leaved woodland and
grassland.
Key birds: *Spring/summer:* Spotted Flycatcher,
Marsh Tit and warblers. *Winter:* Redwing,
Fieldfare, Woodcock. *All year:* Raven, Tawny
Owl, Little Owl, Green and Greater Spotted
Woodpeckers, common woodland species.
Other notable flora and fauna: Fantastic show
of bluebells in May. Autumn fungi. Silver-
washed fritillary butterfly among 23 species
recorded.

Contact: BBOWT, 01865 77 5476;
e-mail: info@bbowt.org.uk
www.bbowt.org.uk/reserves/Foxholes

4. OTMOOR NATURE RESERVE

RSPB (Central England Office).
Location: Sat nav: OX3 9TD (Otmoor Lane). SP 570
126. Car park seven miles NE of Oxford city centre.
From J8 of M40, take A40 W to Wheatley, then B4027.
Take turn to Horton-cum-Studley, then first L to
Beckley. After 0.67 miles turn R (before the Abingdon
Arms public house). After 200 yards, turn L into
Otmoor Lane. Car park at the end of lane (approx
one mile).
Access: Open dawn-dusk. No entry fee. No dogs
allowed on the reserve visitor trail (except public
rights of way). In wet conditions, the visitor route can
be muddy and wellingtons are essential.
Facilities: Limited. Small car park with cycle racks,
visitor trail (3 mile round trip) and two screened
viewpoints. The reserve is not accessible by coach
and is unsuitable for large groups.
Public transport: None.
Habitats: Wet grassland, reedbed, open water.
Key birds: *Summer:* Breeding birds include Cetti's
and Grasshopper Warblers, Lapwing, Redshank,
Curlew, Snipe, Yellow Wagtail, Shoveler, Gadwall,
Pochard, Tufted Duck, Little and Great Crested
Grebes. Hobby breeds
locally. *Winter:* Wigeon,
Teal, Shoveler, Pintail,
Gadwall, Pochard, Tufted
Duck, Lapwing, Golden
Plover, Hen Harrier,
Peregrine, Merlin.
*Autumn/
spring*

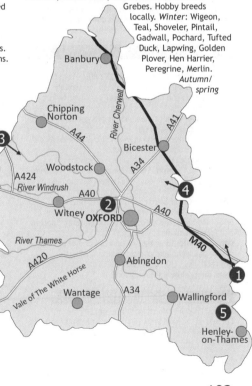

103

passage: Marsh Harrier, Short-eared Owl, Greenshank, Green Sandpiper, Common Sandpiper, Spotted Redshank and occasional Black Tern.
Contact: RSPB, c/o Folly Farm, Common Road, Bexley, OX3 9YR. 01865 351 163.

5. WARBURG NATURE RESERVE

Berks, Bucks & Oxon Wildlife Trust.
Location: Sat nav: RG9 6BL. SU 717 879. Leave Henley-on-Thames NW on A4130. Turn R at end of Fair Mile onto B480. Take L fork in Middle Assendon. After 1 mile, follow road round to R at grassy triangle, car park is on R after 1 mile.
Access: Open all year — visitor centre opens 9am-5pm. Dogs on leads please. In some areas, only guide dogs allowed. Mobility vehicle available - book before visiting.
Facilities: Visitor Centre, toilets, car park, two

hides, one with disabled access, children's Nature Detectives Trail, nature trail, picnic benches, leaflets. Visitors with disabilities and groups should contact the warden before visits. Car park not suitable for coaches, only mini-buses.
Habitats: Scrub, mixed woodland, chalk grassland, ponds.
Key birds: *All year:* Sparrowhawk, Red Kite, Treecreeper, Nuthatch, Tawny Owl. *Spring/summer:* Occasional Firecrest. Warblers include Whitethroat and Lesser Whitethroat. *Winter:* Redpoll, Siskin, sometimes Crossbill, Woodcock.
Other notable flora and fauna: Good for orchids (15 species), butterflies (inc purple hairstreak and silver-washed fritillary) and common deer species.
Contact: Warburg Nature Reserve, 01491 642 001; e-mail: info@bbowt.org.uk
www.bbowt.org.uk/reserves/Warburg-Nature-Reserve

Shropshire

LYING along the Welsh border, Shopshire's habitats range from upland moorland with its Red Grouse and Ring Ouzels to fertile lowland valleys, extensive farmland and mixed woodland. The cluster of waters near Ellesmere attract winter wildfowl and gulls while Venus Pools, Wood Lane and Chelmarsh are the county's chief wader-watching sites.

1. CLUNTON COPPICE

Shropshire Wildlife Trust.
Location: Sat nav: SY7 0HL. SO 342 806. From Craven Arms, take B4368 to Clunton village, go straight over bridge and up the hill to small car park just before reserve sign.
Access: Open at all times. Access along road and public rights of way only.
Facilities: Limited parking in small quarry entrance on R, or opposite The Crown pub.
Public transport: Buses between Craven Arms and Clun stop at Clunton. Steep one mile walk to reserve.
Habitats: One of the county's largest sessile oak woods. Good for ferns, mosses and fungi.
Key birds: Great Spotted Woodpecker, Buzzard and Raven regular. *Spring/summer:* Wide range of woodland birds, inc. Redstart, Wood Warbler, Spotted and Pied Flycatchers, Woodcock.
Other notable flora: Hairy woodrush and bromerape, sessile oak woodland plants, bluebell, bilberry.
Contact: Trust HQ, 01743 284 280.
www.shropshirewildlifetrust.org.uk

2. FENN'S WHIXALL AND BETTISFIELD MOSSES

Natural England (North Mercia Team).
Location: Sat nav: SY13 3NY (Fenn's Bank). Located four miles SW of Whitchurch, to the S of A495 between Fenn's Bank, Whixall and Bettisfield.

Roadside parking at entrances, car parks at Morris's Bridge, Roundthorn Bridge, World's End and a large car park at Manor House. Disabled access by prior arrangement along the railway line.
Access: Permit required except on Mosses Trail routes.
Facilities: Information panels at main entrances and leaflets are available when permits are applied for. Three interlinking Mosses Trails explore the NNR and canal from Morris's and Roundthorn bridges.
Public transport: Bus passes nearby. Railway two miles away.
Habitats: 2,000 acres of raised peatland meres and mosses.
Key birds: *Spring/summer:* Breeding Teal, Mallard, Nightjar, Hobby, Curlew, Tree Sparrow. Hobbies hunt

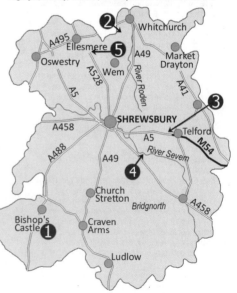

NATURE RESERVES - CENTRAL ENGLAND

here. *All year*: Kingfisher, Skylark, Linnet. *Winter*: Short-eared Owl.
Other notable flora and fauna: Water vole, brown hare, polecat, adder, 2,000 species of moth, 27 species of butterfly, nationally important for dragonflies, inc white-faced darter and yellow-spot chaser.
Contact: Natural England, Attingham Park, 01743 282 000; e-mail: north.mercia@natural-england.org.uk

3. PRIORSLEE LAKE

Severn Trent Water/Friends of Priorslee Lake
Location: Sat nav: TF2 9CQ. SJ 725 094. In Telford between M54 and A5. Leave M54 going north (B5060) at junction 4 and park in lay-by (100 yards from J4) overlooking the lake. Alternatively park without blocking gates by Water Sports Association entrance gate at the end of Teece Drive, Priorslee, Telford. The Flash, Priorslee is a slightly smaller lake half a mile distant. Follow the stream that comes in at the western end of Priorslee Lake or head for Derwent Drive, Priorslee.
Access: Open at all times. Footpath around lake but can be muddy when wet.
Facilities: None.
Public transport: No. 24 bus from Telford town centre bus station, 3 miles from site, goes via train station, 2 miles.
Habitats: A man-made balancing lake, surrounded by woodland, rough grassland and three reedbeds on northern side.
Key birds: More than 155 species recorded (41 breeding). *Winter*: A nearby landfill site makes Priorslee Lake a magnet for gulls and the site has a good track record for Yellow-legged, Caspian and white-winged gulls. Check the wildfowl for less common species such as Goosander and Pintail. Bittern and Snipe have been recorded in reedbeds. Finches, tits (including Willow), Redpoll, Siskin in woodland. *Summer*: Warblers, including Reed and Sedge Warbler.
Other notable flora and fauna: Wide range of butterflies, dragonflies and other insects. Southern marsh, bee and common spotted orchids.
Contact: Richard Camp, FoPL Co-ordinator, 01952 247 783; e-mail: mail@richardcamp.co.uk.
Friends Website: www.priorslee.org.uk

4. VENUS POOL

Shropshire Ornithological Society.
Location: Sat nav: SY5 6JT. SJ 548 062. 6 miles SE of Shrewsbury in angle formed by A458 and minor road leading S to Pitchford. Entrance is half a mile along minor road which leaves A458 half a mile (0.8 km) SE of Cross Houses.
Access: Public access includes four hides. Please keep to footpaths shown on notice boards at both entrances. Wheelchair-friendly paths to two public hides and Lena's Hide overlooking feeding station. Dogs not allowed.
Facilities: Car park with height barrier. Five hides (two for SOS members only). Information boards.
Public transport: Shrewsbury-Bridgnorth buses stop at Cross Houses, a one mile walk from Venus Pool, partly along busy main road.
Habitats: Approx 27 hectares site. Pool, several islands, open shoreline, marshy grassland, hedgerows, scrub and woodland. Species-rich meadows, field growing bird-friendly crops.
Key birds: Noted for wintering wildfowl and passage waders, plus occasional county rarities, including Black-necked Grebe, Purple Heron, Spoonbill, Red Kite and Woodlark. *All year*: Common ducks and waterfowl, passerines, including Tree Sparrow. *April-June*: Passage waders include Curlew, Ringed Plover, Dunlin, Redshank, Green and Common Sandpipers, and both godwits. Passage Black Tern. Breeding Oystercatcher, Little Ringed Plover, Lapwing, warblers, hirundines. *July-September*: Wader passage can include Little Stint, Greenshank, Green, Wood, Curlew and Common Sandpipers, and possible rarities. *October-March*: Occasional wintering Bittern. Geese include occasional White-fronted. Ducks include Wigeon, Teal, Pintail, Shoveler, Pochard, Goosander (up to 50 in evening roosts) and occasional Goldeneye. Water Rail, vagrant raptors and owls, winter thrushes and large passerine flocks including Lesser Redpoll, Linnet, Tree Sparrow, Reed Bunting and Yellowhammer.
Contact: www.shropshirebirds.com/venus_pool/venuspool.htm

5. WOOD LANE

Shropshire Wildlife Trust.
Location: Sat nav: SY12 0HY. SJ 424 328. Take the Colemere road, off A528 at Spunhill, 1 mile SE of Ellesmere. Car park is 0.75 miles down on R.
Access: Open at all times. Visit Trust website to apply on-line for permit to use hides. Reserve accessible to people of all abilities.
Facilities: Car parks signposted. Two hides (permit only).
Habitats: Gravel pit restored by Tudor Griffiths.
Key birds: 168 species recorded since 1999. *Summer*: Breeding Sand Martin, Lapwing, Little Ringed Plover, Yellowhammer and Tree Sparrow. Osprey platforms erected to tempt over-flying birds. Popular staging post for waders (inc. Redshank, Greenshank, Ruff, Dunlin, Little Stint, Green and Wood Sandpiper). *Winter*: Large flocks of Lapwing, plus Curlew and common wildfowl.
Other notable fauna: Good range of dragonflies.
Contact: Trust HQ, 01743 284 280.

Staffordshire

OUTSIDE its urban areas, the county can offer Red Grouse on the northern moors, as well as Lesser Spotted Woodpeckers, Pied Flycatchers and other songbirds at RSPB Coombes Valley. Cannock Chase is good for Nightjars, Woodlark and Goshawk, and often has wintering Great Grey Shrikes. Belvide, Blithfield and Croxall Lakes are the best reservoirs to work for wintering birds.

1. BELVIDE

British Waterways Board/West Midland Bird Club.
Location: Sat nav: ST19 9LX. SJ 870 099. Entrance and car park on Shutt Green Lane, Brewood, seven miles NW of Wolverhampton.
Access: Access only by permit from the West Midland Bird Club (free for members, otherwise £20).
Facilities: Five hides (3 with wheelchair access), hard surface paths. Parking for 25-30 cars (lock combination issued to permit holders).
Public transport: Wolverhampton buses (3 and 877) and Walsall service (6) all stop at Kiddermore Green (eight minute walk to reserve).
Habitats: Reservoir with marsh, reedbeds, woodland and scrub.
Key birds: Wintering wildfowl, inc Great Northern Diver, Bewick's Swan and Goosander. Winter gull roost sometimes includes Glaucous or Iceland Gulls. Breeding and passage waders (up to 12 species in a day when conditions are right) and terns. Warblers breed in reedbeds and hedgerows. Recent scarcities include Sabine's Gull, White-winged and Whiskered Tern and Yellow-browed Warbler.
Other notable fauna: Dragon and damselflies.
Contact: WMBC Permit Secretary, 147 World's End Lane, Quinton, Birmingham B32 1JX.
E-mail: permits@westmidlandbirdclub.com. For other info: belvide@westmidlandbirdclub.com
www.westmidlandbirdclub.com/belvide

2. BLITHFIELD RESERVOIR

South Staffs Water/West Midland Bird Club
Location: Sat nav: WS15 3NJ. SK 058 237. View from causeway on B5013 (Rugeley/Uttoxeter). Close to village of Abbots Bromley. Look for signposts to Blithfield Education Centre.
Access: For members of WMBC only or one-off group permit. Further details from secretary@westmidlandbirdclub.com.
Facilities: Free car park, toilets. Walk 1 has partial wheelchair access.
Public transport: None. **Habitats:** Large reservoir.
Key birds: More than 250 species recorded. *Winter*: Good populations of wildfowl (inc. Bewick's Swan, Goosander, Goldeneye), large gull roost (can inc. Glaucous, Iceland, Mediterrean and Caspian). Passage terns (Common, Arctic, Black) and waders, esp. in autumn (Little Stint, Curlew Sandpiper, Spotted Redshank regular).
Contact: WMBC Secretary: e-mail:secretary@westmidlandbirdclub.com

3. COOMBES VALLEY

RSPB (Midlands Regional Office).
Location: Sat nav: ST13 7EU. SK 009 534. Three miles SE of Leek. From Leek take A523 towards Ashbourne. After Bradnop, turn R on minor road (cross a railway line) to Apesford and follow signs to reserve.
Access: Open daily 9am to 9pm or dusk (except Dec 25), no charge. Free parking. Coach groups welcome by prior arrangement. Only guide dogs allowed off public footpaths. Most trails unsuitable for disabled visitors.
Facilities: Information centre (closes at 5pm), toilets and hot drinks. Two nature trails with eight benches.
Public transport: 108 bus from Leek to Ashbourne, twice daily stops 1.2 miles from reserve, walk towards Ashbourne then take first R, cross railway and continue to reserve.
Habitats: Steep-sided valley with sessile oak woodland, unimproved pasture and meadow.
Key birds: *Spring*: Displaying Woodcock, drumming Great Spotted Woodpeckers and common woodland species are joined by migrant Pied and Spotted Flycatchers, Redstart, Tree Pipit, Grey Wagtail and Wood Warbler. *Jan-Mar*: Displaying birds of prey. *Autumn/winter*: Lesser Redpoll, Siskin, winter thrushes.
Other notable flora and fauna: Bluebells, various butterflies, slow worm.
Contact: Reserve warden. 01538 384 017; e-mail: coombes.valley@rspb.org.uk

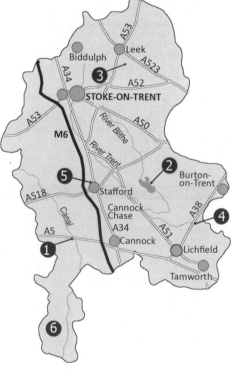

4. CROXALL LAKES

Staffordshire Wildlife Trust.
Location: Sat nav: WS13 8QX. SK 190 139. From Lichfield head N on A38, following signs for National Memorial Arboretum. At NMA entrance, continue over river bridge and turn left on second track into car park.
Access: Open at all times, except to restricted areas. Surfaced access to track, leading to hide overlooking main lake. Wheelchair ramps for both hides but woodland path is uneven. Kissing gate at entrance wide enough for wheelchairs. Restricted areas for dog walkers.
Facilities: Small car park, two bird hides.
Public transport: Bus services from Lichfield to Alrewas (1.2 miles from reserve).
Habitats: Two large lakes formed from gravel pits at the junction of Rivers Tame, Trent and Mease, plus shallow pools, wader scrapes and reedbeds.
Key birds: *Winter:* Substantial numbers of wildfowl, inc Wigeon, Teal, Goldeneye, Shoveler and occasional Smew. Between Nov and Jan, Short-eared Owls hunt over rough ground. *Spring/summer:* Nesting species include grebes, plus waders such as Redshank, Oystercatcher, Ringed Plover and Lapwing. Other species on passage.
Other notable flora and fauna: Otters, water voles and harvest mice all present but dragonflies will be easier to see.
Contact: Trust HQ 01889 880 100; e-mail:info@staffs-wildlife.org.uk

5. DOXEY MARSHES

Staffordshire Wildlife Trust.
Location: Sat nav: ST16 1PU. SJ 903 250. On W side of Stafford town centre, just off A513 (Eccleshall Road) from Junction 14 on the M6. Parking by play park at end of Wootton Drive/ Creswell Farm Drive.
Access: Open at all times. Most of site accessible by wheelchair. Dogs on leads in sensitive areas.
Facilities: One hide, three viewing platforms.
Public transport: Buses and trains to Stafford town centre, walk upstream from Sainsbury's supermarket along River Sow to reserve entrance.
Habitats: Designated SSSI for wet meadow habitats. Marsh, pools, reedbeds, hedgerows, reed sweet-grass swamp
Key birds: More than 200 species (80 breeding) recorded. *Spring/summer:* Breeding Lapwing, Redshank, Little Ringed Plover, Oystercatcher, Shelduck, warblers, Skylark, Water Rail. *Autumn/ Winter:* Snipe, Jack Snipe, Goosander, other wildfowl, Passage waders, vagrants
Other notable flora and fauna: Otter, harvest mouse, water shrew, noctule bat, musk beetle, reed-sweet grass.
Contact: Staffordshire Wildlife Trust, 01889 880 100; e-mail:info@staffs-wildlife.org.uk

6. HIGHGATE COMMON

Staffordshire Wildlife Trust.
Location: Sat nav: DY7 5BS (Highgate Road). SO 836 895. From A449 at Himley take B4176 towards Bridgnorth. After approx 1 mile, turn left at traffic lights onto Wombourne Rd, signposted towards Swindon. Continue through Swindon, along Chasepool Rd. At the T Junction turn R onto Camp Hill Road. About 1 mile after Camp Farm, take 1st L then R at the T junction onto Highgate Rd. Take 1st entrance on R.
Access: Several car parks, network of paths.
Facilities: Public toilets at Warden's Office (restricted opening hours).
Public transport: None.
Habitats: Lowland heath with broadleaf woodland.
Key birds: Cuckoo, Green Woodpecker, Stonechat, Tree Pipit, Skylark, Yellowhammer.
Other notable flora and fauna: More than 5,000 species of insect recorded, including several red data book species of bee and wasp, also glow worm and common lizard.
Contact: Trust HQ, 01889 880 100.

Warwickshire and West Midlands

Warwickshire's river valleys and gravelpits are crucially important for breeding and passage birds. Tame Valley sites such as Kingsbury, Ladywalk and the Sandwell reserves attract passage waders while Brandon Marsh, HQ for the local Wildlife Trust, is important for breeding Cetti's and Grasshopper Warblers. The Trust manages 56 nature reserves.

1. BRANDON MARSH

Warwickshire Wildlife Trust.
Location: Sat nav: CV3 3GW. SP 386 761. Three miles SE of Coventry, 200 yards SE of A45/A46 junction (Tollbar End). Turn E off A45 (just after Texaco garage) into Brandon Lane. Reserve entrance signposted 1.25 miles on R.
Access: Visitor centre open weekdays (9am to 4.30pm), weekends (10am to 4pm). Only Trust members can visit site outside these hours. Entrance charge £2.50 (free to Wildlife Trust members). Wheelchair access to nature trail and Wright hide. No dogs. Parking for 2 coaches.
Facilities: Visitor centre, toilets, tea-room (open daily 10am-3pm weekdays, 10am-4pm weekends), nature trail, seven hides.
Public transport: Bus service from Coventry to Tollbar End then 1.25 mile walk. Tel Travel West Midlands 02476 817 032 for bus times.
Habitats: Ten pools, together with marsh, reedbeds, willow carr, scrub and small mixed woodland in 260 acres, designated SSSI in 1972.

NATURE RESERVES - CENTRAL ENGLAND

Key birds: More than 230 species recorded. *Spring/summer*: Garden and Grasshopper Warblers, Whitethroat, Lesser Whitethroat, Hobby, Little Ringed Plover, Whinchat, Wheatear. *Autumn/winter*: Bittern (last three winters), Dunlin, Ruff, Snipe, Greenshank, Green and Common Sandpipers, Wigeon, Shoveler, Pochard, Goldeneye, Siskin, Redpoll. *All year*: Cetti's Warbler, Kingfisher, Water Rail, Gadwall, Little Grebe, Buzzard.
Other notable flora and fauna: Badger, otter, great crested newt. More than 20 species of butterfly and 18 species of dragonfly recorded. Almost 500 plants species listed on www.brandonbirding.co.uk
Contact: Visitor centre hotline 02476 308 999; e-mail: enquiries@wkwt.org.uk

2. COOMBE COUNTRY PARK

Coventry City Council.
Location: Sat nav: CV3 2AB. SP 402 795. At Binley, five miles E of Coventry centre, on B4027 Coventry to Brinklow road.
Access: Park open every day, car parks from 8am to dusk. Visitor centre closed on Dec 25/26 and Jan 1. Entry by foot is free. Pay-and-display parking. Paths mainly hard surfaces accessible for wheelchairs. Manual wheelchairs can be hired for a £5 returnable deposit.
Facilities: Visitor centre (10am opening), toilets, including disabled, café, bird hide, gift shop, picnic benches and wildflower meadow (March to September).
Public transport: By rail: To Coventry City Centre, 20 minute bus journey to park. By bus: No 585 Mike de Courcey Travel (for timetable ring 024 7630 2656).
Habitats: 500 acres of parkland, lake, woodland and formal gardens.
Key birds: Large heronry (50+ nests) on lake island, plus many Cormorants. Lesser Spotted Woodpecker and Marsh Tit top the list of woodland species.
Other notable flora and fauna: More than 250 species of plant, including lesser celandine, foxglove, bluebell, red campion and herb robert. Mammals include wood mouse and muntjac deer.
Contact: Coombe Country Park, 02476 453 720; e-mail: coombe.countrypark@coventry.gov.uk

3. DRAYCOTE WATER

Severn Trent Water.
Location: Sat nav: CV23 8AB. SP 460 700. Reservoir and 20-acre country park situated near Dunchurch, 3.5 miles SW of Rugby off the A426.
Access: Open all year, except Dec 25. Access to reservoir on foot or bicycle only. Cars must stop at pay-and-display car park. Disabled parking allowed at Toft, close to bird hide. Paths good for wheelchairs. Dogs only in Country Park.
Facilities: Newly-refurbished visitor centre, with toilets. Five mile road surrounding reservoir. One bird hide.
Habitats: Very large storage reservoir, surrounded by grassland and wooded areas.
Key birds: *Winter:* A wide range of common wildfowl species, plus regular sightings of less common species such as Smew, Black-necked Grebe and Scaup. Gull roost can number in excess of 50,000 birds, with white-winged gulls seen regularly. *Spring and autumn:* Birds on passage include waders, Black and Arctic Terns and Ospreys. Farm and woodland species in surrounding countryside all year round.
Contact: Draycote Water, Kites Hardwick, Warwickshire CV23 8AB. 01788 811 107; e-mail: visitor.sites@severntrent.co.uk.

4. KINGSBURY WATER PARK

Warwickshire County Council.
Location: Sat nav: B76 0DY. SP 203 960. Signposted `Water Park' from J9 M42 and A4097 NE of Birmingham.
Access: Open all year except Dec 25 (generally 8am to dusk, 5.30am in June and July). Pay on entry car park or annual permits in advance online.
Facilities: Four hides, two with wheelchair access overlooking Cliff Pool nature reserve. Miles of flat surfaced footpaths, loan scheme for mobility scooters. Cafes, Information Centre with gift shop (open 9.30am to 4.30pm weekdays; 9am to 5pm weekends and bank holidays).
Public transport: Call for advice.
Habitats: Open water; numerous small pools, some with gravel islands; gravel pits; silt beds with

reedmace, reed, willow and alder; rough areas and grassland.
Key birds: 230 species recorded, inc Kingfisher. *Summer:* Breeding warblers (nine species), Little Ringed Plover, Great Crested and Little Grebes. Shoveler, Shelduck and a thriving Common Tern colony. Passage Ospreys, Hobbies, waders (esp. spring). *Winter:* Wildfowl, Short-eared Owl.
Other notable flora and fauna: Orchids.
Contact: Kingsbury Water Park, 01827 872 660; e-mail: parks@warwickshire.gov.uk
www.warwickshire.gov.uk/park

5. LADYWALK RESERVE

CEGB/West Midland Bird Club
Location: Sat nav: B46 2BS. SP 212 917. Former site of Hams Hall power station, situated in Tame Valley ten miles from Birmingham city centre. From junction 9 of M42, head south on A446 to Hams Hall Distribution Centre. Follow Faraday Avenue to reserve. WMBC members can use secure car park near to Sainsbury's warehouse.
Access: Enter site by footbridge. Reserve open only to WMBC members, but other groups can organise visits with club sec. Non-members can observe site from public footpaths east of River Tame. No easy access on site for disabled visitors. Display permits on dashboard if using secure car park. Dogs not allowed.
Facilities: Six hides, including elevated River Walk Hide. Other screens for close-up viewing. Circular footpath (1.6 miles).
Public transport: Buses for Birmingham Airport (17 and 717 from Nuneaton) and 777 (from Coleshill) stop in Faraday Avenue.
Habitats: 125 acres of floodland, reedbed and woodland within a loop of The River Tame.
Key birds: More than 200 species recorded. *Winter:* Hundreds of wildfowl, inc Wigeon, Teal, Shoveler, Goldeneye and Goosander. Water Rail and Woodcock regular and lots of small bird activity at the feeding stations. Up to four Bitterns in recent years, plus Siskin, Redpoll and winter thrushes. *Spring/summer:* Passage waders inc Greenshank, Curlew, godwits and plovers, plus many hirundines and other migrants.
Other notable flora and fauna: Five species or orchid, including the county's only known colony of marsh hellibore. Also locally rare yellow bird's nest. Butterflies are plentiful and 16 species of dragonfly recorded.
Contact: WMBC permit secretary: Barbara Oakley, 147 Worlds End Lane, Quinton, Birmingham B32 1JX. E-mail: permits@westmidlandbirdclub.com

6. MIDDLETON LAKES

RSPB (Midlands Regional Office).
Location: Sat nav: B78 2AE. SP 192 967. Reserve lies in the Tame Valley, S of Tamworth, next to Middleton Hall. Leave M42 at J9 onto A446, then A4091 and finally into Bodymoor Heath Road.
Access: Open dawn till dusk daily. Free for RSPB members, £2 parking fee for non-members. Surfaced path from car park to Middleton Hall and heronry.

Other paths are unsurfaced but generally flat. Playmeadow Trail has partial wheelchair access. Car parking for 30 and bike racks on site. Dogs allowed in leads in parts of the site.
Facilities: Three viewing platforms and three viewing screens. Lookout hide open to view northern scrapes (see RSPB website for lock combination number). Four trails, ranging from 500m to 3km in length. Nearest toilets at Middleton Hall.
Public transport: No local bus service. Wilnecote train station is 2.5 miles from the reserve.
Habitats: This former quarry now boasts lakes, reedbeds, meadows and woodland areas.
Key birds: *All year:* Barn Owls are regularly seen and Cetti's Warbler frequently heard. *Spring/summer:* 100-strong heronry, plus common migrant warblers, Lapwing, hirundines and woodland species. *Winter:* Lesser Spotted and Great Spotted Woodpeckers and Willow Tit on the feeders, plus peak numbers of wildfowl and waders. Raptors include Hen and Marsh Harriers, Merlin, Peregrine and Short-eared Owl.
Other notable wildlife: Bluebells and spring flowers, grass snake, common butterflies and moths.
Contact: Call reserve on 01827 259 454; e-mail: middletonlakes@rspb.org.uk

7. ROUGH WOOD CHASE LNR

Walsall Metropolitan Borough Council.
Location: Sat nav: WV12 5NH. SJ 984 007. Reserve composed of six sites on W edge of Walsall Borough. From M6 (Jt 10) head for Willenhall and A462. Turn right into Bloxwich Road North and right again into Hunts Lane. Car park on bend.
Access: Open all year.
Facilities: Circular nature trail linking all sites.
Public transport: 369 Walsall and Willenhall, 364 Walsall and Coppice Farm and 341 Walsall and Willenhall.
Habitats: 70 acres of oakwood, significant for West Midlands. Sneyd reservoir, meadows, ponds, pools, marsh and scrubland.
Key birds: Great Crested and Little Grebes on pools in the north end of Chase. Breeding Jay and Sparrowhawk. Common woodland species all year and warblers in summer.
Other notable flora and fauna: Great crested and smooth newts, water vole, various dragonfly species, purple hairstreak, brimstone and small heath butterflies.
Contact: Morgan Bowers, Senior Countryside Ranger 01922 654 220; e-mail: bowersm@walsall.gov.uk

8. SANDWELL VALLEY COUNTRY PARK

Sandwell Metropolitan Borough Council.
Location: Sat nav: B71 4BG (Salter's Lane). Entrances at SP 012 918 and SP 028 992. Located approx. 1 mile NE of West Bromwich town centre. Main entrance off Salters Lane or Forge Lane.
Access: Car parks open 8am to sunset. Wheelchair access to Priory Woods LNR, Forge Mill Lake LNR and other parts of the country park.

Facilities: 1,700 acre site. Visitor centre, toilets, café at Sandwell Park Farm (10am-4.30pm). Good footpaths around LNRs and much of the country park. Coach parking by appointment. Also 20 acre RSPB reserve (see below).
Public transport: West Bromwich bus station and central metro stop. (Traveline 0871 200 2233).
Habitats: Pools, woodlands, grasslands, including three Local Nature Reserves.
Key birds: Wintering wildfowl including regular flock of Goosander, small heronry. *All year:* Grey Heron, Great Crested Grebe, Lapwing, Reed Bunting, Great Spotted and Green Woodpeckers, Sparrowhawk, Kestrel. *Spring:* Little Ringed Plover, Oystercatcher, up to 8 species of warber breeding, passage migrants. *Autumn:* Passage migrants. *Winter:* Goosander, Shoveler, Teal, Wigeon, Snipe.
Other notable flora and fauna: Common spotted and southern marsh orchid. Ringlet butterfly. Water vole, weasel.
Contact: Senior Countryside Ranger, Sandwell Park Farm, 01215 530 220 or 2147.

9. SANDWELL VALLEY RSPB

RSPB (Midlands Regional Office).
Location: Sat nav: B43 5AG. SP 035 928. Great Barr, Birmingham. Follow signs S from M6 J7 via A34. Take R at 1st junction onto A4041. Take 4th

L onto Hamstead Road (B4167), then R at 1st mini roundabout onto Tanhouse Avenue.
Access: 800 metres of paths accessible to assisted and powered wheelchairs with some gradients (please phone for further information). Dogs on leads. Car parks closed on Mon and Thurs.
Facilities: Visitor centre still unavailable following fire in 2010 — toilets, refreshments and car parking at Forge Mill Farm (15 minute walk). Viewing screens. Phone centre for details on coach parking. Lakeside hide and car park are open (10.30am-1pm Tue-Fri), (10.30am-3.30pm Sat-Sun), at other times the reserve is open to pedestrians. More facilities are being added.
Public transport: Bus: 16 from Corporation Street (Stand CJ), Birmingham City Centre (ask for Tanhouse Avenue). Train: Hamstead Station, then 16 bus for one mile towards West Bromwich from Hamstead (ask for Tanhouse Avenue).
Habitats: Open water, wet grassland, reedbed, dry grassland and scrub.
Key birds: *Summer:* Lapwing, Little Ringed Plover, Reed Warbler, Whitethroat, Sedge Warbler, Willow Tit. *Passage:* Sandpipers, Yellow Wagtail, chats, Common Tern. *Winter:* Water Rail, Snipe, Jack Snipe, Goosander, Bullfinch, woodpeckers and wildfowl.
Contact: Sandwell Valley RSPB Reserve, 01213 577 395; e-mail: sandwellvalley@rspb.org.uk

Worcestershire

THE LARGELY rural county has only one sizeable reservoir — Bittell — but there are excellent wetlands to explore at Upton Warren and Bredon's Hardwick. For the widest range of woodland species, the best area is the Wyre Forest west of Kidderminster, but the Wildlife Trust owns or manages 70 reserves covering a wide range of habitats.

1. KNAPP & PAPERMILL

Worcestershire Wildlife Trust.
Location: Sat nav: WR6 5HR. Take A4103 SW from Worcester; R at Bransford roundabout then L towards Suckley and reserve is approx three miles (do not turn off for Alfrick). Park at Bridges Stone lay-by (SO 751 522), cross road and follow path to the Knapp House.
Access: Open daily. Large parties should contact Warden in advance. Paths steep and uneven.
Facilities: Nature trail, small visitor centre with toilets, wildlife garden, Kingfisher viewing screen.
Public transport: None.
Habitats: Broadleaved woodland, unimproved grassland, fast stream, old orchard in Leigh Brook Valley.
Key birds: *Summer:* Breeding Grey Wagtail and Dipper, Nuthatch and common woodland species, Kingfisher, Spotted Flycatcher (nests in private garden), all three woodpeckers. Buzzard, Sparrowhawk and Redstart also occur.

Other notable flora and fauna: Otters have returned recently. Good numbers of dragonflies and butterflies (30 species recorded) on all three meadows include holly blue, purple hairstreak and white admiral. Bluebells, green-winged and spotted orchids.
Contact: The Warden, Knapp and Papermill reserve, The Knapp, Alfrick WR6 5HR. 01905 754 919; enquiries@worcestershirewildlifetrust.org

2. MALVERN HILLS

Malvern Hills Conservators.
Location: Sat nav: WR13 6HR (British Camp car park). SO 756 402. An eight-mile-long range of hills and commons lying S and W of Great Malvern, covering approx 3,000 acres. Best birding areas include Castlemorton Common and Midsummer Hill.
Access: Open all year. Charge for car parks is £2 per day or £25 for year-long permit.
Facilities: Public toilets with disabled access opposite British Camp car park (A449 Worcester Road). Two easy-access trails at Earnslaw (400 metres long) and Blackhill (200 metres long).
Habitats: Grassland on hilltops, mixed woodland, scrub, quarries, small reservoirs and lakes.
Key birds: Raptors include Buzzard, Sparrowhawk, Peregrine and Hobby. Ravens nest in quarries and spring passage migrants include Wheatear, Ring Ouzel (best in Happy Valley between Worcestershire Beacon and North Hill) and more rarely, Dotterel. Autumn sees a good range of migrants heading south. Wooded areas hold all the expected common species, plus

NATURE RESERVES - CENTRAL ENGLAND

breeding warblers and flycatchers, all three woodpeckers and Tree Pipits on woodland edges. A few Nightingales hang on in areas of dense scrub, which also hold chats, pipits and Linnets. A winter highlight is Snow Bunting on the highest hills.

Other notable flora and fauna: Lesser horseshoe and barbastelle bats, polecat, 25 species of butterfly recorded, inc high brown fritillary. Broad range of plants include blinks, crosswort and common spotted orchid.

Contact: Malvern Hills Conservators, Manor House, Grange Road, Malvern WR14 3EY. Tel: 01684 892 002; e-mail: conservators@malvernhills.org.uk

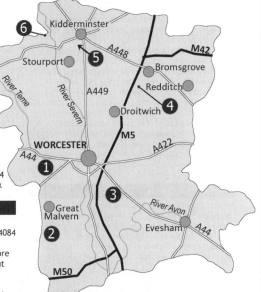

3. TIDDESLEY WOOD NATURE RESERVE

Worcestershire Wildlife Trust.

Location: Sat nav: WR10 2AD. SO 929 462. Take B4084 from Pershore towards Worcester. Turn L towards Besford and Croome near town boundary just before the summit of the hill. Entrance is on L after about 0.75 miles.

Access: Open all year except Dec 25. Cycles and horses only allowed on the bridleway. Dogs on leads. Avoid military firing range in SW corner of wood, marked by red flags. Do not enter NE plot, which is private property. Main ride stoney, with some potholes. Small pathways difficult if wet. Coach parking by appointment.

Facilities: Information board. Circular trail around small pathways. Car park off B4084 (signposted to Besford and Croome).

Public transport: First Midland Red services.

Habitats: Ancient woodland, conifers.

Key birds: All year: Coal Tit, Goldcrest, Sparrowhawk, Willow Tit, Marsh Tit. Spring: Chiffchaff, Blackcap, Cuckoo. Winter: Redwing, Fieldfare.

Other notable flora and fauna: Dragonflies including club-tailed and white-legged damselflies. Good for butterflies, including white admiral, peacock and gatekeeper. Important invertebrates include nationally rare noble chafer beetle which has been recorded here for many years.

Contact: Trust HQ, 01905 754 919: e-mail: enquiries@ worcestershirewildlifetrust.org

4. UPTON WARREN

Worcestershire Wildlife Trust.

Location: Sat nav: B61 7ER (Outdoor Education Centre). SO 936 677. Two miles S of Bromsgrove on A38. Leave M5 at junction 5 and head N on A38, turning third exit and first roundabout.

Access: Christopher Cadbury Wetland Reserve consists of Moors Pools (freshwater) and Flashes Pools (saline). Always open except Dec 25. Park in education centre car park. Free for Trust members, or £3 day permit from Trust centre at Smite, education centre or volunteers on site. Disabled access to hides

at Moors Pools only by prior arrangement. No dogs.

Facilities: Six hides, maps at entrances, paths can be very muddy. Coach parking at sailing centre by previous booking.

Public transport: Birmingham/Worcester buses pass reserve entrance.

Habitats: Fresh and saline pools with muddy islands, some woodland and scrub.

Key birds: Winter: Wildfowl, Bittern, Water Rail, Snipe. Spring/autumn: Passage waders. Summer: Breeding Avocet, Redshank, Little Ringed Plover, Oystercatcher, Common Tern, Sedge, Reed, Grasshopper and Cetti's Warblers. Hobby nearby.

Other notable flora and fauna: Saltmarsh plants, dragonflies.

Contact: Trust HQ, 01905 754 919: e-mail: enquiries@ worcestershirewildlifetrust.org

5. WILDEN MARSH

Worcestershire Wildlife Trust.

Location: Sat nav: DY13 9JT. SO 825 730. S of Kidderminster. Take A449 S from Kidderminster. At junction with A442 go straight across roundabout into Wilden Lane, a very busy road with few parking spaces, so park carefully in lay-by.

Access: Enter over stile at gated entrance next to southern lay-by. Please obey signs to leave certain areas undisturbed. No access to northern part of the site. Gated entrances are open at all times. This reserve is complex and new visitors should consult a map. Secure cattle gates at all times. Beware boggy areas, steep banks by the River Stour and deep ditches.

Facilities: None. Limited parking on Wilden Lane.
Public transport: Nearest bus stop at Wilden, half mile from reserve.
Habitats: Dry and marshy fields with small alder and willow woods, reedbeds and many drainage ditches.
Key birds: 192 bird species have been recorded since 1968 and about 70 breed, including Yellow Wagtail, nine species of warblers and Redshank. Wintering area for Water Pipits, though numbers have declined recently.
Other notable fauna: Plants include southern marsh orchids, marsh cinquefoil, marsh arrow-grass, marsh pennywort and lesser water parsnip.
Contact: Trust HQ, 01905 754 919; e-mail: enquiries@worcestershirewildlifetrust.org

6. WYRE FOREST NNR

Natural England/Worcs Wildlife Trust.
Location: Sat nav: DY12 3AA (Fred Dale Reserve car park). SO 750 760. 0.5 miles NW of Bewdley (on the A456) and 4.5 miles W of Kidderminster.
Access: Observe reserve signs and keep to paths.
Facilities: Toilets and refreshments (with disabled access). Several waymarked trails in (some suitable for wheelchair users) as well as regular guided walks, also family cycle routes through the reserve.
Public transport: The nearest train station is in Kidderminster. Local bus services between Bewdley and Kidderminster are provided by First Group (0871 200 2233).
Habitats: Oak forest, conifer areas, birch heath, lowland grassland, stream.
Key birds: Breeding birds include Redstart, Pied Flycatcher, Wood Warbler, Buzzard and Raven, with Dipper, Grey Wagtail and Kingfisher found on the larger streams.
Other notable flora and fauna: Mammals include, fallow, roe and muntjac deer, polecat, otter and mink, yellow-neck mouse, dormouse, voles and water shrew. Several bat species including pipistrelle and Daubenton's. Important site for invertebrates including England's largest colony of pearl-bordered fritillary butterflies.
Contact: Wyre Forest NNR, Natural England Office, Lodge Hill Farm, Dowles Brook, Bewdley DY12 2LY; 01299 400 686.

Eastern England

Bedfordshire, Cambridgeshire, Essex, Hertfordshire, Norfolk, Suffolk

Bedfordshire

THOUGH one of England's smallest counties, Bedfordshire is not devoid of birding interest. Blows Down is one of the best southern sites in to see Ring Ouzels on spring passage. Intense observer coverage at the RSPB's HQ at The Lodge, Sandy, has produced a series of excellent records. Exploring Country Parks such as Priory and Harold-Odell is best early in the morning before the dog-walkers are out.

1. BLOW'S DOWNS

Beds, Cambs & Northants Wildlife Trust.
Location: Sat nav: LU5 4AE. TL 030 215. On the outskirts of Dunstable. Take A5065 from W of Luton, cross M1, take first exit at roundabout, park with care on verge. Can also walk half mile from Dunstable centre to W entrance at Half Moon Lane off A5.
Access: Open all year, not suitable for wheelchairs due to steep slopes.
Facilities: None. Park on road verge.
Public transport: None.
Habitats: SSSI, chalk downland, scrub and grassland, that is a traditional resting place for incoming spring migrants.
Key birds: *Winter:* Lapwing, Meadow Pipit, Skylark. *Spring/autumn:* Ring Ouzel, Wheatear, Whinchat, Black Redstart, Stonechat, Willow Warbler.
Other notable flora and fauna: Chalkhill blue, brown argus and marbled white butterflies. Plants include small scabious, burnet-saxifrage, squinancywort, great pignut, common spotted and bee orchids.
Contact: Trust Bedfordshire office HQ, 01234 364 213, 01954 713 500; e-mail: bedfordshire@wildlifebcnp.org www.wildlifebcn.org

2. FLITWICK MOOR

Beds, Cambs & Northants Wildlife Trust.
Location: Sat nav: MK45 5BP. TL 046 354. E of Flitwick. From Flitwick town centre (Tesco roundabout) on A5120, cross railway bridge, R at roundabout, immediately L into King's Road. After 500m, L into Maulden Road towards A507. After quarter mile R at Folly Farm, follow track to small car park. Also footpath to reserve from Moor Lane.
Access: Open all year.
Facilities: Car park. Please stick to public paths.
Public transport: Frequent buses (United Counties) from Bedford and Luton to Flitwick, or take train to Flitwick and then three-quarter mile walk.
Habitats: SSSI. Important wetland for the area, blend of fen, meadow, wet woodland and fragile peaty soil. Supports mosses ferns and flowers.
Key birds: *Winter:* Siskin, Water Rail, Great Spotted Woodpecker. *Spring:* Lesser Spotted Woodpecker,

Willow Warbler, Blackcap. *Summer*: Water Rail, Grasshopper and Garden Warblers, Cuckoo. *Autumn*: Brambling.
Other notable flora and fauna: Good variety of butterflies and dragonflies, plus chimney sweeper moth and conehead bush cricket. Plants include ten species of sphagnum moss, marsh pennywort, black knapweed, water figwort plus fly agaric and yellow brain fungus in autumn.
Contact: Reserves manager 01234 364 213; e-mail: bedfordshire@wildlifebcn.org

3. THE LODGE

RSPB (Central England Office).
Location: Sat nav: SG19 2DL. TL 191 485. Reserve lies 1 mile E of Sandy, signposted from the B1042 road to Potton.
Access: Reserve open daily 7am to 9pm (or sunset when earlier); shop 9am to 5pm weekdays, 10am to 5pm weekends and bank hols. Non-members: £5 per motor vehicle. Dogs only allowed on bridleway.
Facilities: Five miles of nature trails. One bridleway (half mile) and gardens are wheelchair/pushchair accessible. One hide (wheelchair accessible), 50 yards from car park. Coach parking at weekends by arrangement. Refreshments at shop. Toilets (in disabled).
Public transport: Buses to Sandy Market Square from Bedford, infrequent service. One mile walk or cycle from centre of Sandy or half mile from Sandy railway station, in part along trail through heathland restoration.
Habitats: This 180-hectare reserve is a mixture of woodland, heathland and acid grassland and includes the formal gardens of the RSPB's UK headquarters. New areas being restored to heathland.
Key birds: *Spring/summer*: Hobby, Spotted Flycatcher, breeding common woodland species and warblers. *All year*: Woodpeckers, woodland birds. *Winter*: Winter thrushes, woodland birds.
Other notable flora and fauna: Natterjack toads, rare heathland insects. Particularly good site for fungi, and lichens. Garden pools are good for dragonflies.
Contact: RSPB The Lodge Shop 01767 680 541; e-mail: thelodgereserve@rspb.org.uk

4. MARSTON VALE MILLENIUM COUNTRY PARK

Marston Vale Trust.
Location: Sat nav: MK43 0PS. TL 004 417. SW of Bedford off A421 at Marston Moretaine. Only five mins from J13 of M1 along A421 towards Bedford.
Access: Pedestrian access to park at any time. Forest centre open summer 10am to 6pm, winter 10am to 5pm. Forest Centre and car park closed Dec 25/26 and Jan 1. No dogs in wetlands. Entry charge for wetland reserve. Main 8km trail and 2km Wetland Trail surfaced for wheelchair and pushchair access. Coach parking available.
Facilities: Cafe bar, gift shop, art gallery. Free parking. The 2km wetland trail is a level path with a compacted, loose stone surface inc two hand gates

with top latches.
Public transport: Trains to Millbrook and Stewartby station, 20 minute walk to Forest Centre.
Habitats: Millenium Country Park covers 555 acres and includes the 210-acre Stewartby Lake which attracts birds when smaller waters are frozen. Reedbeds, woodland, hawthorn scrub, ponds and wet grassland.
Key birds: *Winter*: Bittern, Peregrine, Siskin, Redpoll, Stonechat, Snipe, gulls inc Caspian, Yellow-legged and Mediterranean Gulls, thrushes, wildfowl (Gadwall, Shoveler, Pochard, Teal and Tufted Duck), Little and Great Crested Grebes. Rarer species can include divers, grebes, Common Scoter, Smew and Scaup. *Spring*: Passage waders and terns (Black, Sandwich and Arctic Terns), hirundines, Wheatear, Whinchat, Osprey and Little Gull. Yellow Wagtail and Garganey occasionally breed.
Summer: Ten species of breeding warblers, Hobby, Turtle Dove, Nightingale, Bearded Tit, Cuckoo, Barn Owl, Marsh Harrier, Water Rail, Kingfisher and common wildfowl. *Autumn*: Passage waders and terns. *Rarities*: Glossy Ibis, Laughing Gull, Caspian Gull, Manx Shearwater, Purple Heron and White Stork.
Other notable flora and fauna: Dingy and grizzled skipper butterflies, excellent for dragonflies. Also otter and brown hare, plus bee and pyramidal orchids and stoneworts.
Contact: Forest Centre, 01234 767 037; e-mail: info@marstonvale.org; www.marstonvale.org

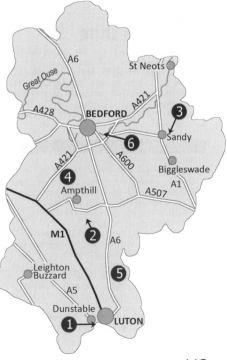

5. PEGSDON HILLS RESERVE

Beds, Cambs & Northants Wildlife Trust.
Location: TL 120 295. 5 miles W of Hitchin. Take B655 from Hitchin towards Barton-le-Clay. Turn R at Pegsdon then immediately L and park in lay-by. Reserve entrance across B655 via footpath.
Access: Open all year. Dropping off point for coaches only.
Facilities: None.
Public transport: Luton to Henlow buses (United Counties) stop at Pegsdon.
Habitats: Chalk grassland, scrub and woodland.
Key birds: *Winter*: Brambling, Stonechat, winter thrushes, raptors including Buzzard. *Spring*: Wheatear, Ring Ouzel, Tree Pipit, Yellowhammer. *Summer*: Turtle Dove, Grey Partridge, Lapwing, Skylark.
Other notable flora and fauna: Dark green fritillary, dingy and grizzled skippers, chalkhill blue, brown argus and small heath butterflies. Glow worms. Plants include pasqueflower in spring, fragrant and common spotted orchids.
Contact: Bedfordshire office 01234 364 213; e-mail: bedfordshire@wildlifebcn.org www.wildlifebcn.org

6. PRIORY COUNTRY PARK

Bedford Borough Council.
Location: Sat nav: MK41 9DJ. TL 071 495. 1.5 miles SE from Bedford town centre. Signposted from A4280 and A421. Entry point to new 'River Valley Park'

Access: Park and hides open at all times. No access to fenced/gated plantations.
Facilities: Toilets and visitor centre open daytime, all-year-round disabled access on new path around lake. Hides, nature trails, labyrinth, Premier Inn for meals, accommodation.
Public transport: Stagecoach (01604 676 060) 'Blue Solo 4' every 20 mins. Mon-Sat. Alight 1st stop Riverfield Drive (200 m). Rail station at Bedford (approx 2.5 miles)
Habitats: Lakes, reedbeds, scrub and woodland, meadows adjoining Great Ouse.
Key birds: 212 species recorded. Good numbers/variety of winter wildfowl, varied mix of spring passage species, with breeding warblers and woodpeckers, augmented by feeding terns, hirundines and raptors lakeside. *Winter*: Grebes, Pochard, Shoveler, Gadwall, Merlin, Water Rail, gulls, thrushes, Chiffchaff, corvids, buntings. *Passage*: Raptors, waders, terns, pipits. *Summer*: Hobby, Turtle Dove, Swift, hirundines, *acrocephalus* and *sylvia* warblers. *All year*: Cormorant, Little Egret, Grey Heron, Stock Dove, woodpeckers, Kingfisher, Grey Wagtail, Treecreeper, Goldfinch, Bullfinch.
Other notable flora and fauna: 23 species of dragonfly, incl small red-eyed damsel and hairy hawker. 20 species of butterfly. Large plant list. Fox, muntjac and otter.
Contact: Jon Bishop, Wardens Office, Visitor Centre, Priory CP, Barkers Lane, Bedford, MK41 9SH. 01234 211 182.

Cambridgeshire

THE NENE and Ouse Washes are superb for wintering wildfowl, owls and raptors, with the former also offering the chance of Cranes, breeding Black-tailed Godwits, Spotted Crakes plus introduced Corncrakes in summer. Grafham Water attracts plenty of scarce species, while Paxton Pits is probably the best place in the country to actually see Nightingales.

1. FEN DRAYTON LAKES

RSPB (Eastern England Office).
Location: Sat nav: PE27 4TR. TL 341 699. NW of Cambridge. Leave A14 at Junction 28; follow signs to Swavesey. Turn L in Boxworth End (signed to Fen Drayton). Turn R onto minor road (signed to Swavesey), then L into entrance to Fen Drayton Lakes. Follow signs to car park.
Access: Open at all times. Dogs only allowed on public footpaths and bridleways. Disabled birders can get car access to one viewing screen.
Facilities: Five viewing screens, one hide and three open viewing shelters. Ten-mile network of trails. Information boards give access details. Free trail guides and events leaflets are available from the Elney car park.
Public transport: Cambridgeshire Guided Bus service between Huntingdon and Cambridge (runs every ten

mins) has a request stop in the reserve.
Habitats: A complex of lakes (former gravel workings) and traditional riverside meadows next to the River Great Ouse).
Key birds: At least 213 species have been recorded in the area with some 65 species being regular breeders, including Common Tern. Hobby, waders on passage. Rarities include Great White Egret, Purple Heron, Glossy Ibis, Common Crane, Red-Footed Falcon, Honey Buzzard and Whiskered Tern. Bitterns are now a regular sight, with Holywell Lake and Elney Lake being the favoured sites. *Winter*: Nationally important numbers of Gadwall and Coot.
Other notable fauna: Good site for butterflies, dragonflies and mammals.
Contact: Fen Drayton, 01954 233 260; e-mail: fendraytonlakes@rspb.org.uk

2. FERRY MEADOWS COUNTRY PARK

Nene Park Trust.
Location: Sat nav: PE2 5UU (Ham Lane). TL 145 975. Three miles W of Peterborough city centre and two miles E of A1. On all major routes into city, follow brown tourist signs for Nene Park or country park symbol. Also signposted on Oundle Road (A605).
Access: Open all year, 7am to dusk (summer), 8am until sunset in winter. Electric scooters and wheelchair available for loan — call to book in advance. Coach parking free at all times. Car parking

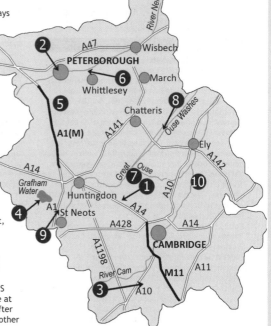

charge (£4) applies at weekends and Bank Holidays between March and Oct.

Facilities: Car park, visitor centre (opens 10am), toilets (inc disabled), café, two wheelchair-accessible hides in nature reserve area. Hard surface paths in park's central areas, but steep slopes in Bluebell Wood.

Public transport: Stagecoach X14 stops on A605 by Notcutts Nursery. Half mile walk to park entrance. Tel. Traveline 0870 6082 608 or www.traveline.org.uk

Habitats: Lakes, meadows, scrub, broadleaved woodland and small wetland nature reserve.

Key birds: *All year*: Good selection of woodland and water birds, Kingfisher. *Spring*: Terns, waders, Yellow Wagtail. *Winter*: Grebes, gulls, Siskin, Redpoll, Water Rail.

Other notable flora and fauna: Bluebell, wood anemone, wild garlic in woodland.

Contact: Visitor Services Officer, Nene Park Trust, 01733 234 193; www.nene-park-trust.org.uk e-mail: visitor.services@ neneparktrust.org.uk

3. FOWLMERE

RSPB (Eastern England Office).

Location: Sat nav: SG8 6EZ. TL 406 461. 7 miles S of Cambridge. From A10, turn towards Fowlmere at Fowlmere-Shepreth crossroads (no RSPB sign); after 1 mile, turn R by cemetery (RSPB sign); after another 0.6 mile, turn L into reserve.

Access: Access at all times along marked trail. Dogs only on private track on eastern boundary. Donations requested from non-RSPB members.

Facilities: 1.8 miles of trails. Three hides, visitor centre and toilets. Space for one coach, prior booking essential. Wheelchair access to one hide, toilet and some of the trails.

Public transport: Shepreth railway station 2 miles. By bus: Dunsbridge Turnpike (outside Country Homes & Gardens), 1 mile. Walk towards Melbourn; after 300 m, cross road and turn left on to single track road to Fowlmere (beware of traffic); after 0.75 mile (1.2 km), turn right into reserve (RSPB sign).

Habitats: Reedbeds, meres, woodland, scrub.

Key birds: *Spring/summer*: Little Grebe, Turtle Dove, ten breeding warblers. *All year*: Water Rail, Kingfisher, Reed Bunting. *Autumn*: Yellowhammer, Corn Bunting. *Winter*: Snipe, Water Rail, raptors.

Other notable flora and fauna: Healthy population of water shrews and otters. 18 species of dragonfly.

Contact: Fowlmere, 01763 208 978; e-mail:fowlmere@rspb.org.uk

4. GRAFHAM WATER

Beds, Cambs & Northants Wildlife Trust.

Location: Sat nav: PE28 0DW (West Perry car park). TL 143 671. Follow signs for Grafham Water from A1 at Buckden or A14 at Ellington. Follow B661 road towards Perry and Staughtons to West Perry. As you leave village, Anglian Water's Mander car park is signposted on R.

Access: Open all year. Dogs barred in wildlife garden only, on leads elsewhere. Car parking £2 for day ticket.

Facilities: Six bird hides in nature reserve, three in bird sanctuary area. Two in wildlife garden accessible to wheelchairs. A further hide overlooks islands and scrapes in the settlement lagoons. Cycle track through reserve also accessible to wheelchairs. Visitor centres at Mander and Plummer car parks with restaurants, shops and toilets. Disabled parking. Use Plummer car park for lagoons and Marlow car park for dam area (good for waders and vagrants).

Public transport: None.

Habitats: Open water, lagoons, reedbeds, open water, wet mud and willow carr, ancient and plantation woodland, scrub, species-rich grassland.

Key birds: *Resident*: Common woodland birds, wildfowl. *Winter*: Waders including Common Sandpiper and Dunlin, Great Crested Grebe. Wildfowl including large flocks of common species, plus Shelduck, Goldeneye, Goosander and Smew, gulls (can be up to 30,000 roosting in mid-winter). *Spring/summer*: Breeding Nightingale, Reed, Willow and Sedge Warblers, Common and Black Terns. *Autumn*: Passage waders. *Rarities*: Have included Wilson's Phalarope (2007), Ring-necked Duck, Great Northern Diver, Glaucous, Iceland and Mediterranean Gulls.

Other notable flora and fauna: Bee,common spotted and early purple orchids, common twayblade (in woods), cowslip. Common blue and marbled white butterflies, dragonflies including broad-bodied chaser, voles, grass snakes.

Contact: Grafham Water Nature Reserve, 01480 811 075; grafham@wildlifebcn.org

5. THE GREAT FEN

BC&N Wildlife Trust/Natural England/Environment Agency/Hunts District Council
Location: Sat nav: PE26 2RS. TL 245 848 (Ramsey Heights), plus Holme Fen NNR and Woodwalton NNR (Chapel Road, Ramsey Heights), south of Peterborough, lying between the A1 in the west and Ramsey. B660 runs through the centre of Great Fen.
Access: Open access at all times to three visitor sites with views over farmland linking the reserves. Eventually Great Fen will occupy 9,000 acres. No dogs allowed. Wheelchair access difficult on grassy rides.
Facilities: Countryside Centre at Ramsey Heights site. Three elevated bird hides at Woodwalton reached via steps. One bird hide at Holme Fen. Grassed paths at Woodwalton and Holme Fens. New Decoy visitor information point.
Public transport: Limited bus service between Peterborough and Ramsey stops at end of Chapel Road, half mile from Countryside Centre.
Habitats: Pools formed from clay pits at Ramsey Heights; extensive birch forest (largest in lowland Britain) and reedbed at Holme Fen; mixed woodland, open waters, fen and grassland at Woodwalton.
Key birds: Wide variety of common wildfowl, plus Kingfisher, Grey Heron, Bittern and wintering Goosander on meres. Hen Harriers visit in winter while Marsh Harriers breed in reedbed, along with Bearded Tit and Cetti's Warbler. Common Crane observed in recent years. Wet meadows at Darlow's Farm attractive to breeding Lapwing, Snipe and Redshank and wintering Whooper and Bewick's Swans.
Other notable flora and fauna: Great crested newt and rare beetles at ramsey heights; otter, hare, deer species, water vole; scarce chaser dragonfly, small copper and white admiral butterflies. Wide variety of bog and heath plants.
Contact: Great Fen Team - 01487 710 420; e-mail: info@greatfen.org www.greatfen.org.uk

6. NENE WASHES

RSPB (Eastern England Office).
Location: Sat nav: PE7 2DD. TL 318 991. Reserve is 8 miles E of Peterborough, and NE of Whittlesey. Car park at end of Eldernell Lane, N off A605 east of Coates. There is currently no signposting to reserve.
Access: Open at all times along South Barrier Bank, accessed at Eldernell. Group visits along central path by arrangement. No access to fields or for wheelchairs along bank.
Facilities: Small car park – one coach max – at end of Eldernell Lane. No toilets or hide. Nene Valley Way path offers elevated views over reserve.
Public transport: Stagecoach Bus runs on A605, alight at Coates, walk down Eldernell Lane. 01733 554 575.
Habitats: Wet grassland with ditches. Often flooded.
Key birds: *Spring/early summer:* Corncrake release scheme, plus Spotted Crake. UK's top site for breeding Black-tailed Godwit. Other breeding

waders inc Lapwing, Redshank and Snipe. Duck (inc Garganey), Marsh Harrier, Hobby, Yellow Wagtail and Tree Sparrow. *Autumn/winter:* Waterfowl in large numbers (inc Bewick's Swan, Pintail, Shoveler), Barn and Short-eared Owls, Hen Harrier, Common Crane, roost of up to 20 Marsh Harriers.
Other notable flora and fauna: Water vole, otter, water violet, flowering rush and fringe water lily.
Contact: Charlie Kitchin, RSPB Nene Washes, 21a East Delph, Whittlesey, Cambs PE7 1RH. 01733 205 140.

7. OUSE FEN

RSPB (Eastern England office)/ Hanson.
Location: Sat nav: PE27 4TA. TL 348 729. Located at Needingworth, near St Ives. Leave Junction 26 of A14 onto A1096 London Road. Go straight over three roundabouts. At the fourth take third exit (A1123). Cross over the next roundabout and take next right-hand turn onto Bluntisham Road. After 400m, turn left into the reserve.
Access: Open at all times. Free parking. One Blue Badge space. Guide dogs welcome.
Facilities: Two waymarked visitor trails. Two viewpoints (one screened). No visitor centre or toilets.
Public transport: Whippet Buses run from St Ives to Needingworth (Nos 21/22 offer limited services Monday to Friday). From village bus stop follow Bluntisham Road east for 1 km until signpost for reserve on the right. Call Traveline on 0870 6082 608.
Habitats: A working sand and gravel quarry being developed into a vast nature reserve with open water, grassland and potentially the UK's largest reedbed.
Key birds: *Spring/summer:* Breeding Great Crested Grebe, Skylark, Marsh Harrier, Black-headed Gull, Reed Bunting, Bearded Tit and incoming migrants such as Reed and Sedge Warblers, hirundines, Black-tailed Godwit, Ruff, Garganey, Common Tern and Hobby. *Autumn:* Passage waders inc Green Sandpiper, increasing numbers of common wildfowl and incoming winter thrushes. *Winter:* Good numbers of Mute Swan, Gadwall, Tufted Duck, Wigeon and Pochard and regular sightings of Smew. Large numbers of Little Egret, plus flocks of tits, finches and buntings. Barn Owl and Bittern regular, plus occasional Short-eared Owl, Hen Harrier and Peregrine.
Other notable flora and fauna: Brown hare, roe and muntjac deer. Wide range of butterfly and dragonfly species.
Contact: RSPB Ouse Fen 01954 233 260.

8. OUSE WASHES

RSPB (Eastern England Office).
Location: Sat nav: PE15 0NF. TL 471 860. Between Chatteris and March on A141, take B1093 to Manea. Reserve signposted from Manea. Reserve office and visitor centre located off Welches Dam.
Access: Access from visitor centre (open 9am-5pm daily except Dec 25/26). Hides open at all times. Welches Dam to public hides approached by marked paths behind boundary bank. No charge. Dogs on leads. Disabled access to Welches Dam hide, 350

yards from car park. Groups welcome, but large coaches (36+ seats) cannot traverse final bend to reserve.
Facilities: Car park (inc 2 disabled bays) and toilets. Space for up to two small coaches. Ten hides overlook reserve: nearest 350 yards from visitor centre (with disabled access) up to 1.8 miles from visitor centre. Boardwalk over pond is good for dragonflies in summer.
Public transport: None to reserve entrance. Buses and trains stop at Manea, three miles from reserve.
Habitats: Lowland wet grassland — seasonally flooded. Open pool systems in front of some hides, particularly Stockdale's hide.
Key birds: *Summer:* Around 70 species breed including Black-tailed Godwit, Lapwing, Redshank, Snipe, Shoveler, Gadwall, Garganey and Spotted Crake. Also Hobby and Marsh Harrier. *Autumn:* Passage waders including Wood and Green Sandpipers, Spotted Redshank, Greenshank, Little Stint, plus terns and Marsh and Hen Harriers. *Winter:* Large number of wildfowl (up to 100,000 birds) including Bewick's and Whooper Swans, Wigeon, Teal, Shoveler, Pintail, Pochard.
Other notable flora and fauna: Good range of dragonflies, butterflies and fenland flora.
Contact: Site Manager, Ouse Washes Reserve, 01354 680 212; e-mail: ouse.washes@rspb.org.uk

9. PAXTON PITS NATURE RESERVE

Huntingdonshire District Council/Friends of Paxton Pits.
Location: Sat nav PE19 6ET. TL 196 629. Access from A1 at Little Paxton, two miles N of St Neots. Reserve signposted from edge of Little Paxton.
Access: Free entry. Open 24 hours. Visitors' centre open 7 days a week. Dogs allowed under control. Heron trail suitable for wheelchairs during summer. Coaches and group visits by arrangement.
Facilities: Wheelchair-accessible visitor centre (open most days) sells books, bird feeders and seed etc, plus light refreshments. Toilets (including disabled) available when visitor centre is open. Two bird hides (always open), marked nature trails.
Public transport: Buses run from St Neots and Huntingdon to Little Paxton (enquiries 0845 045 5200). The nearest train station is St Neots (enquiries 0845 748 4950).
Habitats: Grassland, scrub, lakes. Site, currently 78 hectares, is due to be expanded over the next 10 years, to include extensive reedbed.

Key birds: *Spring/summer:* Nightingale, Kingfisher, Common Tern, Sparrowhawk, Hobby, Grasshopper, Sedge and Reed Warblers, Lesser Whitethroat. Large Cormorant colony. *Winter:* Smew, Goldeneye, Goosander, Gadwall, Pochard.
Other notable flora and fauna: Wildflowers, butterflies (27 species recorded) and dragonflies (21 species regularly seen) are in abundance. Along the meadow trail there are common spotted orchids. Bee orchids are found around the car park. Otters are known to use the reserve.
Contact: The Rangers, Paxton Pits Nature Reseve, High Street, Little Paxton, St Neots, Cambs PE19 6ET. 01480 406 795; www.paxton-pits.org.uk
e-mail: paxtonpits@huntingdonshire.gov.uk

10. WICKEN FEN NNR

The National Trust.
Location: Sat nav: CB7 5XP (Lode Lane, Wicken, Nr Ely). TL 563 705. Lies 17 miles NE of Cambridge and ten miles S of Ely. From A10 drive E along A1123.
Access: Reserve open daily except Dec 25. Entry fee for non-members of NT. Visitor centre and shop open daily (10am to 5pm or dusk during winter months). Cafe open daily March to Oct, Weds to Sun Nov to Feb. Boardwalk suitable for wheelchairs, with 2 hides. Disabled toilets.
Facilities: Toilets, visitor centre, café, nine wildlife hides (three equipped for wheelchairs), boardwalk, footpaths, cycle route (NCN Route 11 passes through reserve) , disabled parking in main car park and close to Visitor Centre, coach parking limited (parties need to pre-book). Dragonfly Centre open weekends during the summer months.
Public transport: No buses to Wicken.
Habitats: A wetland of international importance, includes open fen meadows, , sedge fields, grazing marsh, partially flooded wet grassland, reedbed, scrub, woodland.
Key birds: *Spring:* Passage waders and passerines. *Summer:* Marsh Harriers, Hobbies, waders and warblers. *Winter:* Wildfowl, Hen Harriers roost on Sedge Fen, Marsh Harrier, Barn and Short-eared Owls, Bittern, Black-tailed Godwit, Cetti's Warbler.
Other notable flora and fauna: More than 8,500 species recorded: 21 species of dragonfly/damselfly, 27 species of butterfly and 1,200-plus species of moth. Water vole, otter.
Contact: The Visitor Centre, Wicken Fen, 01353 720 274; e-mail: wickenfen@nationaltrust.org.uk www. nationaltrust.org.uk/wickenfen

Essex

ESSEX Wildlife Trust manages 87 nature reserves of varied habitats throughout this huge county. As well as woodland at Epping Forest, the reservoirs at Abberton and Hanningfield, and coastal marshes such as Rainham Marshes RSPB and Old Hall Marshes RSPB, are all rich in birds. Try the migration hotspots at the Naze, a bird observatory at Bradwell and even seawatching along the Thames off Southend Pier.

1. ABBERTON RESERVOIR

Essex Wildlife Trust.
Location: Sat nav: CO2 0EU. TL 962 177. Six miles SW of Colchester on B1026 (Colchester to Maldon). Follow signs from Layer-de-la-Haye or Great Wigborough.
Access: Open daily (9am-5pm) except Dec 25/26.

NATURE RESERVES - EASTERN ENGLAND

Good viewing where roads cross reservoir. Electric wheelchair for hire.

Facilities: New visitor centre includes toilets, viewing verandah, light refreshments and gift shop. Nature trails with panoramic views, two bird hides overlook water, one more in new woodland. Ample parking, including disabled and coaches. Middleditch Wild Play Area.

Habitats: 60 acres on edge of expanding 1,200-acre reservoir. Concrete edges now replaced by wader-friendly muddy margins.

Key birds: *Winter:* Nationally important for Coot, Mallard, Teal, Wigeon, Shoveler, Gadwall, Pochard, Tufted Duck, Goldeneye. Smew, Bittern and Goosander regular. Golden Plover and Lapwing flocks on surrounding fields. *Spring:* Passage waders, terns, birds of prey. *Summer:* Tree-nesting Cormorant colony; raft-nesting Common Tern. Hobby, Yellow Wagtail, warblers, Nightingale, Turtle Dove, Skylark, Corn Bunting. *Autumn:* Red-crested Pochard, waders, rarities.

Other notable flora and fauna: Dragonflies including broad-bodied chaser, small red-eyed damselfly. Butterflies include brown argus and purple hairstreak. Roesel's bush-cricket. Brown hare, smooth newt, wasp spider.

Contact: Centre Manager, Essex Wildlife Trust, Church Road, Layer-de-la-Haye, Colchester. 01206 738172; e-mail:abberton@essexwt.org.uk

2. ABBOTT'S HALL FARM

Essex Wildlife Trust.

Location: Sat nav: CO5 7RZ. TL 963 145. On Blackwater estuary, seven miles SW from Colchester. Turn E off B1026 (Colchester-Maldon road) towards Peldon. Entrance near Great Wigborough, is 0.5 mile on R.

Access: Weekdays (9am-5pm). Two hides with wheelchair ramps. Dogs only in designated area.

Wildlife Trust HQ. Working farm, so please take care.

Facilities: Toilets, three hides, guided walks, fact-sheets, information boards. Many footpaths through active farmland areas.

Public transport: None.

Habitats: Saltmarsh, saline lagoons, grazing marsh, farmland, woodland, freshwater lakes and ponds with Ramsar, SPA and SAC designations.

Key birds: *Winter:* Waders and wildfowl, large roost of Little Egrets. Passage migrants and summer warblers. Skylark, Grey Partridge, Corn Bunting and other farmland species

Other notable flora and fauna: Range of butterflies, reptiles, newts and water vole.

Contact: Trust HQ, 01621 862 960; e-mail: admin@essexwt.org.uk

3. BRADWELL BIRD OBSERVATORY

Essex Birdwatching Society.

Location: Sat nav: CM0 7PN. TM035 085. Located on edge of Bradwell Shell Bank nature reserve, 100 yards S of St Peter's Chapel, Bradwell-on-Sea. Mouth of Blackwater estuary, between Maldon and Foulness.

Access: Open all year. Keep to seawall in breeding season to prevent disturbance.

Facilities: Accommodation for eight in hut; two rooms each with four bunks; blankets, cutlery, etc. supplied.

Habitats: Mudflats, saltmarsh, 30 acres of shellbank.

Key birds: *Winter:* Wildfowl (inc. Brent Geese, Red-throated Diver, Red-breasted Merganser), large numbers of waders (up to 20,000); small numbers of Twite, Snow Bunting and occasional Shore Lark on beaches, also Hen Harrier, Merlin and Peregrine. Good passage of migrants usual in spring and autumn. *Summer:* Small breeding population of terns and other estuarine species, plus Yellow Wagtail, Reed Bunting and Linnet.

Other notable flora and fauna: A variety of dragonflies inc hairy dragonfly and scarce emerald damselfly.

Contact: Graham Smith, 48 The Meads, Ingatestone, Essex CM4 0AE. 01277 354 034.

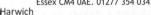

4. FINGRINGHOE WICK

Essex Wildlife Trust.

Location: Sat nav: CO5 7DN. TM 048 193. Reserve signposted from B1025 to Mersea Island, five miles S of Colchester.

Access: Open Tuesday to Sunday all year (9am to 5pm), plus Bank Holidays except Dec 25/26. Entry by suggested donation: adult £2, child £1 and family £5. Dogs on leads limited to dog walk area at edge of reserve

Facilities: Visitor centre: toilets inc: baby changing facilities, easy access toilet. One wheelchair is available. Gift shop, light refreshments, optics, observation room with displays, observatory, car park, seven bird hides,

nature trails. **Public transport:** None.
Habitats: Old gravel pit, large lake, many ponds, sallow/birch thickets, young scrub, reedbeds, saltmarsh, gorse heathland.
Key birds: Up to 200 species recorded. *Autumn/winter*: Brent Goose, waders, Hen Harrier, Little Egret. *Spring*: 40+ male Nightingales. Good variety of warblers in scrub, thickets, and Turtle Dove, Green/Great Spotted Woodpeckers. *Winter*: Little Grebe, Mute Swan, Teal, Wigeon, Shoveler, Gadwall on lake.
Other notable flora and fauna: Swathes of sea lavender in summer among 350 plants on site. Numerous dragonfly and butterfly species.
Contact: Centre Manager, Fingringhoe Wick Visitor Centre, 01206 729 678; www.essexwt.org.uk
e-mail: fingringhoe@essexwt.org.uk

5. HANNINGFIELD RESERVOIR

Essex Wildlife Trust.
Location: Sat nav: CM11 1WT. TQ 725 971. Three miles N of Wickford. Exit off Southend Road (Old A130) at Rettendon onto South Hanningfield Road. Follow this for two miles until reaching the T-junction with Hawkswood Road. Turn R and the entrance to the visitor centre and reserve is one mile on the R.
Access: Open daily (9am-5pm) except Dec 25/26. Voluntary entrance donation. Disabled parking, toilets, adapted hide. No dogs. No cycling.
Facilities: Visitor centre, gift shop, optics, refreshments, toilets, four bird hides, nature trails, picnic area, coach parking, education room.
Public transport: Chelmsford to Wickford bus no 14 to Downham village and walk half mile down Crowsheath Lane.
Habitats: Mixed woodland (110 acres) with grassy glades and rides, adjoining 870-acre Hanningfield Reservoir, designated an SSSI due to its high numbers of wildfowl.
Key birds: *Spring*: Good numbers and mix of woodland warblers. *Summer*: Vast numbers of Swifts, Swallows and martins feeding over the water. Hobby and Osprey. *Winter*: Good numbers and mix of waterfowl. Large gull roost.
Other notable flora and fauna: Spectacular displays of bluebells in spring. Damselflies and dragonflies around the ponds. Grass snakes and common lizards sometimes bask in rides.
Contact: Hanningfield Reservoir Visitor Centre, 01268 711 001; www.essexwt.org.uk

6. OLD HALL MARSHES

RSPB (Eastern England Office).
Location: Sat nav: CM9 8TP. TL 959 122. Overlooks River Blackwater, SW of Colchester. From the A12 take the B1023, via Tiptree to Tolleshunt D'Arcy. Turn L at village maypole then R into Chapel Road (back road to Tollesbury). After approx 1 mile (1.6 km), turn L into Old Hall Lane. Continue up Old Hall Lane, through iron gates, then follow signs straight ahead to car park.
Access: Open 9am-5pm when car park gates are locked. No wheelchair access or facilities. No

coaches. Dogs under control allowed on footpaths.
Facilities: Two trails — one of three miles and one of 6.5 miles. Viewing screens overlooking saline lagoon area at E end of reserve. No visitor centre or toilets (nearest are in Tiptree 6 miles away).
Public transport: Limited bus service to Tollesbury (two miles away). Train to Kelvedon followed by bus to Tollesbury or cycle.
Habitats: 1,560 acres of coastal grazing marsh, reedbed, open water, saline lagoon, saltmarsh and mudflat.
Key birds: *Summer*: Breeding Avocet, Redshank, Lapwing, Pochard, Shoveler, Gadwall, Marsh Harrier, Bearded Tit and Barn Owl. *Winter*: Large assemblies of wintering wildfowl: Brent Goose (4,000 approx), Wigeon, Teal, Shoveler, Goldeneye, Red-breasted Merganser, all the expected waders, Hen Harrier, Merlin, Short-eared Owl and Twite. *Passage*: All expected waders inc Spotted Redshank, Green Sandpiper and Whimbrel. Yellow Wagtail, Whinchat and Wheatear.
Other notable fauna: Brown hare, water vole, hairy dragonfly, scarce emerald damselfly, ground lackey moth, cream spot tiger, white letter hairstreak among 24 recorded butterfly species, yellow meadow ant.
Contact: Site Manager, 01621 869 015; e-mail: oldhallmarshes@rspb.org.uk

7. RAINHAM MARSHES

RSPB (Eastern England office)
Location: Sat nav: RM19 1SZ. TQ 552 792. Off New Tank Hill Road (A1090) in Purfleet, just off the A1306 between Rainham and Lakeside. This is accessible from the Aveley, Wennington and Purfleet junction off A13 and junction 30/31 of M25.
Access: Open Nov 1 – Jan 31 (9.30am-4.30pm). Feb 1 – Oct 31 (9.30am-5pm). Closed Dec 25/26. Entry fee for non-RSPB members (£3 adults, £1.50 children, £9 families). Guided walks — check RSPB website for details. Approx 2.5 miles of boardwalks suitable for wheelchairs and pushchairs. Dogs allowed only on Thames riverside path.
Facilities: Award-winning visitor centre, disabled toilets, car park (seven Blue Badge spaces) on site, picnic area, shop, refreshments available, wildlife garden and children's playground. Two bird hides. Entry charges for non-RSPB members.
Public transport: Route 44 (Ensignbus – 01708 865 656) runs daily between Grays and Lakeside via Purfleet. Nearest train station is Purfleet. Reserve is a 15 min walk.
Habitats: Former MoD shooting range, largest remaining area of lowland wetland along the Thames.
Key birds: *Spring*: Marsh Harrier, Hobby, Wheatear, hirundines and other migrants. *Summer/autumn*: Many waders, including Black-tailed Godwit, Whimbrel, Greenshank, Snipe, Lapwing, Avocet. Yellow-legged Gull. Hunting Merlin and Peregrine. *Winter*: Waders, wildfowl, Water Pipit, Short-eared Owl, Little Egret and Penduline Tit most winters.
Other notable flora and fauna: 21 species of dragonfly, including hairy hawker, scarce emerald

and small red-eyed damselfly. Marsh frog, water vole, water shrew, fox, stoat, weasel, 32 species of butterfly, and 13 species of orthoptera. Deadly nightshade, flowering rush.
Contact: The Warden, The Visitor Centre, 01708 899 840; e-mail: rainham.marshes@rspb.org.uk

8. THURROCK THAMESIDE NATURE PARK

Essex Wildlife Trust/Cory Environmental Trust.
Location: Sat nav: SS17 0RN. TQ 698 806. From Basildon head SW on A13 towards Stanford-le-Hope. Take A1014 exit and follow signs for Walton Hall Farm Museum. Past the museum entrance turn right into Mucking Wharf Road and take single lane entrance road to visitor centre.
Access: Free access daily (9am to 5pm) except Dec 25/26. Good access for wheelchair users to visitor centre, toilet and paths. Dogs must be on leads.
Facilities: Visitor centre with rooftop viewing platform, café, gift shop, toilets (inc disabled). Bird hide overlooks mudflats.
Public transport: No trains or buses within three miles of reserve.
Habitats: Reclaimed landfill site covering 120 acres overlooking Mucking Flats SSSI and the Ramsar-designated Thames estuary. Features saltmarsh, grassland, woodland, ponds and reedbed.
Key birds: Internationally important numbers of Ringed Plover and Avocet and nationally significant numbers of Grey Plover, Dunlin, Redshank and godwits. Also look for wildfowl, Kingfisher, Barn Owl, Reed Bunting, Bearded Tit, Cetti's Warbler and Skylark.
Other notable fauna: Water vole, harvest mouse, shrill carder bee, great crested newt, adder.
Contact: Nature Park 01261 862 960; e-mail: admin@essexwt.org.uk

9. TOLLESBURY WICK MARSHES

Essex Wildlife Trust.
Location: Sat nav: CM9 8RJ. TL 970 104. On Blackwater Estuary eight miles E of Maldon. Follow B1023 to Tollesbury via Tiptree, leaving A12 at Kelvedon. Then follow Woodrolfe Road S towards the marina. Use small public car park at Woodrolfe Green (TL 964 107), 500m before reserve entrance on sea wall. Car park suitable for mini-buses and small coaches.
Access: Open all times along exposed sea wall footpath. Motorised wheelchair access possible to

Block House Bay.
Facilities: Bird hide. Public toilets at Woodrolfe Green car park.
Public transport: Hedingham bus services run to Tollesbury from Maldon, Colchester and Witham — call 01621 869 214 for information.
Habitats: Estuary with fringing saltmarsh and mudflats with some shingle. Extensive freshwater grazing marsh, brackish borrowdyke and small reedbeds.
Key birds: *Winter*: Large numbers of wintering wildfowl and waders, particularly Brent Geese and Wigeon, Lapwing and Golden Plover. Short-eared Owl, Hen Harrier and, increasingly, Marsh Harrier. *Summer*: Breeding Avocet, Redshank, Lapwing, Little Tern, Reed and Sedge Warblers, Reed Bunting, Barn Owl. *Passage*: Whimbrel, Spotted Redshank, Green Sandpiper.
Other notable flora and fauna: Plants include spiny restharrow, grass vetchling, yellow horned-poppy, slender hare's-ear. Hairy dragonfly, Roesel's and great green bush-crickets. Brown hares. Occasional common seals can be seen from the sea wall.
Contact: Reserve Manager 01621 868 628.
www.essexwt.org.uk

10. WRABNESS NATURE RESERVE AND MARSH

Essex Wildlife Trust.
Location: Sat nav: CO11 2TD. TM 167 315. Lies of southern bank of Stour estuary. From B1352 between Bradfield and Wrabness turn down Whitesheaf Lane to reach reserve. Car park is on left just beyond railway bridge.
Access: Open all year. Hard-surfaced path around site suitable for wheelchairs.
Facilities: Car park, footpath, bird hide.
Public transport: Wrabness railway station is a mile walk from reserve on public footpath. Bus service from Colchester to Harwich runs along the B1352.
Habitats: 60-acre site of grazed grassland and open scrub overlooking wader and wildlfowl feeding grounds in Jacques Bay.
Key birds: *Winter:* Internationally important species such as Brent Goose, Shelduck, Wigeon, Pintail, Black-tailed Godwit, Grey Plover, Dunlin, Turnstone and Curlew. Short-eared and Barn Owls hunt over grassland. *Spring/summer:* Nightingale, Whitethroat, Turtle Dove, Bullfinch, Yellowhammer.
Other notable flora and fauna: Wildflowers, plus good range of butterflies and dragonflies.
Contact: Essex Wildlife Trust 01621 862 960.

Hertfordshire

WITH more than 40 nature reserves under its control, the Herts & Middlesex Wildlife Trust can offer residents of the urbanised Home Counties a welcome taste of the countryside. Gravel pits such as those at Amwell and Tring are the best places to watch for birds, the latter holding a special place in the history of British birding as the site where Little Ringed Plovers first bred in this country.

1. AMWELL NATURE RESERVE

Herts Wildlife Trust.
Location: Sat nav: SG12 9SS. TL 376 127. In Lee Valley near Ware. From A10, leave at junction signposted A414 to Harlow. At first roundabout, take B181 to St Margarets and Stanstead Abbotts. On entering

St Margarets, just before railway, turn L on Amwell Lane. Reserve is on the R (signposted).
Access: Open all year. Dragonfly Trail open May-Sept.
Facilities: Three hides, several viewing areas and Dragonfly Trail boardwalk.
Public transport: St Mary's Church, Hoddesdon Road, St Margarets (310, 311, C4) 5 minute walk from railway station. Rail: St Margarets (0.75 miles). From station walk E along B181 to towpath of River Lee Navigation, then walk N for 0.5 miles to reserve.
Habitats: Disused gravel pit with reedbeds and woodland.
Key birds: *Spring/summer*: Ringed Plover, Little Ringed Plover. *Winter*: Smew, other ducks, Bittern. SSSI for wintering Gadwall and Shoveler.
Other notable fauna: Best county site for dragonflies (19 species recorded), otter, nationally scarce marsh dock, plus early and southern marsh orchids.
Contact: Trust HQ, 01727 858 901;
e-mail: info@hmwt.org;
www.hertswildlifetrust.org.uk

2. KINGS MEAD

Herts & Middlesex Wildlife Trust/various owners.
Location: Sat nav: SG12 9XD. TL 349 136. From Ware head SE on A1170 High Street, turn R into Burgage Lane shortly after Ware Museum. Park in public car park. From here pedestrian access is via the River Lee — go over the bridge, turn R and walk 250 yards. Turn L into the reserve.
Access: Open all year.
Facilities: None.
Public transport: Bus stops on Hertford Road (A119). Trains to Ware station (five minute walk to reserve).
Habitats: Largest remaining area of grazed riverside flood meadow in Hertfordshire.
Key birds: 119 species recorded. *Summer*: Skylark, Reed Warbler, Reed Bunting, seven species of breeding warblers, Yellow Wagtail. *Winter/spring*: Gadwall, Shoveler, Wigeon, Teal, Snipe, gulls, waders.
Other notable flora and fauna: 265 species of wildflower, 18 species of dragonfly. Significant population of short-winged conehead.
Contact: Herts & Middlesex Wildlife Trust, 01727 858 901. e-mail: info@hmwt.org
www.hertswildlifetrust.org.uk

3. LEMSFORD SPRINGS

Herts & Middlesex Wildlife Trust.
Location: Sat nav: AL8 7TN. TL 222 123. Lies 1.5 miles W of Welwyn Garden City town centre, off roundabout leading to Lemsford village on B197, W of A1(M). Park in cul-de-sac next to reserve entrance.
Access: Access, via key, by arrangement with warden. Open at all times, unless work parties or group visits in progress. Keep to paths. Dogs on leads. 150m

earth path to hide. Wheelchair access ramp to hide. Coaches welcome and room to park on road, but limit of 30 persons.
Facilities: Two hides, classroom, chemical toilet, paths and bridges. Circular walk.
Public transport: Bus: The Sun Inn, Lemsford Village (36, 61). Nearest railway station Welwyn Garden City (25 minute walk).
Habitats: Former water-cress beds, open shallow lagoons. Stretch of the River Lea, marsh, hedgerows. Nine acres.
Key birds: *Spring/summer*: Breeding warblers, Grey Wagtail, Kestrel, Green Woodpecker. *Autumn/winter*: Green Sandpiper, Water Rail, Snipe, Siskin, Little Egret, occasional Jack Snipe. *All year*: Mandarin Duck, Kingfisher, Grey Heron, Sparrowhawk.
Other notable flora and fauna: Muntjac, fox and stoat. Common butterflies and damselflies in summer.
Contact: Barry Trevis, Warden, 11 Lemsford Village, Welwyn Garden City, Herts, AL8 7TN. 01707 335 517;
e-mail: info@hmwt.org
www.hertswildlifetrust.org.uk

4. MAPLE LODGE

Thames Water/Maple Lodge Conservation Society.
Location: Sat nav: WD3 9SF. TQ 036 925. South of Rickmansworth, close to village of Maple Cross. From M25 junction 17 drive towards Denham/Uxbridge, turn L at traffic lights. Drive down Maple Lodge Close and park in social club car park on the right.
Access: Restricted to members of MLCS. Visits by non-members and groups can be arranged in advance. Site can be boggy — please keep to designated paths.
Facilities: Information centre, toilets. Ten bird hides — two wheelchair-friendly (plus two more when ground is dry).
Winter feeding stations.

121

Public transport: Bus services are available from Rickmansworth train station to Maple Cross.
Habitats: A man-made wetland habitat formed from two gravel pits and a sludge settlement area. Two lakes and a reedbed. Mixed broadleaf plantation on eastern side.
Key birds: Wildfowl throughout year, numbers building in winter. All three woodpeckers, plus variety of finches, thrushes and woodland species. Nesting species include Kingfisher, Tawny Owl, Water Rail and migrant warblers. Snipe, Green and Common Sandpipers on passage. Birds of prey including Sparrowhawk, Hobby, Red Kite and Common Buzzard.
Other notable flora and fauna: 250 species of moth recorded, plus many butterflies and aquatic insects. 125 species of wildflower recorded. Seven of the nine bat species found in Herts recorded.
Contact: Chairman Keith Pursall, 07580 535 986; e-mail: keith@maplelodge.org
www.maplelodge.org Also on Facebook.

5. RYE MEADS

RSPB/Hertfordshire & Middlesex Wildlife Trust.
Location: SG12 8JS. TL 389 103. Take Hoddesdon turn off A10 and follow brown duck signs. Near Rye House railway station.
Access: Open every day 10am-5pm (or dusk if earlier), except Dec 25/26. Gates are locked when the reserve is closed.
Facilities: Disabled access and toilets. Drinks machine, staffed reception, classrooms, picnic area, car park, bird feeding area. Nature trails, 10 hides. RSPB reserve has close-circuit TV on Kingfisher and Common Tern nests in summer. Car parking charge for non members.
Public transport: Rail (Rye House) 370 metres, bus (310) stops 600 metres from entrance.
Habitats: Marsh, willow scrub, pools, scrapes, lagoons and reedbed.
Key birds: *Summer:* Breeding Water Rail, Tufted Duck, Gadwall, Common Tern, Kestrel, Kingfisher, Little Ringed Plover, nine species of warblers. *Winter:* Bittern, Shoveler, Water Rail, Teal, Snipe, Jack Snipe, Redpoll and Siskin. *Autumn:* Birds on passage including Green Sandpiper, Teal and Snipe, plus occasional rarities.
Other notable flora and fauna: Fen vegetation, invertebrates and reptiles.
Contact: RSPB Rye Meads Visitor Centre, 01992 708 383; e-mail: rye.meads@rspb.org.uk
Herts & Middlesex Wildlife Trust, 01727 858 901; e-mail: info@hmwt.org
www.hertswildlifetrust.org.uk

6. THERFIELD HEATH LNR

Therfield Regulation Trust.
Location: Sat nav: SG8 5GB. TL 335 400. Common land SSSI lies west and south of Royston and is accessed from A505 (Baldock Road).
Access: Open at all times.
Facilities: Open downland walks, golf course and

sports fields.
Public transport: Royston railway station a two minute walk from heath.
Habitats: Natural chalk/grass downland.
Key birds: Noted stop-off site for migrants such as Ring Ouzel and Wheatear. *Spring/summer:* Breeding Skylark, Meadow Pipit, Willow Warbler, Whitethroat, Lesser Whitethroat and Grey Partridge. Good selection of raptors seen regularly.
Other notable flora and fauna: 26 species of butterfly recorded, inc increasingly rare chalkhill blue. Several orchid species, plus pasque flower and wide variety of chalk grassland flowers.
Contact: Therfield Regulation Trust; e-mail: clerk. conservators.therfield@gmail.com
Sports bar & café: http://www.roystonheath.co.uk/

7. TRING RESERVOIRS

All four reservoirs – British Waterways/H&M Wildlife Trust/Friends of Tring Res. WTW lagoon – Thames Water/FoTR.
Location: Sat nav: HP23 4NW (Wilstone Res.) SP 903 134). Other reservoirs SP 920 135. WTW Lagoon SP 923 134 adjacent to Marsworth Res. Reservoirs 1.5 miles N of Tring, all accessible from B489 which crosses A41 Aston Clinton by-pass. NB: exit from by-pass only southbound.
Access: Reservoirs open at all times. WTW Lagoon and hide open at all times (by permit from FoTR). Coaches can only drop off and pick up, for advice contact FoTR. Wilstone Res. has restricted height access of 2.1 metres. Disabled access available for Startops and Marsworth Reservoirs from car park, as well as FoTR Lagoon Hide.
Facilities: Café and pubs adjacent to Startops Res. car park, safe parking for cycles. Wilstone Res: Pub 0.5 mile away in village. Cafe and farm shop 0.25 mile from car park. Hides on all reservoirs.
Public transport: Buses from Aylesbury and Tring including a weekend service, tel. 0871 200 2233. Tring Station is 2.5 miles away via canal towpath.
Habitats: Four reservoirs with surrounding woodland, scrub and meadows. Two of the reservoirs have extensive reedbeds. WTW Lagoon with islands and dragonfly scrape, surrounding hedgerows and scrub.
Key birds: *Spring/summer:* Breeding water birds Common Terns and heronry. Regular Hobby, Black Terns and Red Kite, warblers including Cetti's. Occasional Marsh Harrier, Osprey. *Autumn/winter passage:* Waders, occasional White-winged Black Tern. *Winter:* Gull roost, large wildfowl flocks, bunting roosts, Bittern.
Other notable flora and fauna: Black poplar trees, some locally rare plants in damp areas. 18 species of dragonfly include black-tailed skimmer, ruddy darter and emerald damselfly. Holly blue and speckled wood butterflies. Chinese water deer, Daubenton's, Natterer's and both pipistrelle bats.
Contact: Herts & Middsx Wildlife Trust (www.hertswildlifetrust.org.uk)
Friends of Tring Reservoir (www.fotr.org.uk).

Norfolk

ITS EAST COAST location and largely unspoilt coastline ensures Norfolk's reputation as our finest birding county. Whatever the season you can be guaranteed a wide variety of birds, including many vagrants, out-and-out rarities and thousands of over-wintering geese, ducks and waders. This survey details a small selection of popular sites, but the revised 3rd edition of *Best Birdwatching Sites: Norfolk* spotlights more than 85 valuable birding locations.

1. CLEY MARSHES NNR

Norfolk Wildlife Trust.
Location: Sat nav: NR25 7SA. TG 054 441. Situated four miles N of Holt on A149 coast road, half a mile E of Cley-next-the-Sea. Visitor centre and car park on inland side of road.
Access: Open every day, except Dec 24 and 25 as follows: March 1 to 30- (10am-to-4.30pm). March 31 to Oct 26 (10am-5pm), Oct 27 to-Nov 2 (10am to 4.30pm), Nov 3 to Feb 28 (10am to 4pm). Café closes 30 minutes before the centre. Free admission to visitor centre but reserve fee is £5 with Gift Aid. NWT members and children are free. No dogs.
Facilities: Environmentally-friendly visitor centre (wheelchair accessible) incorporates an observation area, interactive interpretation, including remote controllable wildlife camera, café and sales area. Five hides (three with excellent wheelchair access). Audio trail. Wildlife detective bumbags for children, free to hire. Boardwalk and information boards. Reserve leaflet. Regular events.
Public transport: Coasthopper bus service frequently stops outside. Connections for train and bus services at Sheringham. Special discounts to visitors arriving by bus. Call 01603 223 800 for info.
Habitats: Reedbeds, salt and freshwater marshes, scrapes and shingle ridge with international reputation as one of the finest birdwatching sites in Britain.
Key birds: Avocet, Marsh Harrier, Spoonbill, Bearded Tit and large numbers of wintering wildfowl, including Wigeon, Teal, Pintail and Brent Goose. Migrating waders such as Ruff and Temminck's Stint. Many rarities.
Contact: NWT Cley Marshes Visitor Centre, 01263 740 008; e-mail: cley@norfolkwildlifetrust.org.uk www.norfolkwildlifetrust.org.uk

2. HICKLING BROAD NNR

Norfolk Wildlife Trust.
Location: Sat nav: NR12 0BW. TG 428 222. Approx four miles SE of Stalham, just off A149 Yarmouth Road. From Hickling village, follow brown badger tourist signs into Stubb Road at the Greyhound Inn. Follow Stubb Road for another mile and turn R at the end for nature reserve.
Access: Reserve open all year (dawn to dusk). Visitor centre open Easter to Oct (10am-5pm daily. Cost:

adults £4.50 (with Gift Aid), children under 16 and NWT members free. Dogs only allowed on Weaver's Way footpath.
Facilities: Visitor centre, boardwalk trail through reedbeds to open water, birdwatching hides, wildlife gift shop, refreshments, picnic site, toilets, coach parking, car parking, disabled access to broad, boardwalk and toilets. Groups welcome. Water trail boat trips May to Sept (additional charge — booking essential).
Public transport: Morning bus service only Mon-Fri from Norwich (Neaves Coaches) Cromer to North Walsham (Sanders). Buses stop in Hickling village, a 25 minute walk away.
Habitats: Hickling is the largest, wildest Norfolk Broad with reedbeds, grazing marshes and wide open skies.
Key birds: Marsh Harrier, Bittern, warblers. From November to February the raptor roost at Stubb Mill, provides excellent views of raptors flying in to roost. Likely birds include Marsh and Hen Harriers, Merlin, Crane and Pink-footed Goose. *Autumn/winter:* Shoveler, Teal and Goldeneye. *All year:* Bittern, Pochard, Water Rail, Cetti's Warbler, Bearded Tit.
Other notable flora and fauna: Swallowtail butterfly, Norfolk hawker dragonfly, marsh orchid.
Contact: *In season:* Hickling Broad Visitor Centre, 01692 598 276; www.norfolkwildlifetrust.org.uk e-mail: info@norfolkwildlifetrust.org.uk
Out of season: John Blackburn, The Warden's House, Hickling Broad NNR, Stubb Road, Hickling, Norfolk NR12 0BW. 01692 598 292.

3. HOLKHAM NNR

Natural England (Norfolk and Suffolk Team).
Location: Sat nav: NR23 1RJ. TF 890 450. Three miles W of Wells on A149. From Holkham village turn down Lady Ann's Drive (opposite entrance to Holkham Hall) to park. More parking at end of Wells Beach Road in Wells and at Burnham Overy.
Access: unrestricted, keep to paths and off grazing marshes and farmland. Pay-and-display parking.
Facilities: Two hides. Disabled access.
Public transport: Coasthopper bus service every 30 mins in summer. Norbic Norfolk bus information line 0845 3006 116.
Habitats: 4,000 hectares of sandflats, dunes, marshes, pinewoods, reclaimed saltmarsh.
Key birds: *Passage:* Migrants, including Yellow Wagtail, Wheatear, Cuckoo and many unusual species. *Winter:* Wildfowl, inc. Brent (7,000), Pink-footed (20,000) and White-fronted Geese, up to 13,000 Wigeon, Shorelark, Twite and Snow Bunting. *Summer:* Breeding Little Tern, Snipe, Oystercatcher and Ringed Plover. *All year:* Marsh Harrier, Grey Heron, Lapwing, Barn Owl, Kestrel.
Other notable flora and fauna: Seablite bushes, attractive to incoming migrant birds, sea aster and sea lavender. Antlion recently recorded.
Contact: Sarah Henderson, Hill Farm Offices, Main Road, Holkham, Wells-next-the-Sea, NR23 1AB. 01328 800 730; e-mail: s.henderson@holkham.co.uk

NATURE RESERVES - EASTERN ENGLAND

4. HOLME OBSERVATORY

Norfolk Ornithologists' Association (NOA).
Location: Sat nav: PE36 6LQ. TF 717 450. E of Hunstanton, signposted from A149. Access from Broadwater Road, Holme. Reserve and visitors centre are beyond the White House at the end of the track.
Access: Open daily to members dawn to dusk; non-members (9am-5pm) by permit from the Observatory. Parties by prior arrangement. Dogs on leads.
Facilities: Accredited Bird Observatory operating all year for bird ringing, MV moth trapping and other scientific monitoring. Visitor centre, car park and several hides (seawatch hide reserved for NOA members), together with access to beach and coastal path.
Public transport: Coastal bus service (Hunstanton to Sheringham) roughly every 30 mins in summer. Phone Norfolk Green Bus, 01553 776 980.
Habitats: In ten acres of diverse Habitats: sand dunes, Corsican pines, scrub and reed-fringed lagoon make this a migration hotspot.
Key birds: Species list over 320. Ringed species over 150. Recent rarities have included Red Kite, Common Crane, Osprey, Red-flanked Bluetail, Yellow-browed, Pallas's, Arctic and Barred Warblers.
Other notable flora and fauna: Moth trap run March 1 to Oct 31: migrant moths and butterflies recorded yearly.
Contact: Sophie Barker, Holme Bird Observatory, Broadwater Road, Holme, Hunstanton, Norfolk PE36 6LQ. 01485 525 406; e-mail: info@noa.org.uk www.noa.org.uk

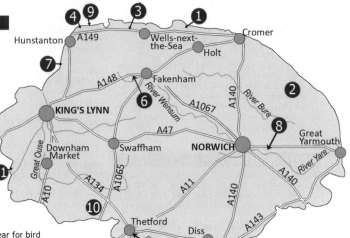

5. NUNNERY LAKES

British Trust for Ornithology.
Location: TL 873 815. On the S edge of Thetford, adjacent to the BTO's headquarters at The Nunnery. Main access point is via Nun's Bridges car park, across pedestrian bridge at TL 874 821.
Access: Open dawn to dusk. Public access along permissive paths. Keep dogs on leads at all times. Call reception in advance to arrange wheelchair access to the lakes and hide.
Facilities: Waymarked paths, information panels, bird hide, boardwalk through wet woodland. Pre-booked coaches can park in grounds.
Public transport: Thetford railway station approx 1 mile (0845 7484 950). Thetford bus terminal approx 0.5 mile (0870 6082 608).
Habitats: Flood meadows, scrape, flooded gravel pits, scrub and woodland.

Key birds: Wide range of species present throughout the year including Grey Heron, Egyptian Goose, Kingfisher, Green Woodpecker. *Spring:* Passage waders, hirundines, Swift, passerines. *Summer:* Warblers, Cuckoo, Oystercatcher, Lapwing, Hobby. *Winter:* Goosander, Teal, Water Rail, Snipe, Siskin.
Other notable flora and fauna: Otter, brown hare, muntjac, grass snake, common lizard. Emperor dragonfly, red-eyed damselfly. Speckled wood and orange tip butterflies. Mossy stonecrop.
Contact: Chris Gregory, The British Trust for Ornithology, The Nunnery, Thetford, Norfolk, IP24 2PU. 01842 750 050; e-mail: chris.gregory@bto.org www.bto.org

6. SCULTHORPE MOOR

Hawk and Owl Trust.
Location: Sat nav: NR21 9GN. TF 900 305. In Wensum Valley, just W of Fakenham, on A148 to King's Lynn. Nature reserve signposted opposite village of Sculthorpe. Follow Turf Moor Road to Visitor Centre.
Access: Open daily including Bank Holidays (except Dec 25 October: April to Oct (8am-6pm), Thurs (8am-dusk). November to March: (8am-4pm). £3.50 suggested donation for adult visitors, children and members free. Guide dogs only.
Facilities: Visitor centre open daily 9am-5pm (4pm in winter), with adapted toilets, hot drinks, interpretive displays and live CCTV coverage from around the reserve. Reserve and 2 hides accessible to wheelchairs and buggies via a mile of boardwalk. Bark chipping path to other hides. Coach parking available.
Public transport: Norfolk Green (01553 776 980 www.norfolkgreen.co.uk) bus X8 Fakenham to King's Lynn stops at end of Turf Moor Road. Sustrans no.1 cycle route runs within 200 metres of Turf Moor Road. Bike racks on site.
Habitats: Wetland reserve, fen containing saw

sedge (a European priority habitat), reedbed, wet woodland, pools, ditches and riverbank.

Key birds: 90 species recorded, including breeding Marsh Harrier, Barn Owl and Tawny Owl, visiting Buzzard, Goshawk, Hobby, Kestrel, Osprey, Sparrowhawk, also Water Rail, Kingfisher, Marsh Tit, Lesser Spotted Woodpecker and Willow Tit.

Other notable flora and fauna: Otter, water vole, roe deer, 19 species of dragonfly/damselfly, butterflies including white admiral, glow-worms.

Contact: The Hawk and Owl Trust, Turf Moor Road, Sculthorpe, Fakenham NR21 9GN. 01328 856 788; e-mail: sculthorpe@hawkandowl.org www.hawkandowl.org/sculthorpe

7. SNETTISHAM

RSPB (Eastern England Office).

Location: Sat nav: PE31 7PS. TF 651 330. Car park two miles along Beach Road, signposted off A149 S of Hunstanton, opposite Snettisham village.

Access: Due to severe damage caused by winter tidal surge only one hide and small part of reserve is safe for public use. Check RSPB website for latest information regarding repairs and access advice.

Habitats: Intertidal mudflats, saltmarsh, shingle beach, brackish lagoons, and unimproved grassland/scrub. Highest tides best for good views of waders.

Key birds: *Autumn/winter/spring:* Waders (particularly Knot, Bar and Black-tailed Godwits, Dunlin, Grey Plover), wildfowl (particularly Pink-footed and Brent Geese, Wigeon, Gadwall, Goldeneye), Peregrine, Hen Harrier, Merlin, owls. Migrants in season. *Summer:* Breeding Mediterranean Gull, Ringed Plover, Redshank, Avocet, Common Tern. Marsh Harrier regular.

Other notable flora and fauna: Yellow horned poppies and other shingle flora along the beach.

Contact: RSPB, 01485 542 689; www.rspb.org.uk e-mail: snettisham@rspb.org.uk

8. STRUMPSHAW FEN

RSPB (Eastern England Office).

Location: Sat nav: NR13 4HS. TG 341 065. Near Brundell, seven miles ESE of Norwich. Follow signposts. Entrance across level-crossing from car park, reached by turning sharp R and R again into Low Road from Brundall, off A47 to Great Yarmouth.

Access: Open dawn-dusk. RSPB members free, adults £3.50, children £1.50, family £7. Guide dogs only. Limited wheelchair access – please phone for advice.

Facilities: Toilets, reception hide and two other hides, two walks, five miles of trails.

Public transport: Brundall train station about one mile from reserve. Bus 17A from Norwich stops 0.5 mile from reserve - First Buses (0845 602 0121).

Habitats: Reedbed and reedfen, wet grassland and woodland.

Key birds: *Summer:* Bittern, Little Egret, Bearded Tit, Marsh Harrier, Hobby, Kingfisher, Cetti's Warbler and other reedbed birds. *Winter:* Bittern, wildfowl, Marsh and Hen Harrier.

Other notable flora and fauna: Rich fen flora: six

species of orchid, inc marsh helleborine and narrow-leaved marsh orchid. Otter, Chinese water deer and water vole. Swallowtail, white admiral and small heath butterflies, Norfolk hawker, scarce chaser and variable damselfly among 20 dragonfly species.

Contact: Tim Strudwick, Staithe Cottage, Low Road, Strumpshaw, Norwich, Norfolk NR13 4HS. 01603 715 191; e-mail: strumpshaw@rspb.org.uk

9. TITCHWELL MARSH

RSPB (Eastern England Office).

Location: Sat nav: PE31 8BB. TF 750 438. E of Hunstanton, signposted off A149.

Access: Reserve and hides open at all times. Wheelchairs available (no charge). All trails suitable for wheelchairs, but beach not accessible due to collapse of boardwalk. Coach parking – pre-booking essential. Car park fee (£5) for non-RSPB members. Dogs allowed only on west bank path.

Facilities: Visitor centre, shop with large selection of optics, birdfood and books, open every day 9.30am-5pm (Nov to Feb, 9.30-4pm). Cafe open 9.30am-4.30pm every day (Nov-mid Feb, 9.30-4pm). Visitor centre and tea-room closed Dec 25/26. Three large hides.

Public transport: Phone Traveline East Anglia on 0871 200 22 33 for times of Coasthopper buses.

Habitats: Freshwater reedbed and fresh water lagoons, extensive salt marsh, dunes, sandy beach with associated exposed peat beds.

Key birds: Diverse range of breeding reedbed and wetland birds with good numbers of passage waders during late summer/autumn. *Spring/summer:* Breeding Avocet, Bearded Tit, Bittern, Marsh Harrier, Reed Sedge and Cetti's Warbler, Redshank, Ringed Plover and Common Tern. *Summer/autumn:* Passage waders including Knot, Wood and Green Sandpiper, Little Stint, Spotted Redshank, Curlew Sandpiper and many more. *Winter:* Brent Goose, Hen/Marsh Harrier roost, Snow Bunting. Offshore Common and Velvet Scoter, Long-tailed Duck, Great Northern and Red-throated Divers.

Other notable flora and fauna: 25 species of butterfly, including all the common species, plus Essex skipper and annual clouded yellow. 21 species of dragonfly, including small red-eyed damselfly. Good diversity of saltmarsh plants including shrubby sea-blite and three species of sea lavender.

Contact: Centre Manager, 01485 210 779; e-mail: titchwell@rspb.org.uk

10. WEETING HEATH

Norfolk Wildlife Trust.

Location: Sat nav: IP26 4NG. TL 756 881. Weeting Heath is signposted from the Weeting-Hockwold road, two miles W of Weeting near to Brandon in Suffolk. Nature reserve can be reached via B1112 at Hockwold or B1106 at Weeting.

Access: Open daily from Apr-Sep. Cost: £4.00 with gift aid, £3.50 without, children free. NWT members free. Disabled access to visitor centre and hides.

Facilities: Visitor centre open daily Apr-Aug,

birdwatching hides, wildlife gift shop, refreshments, toilets, coach parking, car park, groups welcome (book first).
Public transport: Train services to Brandon and bus connections (limited) from Brandon High Street.
Habitats: Breckland, grass heath.
Key birds: Stone Curlew, migrant passerines, Wood Lark, Spotted Flycatcher.
Contact: *In season:* The Summer Warden, Weeting Heath, Hockwold Road, Weeting, Brandon, Norfolk; 01842 827 615. *Out of season:* Darrell Stevens, Norfolk Wildlife Trust, Bewick House, 22 Thorpe Road, Norwich NR1 1RY. 01603 625 540; e-mail: info@ norfolkwildlifetrust.org.uk
www.norfolkwildlifetrust.org.uk

11. WELNEY WETLAND CENTRE

The Wildfowl & Wetlands Trust.
Location: Sat nav: PE14 9TN. TL 546 944. Hundred Foot Bank, ten miles N of Ely, signposted from A10 and A1101. Check if A1101 is flooded in winter before setting off.
Access: Open daily except Dec 25. Open Nov to Feb (Mon-Wed 10am to 5pm, Thurs-Sun 10am to 8pm); Mar to Oct (Mon-Sun 9.30am to 5pm). Free admission to WWT members (see website for ticket prices for non-WWT members) Wheelchair accessible. Access roads and paths to remote hides may be flooded so

check before visiting. No dogs allowed.
Facilities: Visitor centre (wheelchair-friendly). Cafe opening times: Winter: Mon to Fri 10am to 4.30pm; Sat & Sun 10am to 6pm. Summer: 10am to 4.30pm daily (changing to 10am - 4pm daily from April 1). Large, heated observatory, additional 5 hides. Free parking and coach parking. Blue Badge parking, wheelchairs for hire (1 electric scooter and 2 manual chairs), lifts, disabled toilets, ramps.
Public transport: None.
Habitats: 1,000 acres of washland reserve, spring damp meadows, winter wildfowl marsh (SPA, Ramsar site, SSSI, SAC). Additional 200 acres of recently created wetland habitat next to visitor centre.
Key birds: Large numbers of wintering wildfowl are replaced by breeding waders, terns and warblers. *Winter:* Bewick's and Whooper Swans, wintering wildfowl e.g. Wigeon. *Spring/summer:* Common Tern, Avocet, Lapwing, Black-tailed Godwit, House Martin, occasional rarities.
Other notable flora and fauna: Purple loosestrife, meadow rue, mixed grasses. Dragonflies include scarce chaser, emperor, banded demoiselle, small red-eyed damselfly. Approx. 400 species of moth including goat moth. Butterflies include brown argus.
Contact: WWT Welney, 01353 860 711; e-mail: info. welney@wwt.org.uk
www.wwt.org.uk/visit/welney/plan-your-visit/

Suffolk

SUFFOLK hosts more Breckland sites than neighbouring Norfolk and there are other inland locations good for birds among the Wildlife Trust's 52 reserves. However, it is the coastal hotspots such as Minsmere, Landguard Bird Observatory, Walberswick and Dunwich Heath that tend to get most attention from visiting birders.

1. BENACRE BROAD NNR

Natural England (Suffolk team)
Location: Sat nav: NR34 7JW (Covehithe). TM 528 827. On coast S of Kessingland. From A12 take minor road to Covehithe at Wrentham. Park near Covehithe church.
Access: Open at all times on permissive paths. Clifftop from Covehithe unstable, so walk with care. If sea has breached sandbar it is not possible to reach bird hide from the north. Telescope needed for best views. Dogs on lead.
Facilities: Elevated bird hide on southern edge of Broad.
Public transport: None.
Habitats: Coastal woodland, saline lagoons, reedbeds and heathland covering 393 hectares.
Key birds: 100 species of breeding bird, inc Marsh Harrier, Bearded Tits, Water Rail and wildfowl. Bittern breeds irregularly. Woodlark, Hobby and Wheatear breed on heathland areas and Little Terns fish off the coast. *Winter:* Shorelark possible on cliff-top areas,

winter thrushes.
Other notable flora and fauna: Lagoon shrimp, starlet sea-anemone, yellow-horned poppy, grey hair grass.
Contact: Adam Burrows, Senior Reserve Manager, Natural England, 01502 676 171; e-mail: enquiries.east@naturalengland.org.uk

2. BOYTON & HOLLESLEY MARSHES

RSPB (Eastern England Office).
Location: Sat nav: IP12 3LR. TM 387 475. Two grazing marshes in lower reaches of Alde-Ore Estuary, approx. seven miles E of Woodbridge. Follow B1084 to Butley. Turn R and follow to Capel St. Andrew before turning L towards Boyton village. Approximately 0.25 mile before village, bear L down concrete track on sharp right-hand turn.
Access: Open at all times. Entrance free but donations welcome. Public footpath on site not suited to wheelchair use. Dogs only on public footpaths.
Facilities: Car park at Boyton (eight spaces only). For Hollesley park at Shingle Street. No toilets or hides at either site. Information boards at both sites.
Public transport: Route 160 (Ipswich-Bealings-Woodbridge-Orford)/bus stops at Boyton village. Reserve is located 0.5 mile NE of village.
Habitats: 57 ha of coastal grazing marsh and saltmarsh on the lower Alde-Ore estuary.
Key birds: *Spring:* Breeding waders and wildfowl, such as Lapwing, Avocet, Shoveler and Gadwall. Spring migrants inc Yellow Wagtail and Whitethroat.

Barn and Little Owls. *Autumn:* Wintering wildfowl such as Teal and Wigeon. Migrating waders inc Whimbrel, Black-tailed Godwit and Greenshank. *Winter:* Wintering wildfowl and wading birds, including Wigeon, Teal, Curlew, Dunlin and Redshank. **Other notable fauna:** Grassland butterflies such as skippers, wall and meadow browns and dragonflies. **Contact:** RSPB Havergate, 01394 450 732; e-mail: havergate.island@rspb.org.uk

3. CARLTON MARSHES

Suffolk Wildlife Trust.
Location: TM 508 920. SW of Lowestoft, at W end of Oulton Broad. From Lowestoft, take A146 towards Beccles and turn R after Tesco garage.
Access: Open during daylight hours. Keep to marked paths. Dogs allowed in some areas, on leads at all times. Car park suitable for coaches.
Facilities: Education centre with disabled toilet. Firm path around part of the marsh, including easy access gates. Disabled access route along the river wall from Oulton Broad to Carlton Marshes. Free car park.
Public transport: Bus and train in walking distance.
Habitats: 120 acres of grazing marsh, peat pools and fen.
Key birds: Wide range of wetland and Broadland birds, including Reed, Sedge and Cetti's Warblers, Bearded Tit, Hobby and Marsh Harrier.
Other notable flora and fauna: Water vole, 15 species of dragonfly including Norfolk hawker, rare water soldier and raft spider. Plants include common spotted and southern marsh orchids.
Contact: Reserve warden, e-mail: carlton.reserve@suffolkwildlifetrust.org Education centre - 01502 564 250.

4. DINGLE MARSHES

Suffolk Wildlife Trust.
Location: Sat nav: IP17 3EN. TM 479 708 (Dunwich beach car park). Eight miles from Saxmundham. Follow brown signs from A12 to Minsmere and continue to Dunwich. Forest car park (hide) TM 467 710. The reserve forms part of the Suffolk Coast NNR.
Access: Open at all times. Access via public rights of way and permissive path along beach. Dogs on lead in

breeding season. Coaches can park on beach car park.
Facilities: Toilets at beach car park, Dunwich. Hide in Dunwich Forest overlooking reedbed, accessed via Forest car park. Circular trail marked from car park.
Public transport: Via Coastlink, Dial-a-ride service to Dingle (01728 833 546) links to buses and trains.
Habitats: Grazing marsh, reedbed, shingle beach, fresh and saline lagoons with forest and heath.
Key birds: *All year:* In reedbed, breeding Bittern, Marsh Harrier, Bearded Tit. *Winter:* Hen Harrier, White-fronted Goose, Wigeon, Snipe, Teal on grazing marsh, Twite. *Summer:* Lapwing, Avocet, Snipe, Black-tailed Godwit, Hobby. Good for passage waders.
Other notable flora and fauna: Site is internationally important for starlet sea anemone — the rarest sea anemone in Britain. Otter and water vole.
Contact: Alan Miller, Suffolk Wildlife Trust; e-mail: alan.miller@suffolkwildlifetrust.org www.suffolkwildlifetrust.org

5. HAVERGATE ISLAND

RSPB (Eastern England Office).
Location: Sat nav: IP12 2NU (Orford quay). TM 425 495. Part of the Orfordness-Havergate Island NNR on the Alde/Ore estuary. Orford is 17km NE of Woodbridge, signposted off the A12.
Access: Pre-booked boat crossings only on first Saturday of every month (10am) and special event weekends (see website). Book in advance through Minsmere RSPB visitor centre, (see below). RSPB members £12, non-members £19. Park in Orford's pay-and-display car park next to quay. Guide dogs only.
Facilities: Toilets, picnic area, five birdwatching hides, viewing platform, visitor trail (approx 2km).
Public transport: Local bus (route 160) from Ipswich to Orford. For timetable info call 0870 608 2608. Bus stop is 0.25 miles from quay.
Habitats: Shallow brackish water, lagoons with islands, Mudflats, saltmarsh.
Key birds: *Summer:* Breeding gulls, terns, Avocet, Shelduck and Oystercatcher. A flock of Spoonbills is present from mid July onwards. *Winter:* Wildfowl and waders including Wigeon, Teal, Pintail, Shoveler, Avocet, Lapwing and Black-tailed Godwit. Also, Short-eared Owl, Marsh Harrier and Barn Owl.
Other notable fauna: Brown hare.
Contact: RSPB Havergate Reserves 01394 450 732; e-mail:Kieren.Alexander@rspb.org.uk

NATURE RESERVES - EASTERN ENGLAND

6. HEN REEDBED NNR

Suffolk Wildlife Trust.
Location: Sat nav: IP18 6SQ. TM 471 771. Three miles from Southwold. Turn off A12 at Blythburgh and follow A1095 for two miles to signposted car park. The reserve forms part of the Suffolk Coast NNR.
Access: Open at all times. No dogs in hides.
Facilities: Two hides overlook Wolsey Creek marsh and two viewing platforms on waymarked trails.
Public transport: Bus service between Halesworth and Southwold.
Habitats: Reedbed, grazing marsh, scrape and estuary.
Key birds: *Spring/summer:* Marsh Harrier, Bittern, Bearded Tit, Hobby, Lapwing, Snipe, Avocet, Black-tailed and Bar-tailed Godwits, Reed and Sedge warblers. *Passage:* Wood and Green Sandpipers. *Winter:* Large flocks of waders on estuary, inc Golden and Grey Plovers, Bar and Black-tailed Godwits, Avocet and Dunlin.
Other notable flora and fauna: Otters and water voles frequently seen. Four-spot chaser and hairy dragonfly, occasional Norfolk hawker. Brown argus butterfly colony close to car park.
Contact: As Dingle Marshes.

7. LACKFORD LAKES NATURE RESERVE

Suffolk Wildlife Trust.
Location: Sat nav: IP28 6HX. TL 803 708. Via track off N side of A1101 (Bury St Edmunds to Mildenhall road), between Lackford and Flempton. Five miles from Bury.
Access: Reserve and hides open dawn to dusk every day. Visitor centre open winter (10am-4pm), summer (10am-5pm) Wed to Sun (closed Mon and Tues). Tea and coffee facilities, toilets. Visitor centre, Kingfisher Trail and 4 hides good for wheelchair access.
Facilities: Visitor centre with viewing area upstairs. Tea and coffee facilities, toilets. Eight hides. Coaches should pre-book.
Public transport: Bus to Lackford village (Bury St Edmunds to Mildenhall service) — walk from church.
Habitats: Restored gravel pit with open water, lagoons, islands, willow scrub, reedbeds.
Key birds: *Winter:* Bittern, Water Rail, Bearded Tit. Large gull roost (20,000+). Wide range of waders and wildfowl (inc. Goosander, Pochard, Tufted Duck, Shoveler). *Spring/autumn:* Migrants, inc. raptors. Breeding Shelduck, Little Ringed Plover and reedbed warblers. Nightingale, Turtle Dove, Hobby in summer and Osprey on passage.
Other notable flora and fauna: Otter. 17 species of dragonfly including hairy and emperor. Early marsh and southern orchid.
Contact: Lackford Lakes Visitor Centre, Lackford, Bury St Edmunds, Suffolk, IP28 6HX. 01284 728 706; e-mail: lackford.reserve@suffolkwildlifetrust.org

8. LAKENHEATH FEN

RSPB (Eastern England Office).
Location: Sat nav: IP27 9AD. TL 722 864. W of Thetford, straddling the Norfolk/Suffolk border. From A11, head N on B1112 to Lakenheath and then two miles further. Entrance is 200 metres after level crossing.
Access: Open dawn to dusk, year round (apart from Dec 24 to Jan 1). Visitor centre and toilets open 9am to 5pm every day. Group bookings welcome. Visitor centre accessible to wheelchair users and a few points on the reserve. £4 car park fee for non-RSPB members. Dogs restricted to public footpaths.
Facilities: Visitor centre, toilets (inc disabled). Coach parking (must book). Four nature trails of varied terrain, but most OK for wheelchairs. Viewpoints. Picnic area with tables. Events programme.
Public transport: On-demand Brecks Bus (Mon to Fri) reaches the reserve from Brandon and Thetford. To book, phone Brecks Bus on 01638 664 304 by noon the weekday before travel. Weekend-only trains on Norwich-Ely service stop in Lakenheath.
Habitats: Reedbed, riverside pools, poplar woods.
Key birds: Principally a site for nesting migrants but ducks and some wild swans in winter. *Spring/summer:* Bittern, Marsh Harrier, Turtle Dove, limited numbers of Golden Oriole, Hobby (up to 40), Grasshopper, Reed and Sedge Warblers. *Autumn:* Harriers, Bearded Tit. *Winter:* Ducks, swans, Common Crane, Peregrine, Barn Owl.
Other notable flora and fauna: More than 15 species of dragonflies and damselflies, inc hairy dragonfly and scarce chaser. Range of fenland plants e.g. water violet, common meadow rue and fen ragwort. Roe deer, otter and water vole.
Contact: David White (Information Officer), Visitor Centre, RSPB Lakenheath Fen, Lakenheath, Norfolk IP27 9AD. 01842 863 400; www.rspb.org.uk/reserves e-mail: lakenheath@rspb.org.uk

9. LANDGUARD BIRD OBERVATORY

Landguard Conservation Trust.
Location: Sat nav: IP11 3TW. TM 283 317. On Landguard peninsula, off View Point Road S of Felixstowe town centre. Housed in wartime emplacements alongside Languard Fort.
Access: Visiting by appointment — e-mail: landguardbo@yahoo.co.uk well in advance to check a volunteer will be available.
Facilities: Migration watch point and ringing station.
Public transport: Buses and trains to Felixstowe centre (1.5 miles away).
Habitats: Adjoining Local Nature Reserve, composed of close grazed turf, raised banks with holm oak, tamarisk, etc.
Key birds: Unusual species and common migrants, especially in spring and autumn. Mediterranean Gull regular on beach. In summer and autumn check for seabird and wildfowl movements offshore.
Other notable flora and fauna: 18 species of dragonfly and 29 species of butterfly have been recorded on the site. Several small mammal species plus sightings of cetaceans and seals off-shore. Nationally rare stinking goosefoot.
Contact: Landguard Bird Observatory, View Point

128

Road, Felixstowe IP11 3TW. 01394 673 782;
e.mail: landguardbo@yahoo.co.uk www.lbo.co.uk

10. MINSMERE

RSPB (Eastern England Regional Office).
Location: Sat nav: IP17 3BY. TM 453 672. Six miles NE
of Saxmundham. From A12 at Yoxford or Blythburgh.
Follow brown tourist signs via Westleton village. Car
park is two miles from village.
Access: Car park and hides open dawn to dusk every
day except Dec 25/26. Visitor centre open 9am-5pm
(9am-4pm Nov-Jan). Shop and tea-room open from
10am. Charge (£8 for adults, under-19s £4) for entry
to reserve, except RSPB members. Free entry to
visitor centre.
Facilities: Car park, hides, toilets (inc disabled
and nappy changing), visitor centre with RSPB
shop and cafe. Volunteer guides. Guided walks and
family events (see website for details). Coaches by
appointment only.
Public transport: Train to Saxmundham or Darsham (5
miles) then Suffolk Coastlink bus (book in advance on
01728 833 526.
Habitats: Coastal lagoons, 'the scrape', freshwater
reedbed, grazing marsh, vegetated dunes, heathland,
arable reversion and woodland.
Key birds: *All year:* Marsh Harrier, Bearde'd Tit,
Bittern, Cetti's and Dartford Warblers, Little Egret,
Green and Great Spotted Woodpeckers. *Summer:*
Breeding Hobby, Avocet, Lapwing, Redshank,
Common, Sandwich and Little Terns, Mediterranean
Gull, Sand Martin, warblers, Nightingale, Nightjar,
Woodlark, Stone Curlew (sometimes visible). *Winter:*
Wildfowl inc White-fronted Goose, Bewick's Swan,
Smew, Hen Harrier (scarce), Water Pipit, Siskin.
Autumn/spring: Passage waders inc Black-tailed
Godwit, Spotted Redshank, Ruff. Regular Wryneck,
Red-backed Shrike, Yellow-browed Warbler.
Other notable flora and fauna: Red and muntjac
deer, otter, water vole, badger. Dragonflies inc
emperor, Norfolk hawker and small red-eyed
damselfly. 27 species of butterflies inc purple and
green hairstreaks and brown argus. Adder. Antlion.
Marsh mallow, southern marsh orchid.
Contact: Reserve Manager, RSPB Minsmere NR, 01728
693 540; e-mail: minsmere@rspb.org.uk

11. NORTH WARREN

RSPB (Eastern England Office).
Location: Sat nav: IP15 5BH. TM 467 575. Directly N
of Aldeburgh on Suffolk coast. Take A1094 to Aldebugh
then follow Thorpe Road towards Thorpeness. Use
signposted main car park on beach.
Access: Open at all times. Pay-and-display car park
on thorpe Road. Please keep dogs on leads. Beach
area suitable for disabled.
Facilities: Three nature trails, leaflet available from
Minsmere RSPB. Toilets in Aldeburgh and Thorpeness.
Three spaces for coaches at Thorpeness beach car
park.
Public transport: Bus service to Aldeburgh. First

Eastern Counties (08456 020 121). Nearest train
station is Saxmundham (six miles away).
Habitats: Grazing marsh, lowland heath, reedbed,
woodland.
Key birds: *Winter:* White-fronted Goose, Tundra
Bean Goose, Wigeon, Shoveler, Teal, Gadwall, Pintail,
Snow Bunting. *Spring/summer:* Breeding Bittern,
Marsh Harrier, Hobby, Nightjar, Woodlark, Nightingale,
Dartford Warbler.
Other notable flora and fauna: Hairy dragonfly,
Norfolk hawker and red-eyed damselfly, green and
purple hairstreak butterflies and southern marsh
orchid.
Contact: As Minsmere above.

12. REDGRAVE & LOPHAM FENS

Suffolk Wildlife Trust.
Location: Sat nav: IP22 2HX. TM 052 803. Five miles
from Diss, signposted and easily accessed from A1066
and A143.
Access: Reserve open all year (10am to 5pm summer,
10am to 4pm winter). Dogs on short leads. Visitor
centre is fully accessible. Five waymarked circular
trails (wheelchair-accessible gates on 'spider' trail).
Trails can be muddy after heavy rain (not wheelchair
accessible).
Facilities: Education centre with café, gift shop and
light refreshments, toilets, including disabled, car
park with coach space. Bike parking area, boardwalk
and viewing platform/short boardwalk.
Public transport: Buses and trains to Diss — Coaches
to local villages of Redgrave and South Lopham from
Diss. Simonds Coaches 01379 647 300 and Galloway
Coaches 01449 766 323.
Habitats: Calcareous fen with open water areas, wet
acid heath, river corridor, scrub and woodland.
Key birds: *All year:* Water Rail, Snipe, Teal, Shelduck,
Gadwall, Woodcock, Sparrowhawk, Kestrel, Great
Spotted and Green Woodpeckers, Tawny, Little
and Barn Owls, Kingfisher, Reed Bunting, Bearded
Tit, Willow and Marsh Tits, Linnet. *Summer:*
Hobby, Blackcap, Chiffchaff, Willow, Reed, Sedge
and Grasshopper Warblers, Spotted Flycatcher,
Whitethroat, Hobby plus large Swallow and Starling
roosts. *Winter/ occcasionals on passage:* Marsh
Harrier, Greenshank, Green Sandpiper, Shoveler,
Pintail, Garganey, Jack Snipe, Bittern, Little Ringed
Plover, Oystercatcher, Wheatear, Stonechat and
Whinchat.
Other notable flora and fauna: Otter, water
vole, roe, muntjac and Chinese water deer, stoat,
pipistrelle and Natterer's bats. Great crested newt,
grass snake, adder, slow worm, common lizard. More
than 300 flowering plants. 27 species of butterflies
inc purple and green hairstreaks and brown argus.
More than 20 species of dragonfly inc emperor, hairy
dragonfly, black-tailed skimmer and scarce emerald
damselfly. Fen raft spider population on site.
Contact: Redgrave and Lopham Fens, 01379 688 333;
e-mail: redgrave.centre@suffolkwildlifetrust.org
www.suffolkwildlifetrust.org

Northern England

Cheshire, Cleveland and Co. Durham, Cumbria, Lancashire, Manchester (Greater), Merseyside, Northumberland, East Yorkshire, North Yorkshire, South Yorkshire, West Yorkshire

Cheshire

FROM THE FELLS and forests bordering the Peak District to the wader-rich coastal sites along the Dee and Mersey estuaries, Cheshire has much to interest birdwatchers, while the Wildlife Trust's 40-plus reserves cover a broad range of habitats of value to flora and fauna.

1. DEE ESTUARY (BURTON MERE WETLANDS)

RSPB Dee Estuary Office (formerly known as Inner Marsh Farm).
Location: Sat nav: CH64 5SF. SJ 319 739. Located on the Wirral. From Chester High Road (A540) follow signs for Burton Mere Wetlands. Turning down Puddington Lane, the reserve's entrance is just outside Burton Village.
Access: Reserve open between 9am and 9pm (or dusk if earlier) each day; visitor centre opens 9.30am to 5pm. £4 admission for non-RSPB members. Guide dogs only.
Facilities: Reception centre and café. Large car park, not suitable for coaches (groups should ring for advice). Two major hides (one in reception building) overlooking pools and wetland area, plus viewing screens. Wheelchair access to footpaths and hides. Toilets including disabled facilities. Picnic tables. Guided walks and binocular hire available.
Public transport: Nearest bus stop at Ness Botanic Gardens, 1.5 miles from reserve. Contact Traveline on 0871 200 2233.
Habitats: Former farm and fishery now converted to wetland and meadow habitats.
Key birds: *All year:* Little Egret. Great Spotted and Green Woodpecker. *Spring/summer:* Avocet, Grasshopper Warbler, Lesser Whitethroat and other commoner warblers, passage Black-tailed Godwit, Spotted Redshank and regular Mediterranean Gull. Hobby, Marsh Harrier, Spoonbill. *Autumn:* Passage waders (inc Little Stint, Ruff, Spotted Redshank, Green, Curlew and Wood Sandpipers). *Winter:* Linnet, Brambling, Fieldfare, Redwing, Whooper and Bewick's Swans, Teal, Water Rail, Hen Harrier.
Other notable flora and fauna: Extensive butterfly list. Pipistrelle, noctule, Daubenton's bats, water vole, wide array of orchids. Red-eyed damselfly.
Contact: Burton Point Farm, Station Road, Burton, Nr Neston CH64 5S8. 0151 353 8478; e-mail: deeestuary@rspb.org.uk

2. DEE ESTUARY (PARKGATE)

RSPB Dee Estuary Office.
Location: Sat nav: CH64 6RL. SJ 273 789. On W side of Wirral, S of Birkenhead. View high tide activity from Old Baths car park near Boathouse pub, Parkgate, off B5135.
Access: Open at all times. Viewing from public footpaths and car parks. Don't walk on saltmarsh — the tides are dangerous and nesting birds should not be disturbed. Dogs allowed only on footpaths.
Facilities: Shared car park (closes at 5pm in winter and 8pm in summer), picnic area, group bookings, guided walks, special events, wheelchair access. Toilets at Parkgate village opposite the Square.
Public transport: Bus to Parkgate every hour. Rail station at Neston, two miles from reserve.
Habitats: Estuary, saltmarsh, pools, mud, sand.
Key birds: *Spring/summer/autumn:* Little Egret, Greenshank, Spotted Redshank, Curlew Sandpiper, Skylark, Reed Bunting. *Winter:* Pink-footed Goose, Shelduck, Teal, Wigeon, Pintail, Oystercatcher, Black-tailed Godwit, Curlew, Redshank, Merlin, Peregrine, Water Rail, Short-eared Owl, Hen Harrier.
Other notable flora and fauna: On very high tides, the incoming water displaces several mammal species inc pygmy shrew, water shrew, harvest mouse, weasel and stoat.
Contact: Burton Point Farm, Station Road, Burton, Nr Neston, Cheshire CH64 5SB, 01513 367 681; e-mail: deeestuary@rspb.org.uk

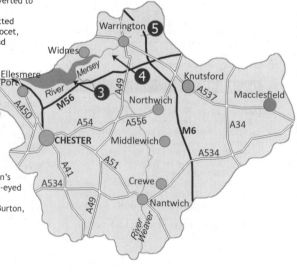

NATURE RESERVES - NORTHERN ENGLAND

3. FRODSHAM MARSH

Manchester Ship Canal Company.
Location: Sat nav: WA6 7BN. SJ 512 779 (Marsh Lane), SJ 520 785 (Weaver Bend/Ship Street). Large area of mixed habitat lying alongside Manchester Ship Canal, SW of Runcorn. Follow Marsh Lane from Frodsham town centre over M56 motorway until it becomes a dirt track. Follow for three miles to small concrete bridge crossing Hoole Pool Gutter.
Access: Open at all times. Park just before concrete bridge and walk along grassy track to barrier gates and then towards vantage points overlooking Rivers Mersey and Weaver. Wheelchair access difficult.
Facilities: None. **Public transport:** None.
Habitats: Saltmarsh, mudflats, embanked tanks to hold river dredgings, reedbeds, farmland and river.
Key birds: More than 20 species of wader recorded, including large flocks of Black-tailed Godwit, Dunlin and Redshank. *Winter:* Wildfowl, inc Whooper Swan, Pinkfeet, Shelduck, Pochard, Pintail, Wigeon and other common species, Raven, Short-eared Owl, Hen Harrier, Peregrine. Passage migrants inc wagtails, pipits, terns, Garganey, Wheatear and Whinchat. *Summer:* Breeding Oystercatcher, Ringed and Little Ringed Plovers, Grasshopper, Sedge and Reed Warblers. Hobbies hunt in autumn.
Contact: None.

4. MOORE NATURE RESERVE

FCC Environment.
Location: Sat nav: WA4 6XE. SJ 577 854. SW of Warrington, via A56 Warrington-to-Chester road. At traffic lights at Higher Walton, follow signs for Moore. Take Moore Lane over swing bridge to reserve.
Access: Open all year. One hide suitable for wheelchairs, other parts of site unsurfaced or gravel paths.
Facilities: Car park, coaches by prior arrangement. Paths, ten bird hides, bird feeding area. Guided walks available on request. See website for wildlife events throughout the year.
Public transport: 62 and 66 buses from Warrington and Runcorn stop in Moore village, less than 1km from reserve. Call 0870 608 2608 for times.
Habitats: Almost 200 acres of wetland, woodland, grasslands, five pools.

Key birds: More than 130 species every year, inc. occasional rarities. *Spring/summer:* Breeding wildfowl and waders, warblers. *Autumn/winter:* Wide variety of wildfowl, Bittern. Also good for gulls, woodpeckers, owls (all five UK species recorded) and raptors. See website for list and latest sightings.
Other notable flora and fauna: Wildfowers including some rarities. Great crested newt.
Contact: The Site Manager, Moore Nature Reserve, 01925 444 689; www.facebook.com/moorenr
e-mail: paul.cassidy@fccenvironment.co.uk
www.fccenvironment.co.uk/moorenaturereserve/

5. WOOLSTON EYES

Woolston Eyes Conservation Group.
Location: SJ 654 888. E of Warrington between the River Mersey and Manchester Ship Canal. Off Manchester Road down Weir Lane or from Latchford to end of Thelwall Lane. Do not park at the bottom end of Weir Lane.
Access: Open all year. Permits required from Chairman, £10 each, £20 per family (see address below).
Facilities: Toilets located at No 3 bed.
Public transport: Buses along A57 nearest stop to Weir Lane, or Thelwall Lane, Latchford. The bus to Weir Lane, Martinscroft (to access reserve from the N) is No3 from Central Station, Warrington. To access reserve from S take either No1 or No2 bus to Westy, Whitley Avenue and walk to the East end of Thelwall Lane. For further info go to www.warrington borough transport.co.uk
Habitats: Wetland, marsh, scrubland, wildflower meadow areas.
Key birds: Breeding Black-necked Grebe, warblers (including Grasshopper Warbler), all raptors (Merlin, Peregrine, Marsh Harrier). SSSI for wintering wildfowl, many duck species breed.
Other notable flora and fauna: 19 mammal species recorded, plus 241 species of lepidoptera, four species of bat. Wide variety of butterflies and 22 species of dragonfly. Notable plants include marsh and bee orchids, helleborine, snakeshead fritillary and cowslip.
Contact: BR Ankers, Chairman, 9 Lynton Gardens, Appleton, Cheshire, WA4 1PD. 01925 267 355. Please enclose A5 S.A.E. for reply. www.woolstoneyes.co.uk

Cleveland /Co Durham

THE ACCLAIMED site guide by Brian Unwin (see page 218) underlines the tremendous birding potential of these two adjoining counties. While coastal sites such as Hartlepool Headland and Whitburn pull in rarities and regular migrants, there are many rewards in the unspoiled inland areas too.

1. BEACON HILL/HAWTHORN DENE MEADOW

Durham Wildlife Trust and National Trust.
Location: Sat nav: SR7 8SH. NZ 427 458. Hawthorn

Dene and Meadow located between Easington and Seaham on Durham coast. Leave A19 at Easington or Seaham and join B1432 to Hawthorn village. From N end of village, follow minor road E, signposted 'Quarry Traffic'. After quarter mile, road ends at two metal gates. Park on grass verge on opposite side to cottage. Access is by foot taking the right-hand path. Access to Beacon Hill (NZ 440 455) is along Coastal Footpath or through southern end of Hawthorn Dene.
Access: Open all year, dogs on leads in spring.
Facilities: Information point. Footpaths.
Public transport: Regular bus services from Durham to Hawthorn.
Habitats: Extensive area of semi-natural habitat

NATURE RESERVES - NORTHERN ENGLAND

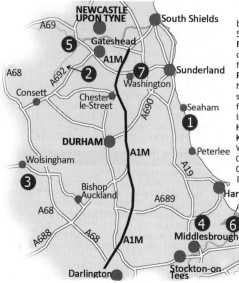

both accessible to wheelchairs from Swalwell centre. Shopmobility scooters can be hired here.
Facilities: Toilets at Thornley and Swalwell visitor centres. Hides at Far Pasture Ponds and Thornley feeding station.
Public transport: 45, 46, 46A, 47/47A/47B buses from Newcastle/Gateshead to Swalwell/Rowlands Gill. Bus stop Thornley Woodlands Centre. (Regular bus service from Newcastle). Information from Nexus Travel Information, 0919 203 3333. www.nexus.org.uk
Habitats: Mixed woodland, river, ponds, meadows.
Key birds: *Summer:* Red Kite, Grasshopper Warbler, Lesser Whitethroat, Kingfisher, Dipper, Great Spotted and Green Woodpeckers, Blackcap, Garden Warbler, Nuthatch. *Winter:* Teal, Tufted Duck, Brambling, Marsh Tit, Bullfinch, Siskin, Great Spotted Woodpecker, Nuthatch, Goosander, Kingfisher.
Other notable flora and fauna: Otter, roe deer, badger, woodland flowers.
Contact: Thornley Woodlands Centre, 01207 545 212; e-mail: countryside@gateshead.gov.uk
www.gatesheadbirders.co.uk
www.gateshead.gov.uk

situated on magnesian limestone escarpment. Steep-sided ravine woodland and limestone grassland.
Key birds: *Summer:* Skylark (important conservation site), Twite, Linnet, Yellowhammer, Goldfinch, Whitethroat, Blackcap, Wren, Long-tailed Tit, Grasshopper Warbler, Reed Bunting, Green Woodpecker, Kestrel, Sparrowhawk. *Winter:* Wide variety of waders inc Turnstone, Purple Sandpiper, Redshank, Curlew, Oystercatcher. Seabirds inc Red-throated Diver, Common Scoter, Guillemot, Cormorant and Great Crested Grebe. *Passage:* Wheatear, Fieldfare, Redwing, Waxwing, Buzzard, Ringed Plover, Dunlin, Knot, Lapwing.
Other notable flora and fauna: Good variety of butterflies. Snowdrops, bluebells and numerous species of orchid, including early purple, bird's nest, lesser butterfly and bee orchids. Roe deer, badger and brown hare.
Contact: Durham Wildlife Trust, 0191 584 3112.
e-mail: mail@durhamwt.co.uk www.durhamwt.co.uk

2. DERWENT WALK COUNTRY PARK & DERWENTHAUGH PARK

Gateshead Council.
Location: Sat nav: NE39 1AU (Thornley Woodlands Centre). NZ 178 604. Along River Derwent, four miles SW of Newcastle and Gateshead. Several car parks along A694. Derwent Walk follows old railtrack bed for 11 miles from Swalwell to Consett.
Access: Site open all times. Thornley visitor centre near Rowlands Gill open Mon-Fri (10am-2pm), weekends and Bank Holidays (1pm-4pm). Keys for hides from Thornley Woodlands Centre. Swalwell visitor centre open daily (9am-4pm). Both centres are closed on Bank Holidays and between Christmas and New Year. Derwent Walk and Derwenthaugh Parks

3. HAMSTERLEY FOREST

Forestry Commission.
Location: Sat nav: DL13 5NL (Forest Drive car park). NZ 053 277. Ten miles W of Bishop Auckland. Main entrance is five miles from A68, S of Witton-le-Wear and signposted through Hamsterley village and Bedburn.
Access: Open all year. £3 toll charge (£5 on Bank Holiday weekends). Forest drive and car park close 8pm (5pm in winter). Information point open daily (9am to 5pm) and cafe open April to October (10am to 5pm) and weekends only Nov-March (11am to 4pm). Visitors should not enter fenced farmland.
Facilities: Visitor centre, tea-room, toilets, shop, access for disabled. Cycles for hire.
Public transport: None.
Habitats: Commercial woodland, mixed and broadleaved trees.
Key birds: *Spring/summer:* Willow Warbler, Chiffchaff, Wood Warbler, Redstart, Pied Flycatcher. *Winter:* Crossbill, Redwing, Fieldfare. *All year:* Jay, Dipper, Green Woodpecker.
Other notable flora: Hay meadows have wide variety of plants including globe flower.
Contact: Forestry Commission, 01434 220 242; e-mail: enquiries.hamsterley@forestry.gsi.gov.uk

4. SALTHOLME

RSPB.
Location: Sat nav: TS2 1TP. NZ 502 231. North of River Tees between Middlesbrough and Billingham. From A19, take A689 north of Stockton and then A1185. After four miles join A178 at mini roundabout. Take third exit and reserve is 250 yards on right.
Access: Open every day except Dec 25. £3 per car for non-members. RSPB members, users of public

More detailed reports on 54 sites in Cleveland and Co. Durham in *Best Birdwatching Sites: North-East England,* available from Buckingham Press Ltd

transport and cyclists free. Opening hours: Apr 1 to Sept 30 (10am-5pm), Oct 1 to Mar 31 (10am-4pm). Dogs only allowed in small exercise area.

Facilities: Award-winning visitor centre with tea-room (open to 4pm each day) and shop, large car park, including Blue Badge spaces and coach parking. Toilets (inc disabled), picnic area. Bound gravel surfaces to four nature trails ¬ wheelchair users may need assistance to reach the three bird hides. Walled garden designed by TV gardener Chris Beardshaw.

Public transport: Stagecoach No1 from Hartlepool stops outside reserve.

Habitats: Wet grasslands, reedbeds, pools with tern islands, wader scrapes.

Key birds: *All year:* Lapwing, Peregrine, Water Rail. *Spring/summer:* Breeding Great Crested Grebe, common wildfowl, hirundines, Snipe, Skylark, Yellow Wagtail, large colony of Common Terns. *Autumn:* Varied waders inc Black-tailed Godwits and Green Sandpipers, occasional rarer species. *Winter:* Large numbers of wildfowl and waders, inc impressive flocks of Golden Plover and Lapwing.

Contact: The Warden, Saltholme, 01642 546 625; e-mail: saltholme@rspb.org.uk; www.rspb.org.uk/reserves

5. SHIBDON POND

Gateshead Council/Durham Wildlife Trust.

Location: Sat nav: NE21 5LU. NZ 192 628. E of Blaydon, S of Scotswood Bridge, close to A1. Car park at Blaydon swimming baths. Open access from B6317 (Shibdon Road).

Access: Open at all times. Disabled access to hide.

Facilities: Hide in SW corner of pond.

Public transport: At least six buses per hour from Newcastle/Gateshead to Blaydon (bus stop Shibdon Road). Nexus Travel Line (0191 232 5325).

Habitats: Pond, marsh, scrub and damp grassland.

Key birds: *Winter:* Large numbers of wildfowl, Water Rail, occasional white-winged gulls. *Summer:* Reed Warbler, Sedge Warbler, Lesser Whitethroat, Grasshopper Warbler, Water Rail. Roosts of terns and Cormorants. *Autumn:* Passage waders and wildfowl, Kingfisher.

Other notable fauna: 17 species of butterfly, inc dingy skipper. Nine species of dragonflies inc ruddy darter, migrant hawker. Otter, great crested newt.

Contact: Thornley Woodlands Centre, 1209 545 212; e-mail: countryside@gateshead.gov.uk www.gatesheadbirders.co.uk

6. TEESMOUTH NNR

Natural England (Northumbria Region).

Location: Two components, centred on NZ 535 276 and NZ 530 260, three and five miles S of Hartlepool, E of A178. Access to northern component from car park at NZ 533 282, 0.5 miles E of A178. Access to southern part from A178 bridge over Greatham Creek at NZ 509 254. Car park adjacent to A178 at NZ 508 251. Both car parks can accommodate coaches.

Access: Open at all times. In northern component, no restrictions over most of dunes and North Gare Sands (avoid golf course, dogs must be kept under close control). In southern component, easy-access path to public hides at NZ 516 255 and NZ 516 252 (no other access).

Facilities: Nearest toilets at Seaton Carew, one mile to the N and RSPB Saltholme (one mile to S). Easy-access path and hides (see above), interpretive panels and leaflet. Teesmouth Field Centre (Tel: 01429 853 847).

Public transport: Half-hourly bus service (service 1) operates Mon-Sat between Middlesbrough and Hartlepool (hourly on Sundays), along A178, Stagecoach Hartlepool, Tel: 01429 267 082. Seaton Carew train station is 2km from North Gare car park.

Habitats: Grazing marsh, dunes, intertidal flats.

Key birds: Passage and winter wildfowl and waders. Passage terns and skuas in late summer. Scarce passerine migrants and rarities. *Spring/summer:* Breeding Ringed Plover, Lapwing, Oystercatcher, Redshank and Snipe. *Winter:* Internationally important numbers of waterbirds, inc waders and Shelduck. Merlin, Peregrine, Snow Bunting, Twite, divers, grebes.

Other notable flora and fauna: Northern component has large marsh orchid populations in damp dune grassland. Colony of 100 common seals at Seal Sands (pups born in late June).

Contact: Senior Reserve Manager: 01429 853 325/0300 060 1729; e-mail: mike.leakey@naturalengland.org.uk www.naturalengland.org.uk

7. WASHINGTON

The Wildfowl & Wetlands Trust.

Location: Sat nav: NE38 8QU. NZ 329 560. On N bank of River Wear, four miles E of A1(M), sign-posted from A195, A19, A182 and A1231.

Access: Open all year except Dec 25: 9.30am to 5.30pm (summer), 9.30am to 4.30pm (winter). Free to WWT members. Admission charge for non-members. Guide dogs only. Good access for people with disabilities.

Facilities: Visitor centre, toilets, parent and baby room, range of hides. Shop and café.

Public transport: Buses to Waterview Park (250 yards

walk to Washington), from Sunderland, Newcastle-upon-Tyne, Durham and South Shields. Tel: 0845 6060 260 for details.
Habitats: Wetlands, woodland and meadows.
Key birds: *Spring/summer*: Nesting colony of Grey Heron, other breeders include Common Tern, Avocet, Oystercatcher, Lapwing. *Winter*: Bird-feeding station visited by Great Spotted Woodpecker, Bullfinch, Jay and Sparrowhawk. Goldeneye and other ducks.
Other notable flora and fauna: Wildflower meadows hold cuckoo flower, bee orchid and yellow rattle. Dragonfly and amphibian ponds.

Cumbria

SITES along the Solway coast tend to hog the limelight when it comes to bird sightings, but the Lake District can still offer a typical range of upland birds, plus one Golden Eagle still hanging on at Haweswater and an Osprey watchpoint at Lake Bassenthwaite. In all, the county's Wildlife Trust manages 43 reserves, of which 36 are open to visitors.

1. CAMPFIELD MARSH

RSPB (Northern England office).
Location: Sat nav: CA7 5AG. NY 197 615. At North Plain Farm, on S shore of Solway estuary, W of Bowness-on-Solway. Signposted on unclassified coast road from B5307 from Carlisle.
Access: Open at all times, no charge. Car park at North Plain Farm. Disabled visitors can drive to wheelchair-friendly hide to view high-tide roosts. Grassed paths can be muddy.
Facilities: Small visitor centre at North Plain. One hide overlooking wetland areas, four viewing screens along nature trail (3 miles). Three lay-bys over wader roosts on saltmarsh.
Public transport: Bus No 93 from Carlisle terminates at reserve's eastern end — 1.5 mile walk to North Plain Farm.
Habitats: Saltmarsh/intertidal areas, open water, peat bog, wet grassland.
Key birds: *Winter*: Waders and wildfowl include Barnacle and Pinkfooted Geese, Shoveler, Scaup, Grey Plover. *Spring/summer*: Breeding Lapwing, Curlew, Redshank, Snipe, Tree Sparrow and warblers. *Spring and autumn*: Passage waders such as Black-tailed Godwit, Whimbrel. Look for Pomarine, Arctic, Great and Long-tailed Skuas over the Solway. *Autumn/winter*: Up to 10,000 Oystercatchers among large roosting wader flocks. Hen Harrier.
Other notable flora and fauna: Roe deer, brown hare. Bog rosemary, bog asphodel, sundews and cotton grass. Large numbers of dragonflies (inc azure and emerald damselflies and four-spotted chaser).
Contact: North Plain Farm, Bowness-on-Solway, Wigton, Cumbria, CA5 5AG. 01697 351 330;
e-mail: campfield.marsh@rspb.org.uk
www.rspb.org.uk

2. DRUMBURGH MOSS NNR

Cumbria Wildlife Trust.
Location: Sat nav: CA7 5DW. NY 255 586 (OS Landranger 85). From Carlisle city centre, head W on B5307 to Kirkbride. After about one mile, turn R to Burgh by Sands. Follow road for 7.5 miles to Drumburgh village. Turn L by post box, continue down track and park on R past Moss Cottage.
Access: Open all year. Difficult terrain, so it is best to walk on paths or waymarked routes.
Facilities: None.
Public transport: Bus service between Carlisle and Bowness-on-Solway stops in Drumburgh.
Habitats: One of four raised bogs south of Solway (rated best in England), woodland, wet heath, grassland.
Key birds: *Summer*: Red Grouse, Curlew, Redshank and Grasshopper Warbler all breed. *Winter*: Geese from the Solway, plus Short-eared Owl.
Other notable flora and fauna: Large heath butterfly, emperor moth, adder and lizards, roe deer, brown hare. Specialist plants include 13 species of sphagnum moss, sundews, cotton grass and bog rosemary.
Contact: Trust HQ, 01539 816 300;
e-mail: mail@cumbriawildlifetrust.org.uk
www.cumbriawildlifetrust.org.uk

3. HAWESWATER

RSPB and United Utilities.
Location: Sat nav: CA10 2QT (Haweswater car park). NY 469 108. For the eagle viewpoint, go to Bampton village, 10 miles S of

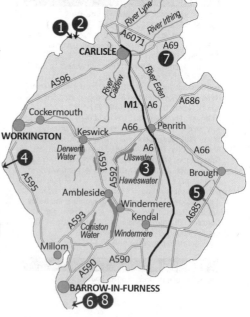

Penrith and five miles NW of Shap. From Bampton, head S towards Haweswater reservoir. Drive down unclassified road alongside Haweswater reservoir, the road ends at a car park. From here you will need to walk.
Access: Visitors are asked not to go beyond the viewpoint, which is always open. There is no wheelchair access. Car park fills quickly in summer, so arrive early.
Facilities: Golden Eagle viewpoint, manned Sat/Sun, plus bank holidays, Apr to end Aug (11am-4pm), telescopes available. There is no coach parking or toilets.
Habitats: Fells with rocky streams, steep oak and birch woodlands.
Key birds: *Upland breeders*: Golden Eagle, Peregrine, Raven, Ring Ouzel, Curlew, Redshank, Snipe. *Woodlands*: Pied Flycatcher, Wood Warbler, Tree Pipit, Redstart, Buzzard, Sparrowhawk. Breeding Goosander on reservoir. Large gull roost in winter.
Other notable fauna: Red deer, red squirrel.
Contact: RSPB Office, 01931 713 376; e-mail: haweswater@rspb.org.uk

4. ST BEES HEAD

RSPB (Northern England).
Location: Sat nav: CA27 0ET. NX 959 118. S of Whitehaven via the B3545 road to St Bees village. Car park at end of Beach Road.
Access: Open at all times, no charge. Access via coast-to-coast footpath. The walk to the viewpoints is long and steep in parts. Dogs only on public footpaths.
Facilities: Copeland Borough Council pay-and-display car park and toilets next to reserve. Three viewpoints overlooking seabird colony. Cliff-top path for nearly three miles.
Public transport: Nearest trains at St Bees (0.5 mile). No bus services.
Habitats: Three miles of sandstone cliffs up to 300 ft high.
Key birds: *Summer*: Largest seabird colony on W coast of England: Guillemot, Razorbill, Puffin, Kittiwake, Fulmar and England's only breeding pairs of Black Guillemot (around Fleswick Bay). Linnet, Stonechat, Whitethroat and Rock Pipit in cliff-top heath areas.
Contact: RSPB, North Plain Farm, Bowness-on-Solway, Wigton, Cumbria CA7 5AG. 01697 351 330; e-mail: stbees.head@rspb.org.uk www.rspb.org.uk

5. SMARDALE GILL NNR

Cumbria Wildlife Trust.
Location: Sat nav: CA17 4HG. NY 727 070. NNR occupies a 6km stretch of the disused railway between Tebay and Darlington. Approx 2.5 miles NE of Ravenstonedale on A685 or 0.5 miles S of Kirkby Stephen station. Take turning signed to Smardale. Cross over railway and turn L to junction, ignoring turn to Waitby. Cross over railway and turn L at junction ignoring sign for Smardale. Cross disused

railway, turn L immediately and L again to car park.
Access: Railway line is open to all, non-members should obtain a permit before visiting other parts of the reserve.
Facilities: None.
Public transport: Train: nearest station Kirkby Stephen. Buses from here to Kendal, Brough and Sedburgh.
Habitats: Limestone grassland, river, ancient semi-natural woodland, quarry.
Key birds: *Summer*: Redstart, Pied Flycatcher and commoner woodland species. *All year*: Usual woodland birds, Buzzard, Sparrowhawk, Raven, Green Woodpecker and Dipper.
Other notable flora and fauna: Scotch argus, northern brown argus, common blue and dark green fritillary butterflies. Fragrant orchid, common rockrose, bluebell and bloody cranesbill. Red squirrel.
Contact: Trust HQ, 01539 816 300; e-mail: mail@cumbriawildlifetrust.org.uk

6. SOUTH WALNEY

Cumbria Wildlife Trust.
Location: Sat nav: LA14 3YQ. SD 225 620. Six miles S of Barrow-in-Furness. From Barrow, cross Jubilee Bridge onto Walney Island, turn L at lights. Continue through Biggar village to South End Caravan Park. Follow road for 1 mile to reserve.
Access: Open daily (10am-5pm, 4pm in winter) plus Bank Holidays. No dogs except assistance dogs. Day permits: £3 adults, £1 children. Cumbria Wildlife Trust members free.
Facilities: Toilets, nature trails, eight hides (two are wheelchair accessible), 200m boardwalk. Electric wheelchair for hire. Coach parking available.
Public transport: Bus service as far as Biggar.
Habitats: Shingle, lagoon, sand dune, saltmarsh.
Key birds: *Spring/autumn*: Passage migrants inc Wheatear, Redstart, Goldcrest and Willow Warbler. *Summer*: 14,000 breeding pairs of Herring, Greater and Lesser Black-backed Gulls, Shelduck, Eider. *Winter*: Teal, Wigeon, Goldeneye, Redshank, Greenshank, Curlew, Oystercatcher, Knot, Dunlin, Merlin, Short-eared Owl, Twite.
Other notable flora and fauna: 450 species of flowering plants. Natterjack toad at North Walney.
Contact: The Warden, South Walney Nature Reserve, Walney Island, Barrow-in-Furness LA14 3YQ. 01229 471 066; e-mail: mail@cumbriawildlifetrust.org.uk

7. TALKIN TARN COUNTRY PARK

Carlisle City Council.
Location: Sat nav: CA8 1HN. NY 544 591. Twelve miles E of Carlisle. From A69 E at Brampton, head S on B6413 for two miles. Talkin Tarn is on E just after level crossing.
Access: All year. Wheelchair access around tarn, Tearoom has lift. Coaches welcome.
Facilities: Tearoom open all year (10.30am-4pm). Mon - Wed, takeaway only, during winter. Dogs allowed on outdoor balcony. Toilet facilities. Angling by day

permit (with closed season).
Public transport: Bus: infrequent. Tel: 0870 608 2608.
Train: nearest station is Brampton Junction. Tel: 0845
748 4950. One mile away by footpath.
Habitats: Natural glacial tarn, mature oak/beech
woodland, orchid meadow (traditionally managed),
wet meadow and farmland.
Key birds: *Spring/summer*: Pied Flycatcher, Spotted
Flycatcher, Redstart, Chiffchaff, Wood Warbler.
Winter: Grebes, Smew, Long-tailed Duck, Goosander,
Gadwall, Wigeon, Brambling, swans.
Other notable flora and fauna: Common blue
damselfly, common darter, small copper butterfly,
otter, red squirrel.
Contact: Greenspaces Team, Carlisle City County,
Civic Centre, Carlisle CA3 8QG. 01228 817 200;
e-mail: parks@carlisle.gov.uk

8. WALNEY BIRD OBSERVATORY

Location: Sat nav: LA14 3YQ. Walney Island, south of
Barrow-in-Furness.
Access: Several areas, notably the golf course and
airfield, are restricted but the island's narrow width
means most sites are viewable from the road or
footpaths.

Facilities: Monitoring and ringing of breeding and
migrant, with ringing opportunities for qualified
visitors. For availability write to Walney Bird
Observatory (address below).
Public transport: Barrow-in-Furness connects to the
rail network and local bus routes serve Walney Island.
Routes 1 and 1A cover the central area while 6 and
6A cover the north end of the island. No bus route to
southern end.
Habitats: Estuarine, maritime, dunes, freshwater and
brackish pools, scrub and farmland.
Key birds: Renowned Eider and gull colonies at south
end. The winter months provide a wildfowl and wader
spectacular across the island. Migrants aplenty appear
during both passage periods — the island has a proven
pedigree for attracting rare and unusual species.
Other notable flora and fauna: Famed for Walney
geranium, but also important for coastal shingle
species such as sea holly, sea rocket and sea kale.
More than 500 species of moth recorded, inc sand
dune specialities such as coast dart and sand dart.
Contact: Walney Bird Observatory, Coastguard
Cottages, Walney Island, Barrow-in-Furness, Cumbria
LA14 3YQ.

Lancashire

THE COUNTY'S mosses attract huge numbers
of wintering Pink-footed Geese, Bewick's and
Whooper Swans, while tens of thousands of waders
winter in Morecambe Bay. A series of estuaries are
attractive to wildfowl and waders. Inland, Pendle
Hill attracts regular Dotterel on spring passage.

1. BROCKHOLES

Lancashire Wildlife Trust.
Location: Sat nav: PR5 0AG. SD 589 309. Site in
Preston New Road, Samlesbury, which first opened in
2011, is adjacent to junction 31 of the M6. From S
take A59 towards Blackburn and then first exit, signposted to reserve, and follow under the southbound
slip road north of River Ribble.
Access: Open 10am to 5pm (April to Oct), 4pm for
rest of year. Most paths are surfaced and wheelchair-
friendly. £10 refundable deposit for keys to access
gates bypassing kissing gates. 16 blue badge parking
spaces. Car park charges, but free coach parking.
Guided tours need to be booked. No dogs.
Facilities: Floating World is a cluster of buildings
made from sustainable materials and housing a village
store and gift shop, restaurant (free wi-fi access), and
adapted toilets. Bird hides.
Public transport: Stagecoach No59 or Transdev
Lancashire United X80/280 buses between Preston,
Blackburn and Accrington stop at Tickled Trout Motel
by M6.
Habitats: Created from disused gravel pits, the site
alongside the River Ribble now features open water,

reedbeds, wet grassland and woodland.
Key birds: *Spring/summer*: Breeding Great Crested
Grebe, Lapwing, Redshank, Reed and Sedge Warblers,
Reed Bunting, Skylark. *Winter*: Good for wildfowl, inc
Pochard, Pintail, Goldeneye and Teal. Passage waders
inc Turnstone, Grey Plover, Greenshank, Whimbrel,
Curlew, Wood, Green and Curlew Sandpipers and
Black-tailed Godwit.
Other notable flora and fauna: Brown hawker and
emperor dragonflies.
Contact: info@brockholes.org or phone 01772 872
000.

2. HEYSHAM NR & BIRD OBSERVATORY

Wildlife Trust for Lancashire, Manchester and North
Merseyside/EDF Energy Estates.
Location: Sat nav: LA3 2UP (Duke of Rothesay pub).
SD 407 601 W of Lancaster. Take A683 to Heysham
port. Turn L at traffic lights by Duke of Rothesay pub,
then turn R after 300m.
Access: Gate to reserve car park open 10am to 6pm
(dusk in winter). Pedestrian access at all times.
Limited disabled access. Dogs barred on main reserve
but an extensive off-lead area is nearby.
Facilities: Map giving access details at the reserve car
park. No manned visitor centre or toilet access, but
someone usually in reserve office, next to the main
car park, in the morning. Check heyshamobservatory.
blogpot.com for virtually daily updates, plus detailed
map at the bottom of the page. Read blogsite sidebar
for latest on access around the harbour area.
Public transport: Train services connect with
nearby Isle of Man ferry terminal. Plenty of buses to

NATURE RESERVES - NORTHERN ENGLAND

Lancaster from various Heysham sites within walking distance (ask for nearest stop to the harbour).
Habitats: Varied: wetland, acid grassland, alkaline grassland, foreshore.
Key birds: Passerine migrants in the correct conditions. Good passage of seabirds in spring, especially Arctic Tern. Storm Petrel and Leach's Petrel during strong onshore (SW-WNW) winds in midsummer and autumn respectively. Good variety of breeding birds (e.g. eight species of warbler on the reserve itself). Two-three scarce land-birds each year, most frequent being Yellow-browed Warbler.
Other notable flora and fauna: Notable area for dragonflies: red-veined darter has bred for several years at nearby Middleton Community Woodland main pond SD 418 592 (mid June to mid July). Bee orchid.
Contact: Reserve Warden, Heysham Nature Reserve. 01524 855 030. Annual report from Leighton Moss RSPB reserve shop. www.lancswt.org.uk http://heyshamobservatory.blogspot.com

3. LEIGHTON MOSS

RSPB (Northern England).
Location: Sat nav: LA5 0SW. SD 478 750. Four miles NW of Carnforth, Lancs. Leave M6 at J35. Take the A6 N towards Kendal and follow brown signs for Leighton Moss off A6.
Access: Reserve open daily dawn-dusk. Visitor centre open 9.30am to 5pm (4.30pm Dec-Jan inclusive except dec 25). Free for RSPB members or those arriving by public transport or bike (you also get 10% discount in café). Non-members pay £5 (adult), £3 (concessions), £1 (children). Dogs restricted to Causeway public footpath.
Fa-

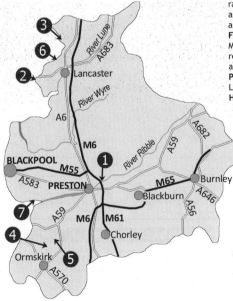

cilities: Visitor centre, shop, cafe and toilets, disabled toilet. Nature trails and seven hides (four have wheelchair access), plus two hides at saltmarsh pools. Stairlift to café for those with mobility issues. Binoculars for hire.
Public transport: Silverdale train station (on Manchester Airport to Barrow line) is 250 metres from reserve. Shuttle bus service meets trains and takes passengers to Silverdale village. Call Traveline on 0871 200 2233, or visit http://www.lancashire.gov.uk
Habitats: Reedbed, shallow meres and woodland. Saltmarsh pools approx 1 mile.
Key birds: *All year:* Bittern, Bearded Tit, Water Rail, Shoveler, Gadwall, Marsh Tit, Little Egret. *Summer:* Breeding Marsh Harrier, Reed and Sedge Warbler. Avocet at saltmarsh pools. *Passage:* Good numbers of Black-tailed Godwits in spring with Greenshank, Ruff and godwits in autumn. *Winter:* Large flocks of Starlings roosting, hunting Peregrine and Merlin terrorise overwintering wildfowl.
Other notable flora and fauna: Otter, red deer.
Contact: RSPB Leighton Moss Nature Reserve, Myers Farm, Silverdale, Carnforth, LA5 0SW. 01524 701 601; e-mail: leighton.moss@rspb.org.uk

4. MARTIN MERE

The Wildfowl & Wetlands Trust.
Location: Sat nav: L40 0TA. SD 428 145. Off Fish Lane, Burscough, six miles N of Ormskirk via Burscough Bridge (A59). 20 miles from Liverpool and Preston.
Access: Closed on Dec 25. Opening times: 9.30am-4.30pm (Oct 27 to March); 9.30am-6pm (rest of year). Special dawn and evening events. Guide dogs only. Admission charge for non-WWT members. Special rates for coach parties. Fully accessible to disabled, all hides suitable for wheelchairs. Coach park available.
Facilities: Visitor centre with toilets, gift shop, Mere Side Café, education centre, play area, nature reserve and nature trails, hides, waterfowl collection and sustainable garden.
Public transport Train to Burscough Bridge or New Lane Stations (both 1.5 miles from reserve).
Habitats: Open water, wet grassland, moss, copses, reedbed, parkland.
Key birds: *Winter:* Whooper and Bewick's Swans, Pink-footed Goose, various ducks, Ruff, Black-tailed Godwit, Peregrine, Hen Harrier, Tree Sparrow. *Spring:* Ruff, Shelduck, Little Ringed and Ringed Plovers, Lapwing, Redshank. *Summer:* Marsh Harrier, Garganey, hirundines, Tree Sparrow. Breeding Avocet, Lapwing, Redshank, Shelduck. *Autumn:* Pink-footed Goose, waders on passage.
Other notable flora and fauna: Whorled caraway, golden dock, tubular dropwort, 300 species of moth.
Contact: WWT Martin Mere Wetland Centre, 01704 895 181; e-mail: info.martinmere@wwt.org.uk

5. MERE SANDS WOOD

Wildlife Trust for Lancashire, Manchester and North Merseyside.
Location: Sat nav: L40 1TL. SD 447 157. 12 miles by road from Southport, 0.5 miles off A59 Preston to Liverpool road, in Rufford along B5246 (Holmeswood Road).
Access: Public footpaths open at all times. Visitor centre open 9am to 5pm. No admission charge but £2 donation encouraged. Car park open until 8pm in summer. Three miles of wheelchair-accessible footpaths. All hides accessible to wheelchairs. Guided walks for bird/wildlife groups can be arranged.
Facilities: Visitor centre with toilets (disabled), six viewing hides, three trails, exhibition room, latest sightings board. Feeding stations. Booking essential for two motorised buggies.
Public transport: Bus: Southport-Chorley 347 and Preston-Ormskirk 2B stop in Rufford, 0.5 mile walk. Train: Preston-Ormskirk train stops at Rufford station, one mile walk.
Habitats: 40h inc freshwater lakes, mixed woodland, sandy grassland/heath.
Key birds: 170 species recorded, with 60 known to have bred. *Winter:* Regionally important for Teal and Gadwall, good range of waterfowl inc Mandarin and Goosander, Kingfisher. Feeding stations attract Tree Sparrow, Bullfinch, Reed Bunting, Water Rail. *Woodland:* Lesser Spotted Woodpecker, Willow Tit, Treecreeper, Nuthatch. *Summer:* Kingfisher. *Passage:* Most years, Osprey, Crossbill, Green Sandpiper, Greenshank.
Other notable flora and fauna: 18 species of dragonfly recorded annually, broad bucker fern, plus more than 200 species of fungi.
Contact: Reserve Manager, Mere Sands Wood Nature Reserve, 01704 821 809; www.lancswt.org.uk
e-mail: lbeaton@lancswt.org.uk

6. MORECAMBE BAY (HEST BANK)

RSPB (Northern England).
Location: Sat nav: LA2 6HN. SD 467 666. Two miles N of Morecambe at Hest Bank. Access car park from Hest Bank level crossing off A5105.
Access: Open at all times. Do not venture onto saltmarsh or intertidal area, as there are dangerous channels and quicksands. Paths from car park too rough for wheelchairs. Dogs allowed.
Facilities: Viewpoint and toilets at local council car park. Guided walks programme.
Public transport: No 5 bus runs between Carnforth and Morecambe. Tel: 0870 608 2608. Nearest rail station is Morecambe (three miles from reserve).
Habitats: Saltmarsh, estuary.
Key birds: 250,000 waders and wildfowl spend winter on Britain's second-most important estuary site. *Winter:* Wildfowl (Pintail, Shelduck, Wigeon) and waders. This is an important high tide roost for Oystercatcher, Curlew, Redshank, Dunlin and Bar-tailed Godwit.
Contact: RSPB Leighton Moss & Morecambe Bay Nature Reserves, 01524 701601;
e-mail: leighton.moss@rspb.org.uk
www.rspb.org.uk/morecambebay

7. RIBBLE ESTUARY

Natural England (Cheshire to Lancashire Coastal Team).
Location: SD 380 240. Lies 7km W of Preston, stretching on both sides of River Ribble as far as Lytham and Crossens. Take A584 and minor roads for north bank and A59 and minor roads for the southern side.
Access: Public footpaths open at all times, but no access to saltmarsh itself.
Facilities: No formal visiting facilities. Ribble Discovery Centre is at Fairhaven Lake (5km W of Lytham). RSPB Marshside, adjacent to NNR, has hides, parking and information boards.
Public transport: For bus service information visit: www.stagecoachbus.com
Habitats: Ramsar and SPA designation for one of England's largest areas of saltmarsh, and mudflats.
Key birds: High water wader roosts of Knot, Dunlin, Black-tailed Godwit, Oystercatcher and Grey Plover are best viewed from Southport, Marshside, Lytham and St Annes. Pink-footed Geese and wintering swans are present in large numbers Oct-Feb on Banks Marsh and along River Douglas respectively. Banks Marsh can be viewed from the public footpath which runs along the sea defence embankment from Crossens Pumping Station to Hundred End. The large flocks of Wigeon, for which the site is renowned, can be seen on high tides from Marshside but feed on saltmarsh areas at night. Good numbers of raptors also present in winter.
Contact: Senior Reserve Manager, Natural England, Ribble Estuary NNR, 01704 578 774;
e-mail: dave.mercer@naturalengland.org.uk

Manchester, Greater

FOR A largely urban area, there are good places for birdwatching. Pennington Flash is the area's best all-round birding site, while Peregrines and Black Redstarts breed in the city centre and urban regeneration has cleaned up the water to such an extent that increasing numbers of ducks are wintering in Salford Docks. Etherow CP holds Dipper, Grey Wagtail, Pied Flycatcher and all three woodpeckers.

BROAD EES DOLE (SALE WATER PARK)

Mersey Valley Countryside Warden Service
Location: Sat nav: M32 9UP. SJ 799 933. Local Nature Reserve located close to visitor centre in Sale Water

Park, Trafford. Access from Junction 6 of M60, following signs for Trafford Water Sports Centre. **Access:** No paths within the reserve, so view from perimeter paths. Sale Water Park visitor centre car park off Rifle Road. Walk to reserve by following track behind visitor centre.
Facilities: Small concrete bird hide overlooks site.
Habitats: Wetland site with water levels managed to provide feeding and breeding opportunities for a variety of birds such as herons, Kingfisher, Little Ringed Plover and Lapwing.
Key birds: Important site for migratory species and waders inc Snipe and Jack Snipe. Winter wildfowl inc Mallard, Gadwall, Teal, Coot, Moorhen in LNR, wider variety on main lake of Water Park.
Other notable flora and fauna: Spotted orchid, smooth and great crested newts. Variety of fish on main lake in Sale Water Park.
Contact: MVCWS, 0161 881 5639;
e-mail: info@merseyvalley.org.uk
www.merseyvalley.org.uk

ETHEROW COUNTRY PARK

Stockport Metropolitan Borough Council.
Location: Sat nav: SK6 5JD. SJ 965 908. Site lies at the halfway point on the 12-mile Valley Way Footpath which links Stockport and Woolley Bridge. Situated at Compstall on B6104 near Romiley, Stockport.
Access: Park land open at all times; permit required for conservation area. Keep to paths.
Facilities: Reserve area has SSSI status. One bird hide, nature trail, visitor centre, café and toilets, scooters for disabled. Check opening times for facilities prior to arrival 0161 427 6937. Good parking but charges are in operation.
Public transport: There is a good bus service from Stockport, one route coming through Romiley and one coming through Marple. Bus numbers are 383 & 384. The nearest train stations are at Romiley and Marple Bridge.
Habitats: River Etherow, woodlands, marshy area, ponds and surrounding moorland.
Key birds: More than 100 species recorded, inc Sparrowhawk, Buzzard, Dipper, all three woodpeckers, Pied Flycatcher, warblers. *Winter:* Brambling, Siskin, Water Rail. Frequent sightings of Merlin and Raven over hills.
Other notable flora and fauna: 200 species of plant.
Contact: John Rowland, Countryside Officer for Stockport via 0161 217 611;
e-mail: stockportdirect@stockport.gov.uk

HOLLINGWORTH LAKE

Hollingworth Lake/Rochdale MBC.
Location: Sat nav: OL15 0AQ. SD 939 153 (visitor centre). On outskirts of Littleborough, 4 miles NE of Rochdale, signposted from A58 Halifax Road and J21 of M62 (B6225 to Littleborough).
Access: Open access to lake and surroundings.
Facilities: Cafes, hide, trails and education service, car parks, coach park by prior arrangement. Free

wheelchair hire, disabled toilets and baby changing facilities, fishing. Visitor centre open 10am to 3.30pm, Friday to Tuesday. Toilets and café open at 9.30am.
Public transport: Bus Nos 452, 450. Train to Littleborough or Smithy Bridge.
Habitats: Lake (116 acres, includes 20 acre nature reserve), woodland, streams, marsh, willow scrub.
Key birds: *All year:* Great Crested Grebe, Kingfisher, Lapwing, Little Owl, Bullfinch, Cormorant. Occasional Peregrine, Sedge Warbler, Water Rail, Snipe. *Spring/ autumn:* Passage waders, wildfowl. *Summer:* Reed Bunting, Dipper, Common Sandpiper, Curlew, Oystercatcher, Black Tern, 'Commic' Tern, Grey Partridge, Blackcap. *Winter:* Goosander, Goldeneye, Siskin, Redpoll, Golden Plover.
Contact: The Ranger, Hollingworth Lake Visitor Centre, Rakewood Road. 01706 373 421;
e--mail: holl.lakecp@rochdale.gov.uk
www.rochdale.gov.uk

PENNINGTON FLASH COUNTRY PARK

Wigan Leisure and Culture Trust.
Location: Sat nav: WN7 3PA. SJ 640 990. One mile from Leigh town centre and well signposted from A580 East Lancashire Road. Main entrance on A572 (St Helens Road).
Access: Park is permanently open. Five largest hides, toilets and information point open 9am-dusk (except Christmas Day). Main paths flat and suitable for disabled. Main car park pay & display with coach parking available if booked in advance.
Facilities: Toilets (including disabled) and information point. Total of eight bird hides. Site leaflet available and Rangers based on site. Group visits welcome but please book in advance.
Public transport: Only 1 mile from Leigh bus station. Several services stop on St Helens Road near entrance to park. Tel: 01942 883 501 for more details.
Habitats: Lowland lake, ponds and scrapes, fringed with reeds, rough grassland and young woodland.
Key birds: Waterfowl all year, waders (14-plus species) and terns (4-plus species) mainly on passage in both spring and autumn. Breeding birds include nine species of warbler. Feeding station attracts Willow Tit, Stock Dove and up to 40 Bullfinches all year. Large gull roost in winter. More than 240 species recorded, including seven county firsts in the last decade alone.
Other notable flora and fauna: Several species of orchid, including bee orchid. Wide variety of butterflies and dragonflies.
Contact: Site Manager, Pennington Flash CP. 01942 605 253; e-mail: pfcp@wlct.org; www.wlct.org/open-spaces/parks/park-information.htm

WIGAN FLASHES

Lancashire Wildlife Trust/Wigan Council.
Location: Sat nav: WN3 5NY (Hawkley Hall school). D 580 035. Leave M6 at J25 head N on A49, turn R on to Poolstock Lane (B5238). There are several entrances

to the site; at end of Carr Lane near Hawkley Hall School; one off Poolstock Lane; two on Warrington Road (A573). Also accessible from banks of Leeds and Liverpool Canal.

Access: Free access, open at all times. Areas suitable for wheelchairs. Paths (10km in total) being up-graded. Access for coaches: contact reserve manager for details.

Facilities: Six hide screens. Poolstock Lane car park has 300 spaces.

Public transport: 610 bus (Hawkley Hall Circular). Local timetable info - call 0161 228 7811.

Habitats: Open water (eight flashes) with reedbed, wet woodland and rough grassland.

Key birds: More than 200 species recorded. Black Tern on migration. *Summer*: Nationally important for Reed Warbler and breeding Common Tern. Willow Tit, Cetti's and Grasshopper Warblers, Kingfisher. *Winter*: Wildfowl, especially diving duck and Gadwall. Bittern (especially winter).

Other notable flora and fauna: Interesting orchids, with the six species including marsh and dune helleborine. One of the UK's largest feeding assemblage of noctule bats. Water vole. Eighteen species of dragonfly which has included red-veined darter.

Contact: Mark Champion, Lancashire Wildlife Trust, Highfield Grange, Wigan, Lancs WN3 6SU. 01942 233 976; e-mail: wiganflashes@lancswt.org.uk

Merseyside

SEAFORTH DOCKS has a good reputation for rare gulls, while north-westerly gales in autumn bring Leach's Petrels to the tip of the Wirral peninsula, probably the best place in Britain to see them away from their breeding sites.

1. DEE ESTUARY

Metropolitan Borough of Wirral.

Location: Sat nav: CH60 9JS. SJ 255 815. Leave A540 Chester to Hoylake road at Heswall and head downhill (one mile) to the free car park at the shore end of Banks Road. Heswall is 30 mins from South Liverpool and Chester by car.

Access: Open at all times. Best viewpoint 600 yards along shore N of Banks Road. No disabled access along shore, but good birdwatching from bottom of Banks Road. Arrive 2.5 hours before high tide. Coach parking available.

Facilities: Information board. No toilets in car park. Wirral Country Park Centre three miles N, off A540 has toilets, hide, café, kiosk (all accessible to wheelchairs). Sheldrakes Restaurant, at the end of Banks Road, has an outside terrace overlooking the foreshore. Tel 0151 342 1556.

Public transport: Bus service to Banks Road car park from Heswall bus station, or bus to Irby village, then walk one mile. Mersey Travel (0151 236 7676).

Habitats: Saltmarsh and mudflats.

Key birds: *Autumn/winter*: Large passage and winter wader roosts – Redshank, Curlew, Black-tailed Godwit, Oystercatcher, Golden Plover, Knot, Shelduck, Teal, Red-breasted Merganser, Peregrine, Merlin, Hen Harrier, Short-eared Owl. Smaller numbers of Pintail, Wigeon, Bar-tailed Godwit, Greenshank, Spotted Redshank, Grey and Ringed Plovers, Whimbrel, Curlew Sandpiper, Little Stint, occasional Scaup and Little Egret.

Contact: Wirral Country Park Visitors Centre, Station Road, Thustaston, Wirral CH61 0HN. 0151 648 4371; e-mail: wirralcountrypark@wirral.gov.uk

2. HILBRE ISLAND LNR

Metropolitan Borough of Wirral.

Location: Sat nav: CH48 0QA (Dee Lane, West Kirby). SJ 184 880. Three tidal islands in the mouth of the Dee Estuary. Park in West Kirby on A540 Chester-to-Hoylake road, 30 minutes from Liverpool, 45 minutes from Chester. Follow the brown Marine Lake signs to Dee Lane pay & display car park or free parking along the promenade. Coach parking available at West Kirby.

Access: Two mile walk across sands from Dee Lane slipway. No disabled access. Do not cross either way within 3.5 hours of high water — tide times and suggested safe route on noticeboard at slipway. Call 0151 632 4455 for advice on tide times. Permit required for groups of six and above (apply to Wirral Visitor Centre).

Facilities: Hilbre Bird Observatory by prior appointment only. Composting toilets on the main island (Hilbre) and at Wirral Sailing Centre (end of Dee Lane, West Kirby). Leaflets and tide times from Thurstaston Visitor Centre.

Public transport: Bus and train station (from Liverpool) within 0.5 mile of Dee Lane slipway. Contact Mersey Travel, 0151 236 7676.

Habitats: Sandflats, rocky shore and open sea.

Key birds: *Late summer/autumn:* Seabird passage — Gannets, terns, skuas, shearwaters and after NW gales good numbers of Leach's Petrel. *Winter:* Wader roosts at high tide, Purple Sandpiper, Turnstone, sea ducks, divers, grebes. Passage migrants.

Other notable flora and fauna: Nationally scarce rock sea-lavender and sea spleenwort. Field vole, grey seal. Whales and dolphins seen offshore.

Contact: As Dee Estuary (above).

3 . MARSHSIDE

RSPB (Northern England).

Location: Sat nav: PR9 9PJ. SD 353 205. From Southport, follow minor coast road Marine Drive N (1.5 miles from Southport Pier) to small car park by sand works.

Access: Open 8.30am to 5pm (dusk in winter) all year. Guide dogs only. Coach parties please book in advance. No charges but donations welcomed. Park in Sefton Council car park along Marine Drive.

Facilities: Information centre, toilets (inc disabled), two hides (one heated) and trails accessible to wheelchairs. Two viewing screens and a viewing platform.

Public transport: Bus service to Elswick Road/ Marshside Road half-hourly, bus No 44, from Lord Street. Contact Traveline (0870 608 2608).

Habitats: Coastal grazing marsh and lagoons.

Key birds: *Winter:* Pink-footed Goose, wildfowl, waders, raptors inc Peregrine, Merlin, Sparrowhawk and Kestrel. *Spring:* Breeding waders, inc. Avocet and wildfowl, Garganey, migrants. *Autumn:* Migrants. *All year:* Black-tailed Godwit.

Other notable flora and fauna: Hares, various plants including marsh orchid, migrant hawker dragonfly.

Contact: Marshside RSPB Reserve, 01704 226 190.

4. NORTH WIRRAL COASTAL PARK

Friends of North Wirral Coastal Park.

Location: Sat nav: CH46 4TA. SJ 241 909. Located between the outer Dee and Mersey Estuaries. From Moreton take A553 E. then A551 N. Turn left onto Tarran Way South then R onto Lingham Lane. Parking available by lighthouse. Foreshore can be viewed from footpath which runs alongside.

Access: Open at all times.

Facilities: Visitor centre, eight car parks, three toilet blocks (one summer-only), extensive footpath network and public bridleways, four picnic areas.

Public transport: The area being served by Grove Road (Wallasey), Leasowe, Moreton, and Meols Merseyrail Stations, and with bus routes along Leasowe Road, Pasture Road and Harrison Drive.

Habitats: Saltmarsh.

Key birds: Important as a feeding and roosting site for passage and wintering flocks of waders, wildfowl, terns and gulls. Wintering populations of Knot (20,000+), Bar-tailed Godwit (2,000+) and Dunlin (10,000). Redshank (1,000+) and Turnstone (500+) feed on the rocky shore at Perch Rock and on the rocky sea walls. Oystercatcher (500+), Curlew, Grey Plover and Black-tailed Godwit also regularly roost here in relatively high numbers. Small populations of wildfowl, including Common Scoter, Scaup and Goldeneye, Red-throated Divers and Great Crested Grebes also frequently winter on this site.

Other notable flora and fauna: Sea holly, marram grass, storksbill, burnet rose and rarities like the Isle of Man cabbage can be found. One of two known sites in the world for the very rare British sub-species of the belted beauty moth.

Contact: Friends of North Wirral Coastal Park 01516 785 488;

e-mail: info@friendsofnorthwiralcoastalpark.co.uk

5. SEAFORTH NATURE RESERVE

Wildlife Trust for Lancs, Manchester and N Merseyside.

Location: Sat nav: L21 1JD. SJ 318 971. Five miles from Liverpool city centre. From M57/M58 take A5036 to docks. Enter via Liverpool Freeport entrance in Crosby Road South.

Access: Organised groups must contact reserve office (see below) at least seven days in advance of their planned trip. Coaches welcome. Wildlife Trust members can apply for permits from the Trust but must pick them up in person from Port Police.

Facilities: Toilets at visitor centre when open, three hides.

Public transport: Train to Waterloo or Seaforth stations from Liverpool. Buses to dock gates from Liverpool.

Habitats: Saltwater and freshwater lagoons, scrub grassland and small reedbed.

Key birds: Noted site for Little Gull on passage (Apr), plus Roseate, Little and Black Terns. Breeding and passage Common Tern (Apr-Sept). Passage and winter waders and gulls – 15 species of gull recorded, with Ring-billed annual and Mediterranean seen almost daily. Passage passerines, especially White Wagtail, pipits and Wheatear, plus a sprinkling of vagrants.

Contact: Seaforth Nature Reserve, Port of Liverpool, L21 1JD. 0151 9203 769. www.lancswt.org.uk

Contact: As Dee Estuary (above).

Northumberland

THIS IS A STUNNING county, with a fantastic range of habitats. The seabird colonies on the Farne Islands are world famous, while Holy Island (Lindisfarne) attracts a range of migrants in spring and autumn, plus huge numbers of wintering birds. Kielder Forest is good for Crossbills and raptors, including Goshawk. The nearby moors hold a good selection of upland species.

1. DRURIDGE POOLS – CRESSWELL POND

Northumberland Wildlife Trust.
Location: Two sites lying on coast between Newbiggin and Amble, off A1068. 1: Sat nav: NE61 5EG for Druridge Pools (NZ 275 963). Roadside parking next to NT's Druridge Links site. 2: Cresswell Pond (NZ 283 944). Park at bottom of track to Blakemoor Farm. Half mile N of Cresswell.
Access: 1: Access along public footpath or short path to screen. 2: Access along short path from farm track. Wheelchair users can view northern part of Cresswell Pond from public footpath or roadside. Dogs on leads.
Facilities: 1: Three hides: 2: Hide.
Public transport: 1: Arriva X18 to Widdrington village (2 miles). 2: Arriva 1 to Cresswell village.
Habitats: 1: Deep lake and two wet meadows with pools behind dunes. 2: Shallow brackish lagoon behind dunes fringed by saltmarsh and reedbed, some mudflats.
Key birds: 1: Especially good in spring. Winter and breeding wildfowl (mostly Wigeon and Teal); passage and breeding waders. 2: Good for waders, esp. on passage. Most northly recorded of breeding Avocets in 2011. Pinkfooted Geese in winter, plus wildfowl.
Other notable flora and fauna: The sheltered sunny banks are good for a range of butterflies and dragonflies in summer at Druridge Pools. Otters are often seen by the lakes.
Contact: Northumberland Wildlife Trust, 01912 846 884; e-mail: mail@northwt.org.uk www.nwt.org.uk

2. EAST CHEVINGTON

Northumberland Wildlife Trust.
Location: Sat nav: NE61 5BX. NZ 270 990. Near Red Row, overlooking Druridge Bay, off A 1068 between Hauxley and Cresswell.
Access: Main access from overflow car park at Druridge Bay Country Park (signpost from main road).
Facilities: Four public hides, café, toilets and information at Country Park (County Council). ID boards for coastal plants.
Public transport: Arriva X18 to Red Row (1 mile).
Habitats: Ponds and reedbeds created from former open cast coal mine. Areas of scrub and grassland.
Key birds: Large numbers of wildfowl, including Greylag and Pinkfooted Geese in winter. Breeding Skylark, Stonechat, Reed Bunting, plus Reed, Sedge and Grasshopper Warblers. Capable of attracting rarities at any time of year. Marsh Harriers bred in 2009 (first county record for 130 years).

Other notable flora and fauna: Coastal wildflowers and in grassland, dyer's greenweed.
Contact: Northumberland Wildlife Trust, 01912 846 884; e-mail: mail@northwt.org.uk

3. FARNE ISLANDS

The National Trust.
Location: Sat nav: NE68 7SS (Seahouses). NU 230 370. Access by boat from Seahouses Harbour, which is reached from A1.
Access: Apr, Aug-Oct: Inner Farne 10.30am to 6pm. May-Jul: Staple Island 10.30am to 1.30pm, Inner Farne: 1.30pm to 5pm. Disabled access possible on Inner Farne, telephone Property Manager for details. Dogs allowed on boats but not on islands. NT fees for visiting islands do not include boatmens' fees.
Facilities: Toilets on Inner Farne.
Public transport: Nearest rail stations at Alnmouth and Berwick. Hourly Travelsure buses between Budle and Beadnell Bays (Mon-Sat). Call 01665 720 955.
Habitats: Maritime islands – between 15-28 depending on height of tide.
Key birds: 18 species of seabirds/waders, four species of tern (including Roseate), 40,000-plus pairs of Puffin, 33,000 pairs of Guillemot, 4,000 Kittiwake, 800 Eider, 500 Razorbill, Rock Pipit, Pied Wagtail etc.
Contact: David Steel, Farne Islands, Seahouses NE68 7SR. 01289 389 244.
e-mail: farneislands@nationaltrust.org.uk

4. KIELDER WATER AND FOREST PARK

Forestry Commission.
Location: Sat nav: NE48 1ER (Kielder Castle). NY 632 934. Kielder Castle is situated at N end of Kielder Water, NW of Bellingham, 30 miles from Hexham.
Access: Forest open all year. Toll charge £3 on 12-mile forest drive (rough surface). Forest drive is closed from November to end April due to weather conditions and lack of mobile phone signal throughout. Car parking facilities at Kielder Castle and overflow behind the Angler's Arms pub. Price for 24 hours parking is £4. Ticket transferable for all car parks on south shore of Kielder Reservoir.
Facilities: Kielder Castle Information Centre, free exhibition, licensed Kielder Castle Café with live wildlife viewing screens, access for disabled and toilets including baby changing facilities. Kielder Cycle Centre and bike wash, post office/local shop, Angler's Arms pub, youth hostel, camp site, No 27 B&B and 24 hour (pay by card) garage. The 1 mile multi-access Duke's Trail includes an arboretum and hide where red squirrels can usually be viewed. Nature reserve and dipping pond at Bakethin Nature Reserve. Many walking and mountain biking trails start from Kielder Castle, ask staff at the Information Centre for more info.
Public transport: Buses 880/714: Check with local transport operators before travel; Snaith's Travel and Tyne Valley Coaches.
Habitats: Commercial woodland, coniferous and broadleaved trees.

Key birds: Successful Osprey breeding programme since 2009. *Spring/summer*: Goshawk, Raven, Chiffchaff, Willow Warbler, Redstart, Siskin. *Winter*: Crossbill, Siskin and winter thrushes. *Resident*: Jay, Nuthatch, Dipper, Great Spotted Woodpecker, Green Woodpecker, Tawny Owl, Song Thrush, Goldcrest.
Other notable flora and fauna: Impressive display of northern marsh orchids at entrance to Kielder Castle. Red squirrel, badger, otter, roe deer, seven species of bat.
Contact: Forestry Commission, 01434 250209.
e-mail: kieldercastle@forestry.gsi.gov.uk

5. LINDISFARNE NATIONAL NATURE RESERVE

Natural England (Northumbria Team).
Location: Sat nav: TD15 2SS. NU 090 430. Island access lies two miles E of A1 at Beal, signposted to Holy Island, 10 miles S of Berwick-on-Tweed.
Access: Causeway floods at high tide, so check when it is safe to cross. Some restricted access (bird refuges). Coach parking available on Holy Island.
Facilities: Toilets, visitor centre in village. Hide on island (new hide with disabled access at Fenham-le-Moor). Self-guided trail on island.
Public transport: Irregular bus service to Holy Island, mainly in summer. Main bus route follows mainland boundary of site north-south.
Habitats: Dunes, sand, mudflats and saltmarsh, rocky shore and open water..
Key birds: *Passage and winter*: Wildfowl and waders, including Pale-bellied Brent Goose, Long-tailed Duck and Whooper Swan. Rare migrants.
Other notable flora and fauna: Butterflies include dark green fritillary (July) and grayling (August). Guided walks advertised for nine species of orchid including coralroot and Lindisfarne helleborine.
Contact: Reserve Manager, Beal Station, Berwick-on-Tweed, TD15 2SP. 01289 381 470.

6. PRESTWICK CARR

Northumberland Wildlife Trust.
Location: Sat nav: NE20 9UD (Prestwick). NZ 192 733. Seven miles NW of Newcastle city centre between Dinnington and Pontesland. Take A696 from A1 western bypass for three miles and take minor road to Prestwick hamlet. Park on minor roads north of Prestwick and Dinnington.
Access: Restricted to minor roads and a bridleway across the carr. No access to northern section when military firing range between Prestwick Mill Farm and Berwick Hill is in use.
Facilities: Viewing platform and interpretation.
Habitats: SSSI designation for section of lowland raised mire, woodland, farmland.
Public transport: Bus service 45 runs between Newcastle Haymarket and Dinnington (0.75 mile walk to carr's eastern end).
Key birds: A noted raptor watchpoint: 2010's White-tailed Eagle became 14th bird of prey species recorded since 1990s. Hen Harriers are regular between Oct and Jan, along with Merlin and Peregrine. Barn,

Little, Tawny and Long-eared Owls all nest and Short-eared Owls hunt in winter. Waders occur in large numbers at passage times if carr is flooded. Water Rail, Kingfisher, Stonechat, Whinchat and Willow Tit are resident with a good range of summer migrants, including Grasshopper Warbler.
Contact: Trust HQ, 01912 846 884;
e-mail: mail@northwt.org.uk

7. WHITELEE MOOR

Northumberland Wildlife Trust.
Location: Sat nav: TD8 6PT (Carter Bar). NT 690 065. Reserve located at head of Redesdale, south of A68 Newcastle to Jedburgh road where it crosses Scottish Border at Carter Bar.
Access: Park at tourist car park at Carter Bar and on lay-bys on forest track at reservoir end. A public footpath along old track to Whitelee Limeworks and then southwards extends to site's southern boundary and eastwards to link up with a bridleway from White Kielder Burn to Chattlehope Burn. Additional access on foot via Forestry road near eastern corner of reserve. Reserve is remote and wild, so hill-walking experience needed if attempting long walks.
Facilities: Car park and lay-bys.
Habitats: Active blanket bog and heather heath.
Key birds: The River Rede and its tributaries add to the habitat and bird diversity. Notable breeding birds include Merlin and Stonechat. Black Grouse, Skylark, Meadow Pipit, Dunlin, Curlew, Golden Plover, Grey

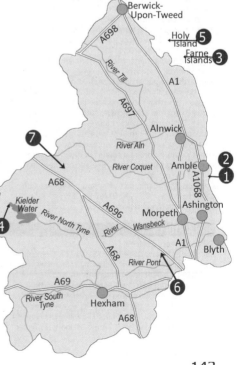

143

Wagtail, Dipper and Ring Ouzel regularly visit the reserve.

Other notable flora and fauna: Otters often hunt along the Rede and a herd of feral goats may be seen. **Contact:** Trust HQ, 01912 846 884; e-mail: mail@northwt.org.uk www.nwt.org.uk

Yorkshire, East Riding

COASTAL birding dominates here: Bempton Cliffs is probably the best seabird colony in England, with Puffins in front of your face and a Gannetry to boot. Two headlands — Flamborough Head and Spurn Point — attract migrants, including scarce vagrants, in autumn. Book a boat trip from Bridlington to see shearwaters and skuas in autumn.

1. BEMPTON CLIFFS

RSPB (Northern England).
Location: Sat nav: YO15 1JF. TA 197 738. Near Bridlington. Take Cliff Lane N from Bempton village off B1229 to car park and visitor centre.
Access: Visitor centre open year round (9.30am to 5pm Mar - Oct; 9.30am to 4pm Nov - Feb). Car parking fee for non-RSPB members £5 for cars, £8 for minibuses and £10 for coaches). Cliff-top public footpath with two observation points accessible for wheelchair users. Dogs on leads.
Facilities: Visitor centre, toilets inc disabled, light refreshments, five cliff-top observation points, picnic area, limited coach parking. Four miles of stunning chalk cliffs, highest in county. Short farmland footpath. Binoculars for hire.
Public transport: Bempton railway station (limited service) 1.5 miles — irregular bus service to village 1.25 miles from reserve.
Habitats: Seabird nesting cliffs, farmland, grassland, coastal scrub.
Key birds: Largest mainland seabird colony in UK; only Gannet colony in England. Birds present January to October with numbers peaking in excess of 200,000 between Apr and Jun. Includes Kittiwake, Gannet, Puffin, Guillemot, Razorbill and Fulmar. Nesting Tree Sparrow and Corn Bunting. Passage skuas, shearwaters, terns and passerine migrants.
Other notable flora and fauna: Harbour porpoise and grey seal regularly offshore. Bee and northern marsh orchids can occur.
Contact: RSPB Bempton Cliffs Nature Reserve, Cliff Lane, Bempton YO15 1JF. 01262 851 179; e-mail: bempton.cliffs@rspb.org.uk

2. BLACKTOFT SANDS

RSPB (Northern England).
Location: Sat nav: DN14 8HL. SE 843 232. Eight miles E of Goole. Follow brown tourist signs on minor road between Ousefleet and Adlingfleet.
Access: Reserve open 9am-9pm or dusk if earlier throughout year. Reception hide open daily 9am to 4pm (April to Oct) and at weekends and selected weekdays outside this period. RSPB members free, £4 permit for non-members, £3 concessionary, £1 under-16s, £7 family. Guide dogs only.
Facilities: Car park, toilets, visitor centre, six hides with wheelchair spaces, one viewing screen, footpaths suitable for wheelchairs. Binoculars for hire.
Public transport: Goole/Scunthorpe bus 357 (Sweynes' Coaches) stops outside reserve entrance). Visit: www.sweyne.co.uk for details.
Habitats: Second largest tidal reedbed in UK, saline lagoons, lowland wet grassland, willow scrub.
Key birds: 270 species recorded. *Summer:* Breeding Avocet (up to 40 pairs), Tree Sparrows (approx 28 pairs), Marsh Harrier, Bittern, Bearded Tit, passage waders (exceptional list inc many rarities), up to 350 pairs of Reed Warblers, 250 pairs of Sedge Warblers. *Winter:* Hen Harrier, Merlin, Peregrine, wildfowl.
Other notable flora and fauna: Good place to see water vole. Small number of dragonflies and damselflies including black-tailed skimmer, four-spotted chaser, large red damselfly. Marsh sow thistle easily seen from footpaths in summer. Rare brown-veined wainscot moth.
Contact: Visitor Development Officer, Blacktoft Sands RSPB reserve, Hillcrest, Whitgift, Nr Goole DN14 8HL. 01405 704 665; e-mail: blacktoft.sands@rspb.org.uk

3. FLAMBOROUGH CLIFFS

Yorkshire Wildlife Trust.
Location: Sat nav: YO15 1BJ. TA 239 720. The reserve is part of Flamborough headland, approx 4 miles NE of Bridlington. From Bridlington take B1255 to Flamborough and follow the signs for the North Landing.
Access: Open all year. Car park at North Landing gives access to both parts of the reserve. Paths not suitable for wheelchairs.
Facilities: Car park (pay and display), trails, refreshments available at café at North Landing (open Apr-Oct 10am-5pm), toilets.
Public transport: Flamborough is served by buses from Bridlington and Bempton. Phone 01482 222 222 for details.
Habitats: Coastal cliffs, species-rich rough grassland and scrub, farmland. Spectacular views of this chalk coastline and living seas beyond.
Key birds: *Summer:* Nesting Puffin, Guillemot, Razorbill, Kittiwake, Shag, Fulmar, Skylark, Meadow Pipit, Linnet, Whitethroat, Yellowhammer, Tree Sparrow, occasional Corn Bunting. Thornwick reedbeds hold Reed and Sedge Warblers and Reed Buntings. *Passage migrants:* Fieldfare, Redwing and occasional rarities such as Wryneck and Red-backed Shrike. *Autumn:* Passage divers, grebes and seaduck.
Other notable flora and fauna: Pyramidal and northern marsh orchids, harebell, thrift on cliff tops. Migrant butterflies such as small skipper and painted lady.

Contact: Yorkshire Wildlife Trust, 01904 659 570; e-mail: info@ywt.org.uk www.ywt.org.uk

4. HORNSEA MERE

Wassand Hall.
Location: Sat nav: HU18 1AX. Hornsea lies 12 miles E of Beverley on B1244. Enter town, onto Southgate then take signposted road to car park at Kirkholme Point.
Access: Mere is owned by the nearby Wassand Hall estate, which opens to the public on selected days throughout the year. Mere footpath open all year during the day (see notices for closing times). View from footpath along southern edge. Dogs on leads.
Facilities: Café on site (limited opening in winter), toilets.
Habitats: Yorkshire's largest body of freshwater, located 1km inland from the coast. Edged by reedbeds and woodland.
Key birds: Common wildfowl throughout the year, but in winter there is always the chance of divers, grebes, Long-tailed Duck, Goosander and Pintail. *Spring and autumn passage:* Marsh Harrier, Osprey, Little Gull, terns, White and Yellow Wagtails, Wheatear, plus rarer species.
Contact: www.wassand.co.uk

5. LOWER DERWENT VALLEY NNR

Natural England/Yorkshire Wildlife Trust/Countryside Trust.
Location: Sat nav: YO19 6FE (Bank Island). Six miles SE of York, stretching 12 miles S along River Derwent from Newton-on-Derwent to Wressle and along Pocklington Canal. Visitor facilities at Bank Island (SE 691 448), Wheldrake Ings YWT (SE 691 444 see separate entry — page 174), Thorganby (SE 692 418) and North Duffield Carrs (SE 697 367).
Access: Open all year. No dogs. Disabled access at North Duffield Carrs.
Facilities: Bank Island — two hides, viewing tower. Wheldrake Ings — four hides. Thorganby — viewing platform. North Duffield Carrs — two hides and wheelchair access. Car parks at all sites. Bicycle stands in car parks at Bank Island and North Duffield Carrs.
Public transport: Bus from York/Selby — contact First (01904 622 992). Train station at Wressle.
Habitats: SPA and Ramsar site composed of flood and hay meadows, swamp, open water and alder/willow woodland.
Key birds: More than 80 species recorded in recent times.
Spring/summer: Breeding wildfowl and waders, incl. Garganey, Snipe and Ruff, plus Corncrake and Spotted Crake. Barn Owl and warblers.
Winter/spring: Bittern, 20,000-plus waterfowl

including Whooper Swan, wild geese, Teal and Wigeon. Large gull roost, incl. white-winged gulls. Also passage waders, incl. Whimbrel.
Other notable flora and fauna: Pocklington Canal is particularly good for a wide range of aquatic plants and animals. Noctule, Daubenton's and pipistrelle bats regularly recorded. Water vole, pygmy shrew and brown hare.
Contact: Senior Reserve Manager, Natural England Yorkshire and Humber Region, 01904 449589; www.naturalengland.org.uk
Pocklington Canal: www.pocklington.gov.uk/pcas

6. NORTH CAVE WETLANDS

Yorkshire Wildlife Trust.
Location: Sat nav: HU15 2LY. SE 888 328. NW of North Cave village, approx 10 miles W of Hull (SE 886 328). From junction 28 of M62, follow signs to North Cave on B1230. In village, turn L and follow road to next crossroads, then go L, then and park in Dryham Lane.
Access: Open all year with car parking on Dryham Lane. Part of circular footpath is suitable for all abilities. No dogs in reserve.
Facilities: Five bird-viewing hides including unique straw bale constructions, four are accessible to wheelchair users. Portaloo available on site and Wild Bird Café open each day on Dryham Lane, adjacent to reserve.
Public transport: Buses serve North Cave from Hull and Goole: telephone 01482 222 222 for details.
Habitats: Former gravel pits have been converted into various lagoons for wetland birds, including one reedbed. There are also, scrub and hedgerows, and since 2010 a large area of wet grassland.
Key birds: More than 200 species recorded. Breeding birds inc Great Crested Grebe, Gadwall, Pochard, Sparrowhawk, Avocet, Little Ringed and Ringed

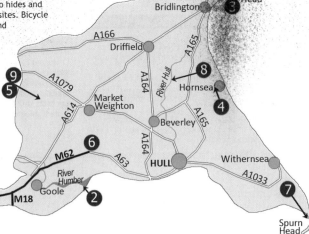

Plover, Oystercatcher, Sedge Warbler and Reed Bunting. Large numbers of Sand Martins feed over reserve in summer. Wintering wildfowl and waders include Golden Plover, Dunlin, Ruff and Redshank. Tree Sparrow.
Other notable flora and fauna: Water vole, dragon and damselflies, several butterfly species inc small colony of brown argus.
Contact: Yorkshire Wildlife Trust, 01904 659 570; e-mail: info@ywt.org.uk

7. SPURN NNR

Yorkshire Wildlife Trust.
Location: Sat nav HU12 0UH. Entrance Gate TA 419 149. 26 miles from Hull. Take A1033 from Hull to Patrington then B1445 from Patrington to Easington and unclassified roads on to Kilnsea and Spurn Point.
Access: Normally open at all times. Vehicle admission fee. No charge for pedestrians. No dogs allowed under any circumstances, not even in cars. Coaches by permit only (must be in advance).
Facilities: Reserve open all year. Blue Bell café open daily. Visitor centre, four hides. Public toilets in Blue Bell car park.
Public transport: Nearest bus service is at Easington (3.5 miles away). 2011 Sunday service to the Point, hail and ride, Easter to last weekend of October.
Habitats: Sand dunes with marram and sea buckthorn scrub. Mudflats around Humber Estuary.
Key birds: *Spring:* Many migrants on passage and often rare birds such as Red-backed Shrike, Bluethroat etc. *Summer:* Little Terns feed offshore. *Autumn:* Passage migrants and rarities such as Wryneck, Pallas's Warbler. *Winter:* Large numbers of waders, Shelduck and Brent Geese, plus Merlin and Peregrine.
Other notable flora and fauna: Unique habitats and geographical position makes Spurn a very interesting site in Yorkshire for butterflies (25 species recorded) and moths.
Contact: Outer Humber Officer, Spurn NNR, Blue Bell, Kilnsea, Hull HU12 0UB; e-mail: info@ywt.org.uk

8. TOPHILL LOW NATURE RESERVE

Yorkshire Water.
Location: Sat nav: YO25 9RH. TA 071 482. Located SE of Driffield and signposted from village of Watton on A164.
Access: Open daily (9am-6pm). Charges: £3.30 per person. £1.50 concessions. Provision for disabled visitors (paths, ramps, hides, toilet etc). Coaches welcome.
Facilities: Toilets open daily. 12 hides (eight with wheelchair access), paths and sightings board.
Public transport: None.

Habitats: Open water (two reservoirs), marshes, wet grassland, wader scrapes, woodland and thorn scrub.
Key birds: 160 species annually. *Winter:* SSSI for wildfowl, plus one of the UK's largest Black-headed and Common Gull roosts. Regular wintering Bittern and Smew. Active feeding station with Marsh and Willow Tit. *Spring/early summer:* Hirundines, Black Tern and Black-necked Grebe. Breeding Little Ringed Plover, Common Tern, Kingfisher and Barn Owl with variety of warblers. *Late summer/autumn:* Up to 20 species of passage wader.
Other notable flora and fauna: 400+ Sp. flora, 365+ Sp. fungi 16 Sp.odonata inc. hairy hawker. Grass snake, otter, water vole, great crested newt and roe deer.
Contact: Richard Hampshire, Tophill Low Nature Reserve, Hutton Cranswick, Driffield, East Yorkshire YO25 9RH. 01377 270 690. e-mail:richard.hampshire@yorkshirewater.co.uk, www.tophilllow.blogspot.com. Twitter @tophilllow

9. WHELDRAKE INGS

Yorkshire Wildlife Trust.
Location: Sat nav: YO19 6FE (Ings Lane car park). SE 691 449. From York by-pass (A64) head S on A19 towards Selby for 1.2 miles, then turn left on Wheldrake Lane. Drive through Wheldrake village and turn sharp right to reach Natural England's Bank Island car park.
Access: Open at all times, but entrance road to YWT Wheldrake car park (Ings Lane) can be flooded in winter. Free admission and parking. Paths and hides not suitable for wheelchairs. No dogs allowed.
Facilities: Four hides. Sightings board in Bank Island car park. RADAR key toilets at Bank Island car park.
Public transport: York to Selby buses stop 25 metres from entrance road on Thorganby Road.
Habitats: Flooded meadows and pools, riverside vegetation.
Key birds: A noted site for large numbers of wintering wildfowl, inc Shelduck, Pintail and Goldeneye among the commoner species. Records of Hen Harrier, Whooper and Bewick's Swans, Little Egret. *Spring passage:* Garganey, Little Gull, terns and Wheatear. *Summer:* Breeding waders, plus Turtle Dove, Yellow Wagtail, hirundines and migrant warblers. *Autumn:* Passage waders, Hobby and wildlfowl. Kingfisher, Little and Barn Owl are among a long list of resident species.
Other notable flora and fauna: Internationally important community of meadow plants.
Contact: Yorkshire Wildlife Trust 01904 659 570; e-mail: info@ywt.org.uk

Yorkshire, North

SEAWATCHING in autumn from Filey Brigg can produce a range of skuas and shearwaters, with divers and grebes becoming more noticeable as the season progresses. The North York Moors hold breeding waders, chats, raptors and Red Grouse. There are several areas to explore in the Lower Derwent Valley, with first class birding throughout the year.

1. COATHAM MARSH

Tata Steel/Tees Valley Wildlife Trust.
Location: Sat nav TS10 5BQ (Tod Point Road). NZ 586 247 for car park. Located on W edge of Redcar, off A1085. At crossroads with Kirkleatham Lane, turn left and travel to next mini roundabout. Turn left onto Tod Point Road and continue over the railway bridge. The reserve is on the left.
Access: Reserve is open throughout daylight hours. Please keep to permissive footpaths only.
Facilities: Good footpaths around site, but section along The Fleet prone to winter flooding. Nearest toilets on Redcar seafront.
Public transport: Very frequent bus service between Middlesbrough and Redcar. Nearest stops are in Coatham 0.25 mile from reserve (Arriva tel 0871 200 2233). Redcar Central Station one mile from site. Frequent trains from Middlesbrough and Darlington.
Habitats: 54 hectares of freshwater pools, lakes, reedswamp.
Key birds: *Spring/autumn*: Wader passage (including Wood Sandpiper and Greenshank). *Summer*: Passerines (including Sedge Warbler, Yellow Wagtail). *Winter*: Large numbers of common ducks (plus Smew). *Occasional rarities*: Water Rail, Great White Egret, Avocet, Bearded Tit and Bittern.
Other notable flora and fauna: Lime-rich soil good for wildflowers, including northern marsh orchid. Insects include migrant hawker dragonfly.
Contact: Steve Ashton, Tees Valley Wildlife Trust, 01287 636 382; e-mail: info@teeswildlife.org
www.teeswildlife.org

2. FILEY BRIGG BIRD OBSERVATORY / THE DAMS

FBOG/Yorkshire Wildlife Trust (The Dams).
Location: Sat nav: YO14 0DG (The Dams). TA 106 807. Two access roads into Filey from A165 (Scarborough to Bridlington road). Filey Dams is a nature reserve within the Observatory's recording area.
Access: Opening times – no restrictions. Dogs only in Parish Wood and The Old Tip (on lead). Coaches welcome. Park at the end of Wharfedale Road (Dams), Sycamore Avenue (Parish Wood/Tip) or in North Cliff Country Park (Brigg).
Facilities: Wheelchair access to the Main Hide (dams). Two open-access hides at The Dams, one on The Brigg (for FBOG members only). Toilets in Country Park (Apr-Nov 1) and town centre. Nature trails at The Dams, Parish Wood/Old Tip. Cliff top walk for seabirds along Cleveland Way.

Public transport: All areas within a mile of Filey railway station. Trains into Filey tel. 08457 484 950; buses into Filey tel. 01723 503 020
Habitats: The Dams – two freshwater lakes, fringed with some tree cover and small reedbeds. Parish Wood – a newly planted wood which leads to the Old Tip, the latter has been fenced (for stock and crop strips) though there is a public trail. Carr Naze has a pond and can produce newly arrived migrants.
Key birds: *The Dams:* Breeding and wintering water birds, breeding Sedge Warbler, Reed Warbler and Tree Sparrow. *The Tip:* Important for breeding Skylark, Meadow Pipit, common warblers and Grey Partridge. *Winter:* Buntings, including Lapland. *Seawatch Hide (Jul-Oct):* All four skuas, shearwaters, terns. *Winter:* Divers and grebes. *Rocket Pole Field:* A new project should encourage breeding species and wintering larks, buntings etc. Many sub-rare/rare migrants possible at all sites.
Contact: e-mail: secretary@fbog.co.uk
www.fbog.co.uk

3. FYLINGDALES MOOR CONSERVATION AREA

Hawk and Owl Trust/Strickland Estate/Fylingdales Moor ESS Co Ltd.
Location: Sat nav: YO22 4UL (car park). NZ 947 003. Conservation area covers 6,800 acres within National Park off A171 S of Whitby, stretching between Sneaton High Moor (Newton House Plantation) and the coast at Ravenscar.
Access: Open access. Parking (inc coaches) available at Jugger Howe lay-by (NZ 947 003) on A171.
Facilities: Numerous footpaths including Jugger Howe Nature Trail, Lyke Wake Walk and Robin Hood's Bay Road.
Public transport: Half-hourly Arriva buses (No. 93 and X93) between Scarborough and Whitby, nearest stop at Flask Inn (approx. 1 mile N of Jugger Howe lay-by). 0191 281 1313 for timetable information or visit: www.arrivabus.co.uk or www.hawkandowl.org. fylingdales
Habitats: Heather moorland (former grouse moor), with scattered trees, wooded valleys and gulleys. Managed exclusively for wildlife and archaeological remains, the moor is an SSSI and SPA (Merlin and Golden Plover) and a Special Area of Conservation.
Key birds: More than 80 common bird species, plus rare and endangered breeding birds such as harriers, Merlin, Golden Plover, Red Grouse, Curlew, Wheatear, Stonechat, Whinchat, Skylark, Marsh Tit, Willow Tit, Linnet, Bullfinch, Reed Bunting and Yellowhammer. The moor is also home to Kestrel, Lapwing, Snipe, Cuckoo, Meadow Pipit, Grey Wagtail and Wood Warbler and visited by Peregrine.
Other notable flora and fauna: Otter, roe deer, brown hare, stoat, weasel and badger. Important for water vole. Three species of heather, plus cranberry, cowberry, moonwort and, in wetter parts, bog myrtle, lesser twayblade, bog asphodel, butterwort, marsh helleborine, and sundews can be found. Also rare orchids and sedges. Insect species include large heath and small pearl-bordered fritillary butterflies

147

and emperor moth.
Contact: Chris Hansell, The Hawk and Owl Trust
01751 417 398; e-mail: chris.hansell@
hawkandowl.org
www.hawkandowl.org

4. NOSTERFIELD LNR

Lower Ure Conservation
Trust.
Location: Sat nav:
DL8 2QZ. SE 278 795.
Six miles N of Ripon,
between West Tanfield
and Nosterfield E of A6108
(Ripon to Masham road) and
approx 4 miles W of A1.
Access: Open all year. Lower
viewing area beyond car park
permits viewing from cars only.
Footpath (1,500 metres) is fully
wheelchair-friendly. Dogs (on short leads)
on most of footpath network. Coaches: book in
advance.
Facilities: Two disabled-friendly hides, interpretation
panels (main hide), comfortable 'woolly' seats,
lowered windows for wheelchair users. No other on-
site facilities.
Public transport: Irregular buses from Ripon and
Masham stop at West Tanfield (half mile walk to
reserve).
Habitats: Wetland grassland and open water. Also
Magnesian limestone grassland, gravel banks,
hedgerows and scrub.
Key species: Annually 150 species recorded — more
than 225 species recorded overall (including rarities).
Spring/autumn: Up to 30 wader species recorded
annually, also terns. *Summer:* Breeding species
include Redshank, Lapwing, Avocet, Oystercatcher,
Curlew, Ringed Plover, Mediterranean Gull, Shoveler,
Gadwall, Barn Owl, Skylark, Lesser Whitethroat, Tree
Sparrow, Linnet, Reed Bunting. *Autumn:* Passage
waders including regular Pectoral Sandpiper. *Winter:*
Wildfowl (Wigeon, Teal, Greylag and rarer geese),
waders (Golden Plover, Lapwing, Curlew) and
Peregrine.
Other notable flora and fauna: Specialist grassland
and wetland flora, including seven species of orchid,
mudwort, yellow rattle, golden dock. Butterflies
include white-letter hairstreak, brown argus, wall
and large colony of common blue. Dragonflies include
emperor, black-tailed skimmer, red-veined darter (has
bred). At least 480 species of moths have now been
recorded. Also, brown hare and water shrew.
Contact: e-mail:luct@luct.org.uk www.luct.org.uk
Follow site on Twitter: @NosterfieldLNR

5. TIMBLE INGS

Yorkshire Water.
Location: Sat nav: LS21 2PP. SE 170 542 (parking
opposite Anchor Farm). Large area of upland
woodland west of Harrogate, north of Otley. Off the
A59 south of Blubberhouses, near Timble village.
Access: Open at all times, all year.
Facilities: Toilets, cafes, pubs, coach parking all
nearby. Hard forest tracks.
Public transport: None.
Habitats: Pine, larch and spruce woodland and nearby
reservoir. SW corner of wood a good place to observe
visible migration in autumn.
Key birds: Bradford OG species list stands at
134. Habitat management work by Yorkshire
Water makes site attractive to Long-eared and
Tawny Owls, Nightjars and Tree Pipits. Buzzards
now nest and Red Kites seen regularly. Goshawk
numbers in decline. *Summer:* Breeding species inc
Redpoll, Siskin, Crossbill, Woodcock, Redstart and
GrasshopperWarbler. Short-eared Owls hunt adjacent
moorland. *Winter:* Fieldfare, Redwing, Brambling,
occasional Waxwings and Hawfinches.
Other notable flora and fauna: Roe deer, badger,
brown hare, shrew, vole and mouse species (all
detected from owl pellets). Ponds attractive to
amphibians and dragonflies, inc broad-bodied chaser,
emperor and black darter.
Contact: Recreation Officer, Yorkshire Water
e-mail:Geoff.D.Lomas@yorkshirewater.co.uk
www.yorkshirewater.co.uk (turn to recreation page).

Yorkshire South & West

CONSIDERING the number of industrial towns in the area, such as Sheffield, Barnsley and Doncaster, South Yorkshire still manages to offer birdwatchers a surprising number of interesting wildlife sites. Places such as RSPB Fairburn Ings (right next to the A1), Potteric Carr, RSPB Old Moor reserve and its near neighbour, Bolton Ings, all have year-round interest.

1. BOLTON INGS (DEARNE VALLEY)

RSPB (Northern England)
Location: Sat nav: S73 0YF. SE 425 020. Park at RSPB Old Moor and walk east along Trans-Pennine Trail to Bolton Ings. By car, Old Moor is just off Manvers Way (A633). From the M1, take junction 36 then follow the A6195. From the A1M, take junction 37 then follow the A635 towards the A6195.
Access: Open all year round. Dearne Way footpath and Trans-Pennine Trail open at all times, but not suitable for wheelchair users. Dogs only on public footpaths.
Facilities: Cormorant View hide. More facilities at RSPB Old Moor.
Public transport: Wombwell and Swinton train stations approximately 3 miles from reserve. Buses run to Old Moor reserve from Barnsley, Doncaster and Meadowhall – call Traveline on 01709 515 151 for details. Trans-Pennine Trail runs along southern edge of reserve.
Habitats: 43 hectares of reedbed and scrub. Excellent warbler habitat.
Key birds: *All year:* Kingfisher, Grey Heron. *Winter:* Stonechat. *Spring/summer:* Reed Bunting. breeding waders and warblers, Cuckoo, Garganey. Avocets and Spoonbills also recorded. *Autumn:* Passage waders

including Greenshank, Green Sandpiper, Golden Plover. *Winter:* Wildfowl, including Goosander, Wigeon and Teal.
Other notable flora and fauna: Dragonflies inc. banded demoiselle, brown hare.
Contact: RSPB Old Moor, Old Moor Lane, Wombwell, Barnsley, South Yorkshire, S73 0YF. 01226 751 593; e-mail: old.moor@rspb.org.uk

2. DENABY INGS

Yorkshire Wildlife Trust.
Location: Sat nav: S64 0JJ (Pastures Rd, off A6023 near Mexborough). SE 496 008. Proceed along Pastures Road for 0.5 miles and watch for a sign on R marking entrance to car park. Climb flight of concrete steps to enter reserve.
Access: Open all year. Dogs on leads OK.
Facilities: Car park, two hides, interpretation panels, circular trail.
Public transport: None.
Habitats: Hay meadows, open water, deciduous woodland, marsh, willows.
Key birds: *Spring/summer:* Waterfowl, Barn Owl, Tawny Owl, Sand Martin, Swallow, Whinchat, Grasshopper Warbler, Lesser Whitethroat, Whitethroat, other warblers, Kingfisher. *Passage:* Waders, Common, Arctic and Black Terns, Redstart, Wheatear. *Winter:* Whooper Swan, wildfowl, Jack Snipe and other waders, Grey Wagtail, Fieldfare, Redwing, Brambling, Siskin. *All year:* Corn Bunting, Yellowhammer, all three woodpeckers, common woodland birds, possible Willow Tit.
Contact: Yorkshire Wildlife Trust 01904 659 570; e-mail:info@ywt.org.uk; www.ywt.org.

3. FAIRBURN INGS

RSPB (Northern England).
Location: Sat nav: WF10 2BH. SE 451 277. 12 miles from Leeds, six miles from Pontefract, 3 miles from Castleford, situated next to A1246 from J42 of A1.
Access: Reserve and hides open every day except Dec 25/26. Centre and shop open each day (9am to 5pm between March and Oct, 4pm for rest of year). Dogs on leads welcome. Boardwalks leading to Pickup Pool, feeding station and Kingfisher viewpoint are all wheelchair-friendly. Car parking free for RSPB members and disabled drivers. Dogs on leads welcome.
Facilities: Five hides open at all times. Two public trails (one accessible to wheelchairs). Toilets open 9am-5pm. Disabled toilets and baby-changing facilities. Hot and cold drinks, snacks available. Wildlife garden, pond-dipping and mini beast areas, plus duck feeding platform. Coach parking for club visits.
Public transport: Nearest train stations are Castleford, Micklefield and Garforth. No bus service.
Habitats: Open water, wet grassland, marsh

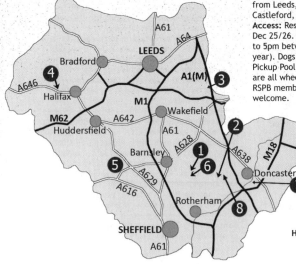

and fen scrub, reedbed, reclaimed colliery spoil heaps.
Key birds: *All year:* Tree Sparrow, Kingfisher, Willow Tit, Green Woodpecker, Bullfinch. *Winter:* Smew, Goldeneye, Goosander, Wigeon, Peregrine. *Spring:* Osprey, Little Gull, Wheatear, five species of tern inc annual Black Tern, Garganey, Little Ringed Plover. *Summer:* Nine species of breeding warbler, Grey Heron, Gadwall, Little Ringed Plover. *Autumn:* Thousands of waders on passage inc Green Sandpiper, Little Ringed Plover and Black-tailed Godwit.
Other notable flora and fauna: Brown hare, harvest mouse, roe deer, Leisler's and Daubenton's bats, 28 species of butterfly and 20 species of dragonfly.
Contact: Laura Bentley, Visitor Services Manager, Fairburn Ings Visitor Centre, 01977 628 191; e-mail: fairburnings@rspb.org.uk

4. HARDCASTLE CRAGS

National Trust.
Location: Sat nav: HX7 7AA (Midgehole car park) or HX7 7AZ (Clough Hole car park). SD 988 291. From Hebden Bridge follow National Trust signs to A6033 Keighley Road. Follow for 0.75 miles. Turn L at the National Trust sign to car parks. Alternate pay-and-display car park at Clough Hole on Widdop Road, Heptonstall.
Access: Open all year. NT car park charges. Admission: no charge for NT members and disabled badge holders. Non-members: £3.60, child £1.60, family £9.
Facilities: Two small car parks, cycle racks and several way-marked trails. Gibson Mill visitor centre (not NT property) has toilets, café, exhibitions. No mains services — in extreme conditions mill may be closed for health and safety reasons.
Public transport: Trains to Hebden Bridge from Manchester or Leeds every 30 minutes. Call 08457 484 950. Weekday buses every 30 minutes to Keighley Road, then 1 mile walk to Midgehole. Summer weekend bus 906 Widdop-Hardcastle Crags: 0113 245 7676.
Habitats: 400 acres of unspoilt wooded valleys, ravines, streams, hay meadows and moorland edge.
Key birds: *Spring/summer:* Cuckoo, Redstart, Lesser Whitethroat, Garden Warbler, Blackcap, Wood Warbler, Chiffchaff, Spotted Flycatcher, Pied Flycatcher, Curlew, Lapwing, Meadow Pipit. *All year:* Sparrowhawk, Kestrel, Green, Greater Spotted and Lesser Spotted Woodpeckers, Tawny Owl, Barn Owl, Little Owl, Jay, Coal Tit, Dipper, Grey Wagtail and other woodland species. Goshawk in Crimsworth Dean.
Other notable flora and fauna: Northern hairy wood ant, moss carder bee, tree bumble bee, killarney fern, brittle bladder fern, roe deer and eight species of bat.
Contact: National Trust, Hardcastle Crags, 01422 844 518; e-mail: hardcastlecrags@nationaltrust.org.uk

5. INGBIRCHWORTH RESERVOIR

Yorkshire Water.
Location: Sat nav: S36 7GN. SE 217 058. Leave M1 at junction 37 and take A628 towards Manchester. After five miles turn R at roundabout onto A629 Huddersfield road. Drive 2.5 miles to Ingbirchworth and at The Fountain Inn, turn L, then bear L to cross the dam, proceed straight forward onto the track leading to the car park.
Access: Open all year. One of the few reservoirs in the area with footpath access.
Facilities: Car park, picnic tables.
Public transport: None.
Habitats: Reservoir, small strip of deciduous woodland.
Key birds: *Spring/summer:* Whinchat, warblers, woodland birds, House Martin. *Spring/autumn passage:* Little Ringed Plover, Ringed Plover, Dotterel, other waders, Common Tern, Arctic Tern, Black Tern, Yellow Wagtail, Wheatear. *Winter:* Wildfowl, Golden Plover, waders, occasional rare gull such as Iceland or Glaucous, Grey Wagtail, Fieldfare, Redwing, Brambling, Redpoll.
Other notable flora: Woodland wildflowers, inc bluebells.
Contact: www.yorkshirewater.co.uk (recreation page) e-mail: Geoff.D.Lomas@yorkshirewater.co.uk

6. OLD MOOR (DEARNE VALLEY)

RSPB (Northern England).
Location: Sat nav: S73 0YF. SE 422 022. By car, Old Moor is just off Manvers Way (A633). From the M1, take junction 36 then follow the A6195. From the A1M, take junction 37 then follow the A635 towards the A6195.
Access: Visitor centre and cafe open daily, except Dec 25/26 (9.30am to 5pm from Feb to end of Oct), (9.30am to 4pm Nov to end of Jan). Reserve is open until 8pm from April to Oct. RSPB Members free, adult non-members £4, family £8, children £2, concessions £2.50. Guide dogs only.
Facilities: Visitor centre, café, shop, education and meeting rooms. Accessible toilets. Two trails with seven hides, all suitable for wheelchair users. Two viewing screens. Mobility scooter for hire.
Public transport: Buses run to Old Moor reserve from Barnsley, Doncaster and Meadowhall — Traveline (01709 515 151).
Habitats: Lakes and flood meadows, wader scrape and reedbeds. **Key birds:** *All year:* Kingfisher, Little Owl. *Winter:* Large numbers of wildfowl, spectacular flocks of Lapwing and Golden Plover (up to 8,000 birds), Peregrine, Tree Sparrow in garden feeding area. *Summer:* Breeding Bittern, Sand Martin waders, inc Little Ringed Plover and drumming Snipe, migrant warblers and wildfowl.
Other notable flora and fauna: Water vole, brown hare, weasel, pygmy shrew, wildflowers including orchids and adders tongue fern.
Contact: RSPB Old Moor, 01226 751 593; e-mail: old.moor@rspb.org.uk www.rspb.org.uk

7. POTTERIC CARR

Yorkshire Wildlife Trust.
Location: Sat nav: DN4 8DB. SE 589 007. From M18 junction 3 take A6182 (Doncaster) and at first traffic lights turn right. Entrance and car park are on right after 50m.
Access: Open daily 9am-5pm. Obtain ticket on arrival, YWT members free; Single £4; family £7.50 (up to two adults / three children); concession £2.50; child £2. Groups of ten or more should book in advance. Guide dogs only.
Facilities: Around 8 km of paths (5 km accessible to wheelchairs, unassisted), 14 viewing hides (10 suitable for disabled) and tea-rooms open daily (10am to 4pmin winter and 11am to 5pm in summer) with hot and cold drinks, snacks and meals. Toilets at entrance reception, in tea-rooms (during opening times) and outside.
Public transport: Nearest railway station is Doncaster. From Frenchgate Interchange, take bus number 72 or 75, and alight at B&Q on Woodfield Way. Cross White Rose Way, walk down Mallard Way. Cross car park to reserve entrance in Sedum House.
Habitats: Flood plain of River Tome, with reed fen, subsidence ponds, artificial pools, grassland, woodland.
Key birds: 102 of recorded 230 species have bred on site. Nesting waterfowl (inc. Shoveler, Gadwall, Pochard), Water Rail, Kingfisher, all three woodpeckers, Lesser Whitethroat, Reed and Sedge Warblers, Willow Tit. *Passage/winter*: Bittern, Marsh Harrier, Black Tern, waders, wildfowl.
Other notable flora and fauna: 20 species of dragonfly recorded, 28 species of butterfly including purple hairstreak and dingy skipper. Palmate and great crested newt. Common spotted and bee orchids.
Contact: Potteric Carr Nature Reserve, 01302 570 077; e-mail: potteric.carr@ywt.org.uk www.ywt.org.uk

8. SPROTBOROUGH FLASH/DON GORGE

Yorkshire Wildlife Trust.
Location: Sat nav: DN5 7NB (postcode for Boat Inn). SE 530 077. Leave A1(M) at junction 36 onto A630 towards Rotherham. After 0.8km, turn R at traffic lights to Sprotborough. After approx 1.6km the road drops down into Don Gorge. Cross a bridge over river, then another over a canal, turn immediately L. Public car park on left next to toll house in Nursery Lane.
Access: Open all year.
Facilities: Three hides (two accessible to wheelchairs), footpaths, interpretation panels.
Public transport: River bus from Doncaster in summer months. Bus service from Doncaster to Sprotbrough village (10 minute walk to reserve).
Habitats: Limestone gorge, woodland, limestone grassland on plateau and open water.
Key birds: *Summer*: Hirundines, Lesser Whitethroat, Whitethroat, Garden Warbler, Blackcap, Chiffchaff, Willow Warbler, Cuckoo. *Spring/autumn passage*: Little Ringed Plover, Dunlin, Greenshank, Green Sandpiper, waders, Yellow Wagtail. *Winter/all year*: Wildfowl, Water Rail, Snipe, Little Owl, Tawny Owl, all three woodpeckers, thrushes, Siskin, possible Corn Bunting.
Contact: Potteric Carr office 01302 570 077; e-mail:info@ ywt.org.uk

South East England

Berkshire, Buckinghamshire, Hampshire, Kent, London (Greater), Surrey, East Sussex, West Sussex .

Berkshire

DESPITE its proximity to London, Berkshire offers a surprisingly wide range of habitats including heathland and downland. It is the gravel pits that attract the widest range of bird species though, including good numbers of wintering Smew. Increasingly wide areas along the Thames are good for Ring-necked Parakeets.

1. DINTON PASTURES

Wokingham District Council.
Location: Sat nav: RG10 0TH. SU 784 718. From M4's junction 10 head towards Reading, then follow sign to Winnersh on A329. Park is signposted off B3030 between Hurst and Winnersh.
Access: Open all year, dawn to dusk. Car parking charges apply 8am to 6.30pm each day. Dogs allowed. Electric buggies available for disabled visitors.
Facilities: Three hides (one adapted for wheelchairs), information centre, car park, café (open from 8.30am each day), toilets (suitable for wheelchairs). Electric buggies for hire. Various trails between one and three miles in length. Walks leaflet at café.
Public transport: Buses 128 and 129 between Reading and Wokingham stop near main entrance, roughly one an hour. Winnersh rail station is a 15 minute walk.
Habitats: 335 acres of mature gravel pits and banks of River Loddon. Sandford Lake managed for

wildfowl, Lavell's Lake (see below) best for waders and scrub species.

Key birds: *All year:* Kingfisher, Water Rail, Barn Owl. *Spring/summer:* Hobby, Little Ringed Plover, Common Tern, Nightingale, common warblers. *Winter:* Bittern, wildfowl (inc. Goldeneye, Wigeon, Teal, Gadwall), thrushes. Waders include Green and Common Sandpipers, Snipe, Redshank.

Other notable flora and fauna: Water vole, harvest mouse, great crested newt, Loddon pondweed and Loddon lily. 18 species of dragonflies inc emperor, black-tailed skimmer, migrant hawker, white-legged and banded agrion damselfies.

Contact: Dinton Pastures Country Park, 01189 342 016; e-mail: countryside@wokingham.gov.uk www.wokingham.gov.uk/parks/parks/countryparks/dintonpastures/

2. HUNGERFORD MARSH

Berks, Bucks & Oxon Wildlife Trust.
Location: Sat nav: RG17 0JB. SU 333 687. On W side of Hungerford, beside the Kennet and Avon Canal. From town centre, go along Church Street past the town hall. Turn R under the railway. Follow public footpath over swing bridge on the canal near the church. The reserve is separated from Freeman's Marsh by a line of willows and bushes.
Access: Open all year. Please keep to the footpath. Dogs on leads please.
Facilities: Car park.
Public transport: Hungerford railway station half mile from reserve.
Habitats: An idyllic waterside site with chalk stream, water meadows, unimproved rough grazing and reedbed.
Key birds: 120 species recorded. *Spring/summer:* Reed and Grasshopper Warblers. *Winter:* Siskin and Water Rail. *All year:* Common wildfowl, Grey Heron, Kingfisher, Mute Swan, Little Grebe, Reed Bunting, Bullfinch.
Other notable flora and fauna: Water vole, otter and grass snake. Southern marsh orchid, fen bedstraw.
Contact: Berks, Bucks & Oxon Wildlife Trust, 01865 775 476; e-mail: info@bbowt.org.uk www.bbowt.org.ukreserves/Hungerford-Marsh

3. LAVELL'S LAKE

Wokingham District Council.
Location: SU 785 727. Via Sandford Lane off B3030 between Hurst and Winnersh, E of Reading or from Dinton Pastures.
Access: Dawn to dusk. No permit required. Dogs on leads all year.
Facilities: Car park (open 9am to 5pm), two public hides, one with disabled access, one members-only hide (see below), viewing screen.
Public transport: Thames Travel bus services 128/129 run between Reading and Wokingham, stopping outside Dinton Pastures main entrance. Nearest train services are at either Winnersh, or Winnersh Triangle.
Habitats: Ten hectare site composed of gravel pits, two wader scrapes, reed beds, rough grassland,

marshy area, sand martin banks, between River Loddon and Emm Brook. To N of Lavell's Lake gravel pits are being restored to attract birds. The lake at Lea Farm is viewable walking N along the River Loddon from Lavell's Lake over small green bridge. It is on R and can be seen through a viewing screen and a members-only hide for Friends of Lavell's Lake (see www.foll.org.uk). No access.

Key birds: *All year:* Great Crested Grebe, Gadwall, Sparrowhawk, Kingfisher, Red Kite, Buzzard, Cetti's Warbler. *Summer:* Common Tern, Redshank, Lapwing, Hobby, warblers include Reed, Sedge, Whitethroat. *Passage:* Garganey, Little Ringed Plover, Common and Green Sandpiper and Greenshank. *Winter:* Water Rail, Bittern, Little Egret, Teal, Shoveler, Pochard, Goldeneye, occasional Smew and Goosander. Along River Loddon — Siskin, Lesser Redpoll, Fieldfare and Redwing.

Contact: As for Dinton Pastures, 0118 934 2 016.

4. MOOR GREEN LAKES

Lakes Group Moor Green/Blackwater Valley Countryside Partnership
Location: Sat nav: RG40 3TF (free car park in Lower Sandhurst Road, Finchampstead (open 8am to dusk approx). SU 805 628. Alternatively, Horseshoe Lakes free car park in Mill Lane, Sandhurst (SU 820 620).
Access: Reserve closed to all, but can be viewed from footpaths bordering eastern, southern and westerns sides. Paths can be used by wheelchairs, though surface not particularly suitable. Southern path forms part of Blackwater Valley long distance footpath.
Facilities: Two bird hides open to MGLG members (see map on website), four viewing screens available to public. Feeding station viewable from bench on western path.
Public transport: Nearest railway station, Crowthorne on Reading to Gatwick line (First Great Western Trains).
Habitats: Thirty-six hectares (90 acres) in total. Three lakes with gravel islands, beaches and scrapes. River Blackwater, grassland, surrounded by willow, ash, hazel and thorn hedgerows.
Key birds: More than 200 species recorded, with 60 breeding on a regular basis. *Spring/summer:* Little Ringed Plover, Reed Warbler and Hobby. Also Whitethroat, Sedge Warbler, Common Sandpiper. Mandarin Duck, Common Tern and Barn Owl breed on site. Dunlin and Green Sandpiper on passage. *Winter:* Wigeon, Teal, Gadwall and of particular interest, a roost of Goosander on Grove Lake. Little Egret regular, Snipe, Lapwing and Green Sandpiper. Gull roost on adjacent Manor Farm workings includes up to 1,000 Lesser Black-backeds.
Other notable flora and fauna: 31 species of butterfly and 15 species of dragonfly have been recorded. See website for more details.
Contact: Moor Green Lakes Group, e-mail: chairman@mhlg.ork.uk www.mglg.org.ik Blackwater Valley Countryside Partnership, 01252 331 353; e-mail: blackwater.valley@hants.gov.uk www.blackwater-valley.org.uk

NATURE RESERVES - SOUTH EAST ENGLAND

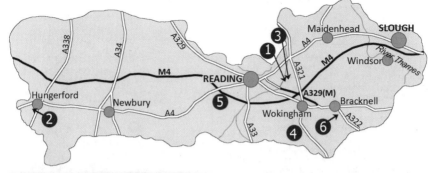

5. THEALE GRAVEL PITS

Theale Area Bird Conservation Group.
Location: Sat nav: RG7 4AP. SU 656 703 (Main Pit).
Group of pits situated between junctions 11 and 12
of the M4, south of Reading. Includes Hosehill Lake
LNR (SU 648 696). From Theale town centre head S on
Station Road and Hanger Road and park in lay-bys in
Dean Copse Road.
Access: Open at all times. Parking for a few vehicles
in lay-bys near Fox & Hounds pub.
Facilities: Tern rafts, Sand Martin bank and
wildflower meadow in Hosehill Lake LNR, together
with information boards and benches on a mile-long
circular walk.
Public transport: Theale railway station within
walking distance of nearest pits.
Habitats: Flooded fields, Kennet & Avon Canal, scrub
and worked-out gravel pits.
Key birds: *Spring/summer:* Migrant warblers,
breeding Nightingale and Common Tern, passage
Arctic and Black Terns, large number of hirundines,
resident Peregrine favours pylon area. *Autumn:*
Dunlin, Common Sandpiper and other waders on
passage. Little Gulls recorded, along with terns
on passage, plus Osprey. *Winter:* Large numbers
of wildfowl, including Goldeneye and Goosander.
Thousands of gulls on nearby Moatlands pit. Bitterns
sometimes recorded in Hosehill Lake LNR reedbed.
Other notable flora and fauna: Good range of
dragonflies and butterflies. Grass vetchling worthy
of note.

Contact: TABCC membership secretary Cathy McEwan
01189 415 792; e-mail: tabcgsec@yahoo.com

6. WILDMOOR HEATH

Berks, Bucks & Oxon Wildlife Trust.
Location: Sat nav: RG45 7PP. SU 843 628. Between
Bracknell and Sandhurst. From Sandhurst shopping
area, take the A321 NW towards Wokingham. Turn
E at the mini-roundabout on to Crowthorne Road.
Continue for about one mile through one set of traffic
lights. Car park is on the R at the bottom of the hill.
Access: Open all year. No access to woodland N of
Rackstraw Road at Broadmoor Bottom. Dogs on a
lead. Not suitable for wheelchairs due to slope of site
and muddy, uneven terrain.
Facilities: Car park.
Public transport: The reserve is one mile north of
Sandhurst railway station.
Habitats: 99-hectares of wet and dry lowland
heath, bog, mixed woodland and mature Scots pine
plantation.
Key birds: *Spring/summer:* Wood Lark, Tree Pipit,
Nightjar, Dartford Warbler, Hobby, Reed Bunting and
Stonechat among 55 species recorded at this site.
Other notable flora and fauna: Dragonflies (20
species recorded), slow worm, adder, grass snake,
common lizard, roe deer. Bog plants inc sundews.
Contact: BBOWT, 01865 775 476;
e-mail:info@bbowt.org.uk
www.bbowt.org.uk/reserves/Wildmoor-Heath

Buckinghamshire

BORDERED by the River Thames to the south and
River Ouse to the north, Buckinghamshire offers
a good selection of woods, lakes and gravel pits.
The high ground of the Chiltern escarpment is an
excellent place to watch Red Kites. There is a good
breeding population of Firecrests in the county.

1. BURNHAM BEECHES NNR

City of London Corporation.
Location: Sat nav: SL1 8PN. SU 950 850. Four
kilometres N of Slough and on W side of A355, running
between J2 of the M40 and J6 of M4. Entry from

A355 via Beeches Road. Also smaller parking areas in
Hawthorn Lane and Pumpkin Hill to the S and Park
Lane to the W.
Access: Open all year, except Dec 25. Main Lord
Mayor's Drive open from 8am-dusk. Beeches Café,
public toilets and information point open 10am to
5pm. Motorised buggy available for hire. Network of
wheelchair accessible roads and paths.
Facilities: Car parks, toilets, café, visitor information
centre. Easy access path network, suitable for
wheelchairs, most start at Victory Cross. Coach
parking.
Public transport: Train: nearest station is Slough on
main line from Paddington. Arriva, First and Jason
Tours bus numbers 74 and 40, tel 0871 200 22 33

(Traveline).
Habitats: Ancient woodland, streams, pools, heathland (Stoke Common), grassland, scrub.
Key birds: *Spring/summer:* Cuckoo, possible Turtle Dove. *Winter:* Siskin, Crossbill, regular large flocks c100 Brambling. Possible Woodcock. *All year:* Mandarin (good population), all three woodpeckers, Sparrowhawk, Marsh Tit, possible Willow Tit, Red Kite and Buzzard.
Other notable flora and fauna: Ancient beech and oak pollards with associated wildlife. Rich array of fungi.
Contact: City of London Corporation, Burnham Beeches Office, Hawthorn Lane, Farnham Common, SL2 3TE. 01753 647 358; e-mail: burnham.beeches@cityoflondon.gov.uk www.cityoflondon.gov.uk

2. CALVERT JUBILEE

Berks, Bucks & Oxon Wildlife Trust.
Location: Sat nav: MK18 2EP. SP 683 250. Near Steeple Claydon, 6.5 miles E of Bicester. Park opposite Greatmoor Sailing Club.
Access: Please keep to network of paths. Surfaced path to bird hide. Guide dogs only.
Facilities: Two hides, small car park.
Public transport: None.
Habitats: Ex-clay pit, railway and landfill site. Now with deep lake, marginal reedbed and scrub habitat.
Key birds: *Summer:* Nesting Common Tern on rafts, Kingfisher, Hobby, warblers and Cuckoo. *Passage migrants:* Black Tern and fly-over waders. *Winter:* Over-wintering wildfowl. Bittern, Water Rail and large gull roost with occasional Glaucous and Iceland Gulls. Rarer birds turn up regularly.
Other notable flora and fauna: Rare butterflies, including dingy and grizzled skippers and black hairstreak. Bee and common spotted orchids.
Contact: BBOWT, 01865 775 476; e-mail: info@bbowt.org.uk www.bbowt.org.uk/reserves/Calvert-Jubilee

3. CHURCH WOOD

RSPB (Midlands Regional Office).
Location: Sat nav: SL2 3XB. SU 971 872. Reserve lies three miles from J2 of M40 in Hedgerley. Park in village, walk down small track beside pond for approx 200m. Reserve entrance is on L.
Access: Open all year, dawn to dusk. Not suitable for wheelchairs. Please keep dogs on leads (April to June).
Facilities: Two marked paths with some inclines. No toilets or car park on site.
Public transport: Bus No 40 from Slough to Hedgerley or No 74 to Farnham Common.
Habitats: Mixed woodland.
Key birds: *Spring/summer:* Red Kite, Buzzard, Blackcap, Garden Warbler, Swallow. *Winter:* Redpoll, Siskin. *All year:* Marsh Tit, Willow Tit, Nuthatch, Treecreeper, Great Spotted and Green Woodpeckers.
Other notable flora and fauna: Wood anenome, wood sorrel, bluebell and other woodland plants. Brimstone, comma, white admiral and peacock

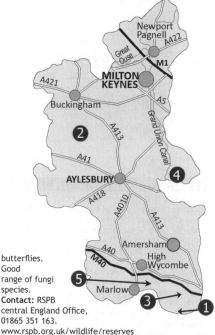

butterflies. Good range of fungi species.
Contact: RSPB central England Office, 01865 351 163. www.rspb.org.uk/wildlife/reserves

4. COLLEGE LAKE

Berks, Bucks & Oxon Wildlife Trust.
Location: Sat nav: HP23 5QG. SP 926 138. Two miles N of Tring on B488, quarter mile N of canal bridge at Bulbourne turn L into gated entrance. Marked with brown tourist signs.
Access: Open Apr-Oct (9.30am-5pm); Nov-Mar (9.30am-4pm), seven days a week. Wheelchair access to some hides and disabled toilets. Electric tramper available for disabled visitors, please phone to book.
Facilities: Large car park, coach park, 11 bird hides, interactive interpretation. Network of wheelchair-friendly paths, visitor centre/gift shop, toilets. Café open 10am to 4pm (Feb to Oct) and 10am to 3pm for rest of year.
Public transport: Tring railway station, two miles walk mostly on canal towpath.
Habitats: Deep lake in former chalk pit, shallow pools, chalk and rough grasslands, scrub.
Key birds: *Spring/summer:* Breeding Lapwing, Redshank and Little Ringed Plover. Sand Martin, Hobby, Common Tern, Skylark and Shelduck. *Winter:* Wildfowl (Wigeon, Shoveler, Teal, Gadwall), waders, inc. Snipe, Peregrine Falcon. Rarer birds turn up regularly.
Other notable flora and fauna: Chalk grassland flowers. Arable Weed Project includes displays of cornflowers in June/July. Butterflies include small blue and green hairstreak. Good numbers of dragonflies (16 species). Brown hare.
Contact: Visitor Centre, College Lake. 01442 826

7740; e-mail: collegelake@bbowt.org.uk
www.bbowt.org.uk/collegelake

5. LITTLE MARLOW GRAVEL PITS

Lefarge Aggregates.
Location: Sat nav: SL8 5PS. SU 880 880. NE of
Marlow from J4 of M40. Use permissive path from
Coldmoorholm Lane to Little Marlow village.
Follow path over a wooden bridge to N end of lake.
Permissive path ends just past the cottages where it
joins a concrete road to sewage treatment works. Be
careful at all times when walking round the lake.
Access: Open all year. Do not enter the gravel works
and watch for heavy traffic when crossing site's

entrance road.
Facilities: Permissive footpath.
Habitats: Gravel pit with sand spit (best viewed from
west bank), lake, scrub.
Key birds: *Spring:* Passage migrants including
Whimbrel, Wheatear, Whinchat, Sand Martin,
Garganey, Hobby. *Summer:* Reedbed warblers,
Kingfisher, wildfowl. *Autumn:* Passage migrants.
Winter: Wildfowl, possible Smew, Goldeneye, Water
Rail, Yellow-legged Gull among large gull flocks,
Lapwing, Snipe.
Contact: Little Marlow Lakes Country Park Community
Partnership: e-mail: littlemarlowlakescountrypark@
hotmail.co.uk

Hampshire

DOMINATED by the New Forest, this huge county
holds many scarce breeding birds including
Honey Buzzard, Goshawk, Red Kite (north of the
county), Firecrest, Hawfinch, Dartford Warbler and
Nightjar, with Great Grey Shrikes regular in winter.
Keyhaven and Farlington Marshes are the best sites
for migrants. Blashford Lakes holds a good selection
of waterbirds including wintering Bitterns.

1. BLASHFORD LAKES

Hampshire & Isle of Wight Wildlife Trust/Wessex
Water.
Location: Sat nav: BH24 3PJ. SU 151 083. From
Ringwood take A338 for two miles towards
Fordingbridge/Salisbury, pass Ivy Lane R and take
next R at Ellingham Cross, into Ellingham Drove. The
main car park for hides is first L (entrance shared
with Hanson works) after 400 yards.
Access: Car park, hides and visitor centre (with
toilets) open daily (9am to 4.30pm) except Dec
25. Paths open outside these hours but no vehicle
access. Dogs not allowed. Groups should book in
advance. RADAR keys needed to open kissing gates
for wheelchairs.
Facilities: Education centre, with toilets. Parking,
footpaths, six hides, viewing screens, toilets and
information including recent sightings board,
webcams. Coach parking by arrangement.
Public transport: X3 Bournemouth-Salisbury bus
service stops at Ellingham Cross, 500yds W of the
main reserve entrance.
Habitats: Flooded gravel pits, areas of wet ancient
woodland, also dry grassland and lichen heath.
Key birds: *Winter:* Up to 5,000 over-wintering
wildfowl, inc. internationally important numbers of
Gadwall. Grey Heron, Little Egret and Bittern. Also
a large gull roost on Ibsley Water. *Spring/summer:*
Breeding birds include Common Tern, Sand Martin (in
artificial bank), Lapwing, Redshank, Oystercatcher,
Kingfisher, Garden Warblers are especially common.
Autumn: Waders on migration including Green and
Common Sandpipers and Greenshank, also Hobby,
Black Tern and passerines.

Other notable flora and fauna: Dragonflies (25
species recorded) including brown hawker, scarce
chaser and large and small red-eyed damselfly. Roe
deer, badgers, otters, foxes, reptiles include adders
and grass snakes.
Contact: Blashford Lakes Centre, 01425 472 760 or
07917 616 695; e-mail: blashfordlakes@hwt.org.uk

2. FARLINGTON MARSHES

Hants & Isle of Wight Wildlife Trust.
Location: Sat nav: PO6 1RN. SU 685 045. North of
Langstone Harbour. Main entrance off roundabout
junction A2030/A27 is a small lane between the A27
westbound and the A2030 leading to Portsmouth.
Access: Open at all times, no charge or permits,
but donations welcome. Dogs on leads at all times.
Wheelchair access via RADAR gates. Short slopes up
to sea wall. Paths mostly level but main track along
the sea wall is very uneven in places pending repair,
and muddy in wet weather.
Facilities: 2.5 mile circular walk around sea wall with
benches every 300m. Information at entrance and
shelter. No toilets. Height barriers on car parks.
Public transport: The 21 service from Portsmouth
Harbour to Havant stops by Farlington Sainsbury's
(north of A27), a 15 + min walk to the reserve.
Contact First bus service on 023 8058 4321. *By train:*
Hilsea station is 1.5 miles from reserve. Contact
South West Trains on 0845 6000 650.
Habitats: Coastal grazing marsh with pools and
reedbed within reserve. Views over intertidal
mudflats/saltmarshes of Langstone Harbour.
Key birds: *Summer:* Breeding waders and wildfowl
(including Lapwing, Redshank and Shelduck) also
breeding Cetti's, Sedge and Reed Warbler, Bearded
Tit. *Late summer:* Passage migrants (Yellow Wagtail,
Whimbrel, etc) and returning waders, chance of
rarities such as Spotted Crake, Curlew Sandpiper,
stints. *Autumn/winter:* Waders and wildfowl, good
numbers of Teal, Wigeon, Pintail, Marsh Harrier,
Short-eared Owl regular visitors. Internationally-
important numbers of Dark-bellied Brent Goose and
Bar-tailed Godwit. Important high tide roost site best
viewed over spring high tide.
Other notable flora and fauna: Corky fruited
waterdropwort, slender hares-ear, southern marsh

NATURE RESERVES - SOUTH EAST ENGLAND

and early marsh orchids. Water vole in ditches.
Contact: Steve Wiltshire, South East Hamshire
Reserves Officer. 01489 774 429. www.hiwwt.org.uk -
go to 'Nature Reserves'.

3. FLEET POND LNR

Hart District Council Service/Fleet Pond Society.
Location: Sat nav: GU51 2RR. SU 824 552. Located
in Fleet, W of Farnborough. The main site car
park, which is free, is off Cove Road B3013/
A327 (follow brown duck signs).
Access: Open all year. Additional free
parking is available in Wellington
Avenue and Chestnut Grove but
limited to two hours. Kenilworth Road
and Westover Road offer unlimited free
parking.
Facilities: Some surfaced paths,
boardwalks in wet areas.
Public transport: Fleet railway station lies
N of site.
Habitats: Largest freshwater lake in
Hampshire, marshes, reedbeds, heathland, wet
and dry woodland.
Key birds: Up to 180 species recorded. *Spring/
autumn:* Migrant waders incl. Little Ringed Plover,
Dunlin, Greenshank, Little Gull, Lesser Spotted
Woodpecker, occasional Kittiwake, terns, Wood
Lark, Skylark, occasional Ring Ouzel, Firecrest, Pied
Flycatcher. *Summer:* Hobby, Common Tern, Tree Pipit,
occasional Red Kite and Osprey. *Winter:* Bittern,
wildfowl, occasional Smew, Snipe, occasional Jack
Snipe, Siskin, Redpoll.
Other notable flora and fauna: Dragonflies and
damselflies in wet areas of marshes and heathlands
(21 species recorded). Butterflies (26 species
recorded), roe deer. More than 400 plant species
include ling and bell heather, phragmites reeds.
Contact: Hart District Council, 01252 623 443;
e-mail: countryside@hart.gov.uk
www.hart.gov.uk

4. LOWER TEST MARSHES

Hampshire & Isle of Wight Wildlife Trust.
Location: Sat nav: SO40 3BR. SU 364 150. Area
bounded by M27, M271 and A35 west of Southampton.
Limited on-road parking near Salmon Leap pub,
Testwood Lane, Totton.
Access: Open at all times. No coach parking facilities.
Disabled access limited. Dogs allowed only on Test
Way footpath.
Facilities: One hide and two screens, all accessible on
foot from Compton Road. Hide open 9am-4pm every
day, screens open at all times. Boardwalk over wetter
areas of site. Another viewpoint at Old Redbridges, an
unsurfaced lay-by off A36.
Public transport: Totton train station and bus stops
within easy walking distance. Tel 01983 827 005 for
bus details.
Habitats: Saltmarsh, brackish grassland, wet
meadows, reedbed, scrapes, meres, estuary.
Key birds: *Summer/breeding:* Kingfisher,

Oystercatcher, Reed Warbler, Cetti's Warbler, Sedge
Warbler, Reed Bunting. *Autumn/winter waders:*
Green Sandpiper, Common Sandpiper, Oystercatcher,
Redshank, Curlew, Black-tailed Godwit, Lapwing.
Winter wildfowl: Wigeon, Teal, Mallard, Shelduck.
Other notable species: Peregrine, Water Pipit. *On
passage:* Osprey, Marsh Harrier, Wood Sandpiper,
Garganey.
Other notable flora and fauna: Good range of
common butterflies. Dragonflies including scarce
chaser, emperor and migrant hawker. Early marsh,
green-winged, southern marsh orchids and green-
flowered helleborine.
Contact: Reserves Officer, Hampshire and Isle of
Wight Wildlife Trust, 02380 667 919;
e-mail: clareb@hwt.org.uk

5. MARTIN DOWN

Natural England (Wiltshire Team).
Location: Sat nav: SP6 3LS. SU 060 201. Fourteen
miles SW of Salisbury, 1km W of Martin village. The N
part of the site is crossed by the A354. A car park is
on the A354 and another at the end of Sillens Lane, a
minor road from Martin village.
Access: Open access, but organised groups of 10+
should book in advance. Car park height barrier of 7ft
6 ins. Coaches only by prior arrangement. Hard flat
track from A354 car park suitable for wheelchairs.
Facilities: Two car parks, interpretative boards.
Public transport: One bus Salisbury/Blandford. Call
01722 336 855 or visit www.wdbus.co.uk
Habitats: Unimproved chalk downland and scrub.
Key birds: *Spring/summer:* Cuckoo, Grey
Partridge, Turtle Dove, warblers, Nightingale.

Winter: Occasional Merlin, Hen Harrier. *All year:* Yellowhammer, Skylark.

Other notable flora and fauna: Species-rich chalk downland with a variety of orchids, plus pasqueflower and milkwort. More than 20 species of butterfly.

Contact: South Wiltshire NNR Office, 0300 060 6000, e-mail: enquiries@naturalengland.org.uk www.naturalengland.org.uk

6. SWANWICK LAKES NATURE RESERVE

Hampshire & Isle of Wight Wildlife Trust.

Location: Sat nav: SO31 7AY. SU 507 099. SE from Southampton. About 2 miles from Bursledon and 7 miles from Fareham. From M27 J8, follow signs to A3024 Southampton and Hamble and then Park Gate A27. At lights by The Navigator pub turn L onto Swanwick Lane. Cross motorway then L onto Sopwith Way. Turn R at mini roundabout by security gates. From J9 follow signs for Southampton A27 up to Park Gate. Take road to Botley. At Elm Tree pub turn L onto Swanwick Lane. After about a mile, turn R onto Sopwith Way. Turn R at mini roundabout by security gates.

Access: Some surfaced paths for wheelchairs, plenty of benches. Groups should contact reserve before visiting. Dogs welcome.

Facilities: Network of surfaced and unsurfaced paths, 3 waymarked trails of varying lengths, frequent benches, fantastic viewpoints, reserve leaflet including a trail guide available. Toilets available when study centre is open.

Public transport: *By train:* About 30 mins walk from Swanwick. From station turn R at end of access road then continue to Elm Tree Pub. Turn L onto Swanwick Lane then continue as above. *By bus:* Several First Group buses stop on A27, at the bottom of Swanwick Lane. www.firstgroup.com/ukbus/hampshire/

Habitats: Mixed woodland, flower-rich meadows and deep lakes.

Key birds: Good range of birds including Little Grebe, Gadwall, Buzzard, Kingfisher, Great Spotted and Green Woodpecker, Nuthatch, Treecreeper, finches and tits.

Other notable flora and fauna: Common butterflies, with occasional silver-washed fritillary and purple emperor, common dragonflies and damselflies and other insects including mining bees. Great crested newts. Common spotted orchid. Rich variety of different fungi. Roe deer.

Contact: Trust HQ, 01489 774 400 or Swanwick Lakes Education Officer, 01489 570 240; e-mail: swanwicklakes@hwt.org.uk

7. TESTWOOD LAKES

Southern Water/HIOW Wildlife Trust.

Location: Sat nav: SO40 3WX. SU 347 155. Take M271 West J2 towards Totton. L at first roundabout, then left onto A36. L at next roundabout onto Brunel Rd. Entrance on L after ¼ mile.

Access: Car parks open 8am to 4pm, winter and 8am to 6pm summer. Surfaced paths around lakes and to hides are relatively flat. Dogs not allowed

in conservation and education areas. RADAR key (available at centre) needed for wheelchair users to get through gates. Mobility vehicle available (please book in advance).

Facilities: Testwood Lakes Centre open 10am to 4pm (Mon to Fri) and 1pm to 4pm on Sundays and most Saturdays in summer. Closes 3pm in winter. Weekday access may not be possible if school groups are in attendance. Two hides and two screens. Hides open 10am-4pm daily. Disabled toilet in Education Centre.

Public transport: Totton rail station is 1.5 miles from the reserve. Bluestar and Wilts & Dorset buses stop ¼ mile from entrance. Tel 01983 827 005.

Habitats: Flooded gravel pits, scrapes, wet and dry grasslands, woodland and hedgerows.

Key birds: *Winter:* Various wildfowl (inc. Tufted Duck, Wigeon, Pochard, Teal, Gadwall, Goosander), Siskin, Hawfinch, Meadow Pipit, Common Sandpiper, Green Sandpiper, Pochard, Redwing, Fieldfare. *Spring:* Shelduck, Sand Martin, Little Ringed Plover, Willow Warbler. *Summer:* Swift, Swallow, Blackcap, Whitethroat. *Autumn:* Wheatear, Yellow Wagtail, Goldfinch.

Other notable flora and fauna: Good range of butterflies. Dragonflies including emperor, scarce chaser, southern and migrant hawker and golden ring.

Contact: Clare Bishop, Trust HQ, 02380 424 206; e-mail: clareb@hwt.org.uk www.hwt.org.uk

8. TITCHFIELD HAVEN NNR

Hampshire County Council.

Location: Sat nav: PO14 3JT. SU 535 025. Located on Cliff Road, Hill Head in Fareham. Reach from A27 and B3334 W of Fareham. Car park adjacent to Hill Head Sailing Club (free for blue badge holders).

Access: Free admission to visitor centre, charge applied for reserve. Open daily all year 9.30am to 5pm (April to Oct) 9.30am to 4pm (Nov to March, except Dec 25 & 26. Public footpath follows derelict canal along W of reserve and road skirts S edge. Guide dogs only.

Facilities: Centre has information desk, toilets, tea room and shop. All six hides are accessible to wheelchair users.

Public transport: Bus stop in Solent Road is within 200 yards of reserve.

Habitats: Covers 369 acres of Lower Meon valley. Shoreline, reedbeds, freshwater scrapes, wet grazing meadows.

Key birds: More than 200 species recorded. *Spring/summer:* Waders (inc. Avocet and Black-tailed Godwit), wildfowl, Common Tern, breeding Cetti's Warbler, Water Rail. *Autumn/winter:* Bittern, Kingfisher, Bearded Tit, Brent Geese, Wigeon, Teal, Shoveler and Snipe.

Other notable flora and fauna: Six species of nationally rare plant, roe deer, badger and pipistrelle bat. Water voles released in 2013. Dragonflies (19 species recorded) and more than 30 species of butterfly.

Contact: Reserve Manager, Titchfield Haven, 01329 662 145; e-mail:titchfield.enquiries@hants.gov.uk

Kent

THIS IS A FABULOUS county for birders. Being so close to France, the shingle spit at Dungeness offers excellent seawatching, an RSPB reserve and bird observatory. There is another observatory at Sandwich Bay, marshes all along the north coast and reedbeds at Stodmarsh. The Isle of Sheppey holds a wide selection of birds of prey in winter.

1. BOUGH BEECH RESERVOIR

Kent Wildlife Trust.
Location: Sat nav: TN14 6LD. TQ 496 494. Lying SW of Sevenoaks, Bough Beech is situated 3.5 miles S of Ide Hill, signposted off B2042.
Access: Visitor centre in Winkhurst Green, Ide Hill open on Weds, Sat, Sun and Bank Holidays between 10am and 5pm and Sundays (10am to 4pm) between November and March. Dogs on leads at all times. Roadside parking.
Facilities: Visitor centre offers hot and cold drinks, gift shop, picnic facilities, toilets (inc disabled). Paths are uneven and can be muddy. Hide overlooks wader scrape.
Public transport: Rail service to Penshurst Station (two miles south).
Habitats: Reserve occupies northern end of the reservoir and adjacent woodland and farmland.
Key birds: Approx 60 species of birds breed in and around the reserve annually, with Tufted Duck, Mandarin and Great Crested Grebe notable among the waterfowl. Little Ringed Plover nest most years. *Autumn:* Good for numbers of waders like Green and Common Sandpipers and Greenshank. Many rarities have been recorded. Ospreys recorded most years. Winter wildfowl numbers are much higher than summer and include Goldeneye and Goosander.
Other notable flora and fauna: Great crested newt, toad, dragonflies (black-tailed skimmer, ruddy darter, emperor, southern aeshna, migrant hawker, red-eyed damselfly), common lizard, Roesel's bush cricket, long-winged conehead, dormouse, water shrew, white admiral butterfly, glow-worm, bats (pipistrelle, Daubenton, noctule, brown long-eared).
Contact: Visitor Centre Manager, Peter Bassett (01732 750 624), Reserve Manager Paul Glanfield (01732 456 407); e-mail: info@kentwildlife.org.uk

2. CLIFFE POOLS

RSPB (South East Region Office).
Location: Sat nav: ME3 7SU (Salt Lane, Cliffe). TQ 722 757. From coastbound A2, take A289 near Strood. From A289 follow signs for Wainscott and Cliffe onto B2000. At T-junction turn L to Cliffe. At crossroads, turn L to Higham. Before you enter Cliffe, take 2nd L after Cliffe sign. Turn L at next T-junction and L again into Salt Road. Car park is on L just past a sharp R bend.
Access: Free admission at all times. Group bookings welcome. Car park open daily from 8.30am-5pm, except Dec 25. Monthly guided walks available. Dogs only on public footpaths.
Facilities: Six viewing points. Public rights of way encircle reserve and bisect it. Pushchair friendly. Secure parking for 40 vehicles.
Public transport: Bus 133 from Chatham, Rochester and Strood stops at Six Bells pub in Cliffe.
Habitats: A mix of saline lagoons, freshwater pools, grassland, saltmarsh and scrub.
Key birds: Massed flocks of waders in winter (more than 9,000 Black-tailed Godwits reported in winter 2013), up to 10,000 Dunlin plus a wide range of wildfowl. A great variety of passage birds in spring and autumn. Breeding species include Lapwing, Redshank, Avocet, Ringed Plover, Shelduck. Also look out for Nightingale, Hobby, Mediterranean Gull and Turtle Dove.
Other notable flora and fauna: Good range of insects (rare bees include shrill carder bee, brown-banded carder bee). Butterflies, inc. marbled white, common blue, Essex skipper and the migrant clouded yellow, grasshoppers and bush crickets, including Roesel's.
Contact: Reserve Manager, 01634 222 480; e-mail:northkentmarshes@rspb.org.uk

3. DUNGENESS NNR

RSPB (South East Region Office).
Location: Sat nav: TN29 9PN. TR 062 197. One mile out of Lydd on the Dungeness Road, turn R for main site. Visitor centre and car park are one mile along entrance track. Entrance to Hanson ARC site and car park is opposite main reserve entrance on L of Dungeness Road.
Access: Open daily (9am to 9pm or sunset when earlier). Visitor centre open (10am to 5pm, or 4pm Nov-Feb). Parties over 12 by prior arrangement. Closed Dec 25 & 26. Charge for non-RSPB members (£3 adults, concessions £1, under-16s £1). Only guide dogs allowed on site.
Facilities: Visitor centre, toilets (including disabled access), six hides (all wheelchair-accessible), viewing screen, two nature trails. Fully equipped classroom/meeting room. Coach parking available. Hide and viewing screen at Hanson ARC site.
Public transport: Limited service. Bus 11 from Ashford stops at reserve entrance on request — one mile walk to visitor centre.
Habitats: Shingle, 90 flooded gravel pits, sallow scrub, newly-extended reedbed on Denge Marsh, wet grassland.
Key birds: *All year:* Bittern, Marsh Harrier, Bearded Tit, Cetti's Warbler *Spring:* Garganey, Little Ringed Plover among a wide variety of waders, Wheatear, Yellow Wagtail, Lesser Whitethroat, Black Redstart. *Autumn:* Migrant waders and passerines, inc large flocks of swallows and martins. *Winter:* Smew, Goldeneye, Black-necked and Slavonian Grebes, Wigeon, Goosander, Bewick's Swan, Marsh and Hen Harriers, plus other raptors.
Other notable flora and fauna: Jersey cudweed, Nottingham catchfly, endemic leafhopper.
Contact: Reserve Manager, 01797 320 588; e-mail: dungeness@rspb.org.uk

4. DUNGENESS BIRD OBSERVATORY

Dungeness Bird Observatory Trust.
Location: Sat nav: TN29 9NA. TR 085 173. Three miles SE of Lydd. Turn south off Dungeness Road at TR 087 185 and continue to end of road, past two lighthouses.
Access: Observatory open throughout the year — wardens on site between March and Nov. No wheelchair access.
Facilities: Accommodation for up to nine people (£15 a night for non-members, £10 for Friends). Apply in writing to the warden or by phone. Bring own sleeping bag/sheets and toiletries. Shared facilities including fully-equipped kitchen. Coach parking available at railway station.
Public transport: Bus service between Rye and Folkestone, numbers 11, 12. Alight at the Pilot Inn, Lydd-on-Sea, a short walk from Observatory. Stagecoach East Kent: Tel: 01227 472 082.
Habitats: Shingle promontory with scrub and gravel pits.
Key birds: Breeding birds include Raven, Wheatear and Black Redstart and seabirds on RSPB Reserve. Important migration site with regular overshoots such as Bee-eater, Purple Heron and Red-rumped Swallow. Excellent seawatching when weather conditions are suitable. Power station outfall, 'The Patch' good for terns and gulls, inc Mediterranean and Yellow-legged.
Other notable flora and fauna: Long Pits are excellent for dragonflies, including small red-eyed damselfly. Moth trapping throughout the year.
Contact: David Walker, Dungeness Bird Observatory, 11 RNSSS Cottages, Dungeness, Romney Marsh, Kent TN29 9NA. 01797 321 309;
e-mail: dungenessobs@vfast.co.uk
www.dungenessbirdobs.org.uk

5. ELMLEY MARSHES NNR

Elmley Conservation Trust.
Location: Sat nav: ME12 3RW. TQ 924 698. From J5 on the M2, follow A249 towards Sheerness. Reserve signposted from the exit for Iwade and Ridham Dock, immediately before the Sheppey bridge. At the roundabout, take second exit onto the old road bridge. On the Isle of Sheppey, after 1.25 miles (2 km), turn R following reserve sign. Follow the rough track for approximately 2 miles (3 km) to the car park at Kingshill Farm.
Access: Open every day (8am-8pm or dusk if earlier) except Tuesdays and Dec 25/26. Honesty box in car park for £5 car park fees. Guide dogs only allowed on reserve. Less mobile visitors may drive closer to the hides.
Facilities: Five hides. Disabled access to Wellmarsh hide. No visitor centre, but owners Philip and Corinne Merricks have pledged to create an extra walk route and more hides. Toilets located in car park 1.25 miles from hides. Pushchair friendly. Uide dogs only.
Public transport: Swale Halt nearest railway station on Sittingbourne to Sheerness line. From there it is a three mile walk to reserve.
Habitats: 3,000 acres of coastal grazing marsh, ditches and pools alongside the Swale Estuary with extensive intertidal mudflats and saltmarsh.
Key birds: *Spring/summer:* Breeding waders — Redshank, Lapwing, Avocet, Yellow Wagtail, passage waders, Hobby. *Autumn:* Passage waders. *Winter:* Spectacular numbers of wildfowl, especially Wigeon and White-fronted Goose. Waders. Hunting raptors — Peregrine, Merlin, Hen Harrier and Short-eared Owl.
Other notable flora and fauna: Water vole.
Contact: 01795 666014/07873 305 368;
e-mail: ect1@live.co.uk

6. NORTHWARD HILL

RSPB (South East Region Office).
Location: Sat nav: ME3 8DS. TQ 768 765. Leave M2 at junction 1 and join A228, signposted to Grain. Reserve is in Cooling Road, adjacent to High Halstow, approx four miles NE of Rochester.
Access: Open all year, dawn to dusk, free access, trails in public area of wood joining Saxon Shoreway link to grazing marsh. Dogs only allowed on Saxon Shoreway. Trails often steep and not suitable for wheelchair users.
Facilities: Four trails vary in length from 0.5 to 4km. The Toddler trail is surfaced and suitable for 'off-road' pushchairs. Four viewpoints with benches. Rough surface in car park, where toilets are located.

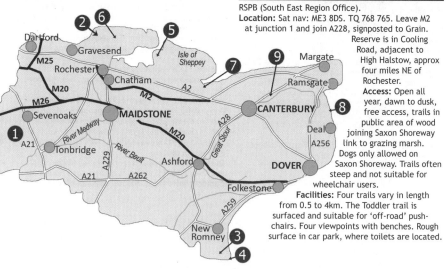

Public transport: Infrequent buses to village of High Halstow, 1.5 miles from reserve. Contact Arriva buses (01634 283 600).
Habitats: Ancient and scrub woodland (approximately 130 acres), grazing marsh (approximately 350 acres).
Key birds: *Spring/summer:* Wood holds UK's largest heronry, with c.100 pairs of Grey Heron and c.50 pairs of Little Egret, breeding Nightingale (1% of UK population), Turtle Dove, scrub warblers and woodpeckers. Marshes — breeding Lapwing, Redshank, Avocet, Marsh Harrier, Shoveler, Pochard. *Winter:* Wigeon, Teal, Shoveler. Passage waders (ie Black-tailed Godwit), raptors, Corn Bunting. Long-eared Owl.
Other notable flora and fauna: Good range of dragonflies over the marsh, white-letter hairstreak butterfly in the woods.
Contact: Jason Mitchell, RSPB North Kent Marshes, 01634 222 480;
e-mail: northkentmarshes@rspb.org.uk

7. OARE MARSHES LNR

Kent Wildlife Trust.
Location: Sat nav: ME13 0QA. TR 01 36 48 (car park). Off Church Road, Oare, two miles N of Faversham. From A2 follow signs to Oare and Harty Ferry.
Access: Open at all times. Car parking opposite the Watch House near seawall. Disabled-only car park 300m from East Flood hide. Access along marked paths only. Dogs on leads.
Facilities: Three hides. Roadside viewpoint of East Hide accessible by wheelchair users. Those with pneumatic tyres can reach seawall path and hide. Small car park, restricted turning space, not suitable for coaches.
Public transport: 333 bus from Feversham, Sittingbourne and Maidstone to Oare Village one mile from reserve. Arriva service (Mon-Sat), Jaycrest (Sun) — call Traveline on 0870 608 2608. Train: Faversham (two miles distance).
Habitats: Ramsar, SPA and SSSI designated site with grazing marsh, freshwater dykes, open water scrapes, reedbed, mudflats, Swale Sea Channel.
Key birds: *All year:* Waders and wildfowl, Little Egret, Marsh Harrier, Water Rail, Barn and Little Owls. *Winter:* Brent Goose, Red-breasted Merganser, Hen Harrier, Merlin, Peregrine, Short-eared Owl, Bittern, Stonechat. Divers, grebes and sea ducks on Swale. *Spring/summer:* Avocet, Garganey, Green, Wood and Curlew Sandpipers, Little Stint, Black-tailed Godwit, Little Tern. Site has a good record for attracting rarities.
Contact: Kevin Duvall, Kent Wildlife Trust, 01622 662 012; e-mail: info@kentwildlife.org.uk
www.kentwildlifetrust.org.uk

8. SANDWICH BAY BIRD OBSERVATORY

Sandwich Bay Bird Observatory Trust.
Location: Sat nav: CT13 9PF. TR 355 575. 2.5 miles from Sandwich, five miles from Deal. A256 to Sandwich from Dover or Ramsgate. Follow signs to Sandwich Station and then Sandwich Bay.
Access: Open daily. Disabled access.
Facilities: New Field Study Centre. Visitor centre, toilets, refreshments, hostel-type accommodation, plus self-contained flat.
Public transport: Sandwich train station two miles from Observatory.
Habitats: Coastal, dune land, farmland, marsh, two small scrapes.
Key birds: *Spring/autumn passage:* Good variety of migrants and waders, especially Corn Bunting. Annual Golden Oriole. Firecrest and Yellow-browed Warbler occur in The Elms. *Winter:* Golden Plover. Breeding residents include Grey Partridge, Stonechat, Stock Dove, Little Owl, Oystercatcher, Littled Ringed Plover.
Other notable flora and fauna: Sand dune plants such as lady's bedstraw and sand sedge. Small heath butterfly, red-veined darter.
Contact: The Secretary, Sandwich Bay Bird Observatory, 01304 617 341; www.sbbot.co.uk
e-mail: sbbot@talk21.co.uk

9. STODMARSH NNR

Natural England (Kent Team).
Location: Sat nav: CT3 4BA (Red Lion, Stodmarsh). TR 222 618. Lies alongside River Stour and A28, five miles NE of Canterbury. Car park in Stodmarsh village.
Access: Open at all times. Keep to paths. No dogs.
Facilities: Fully accessible toilets at the Stodmarsh entrance car park. Five hides (one fully accessible), easy access nature trail, footpaths and information panels. Car park, picnic area and toilets adjoining the Grove Ferry entrance with easily accessible path, viewing mound and two wheelchair-accessible hides.
Public transport: There is a regular Stagecoach East Kent bus service from Canterbury to Margate/ Ramsgate. Alight at Upstreet for Grove Ferry. Hourly on Sun.
Habitats: Internationally-important mix of open water, reedbed (largest in SE England), wet meadows, dry meadows, woodland.
Key birds: *Spring/summer:* Breeding Marsh Harrier, Bearded Tit, Cetti's Warbler, Garganey, Reed, Sedge and Willow Warblers, Nightingale. Migrant Black Tern, Hobby, Osprey, Little Egret. *Autumn:* Large roosts of Swallows, martins and Starlings. *Winter:* Wildfowl, Hen Harrier, Bittern.
Other notable flora and fauna: Nationally rare plants and invertebrates, including shining ram's horn snail.
Contact: David Feast, Natural England, 07767 321 058 (mobile).

London, Greater

PEREGRINES are happily colonising tall city structures such as Tate Modern, Battersea Power Station and the O2 Arena to name but a few. Black Redstarts are present too. Recent attention has been devoted to impressive visible migration over the city. There are many parks to explore and Common Terns now fish along the cleaned-up Thames.

BEDFONT LAKES COUNTRY PARK

Friends of BLCP/Continental Landscapes Ltd.
Location: Sat nav: TW14 8QA (Clockhouse Lane). TQ 080 728. From M25 take junction 13 (A30) towards central London. Continue through Crooked Billet traffic light complex, past Ashford Hospital and take B3003 (Clockhouse Lane) from the Clockhouse roundabout.
Access: Park open (8am to 9pm or dusk, whichever is earlier), all days except Dec 25. Disabled friendly. Dogs on leads. Main nature reserve only open Sun (2pm-4pm). Keyholder membership available (£12 annually) to access reserve at any time.
Facilities: Toilets, information centre, several hides, nature trail, free parking, up-to-date information.
Public transport: Train to Feltham and Ashford. Bus – H26 (Feltham to Hatton Cross) and 116 from Hounslow to Ashford Hospital.
Habitats: North side nature reserve consists of 180 acres of lakes, reedbed, wildflower meadows, wet woodland, scrub.
Key birds: 140 species recorded. *Winter:* Water Rail, Bittern, Smew and other wildfowl, Meadow Pipit. *Summer:* Common Tern, Willow, Garden, Reed and Sedge Warblers, Whitethroat, Lesser Whitethroat, hirundines, Hobby, Blackcap, Chiffchaff, Skylark. *Passage:* Wheatear, Wood Warbler, Spotted Flycatcher, Ring Ouzel, Redstart, Yellow Wagtail.
Other notable flora and fauna: 140 plant species inc bee and pyramidal orchid. Nathusius pipistrelle bat, emperor dragonfly plus other butterflies and dragonflies.
Contact: James Herd, Ranger, BLCP, Clockhouse Lane, Bedfont, Middx, TW14 8QA. 0845 456 2796.
e-mail: bedfont.lakes@continental-landscapes.co.uk

BRENT (WELSH HARP) RESERVOIR

Welsh Harp Conservation Group/British Waterways.
Location: Sat nav: NW9 7BH. In NW london close to junction 1 of M1. A5 (Edgeware Road) runs along eastern edge of site. From A5 turn into Cool Oak Lane and park just behind the bridge separating northern and eastern marshes.
Access: Open access at all times, but key needed to use Main and Heron hides overlooking the eastern marsh (apply to Conservation Group), unless a member is already in situ. Park in Birchen Grove to access Welsh Harp Open Space nature reserve. WHCG and North-East London RSPB Group organises regular Sunday birdwalks.

Facilities: Raised viewing platform and permanently open public hide overlooks northern marsh. Circular walk.
Public transport: Hendon station (Thameslink) is a short walk away take Station Road and West Hendon Broadway to Cool Oak Lane).
Habitats: Reservoir surrounded by marshland, woodland, unimproved grassland and playing fields.
Key birds: More than 250 species recorded. *Spring/ summer:* Breeding Great Crested Grebe, Gadwall, Shoveler, Pochard, Common Tern, woodland species and up to eight species of warbler. A long history of rare birds includes London's first Great White Egret in 1997 and the UK's first Iberian Chiffchaff in 1972. *Winter:* A wide range of wildfowl and gull species.
Other notable flora and fauna: 28 species of butterfly recorded, including marbled white and ringlet, plus 15 species of dragonfly. A noted site for bat species.
Contact: WHCG telephone, 0208 4471 810.

DAGENHAM CHASE LNR

Barking & Dagenham Parks Ranger Service.
Location: Sat nav: RM7 0SS (Millenium Centre). TQ 515 860. Lies in the Dagenham Corridor, an area of green belt between the London Boroughs of Barking & Dagenham and Havering.
Access: Open throughout the year and at all times. Reserve not suitable for wheelchair access. Eastbrookend Country Park which borders The Chase LNR has surfaced footpaths for wheelchair use.
Facilities: Millennium visitor centre in Eastbrookend CP, toilets, ample car parking, Timberland Trail walk.
Public transport: Rail: Dagenham East (District Line) 15 minute walk. Bus: 174 from Romford or Dagenham five minute walk.
Habitats: Shallow wetlands, reedbeds, horse-grazed pasture, scrub and wetland. These harbour an impressive range of animals and plants, including the nationally rare black poplar tree.
Key birds: A haven for birds, with approx 190 different species recorded. *Summer:* Breeding Reed Warbler, Lapwing, Water Rail, Lesser Whitethroat, Little Ringed Plover, Kingfisher, Reed Bunting. *Winter:* Significant numbers of Teal, Shoveler, Redwing, Fieldfare and Snipe dominate the scene. *Spring/ autumn migration:* Yellow Wagtail, Wheatear, Ruff, Wood Sandpiper, Sand Martin, Ring Ouzel, Black Redstart and Hobby regularly seen.
Other notable flora and fauna: 140 plant species, wasp spider, butterflies and dragonflies.
Contact: Ranger service 020 8227 2332

LONDON WETLAND CENTRE

Wildfowl & Wetlands Trust.
Location: Sat nav: SW13 9WT. TQ 228 770. In Queen Elizabeth's Walk, Barnes, less than 1 mile from South Circular (A205). In London Zone 2/3, one mile from Hammersmith.
Access: Winter (9.30am to 5pm: last admission 4pm), summer (9.30am to 6pm: last admission 5pm). Charge

for admission for non-WWT members. Coach parking by arrangement.
Facilities: Visitor centre, hides, nature trails, discovery centre and children's adventure area, restaurant (hot and cold food), cinema, shop, observatory building, six hides (all wheelchair accessible), sustainable gardens, interactive pond zone, three interpretative buildings.
Public transport: Train: Barnes. Tube: Hammersmith then bus 283 (comes into centre). Other buses from Hammersmith are 33, 72, 209; from Richmond, 33.
Habitats: Main lake, reedbeds, wader scrape, open water lakes, wet woodland, grazing marsh.
Key birds: Nationally important numbers of wintering waterfowl, including Gadwall and Shoveler. Important numbers of wetland breeding birds, including grebes, swans, a range of duck species such as Pochard, plus Lapwing, Little Ringed Plover, Redshank, warblers, Reed Bunting and Bittern. Cetti's Warblers remain on site all year round and bred for the first time in 2010. Artifical nesting bank for Sand Martins and rafts for nesting terns. Peregrines which nest on Charing Cross Hospital sighted regularly.
Other notable flora and fauna: Water voles, slow worm, grass snake, common lizard. Seven species of bat, 22 species of dragonfly and 25 of butterfly. Notable plants inc snake's head fritillaries, cowslip, pyramidal and bee orchids.
Contact: London Wetland Centre 020 8409 4400; e-mail: info.london@wwt.org.uk www.wwt.org.uk/london Twitter:@wwtlondon.

SYDENHAM HILL WOOD

London Wildlife Trust.
Location: Sat nav: SE26 6RU. TQ 342 722. Forest Hill, SE London, SE26, between Forest Hill and Crystal Palace, just off South Circular (A205). Entrances at Crescent Wood Road and Coxs Walk.
Access: Open at all times, no permits required. Some steep slopes, so wheelchair access is difficult.
Facilities: Nature trail, information boards. No toilets.
Public transport: Train stations: Forest Hill (from London Bridge) or Sydenham Hill (from Victoria). Buses 363, 202, 356, 185, 312, 176, P4. Call Transport for London 0207 5657 299 for details.
Habitats: Ancient woodland, reclaimed Victorian gardens, meadow and small pond.
Key birds: Woodland and gardens species all year round. *All year:* All three woodpeckers, Tawny Owl, Kestrel, Sparrowhawk, Goldcrest, Nuthatch, Treecreeper, Stock Dove. *Summer:* Blackcap, Chiffchaff, Willow Warbler. *Winter:* Fieldfare, Redwing.
Other notable flora and fauna: Five species of bat, including noctule and brown long-eared. Bluebell, wood anemone, dog violet and primrose. Oak and hornbeam. Speckled wood, comma, painted lady and orange-tip butterflies.
Contact: Centre for Wildlife Gardening 020 7252 9186.

Surrey

LONDON'S urban sprawl has now enveloped much of northern Surrey, but reservoirs and the sewage farm at Beddington offer opportunities for birders. To the west of the county, heathland at Thursley Common and around Frensham are good for the likes of Nightjar, Hobby, Woodlark and Dartford Warbler.

nationally rare Dartford Warbler, Hobby and Nightjar. Other notable birds include Yellowhammer, Stonechat, Linnet and Skylark.
Other notable flora and fauna: More than 350 flowering plants, 25 species of mammal, 29 species of butterfly inc silver-studded blue and 22 species of dragonfly all recorded.
Contact: Surrey Wildlife Trust 01483 795 440 or e-mail: info@surreywt.org.uk

1. CHOBHAM COMMON NNR

Surrey Wildlife Trust.
Location: Sat nav: GU24 8TU. SU 971 644 (Staple Hill car park). From J3 of M3 head N on A322 and A30 in direction of Sunningdale. Car park in Staple Hill Road leading off from B383 Windsor Road.
Access: Open at all times.
Facilities: Three self-guided trails, six car parks with information boards. Site leaflet available from rangers.
Public transport: Hourly buses from Woking to Chobham, stopping in Bowling Green Road, just S of Common. Also services to Sunningdale from Ascot, Windsor, Camberley and Staines. Sunningdale railway station is 600 metres from NW corner of Common.
Habitats: Largest NNR in southern England. Lowland wet and dry heath, with 30 pools, mixed broadleaf and pine woodlands.
Key birds: More than 115 species recorded, including

2. FARNHAM HEATH

RSPB (South East Region Office).
Location: Sat nav: GU10 2DL. SU 859 433. Take B3001 SE from Farnham. Take the R hand fork, signposted Tilford, immediately past level crossing. Keep to that road. Just outside Tilford village look for sign to the Rural Life Centre. Entrance is on the R after 0.5 mile.
Access: Reserve open at all times. Car park opens 9.30 am weekdays and 10.30 am weekends. Park in lay-bys on adjacent roads outside those hours. Rural Life Centre open Weds to Sun between April and Sept and Weds, Thurs and Sun for rest of year. Tea room opens at 11 am.
Facilities: Large grass car park, shared with Rural Life Centre. No height barrier, but gates may be locked outside opening hours. No bike racks. Toilets (including disabled), picnic area, refreshments. Group bookings accepted, guided walks available. Good for walking, pushchair friendly. Three way-marked trails.

Public transport: Bus 19 (Farnham to Hindhead service) stops in Millbridge village, outside entrance to Pierrepont House. Reserve is a mile away, along Reeds Road (follow signs to the Rural Life Centre).
Habitats: Heathland and pine woodland.
Key birds: *Spring*: Blackcap, Tree Pipit, Woodcock, Woodlark. *Summer*: Woodcock and Nightjar, woodland birds, including Stock Dove and Green and Great Spotted Woodpeckers. *Winter*: Crossbills in pine woods, winter finches, including Brambling around the feeders, winter thrushes.
Other notable flora and fauna: Fungi — more than 150 species. Bats in summer. Sand lizard, plus a range of butterflies inc grayling.
Contact: Mike Coates, c/o The Rural Life Centre, 01252 795 632; e-mail: farnham.heath@rspb.org.uk

3. FRENSHAM COMMON & COUNTRY PARK

Waverley BC and National Trust.
Location: Sat nav: GU10 3BT (Frensham main car park SU 856 418) or Bacon Lane car park, Churt (SU 843 403). Common (1,000 acres in area) lies on either side of A287 between Farnham and Hindhead.
Access: Open at all times. Car park (locked 9pm-9am). Keep to paths. Dogs on leads during breeding season.
Facilities: Car parks at Great and Little Ponds (free on weekdays). Information rooms, toilets (inc disabled) and refreshment kiosk at Great Pond.
Public transport: Stagecoach bus 19 from Farnham to Haslemere stops at Frensham Pond Lane (no Sunday service).
Habitats: Dry and humid heath, woodland, two large ponds, reedbeds.
Key birds: *Summer*: Dartford Warbler, Woodlark, Hobby, Nightjar, Common Tern, Stonechat, Spotted Flycatcher, Sedge and Reed Warblers, Reed Bunting. *Winter*: Wildfowl (inc. occasional Smew), Bittern, Great Grey Shrike.
Other notable flora and fauna: Tiger beetle, purple hairstreak and silver-studded blue butterflies, sand lizard, smooth snake.
Contact: The Rangers Office, 01252 792 416.

4. LIGHTWATER COUNTRY PARK

Surreyheath Council.
Location: Sat nav: GU18 5RG. SU 921 622. From J3 of M3, take the A322 and follow brown Country Park signs. From Guildford Road in Lightwater, turn into The Avenue. Entrance to the park is at the bottom of the road.
Access: Open all year, dawn-dusk. Check opening times for Heathland Visitor Centre.
Facilities: Car park, toilets, waymarked trails with leaflets available.
Public transport: Train: Bagshot two miles. Tel SW Trains 0845 6000 650. Arriva Bus: No 34 stops at

Lightwater village Tel: 01483 306 397.
Habitats: Heathland, woodland, three ponds and meadows.
Key birds: *All year*: All three woodpeckers, Goldcrest in woods, Coot, Moorhen, Grey Heron and Kingfisher on ponds. *Summer*: Nightjar, Willow Warbler, Chiffchaff, Blackcap, Whitethroat. *Winter*: Fieldfare, Redwing, Siskin.
Other notable flora and fauna: Ox-eye daisies, knapweed and common spotted orchid in meadow, heathers and gorse species on heath. Wood ant nests in woodlands. Range of dragonflies and butterflies.
Contact: Surreyheath Ranger Service, Lightwater Country Park 01276 707 166; e-mail: rangers@surreyheath.gov.uk; www.surreyheath.gov.uk

5. THURSLEY COMMON NNR

Natural England (NNR Delivery Team South East).
Location: Sat nav: GU8 6LN. SU 900 417. From Guildford, take A3 SW to B3001 (Elstead/Churt road). Use the Moat car park, S of Elstead village.
Access: Open access. Parties must obtain prior permission.
Facilities: Boardwalk in wetter areas along the Heath Trail (2.25 miles in length).
Public transport: None.
Habitats: Wet and dry heathland, woodland, bog.
Key birds: *Winter*: Hen/Marsh Harriers, Great Grey Shrike and passage/migrant waders such as Redshank, Greenshank, Wood and Common Sandpipers. *Summer*: Hobby, Woodlark, Lapwing, Stonechat, Curlew, Snipe, Nightjar, Spotted Flycatcher, Redstart, Crossbill.
Other notable flora and fauna: Large populations of silver-studded blue, grayling and purple emperor butterflies can be seen here, alongside 26 recorded dragonfly species. Sandier sites on the reserve provide homes for many species of solitary bees and wasps and tiger beetles. Damp areas support carnivorous sundews and a large population (in the thousands) of early marsh orchid.
Contact: James Giles, Natural England, T01483 307 703; e-mail: james.giles@naturalengland.org.uk
www.naturalengland.org.uk

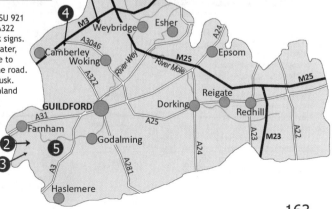

Sussex, East

THE AREA around Rye Harbour and nearby Pett Level guarantees a good day's birdwatching, with an interesting mix of wildfowl, waders, raptors, terns and Bitterns, depending on the season. If you enjoy finding your own migrants, then a spring or autumn visit to Beachy Head is a must. Ashdown Forest offers a fine mix of woodland heathland birds.

1. CASTLE WATER, RYE HARBOUR

Sussex Wildlife Trust.
Location: Sat nav: TN31 7TU. TQ 942 189. Local Nature Reserve is one mile SE of Rye along Harbour Road. The Trust manages 88 hectares around Castle Water, while the Environment Agency is responsible for the Beach reserve and Rye Harbour Farm.
Access: Open at all times, entry is free. Information centre at Limekiln Cottage open every day 10am-4pm when volunteers are available. Site is flat with some wheelchair access to all four hides, although there are stiles where the sheep are grazing the fields.
Facilities: Information centre, large car park at Rye Harbour with nearby toilets. Replacement wader pool hide now open.
Habitats: Large area of intertidal saltmarsh, marsh, drainage ditches, shingle ridges, pits, sand, scrub, woodland.
Key birds: Many birds occur here in nationally important numbers, such as Shoveler and Sanderling in the winter and breeding Little Tern and Mediterranean Gull. Nesting Black-headed Gull colony, Common and Sandwich Terns and a good range of waders and ducks. Barn and Short-eared Owls.
Other notable flora and fauna: The saltmarsh supports such unusual plants as sea-heath and marsh mallow, and even highly specialised insects including the star-wort moth and saltmarsh bee.
Contact: Sussex Wildlife Trust, 01273 492 630; e-mail: enquiries@sussexwt.org.uk - www.sussexwt.org.uk

2. LULLINGTON HEATH NNR

Natural England (South Downs Team).
Location: Sat nav: BN26 5RH. TQ 525 026. Seven miles NW of Eastbourne, between Jevington and Litlington, on northern edge of Friston Forest.
Access: Via footpaths and bridleways. Site open for access on foot.
Facilities: None. Nearest toilets/refreshments at pubs in Jevington, Litlington or Seven Sisters CP, 2km to S.
Public transport: Nearest bus stop is Seven Sisters Country Park. Phone Brighton & Hove services on 01273 886 200;

e-mail: info@buses.co.uk or visit http://www.buses.co.uk/travel/service.aspx?serviceid=1233
Habitats: Grazed chalk downland and heath, with mixed scrub and gorse.
Key birds: *Summer:* Breeding Nightingale, Turtle Dove, Nightjar and diverse range of grassland/scrub-nesting species. Passage migrants include Wheatear, Redstart, Ring Ouzel. *Winter:* Raptors (inc. Hen Harrier), Woodcock.
Other notable flora and fauna: Bell heather, ling and gorse on chalk heath; orchid species in grassland.
Contact: East Sussex NNRs, Natural England, 07971 974 401; e-mail: malcolm.emery@naturalengland.org.uk or Reserve Manager 07825 386 620; e-mail: lou.parkinson@naturalengland.org.uk For a leaflet of the site, visit: http://www.naturalengland.org.uk/ourwork/conservation/designations/nnr/1006097.aspx

3. OLD LODGE RESERVE

Sussex Wildlife Trust.
Location: Sat nav: TN22 3JD. TQ 469 306. A Local Nature Reserve within the much larger Ashdown Forest on W side of B2026 between Maresfield and Hartfield, about 0.75 miles N of junction with B2188 at Kings Standing.
Access: Open all year on well-marked nature trail leading from car park. Dogs must be kept on leads between Jan-end Sept and when livestock is present.
Facilities: Car park, well-marked nature trail. Steep paths.
Public transport: None.
Habitats: Heath, pine and deciduous woodlands covering 76 hectares.
Key birds: *All year:* Heathland specialists inc Dartford Warbler. *Spring/summer:* Breeding Nightjar, Woodcock, Redstart, Woodlark, Tree Pipit, Stonechat. *Autumn/winter:* Raven, Crossbill.
Other notable flora and fauna: Good for dragonflies including black darter, golden ringed and small red damselfly. Small colony of silver-studded blue butterflies.

Contact: Sussex Wildlife Trust, 01273 492 630;
e-mail: enquiries@sussexwt.org.uk

4. RYE HARBOUR

Rye Harbour LNR Management Committee.
Location: Sat nav: TN31 7TU. TQ 941 188. One mile
from Rye off A259 signed Rye Harbour. From J10 of
M20 take A2070 until it joins A259.
Access: Open at all times by footpaths. Organised
groups please book.
Facilities: Car park in Rye Harbour village.
Information kiosk in car park. Shop, two pubs, toilets
and disabled facilities near car park, four hides
(wheelchair access), information centre open most
days (10am-4pm) by volunteers.
Public transport: Train stations at Rye and
Winchelsea, (08457 484 950), bus (0870 608 2608),
tourist information (tel: 01797 226 696).

Habitats: Sea, sand, shingle, pits, saltmarsh and
grassland.
Key birds: Seventy of the 279 recorded species
have bred on the reserve. *Spring:* Passage waders,
especially roosting Whimbrel. *Summer:* Turtle Dove,
Breeding terns (3 species), waders (7 species), gulls
(6 species inc Mediterranean), Garganey, Shoveler,
Cetti's Warbler, Bearded Tit, Wheatear. *Winter:*
Wildfowl, inc Smew and nationally important numbers
of Shoveler, Water Rail, Bittern.
Other notable flora and fauna: Good shingle flora
including endangered least lettuce and stinging
hawksbeard. Excellent range of dragonflies including
breeding red-veined darter and scarce emerald
damselfly.
Contact: Barry Yates, (Manager), 01797 227 784;
e-mail: rhnr.office@eastsussex.gov.uk
www.wildrye.info

Sussex, West

PAGHAM HARBOUR is worth a visit at any time of
year. Nearby Selsey Bill is good for migrants and
there is a noticeable skua passage in the spring.
The WWT reserve at Arundel is good for Mandarins
and Cetti's Warblers, while further inland, RSPB
Pulborough Brooks holds important numbers of
wintering wildfowl including the chance of Bewick's
Swans.

1. ADUR ESTUARY

RSPB (South East Region Office).
Location: Sat nav: BN43 5EE. TQ 215 049. On W side
of Shoreham-on-Sea: view from Coronation Green,
situated near town centre or footbridge linking High
Street and Riverside Road.
Access: No direct access to reserve areas, but good
views from riverside paths between footbridge in
Shoreham town centre and A259 Norfolk bridge
(car park). Free public car park at the Council's
recreational field on N side of A259.
Facilities: None.
Public transport: Trains: Shoreham-by-Sea. Bus:
Shoreham-by-Sea town centre. Brighton and Hove
buses (01273 886 200) less than one mile away.
Habitats: Mudflats and saltmarsh.
Key birds: A small area but a haven for waders and
wildfowl. *Spring/summer:* Little Egret, Turnstone,
Ringed Plover, Dunlin, Redshank, Common and
Sandwich terns. *All year:* Oystercatcher. *Winter:*
Good range of gulls, Kingfisher and several wader
species.
Contact: RSPB, 01273 775 333;
e-mail: pulborough.brooks@rspb.org.uk
www.rspb.org.uk/adurestuary

2. ARUNDEL WETLAND CENTRE

Wildfowl and Wetland Trust.
Location: Sat nav: BN18 9PB. TQ 020 081. Centre on

Mill Road clearly signed from Arundel, just N of A27.
Access: Summer (9.30am-5.30pm), winter (9.30am-
4.30pm). Closed Dec 25. Approx 1.5 miles of level
footpaths, suitable for wheelchairs. Guide dogs only.
Admission charges for non-WWT members.
Facilities: Visitor centre, restaurant, shop, hides,
picnic area, seasonal nature trails. Eye of The Wind
Wildlife Gallery. Corporate hire facilities. Electric
boat safaris. Manual wheelchairs available.
Public transport: Arundel station, 15-20 minute walk.
Tel: 01903 882 131. Buses from Brighton and Worthing
(route 700) to Arundel (one mile walk to reserve).
Habitats: Site covers 65 acres with lakes, wader
scrapes, reedbed.
Key birds: *All year:* All three woodpeckers,
Kingfisher. *Summer:* Nesting Redshank, Lapwing,
Oystercatcher, Common Tern, Sedge, Reed and Cetti's
Warblers, Peregrine, Hobby. *Winter:* Teal, Wigeon,
Reed Bunting, Water Rail, Cetti's Warbler and
occasionally roosting Bewick's Swan.
Other notable flora and fauna: Bee orchid, water
shrew, palmate and smooth newt, grass snake, six
species of bat.
Contact: WWT Arundel Wetland Centre, Mill Road,
Arundel. 01903 883 355;
e-mail: info.arundel@wwt.org.uk

3. CHICHESTER HARBOUR

Chichester Harbour Conservancy.
Location: West of Chichester, with various viewing
points along 47 miles of coastline to Hayling Island.
East Head/ West Wittering good places for birding
from A27 S of Chichester, follow brown signs for West
Wittering Beach. Sandy Point Nature Reserve occupies
the SE corner of Hayling Island but can only be visited
on guided walks.
Access: Five paths suitable for wheelchairs: Cobnor
Point/ Itchenor/ Prinsted/ North Common, Northney/
Sandy Point, Hayling Island. All-terrain wheelchair can
be hired (call 01243 514 143).
Facilities: Wheelchair-accessible viewing platform

and toilet at Itchenor. RADAR-key tilet at Dell Quay.
Public transport: Contact Stagecoach South on 0871
200 2233 for information on services.
Habitats: Deep saltwater channels, mud banks, sand
dunes and shingle.
Key birds: Internationally-important for birds,
with an estimated 55,000 birds a year residing or
passing through the harbour each year. *Autumn/
winter:* Waders inc Golden Plover, Lapwing,
Curlew, Whimbrel, Black- and Bar-tailed Godwits,
Oystercatcher, Turnstone, Snipe, Dunlin and
Sanderling. Up to 10,000 Brent Geese, Red-breasted
Merganser and common wildfowl species. Kingfisher,
Short-eared owl, Hen Harrier, Linnet and Skylark.
Spring/summer: Little, Sandwich and Common Terns
all breed. Dartford Warbler breeds at Sandy Point NR.
Other notable flora and fauna: Harbour seal, water
vole, stoat, marsh samphire, sea purslane, sea
lavender and sea aster.
Contact: Friends of Chichester Harbour, Harbour
Office, Itchenor, PO20 7AW. 01243 512 301;
e-mail: secretary@friendsch.org
www.friendsch.org

4. KINGLEY VALE NNR

Natural England (Sussex Downs Team).
Location: Part of South Downs National Park. Sat
nav: PO18 9BN for the local church. Continue west
past church to reserve car park 100m down the hill.
SU 825 088 (West Stoke car park, 1km from reserve
entrance). Approx five miles NW of Chichester town
centre (as the crow flies). Travel N from Chichester
on A286 to Lavant, then turn L (W) by the church on
to Downs Road. Follow to West Stoke. Turn R at the
junction after the church to West Stoke car park.
Access: Via a footpath from reserve car park,
bridleway access is via Woodend. No permits
required, no disabled access. All dogs on a lead
to protect grazing stock, nesting birds and other
sensitive wildlife.
Facilities: Nature trail (posts 1-24) and an unmanned
information centre, leaflets and nature trail guides
can be downloaded from http://www.naturalengland.
org.uk/ourwork/conservation/designations/
nnr/1006085.aspx No toilets, but plenty of trees and
bushes!
Public transport: Nearest railway station approx five
miles walking distance. Nearest main bus route just
over one mile on A286 at Mid Lavant. No 60 from
Chichester Bus Station next to the Rail Station.
Habitats: Greatest yew forest in western Europe
(more than 30,000 yew trees). Chalk grassland, mixed
oak/ash woodland and scrub. Chalk heath.
Key birds: *Spring/summer:* Nightingale, Whitethroat,
Blackcap, Lesser Whitethroat. *Autumn/winter:* Hen
Harrier on migration, Buzzard, Hobby on migration,
Red Kite, Barn and Tawny Owls, Hawfinch, Ravens,
Goldcrest, Firecrest, Redwing, Fieldfare, Osprey
(passing over on migration), Green Woodpecker,
Nuthatch, Bullfinch, Treecreeper, Woodcock.
Other notable flora and fauna: Ancient yew trees,

yellow meadow ant, 39 recorded species of butterfly
inc brown argus and chalkhill blue, 11 species of
orchid, brown hare, dormice, bats.
Contact: Natural England, 01243 575 353; e-mail:
enquiries.southeast@naturalengland.org.uk
www.naturalengland.org.uk

5. PAGHAM HARBOUR

West Sussex County Council/RSPB.
Location: Sat nav: PO20 7NE. SZ 857 966. Five miles S
of Chichester on B2145 towards Selsey. After 0.5miles
turn R at first roundabout still following Selsey. Look
for entrance just after leaving Sidlesham after speed
limit increases to 50mph.
Access: Sidlesham Ferry and Church Norton car parks
open at all times. Dogs must be on leads. Disabled
trail with accessible hide. All groups and coach
parties must book in advance.
Facilities: Visitor Centre open most of the week
throughout the year (10am-4pm) but check first
(closed Dec 25 and 26). Toilets (including disabled),
three hides (only Ferry Pool hide accessible to
wheelchairs) and several other viewpoints, one
nature trail.
Public transport: Bus 51 (Chichester to Selsey) stops
by visitor centre.
Habitats: Mudflats, intertidal saltmarsh, shingle
beaches, lagoons and farmland.
Key birds: *Spring:* Passage migrants (warblers,
hirundines, Wheatear). *Summer:* Breeding Little and
Common Terns. *Autumn:* Passage waders inc Curlew
Sandpiper, Ruff and Little Stint, other migrants, inc
Pied and Spotted Flycatchers, incoming wildfowl
species. *Winter:* 20,000 birds inc Brent Goose,
Slavonian Grebe, wildfowl and waders. *All year:*
Little Egret.
Other notable flora and fauna: Common and grey
seals (winter). Wide range of grasses, butterflies and
dragonflies (inc emperor, broad-bodied chaser and
hairy dragonfly).
Contact: Reserve Manager 01243 641 508; e-mail:
pagham.harbour@rspb.org.uk

6. PILSEY AND THORNEY ISLANDS

RSPB (South East Region Office).
Location: Sat nav. PO10 8HS. SU 766 051. W of
Chichester. Take A259 and park in Prinstead, near
Emsworth. Walk over sea walls to view both Thorney
and Pilsey islands.
Access: No vehicle access to Thorney Island, viewing
from footpaths only. Pilsey Island can also be viewed
from 5.5.mile coastal path (the Sussex Border Path)
that runs around the Thorney Island MoD base. Long,
exposed walk.
Facilities: None.
Habitats: Intertidal sandflats and mudflats, fore
dunes and yellow dunes, bare and vegetated shingle
and saltmarsh.
Key birds: The reserve, together with the adjacent
area of Pilsey Sand, forms one of the most important
pre-roost and roost site for passage and wintering

NATURE RESERVES - SOUTH EAST ENGLAND

waders in the area. Brent Geese in winter, plus Merlin and Peregrine possible. *Summer:* Breeding Sandwich and Common Terns. Ringed Plovers and Osprey possible. *Autumn:* Passage wader numbers increase and Brent Geese return in Oct.
Contact: Site Warden, 01798 875 851; e-mail: pilsey.island@rspb. org.uk

7. PULBOROUGH BROOKS

RSPB (South East Region Office).
Location: Sat nav: RH20 2EL. TQ 058 164. Part of South Downs National Park, signposted on A283 between Pulborough (via A29) and Storrington (via A24). Two miles SE of Pulborough.
Access: Visitor centre open daily (9.30am-5pm) except Dec 25/26. Nature trail and hides (sunrise to sunset), closed Dec 25. Admission fee for nature trail (£5 for adults, £2 children: free to RSPB members). No dogs. All hides accessible to wheelchair users, though strong helper is needed.
Facilities: Visitor centre (incl RSPB shop, tea room with terrace, displays, toilets). Nature trail, four hides and additional viewpoints. Large car park including coach area. Play and picnic areas. An electric buggy is available for free hire,.
Public transport: Two miles from Pulborough train station. Connecting bus service regularly passes reserve entrance (not Sun). Compass Travel (01903 690 025). Cycle stands.
Habitats: Lowland wet grassland (wet meadows and ditches). Restored heathland, hedgerows, scrub and woodland.
Key birds: *Winter:* Thousands of wintering wildfowl and waterbirds, Bewick's Swan. Peregrine, Hen Harrier, Merlin and Short-eared Owl hunt regularly. *Spring/summer:* Breeding wading birds and songbirds (inc Lapwing and Nightingale), Hobby, Nightjar, Woodlark, Lesser-spotted Woodpecker, Barn Owl. *Autumn:* Passage wading birds, Redstart, Whinchat, Yellow Wagtail, incoming wildfowl species.
Other notable flora and fauna: Good range of butterflies and dragonflies (inc emperor, four-spotted chaser and downy emerald).
Contact: The Administrator, 01798 875 851; e-mail: pulborough.brooks@rspb.org.uk www.rspb.org.uk/pulboroughbrooks

8. WARNHAM LNR

Horsham District Council.
Location: Sat nav: RH12 2RA. TQ 167 324. One mile NW from Horsham town centre on B2237, just off A24 'Robin Hood' roundabout.
Access: Open all year (except Dec 25 and 26) Mar -

Oct (10am-6pm), Nov-Feb (10am-5pm). Day permits: Adults £1.50, children under 16 free. Annual permits also available. No dogs or cycling allowed. Good wheelchair access over most of the Reserve.
Facilities: Free access to visitor centre and café. Stag beetle loggery. Ample car park — coaches by request. Toilets (including disabled), four hides, reserve leaflets, millpond nature trail, bird feeding station, wader scrapes, boardwalks, benches and hardstanding paths.
Public transport: One mile from Horsham Railway Station, along Hurst Road, with a R turn onto Warnham Road. Buses from 'CarFax' in Horsham Centre stop within 150 yards of the reserve. Travel line, 0870 608 2608.
Habitats: Site of 92 acres includes 17 acre millpond, reedbeds, marsh, meadow and woodland (deciduous and coniferous).
Key birds: *Summer:* Common Tern, Kingfisher, woodpeckers, Mandarin Duck, Marsh Tit, Goldcrest, hirundines, Hobby, warblers. *Winter:* Cormorant, gulls, Little Grebe, Water Rail, Brambling, Siskin, Lesser Redpoll, thrushes and wildfowl. *Passage:* Waders, pipits, terns and hirundines.
Other notable flora and fauna: Extensive invertebrate interest, including 33 species of butterfly and 25 species of dragonfly. Mammals including harvest mouse, water shrew and badger. More than 450 species of plant, including broad-leaved helleborine and common spotted orchid.
Contact: The site manager, 01403 256 890; e-mail:jacob.everitt@horsham.gov.uk www.hdcwildlifesightings.blogspot.co.uk

South West England

Cornwall, Devon, Dorset, Somerset, Wiltshire

Cornwall

LOCATION, location, location.... Cornwall is ideally placed to attract overflying migrants in both spring and, particularly, autumn. For full coverage of migrant hotspots near Land's End such as Cot and Nanquidno Valleys see *Best Birdwatching Sites: Cornwall & Scilly*. Headlands at St Ives and Porthgwarra are ideal for autumn seawatching, while Choughs are recolonizing the Lizard.

1. CROWDY RESERVOIR

South West Lakes Trust.
Location: Sat nav. PL32 9XJ. SX 13 834. Follow signs from A39 at Camelford to Davidstow Airfield and pick up signs to reservoir. On edge of forestry plantation, park in pull-in spot near cattle grid. A track leads to a hide via stiles. Main car park located a little further down the lane.
Access: Open all year. No wheelchair access on tracks.
Facilities: Hide accessed from car park along rough track. **Public transport:** None.
Habitats: Reservoir, bog, moorland, forestry.
Key birds: *Spring*: Passage migrants, inc Wheatear, Whimbrel, Ruff. *Summer*: Black-headed Gull, Grasshopper, Reed and Sedge Warblers, returning waders. *Autumn*: Waders, raptors possible inc Peregrine, Goshawk, Merlin. *Winter*: Wild swans, wildfowl, possible Smew. Golden Plover, Woodcock, Fieldfare, Redwing.
Other notable flora: Mire floral communities.
Contact: South West Lakes Trust, 01566 771 930. www.swlakestrust.org.uk

2. HAYLE ESTUARY

RSPB (South West England Office).
Location: Sat nav: TR27 6JF. SW 551 364. In town of Hayle. Follow signs to Hayle from A30. Take B3301 through Hayle past the Tempest factory, turn L into Chenells Rd and R into Ryans Field. See website for access to other points on the reserve.
Access: Open at all times. No permits required. No admission charges. Not suitable for wheelchair users. Dogs on leads restricted to public footpaths. Sorry — no coaches.
Facilities: Eric Grace Memorial Hide overlooks Ryan's Field, but birds here only at high tide. Nearest toilets in town of Hayle. No visitor centre but information board at hide. Circular walk around Ryan's Field and public footpath around Carnsew Pool.
Public transport: Western Greyhound bus services 501 (summer only, not Saturdays) or 515 (not Sundays). Nearest bus stop for Carnsew Pool is in Foundry Square, Hayle (450 metres away). Call 0871 200 2233 for details. Nearest rail station at St Erth

(one mile away).
Habitats: Intertidal mudflats, saltmarsh, lagoon and islands, sandy beaches and sand dunes.
Key birds: *Winter*: Large numbers of wildfowl and waders. Top UK site for over-wintering Ring-billed Gull, but they don't visit every year. Range of gulls, Kingfisher, Great Northern Diver. *Spring/summer*: Migrant waders, breeding Shelduck. *Autumn*: Rare waders, often from N America. Terns, gulls (inc Mediterranean).
Contact: RSPB South West Regional Office, 01736 360 624; e-mail: hayle.estuary@rspb.org.uk

3. HELMAN TOR NATURE RESERVE

Cornwall Wildlife Trust.
Location: Sat nav: PL30 5DU. SX 062 615 (The Barn, Lower Gurtla). Large wetland complex incorporating Breney Common and Red Moor Memorial Reserve. 2.5 miles S of Bodmin. From A30/A391 (Innis Downs) roundabout south of Bodmin, turn N to Lanivet and take first right under A30 bridge. For Breney Common entrance, turn R at Reperry Cross, then L fork to Trebell Green and on towards Gurtla. The entrance track is on the left in Gurtla, after the Methodist church, opposite The Barn.
Access: Open at all times but please keep to paths. Disabled access from small car park at Breney. Small car park at Helman Tor. Wilderness Trail can be very muddy after heavy rain.
Facilities: Wilderness trail from Helman Tor. Boardwalk sections the only suitable surface for wheelchairs, but can be slippery when wet.
Public transport: None.
Habitats: Huge site (536 acres) includes wetland, grassland, heath and scrub.
Key birds: Willow Tit, Nightjar, Tree Pipit, Sparrowhawk, Lesser Whitethroat, Curlew.
Other notable flora and fauna: Royal fern, sundews and other bog plants. Butterflies (inc marsh and small pearl-bordered fritillaries, silver-studded blue).
Contact: Sean O'Hea, Cornwall Wildlife Trust, 01872 273 939; e-mail: info@cornwt.demon.co.uk www.cornwallwildlifetrust.org.uk

4. MARAZION MARSH

RSPB (South West England Office).
Location: Sat nav: TR17 0AA. SW 510 312. Reserve is one mile E of Penzance, 500 yards W of Marazion. Entrance off seafront road near Marazion.
Access: Open at all times. Park in privately operated car parks within walking distance. Free admission. Not suitable for wheelchair users. Dogs on leads please. Sorry — no coaches.
Facilities: No toilets or visitor centre. Viewing bay on seafront pavement overlooks pools and reedbeds of the sanctuary area. Nearest toilets in Marazion and seafront car park.

Public transport: First Group Nos 2, 7 and 8, plus Sunset Bay2Bay service 340 from Penzance. Call 0871 200 2233 for details.
Habitats: Wet reedbed, willow carr.
Key birds: More than 250 species recorded. *Winter*: Wildfowl, Snipe, occasional Bittern, impressive pre-roost flocks of Starlings up to New year attract Buzzards and Sparrowhawks. *Spring/summer*: Breeding Reed, Sedge and Cetti's Warblers, herons, swans. *Autumn*: Large roost of Swallows and martins in reedbeds, migrant warblers and Water Rail.
Other notable flora and fauna: Up to 22 species of dragonfly, plus 500 species of vascular plants, inc lawn camomile and yellow flag.
Contact: RSPB 01736 711 682; e-mail: marazion. marsh@rspb.org.uk

5. NARE HEAD

National Trust.
Location: Part of the NT's Roseland estate. Sat nav: TR2 5PH. SW 92 2 379 (Nare Head car park). Approx ten miles SE of Truro. from A390 head S on A307 to two miles S of Tregony just past the garage. Follow signs to Veryan then L signposted to Carne. Go straight over at crossroad, following Carne and Pendower. Turn L on a bend following NT signs for Nare Head. Bearing R, cross over a cattle grid to the car park. From the garage, Nare Head is about four miles.
Access: Open all year. Approach cliff edges with care as they are unstable.
Facilities: Car park.
Habitats: Headland, open sea.
Key birds: *Spring/summer*: Razorbill, Guillemot, Shag, Sandwich, Common and Arctic Terns, possible Whimbrel, Fulmar, occasional Chough. *Winter*: Black-throated and Great Northern Divers. Red-throated Diver possible. Common Scoter, Velvet Scoter, Slavonian, Black-necked and Red-necked Grebes.
Contact: National Trust, Lanhydrock House, Lanhydrock, Cornwall, PL30 4DE. 01872 580 553; e-mail: roseland@nationaltrust.org.uk

6. STITHIANS RESERVOIR

South West Lakes Trust.
Location: Sat nav: TR16 6NW (Golden Lion Inn). SS 715 365. Signposted from B3297 S of Redruth.
Access: Good viewing from causeway.
Facilities: New hide near main centre (opposite the Golden Lion Inn) open to all. Two other hides for members of CBWPS. Footpath around reservoir.
Habitats: Open water, marshland.
Key birds: County's best open water site for winter wildfowl. Winter gull flocks inc Mediterranean. Good for waders such as Common, Green and Wood Sandpipers, plus rarities, eg. Pectoral and Semipalmated Sandpipers, Lesser Yellowlegs. Passage birds can inc Osprey, Black Tern, Garganey. Good track record for rarities — records inc

Wilson's Phalarope, Caspian Tern, White-rumped Sandpiper, and Black Kite.
Contact: South West Lakes Trust, Centre Manager, 01209 860 301. www.swlakestrust.org.uk

7. TAMAR ESTUARY

Cornwall Wildlife Trust.
Location: Sat nav: PL12 6LJ (China Fleet Club). SX 431 614 (Landulph section). SX 436 627 (Cargreen). From Plymouth head W on A38. Access parking at Cargreen and Landulph from minor roads off A388.
Access: Open at all times. Footpath from Cargreen to Landulph. Access two bird hides from China Fleet Club car park, Saltash. Follow path alongside golf course — do not walk on course itself. Combination number for hide locks available at club reception.
Facilities: Two hides on foreshore, first (0.25 miles from car park) overlooks estuary, second (0.5 miles) has excellent views across Kingsmill Lake.
Habitats: 269 acres of tidal mudflat with some saltmarsh.
Key birds: *Winter*: Large number of Avocet (Oct to March), Snipe, Black-tailed Godwit, Redshank, Dunlin, Curlew, Whimbrel, Spotted Redshank, Green Sandpiper, Golden Plover, Kingfisher. *Spring/summer*: Breeding Shelduck.
Contact: Reserves manager 07866 430 086; e-mail: peter@cornwt.demon.co.uk
www.cornwallwildlifetrust.org.uk

8. TAMAR LAKES

South West Lakes Trust.
Location: Sat nav: EX23 9SB. SS 295 115. Site lies E of A39, N of Bude. Follow brown tourist signs from Holsworthy or Kilkhampton.
Access: Open all year. Limited wheelchair access. Pay-and-display car parks. Sailing and other watersports means Upper Lake is limited for birding. Nature reserve is located on Lower lake.

Facilities: Bird hides at both lakes. Café (limited opening) at Upper Tamar. Toilets at Upper open all year, those at Lower only open in summer. Trail leaflet available from café.
Public transport: None.
Habitats: Two freshwater lakes, plus swamp, scrub and grassland.
Key birds: *All year:* Great Crested Grebe, Black-headed Gull, Kingfisher, Willow Tit, Reed Bunting.

Spring: Black Tern. *Summer:* Breeding Sedge, Reed and Willow Warblers and House Martin.*Winter:* Moderate numbers of wildfowl, inc Wigeon and Teal and gulls.
Other notable flora and fauna: Badger, roe deer, otter, southern marsh orchid, wood white butterfly, grass snake.
Contact: Site warden, Upper Tamar Lakes Visitor Centre, 01288 321 262.

Devon

EXMOOR, with wonderful wooded valleys attractive to birds, is the prettier of the county's two National Parks, whereas Dartmoor is much bleaker. Red-backed Shrikes are attempting to re-establish themselves on Exmoor. The island of Lundy in the Bristol Channel is good for vagrants. Look for waders around Exminster Marshes while the southern coast holds localised but increasing pockets of Cirl Buntings.

1. AYLESBEARE COMMON

RSPB (South West England Office).
Location: Sat nav: EX10 0DF. SY 057 898. Five miles E of J30 of M5 at Exeter, 0.5 miles past Halfway Inn on B3052. Turn R to Hawkerland, car park is on L. The reserve is on the opposite side of the main road.
Access: Open all year. One track suitable for wheelchairs and pushchairs. Dogs only on public footpaths.
Facilities: Car park, two nature trails, picnic area, group bookings, guided walks and special events. Disabled access via metalled track to private farm. No toilets or viewing facilities.
Public transport: Buses (Exeter to Sidmouth, 52A, 52B). Request stop at Joneys Cross (reserve entrance). Tel: 01392 427 711.
Habitats: Heathland, wood fringes, streams and ponds.
Key birds: *All year:* Dartford Warbler, Buzzard, Yellowhammer. *Spring/summer:* Hobby, Nightjar, Tree Pipit, Stonechat. *Winter:* Possible Hen Harrier.
Other notable flora and fauna: Good range of dragonflies and butterflies.
Contact: Toby Taylor, Hawkerland Brake Barn, Exmouth Road, Aylesbeare, Nr Exeter, Devon EX5 2JS. 01395 233 655; e-mail: aylesbeare.common@rspb.org.uk

2. BERRY HEAD NNR

Torbay Coast & Countryside Trust.
Location: Sat nav: TQ5 9AP (Berry Head car park). SX 940 561. Signposted from Brixham on minor roads from A3022 and A379. Located at end of Gillard Road, past Landscove Holiday Village.
Access: Open all year. Guardhouse visitor centre open Easter to Oct (Tues to Sun 10am to 4pm; Mon 1pm to 4pm). Sundays only for rest of year. Wheelchair-friendly 300m path from car park to visitor centre

and café.
Facilities: Pay-and-display car park. Visitor centre (CCTV images of nesting seabirds), café and toilets. Two mobility vehicles for hire (pre-book). Bird hide overlooking cliffs.
Public transport: Bus 17 from Brixham to Victoria Road (Half mile walk to Berry Head: some steep sections). Torbay Coastpath runs from Torquay.
Habitats: Limestone cliffs (200ft), grassland, quarry.
Key birds: *All year:* Cirl Buntings (in flocks in autumn), Peregrine (hunting in quarry area), Fulmar, Greenfinch. *Spring/summer:* Up to 1,000 nesting Guillemots on cliffs below Southern Fort. Well-known as a migrant watchpoint.
Other notable flora and fauna: Limestone flora inc eight species of orchid, small hare's-ear. Harbour porpoise, common dolphin, greater and lesser horseshoe bats (walks arranged), bloody nose beetle and range of butterflies.
Contact: Tel: 01803 882 619; e-mail: berryhead@countryside-trust.org.uk

3. BOVEY HEATHFIELD

Devon Wildlife Trust.
Location: Sat nav: TQ12 6TU. SX 823 765. On the outskirts of Bovey Tracey on SE edge of Dartmoor. From A382 Bovey Straight take Battle Road into Heathfield Industrial estate. Turn L into Cavalier Road, then Dragoon Close – the reserve is along a gravel path.
Access: Open all year. Dogs allowed on leads. Please keep to paths. Rough paths not suitable for wheelchairs. No coach access.
Facilities: Information hut open when warden is on site. Circular way-marked path and viewpoint.
Public transport: Exeter to Plymouth buses stop at Drum Bridge, a 20 min walk to reserve.
Habitats: Mix of wet and dry lowland heath, surrounding by secondary woodland covering 58 acres. Contains numerous ponds.
Key birds: Breeding Nightjar, Tree Pipit, Stonechat and Dartford Warbler, plus commoner species such as Skylark, Linnet and Yellowhammer.
Other notable flora and fauna: Heathers, wet and dry heathland plants, more than 60 endangered insect species, plus grayling and green hairstreak butterflies, slow worm, adder and grass snake.
Contact: Devon Wildlife Trust, Cricklepit Mill, Commercial Road, Exeter, EX2 4AB. 01392 279 244; e-mail: contactus@devonwildlife trust.org

NATURE RESERVES - SOUTH WEST ENGLAND

4. BOWLING GREEN MARSH

RSPB (South West England Office).
Location: Sat nav: EX3 0EN (Holman Rd car park). SX 971 875. On the E side of River Exe, four miles SE of Exeter in Bowling Green Road, Topsham.
Access: Open at all times. Please park at the Holman Way or The Quay public car parks in Topsham village, not in the lane by the reserve. Blue Badge parking space near hide.
Facilities: RSPB shop at Darts Farm, 1.5km from reserve, east of Topsham across River Clyst. Weekly guided walks from Darts Farm. Nearest RADAR toilets at The Quay car park. Wheelchair-friendly bird hide and viewing platform. Bowling Green hide being refurbished, so check to see if it is closed before visiting.
Public transport: Exeter to Exmouth railway has regular (every 30 mins) service to Topsham station (one mile from reserve). Stagecoach Devon 57 (Mon-Sat every 12 mins, Sun every half-hour) from Exeter to Topsham stops at Elm Grove Road (1km from reserve). Call Traveline 0871 200 2233.
Habitats: Coastal grassland, open water/marsh.
Key birds: *Winter*: Large numbers of Wigeon, Shoveler, Teal, Black-tailed Godwit, Curlew, Golden Plover. Also Avocet and Brent Geese. *Spring*: Shelduck, passage waders inc Ringed Plover, Little Stint, Ruff and sandpipers, Whimbrel, passage Garganey and Yellow Wagtail. *Summer*: Tern roosts, high tide wader roosts contain many passage birds. *Autumn*: Wildfowl, Peregrine, wader roosts.
Other notable fauna: Hairy dragonfly, wasp spider.
Contact: RSPB, Darts Farm Shopping Village, Clyst St. George, Exeter EX3 0QH. 01392 879 438 or the reserve on 01392 824 614; www.rspb.org.uk

5. BURRATOR RESERVOIR

South West Lakes Trust.
Location: Sat nav: PL20 6PE. SX 568 689. On south side of Dartmoor, 10 miles NE of Plymouth, off A386 (Tavistock road). At Yelverton take B3212 towards Princeton. Turn R at Burrator Inn and follow signs to reservoir.
Access: Open all year. Free parking areas around reservoir. Main route, though suitable for disabled, is also used by motorists and cyclists. There are about 25 stiles on minor routes.
Facilities: Toilets (including disabled at new visitor centre opposite Burrator Lodge). Snacks and ice-creams available during summer.
Public transport: Bus: daily from Plymouth to Dousland (a short walk from the reservoir). No 82 Western National or No 48 (Sun). Tel: 01752 402 060. Train: nearest station is Plymouth. 08457 484 950.
Habitats: Pine forests, wooded streams, open moorland scrub.
Key birds: *Winter*: Goosander, Dipper, Grey Wagtail, Green Sandpiper, Brambling, Crossbill, Siskin, Redpoll. *All year*: All three woodpeckers, Buzzard, Sparrowhawk, Kestrel, Barn Owl, Tree Sparrow.
Other notable flora and fauna: Marsh fritillary butterfly, dragonflies and damselflies, particularly in the arboretum, bats (various species), otter.
Contact: South West Lakes Trust, Lidn Park, Quarry Crescent, Pennygillam Industrial Estate, Launceston, Cornwall PL15 7PF. 01822 855 700. www.swlakestrust.org.uk

6. DAWLISH WARREN NNR

Teignbridge District Council.
Location: Sat nav: EX7 0NF. SX 983 788. At Dawlish Warren on S side of Exe estuary mouth. Turn off A379 at sign to Warren Golf Club, between Cockwood and Dawlish. Turn into car park adjacent to Lea Cliff Holiday Park. Pass under tunnel and turn L away from amusements. Park at far end of car park and pass through two pedestrian gates.
Access: Open public access, but avoid mudflats. Also avoid beach beyond groyne nine around high tide due to roosting birds. Parking charges. No dogs on beach or dunes between ninth groyne at any time (including the hide).
Facilities: Visitor centre (tel 01626 863 980) open most weekends (1pm to 4pm in winter, 2pm-to 5pm in summer). In summer also open Wed to Fri (2pm to 4pm). Toilets at entrance tunnel and in resort area only. Bird hide one mile NE of visitor centre open at all times — best around high tide.
Public transport: Train station at site, also regular bus service operated by Stagecoach.
Habitats: High tide roost site for wildfowl and waders of Exe estuary on mudflats and shore. Dunes, dune grassland, woodland, scrub, ponds.
Key birds: *Winter*: Waders and wildfowl in large numbers. Also good for divers and Slavonian Grebe offshore. *Summer*: Particularly good for terns. Excellent variety of birds all year, especially on migration.
Contact: Visitor centre: 01626 863 980. Teignbridge District Council: 01626 215 884 (answerphone). www.teignbridge.gov.uk

7. EAST DARTMOOR WOODS & HEATHS NNR

Natural England.
Location: Sat nav: TQ13 9LJ (Yarner Wood). SX 778 787. The NNR is two miles from Bovey Tracey on road to Becky Falls and Manaton. Road continues across Trendlebere Down, where there are roadside car parks and adjacent paths.
Access: Yarner Wood car park open from 8.30am-7pm or dusk if earlier. Outside these hours, access on foot from Trendlebere Down. Dogs welcome under close control.
Facilities: Information/interpretation display and self-guided trails available in Yarner Wood car park also hide with feeding station (Nov-Mar).
Public transport: Carmel Coaches No 671 (Okehampton to Newton Abbot) stops at Manaton.
Habitats: The reserve consists of three connected sites (Yarner Wood, Trendlebere Down and Bovey Valley Woodlands) totalling 365 hectares of upland oakwood and heathland.

NATURE RESERVES - SOUTH WEST ENGLAND

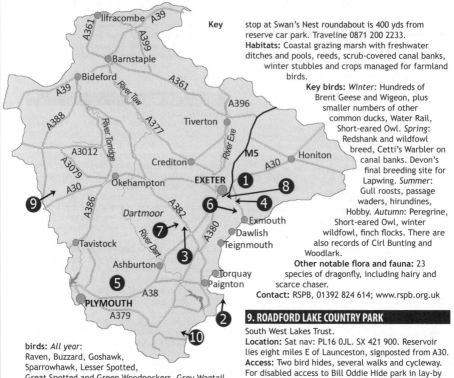

Key stop at Swan's Nest roundabout is 400 yds from reserve car park. Traveline 0871 200 2233.
Habitats: Coastal grazing marsh with freshwater ditches and pools, reeds, scrub-covered canal banks, winter stubbles and crops managed for farmland birds.
Key birds: *Winter*: Hundreds of Brent Geese and Wigeon, plus smaller numbers of other common ducks, Water Rail, Short-eared Owl. *Spring*: Redshank and wildfowl breed, Cetti's Warbler on canal banks. Devon's final breeding site for Lapwing. *Summer*: Gull roosts, passage waders, hirundines, Hobby. *Autumn*: Peregrine, Short-eared Owl, winter wildfowl, finch flocks. There are also records of Cirl Bunting and Woodlark.
Other notable flora and fauna: 23 species of dragonfly, including hairy and scarce chaser.
Contact: RSPB, 01392 824 614; www.rspb.org.uk

9. ROADFORD LAKE COUNTRY PARK

South West Lakes Trust.
Location: Sat nav: PL16 0JL. SX 421 900. Reservoir lies eight miles E of Launceston, signposted from A30.
Access: Two bird hides, several walks and cycleway. For disabled access to Bill Oddie Hide park in lay-by at SX 435 929.
Facilities: Visitor centre, cafe and toilets. Two bird hides. Pay-and-display car parks.
Public transport: Carmel Coaches' Friday-only service from Halwill Junction to Tavistock stops as Broadwoodwidger (short walk to hide).
Habitats: Reservoir of 295ha (northern third designated Special Protection Zone to benefit birds), surrounded by marsh, scrub and fields.
Key birds: County's top inland site for wildfowl (up to 2,000 birds in winter). Small wader passage in autumn depending on water levels. Internationally important site for Lesser Black-backed Gulls. Good record of attracting rarities.
Other notable flora and fauna: Hazel dormouse, various bat species.
Contact: Friends of South West Lakes Trust 01566 771 930.

birds: *All year*: Raven, Buzzard, Goshawk, Sparrowhawk, Lesser Spotted, Great Spotted and Green Woodpeckers, Grey Wagtail and Dartford Warbler (on Trendlebere Down). *Spring/summer*: Pied Flycatcher, Wood Warbler, Redstart, Tree Pipit, Linnet, Stonechat, Cuckoo, Whitethroat, Skylark and Nightjar on heaths. *Autumn/winter*: Good range of birds with feeding at hide, inc Siskin, Redpoll, plus Hen Harrier on Trendlebere Down.
Other notable flora and fauna: Good range of butterflies, inc fritilleries and grayling.
Contact: Site Manager, Natural England, Yarner Wood, 01626 832 330; www.natural-england.org.uk

8. EXMINSTER & POWDERHAM MARSHES

RSPB (South West England Office).
Location: Sat nav: EX6 8DZ (Swan's Nest Inn). SX 954 872. Five miles S of Exeter on W bank of River Exe. Marshes lie between Exminster and the estuary. Powderham Marsh accessed from car park behind Swan's Nest Inn (A379).
Access: Open at all times (except permissive path at Powderham). No dogs at Powderham Marshes.
Facilities: No toilets or visitor centre at either site — refreshments and toilets at Swans Nest Inn and Turf pub. Information in RSPB car park (Exminster site) and marked footpaths across reserve. Exminster circular walk takes 90 minutes. Three viewing screens.
Public transport: Exeter to Newton Abbot No2 bus

10. SLAPTON LEY NNR

Field Studies Council/Natural England
Location: Sat nav: TQ7 2QP (field centre). SX 825 440. The largest freshwater lake in SW England, which lies S of Dartmouth on the south coast, is separated from Start Bay by a shingle bank which carries A379.
Access: Pay-and-display car parks off A379 at Torcross

172

and Slapton Sands. Higher Ley is closed to the public, but can be viewed from public footpath.
Facilities: Hides overlooking Torcross and Stokely Bay areas of the lagoon and surrounding backdrops. Beach trailer with information in Memorial car park in school holiday (Sat to Thurs). Slapton Field Centre offers residential courses.
Public transport: First Group 93 bus from Plymouth and Kingsbridge to Slapton stops outside field centre.
Habitats: Freshwater lake, reedbeds, marsh and woodland.
Key birds: Good seawatching in favourable conditions in spring and autumn, plus migrants on passage.

Large gathering of Swallows in autumn roosts. *Winter:* Divers and grebes on sea, Bittern at Higher Ley. Diving ducks and grebes on Lower Ley. *Spring/summer:* Migrant warblers. *All year:* Up to four pairs of Cirl Bunting, Cetti's Warbler (around 40 singing males each year). Most south-westerly population of Great Crested Grebe.
Other notable flora and fauna: UK's only site for strapwort. Badger, otter, dormouse, 2,000 species of fungi.
Contact: 01548 580 466;
e-mail: enquiries.sl@field-studies-council.org

Dorset

DORSET is established as one of England's top six birding counties. Weymouth makes a splendid base, with two RSPB reserves — Lodmoor and Radipole — in the town itself. From there you can visit the bird observatory and migration hotspot of Portland and The Fleet and Jurassic coast to the west. Heathland, such as Arne RSPB, is good for Dartford Warblers and Nightjars. Studland Bay holds all three divers and five grebe species in winter.

1. ARNE

RSPB (South West England Office).
Location: Sat nav: BH20 5BJ. SY 971 876. Head S from Wareham over the causeway, turn off A351 at Stoborough.
Access: Open 8.30am to dusk. Car park (free for RSPB members) at beginning of Stoborough village. Shipstal Point and Coombe Birdwatchers' trails open all year. Coombe birdwatchers' screen on Middlebere Channel overlooks estuary. Visitor centre open all year except Dec 25/26. Limited wheelchair access on trails. Coaches and escorted parties by prior arrangement.
Facilities: Information centre offers hot drinks. Toilets in car park. Five signposted trails for different abilities. Two hides, one viewpoint and two viewing screens. Visitor hut (no toilets).
Public transport: None to reserve. Nearest train station is Wareham (4 miles from reserve), but 10% discount on cycle hire for RSPB members (call Purbeck Cycle Hire, based at station, on 01929 556 601).
Habitats: Lowland heath, woodland, reedbed and saltmarsh, extensive mudflats of Poole Harbour.
Key birds: *All year:* Dartford Warbler, Little Egret, Stonechat. *Winter:* Brent Goose flocks part of the 30,000 birds which use the harbour, including grebes, divers, Long-tailed Duck, Eider and Scaup. Hen Harrier, Marsh Harrier, Black-tailed Godwit, winter thrushes and finches. *Summer:* Nightjar, Sandwich and Common Terns, Barn Owl, hirundines, warblers. *Passage:* Hobby, Spotted Redshank, Whimbrel, Greenshank, Osprey.
Other notable flora and fauna: Sika deer, all six species of UK reptile, silver-studded blue and 32

other butterflies, 23 dragonflies, 850 moths and 500 flowering plants.
Contact: Arne Nature Reserve, RSPB Work Centre, 01929 553 360: e-mail: arne@rspb.org.uk
www.rspb.org.uk/reserves/guide/a/arne/

2. BROWNSEA ISLAND NATURE RESERVE

Dorset Wildlife Trust/National Trust.
Location: Sat nav: PH15 1HP (Poole Quay). SZ 028 878. Half hour boat rides from Poole Quay with Greenslade Pleasure Boats (01202 631 828) and Brownsea Island Ferries (01929 462 383). Ten minutes from Sandbanks Quay (next to Studland chain-ferry).
Access: Island open March 23 to Nov 2 (10am to 5pm). Free admission to nature reserve for DWT members (show card to NT staff), but landing fee must be paid if visiting rest of island. Assistance dogs only.
Facilities: Toilets, information centre, café, gift shop secondhand book shop, five hides, nature trail. Red squirrel CCTV coverage.
Public transport: Poole rail/bus station for access to Poole Quay and boats. Tel: 01202 673 555.
Habitats: Saline lagoon, reedbed, lakes, coniferous and mixed woodland covering 101 hectares.
Key birds: *Spring:* Avocet, Black-tailed Godwit and other waders, Water Rail, gulls and wildfowl. *Summer:* Common and Sandwich Terns, Yellow-legged Gull, Little Egret, Little Grebe, Golden Pheasant. *Autumn:* Curlew Sandpiper, Little Stint.
Other notable flora and fauna: Red squirrel (up to 200 on island), water vole, Bechstein's bat found 2007. Good range of butterflies and dragonflies.
Contact: Dorset Wildlife Trust, 01202 709 445.

3. DURLSTON NNR & COUNTRY PARK

Dorset County Council.
Location: Sat nav: BH19 2JL. SZ 032 774. Located in Lighthouse Road, Swanage, one mile S of town centre (signposted).
Access: Open between sunrise and sunset. Visitor centre open weekends and holidays during winter and daily in other seasons.
Facilities: Guided walks, new visitor centre located in Durlston Castle features café, toilets, exhibitions, art displays and shop. hide, waymarked trails.

Public transport: Durlston shuttle bus runs between May 27 and September 30 (half-hourly from Swanage railway station and pier).
Habitats: 280 acres of sea cliffs, woodland, grassland, hedges, cliff, meadows and downland.
Key birds: Cliff-nesting seabird colonies including Guillemot, Fulmar, Razorbill and Shag; good variety of scrub and woodland breeding species; spring and autumn migrants (especially important location for visible migration in autumn). Also good for seabirds on passage; seawatching esp. Apr/May and Aug/Nov. *All year:* Peregrine, Kestrel, Raven, woodland species.
Other notable flora and fauna: 34 species of butterfly and 800 species of moth and 500+ species of flowering plants, inc nine species of orchid. Bottle-nose dolphin.
Contact: The Ranger, Durlston Country Park, 01929 424 443, e-mail: info@durlston.co.uk
www.durlston.co.uk

4. GARSTON WOOD

RSPB (South West England Office).
Location: Sat nav: SP5 5PA (postcode for Dean Lane). SU 003 194. SW from Salisbury. From A354 take turn to Sixpenny Handley then take Bowerchalke road (Dean Lane). Proceed for approximately 1.5 miles on single-track road (with passing places). Garston Wood car park on L of road.
Access: Open at all times. Two nature trails accessible to pushchairs but terrain is best in dry weather. Dogs on leads only on public footpaths and bridleways.
Facilities: Car park, reserve leaflet, picnic area, group bookings accepted, guided walks available, remote location, good for walking, pushchair friendly. No toilets or catering facilities.
Public transport: From Salisbury bus station, take Wilts and Dorset 184 service to Sixpenny Handley (Roebuck Inn). One mile walk to reserve.
Habitats: Actively-managed ancient woodland includes large area of coppiced hazel and maple. Other habitats include oak woodland, scrub and mixed plantation, with important features such as glades, rides and dead wood.
Key birds: Common woodland birds plus Turtle Dove and migrant warblers including Blackcap, Willow Warbler, Garden Warbler and Nightingale. Spotted Flycatcher. Raptors include Buzzard, Sparrowhawk and Goshawk. Winter thrushes.
Other notable flora and fauna: Bluebells and spring flowers. Butterflies, including silver-washed fritillary and elusive white admiral. Adders can be seen on the ride side. Good range of fungi. Fallow deer.

Contact: Phone RSPB on 01929 553 360; e-mail: garston.wood@rspb.org.uk

5. HAM COMMON LNR

Poole Borough Council.
Location: Sat nav: BH15 4L (for Hamworthy Pier). SY 980 902. W of Poole. In Hamworthy, take the Blandford Road S along Lake Road, W along Lake Drive and Napier Road, leading to Rockley Park. Park in the beach car park by Hamworthy Pier or Rockley Viewpoint car park, off Napier Road, opposite the entrance to Gorse Hill Central Park.
Access: Open all year. Not suitable for coaches.
Facilities: Toilets at Lake Drive car park near Hamworthy Pier at eastern end of reserve.
Habitats: 32-acre LNR consisting of damp and dry heathland, scrub, reedbeds, freshwater lake. Views over Wareham Channel and Poole Harbour.
Key birds: *Spring/summer:* Stonechat, Dartford Warbler. *Winter:* Brent Goose, Red-breasted Merganser, occasional divers, rarer grebes, Scaup. Waders inc Whimbrel, Greenshank and Common Sandpiper. *All year:* Little Egret.
Other notable flora and fauna: Up to 34 species of butterfly, 25 dragonflies and all six British reptile species.
Contact: Poole Borough Council, 01202 265 265; e-mail: environment@poole.gov.uk
http://www.boroughofpoole.com/environment/countryside/ham-common-nature-reserve/

6. LODMOOR NATURE RESERVE

RSPB (South West England Office).
Location: Sat nav: DT4 7SX (Country Park). SY 688 809. Adjacent Lodmoor Country Park, NE of Weymouth, off A353 to Wareham.

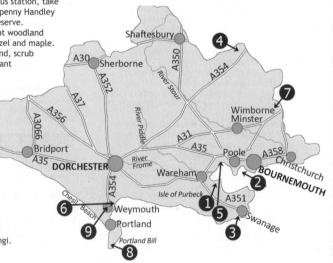

Access: Free entry at all times.
Facilities: One viewing shelter, Three nature trails mostly accessible to wheelchairs. No visitor centre or toilets. Three pay-and-display car parks. Blue Badge spaces at Country Park.
Public transport: Nearest bus stop (without shelter) Preston Beach Road, 300 m away. Buses 4/4b, 31 and X53. Details from First Buses: 0870 0106 022.
Habitats: Marsh, shallow pools, large reedbed and scrub, remnant saltmarsh.
Key birds: *All year:* Little Egret, Kingfisher, Cetti's Warbler, Bearded Tit. *Spring/summer:* Large tern colony, warblers (including Reed, Sedge, Grasshopper), Hobby. *Winter:* Wildfowl, waders, Bittern, Marsh Harrier. *Passage:* Waders (inc Black-tailed Godwit, Green and Wood Sandpipers) and other migrants.
Contact: Nick Tomlinson, RSPB Visitor Centre, Swannery Car Park, 01305 778 313;
e-mail:weymouth.reserves@rspb.org.uk

7. MOORS VALLEY CP & RINGWOOD FOREST

East Dorset Council/Forestry Commission.
Location: Sat nav: BH24 2ET. On Horton Road, Ashley Heath.Two miles W of Ringwood, well-signposted from Ashley Heath roundabout (junction of A31 and A338) between Ringwood and St Leonards.
Access: Open every day (except Dec 25) 8am-8pm (June to Aug), 5pm close Sept to March. Visitor centre open 9am to 4.30pm daily. Many trails wheelchair friendly.
Facilities: Visitor centre, toilets, tea-room, country shop. Coach parking. Way-marked trails are in good condition. Pay-and-display car parks (free for Blue Badge holders).
Public transport: Wilts and Dorset No 38 bus service stops at Castleman Trailway — one mile walk to visitor centre (01988 827 005) or visit: www.wdbus.co.uk
Habitats: River, wet meadow, lakes, scrub, broad-leaved woodland, large coniferous forest, golf course.
Key birds: *Spring/summer:* Cuckoo, Nightjar, Sand Martin, Tree Pipit, Whitethroat. Occasional Woodlark, Sedge Warbler. *Winter:* Teal, Pochard, Gadwall, Snipe, Redpoll. Occasional Brambling, Goosander. *Passage:* Whimbrel, Common Sandpiper, waders. *All year:* Buzzard, Lapwing, Woodcock, Little Owl, Grey Wagtail, Kingfisher, Dartford Warbler, Crossbill, usual woodland species.
Other notable flora and fauna: 20 species of dragonfly. Good numbers of butterflies and other invertebrates. Roe deer, muntjac, badger, fox, rabbit, grey squirrel, adder, slow worm.

Contact: Moors Valley Country Park, 01425 470 721, e-mail: moorsvalley@eastdorset.gov.uk
www.moors-valley.co.uk

8. PORTLAND BIRD OBSERVATORY

Portland Bird Observatory (registered charity).
Location: Sat nav: DT5 2JT. SY 681 690. Six miles S of Weymouth beside the road to Portland Bill.
Access: Open at all times. Parking only for members of Portland Bird Observatory. Self-catering accommodation for up to 20. Take own towels, sheets, sleeping bags.
Facilities: Displays and information, toilets, natural history bookshop, equipped kitchen.
Public transport: Bus service from Weymouth (First Dorset Transit Route 1).
Habitats: World famous migration watchpoint. Scrub and ponds.
Key birds: *Spring/autumn:* Migrants, including many rarities. *Summer:* Breeding auks, Fulmar, Kittiwake. Large numbers of Mediterranean Gulls at Ferrybridge, plus wide range of seabirds. A total of 355 species recorded.
Contact: Martin Cade, 01305 820 553;
e-mail: obs@btinternet.com
www.portlandbirdobs.org.uk

9. RADIPOLE LAKE

RSPB (South West England Office).
Location: Sat nav: DT4 7TZ. SY 671 804. In Radipole Park Drive, Weymouth. Enter from Swannery car park (pay-and-display) on footpaths.
Access: Visitor centre and nature trail open every day, summer (9am-5pm), winter (9am-4pm). Hide open (8.30am-4.30pm). Permit (available from visitor centre) required by non-RSPB members. Dogs on leads.
Facilities: Network of paths, one hide, one viewing shelter (both wheelchair-friendly). Information centre contains café and disabled toilets.
Public transport: Reserve is 400m from train station serving London and Bristol.
Habitats: Lake, reedbeds.
Key birds: *Winter:* Wildfowl (many Pochard), Water Rail, Bittern, pre-roost gatherings of Pied Wagtails. *Spring/summer:* Hirundines arrive. Breeding reedbed warblers (including Cetti's), Bearded Tit, passage waders and other migrants. Garganey regular in spring while Hobbies hunt later in season. Good for rarer gulls.
Contact: Nick Tomlinson, RSPB Visitor Centre, Swannery Car Park, Weymouth, DT4 7TZ. 01305 778 313; e-mail: weymouth.reserves@rspb.org.uk

Somerset

EXTENSIVE habitat restoration work since the 1980s has boosted bird breeding success in the Somerset Levels and Common Cranes hatched at Slimbridge are being released in the area. Somerset is attractive to wildfowl and waders in autumn and winter thanks to a mild climate and its link to the Bristol Channel.

1. BREAN DOWN

National Trust (North Somerset).
Location: Sat nav: TA8 2RR. ST 290 590. 182 map. 100m high promontory jutting into Bristol Channel five miles N of Burnham-on-Sea. From junction 22 of M5, head for Weston-super-Mare on A370 and then head for Brean at Lympsham.
Access: Open all year (free of charge). Dogs on lead. Steep slope not recommended for wheelchair-users.
Facilities: Café/shop at bottom of Brean Down. Toilet (disabled) at café.
Public transport: Call Tourist Information Centre for details 01934 888 800 (bus services differ in winter/summer).
Habitats: Extension of the Mendips' hard limestone, featuring calcareous grassland, scrub and steep cliffs.
Key birds: *All year:* Peregrine, Raven. *Summer:* Blackcap, Garden Warbler, Whitethroat, Stonechat. *Winter:* Curlew, Shelduck, Dunlin on mudflats. *Passage:* Skuas, shearwaters, divers, Gannet, gulls, waders and passerines.
Other notable flora and fauna: Chalkhill blue, marbled white and commoner butterflies. Extremely rare white rock rose in June. Somerset hair grass, dwarf sedge.
Contact: The National Trust, 01934 844 518; e-mail: breandown@nationaltrust.org.uk

2. BRIDGWATER BAY NNR

Natural England (Dorset and Somerset Team).
Location: ST 270 470. Five kilometres N of Bridgwater and extends to Burnham-on-Sea. Take junction 23 or 24 off M5. Turn N off A39 at Cannington and take minor roads to car park at Steart.
Access: Hides open every day except Dec 25. Permits needed for Steart Island (by boat only). Dogs on leads. Disabled access to hides only by arrangement, other areas accessible.
Facilities: Car park, interpretive panels and leaflet dispenser at Steart — follow footpath approx 0.5 miles to tower hide and five other hides at mouth of River Parrett. No toilets within reserve.
Public transport: Train and bus stations in Bridgwater. First Group buses on A39 stop at Stockland Bristol, 2km SW of Steart (www.firstgroup.com).
Habitats: Parrett River estuary, intertidal mudflats, saltmarsh totalling 2,559ha.
Key birds: *All year:* Approx 200 species recorded on this Ramsar and SPA site. Wildfowl includes large population of Shelduck (Europe's second largest moulting ground with up to 2,000 birds in July) and nationally important numbers of Wigeon. Internationally important numbers of Whimbrel and Black-tailed Godwit. Resident Curlews, Avocets and Oystercatchers joined by many other waders on passage. Good for birds of prey. *Spring/autumn:* Passage migrants, including occasional vagrants. *Winter:* Raptors inc Peregrine, harriers and Short-eared Owls. Large numbers of waders and wildfowl.
Other notable flora and fauna: Saltmarsh flora. Rare invertebrates include great silver water beetle, aquatic snail and hairy dragonfly.
Contact: Senior Reserves Manager, Natural England, 0300 060 2570, www.naturalengland.org.uk

3. CATCOTT COMPLEX NATURE RESERVES

Somerset Wildlife Trust.
Location: Five reserves — Catcott Lows, North, Heath, South and Fen — now managed together. ST 400 414 (Catcott Lows). Access from Catcott Broad Drove (Sat nav TA7 8NQ), approx one mile N of Catcott village (off A39 from junction 23 of M5).
Access: Open at all times.
Facilities: Car park at reserve entrance. River Parrett Trail passes through reserve. Two hides at Catcott Lows (one wheelchair-accessible).
Public transport: None.
Habitats: Wet meadows with winter flooding and summer grazing.
Key birds: *Winter:* Wigeon, Teal, Pintail, Shoveler, Gadwall, Bewick's Swan, Peregrine and other raptors. Siskins and Redpolls in alders. *Spring:* Nationally important numbers of roosting Whimbrels, plus passage Greenshank, Ruff and Black-tailed Godwits. *Summer:* Breeding Lapwing, Snipe, Redshank, Yellow Wagtail, warblers. *All year:* Little Egret, Kingfisher, Cetti's Warbler, Reed Bunting.
Other notable flora and fauna: Otter, roe deer, great crested newt, rare dragonflies, threatened saw sedge.
Contact: Somerset Wildlife Trust. 01823 652 400; e-mail: enquires@somersetwildlife.org

4. CHEW VALLEY LAKE

Avon Wildlife Trust/Bristol Water Plc.
Location: Sat nav: BS40 6HN (AWT reserve at Herriott's Pool). ST 570 600. Nine miles S of Bristol. Take B3114 south from Chew Stoke, bear L for West Harptree and head NE on A368. View reserve from causeway at Herriott's Bridge where there is car parking.
Access: Roadside viewing at Herons Green Bay. Permit needed for access to hides (five at Chew, two at Blagdon) — apply to Bristol Water, Recreation Department, Woodford Lodge, Chew Stoke, Bristol BS18 8SH. Tel/Fax 01275 332 339. Parking for coaches available.
Facilities: Grebe Trail (1.2km long) has hard surface suitable for wheelchairs. Unsurfaced Bittern Trail (1.5km) leads to hide but can be muddy. No dogs on this section. Chew tea-shop open 10.30am to 5.30pm

(mid-March to Oct 31; 4.30pm close for rest of year).
Public transport: Traveline, 0870 6082 608.
Habitats: Largest artificial lake in SW England with important reedbed.
Key birds: More than 270 species recorded – often attracts rarities. *Winter and passage*: Wildfowl include important numbers of Shoveler, Gadwall, Teal and Tufted Duck. Large numbers of Goosander, Great Crested Grebe and Cormorant, with the grebe numbers often the highest in Britain in autumn. Plus Bewick's Swan, Goldeneye, Smew, Ruddy Duck. Huge winter gull roost (up to 50,000+), mostly Black-headed, Common and Mediterranean Gull. *Summer*: Breeding Great Crested and Little Grebes, Gadwall, Tufted Duck, Shoveler, Pochard, Reed Warbler. Hobbies in late summer. When the water level is low, mud can attract waders such as Dunlin, Ringed Plover and Green Sandpiper.
Other notable flora and fauna: Ruddy darter and migrant hawker dragonflies.
Contact: Avon Wildlife Trust HQ or Bristol Water Recreation Dept, 01275 332 339;
e-mail: mail@avonwildlifetrust.org.uk
www.avonwildlifetrust.org.uk

5. DUNKERY & HORNER WOOD NNR

National Trust.
Location: Sat nav: TA24 8HY. SS 920 469 (Horner Wood). On northern boundary of Exmoor, 7km south of Minehead. Take A39 W to a minor road 0.8km E of Porlock signposted to Horner. Park in village car park.
Access: Open all year. Car parking in Horner village, West Luccombe and Webber's Post, 150 miles of footpaths. Webber's Post circular walk suitable for wheelchairs. Rugged terrain to reach Dunkery Beacon.
Facilities: Tea-room and toilets. Walks leaflets available from Selworthy shop on Selworthy Green. Interpretation boards in car parks.
Public transport: First Group bus between Porlock and Minehead passes close to reserve.
Habitats: Ancient oak woodland, moorland covering 1,604ha.
Key birds: *Spring/summer*: Wood Warbler, Pied Flycatcher, Redstart, Stonechat, Whinchat, Tree Pipit, Dartford Warbler possible. *All year*: Dipper, Grey Wagtail, woodpeckers, Buzzard, Sparrowhawk.
Other notable flora and fauna: Woodland holds 14 of the UK's species of bat. Silver-washed and heath fritillary butterflies.
Contact: National Trust, 01643 862 452; e-mail: holnicote@ nationaltrust.org.uk
www.nationaltrust.org.uk

6. GREYLAKE

RSPB (South West England Office).
Location: Sat nav: TA7 0JD (Othery). ST 399 346. Off A361 Taunton to Glastonbury road, between Othery and Greinton.
Access: Open all year, dawn to dusk, free admission. Guide-dogs only. Wheelchair users can access a 700 metre-long boardwalk and viewing hide.
Facilities: Information centre, but no toilets or catering facilities. Two nature trails (only one surfaced), interpretive signs. Hide on easy-access trail, viewing screen on reedbed loop trail. No toilets.
Public transport: Bus No 29 (First Group) stops one mile along main road at Greinton phone box, but drivers may stop at reserve on request. Hatch Green No 16 bus from Bridgwater makes request stops.
Habitats: A large wet grassland reserve bought by RSPB in 2003. Formerly arable farmland.
Key birds: *Spring/summer*: Kingfisher, Grey Heron, Little Egret and breeding Garganey, Snipe, Lapwing, Redshank, Skylark, Meadow Pipit, Yellow Wagtail. *Autumn*: Green Sandpiper, waders on passage. *Winter*: Waders, wildfowl (including Lapwing, Golden Plover, Shoveler, Pintail, Teal and Wigeon). Peregrine, Hen Harrier.
Other notable fauna: Roe deer, water vole, stoat, otter, dragonflies including four-spotted chaser.
Contact: Site Manager, 01458 252 805;
e-mail: greylake@rspb.org.uk
www.rspb.org.uk/reserves/guide/g/greylake

7. HAM WALL

RSPB (South West England Office).
Location: Sat nav: BA6 9SX. ST 449 397. W of Glastonbury. From A39 turn N in Ashcott and follow road onto the moor. After three miles pass Church Farm Horticultural building. Shortly after, at metal bridge, reserve is opposite side of road to Shapwick Heath NNR.

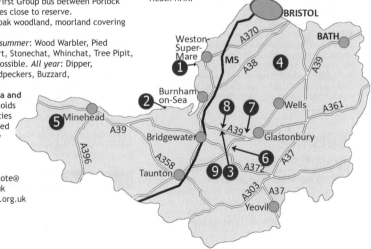

Access: Open all year. 2m height restriction on car park. Coach parking available at Avalon Marshes Centre, Shapwick Road. Dogs only on public footpaths and disused railway line. Wheelchair users can access viewing areas from main track (use RADAR key). Other rougher tracks cover 3.8 miles.
Facilities: Two open-air viewing platforms, five roofed viewing screens and one raised hide. Height-restricted car park in Ashcott Road (shared with Natural England). Two nature trails.
Public transport: By bus: Service to St Mary's Road, Meare (approx 1.2 miles from reserve entrance).
Habitats: 200-plus hectare wetland, including region's largest reedbed.
Key birds: *All year:* Bittern (first breeding in county for 40 years), Cetti's Warbler, Water Rail, Barn Owl. *Spring/summer:* Migrant warblers, hirundines, Hobby, Whimbrel, sandpipers. *Autumn:* Migrant thrushes, Lesser Redpoll, Siskin, Kingfisher, Bearded Tit. *Winter:* Million-plus Starling roost, plus large flocks of ducks, Bittern, Little Egret, Peregrine, Merlin, Short-eared Owl.
Other notable flora and fauna: Otter, roe deer, water vole, dragonflies, butterflies.
Contact: RSPB Ham Wall 1458 860 494;
e-mail: ham.wall@rspb.org.uk

8. SHAPWICK MOOR

Hawk and Owl Trust.
Location: Sat nav: BA6 9TT (Peat Moors Centre). ST 417 398. On Somerset Levels. From J23 on M5 take A39 towards Glastonbury, after 6 miles turn N onto minor road, signed Shapwick. Continue straight over crossroads, through Shapwick village, towards Westhay, turn L at T-junction following signs for Peat Moors Centre, park here. Reserve is about half way between centre and Shapwick village.
Access: Open all year (except Dec 25). Access only along public footpaths and permissive path. Dogs on leads only.
Facilities: Information panels. Public toilets at nearby Avalon Marshes Centre (ST 425 414), none on site.
Public transport: Train to Bridgwater, then First Bus (01278 434 574) No 375 Bridgwater-Glastonbury, to Shapwick village. Sustrans National Route 3 passes through Shapwick village.
Habitats: A wet grassland reserve covering 134 acres. Grazing pasture, hay meadows with rough grass edges, fen, open ditches, pollard willows and hedges.

Key birds: *Spring/summer:* Hobby, Barn Owl, Reed Bunting and Cetti's Warbler. Whimbrel and other waders on passage. Passerines such as Skylark, Bullfinch, Greenfinch and Yellowhammer. *Autumn/winter:* Flocks of finches, Snipe, Shoveler, Gadwall, Stonechat, Brambling. Peregrine and harriers may fly over. *All year:* Buzzard, Kestrel, Sparrowhawk, Kingfisher, Lapwing, Grey Heron, Mute Swan.
Other notable fauna: Roe deer, brown hare, stoat, badger, otter and water vole.
Contact: Hawk and Owl Trust, 0844 984 2824;
e-mail: enquiries@hawkandowl.org
www.hawkandowl.org

9. SWELL WOOD

RSPB South West England Office).
Location: Sat nav: TA3 6PX. ST 360 238. Reserve lies 11 mile E of Taunton. From A378 Langport road, take minor road one mile E of Fivehead.
Access: Swell Wood car park and heronry hide open all year (dawn to dusk). Coach parking in lay-by across main road. Heronry hide and part of woodland trail are wheelchair accessible.
Facilities: Heronry hide, two nature trails: Scarp Trail (only path accessible to dogs) links to public footpaths, disabled parking area.
Public transport: First Group Somerset & Avon bus 54 from Taunton stops at Swell — take Scarp Trail to reserve. WebberBus 38/37 accessible to wheelchairs and will make request stop.
Habitats: Semi-natural ancient oak woodland and views across wet grassland from woodland trails. Part of the Somerset Levels and Moors.
Key birds: Largest heronry in SW England with up to 100 pairs of Grey Herons and small number of Little Egrets. *Spring/summer:* Breeding Buzzard, Bullfinch, Spotted Flycatcher, Song Thrush, warblers such as Chiffchaff, Blackcap and Garden Warbler. *On escorted walks:* Curlew, Snipe, Sedge Warbler, Yellow Wagtail, Skylark, Nightingale. *Autumn:* Green Woodpecker, Robin, Wren, Coal Tit. *Winter:* Long-tailed Tit, Treecreeper, Great Spotted Woodpecker, Nuthatch.
Other notable flora and fauna: Roe deer, dormouse, woodland flora such as bluebells, wood anemone, lesser celandine, plus dragonflies, damselflies, butterflies.
Contact: Site Manager, 01458 252 805;
e-mail: swell.wood@rspb.org.uk

Wiltshire

WILTSHIRE'S position away from the coast limits its range of birds but the Wildlife Trust maintains more than 40 reserves throughout the county. The chalk downlands of Marlborough Downs and the extensive Salisbury Plain are internationally threatened habitats. The Army's use of Salisbury Plain limits human access which helps birds, and for this reason the area has been selected for the experiment to re-introduce Great Bustards to Britain.

LANGFORD LAKE

Wiltshire Wildlife Trust.
Location: Sat nav: SP3 4PA. SU 037 370. Nr Steeple Langford, S of A36, approx eight miles W of Salisbury. In centre of village, turn S into Duck Street,

signposted Hanging Langford. Langford Lakes is first L just after a small bridge.
Access: Opened to the public in Sept 2002. Main gates open during the day — ample parking. Advance notice required for coaches. No dogs.
Facilities: Visitor centre, toilets, education centre. Four hides, all accessible to wheelchairs. Cycle stands provided (250m from Wiltshire Cycleway between Great Wishford and Hanging Langford).
Public transport: Nearest bus stop 500m - X4 Service between Salisbury and Warminster.
Habitats: Four former gravel pits, with newly created islands and developing reed fringes. 12 ha (29 acres) of open water; also wet woodland, scrub, chalk river. Great Meadow wetland opened in 2012.
Key birds: More than 150 species recorded. *Summer*: Breeding Coot, Moorhen, Tufted Duck, Pochard, Gadwall, Little Grebe, Great Crested Grebe. Also Kingfisher, Common Sandpiper, Grey Wagtail, warblers (8 species). *Winter*: Common Wildfowl, sometimes also Bittern, Wigeon, Shoveler, Teal, Water Rail, Little Egret, Bittern. *Passage*: Sand Martin, Green Sandpiper and other waders, Black Tern.
Other notable flora and fauna: Otter, water vole, water shrew. Spawning salmon and trout in river.
Contact: Wiltshire Wildlife Trust, Devizes, 01380 725670; e-mail: info@wiltshirewildlife.org

RAVENSROOST WOOD COMPLEX

Wiltshire Wildlife Trust.
Location: Sat nav: SN16 9RL. SU 023 877 (Ravensroost Wood car park). NW of Swindon. Take B4696 Ashton Keynes road N from Wootton Bassett. After two miles take second turn L to Minety. Go straight on when main road turns R. Go straight over next crossroads and car park is on R after quarter mile.
Access: Wood connects to Ravensroost and Avis Meadows, Distillery and Warbler Meadows and all sites are open at all times.
Facilities: Small car park, small shelter.
Habitats: Woodland, both coppice and high oak forest, and ponds. Surrounding meadows rich in wildflowers.
Key birds: Breeding Willow Warblers, Blackcap, Chiffchaff and Garden Warblers. In winter mixed flocks of Nuthatches, tits and Treecreepers move noisily through the wood and Woodcock can be flushed from wet, muddy areas.
Other notable flora and fauna: Butterflies include silver-washed fritillary and white admiral. Good display of spring bluebells, wood anemone, wood sorrel, sanicle, violet and primrose. In summer, common spotted, early purple and greater butterfly orchids, hemp agrimony and betony.
Contact: Wiltshire Wildlife Trust, Devizes, 01380 725670.
e-mail: info@wiltshirewildlife.org
www.wiltshirewildlife.org

SAVERNAKE FOREST

Savernake Estate Trustees.
Location: Sat nav: SN8 3HP. From Marlborough the A4 Hungerford road runs along side of forest. Two pillars mark Forest Hill entrance, 1.5 miles E of A346/A4 junction. The Grand Avenue leads straight through the middle of the woodland to join a minor road from Stibb.
Access: Privately owned but open all year to public. Visitors can drive along main avenues, but all roads are closed on first working day of the year.
Facilities: Car park, picnic site at NW end by A346. Only enter fenced-off areas if there is a footpath.
Habitats: Ancient woodland, with one of the largest collections of veteran trees in Britain. Beech avenue (4 miles in length) longest in UK. Designated SSSI for its lichens and fungi.
Key birds: *Spring/summer*: Garden Warbler, Blackcap, Willow Warbler, Chiffchaff, Wood Warbler, Redstart, occasional Nightingale, Tree Pipit, Spotted Flycatcher. *Winter*: Finch flocks possibly inc Siskin, Redpoll, Brambling and Hawfinch. *All year*: Sparrowhawk, Buzzard, Red Kite, Woodcock, owls, all three woodpeckers, Marsh Tit, Willow Tit, Jay and other woodland birds.
Other notable flora and fauna: Rare lichens and fungi, all main deer species, badgers, foxes.
Contact: Savernake Estate: 01672 512 161; e-mail: savernakeestate@hotmail.com
www.savernakeestate.co.uk

SWILLBROOK LAKES

Hills Group/Wiltshire Wildlife Trust
Location: Sat nav: SN16 9QA. SU 018 934. NW of Swindon. Also known as Lakes 46 and 48 of Cotswold Water Park. From A419 Swindon to Cirencester road, turn L onto Cotswold Water Park Spine Road. Cross B4696 South Cerney/Ashton Keynes road, take next L, Minety Lane, after about 1.5 miles. Park in gateway either side of road, after about 0.5 miles. Swillbrook Lakes nature reserve and information board is on E side of road.
Access: Open at all times. Adjacent to Clattinger Farm, a Wilts Wildlife Trust reserve.
Facilities: Footpath along N and E sides of lakes. Nearest toilets in Keynes Country Park.
Habitats: Gravel pits with shallow pools, rough grassland and scrub around edges.
Key birds: *Winter*: Wildfowl (inc. Gadwall, Pochard, Smew, Goosander, Goldeneye). *Summer*: Breeding Nightingale, Garden, Reed and Sedge Warblers, Blackcap, Cetti's Warbler, Sand and House Martins, Swallow. One of the best sites for Hobby and Nightingale in Cotswold WP.
Other notable flora and fauna: 13 species of dragonfly including downy emerald and lesser emperor in recent years.
Contact: www.waterpark.org

Scottish Border Counties

Borders, Dumfries & Galloway

Borders

OFTEN overlooked as birders head for the Highlands, counties in the Borders do have many good sites for birds. St Abb's Head holds a large summer seabird colony, while migrants move past in spring and autumn. Ospreys have recently moved into the area and can often be seen fishing at Duns Castle. Water Rails breed at Yetholm Loch, which is also good for wildfowl.

1. BEMERSYDE MOSS

Scottish Wildlife Trust.
Location: NT 614 340. Located eight miles E of Melrose. From here head S on A48 to St Boswells, then take B6404 across the Tweed into minor road to Maidenhall. At T-junction turn right and reserve is half mile ahead.
Access: Open at all times. Limited parking in lay-by on southern edge of loch.
Facilities: Boardwalk leads to wheelchair-friendly bird hide.
Habitats: Long narrow strip of marsh, willow scrub and open water.
Key birds: Breeding birds include Black-necked Grebe, Lapwing, Curlew, Spotted Flycatcher, Tree Sparrow, Yellowhammer, Reed Bunting, Grasshopper Warbler and up to 15,000 pairs of Black-headed Gulls. Good range of wintering wildfowl including large numbers of Wigeon and Greylag Goose.
Other notable flora and fauna: Otter, water vole.
Contact: SWT headquarters, 01313 127 765. www.scottishwildlifetrust.org.uk

2. DUNS CASTLE RESERVE

Scottish Wildlife Trust.
Location: Sat nav: TD11 3NW. NT 778 550. Duns lies W of Berwick-upon-Tweed. From town centre head N on Castle Street and North Castle Street. Alternatively drive N on A6112 for one mile and turn left on B6365 to car park on northern edge of reserve.
Access: Reserve covering 400 acres open all year.
Facilities: Network of well-marked paths, some suitable for wheelchair access.
Habitats: Two man-made lochs (Hen Poo and Mill Dam) and woodland.
Key birds: Woodland birds such as Green and Great Spotted Woodpeckers, Goldcrest and Redstart (summer), waterfowl.
Other notable flora and fauna: Red squirrel, roe deer, occasional otter. Woodland rich in wild flowers.
Contact: SWT headquarters, 01313 127 765. www.scottishwildlifetrust.org.uk

3. ETTRICK MARSHES

Forestry Commission/Borders Forest Trust.
Location: Sat nav: TD7 5HU (Honey Cottage caravan park). Sited in Ettrick Valley, off B7009, approx 16 miles SW from Selkirk.
Access: Open at all times. Best access from Honey Cottage car park.
Facilities: Three car parks, network of footpaths and board walk. Can be flooded after heavy rain.
Habitats: Floodplain mosaic of woodland, wetland, grass and open water of national conservation importance covering 125ha.
Key birds: Eighty species recorded. Goosander, Kingfisher, Buzzard, Crossbill and Dipper seen all year, with occasional Goshawk and Osprey. Summer species include Redstart, Sedge Warbler and Sand Martin.
Other notable flora and fauna: Red squirrel, otter. Moths and plants at northern edge of range.
Contacts: Borders Forest Trust 01835 830 750; enquiries@bordersforesttrust.org

4. GUNKNOWE LOCH AND PARK

Scottish Borders Council.
Location: Sat nav: TD1 3RP. NT 518 345. At Tweedbank, 3.2km from Galashiels on the A6091. Park at Gunknowe Loch or Abbotsford House visitor centre.
Access: Open all year. Surfaced paths suitable for wheelchair use.
Facilities: Car park, information boards, paths in park. Visitor centre, café and toilets at Abbotsford House.
Public transport: Tweedbank is on the Melrose-to-Peebles bus route.
Habitats: River, man-made loch, parkland, scrub, woodland.
Key birds: *Spring/summer:* Grey Wagtail, Kingfisher, Sand Martin, Blackcap, Sedge and Grasshopper Warblers. *Passage:* Yellow Wagtail, Whinchat, Wheatear. *Winter:* Thrushes, Brambling, Wigeon, Tufted Duck, Pochard, Goldeneye. *All year:* Great Spotted and Green Woodpeckers, Redpoll, Goosander,

possible Marsh Tit.
Contact: Ranger Service 01835 825 060.
www.scotborders.gov.uk

5. ST ABBS HEAD

National Trust for Scotland.
Location: Sat nav: TD14 5QF. NT 913 674 (car park) for car park and bus stop. Lies five miles N of Eyemouth. Follow A1107 from A1.
Access: Reserve open all year. All-ability path to viewpoint at Starney Bay. Well behaved dogs welcome; please ensure droppings are taken home. Coach parking at Northfield Farm by prior arrangement.
Facilities: Visitor centre and toilets (inc disabled) open daily Apr-Oct.
Public transport: Nearest rail station is Berwick-upon-Tweed, bus service from Berwick.
Habitats: Cliffs, coastal grasslands and freshwater loch.
Key birds: *Apr-Aug:* Seabird colonies with large numbers of Guillemot and Kittiwake; also Shag, Razorbill, Fulmar. *Apr-May and Sept-Oct:* Good autumn seawatching.
Other notable flora and fauna: Common rock-rose, purple milk-vetch, spring sandwort. Northern brown argus butterfly.
Contact: Liza Cole, Ranger's Office, 01890 771 443. www.nts.org.uk, www.stabbrangers.blotspot.com and St Abb's Head NNR page on Facebook

Dumfries and Galloway

THE SOLWAY holds nationally important numbers of wintering Barnacle Geese, with WWT Caerlaverock and RSPB Mersehead being prime sites. Ospreys and Red Kites are colonising and there is a chance of a Golden Eagle over upland areas or Hen Harrier on moorland. The Mull of Galloway has fine seabird cliffs, while the Ken/Dee Marshes hold Willow Tit and Nuthatch.

6. CAERLAVEROCK WETLAND CENTRE

The Wildfowl & Wetlands Trust.
Location: Sat nav: DG1 4RS. NY 051 656. Overlooks the Solway. From St Michael's church in Dumfries take B725 towards Bankend, following tourist signs. Also signposted from A75 W of Annan.
Access: Open daily (10am-5pm), except Dec 25. Charge for non-WWT members. Assistance dogs only.
Facilities: 20 hides, heated observatory, four towers, Salcot Merse Observatory, sheltered picnic area. Self-catering accommodation and camping facilities. Nature trails in summer. Old Granary visitor building; coffee shop serving light meals and snacks; bookshop; optics for sale. Theatre/conference room. Binoculars for hire. Parking for coaches.
Public transport: Bus 6A from Dumfries stops 30 mins walk from reserve. Stagecoach 01387 253 496.
Habitats: Saltmarsh, grassland, wetland.
Key birds: *Winter:* Wildfowl esp. Barnacle Geese

(max 40,000), Pink-footed Geese and Whooper Swans. *Summer:* Osprey (web-cam on nest), Barn Owl, Skylark, Tree Sparrow, migrant warblers.
Other notable flora and fauna: Natterjack toad, badger, tadpole shrimp, bats. Northern marsh, common spotted and twayblade orchids.
Contact: WWT Caerlaverock, 01387 770 200; e-mail: info.caerlaverock@wwt.org.uk; wwt.org.uk

7. CROOK OF BALDOON

RSPB (Scotland).
Location: NX 442 530. Four miles south of Wigtown. From Wigtown, head south along the A714. Go through Bladnoch, then take the minor road to the left (at the Penkiln Sawmill sign); follow this road straight down to the Crook of Baldoon car park – ignore left hand turns along this road.
Access: Open at all times. Dogs under close control. Site not currently suitable for disabled.
Facilities: Car park and picnic tables.
Public transport: None.
Habitats: Saltmarsh, wet grassland (other wetland features under development).
Key birds: *Winter:* Pink-footed Goose, Barnacle Goose, Golden Plover, Curlew, Lapwing, Hen Harrier, Peregrine Twite. *Summer:* Lapwing, Redshank, Skylark, Osprey, Linnet, Wheatear.
Other notable flora and fauna: Thrift, sea-lavender.
Contact: Crook of Baldoon, 01988 402 130; e-mail: crookofbaldoon@rspb.org.uk.

8. KEN-DEE MARSHES

RSPB (Scotland).
Location: Sat nav: DG7 2NJ. NX 699 684. Six miles from Castle Douglas. Off the A762 (N of Laurieston) or B795 (at Glenlochar), parking at the Mains of Duchrae.
Access: From car park at entrance to Mains of Duchrae farm. Open during daylight hours. Dogs must be under close control.
Facilities: Two hides (one is wheelchair-accessible), viewing platform, nature trails. Three miles of trails available, limited parking for elderly and disabled next to first hide. Part of Red Kite trail.
Public transport: None.
Habitats: Marshes, woodlands, open water.
Key birds: *All year:* Mallard, Grey Heron, Buzzard, Nuthatch, Willow Tit. *Spring/summer:* Lapwing and Curlew nest on farmland. Pied Flycatcher, Redstart, Tree Pipit, Sedge Warbler. *Winter:* Greenland White-fronted and Greylag Geese, raptors (Hen Harrier, Peregrine, Merlin, Red Kite).
Other notable flora and fauna: Red squirrel, roe deer, otter.
Contact: RSPB Ken-Dee Marshes, 01988 402 130. www.gallowaykitetrail.com

9. MERSEHEAD

RSPB (Scotland).
Location: Sat nav: DG2 8AH. NX 928 566. From

Dumfries take A710 S for about 16 miles. Reserve is signposted from New Abbey and then on L just before Caulkerbush village. Single track road with passing places runs for a mile to car park, adjacent to visitor centre. From Castle Douglas, take A745, then A711 to Dalbeattie. Follow signs from Dalbeattie before joining A710.
Access: Wheelchair-friendly hides and trails open at all times.
Facilities: Visitor centre with viewing room, refreshments and toilets (open 10am to 5pm). Blue Badge parking spaces within 400m of hides and 20m from visitor centre.
Public transport: None.
Habitats: Wet grassland, arable farmland, saltmarsh, inter-tidal mudflats.
Key birds: *Winter:* Up to 9,500 Barnacle Geese, 4,000 Teal, 2,000 Wigeon, 1,000 Pintail, waders (inc. Dunlin, Knot, Oystercatcher). *Summer:* Breeding birds include Lapwing, Redshank, Skylark.
Other notable flora and fauna: Natterjack toad.
Contact: RSPB Mersehead, 01387 780 579; e-mail: mersehead@rspb.org.uk

10. MULL OF GALLOWAY

RSPB (Scotland).
Location: Sat nav: DG9 9HP. NX 156 305. Most southerly tip of Scotland – follow brown signs for five miles from village of Drummore, S of Stranraer.
Access: Open at all times. Blue Badge parking by centre. No wheelchair access to foghorn viewing platform overlooking seabird colonies or circular trail. Centre open between Apr-Oct.
Facilities: Visitor centre, toilets, nature trails, CCTV on cliffs. Small shop at neighbouring Gallie Craig café (not RSPB).
Public transport: None.
Habitats: Sea cliffs, coastal heath.
Key birds: *Spring/summer:* Guillemot, Razorbill, Kittiwake, Black Guillemot, Puffin, Fulmar, Raven, Wheatear, Rock Pipit, Twite. Migrating Manx Shearwater. *All year:* Peregrine.

Contact: RSPB Mull of Galloway, 01988 402 130; e-mail: mullofgalloway@rspb.org.uk

11. WIGTOWN BAY LNR

Dumfries & Galloway Council.
Location: Sat nav: DG8 9JH. NX 465 545. Between Wigtown and Creetown, S of Newton Stewart. The A75 runs along E side, with A714 S to Wigtown and B7004 providing superb views of the LNR.
Access: Reserve open at all times. The hide is disabled-friendly. Main accesses: Roadside lay-bys on A75 near Creetown and parking at Martyr's Stake and Wigtown Harbour. All suitable for coaches. Visitor Centre in Wigtown County Building has coach parking plus full disabled access, including lift and toilets.
Facilities: Hide at Wigtown Harbour overlooking River Bladnoch, saltmarsh and fresh water wetland has disabled access from harbour car park. Another hide at Martyr's Stake car park. CCTV of Ospreys breeding in Galloway during summer and wetland birds in winter. Open Mon-Sat 10am-5pm, later some days; Sun 2pm-5pm.
Public transport: Travel Information Line 08457 090 510 (local rate 9am-5pm Mon-Fri). Bus No 415 for Wigtown and W side. Bus No 431 or 500 X75 for Creetown and E side.
Habitats: The largest LNR in Britain at 2,845hr features an estuary with extensive saltmarsh/merse and mudflats plus a freshwater wetland at Wigtown Harbour.
Key birds: *Winter:* Internationally important for Pink-footed Goose, nationally important for Curlew, Whooper Swan and Pintail, with major gull roost and other migratory coastal birds. Small Twite flock. *Summer:* Breeding Osprey, Peregrine, waders and duck.
Other notable flora and fauna: Fish including smelt and shad. Lax-flowered sea-lavender, sea aster.
Contact: Visitor Centre 01988 402 673, Keith Kirk, Countryside Ranger, 01556 505 479, (M)07850 157 661; e-mail:keith.kirk@dumgal.gov.uk
www.dgcommunity.net/wblr

Central Scotland

Argyll, Ayrshire, Clyde, Fife, Forth, Lothian

Argyll

TWO ISLANDS take the birding honours for this region. Islay is renowned for its wintering wildfowl, including huge numbers of Barnacle and White-fronted Geese. Choughs, raptors and Corncrakes are other island specialities. The island of Mull is home to the highest breeding densities of Golden Eagle and White-tailed Eagles in Britain.

1. COLL RESERVE

RSPB (Scotland)
Location: Sat nav: PA34 4LW (Oban harbour). NM 167 563. By ferry from Oban to island of Coll. Take the B8070 W from Arinagour for five miles. Turn R at Arileod. Continue for about one mile. Park at end of the road. Reception point at Totronald.
Access: Open all year. A natural site with unimproved

paths not suitable for wheelchairs. Please avoid walking through fields and crops.
Facilities: Car park, information bothy at Totronald, guided walks in summer. Corncrake viewing bench.
Public transport: None.
Habitats: Sand dunes, beaches, machair grassland, moorland, farmland.
Key birds: *Spring:* Great Northern Diver offshore. Corncrakes arrive in late April. Displaying waders, inc Redshank, Lapwing, Snipe. *Summer:* Auks offshore, plus Gannet, shearwaters and terns. *Autumn:* Barnacle and Greenland White-fronted Geese arrive, thrushes on passage. Waders inc Purple Sandpiper. *Winter:* Long-tailed Duck, divers offshore. Hunting Hen Harrier and Merlin. Twite.
Other notable flora and fauna: Good for ceteceans and basking shark. Otter, 300-plus machair wildflowers inc rare orchids, great yellow bumblebee.
Contact: RSPB Coll Nature Reserve, 01879 230 301.

2. LOCH GRUINART, ISLAY

RSPB (Scotland)
Location: Sat nav: PA44 7PR. NR 275 672. Sea loch on N coast of Islay, seven miles NW from Bridgend.
Access: Two hides and trails with viewpoints open all hours. Visitor centre open daily (10am-5pm), disabled access to south hide, viewing area and toilets. Assistance required for wheelchair users. Car parking at centre and start of trails. Coach parking at visitor centre only. No dogs in hides please. On trails dogs must be kept under close control.
Facilities: Toilets (inc disabled), visitor centre (offers hot drinks), two hides, two trails. Trails car park, opposite the viewpoint, is level and made from rolled stone. Group bookings accepted. Weekly guided walks every Thursday at 10am (April to Oct)
Public transport: Nearest bus stops 3 miles from reserve.
Habitats: Lowland wet grasslands, sea loch, farmland, moorland.
Key birds: *Oct-Apr:* Large numbers of Barnacle and White-fronted Geese, plus other wildfowl and waders. *May-Aug:* Breeding and displaying waders and Corncrake. *Sept-Nov:* Many passage migrants and arriving wildfowl. Birds of prey are present all year, esp Hen Harrier and Peregrine, while Chough can be seen feeding in nearby fields. *Spring:* Displaying Snipe, Lapwing, Curlew and Redshank.
Other notable flora and fauna: Otter, red and roe deer. Marsh fritillary butterflies during May and June.
Contact: RSPB Scotland, 01496 850 505;
e-mail: loch.gruinart@rspb.org.uk;

3. MACHRIHANISH SEABIRD OBSERVATORY

Nancie Smith/ Eddie Maguire (sponsored by SNH).
Location: Sat nav: PA28 6PY. NR 628 209. Southwest Kintyre, Argyll. Six miles W of Campbeltown on A83, then B843.
Access: Daily April-Oct. Wheelchair access. Dogs welcome. Parking for three cars. Digiscoping facilities

include electricity and monitor.
Facilities: Seawatching hide, toilets in nearby village. Coach parking.
Public transport: Regular buses from Campbeltown (West Coast Motors, tel 01586 552 319).
Habitats: Marine, rocky shore and upland habitats.
Key birds: *Summer:* Golden Eagle, Peregrine, Storm Petrel and Twite. *Autumn:* Passage seabirds and waders. On-shore gales often produce inshore movements of Leach's Petrel and other scarce seabirds, including Balearic Shearwater, Sabine's Gull and Grey Phalarope. *Winter:* Great Northern Diver, Purple Sandpiper, Ruddy Turnstone with occasional Glaucous and Iceland Gulls.
Other notable flora and fauna: Grey and common seals, otter, wild goat.
Contact: Eddie Maguire, Warden, 07919 660 292;
e-mail: machrihanishbirds@btinternet.com
www.machrihanishbirdobservatory.org.uk/

4. MULL EAGLE WATCH

RSPB Scotland/Forestry Commission Scotland/SNH/ MICT/Police Scotland.
Location: NM 480 303 (rendezvous point). New watchpoint on northern shore of Loch Scridain, in the western part of Mull.
Access: Visitors will follow ranger in own cars from rendezvous point roughly 0.5km up the Forestry Commission Scotland track at Glen Seilisdeir off B8035 Salen/Kinloch scenic route. Booking places on trips is essential. Charge for all adults except Mull residents, under-16s half price. Trips run at 10am and 1pm Monday to Friday (March 25 to autumn).
Facilities: Purpose-built hide for observing nesting White-tailed Eagles. No toilet facilities.
Habitats: Large sea loch with tidal mudflats at its head (Loch Beg).
Key birds: Apart from the White-tailed Eagles, other raptors in the area include Golden Eagle, Hen Harrier and Buzzard. In winter and early spring it is possible to see three species of diver, Slavonian Grebe, Red-breasted Merganser and Eider in the loch. Otter sightings are common here. Waders can be seen on muddy areas at any time of year.
Contact: To book a trip call the Visit Scotland Information Centre, Craignure on 01680 812 556.

Ayrshire

A RUGGED coastline, combined with river valleys and inland woodland means Ayrshire has many potentially good birding opportunities, though its best known site is the island of Ailsa Craig, which boasts a huge gannetry, together with plenty of other breeding seabirds. Don't miss Martnaham Loch (good for wildfowl and a range of common species) or Turnberry Point (seawatching, plus Twite). The shore at Barassie and Troon sees a large build-up of waders in autumn, plus white-winged gulls in winter.

5. AILSA CRAIG

RSPB (Scotland).
Location: NX 020 998. Island is nine miles offshore, nearest town on mainland is Girvan.
Access: Accessible only by boat: MFV Glorious (tel: 01465 713 219) or Kintyre Express (tel: 01294 270 160) from Girvan during summer. Also from Campbeltown by Mull of Kintyre Seatours' fast rib (07785 542 811).
Facilities: None.
Public transport: None.
Habitats: Volcanic plug (338metres high) provides nest sites for seabirds.
Key birds: Ailsa Craig hosts the third largest gannetry in the UK and supports 73,000 breeding seabirds, including Guillemont, Razorbill, Puffin, Black Guillemot, Kittiwake and up to 36,000 pairs of Gannets. Twite can also be found here.
Other notable flora and fauna: Slow worm.
Contact: RSPB, 0141 331 0993;
e-mail: glasgow@rspb.org.uk

6. CULZEAN CASTLE COUNTRY PARK

National Trust for Scotland.
Location: Sat nav: KA19 8LE. NS 234 103. 12 miles SW of Ayr on A719.
Access: Country Park open all year 9am to dusk. Restaurant/shops open daily (Apr-Oct) and weekends Nov-March. Access leaflet available. Admission charges for Country Park.
Facilities: Car park, visitor centre, children's playground, picnic areas, 21 miles of footpath and estate tracks, ranging from unsurfaced woodland paths to metalled roads.
Public transport: Stagecoach bus No 60 (Ayr to Girvan) stops at site entrance. One mile walk downhill to visitor centre and castle.
Habitats: Shoreline, parkland, woodland, gardens, streams, ponds.
Key birds: *All year:* Good populations of common woodland species, inc Jay, Great Spotted Woodpecker and thrushes. *Spring/summer:* Arriving migrants, esp Blackcap, Chiffchaff and Willow Warbler. Nesting Raven and Gannet on cliffs, Gannet and terns offshore. *Autumn/winter:* Regular flocks of Redwing and Fieldfare, Waxwing, crossbills. Wildfowl on pond inc Little Grebe, Tufted Duck, Goldeneye. Offshore divers and Eider.
Other notable fauna: Roe deer, otter, water vole, several species of bat. Shoreline SSSI rich in rock pool life.
Contact: Culzean Ranger Service 0844 493 2148;
e-mail: culzean@nts.org.uk

Clyde

THE FALLS OF CLYDE Scottish Wildlife Trust reserve has a well-known Peregrine watchpoint, with Dippers and Kingfishers along the river. Whinchats and several species of warbler breed at Baron's Haugh, with a good autumn passage of waders there. RSPB Lochwinnoch offers a good selection of commoner species throughout the year.

7. BARON'S HAUGH

RSPB (Scotland).
Location: Sat nav: ML1 2SG. NS 756 553. On SW edge of Motherwell, overlooking River Clyde. Use Adele Street, then lane off North Lodge Avenue.
Access: Open all year. Most paths suitable for wheelchairs, except circular nature trail, which has some steep sections.
Facilities: Four hides, information board in car park. Disabled access along some of the Clyde walkway but it is difficult due to erosion — ring for details.
Public transport: Airbles train station, with frequent services from Glasgow Central is about 15 minutes' walk. Bus 245 from Motherwell stop in Adele Street (half mile from reserve).
Habitats: Marshland, flooded areas, woodland, parkland, meadows, scrub, river.
Key birds: *Summer:* Breeding Gadwall, warblers (inc. Garden, Grasshopper); Whinchat, Common Sandpiper, Kingfisher, Sand Martin. *Autumn:* Excellent for waders (22 species). *Winter:* Whooper Swan, Pochard, Wigeon, Sparrowhawk.
Contact: RSPB, 0141 331 0993;
e-mail: baronshaugh@rspb.org.uk

8. FALLS OF CLYDE

Scottish Wildlife Trust.
Location: Sat nav: ML11 9DB (visitor centre). NS 881 423. Reserve covers both sides of Clyde Gorge from New Lanark to Bonnington Weir, approx one mile S of Lanark. From Glasgow travel S on M74 until junction 7, then along A72, following brown signs for New Lanark.
Access: Reserve open daily. From New Lanark car park, walk into village, through the iron gates and down steps to the right of the New Lanark Visitor Centre. Follow road to the Falls of Clyde Visitor Centre. Reserve terrain too steep for wheelchairs, but visitor centre is wheelchair friendly, inc toilet facilities.
Facilities: Visitor centre open daily 10am-4pm. Admission charge for non-SWT members (£3). Peregrine watch site open from Mar-Jun. Woodland trails and a range of guided walks inc self-guided, wildflower trail and badger watches.
Public transport: Scotrail trains run to Lanark. Local bus service from Lanark to New Lanark stops near reserve.
Habitats: Reserve stretches along both sides of an ancient gorge, with waterfalls, meadow and wet woodland.
Key birds: Over 100 species of birds, unrivalled views of breeding Peregrines. Others inc Kingfisher, Dipper, Jay, Spotted Flycatcher and Goosander.
Other notable flora and fauna: Badgers, otters, bats and wildflowers.
Contact: Falls of Clyde Visitor Centre 01555 665 262;
e-mail: fallsofclyde@swt.co.uk www.swt.org.uk

NATURE RESERVES - CENTRAL SCOTLAND

9. LOCHWINNOCH

RSPB (Scotland).
Location: Sat nav: PA12 4JF.
NS 358 582. 18 miles SW of Glasgow,
adjacent to A760 Largs Road, off the
A737 (Irvine Road). Leave
M8 at junction 28A.
Access: Open every day
except Christmas and
Boxing Day, Jan 1 and Jan
2. (10am-5pm).
Facilities: Visitor centre,
tea-room, shop, binocular hire.
Two trails, one two hides and toilets
all accessible to disabled visitors.
Public transport: Rail station
adjacent, bus services on A737 more
than half-mile from reserve.
Habitats: Shallow lochs, marsh, mixed
woodland.
Key birds: *Winter:* Wildfowl (esp. Whooper Swan,
Wigeon, Goosander, Goldeneye and occasional
Smew). Hen Harrier and Kingfisher regular. *Passage:*
Occasional migrants inc. Whimbrel, Greenshank.
Summer: Breeding Great Crested Grebe, Water Rail,
Sedge and Grasshopper Warblers, Reed Bunting.
Other notable fauna: Possible otters, roe deer, small
mammals, butterflies, moths and dragon/damselflies.
Contact: RSPB Nature Reserve Centre, 01505 842
663; e-mail: lochwinnoch@rspb.org.uk
www.rspb.org.uk/lochwinnoch

Fife

WINTERING flocks of seaducks off Ruddons Point
often hold a few Surf Scoters among the more
numerous Common and Velvet Scoters, while Fife
Ness is good for seawatching and autumn migrants.
The Eden Estuary holds good numbers of wildfowl
and waders throughout the year but especially
in winter. Tentsmuir offers an unusual mix of
woodland and coastal habitats.

10. EDEN ESTUARY LNR

Fife Coast and Countryside Trust.
Location: Sat nav: KY16 0UJ. NO 447 191 (centre of
site). Reserve centre off main street in Guardbridge,
two miles from St Andrews on A91, and from Leuchars
via Tentsmuir Forest off A919 (4 miles). Use Outhead
at St Andrews, off West Sands beach, to access
Balgove Bay.
Access: Eden Estuary Centre, Guardbridge (keypad
number available from ranger service) open 9am to
5pm all days except Dec 25, 26, 31 and Jan 1. Evans
Hide: at GR 483 183, parking at Pilmuir Links golf
course car park. Combination number required from
ranger service.
Facilities: Visitor centre at Guardbridge. Viewing
platform and picnic area at Outhead. Evans Hide at
Balgove Bay (number from Ranger Service).
Public transport: Leuchars train station (1.5 miles),

regular bus service from Cupar and
Dundee. Tel 08457 484 950.
Habitats: Intertidal mudflats, saltmarsh,
river, reed, sand dunes and wetland covering
891ha. Scotland's third oldest reserve.
Key birds: *Winter and passage:* Significant numbers
of waders and wildfowl. Outer estuary good for
seaduck such as scoters, Eider and Long-tailed Duck,
plus Gannet, terns and skuas. Mudflats ideal for
godwits, plovers, sandpipers, Redshank and Shelduck.
River good for Kingfisher, Common Sandpiper and
Goosander. Surrounding area attracts Short and Long-
eared Owls, Peregrine, Marsh Harrier, White-tailed
Eagle and Merlin. Osprey are regular visitors.
Other notable flora and fauna: Northern marsh
orchid, dune grasses and herbs. Harbour and grey
seal, bottle-nosed dolphin, porpoise, brown hare,
stoat and otter. Butterflies include comma, grayling,
small pearl-bordered, dark green fritilliary, painted
lady and orange tip.
Contact: Ranald Strachan, Fife Ranger Service, 01592
656 080, 07985 707 593.
e-mail: Ranald.Strachan@fifecountryside.co.uk

11. ISLE OF MAY NNR

Scottish Natural Heritage.
Location: NT 655 995. Small island lying six miles off
Fife Ness in the Firth of Forth.
Access: Boats run from Anstruther and North Berwick.
Contact SNH for details on 01334 654 038. Keep
to paths. Those using Observatory accommodation
should note delays are possible, both arriving and
leaving, because of weather.
Facilities: No dogs; no camping; no fires. Prior
permission required if scientific work, photography or
filming is to be carried out.
Public transport: Regular bus service to Anstruther
and North Berwick harbour.
Habitats: Sea cliffs, rocky shoreline.
Key birds: *Early summer:* Breeding auks, gulls and
terns, Kittiwake, Shag, Eider, Fulmar. Over 45,000
pairs of Puffins. *Autumn/spring:* Weather-related
migrations include rarities each year.
Contact: For accomodation: www.isleofmaybirdsobs.

185

org or contact Jonathan Osbourne, The Shieling, Halcombe Crescent, Earlston, Berwickshire TD4 6DA; e-mail: jonathan@osbourn108.fsnet.co.uk. For all other enquiries: SNH, 01463 725 000; www.nnr-scotland.org

Forth

CAMBUS POOLS attracts passage waders and winter wildfowl, while high tide at Kinneil produces good numbers of waders in spring and autumn. The RSPB reserve at Inversnaid is good for Black Grouse, Twite, Redstart, Wood Warbler and Pied Flycatcher. There are large movements of finches and thrushes in autumn. A Red Kite feeding station at Argaty provides visitors with close-up views.

12. CAMBUS POOLS

Scottish Wildlife Trust.
Location: Sat nav: FK10 2PG. NS 846 937. From Stirling, take A907 east towards Alloa. From a roundabout drive 0.6 miles to where the B9096 leads off to Tullibody. Take the minor road (Station Road) right to the small village of Cambus.
Access: Cross River Devon by bridge at NS 853 940 and walk down stream on R bank past bonded warehouses. Open all year. Best viewing around high tide.
Facilities: Bench on S side of western pool.
Public transport: None.
Habitats: Wet grazed grassland, reedbeds and two salty pools.
Key birds: Used extensively by migrants in spring and autumn, inc. wildfowl (Mute and Whooper Swans, Goldeneye, Teal, Shelduck) and waders such as Black-tailed Godwit, Oystercatcher and Greenshank. Gadwall have bred here and Kingfisher is seen regularly. Small birds inc Yellowhammer and Reed Bunting.
Other notable flora and fauna: Brown hare, stoat, short-tailed vole, 115 species of vascular plants. Harbour porpoise seen in Forth.
Contact: SWT headquarters, 01313 127 765. www.scottishwildlifetrust.org.uk/reserve/cambus-pools

Lothian

THOUGH coastal locations usually grab the headlines, the Lammermuir Hills hold a range of upland species. More than 250 species have been recorded at Aberlady Bay, including many thousands of geese in winter. The Seabird Centre at North Berwick is a great place to interest young children, or take a boat out to the gannetry at Bass Rock, while Ferny Ness sees a build-up of Red-necked Grebes in late summer.

13. ABERLADY BAY LNR

East Lothian Council.
Location: Sat nav: EH32 0QB. NT 472 806. From Edinburgh take A198 E to Aberlady. Reserve car park is 1.5 miles E of Aberlady village.

Access: Britain's first ever Local Nature Reserve is open at all times. Please stay on footpaths to avoid disturbance. Disabled access from reserve car park. No dogs please.
Facilities: Small car park and toilets. Notice board with recent sightings at end of footbridge. SOC HQ, Waterston House, located W of Aberlady village. Includes shop, library, hot and cold drinks.
Public transport: First Bus (Edinburgh to N Berwick services 124 X24 and X25 stop close to reserve (request). Nearest train station 4 miles away at Longniddry.
Habitats: Tidal mudflats, saltmarsh, freshwater marsh, dune grassland, scrub, open sea.
Key birds: *Summer:* Breeding birds include Shelduck, Eider, Reed Bunting and up to eight species of warbler. Passage waders inc. Green, Wood and Curlew Sandpipers, Little Stint, Greenshank, Whimbrel, Black-tailed Godwit. *Winter:* Divers (esp. Red-throated), Red-necked and Slavonian Grebes and geese (up to 15,000 Pinkfeet roost); sea-ducks, waders.
Contact: John Harrison, Reserve Warden: e-mail: jharrison@eastlothian.gov.uk; www.aberlady.org

14. BASS ROCK/ SCOTTISH SEABIRD CENTRE

Location: NT 605 875. Island NE of North Berwick. Scottish Seabird Centre is located in North Berwick Harbour (EH39 4SS).
Access: Island is private property. Regular daily sailings from N Berwick or Dunbar around Rock between April and September; local boatman has owner's permission to land individuals or parties by prior arrangement (3 hours on island). Cheaper non-landing trips by boat or RIB (rigid inflatable boat) around Bass Rock and Craigleath run from Mar 29 to Oct.
Facilities: Café, shop, aquaria, telescope deck and toilets at Seabird Centre. No facilities on Bass Rock.
Habitats: Sea cliffs.
Key birds: The spectacular cliffs hold a massive Gannet colony, (with up to 150,000 birds it's the largest in the world), plus Puffin, Guillemot, Razorbill, Kittiwake, Shag, Arctic Tern and Fulmar.
Contact: For details of boat trips call 01620 892 838 or The Scottish Seabird Centre 01620 890 202; e-mail: info@seabird.org www.seabird.org

15. BAWSINCH RESERVE & DUDDINGSTON LOCH

Scottish Wildlife Trust.
Location: Sat nav: EH15 3PX. NT 284 725. Two miles from centre of Edinburgh, below Arthur's Seat. Use car park on Duddingston Road West and Holyrood Park Gate.
Access: Open access to north shore of loch and cavalry ground to SE — best views from Hangman's Rock. Remainder of site and hide only open by prior arrangement with SWT.
Facilities: Hide (SWT members only) with bird and plant lists.
Public transport: Call SWT on 0131 312 7765 for advice.

Habitats: Edinburgh's only natural freshwater loch. Reedbed, marsh, ponds, mixed woodland, flower meadow and scrub. Bawsinch reserve developed from former industrial wasteland.
Key birds: Heronry. Important site for breeding swans, geese, ducks, grebes and Water Rail. *Summer:* Migrants, inc Spotted Flycatcher, hirundines,

warblers, inc occasional Grasshopper Warbler. *Winter:* Roosting wildfowl, gulls and Bittern.
Other notable flora and fauna: Fox, water vole and otter. Damselfly, four species of amphibian.
Contact: SWT headquarters, 01313 127 765.
www.scottishwildlifetrust.org.uk/reserve/bawsinch-and-duddingston

---

Eastern Scotland

Angus & Dundee, Moray & Nairn, NE Scotland, Perth & Kinross

Angus & Dundee

THE ANGUS glens hold a typical range of upland species, including Ring Ouzel, grouse, chats and Golden Eagle. Ospreys fish regularly at RSPB Loch of Kinnordy, while Montreathmont Forest is a mix of coniferous and broadleaved woodland. Montrose Basin is a flagship Scottish Wildlife Trust reserve, with a good selection of wildfowl ever present and waders on passage.

1. LOCH OF LINTRATHEN

Scottish Water/Scottish Wildlife Trust.
Location: Sat nav: DD8 5JH. NO 278 550. Located next to Bridgend of Lintrathen, seven miles W of Kirriemuir. Take B951 and choose circular route on unclassified roads round loch.
Access: Two public hides (one on eastern side of loch is wheelchair-accessible) open 24 hours a day. Rest of reserve is private, but good views possible from unclassified roads.
Facilities: Viewpoint can accommodate five cars. Roadside parking at NO 276 557 off a minor road W of loch. Forest track leads to hide. Second hide (wheelchair accessible) on E side of loch.
Public transport: None.
Habitats: Oligotrophic-mesotrophic loch designated a Ramsar site and SPA because of its value to waterbirds. Surrounded by mainly coniferous woodland in the foothills of Braes of Angus.
Key birds: *Summer:* Grey Heron, Great Crested Grebe and other water birds. Osprey seen occasionally. *Winter:* Internationally-important numbers of Icelandic Greylag Geese (up to 3,000), plus Pink-footed Goose, Goosander, Whooper Swan, Wigeon, Teal and other wildfowl. Birds feed on surrounding farmland during day.
Other notable fauna: Red squirrel, pipistrelle bat.
Contact: Robert Potter, Reserves Manager North East, SWT, 01575 540 396; (M)07920 468 568; e-mail: rpotter@swt.org.uk

2. MONTROSE BASIN LNR

Scottish Wildlife Trust/Angus Council.
Location: Sat nav: DD10 9TA. NO 702 565 (Wildlife

SWT Centre on A92). 1.5 miles from centre of Montrose. Main car park for western end at the Old Mill, Mains of Dun (NN 669 591).
Access: Pick up site map at Visitor Centre, open March 1 to Oct 31 (10.30am to 5pm, 7 days per week) and from Nov 1 to -Feb 28 (10.30am-4pm, Fri, Sat and Sun only). Admission: £4 Adults, £3 Concessions, £7.50 families, SWT members free. Several hides open at all times.
Facilities: Visitor centre, gift shop, fair-trade tea, coffee and snacks, toilets, disabled access to centre, two hides on western half of reserve.
Public transport: Train 1.5 miles in Montrose. Bus stop outside Visitor Centre.
Habitats: Estuary, saltmarsh, reedbeds, farmland.
Key birds: Internationally important for Pink-footed Goose (up to 40,000 arrive Oct), Knot and Redshank. Wintering wildfowl and waders (Curlews at peak numbers in Aug, Dunlin in Feb). Breeding terns, gulls, Shelduck, Goldeneye, Eider (up to 2,000), Grey Partridge in surrounding fields.. Nationally important moulting site for Mute Swan (approx 300 birds).
Contact: Montrose Basin Wildlife Centre, 01674 676 336; e-mail: montrosebasin@swt.org.uk

Moray & Nairn

YEAR-ROUND variety is on offer here, with Lochindorb the best area of moorland to explore, with grouse, raptors, divers and waders all breeding. Roseisle Forest holds Crested Tits and opens out onto Burghead Bay which is superb in winter for seaducks, divers and grebes. Spey Bay can be explored from either side of the river and attracts passage waders, terns, Ospreys, seabirds and wildfowl.

3. CULBIN SANDS

RSPB (Scotland).
Location: Sat nav: IV12 5LF. NH 900 576. Approx 1.5 miles NE of Nairn, overlooking Moray Firth. Use East Beach car park, signed off A96. Follow road through Maggot Road caravan park.
Access: Open at all times. 750m path to Minster's Pool suitable for all abilities.
Facilities: Toilets (inc disabled) and bike racks at car

park. Track along dunes and saltmarsh.
Public transport: Buses stop in St Ninian's Road, Nairn, one mile W of site. Call Rapsons on 0870 608 2608 or Stagecoach on 01862 892 683. Train station in Nairn 1.5 miles W of reserve.
Habitats: Saltmarsh, sandflats, dunes.
Key birds: *Winter*: Flocks of Common Scoter, Long-tailed Duck, Knot, Bar-tailed Godwit, Red-breasted Merganser. Raptors including Peregrine, Merlin and Hen Harrier attracted by wader flocks. Roosting geese, Snow Bunting flocks. *Spring:* Tern flock, esp Sandwich, passage waders. *Summer:* Breeding Eider, Ringed Plover, Oystercatcher. Osprey on passage.
Other notable fauna: Dolphins in Firth. Otters sometimes seen.
Contact: RSPB North Scotland Office, 01463 715 000.

4. SPEY BAY

Scottish Wildlife Trust.
Location: Sat nav: IV32 7NW. NJ 335 657. Eight miles NE of Elgin. From Elgin take A96 and B9015 to Kingston. Reserve is immediately E of village. Car parks at Kingston and Tugnet.
Access: Open all year.
Facilities: Car park, information board. Circular walk at Tugnet.
Public transport: None.
Habitats: Shingle, rivermouth and coastal habitats.
Key birds: *Summer:* Osprey, waders, wildfowl. *Winter*: Seaduck and divers offshore, esp. Long-tailed Duck, Common and Velvet Scoters, Red-throated Diver.
Other notable fauna: Otter, plus dolphin offshore. Good range of dragonflies.
Contact: Robert Potter, SWT, The Kennels, 07920 468 568; e-mail: rpotter@swt.org.uk

NE Scotland

SCOTLAND'S only mainland gannetry is at Troup Head, while RSPB Loch of Strathbeg is the main UK arrival point for Pink-footed Geese and Whooper Swans every autumn. The Ythan Estuary is good for breeding terns, Eiders, and passage and wintering waders. The interior holds typical Highlands species, with the notable exception of Crested Tit.

5. FORVIE NNR

Scottish Natural Heritage.
Location: Sat nav: AB41 8RU (visitor centre). NK 034 289. Including the Ythan Estuary, 12 miles N of Aberdeen. Waterside car park one mile N of Newburgh; visitor centre three miles N of Newburgh.
Access: Reserve open at all times but ternery closed Apr 1 to end of Aug annually. Stevenson Forvie Centre open every day (Apr-Sept) and, outside these months when staff are available. Centre, short trail and hide are wheelchair-accessible.
Facilities: Interpretive display and toilets at Stevenson Forvie Centre. Bird hide, waymarked trails. Coach parking at Waterside car park and Stevenson

Forvie Centre.
Public transport: Bluebird No 63 to Cruden Bay. Ask for the Newburgh or Collieston Crossroads stop. Tel: 01224 591 381.
Habitats: Estuary, dunes, coastal heath.
Key birds: *Spring/summer*: Breeding Eider and terns. Migrant waders and seabirds offshore. *Autumn*: Pink-footed Goose, migrant seabirds, waders and passerines inc occasional scarce species or rarity. *Winter*: Waders and wildfowl, inc Whooper Swan, Long-tailed Duck and Golden Plover.
Other notable flora and fauna: Occasional ceteceans offshore, esp in summer.
Contact: Annabel Drysdale (Reserve Manager), 01358 751 330. www.nnr-scotland.org

6. FOWLSHEUGH

RSPB (Scotland).
Location: Sat nav: AB39 2TP. NO 879 808. Reserve is three miles S of Stonehaven. From A92 take minor road signposted Crawton. Car park just before end of this road.
Access: Unrestricted. Not suitable for wheelchair users. Only assistance dogs allowed.
Facilities: Car park with 12 spaces, 200 yards from reserve. New stone-built viewing shelter at end of footpath. Nearest toilets in Stonehaven.
Public transport: Request bus stop (Stonehaven to Johnshaven route). Mile walk to reserve entrance.
Habitats: Sea cliffs.
Key birds: Spectacular 130,000-strong seabird colony, mainly Kittiwake and Guillemot plus Razorbill, Fulmar and Puffin. Gannet, Eider and skuas offshore, Peregrine regular throughout year. *Autumn*: Red-throated Diver on sea, terns on passage.
Other notable flora and fauna: Grey and common seals, bottle-nosed dolphin regular, white-beaked dolphin and minke whale occasional in summer. Spring flowers, common butterflies and moths.
Contact: RSPB Fowlsheugh Warden, 01346 532 017; e-mail: strathbeg@rspb.org.uk

7. HADDO COUNTRY PARK

Aberdeenshire Council.
Location: Sat nav: AB41 7EQ. NJ 875 345. On the A90 Aberdeen-Peterhead road. After Bridge of Don, turn on to the B999. Continue to Tarves for about 20km and pick up signs for Haddo House.
Access: Grounds open during daylight hours all year. Car park charges April to September.
Facilities: Car parks, display boards, more than 5,000m of surfaced paths, toilets open all year (inc disabled) and bird hides with wheelchair access. Coach parking.
Public transport: Bus: Aberdeen-Tarves stop 3.2km from house. Call Stagecoach on 01224 212 266.
Habitats: Parkland, woodland, wetland, loch, ponds.
Key birds: *Spring/summer*: Osprey, Sedge Warbler, Blackcap, Chiffchaff, Lapwing. *Winter*: Canada and Greylag Geese, Teal, Wigeon, Goldeneye, Goosander, Brambling. *All year*: Buzzard, Sparrowhawk, Grey

NATURE RESERVES - EASTERN SCOTLAND

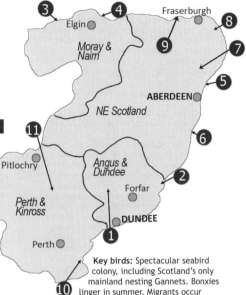

Partridge, Great Spotted Woodpecker, Goosander, Grey Wagtail, Tawny Owl, herons, Cormorant. **Other notable flora and fauna:** Meadow brown, ringlet and common blue butterflies. Fauna includes red squirrels, otters and pipistrelle and Daubenton's bats.
Contact: David Brown, Aberdeenshire Council Ranger Service, 01358 726 417.
e-mail: formartine.ranger@aberdeeshire.gov.uk

8. LOCH OF STRATHBEG

RSPB (Scotland).
Location: Sat nav: AB43 8QN. NK 057 581. Britain's largest dune loch is near Crimond on the A90, nine miles S of Fraserburgh. Reserve signposted from village.
Access: Visitor Centre open daily 9am to 5pm, dusk if earlier.
Facilities: Visitor centre, with toilets and coffee machine. New Willow Hide short walk from centre. Tower Pool hide accessible via 700 metre footpath. Two hides overlooking loch accessed via drive to airfield. Wildlife garden, indoor children's area. Long beach walks from St Combs.
Public transport: Access to whole reserve difficult without vehicle. Buses from Fraserburgh and Peterhead to Crimond, one mile from centre. Details at www.travelinescotland.com.
Habitats: Dune loch with surrounding marshes, reedbeds, grasslands and dunes.
Key birds: Breeding wetland species, passage waders, internationally important numbers of wintering wildfowl. Scarcities year round. Winter: Pink-footed and Barnacle Geese, Whooper Swan, large numbers of duck. Snow Goose and Smew annual. Raptors including Hen and Marsh Harriers. Great Northern Diver offshore. Summer: Common Tern, Water Rail, Corn Bunting. Spring/autumn: Spoonbill, Avocet, Marsh Harrier, Garganey, Little Gull, regular Pectoral Sandpiper. Osprey (seen almost daily), Common Crane (now annual on reserve).
Other notable flora and fauna: Otter, badger, stoat, roe deer. Early purple, butterfly and northern marsh orchids, dark green fritillary butterfly.
Contact: RSPB Loch of Strathbeg, 01346 532 017; e-mail: strathbeg@rspb.org.uk www.rspb.org.uk

9. TROUP HEAD

RSPB (East Scotland).
Location: Sat nav: AB45 3JN. NJ 822 665. Troup Head is between Pennan and Gardenstown on B9031, E along coast from Macduff. It is signposted off B9031. Look for small RSPB signs which direct you to car park past the farm buildings.
Access: Unrestricted, but not suitable for wheelchairs.
Facilities: Parking for small number of cars. Not suitable for coaches. Live pictures are beamed from the reserve to the Macduff Marine Aquarium during the summer.
Public transport: None.
Habitats: Sea cliffs, farmland.

Key birds: Spectacular seabird colony, including Scotland's only mainland nesting Gannets. Bonxies linger in summer. Migrants occur during spring/autumn.
Other notable flora and fauna: Impressive common flower assemblage in spring. Cetaceans possible offshore in summer including minke whale. Brown hare common.
Contact: RSPB Troup Head Warden, 01346 532 017; e-mail: strathbeg@rspb.org.uk

Perth & Kinross

RSPB LOCH LEVEN (formerly known as Vane Farm) is the region's best known reserve and holds huge numbers of wintering geese, ducks and swans. Ospreys fish there too but the well-known watchpoint of Loch of the Lowes offers better views of birds on the nest than RSPB Loch Garten. The Hermitage at Dunkeld is good for woodland species, Dippers and raptors, possibly including Goshawk.

10. LOCH LEVEN (VANE FARM)

RSPB (Scotland).
Location: Sat nav: KY13 9LX. NT 160 990. Part of Loch Leven NNR. Seven miles from Cowdenbeath, signposted two miles E of junction 5 from M90 onto B9097. Drive for approx two miles. Car park on R.
Access: Reserve trails open at all times. Visitor centre open daily (10am-5pm) except Dec 25, 26, Jan 1 and 2. Cost £5 adults, £3 concessions, £1 children, £10 family. Free to RSPB members. Disabled access to shop, coffee shop, observation room area and toilets. Coach parking available. Free car parking. Assistance dogs only.
Facilities: Shop, coffee shop and observation room with four telescopes overlooking Loch Leven and

the reserve. There is a 1.25 mile hill trail through woodland and moorland. Wetland trail with three observation hides. Toilets, including disabled. Binoculars can be hired from shop.
Public transport: Limited bus service (Stagecoach Fife 2043) runs to the reserve from Kinross (4 miles) on Sundays. Contact Stagecoach Fife on 01592 610 686 for further details. Eight-mile cycle path around loch.
Habitats: Wet grassland and flooded areas by Loch Leven. Arable farmland. Native woodland and heath moorland.
Key birds: *Spring/summer*: Breeding and passage waders (including Lapwing, Redshank, Snipe, Curlew), hirundines, Great Crested Grebe, Osprey. Farmland birds (including Skylark and Yellowhammer), Tree Pipit. *Autumn*: Migrating waders on exposed mud. *Winter*: Major fuelling stop for Pink-footed Geese (around 20,000 in late autmn). Also Whooper Swan (6% of Scotland's wintering population), Bewick's Swan, White-tailed Eagle, finch and tit flocks.
Other notable flora and fauna: 237 butterfly and moth species. 25 mammal species including pipstrelle bat and roe deer.
Contact: RSPB Loch Leven, 01577 862 355; e-mail: lochleven@rspb.co.uk

11. LOCH OF THE LOWES

Scottish Wildlife Trust.
Location: Sat nav: PH8 0ES. NO 041 435. Sixteen miles N of Perth, two miles NE of Dunkeld, just off A923 (signposted).
Access: Admission charge for non-members of SWT. Visitor centre open daily March 1 to October 31 (10am-5pm) and Fri-Sun only for rest of year (10.30am-4pm). Observation hide open all year during daylight hours. Crannog hide accessible during visitor centre opening hours. No dogs allowed. Full access for wheelchairs.
Facilities: Visitor centre with exhibition, shop and toilets. Two hides overlooking loch.
Public transport: Railway station at Birnam and Dunkeld, three miles from reserve. Buses to Dunkeld, two miles from reserve.
Habitats: Freshwater loch fringed by areas of fen, reedbeds and semi-natural woodland.
Key birds: Breeding Ospreys (Apr-end Aug) nest 200 metres from hide. Wildfowl and woodland birds.
Other notable fauna: Red squirrels.
Contact: Caroline Hendry, (Manager), Loch of the Lowes, Visitor Centre, 01350 727 337; e-mail: lochofthelowes@swt.org.uk; www.swt.org.uk

Highlands & Islands

Highlands Orkney, Outer Hebrides, Shetland

Highlands

HABITATS found nowhere else in Britain hold a range of scarce species: Dotterel, Ptarmigan and Snow Buntings on the tops, plus Crested Tit, the endemic Scottish Crossbill and Capercaillie are in the Caledonian pine forests. The boggy Flow Country of Caithness and Sutherland attracts breeding Greenshank, Common Scoter and Red- and Black-throated Divers.

Key birds: *All year*: Golden Eagle, Scottish Crossbill, Ptarmigan, Red Grouse, Siskin. *Summer*: Black-throated Diver, Redwing, Snow Bunting. Golden Plover breed on moorland.
Other notable flora and fauna: Wide range of dragonflies, including northern emerald, golden ringed and common hawker. Red deer, pine marten, mountain hare.
Contact: Eoghain Maclean, Reserve Manager, 01445 760 254; e-mail: eoghain.maclean@snh.gov.uk

1. BEINN EIGHE & LOCH MAREE ISLANDS NNR

Scottish Natural Heritage.
Location: NG 990 620. Complex mountain massif by Kinlochewe, Wester Ross, 50 miles from Inverness and 20 miles from Gairloch on A832.
Access: Reserve (UK's oldest NNR) open at all times, no charge. Visitor centre just outside Kinlochewe open Easter-Oct (9am to 5pm).
Facilities: Visitor centre, toilets, woodland, rhyming and mountain trails (self-guided with leaflets from visitor centre). Two trails suitable for all abilities.
Public transport: Very limited.
Habitats: Caledonian pine forest, dwarf shrub heath, mountain tops, freshwater loch shore.

2. CORRIMONY

RSPB (Scotland).
Location: Sat nav: IV63 6TW (Corrimony village). NH 384 303 (car park). Lies 22 miles SW of Inverness between Glen Affric and Loch Ness, off A 831. Park in Corrimony Cairns car park.
Access: Open at all times. Waymarked trail suitable for wheelchairs. Unimproved paths, so terrain may not be suitable for disabled visitors.
Facilities: Way-marked trail (8.5 miles long) passes through farm. Please leave gates as you find them. Guided minibus safaris to see Black Grouse leks in April and May.
Public transport: No 17 bus from Inverness to Cannich stops 1.5 miles from reserve.

Habitats: Pine woodland, moorland, blanket bog covering 1,531 hectares.

Key birds: Black Grouse (more than 30 displaying males), Crested Tit, crossbill species, occasional Golden Eagle and Osprey. Breeding Greenshank, Red Grouse, Black-throated Diver. *Spring/summer:* Tree Pipit, Whinchat, Goosander. *Autumn:* Whooper Swan, Pinkfooted Goose, Woodcock.

Other notable flora and fauna: Red deer, pine marten. Many orchids in July.

Contact: RSPB North Scotland Office, 01463 715 000; e-mail: nsro@rspb.org.uk

3. FORSINARD FLOWS

RSPB (Scotland).

Location: NC 891 425. 30 miles SW of Thurso on A897. From S turn off at Helmsdale (24 miles) or from N coast road (A836) turn 2 miles E of Melvich (14 miles).

Access: Open at all times. Contact reserve office during breeding season (mid-Apr to end Jul) and during deerstalking season (Jul 1 to Feb 15) for advice. Families welcome. Two self-guided trails open all year, disabled viewpoint accessed via farm track on Forsinain Trail. No dogs on Dubh Lochan Trail.

Facilities: Visitor centre situated in Forsinaid station open Easter to Oct 31 (9am-5pm, seven days a week). Hen Harrier nest CCTV. Wheelchair access to centre and toilet. Guided walks Tue and Thu afternoon, May-Aug. Accommodation available locally. Viewpoint on Lochan Trail (not wheelchair accessible).

Public transport: Trains between Inverness and Thurso (08457 484 950) stop at Forsinard three times a day.

Habitats: Blanket bog, upland hill farm.

Key birds: The best time to visit for birds is May-July. Join a guided walk for the best chance of views of Red-throated Diver, Golden Plover, Greenshank, Dunlin, Hen Harrier, Merlin, Short-eared Owl, Dipper. Few birds between Sept-Feb apart from Red Grouse, Golden Eagle, Raven and Buzzard.

Other notable fauna: Red deer, otter,, water vole, azure hawker dragonfly, emperor moth, bog plants including sundews.

Contact: RSPB, Forsinard Flows Reserve, 01641 571 225; e-mail: forsinard@rspb.org.uk

4. HANDA

Scourie Estate/Scottish Wildlife Trust.

Location: NC 138 480. Island accessible by boat from Tarbet, near Scourie — follow A894 N from Ullapool for 40 miles. Continue another three miles, turn L down single track road another three miles to Tarbet.

Access: Open April to Aug inclusive. Boats leave 9.30am-2pm (last boat back 5pm). Dogs not allowed. Ferry tickets £12.50 (adult), £5 (child), with 20% of ticket price going to SWT. Not suitable for disabled due to uneven terrain.

Facilities: Three mile circular path, visitor shelter, compost toilet. Visitors are given introductory talk and a leaflet with map on arrival.

Public transport: Post bus to Scourie (tel 01549 402 357 Lairg Post Office). Train to Lairg (tel 0845 484 950 National Train enquiries). No connecting public transport between Scourie and Tarbet.

Habitats: Sea cliffs, blanket bog and heath, small sandy beaches and coastal grassland.

Key birds: *Spring/summer:* Biggest Guillemot and Razorbill colony in Britain and Ireland. Also nationally important for Kittiwake, Arctic and Great Skuas. Puffin, Shag, Fulmar and Common and Arctic Terns also present.

Contact: Handa Ranger, 07920 468 572; e-mail: handaranger@swt.org.uk

Ferry operators — Roger (07780 967 800) or Paul (07775 625 890).

5. INSH MARSHES

RSPB (Scotland).

Location: Sat nav: PH21 1NS. NN 775 998. In Spey Valley. From A9 take exit to Kingussie. Follow B970 S from village and then beyond Ruthven Barracks. Entrance to reserve is 1km further on. Parking close to viewpoint and opposite entrances to Lynachlaggan and Loch Insh Wood trails.

Access: Open at all times. Disabled access to the information viewpoint. Coach parking available at car park.

Facilities: Unmanned information viewpoint, two hides, three nature trails. Access for disabled to two-level viewpoint only. No toilets.

Public transport: Nearest rail station and bus stop at Kingussie (one mile).

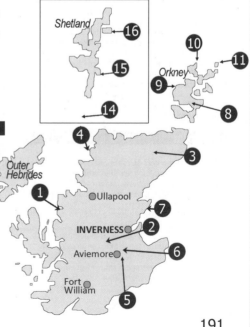

Habitats: More than 1,000 hectares of marshes, woodland, river, open water.
Key birds: *Spring/summer:* Waders (Lapwing, Curlew, Redshank, Snipe), wildfowl (including Goldeneye and Wigeon), Osprey, Wood Warbler, Redstart, Tree Pipit. *Winter:* Hen Harrier, Whooper Swan, Greylag Goose, Teal, Wigeon, other wildfowl.
Other notable flora and fauna: Black darter dragonflies along Invertromie trail plus northern brown argus butterflies. Five species of orchid in Tromie Meadow. Roe deer.
Contact: Pete Moore, 01540 661 518;
e-mail: insh@rspb.org.uk www.visitkincraig.com

6. LOCH GARTEN-ABERNETHY FOREST

RSPB (Scotland).
Location: Sat nav: PH25 3HA. NH 978 183. 2.5 miles from Boat of Garten, eight miles from Aviemore. Off B970, follow 'RSPB Ospreys' road signs (between April 1- Aug 31 only).
Access: Osprey Centre open daily 10am-6pm (Apr to end Aug). Disabled access. Guide dogs only. RSPB members free. Non-members: adults £5, concessions £3, under-16s £2. Family ticket £10 (up to 2 adults and four children). Caper watch fees: RSPB members £1, non-members £3. Dogs on leads please.
Facilities: Osprey Centre overlooking nesting Ospreys, toilets, optics and CCTV live pictures, shop, toilets. Three way-marked trails.
Public transport: Rapsons No34 bus service to Boat of Garten from Aviemore, (ask for Raebreck Junction stop), then 2.5 mile footpath to Osprey Centre. Steam railway to Boat of Garten from Aviemore.
Habitats: Caledonian pine wood.
Key birds: *Spring/summer:* Ospreys nesting from Apr to Aug, Crested Tit, Redstart, Spotted Flycatcher, Tree Pipit, crossbills. Possible views of lekking Capercaillies from the Osprey Centre (Apr to mid-May). On loch look for Goldeneye, Wigeon and Common Sandpiper. *Autumn/winter:* Pinkfeet and Greylag Geese roost on loch, Whooper Swan and various duck species.
Other notable flora and fauna: Red squirrel, roe deer, otter, woodland plants and fungi.
Contact: The Warden, 01479 831 476; e-mail: abernethy@rspb.co.uk

7. UDALE BAY

RSPB (Scotland).
Location: Sat nav: IV7 8LU. NH 712 651. On the Black Isle, one mile W of Jemimaville on the B9163.
Access: Open all year. View wader roost from lay-by. Nearest adapted unisex toilet in Allen Street, Cromarty (one mile away).
Facilities: Wheelchair-accessible hide (no dogs here), large lay-by. No coach parking.
Public transport: No 26 bus stops in Jemimaville six times a day (approx 5 min walk). contact Rapsons, 0870 608 2608 or Stagecoach on 01862 892 683.
Habitats: Mudflat, saltmarsh and wet grassland.
Key birds: *Spring/summer:* 10,000 Pinkfeet on

passage each year, other wildfowl, Oystercatcher, Redshank, waders. Possible Osprey. *Autumn/winter:* Large flocks of wildfowl (approx 10,000 Wigeon), geese, waders (Oystercatcher, Knot, Dunlin and Bar-tailed Godwit join commoner species) and Peregrine.
Contact: RSPB North Scotland Office, 01463 715 000; e-mail: nsro@rspb.org.uk

Orkney

A LACK of managed grouse moors means that Hen Harriers breed here in excellent numbers. Other scarce breeders include Whimbrels, Great and Arctic Skuas and Red-throated Divers. There are excellent seabird colonies such as the one at Marwick Head. North Ronaldsay attracts good numbers of migrants.

8. HOBBISTER

RSPB (East Scotland).
Location: Sat nav: KW17 2RA. HY 395 069 (car park) or HY 382 068 (Waukmill Bay). Overlooking Scarpa Flow 5km W of Kirkwall on A964.
Access: Open access between A964 and the sea. Dogs on leads please. Stout footwear recommended when trails are muddy.
Facilities: A council-maintained footpath to Waulkmill Bay, two car parks. New circular walk from RSPB car park along cliff top and Scapa Flow.
Public transport: Buses along A964 run five times per day. Contact the Visit Orkney on 01856 872 856 for timetables.
Habitats: Orkney moorland, bog, fen, saltmarsh, coastal cliffs, scrub.
Key birds: *Summer:* Breeding Hen Harrier, Merlin, Short-eared Owl, Red Grouse, Red-throated Diver, Eider, Red-breasted Merganser, Black Guillemot. Wildfowl and waders at Waulkmill Bay. *Autumn/winter:* Waulkmill for sea ducks, divers, auks and grebes (Long-tailed Duck, Red-throated, Black-throated and Great Northern Divers, Slavonian Grebe).
Other notable fauna: Otter occasionally seen from Scapa trail. Grey and common seal both possible from footpath looking towards Scapa Flow.
Contact: The Warden, 01856 850 176;
e-mail: orkney@rspb.org.uk

9. MARWICK HEAD

RSPB (East Scotland).
Location: Sat nav: KW17 2NB. HY 229 240. Orkney's largest cliffside seabird colony lies 4 miles N of Skara Brae on W coast of mainland Orkney, near Dounby. Path N from Marwick Bay, or from council car park at Cumlaquoy at HY 232 252 (best for Kitchener Memorial).
Access: Open all year. Rough terrain not suitable for wheelchairs.
Facilities: Cliff top path. Information board in Marwick car park.
Public transport: OCTO bus (tel: 01856 871 536)

operates a 'by request' service to all parts of the west mainland of Orkney.
Habitats: Rocky bay, sandstone cliffs. The Choin low-tide lagoon good for waders and ducks.
Key birds: May-July best for up to 25,000 seabirds. Huge numbers of Kittiwakes and auks, inc. Puffins, also nesting Fulmar, Rock Dove, Raven, Rock Pipit, Short-eared owl.
Other notable fauna: Cetaceans are a possibility from Marwick with porpoise and minke whale occasionally seen. Beach path good place for great yellow bumblebee in Aug.
Contact: The Warden 01856 850 176;
e-mail: orkney@rspb.org.uk

10. NORTH HILL, PAPA WESTRAY

RSPB (East Scotland).
Location: Sat nav: KW17 2BU. HY 495 538. From pier or airfield travel N along main road. From shop/hostel, take road N to junction at Holland Farm and turn R onto main road. Continue past Rose Cottage to reserve entrance.
Access: Access at all times. During breeding season report to summer warden at Rose Cottage, 650 yards S of reserve entrance (01857 644 240) or use trail guide (available in hide).
Facilities: Nature trail (three miles) around Mull Head, hide/info hut. Limited parking. Not suitable for wheelchairs or pushchairs.
Public transport: Orkney Ferries (01856 872 044), Loganair (01856 872 494).
Habitats: Sea cliffs, maritime heath (large by European standards).
Key birds: *Summer:* Close views of colony of Puffin, Guillemot, Razorbill and Kittiwake. Black Guillemot nest under flagstones around reserve's coastline. One of UK's largest colonies of Arctic Tern, also Arctic and Great Skuas. Breeding Lapwing, Redshank and Snipe in grazed areas. Winter: Gannet, Fulmar, Eider and winter thrushes.
Other notable flora and fauna: One of the best areas to see Scottish primrose (*primula scotica*), with two flowering periods that just overlap (May-Aug). Orcas and wahales on migration in autumn. Grey and common seals in winter.
Contact: The Warden at Rose Cottage, Papay Westray DW17 2BU. 01857 644 240 (Apr-Aug only);
e-mail: orkney@rspb.org.uk

11. NORTH RONALDSAY BIRD OBSERVATORY

Location: Sat nav: KW17 2BE. HY 64 52. 35 miles from Kirkwall, Orkney mainland.
Access: Open all year except Christmas.
Facilities: Three star guest house and hostel accommodation, restaurant, cafe, fully licenced, croft walk.
Public transport: Daily subsidised Loganair flights from Kirkwall from Mainland Orkney to North Ronaldsay. 15 minute flight gives stunning views of several islands. See Loganair website (www.loganair.co.uk/reservations/) for full information.
Habitats: Crofting island with a number of eutrophic

and oligotrophic wetlands. Coastline has both sandy bays and rocky shore. Walled gardens concentrate passerines.
Key birds: *Spring/autumn:* Prime migration site including regular BBRC species. Wide variety of breeding seabirds, wildfowl and waders. *Winter:* Waders and wildfowl include Whooper Swan and hard weather movements occur. **Contact:** Alison Duncan, North Ronaldsay Bird Observatory, 01857 633 200; e-mail: alison@nrbo.prestel.co.uk; www.nrbo.co.uk

Outer Hebrides

THESE ISLANDS are the Corncrake stronghold of Britain, though having large numbers of birds doesn't make them any easier to see! There is a strong passage of Long-tailed and Pomarine Skuas past RSPB Balranald in May. The area's ability to attract rare migrants is only just being discovered with recent autumnal trips to Barra turning up trumps.

12. BALRANALD

RSPB (Scotland).
Location: Sat nav: HS6 5DL. NF 706 707. On W coast of North Uist, three miles N of Bayhead. From Skye take ferry to Lochmaddy, North Uist. Drive W on A865 for 20 miles to reserve. Turn off main road at signpost to Houghharry.
Access: Reserve open at all times, no charge. Visitor centre open April to August (9am to 6pm). Dogs on leads. Circular walk not suitable for wheelchairs.
Facilities: Visitor Centre and toilets (disabled access). Marked circular nature trail (three miles). Group bookings welcome.
Public transport: Post bus service (01876 560 244). Caledonian MacBrayne ferries (08705 650 000).
Habitats: Freshwater loch, machair, coast and crofts.
Key birds: *Spring:* Skuas and divers at sea, Purple Sandpiper, Turnstone, Dunlin and other waders on shore. Dotterel. *Summer:* Corncrake, Corn Bunting, Lapwing, Oystercatcher, Dunlin, Ringed Plover, Redshank, Snipe, terns. *Autumn:* Hen Harrier, Peregrine, Greylag Goose. *Winter:* Twite, Snow Bunting, Whooper Swan, Greylag Goose, Wigeon, Teal, Shoveler, sightings of Golden and White-tailed Eagles becoming commoner. *Passage:* Barnacle Goose, Pomarine Skua, Long-tailed Skua.
Other notable flora: Blanket bog and machair plants reach their peak in July. Look for rare great yellow bumblebee on wildflowers Otters in freshwater lochs.
Contact: RSPB 01463 715 000;
e-mail: nsro@rspb.org.uk

13. LOCH DRUIDIBEG NNR

SNH (Western Isles Area).
Location: Sat nav: HS8 5RS. NF 782 378. Lies just N of Kildonan on South Uist. Turn off A865 in Stillgarry at B890 road for Loch Sgioport. Track is 1.5 miles further on — park at side of road.
Access: Open all year. Several tracks and one walk

covering a range of habitats — most not suitable for wheelchairs. Stout footwear essential. Observe Scottish Outdoor Access Code in all areas with livestock. View E part of reserve from public roads but parking and turning areas for coaches is limited.
Facilities: None.
Public transport: Bus stops at reserve. Hebridean Coaches 01870 620 345, MacDonald Coaches 01870 620 288.
Habitats: Covering 1,677ha, the NNR contains freshwater lochs, marshes, machair, coast and moorland.
Key birds: *Summer*: Breeding waders, Corncrake, Black-throated Diver, Greylag Goose, wildfowl, terns and raptors. *Spring and autumn*: Migrant waders and wildfowl. *Winter*: Waders, wildfowl and raptors including Golden Eagle and Hen Harrier.
Contact: SNH Area Officer, 01870 620 238; e-mail: western.isles@snh.gov.uk

Shetland

BRITAIN'S most northerly archipelago is always going to attract large numbers of vagrants, with the observatory on Fair Isle boasting a phenomenal list of species. Seabird colonies here are spectacular and include such unusual species as Leach's Petrels; an overnight stay on Mousa is the best way to catch up with this largely nocturnal species.

14. FAIR ISLE BIRD OBSERVATORY

Fair Isle Bird Observatory.
Location: HZ 2172. Famous island for rarities located SE of mainland Shetland. Regular flights to Sumburgh, Shetland. Daily Direct Flight plane between Tingwall (near Lerwick) and Fair Isle. Enquiries: 01595 840 246. Good Shepherd ferry between Shetland and Fair Isle travels on Tues, Thurs and Sat. 01595 760 363.
Access: Open from end Apr-end Oct. No access restrictions.
Facilities: Public toilets at airstrip and Stackhoull Stores (shop). Accommodation at Fair Isle Bird Observatory includes one room with wheelchair access (phone/e-mail for brochure/details). Guests can join in observatory work and see birds in the hand. Slide shows, guided walks through Ranger Service.
Public transport: Tue, Thurs, Sat — ferry (12 passengers) from Grutness, Shetland. Tel: Neil or Pat Thomson on 01595 760 363. Mon, Wed, Fri, Sat — air (7 seater) from Tingwall, Shetland. Tel: Direct Flight 01595 840 246.
Habitats: Heather moor and lowland pasture/crofting land. Cliffs.
Key birds: Large breeding seabird colonies (auks, Gannet, Arctic Tern, Kittiwake, Shag, Arctic Skua and Great Skua). Many common and rare migrants Apr/May/early Jun, late Aug-Nov.
Other notable flora and fauna: Northern marsh, heath spotted and frog orchid, lesser twayblade, small adders tongue, oyster plant. Orca, minke

whale, white-backed, white-sided and Risso's dolphins. Endemic field mouse.
Contact: Fair Isle Bird Obs, 01595 760 258; e-mail: fibo@btconnect.com; www.fairislebirdobs.co.uk

15. FETLAR

RSPB Scotland.
Location: HU 603 917. Small island lying E of Yell. Take car ferry from Gutcher on Yell to Hamarsness, then drive 6 miles E. Ferry booking advised (01957 722 259).
Access: Apart from the footpath to Hjaltadance circle, Vord Hill, the Special Protection Area is closed mid May to end July. Entry during this period is only by arrangement with warden. Rest of site open at all times. Loch of Funzie can be observed from road.
Facilities: Hide at Mires of Funzie open Apr-Nov. Toilets and payphone at ferry terminal, interpretive centre at Houbie, campsite, shop.
Public transport: None.
Habitats: Serpentine heath, rough hill lane, upland mire.
Key birds: *Summer*: Breeding Red-throated Diver, Eider, Shag, Whimbrel, Golden Plover, Dunlin, Arctic and Great Skuas, Manx Shearwater, Storm Petrel. Red-necked Phalarope on Loch of Funzie (HU 655 899) viewed from road or RSPB hide overlooking Mires of Funzie.
Other notable flora and fauna: Heath spotted orchid and autumn gentian. Otters are common, harbour and grey seals breed.
Contact: RSPB North Isles Warden, 01957 733 246; e-mail: fetlar@rspb.org.uk

16. NOSS NNR

Scottish Natural Heritage (Shetland Office).
Location: HU 531 410. Take car ferry to Bressay from Lerwick and follow signs for Noss (5km). At end of road walk to shore (600 mtrs) where inflatable ferry (passenger only) to island will collect you. If red flag is flying, island is closed due to sea conditions. Information updated daily in season on 0800 107 7818.
Access: Open Tue, Wed, Fri, Sat, Sun (10am-5pm) between late Apr-late Aug. Access by zodiac inflatable. No dogs on ferry. Steep rough track down to ferry. Commercial boat trips around island — call tourist office on 01595 693 434.
Facilities: Visitor centre, toilets. Bike rack/car park on Bressay side. Parking for small coaches.
Habitats: Dune and coastal grassland, moorland, heath, blanket bog, sea cliffs.
Key birds: *Spring/summer*: Breeding Fulmar, Shag, Gannet, Arctic Tern, Kittiwake, Herring and Great Black-backed Gull, Great Skua, Arctic Skua, Guillemot, Razorbill, Puffin, Black Guillemot, Eider, Lapwing, Dunlin, Snipe, Wheatear, Twite plus migrant birds.
Other notable fauna: Grey and common seals, otter, porpoise regularly seen, killer whales annual.
Contact: Glen Tyler, SNH, 01595 693 345;

Eastern Wales

POWYS, formed from the old counties of Breconshire, Radnorshire and Montgomeryshire, is a largely upland rural area with a limited but interesting community of birds. Raptors are prominent, with Hen Harrier, Merlin, Red Kite and Peregrine all well established, while Cors Dyfi has become a successful breeding site for Ospreys.

1. BRECHFA POOL

Brecknock Wildlife Trust.
Location: Sat nav: LD3 0NL (Llyswen). SO 118 377. Travelling NE from Brecon look for lane off A470, 1.5 miles SW of Llyswen; on Brechfa Common, pool is on R after cattle grid.
Access: Open dawn to dusk. Road runs around three-quarters of pool, giving good access.
Facilities: None.
Public transport: None.
Habitats: Marshy grassland, large shallow lake located at a height of 900ft.
Key birds: Good numbers of wintering wildfowl are replaced by breeding gulls and commoner waterfowl. Species recorded inc Teal, Gadwall, Tufted Duck, Shoveler, Wigeon, Little Grebe, Black-headed Gull, Lapwing, Dunlin, Redshank, Kestrel.
Other notable flora: Rare pillwort around pond margins, crowfoot, penny royal and orange foxtail.
Contact: Trust HQ, 01874 625 708;
e-mail: enquiries@brecknockwildlifetrust.org.uk
www.brecknockwildlifetrust.org.uk

2. CORS DYFI NATURE RESERVE

Montgomeryshire Wildlife Trust.
Location: Sat nav: SY20 8SR. SN701 985. Lies 3.5 miles SW of Machynlleth on the A487 Abersytwyth road. Approx 2.5 miles S of Derwenlas, turn right after caravan park.
Access: Open 10am to 6pm between April and Sept and at weekends for rest of year. Programme of special events in winter. Donations welcome to help fund reserve and the Dyfi Osprey Project. Site is wheelchair-accessible apart from elevated bird hide.
Facilities: Visitor centre, small café, elevated hide and toilets (inc disabled). Extensive boardwalk. £1.37 million 360 degree observatory opened in 2014.
Public transport: Nearest bus stop at Llyfnant Valley Bridge is half-mile from reserve.
Habitats: Bog, wet woodland and scrub.
Key birds: Site sprang to national prominence in 2011 when Ospreys bred successfully. *Spring/summer:* Nightjar, Grasshopper, Sedge and Reed Warblers, Snipe, Stonechat, Reed Bunting.
Other notable flora and fauna: Common lizard, four-spotted chaser dragonfly.
Contact: Trust HQ 01938 555 654;
e-mail: janine@montwt.co.uk (for Osprey enquiries).

3. ELAN VALLEY

Dwr Cymru/Welsh Water.
Location: Sat nav: LD6 5HP. SN 928 646 (visitor centre). Three miles SW of Rhayader, off B4518.
Access: Mostly open access. Pay-and-display car park with Blue Badge spaces.
Facilities: Visitor centre, cafe and toilets (open every day except Christmas Day). 10am-5.30pm (1st Mar-31st Oct), 10am-4pm (1st Nov-28th Feb). Nature trails all year and hide at SN 905 617.
Public transport: None.
Habitats: 45,000 acres of moorland, woodland, river and reservoir.
Key birds: *Spring/summer:* Upland birds including Golden Plover and Dunlin. Red Kite, Buzzard, Sparrowhawk, Peregrine, Raven, Green Woodpecker, Grey Wagtail and Marsh Tit are joined in the summer by Pied Flycatcher, Spotted Flycatcher, Wood Warbler, Redstart, Tree Pipit and Cuckoo. *Autumn/winter:* Fieldfare, Redwing, Ring Ouzel, woodpeckers and woodland species.
Other notable flora and fauna: Internationally important oak woodlands. More than 3,000 species of flora and fauna recorded.
Contact: Rangers office, 01597 810 880.
www.elanvalley.org.uk

4. GIGRIN FARM

Location: Sat nav: LD6 5BL. SN 978 676. Farm lies half a mile south of Rhayader, Powys off A470.
Access: Open for kite feeding sessions from 1pm each day, except Dec 25. Feeding at 2pm (winter) and 3pm (summer). No booking required. See website for admission charges. Dogs on leads welcome.
Facilities: Red Kite Shop, five hides (three with disabled access), plus specialist photography hides.
Habitats: 200-acre upland sheep farm rising to 1,200 feet above sea level.
Details: Brilliant views of Red Kites. For the past 20 years, Gigrin has been the official Red Kite feeding station for Wales, helping young birds survive in winter. By attracting large numbers of birdwatchers it relieves pressure on other nest sites in summer.
Key birds: Daily feeds attract a wide range of species including Carrion Crow, Raven, Jackdaw, Buzzard and Red Kite. Kite numbers vary from a few dozen to around 400 when weather is bad. Other feeding stations attract smaller birds such as Brambling, Yellowhammer and Siskin. A 1.5ml trail links to the RSPB Dyffryn reserve while a wetland area attracts wild ducks, Grey Heron and wagtails.
Contact: Chris Powell, Gigrin Farm, South Street, Rhayader, Powys LD6 5BL. 01597 810 243;
www.gigrinfarm.co.uk

5. GILFACH FARM RESERVE

Radnorshire Wildlife Trust.
Location: Sat nav: LD6 5LF (visitor centre). SN 965

NATURE RESERVES - EASTERN WALES

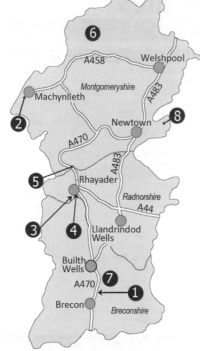

Contact: Reserve manager, 01597 870 301.
e-mail: info@rwtwales.org
www.radnorshirewildlifetrust.org.uk

6. LAKE VYRNWY

Severn Trent/RSPB Mid-Wales Office.
Location: SJ 020 193. Located WSW of Oswestry.
Nearest village is Llanfyllin on A490. Take B4393 to
Llanwddyn and at dam, turn left and left again.
Access: Reserve open all year. Severn Trent's visitor
centre open Apr-Oct (10.30am-5pm), Nov-March
(10.30am-4pm).
Facilities: Toilets, visitor centre, five colour-coded
nature trails, coffee shop, RSPB shop (open 10am to
5pm April to Oct, 4pm rest of year), craft workshops.
Three bird hides, one accessible to wheelchair users.
Public transport: Infrequent bus service to dam.
Habitats: Heather moorland, woodland, meadows,
rocky streams and large reservoir.
Key birds: *All year:* Siskin, Great Spotted
Woodpecker, Buzzard, Raven. *Spring/summer:* Hen
Harrier, Curlew, Cuckoo, Whinchat, Dipper, Kingfisher,
Pied Flycatcher, Wood Warbler, Redstart, hirundines,
Peregrine and Hobby.
Other notable flora and fauna: Mammals include
otter, polecat, brown hare. Golden-ringed dragonflies
frequent in summer.
Contact: Centre Manager, 1691 870 278;
e-mail: vyrnwy@rspb.org.uk

7. PWLL-Y-WRACH

Brecknock Wildlife Trust.
Location: Sat nav: LD3 0DS (Talgarth). SO 165 326.
From Talgarth town centre cross over River Enig, then
take Bell Street and Hospital Road. After 1.5 miles,
reserve is on the right.
Access: Reserve open all year. Please keep to
footpaths. Level, wheelchair-friendly path runs
halfway into site. Elsewhere paths can be muddy and
there are steps. Dogs allowed on leads
Facilities: Information panel in car park.
Public transport: No local services.
Habitats: 17.5 hectares of ancient woodland, river
and spectacular Witches Pool waterfall.
Key birds: Large variety of resident woodland birds,
with migrant boost in spring. Dipper, Kingfisher, Pied
Wagtail, Great Spotted Woodpecker, Chiffchaff, Wood
Warbler, Pied Flycatcher, Mistle and Song Thrushes,
Nuthatch.
Other notable flora and fauna: Otter, dormouse,
bats, common lizard. Early purple and birds' nest
orchids, herb paris, bluebell, wood anenome.
Contact: Brecknock Wildlife Trust, 01874 625 708;
e-mail: enquiries@brecknockwildlifetrust.org.uk
www.brecknockwildlifetrust.org.uk

8. ROUNDTON HILL NNR

Montgomeryshire Wildlife Trust.
Location: Sat nav: SY15 6EL. SO 293 947. SE
of Montgomery. Follow brown duck signs from
Churchstoke on A489, taking minor road towards Old

717. Gilfach is just off the A470, seven miles from
Llangurig. Follow the brown Nature Reserve signs.
The Visitor Centre is one mile across the Reserve.
Parking at Marteg Bridge, three miles N of Rhayader.
Access: Open every day, all year. Disabled access
possible to centre, toilets and purpose-built trail. Full
programme of activities – check website for details.
Facilities: Visitor centre usually open during summer
holidays and some weekends, but this depends on
availability of volunteers. Nestboxes fitted with
cameras, plus pre-recorded footage of badgers and
other mammals. Circular nature trail, short easy-
access trail. Wye Valley Walk and Gwastedyn Church
Trail also pass through reserve.
Public transport: None.
Habitats: Working organic hill farm covering 410
acres, river, oak woods, meadows, hill-land.
Key birds: Of 73 species recorded, 55 breed
regularly. These include Common Sandpiper, Dipper,
Grey Wagtail, Pied and Spotted Flycatchers, Redstart,
Wood Warbler, Tree Pipit, Whinchat, Stonechat,
Linnet, Yellowhammer, Siskin, Redpoll, Marsh and
Willow Tits, Stock Dove, Wheatear, Barn Owl, Raven.
Other visitors include: Curlew, Merlin, Red Kite,
Goshawk, Sparrowhawk, Peregrine, Goosander,
Kingfisher, Reed Bunting.
Other notable flora and fauna: Green hairstreak,
wall brown and ringlet butterflies, mountain pansy,
bloody-nosed beetle. Welsh clearwing moth first
record for Radnorshire.

Churchstoke. After one mile turn R at phone box, then first R.
Access: Open access. Tracks rough in places. Dogs on lead at all times. Uneven tracks not suitable for wheelchairs.
Facilities: Car park. Waymarked trails.
Public transport: Buses to Old Churchstoke, 600 metres from reserve.

Habitats: Ancient hill grassland, woodland, streamside wet flushes, scree, rock outcrops.
Key birds: *All year*: Buzzard, Red Kite, Raven, all three woodpeckers, Tawny Owl, Linnet, Goldfinch.
Spring/summer: Wheatear, Redstart, Whitethroat.
Contact: Trust HQ, 01938 555 654;
www.montwt.co.uk

Northern Wales
Anglesey, Caernarfonshire, Denbighshire, Flintshire, Merioneth

HIGHLIGHTS on Anglesey include a seabird colony and Choughs at South Stack, terns at Cemlyn Bay and waders at Malltraeth. RSPB Valley Lakes and Newborough Warren are all worth exploring too, while Conwy is one of the RSPB's flagship reserves. Smaller inland sites offer a good range of birds.

1. BARDSEY BIRD OBSERVATORY

Bardsey Bird Observatory.
Location: SH 11 21. Private 444 acre island. Twenty minute boat journey from Aberdaron, 15 miles SW of Pwllheli.
Access: Open Mar-Nov. No dogs. Visitor accommodation in 150-year-old farmhouse (two single, two double, two x four bed dorm). To stay at the Observatory contact Alicia Normand (tel 01626 773 908; e-mail; stay@bbfo.org.uk). Day visitors by Bardsey Ferries (07971 760 895)
Facilities: Public toilets available for day visitors. Three hides, one on small bay, two seawatching. Gift shops and payphone.
Public transport: Trains from Birmingham to Pwllheli. Tel: 0345 484 950. Arriva bus from Bangor to Pwllheli. Tel: 0870 6082 608.
Habitats: Sea-birds cliffs viewable from boat only. Farm and scrubland, spruce plantation, willow copses and gorse-covered hillside.
Key birds: *All year*: Chough, Peregrine. *Spring/summer*: Night walks to see Manx Shearwaters (16,000 pairs). Other seabirds. Migrant warblers, chats, Redstart, thrushes. *Autumn*: Masses of common migrants, plus many rarities (in past: Eye-browed Thrush, Lanceolated Warbler, American Robin, Yellowthroat, Summer Tanager).
Other notable flora: Autumn ladies' tresses.
Contact: Steven Stansfield, 07855 264 151;
e-mail: info@bbfo.org.uk; www.bbfo.org.uk

2. CEMLYN

North Wales Wildlife Trust.
Location: SH 332 936. Cemlyn on north coast of Anglesey is signposted from Tregele on A5025 between Valley and Amlwch.
Access: Open all year. Dogs on leads. No wheelchair access. During summer months walk on seaward side

of ridge and follow signs.
Facilities: Car parks at either end of reserve.
Public transport: None within a mile.
Habitats: Brackish lagoon, shingle ridge, salt marsh, mixed scrub.
Key birds: Wintering wildfowl and waders, breeding terns, gulls and warblers, pipits and passing migrants.
Spring: Wheatear, Whitethroat, Sedge Warbler, Manx Shearwater, Whimbrel, Dunlin, Knot and Black-tailed Godwit. *Summer*: Breeding Arctic, Common and Sandwich Terns, Black-headed Gull, Oystercatcher and Ringed Plover. *Autumn*: Golden Plover, Lapwing, Curlew, Manx Shearwater, Gannet, Kittiwake, Guillemot. *Winter*: Little and Great Crested Grebes, Shoveler, Shelduck, Wigeon, Red-breasted Merganser, Coot, Turnstone, Purple Sandpiper.
Other notable flora and fauna: 20 species of butterfly recorded. Sea kale, yellow horned poppy, sea purslane, sea beet, glasswort. Grey seal, harbour porpoise, bottlenose dolphin.
Contact: North Wales Wildlife Trust, 01248 351 541;
e-mail: nwwt@wildlifetrustswales.org
www.northwaleswildlifetrust.org.uk

3. CONNAH'S QUAY POWER STATION RESERVE

E.ON/Deeside Naturalists Society.
Location: Sat nav: CH5 4BP. SJ 275 715. Travel W to end of M56 which then becomes A494. Follow signposts for Flint. Take first slip road to left which joins a large roundabout and turn right onto A548. Continue straight on this road (there are several roundabouts) After crossing the River Dee take first slip road and turn right at the first roundabout and then straight on at second roundabout. Follow the signs for the power station: the reserve entrance is on the left at the next roundabout.
If approaching from the west follow A548, exiting on slip road for Connah's Quay. Turn left at roundabout and follow power station signs.
Access: Advance permit from DNS required (group bookings only). Wheelchair access. Public welcome on open days — see website for details.
Facilities: Field studies centre, five hides.
Public transport: Contact Arriva Cymru on 01745 343 492.
Habitats: Saltmarsh, mudflats, grassland scrub, open

water, wetland meadow.
Key birds: *Summer*: Small roosts of non-breeding estuarine birds. *Winter*: High water roosts of waders and wildfowl including, Black-tailed Godwit, Oystercatcher, Redshank, Spotted Redshank, Curlew, Lapwing, Teal, Pintail and Wigeon.
Other notable fauna: Seventeen species of butterfly.
Contact: Pauline Moulton, Secretary, 01244 313 404; e-mail: secretary@deesidenaturalists.org.uk www.deesidenaturalists.org.uk

4. CONWY

RSPB (North Wales Office).
Location: Sat nav: LL31 9XZ. SH 797 773. On E bank of Conwy Estuary. Access from A55 at exit 18 signposted to Conwy and Deganwy. Footpath and cycleway accessed from Conway Cob.
Access: Open daily (9.30am-5pm). Closed for Christmas Day. Ample parking for coaches. Toilets, buildings and trails accessible to pushchairs and wheelchairs.
Facilities: Visitor centre, gift shop, coffee shop, toilets including disabled. Three hides (accessible to wheelchairs) and three viewing screens. Three trails firm and level, though a little rough in places and wet in winter.
Public transport: Train service to Llandudno Junction, 10 minute walk. Bus service to Tesco supermarket, Llandudno Junction 5 minutes walk. 0871 200 2233.
Habitats: Lagoons, islands, reedbed, scrub, estuary.
Key birds: Wildfowl and waders in winter, warblers and wetland breeding birds in summer. *Spring*: Passage waders, hirundines and wagtails. *Summer*: Lapwing, waterbirds and warblers. *Autumn*: Black-tailed Godwit and other passage waders. *Winter*: Kingfisher, Goldeneye, Water Rail, Red-breasted Merganser, wildfowl, huge Starling roost.
Other notable flora and fauna: Common butterflies through summer, especially common blues. Great display of cowslips in March, bee orchids in summer. Otters seen early mornings.
Contact: Conwy RSPB Nature Reserve, 01492 584 091; e-mail: conwy@rspb.org.uk www.rspb.org.uk/conwy

5. LLYN CEFNI

Welsh Water/ Hamdden Ltd.
Location: Sat nav: LL77 7RQ (Rhosmeirch car park). A reservoir located two miles NW of Llangefni, in central Anglesey. NE section of reservoir managed as nature reserve – entrance at Rhosmeirch SH 451 783. Follow B5111 or B5109 from the village.
Access: Open at all times. Dogs allowed except in sanctuary area. Good footpath (wheelchair accessible) for most of the site, bridges over streams. Walkers can reach reservoir from Dingle nature reserve, Llangefni, on boardwalks and cycle route (one mile).
Facilities: Two picnic sites, good footpath, coach parking at Rhosmeirch car park.
Public transport: Bus 32, 4 (44 Sun only, 52 Thu only). Tel 0871 200 2233 for information.

Habitats: Large area of open water, reedy bays, coniferous woodland, scrub, carr.
Key birds: *Summer*: Sedge and Grasshopper Warblers, Whitethroat, Buzzard, Tawny Owl, Little Grebe, Gadwall, Shoveler, Kingfisher. *Winter*: Waterfowl (Whooper Swan, Goldeneye), Crossbill, Redpoll, Siskin, Redwing. *All year*: Stonechat, Treecreeper, Song Thrush.
Other notable flora and fauna: Northern marsh orchid, rustyback fern, needle spikerush. Banded demoiselle, migrant hawker, golden ringed dragonfly, emerald damselfly. Ringlet, gatekeeper, clouded yellow and wall butterflies. Bloody nose beetle.
Contact: Welsh Water, 01443 452 350.

6. MAWDDACH VALLEY

RSPB (North Wales office).
Location: 1: Coed Garth Gell sat nav: LL40 2TU (village of Bontddu). On north side of Mawddach Estuary, the footpath to the reserve entrance goes from the Fiddler's Elbow carpark at grid ref SH 678 189.
2: Arthog Bog (SH 630 138) is off Dolgellau-to-Tywyn road (A493) west of Arthog. Park at Morfa Mawddach station.
Access: Nature trails are open at all times. Dogs on leads.
Facilities: Nature trails at both sites in Mawddach Valley, plus information boards.
Public transport: Nearest bus stop is Taicynhaeaf on Dolgellau to Barmouth X94 route. Half mile walk to Coed Garth Gell.
Habitats: Oak woodland, bracken and heathland at Coed Garth Gell. Willow and alder scrub and raised bog at Arthog Bog.
Key birds: *At Coed Garth Gell*: Buzzard, Sparrowhawk, Peregrine, Raven, Lesser Spotted Woodpecker, Grey Wagtail, Dipper and Hawfinch are joined in the summer by Pied Flycatcher, Spotted Flycatcher, Wood Warbler, Redstart, Tree Pipit and Cuckoo. *At Arthog Bog*: Buzzard, Sparrowhawk, Peregrine, Raven are seen all year round. Summer migrants include Tree Pipit, Grasshopper Warbler and Cuckoo. In winter flocks of Redpoll and Siskin are common and Red-breasted Merganser, Pintail and Little Egret are on the nearby estuary.
Other notable flora and fauna: Coed Garth Gell has Tunbridge filmy and beech ferns and a wide variety of butterflies. Golden-ringed dragonflies are regular.
Contact: Enquiries via RSPB Ynys-hir reserve, 01654 700 222; e-mail: mawddach@rspb.org.uk

7. SOUTH STACK CLIFFS

RSPB (North Wales Office).
Location: Sat nav: LL65 1YH. RSPB visitor centre SH 218 818, Ellin's Tower information centre SH 206 820. Follow A55 to W end in Holyhead, proceed straight on at roundabout, continue straight on through traffic lights. After another half mile turn L and follow the brown tourist signs for RSPB South Stack.
Access: RSPB car park (no charge) with Blue Badge

parking. 'Access for all' track to viewing area overlooking the lighthouse. Access to Ellin's Tower Seabird Centre gained via staircase. Reserve covered by an extensive network of paths, some of which are not accessible via wheelchair.
Facilities: Free access to RSPB Visitor Centre (open 10am to 5pm daily except Dec 25) and Ellin's Tower which has windows overlooking main auk colony open daily (10am-5pm Easter-Sep). RSPB café closes at 3pm each day. Network of footpaths over coastal and heathland terrain.
Public transport: None.
Habitats: Sea cliffs, maritime grassland, maritime heath, lowland heath.
Key birds: Peregrine, Chough, Fulmar, Puffin, Guillemot, Razorbill, Rock Pipit, Skylark, Stonechat, Linnet, Shag, migrant warblers and passage seabirds.
Other notable flora and fauna: Spathulate fleawort, endemic to South Stack, adders, lizards, porpoise.
Contact: South Stack Visitor Centre, 01407 762 100; e-mail: south.stack@rspb.org.uk
www.rspb.org.uk/southstackcliffs

8. SPINNIES ABER OGWEN

North Wales Wildlife Trust.
Location: Sat nav: LL57 3YH. SH 613 721. From Bangor follow the Tal-y-Bont road from roundabout on A5122 near Penrhyn Castle entrance. Road to reserve is signposted on L after 1km. Reserve can also be approached from a road at Junction 12 off A55. Minor road leads to car park where reserve entrance is signposted
Access: Open all year. Dogs on leads. Keep to the paths. Wheelchair accessible to the main hide.
Facilities: Two hides clearly signposted from the car park, main hide is wheelchair accessible and offers views of Traeth Lafan sands and the Spinnies lagoon. There is a drop-off point at the main entrance. Footpaths are good throughout.
Public transport: Take the 5 or 5X bus from Bangor or Llandudno.
Habitats: Woodland, scrub, grassland, shingle beach mudflats, reed swamp and open water.
Key birds: Autumn/*winter*: Large numbers of wintering wildfowl and waders such as Redshank, Greenshank, Wigeon and Teal. Kingfisher can be seen from Sep-Mar. *Spring/summer*: Red-breasted Merganser, Sandwich Tern, large numbers of Mute Swans, Little Grebe, Blackcap and Sedge Warbler.
Other notable flora and fauna: Broad-leaved helleborine, dog's mercury, bluebells. Red admiral, speckled wood, holly blue, orange tip and small

copper butterflies.
Contact: Chris Wynne, Conservation Officer, 01248 351 541; e-mail: ChrisWynne@wildlifetrustswales.org www.wildlifetrust.org.uk/northwales

9. TRAETH LAFAN LNR

Gwynedd Council.
Location: NE of Bangor, stretching 9.5k to Llanfairfechan. 1: For Traeth Lafan, take minor road from old A55 near Tal-y-Bont (SH 610 710) to Aberogwen car park by coast (SH 614 723). 2: For nearby Morfa Aber Reserve (SH 646 731) follow brown signs from junction 13 of A55.
3: Access to Morfa Madryn Reserve is on foot 1 mile W from Llanfairfechan promenade (SH 679 754).
Access: Open access from 1, 2, and 3. All sites are wheelchair accessible.
Facilities: Public paths. 1: Car park, hides 200m away at Spinnies Reserve. 2: Car park and hide. 3: Car and coach park with toilets and café, hides at reserve.
Public transport: For local bus and train timetables call 0870 60 82 608 or log on to www.gwynedd.gov.uk
Habitats: Intertidal sands and mudflats (2,500ha), wetlands, streams. SPA SAC SSSI and LNR.
Key birds: Third most important area in Wales for wintering waders; of national importance for moulting Great Crested Grebe and Red-breasted Merganser; internationally important for Oystercatcher and Curlew; passage waders; winter concentrations of Goldeneye and Greenshank, and of regional significance for wintering populations of Black-throated, Red-throated and Great Northern Divers and Black-necked and Slavonian Grebes and breeding Lapwings at Morfa Madryn.
Contact: Countryside and Access Unit, 01286 679 827.

Southern Wales

Glamorgan, Gower, Gwent

SUMMER along the Gower coastline will produce breeding seabirds, Peregrines and thousands of Manx Shearwaters offshore. Cardiff Bay is good for passage and wintering waders. The best wetlands are Kenfig Pools — half way between and Cardiff and Swanse a — and the Newport Wetlands Reserve. Both are worth visiting at any time of year.

1. CWM CLYDACH

RSPB Wales.
Location: Sat nav: SA6 5TL. SN 684 026. N of Swansea. Three miles N of J45 on M4, through the village of Clydach on B4291, follow the signs for Craig-cefn-Parc. Car park is close to the New Inn pub.
Access: Open at all times along public footpaths and waymarked trails. Not suitable for wheelchairs. Coach parking not available. Dogs on leads.
Facilities: Two nature trails link to network of public footpaths, car park, information boards.
Public transport: Hourly buses from Swansea stop at reserve entrance.
Habitats: Oak and beech woodland on steep slopes along the banks of the fast-flowing Lower Clydach River.
Key birds: Red Kite, Sparrowhawk, Buzzard, Raven, Green Woodpecker, Dipper and Grey Wagtail are joined in the summer by Spotted Flycatcher, Garden Warbler, Wood Warbler and Cuckoo. In winter Siskin, Lesser Redpoll and Woodcock are regular.
Other notable flora and fauna: Wood sorrel, silver-washed fritillary and speckled wood butterflies. Fungi.
Contact: Reserve warden, 029 2035 3000; e-mail: cymru@rspb.org.uk

2. CWM COL-HUW

The Wildlife Trust of South and West Wales.
Location: Sat nav: CF61 1RF (Cwm Col-Huw car park). SS 957 674. SE from Bridgend, site includes Iron Age fort, overlooking Bristol Channel. From Bridgend take B4265 S to Llanwit Major. Follow beach road from village.
Access: Park in seafront car park. Climb steps. Open all year. **Facilities:** All year toilets and café. Information boards.

Habitats: Unimproved calcareous grassland, woodland, scrub and Jurassic blue lias cliff. Iron Age promontory fort on site.
Key birds: Cliff-nesting House Martin colony, breeding Fulmar, Linnet, Whitethroat. Large autumn passerine passage. Peregrine. Seawatching vantage point. Occasional passing Chough.
Contact: Trust HQ, 01656 724 100; e-mail: info@welshwildlife.org

3. KENFIG NNR

Bridgend County Borough Council.
Location: Sat nav: CF33 4PT. SS 802 811. Seven miles W of Bridgend. From J37 on M4, drive towards Porthcawl, then North Cornelly, then follow signs.
Access: Open at all times. Unsurfaced sandy paths, not suitable for wheelchairs. Flooding possible in winter and spring. Coach parking available.
Facilities: Toilets, hides, free car parking and signposted paths.
Public transport: Local bus service stops at reserve. Call Traveline Cymru for details on 0871 200 2233.
Habitats: 1,300 acre sand dune system, freshwater lake with reeds, numerous wet dune slacks, sandy coastline with some rocky outcrops.
Key birds: *Summer:* Warblers including Cetti's, Grasshopper, Sedge, Reed and Willow Warbler, Blackcap and Whitethroat. *Winter:* Wildfowl, Water Rail, Bittern, grebes.
Other notable flora and fauna: 16 species of orchid, hairy dragonfly, red-veined and ruddy darters, small blue, dark green fritillary, grayling, brown argus butterflies.
Contact: David Carrington, Ton Kenfig, Bridgend, CF33 4PT. 01656 743 386.
e-mail: david.carrington@bridgend.gov.uk

4. LAVERNOCK POINT

The Wildlife Trust of South and West Wales.
Location: Sat nav: CF64 5XQ. ST 181 681 (main entrance). 8km south of Cardiff. Access is from B4267 via Fort Road, signposted Lavernock Point.
Limited parking by gate or in public car park at the end of Fort Road.
Access: Not suitable for wheelchairs as access is via a stile.
Facilities: Information boards.
Public Transport: Bus number 94 from Cardiff to Lavernock.
Habitats: Sea, coastal calcareous grassland and scrub.

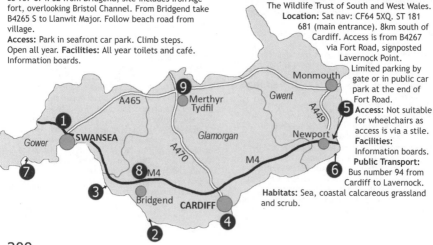

Key birds: Important site for watching bird migrations. In autumn large flocks of Swallow, thrushes and finches. Breeding birds include Whitethroat, Lesser Whitethroat, Bullfinch and Chiffchaff.
Other notable fauna: Butterflies, wild flowers.
Contact: Trust HQ, 01656 724 100; e-mail: info@welshwildlife.org www.welshwildlife.org

5. MAGOR MARSH

Gwent Wildlife Trust.
Location: Sat nav: NP26 3DD (Redwick Road). ST 428 866. Reserve lies to S of Magor. Leave M4 at exit 23, turning R onto B4245. Follow signs for Redwick in Magor village. Take first L after railway bridge. Reserve entrance is half mile further on R.
Access: Open all year. Keep to path. Wheelchair access to bird hide. No dogs please.
Facilities: Hide. Car park, footpaths and boardwalks.
Public transport: Bus no 61 from Newport stops outside reserve.
Habitats: 90 acres of sedge fen, reedswamp, willow carr, damp hay meadows and open water.
Key birds: Important for wetland birds. *Spring*: Reed, Sedge and Grasshopper Warblers, occasional Garganey and Green Sandpiper on passage, Hobby. *Winter*: Teal, Peregrine, Jack Snipe, Snipe, occasional Shoveler and Gadwall, Bittern records in two recent years. *All year*: Little Egret, Little Grebe, Reed Bunting, Cetti's Warbler and Water Rail.
Contact: Gwent Wildlife Trust, 01600 740 600; e-mail: info@gwentwildlife.co.uk

6. NEWPORT WETLANDS NNR

NRW/ RSPB/ Newport City Council.
Location: Sat nav: NP18 2BZ. ST 334 834. SW of Newport. Reserve car park on West Nash Road, just before entrance to Uskmouth power station. From M4 junction 24 take the A48 to Newport Retail Park, turn towards steelworks and follow brown 'duck' signs to the reserve car park.
Access: Free entry 9am to 5pm each day, except Dec 25. Six disabled parking bays. All nature trails are accessible by wheelchair. Dogs only on perimeter footpath.
Facilities: Information centre, tea-rooms (open 10am to 4pm), shop, toilets (inc disabled), viewing screens.
Public transport: The 63 service runs from Newport Bus Station to the reserve daily (exc bank hols).
Habitats: 438 hectares of wet meadows, saline lagoons, reedbed, scrub and mudflats on Severn estuary.
Key birds: *Spring/summer*: Breeding waders such as Lapwing and Oystercatcher, Bearded Tit, Cetti's Warbler, Cuckoo and regular migrants on passage. *Autumn*: Large numbers of migrating wildfowl and waders arrive at the reserve — regulars include Curlew, Dunlin, Ringed Plover, Shoveler. *Winter*: Massive Starling roost (up to 50,000 birds). Bittern, nationally important numbers of Black-tailed Godwit, Shoveler and Dunlin.

Other notable flora and fauna: Badger, wood mouse, otter. Great crested newt. Orchids in spring, 16 species of dragonfly, 23 species of butterfly and around 200 species of moth.
Contact: Newport Wetlands Reserve (NRW) 0300 065 3000; RSPB visitor centre 01633 636 363; e-mail: newport-wetlands@rspb.org.uk

7. OXWICH NNR

NRW(Swansea Office).
Location: Sat nav: SA3 1LS. SS 512 874. From Swansea take A4118 Gower road towards Killay, Parkmill and continue through Nicholaston Oxwich village.
Access: Most of NNR open at all times. Groups can visit some restricted areas by arrangement. No permit required for access to foreshore, dunes, woodlands and facilities.
Facilities: Private car park, summer only. Toilets summer only. Marsh boardwalk and marsh lookout. No visitor centre, no facilities for disabled visitors.
Public transport: Bus service Swansea/Oxwich. First Cymru, tel 01792 580 580.
Habitats: Freshwater marsh, saltmarsh, foreshore, dunes, woodlands.
Key birds: *Summer*: Breeding Reed, Sedge and Cetti's Warblers, Treecreeper, Nuthatch, woodpeckers. *Winter*: Wildfowl.
Contact: NRW, 0300 065 3000; e-mail: enquiries@naturalresourceswales.gov.uk

8. PARC SLIP NATURE PARK

The Wildlife Trust of South and West Wales.
Location: Sat nav: CF32 0EH. SS 880 840. 1km W of Aberkenfig. From junction 36 of M4 take A4063 towards Maesteg, then B4281 (signposted Aberkenfig and Pyle) and follow brown signs to visitor centre in Fountain Road.
Access: Open dawn to dusk. Space for coach parking.
Facilities: Revamped visitor centre with coffee shop (open 10am to 4pm each day except Mondays). Five hides, regular events, interpretation centre. Free car park off Fountain Road. Good access for wheelchairs throughout the site.
Public transport: On Route No 4 of the National Cycle Network. Bus No 63 from Bridgend bus station stops outside the Fountain Inn at the bottom of Fountain Road. Train station at Tondu.
Habitats: Restored opencast mining site, wader scrape, lagoons, grassland, woodland.
Key birds: *Summer*: Breeding Tufted Duck, Lapwing, Skylark. Migrant waders (inc. Little Ringed Plover). Kingfisher, Green Woodpecker. *Winter*: Snipe, Water Rail, Bittern.
Other notable flora and fauna: Twenty species of dragonfly recorded, inc emperor and scarce blue-tailed damselfly. Seven species of orchid, twayblade and broad-leaved helleborine. Great crested newt, harvest mouse, reptiles.
Contact: Trust HQ, 01656 724 100; e-mail: info@welshwildlife.org; www.welshwildlife.org

9. TAF FECHAN

The Wildlife Trust of South and West Wales.
Location: Sat nav: CF48 2HH. SO 033 084, SO 038 075 and SO 045 096 (main entrances). 3km N of Merthyr Tydfil centre. Several entrances along Taff Trail and footpath from Cyfarthfa Park.
Access: Open all year. Not accessible to wheelchairs due to steep terrain and steps.
Facilities: Information boards.
Public Transport: Train station at Merthyr Tydfil

then bus service 25 to Cefn Coed y Cymmer or 33 to Pontsarn.
Habitats: Ancient broadleaved woodland, calcareous grasslands, river gorge and cliffs.
Key birds: Pied Flycatcher, Tawny Owl, Dipper, Kingfisher, Grey Wagtail, Peregrine, Woodcock.
Other notable fauna: Otter, migrating salmon, butterflies.
Contact: Trust HQ, 01656 724 100;
e-mail: info@welshwildlife.org

Western Wales

Carmarthenshire, Ceredigion, Pembrokeshire

A SUMMER boat trip to either Skomer or Skokholm to see the huge seabird colonies, is a must-do outing in summer, but inland, steep wooded valleys are good for Redstarts, Pied Flycatchers, Wood Warblers and Red Kites in spring and summer. For good winter birds head for the National Wetland Centre for Wales in Llanelli.

1. CASTLE WOODS

The Wildlife Trust of South and West Wales.
Location: Sat nav: SA19 6RT (Dinefwr Park). SN 615 217. About 60 acres of woodland overlooking River Tywi, 2km W of Llandeilo town centre, adjacent to Dinefwr Park.
Access: Open all year by footpath from Tywi Bridge, Llandeilo (SN 627 221) or park next to fire station off A40 and walk down Dinefwr Park Drive.
Facilities: Footpaths, mostly too steep for wheelchairs. Bird hide.
Public transport: Buses X13 from Swansea and 280/281 from Carmarthen to Llandovery. Train station in Llandeilo.
Habitats: Old mixed deciduous woodlands, castle.
Key birds: All three woodpeckers, Buzzard, Raven, Sparrowhawk. *Summer:* Pied and Spotted Flycatchers, Redstart, Wood Warbler. *Winter:* On water meadows look for Teal, Wigeon, Goosander, Shoveler, Tufted Duck and Pochard.
Other notable flora and fauna: Fallow deer, badger, butterflies inc silver-washed fritillary.
Contact: Welsh Wildlife Centre, 01239 621 600; e-mail: info@welshwildlife. orgwww.welshwildlife.org

2. CORS CARON NNR

NRW (West Wales Area).
Location: Sat nav: SY25 6JF (car park). SN 690 642. On B4343 two miles N of Tregaron, Ceredigion, NE of Lampeter.
Access: Open access from new car

park on B4343. Circular 4 mile Riverside Walk, shut at times due to flooding/management requirements. Dogs under control on Old Railway Walk, on leads on boardwalk, but not allowed on Riverside Walk.
Facilities: Coach accessible car park with toilets and picnic space. Bird hide on boardwalk, 2nd hide on Old Railway Walk 1.5 miles from car park. Footpath through reserve part of Ystwyth Trail.
Public transport: Infrequent buses (nos T21 and T29) pass Cors Caron.
Habitats: Raised bog, river, fen, wet grassland, willow woodland, reedbed.
Key birds: *Summer:* Lapwing, Redshank, Curlew, Red Kite, Hobby, Grasshopper Warbler, Whinchat, Redpoll, Reed Bunting. *Winter:* Teal, Wigeon, Whooper Swan, Hen Harrier, Red Kite.
Other notable flora and fauna: Small red damselfly among the abundant dragonflies which can be seen from boardwalk. Also adder and common lizard.
Contact: NRW, 0300 065 3000; www.naturalresourceswales.gov.uk/

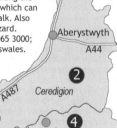

NATURE RESERVES - WESTERN WALES

3. DYFI NNR

NRW (West Wales Area).
Location: Sat nav: SY24 5JZ (Ynyslas visitor centre). SN 640 955. Extensive reserve midway between Machynlleth and Aberystwyth and seaward side of A487, incorporating part of Dyfi estuary, Ynyslas dunes and Borth Bog.
Access: Ynyslas dunes and the estuary have unrestricted access. No access to Borth Bog (Cors Fochno) for casual birdwatching; permit required for study and research purposes. Good views over the bog and Aberleri marshes from W bank of Afon Leri. Public footpaths off A493 E of Aberdyfi, and off B4353 (S of river); minor road from B4353 at Ynyslas to dunes and parking area.
Facilities: NRW visitor centre/shop/toilets at Ynyslas (open 9.30am to 5pm between Easter and end of Sept). No refreshments. Public hide overlooking marshes beside footpath at SN 611 911.
Public transport: Aberystwyth to Tre'r-ddol bus service stops at Borth and Ynyslas.
Habitats: Sandflats, mudflats, saltmarsh, creeks, dunes, raised bog, grazing marsh.
Key birds: *Winter:* Greenland White-fronted Goose, wildfowl, waders and raptors. *Summer:* Breeding wildfowl and waders (inc. Teal, Shoveler, Merganser, Lapwing, Curlew, Redshank).
Contact: NRW 0300 065 3000.

4. GWENFFRWD-DINAS

RSPB Wales.
Location: SN 788 471. North of Llandovery. From A483 take B road signposted to Llyn Brianne Reservoir and then follow signs to reserve, which lies between Cynghordy and Llanwrda.
Access: Public nature trail at Dinas open dawn to dusk. Donation (£1) for parking appreciated.
Facilities: Nature trail including a boardwalk and four benches. Other parts of the trail are rugged. Car park and information board at start of trail. Coach parking can be arranged.
Public transport: None.
Habitats: Hillside oak woods, streams and bracken slopes. Spectacular upland scenery.
Key birds: Upland species such as Red Kite, Buzzard, Peregrine, Raven, Goosander, Dipper and Grey Wagtail are joined in the summer by Pied Flycatcher, Spotted Flycatcher, Wood Warbler, Redstart, Tree Pipit, Common Sandpiper and Cuckoo. Marsh Tit and all three woodpecker species are present.
Other notable flora and fauna: Golden-ringed dragonfly, purple hairstreak, silver-washed fritillary and Wilson's filmy fern.
Contact: RSPB Ynys-hir, 01654 700 222; e-mail: gwenffrwd.dinas@rspb.org.uk

5. NATIONAL WETLANDS CENTRE, WALES

The Wildfowl & Wetlands Trust.
Location: Sat nav: SA14 9SH. SS 533 984. Overlooks the Burry Inlet near Llanelli. Leave M4 at junction 48. Signposted from A484, E of Llanelli.

Access: Open daily 9.30am-5pm, except Dec 24 and 25. Grounds open until 6pm in summer. Centre is fully accessible with disabled toilets. Mobility scooters and wheelchairs are free to hire.
Facilities: Visitor centre with toilets, hides, restaurant, shop, education facilities, free car and coach parking. The centre has level access and hard-surfaced paths.
Public transport: Bus from Llanelli to Lllwydhendy, approx 1 mile from the centre. Telephone Traveline Cymru 0871 200 2233 (7am-10pm daily).
Habitats: Inter-tidal mudflats, reedbeds, pools, marsh, waterfowl collection.
Key birds: Large flocks of Curlew, Oystercatcher, Redshank on saltmarsh. *Winter:* Up to 50,000 waterbirds, including Pintail, Wigeon, Teal. Also Little Egret, Short-eared Owl, Barn Owl, Peregrine.
Other notable flora and fauna: Bee and southern marsh orchids, yellow bartisa. Damselflies and dragonflies, water voles and otters.
Contact: Centre Manager, WWT National Wetlands Centre Wales, 01554 741 087; e-mail: info.llanelli@wwt.org.uk www.wwt.org.uk

6. RAMSEY ISLAND

RSPB Wales.
Location: Sat nav: SA62 6PY (nearest mainland point). SM 706 237. One mile offshore from lifeboat station at St Justinians, two miles west of St Davids, Pembrokeshire.
Access: Open every day, weather permitting, April 1 to Oct 31. RSPB landing fees for non-members, in addition to boat fare. No wheelchair access. Coach and car parking at St Justinians. For boat bookings (sailings at 10am and 12 noon), contact: Thousand Island Expeditions, 01437 721 721; e-mail: sales@thousandislands.co.uk
Facilities: Small RSPB visitor centre/shop selling snacks and hot and cold drinks on island. Toilets a five minute walk uphill from harbour. 3.5 mile self-guiding circular trail on island (rugged in parts) with introduction from resident wardens. Guided walks are also available.
Public transport: Trains to Haverfordwest Station. Hourly buses from Haverfordwest to St Davids and then Celtic Coaster shuttle bus to boat embarkation point (Tel 01348 840 539).
Habitats: Acid grassland, maritime heath, seacliffs.
Key birds: *Spring/summer:* Cliff-nesting auks (Guillemot, Razorbill), Kittiwake, Fulmar, Shag, Stonechat, Wheatear, Skylark, Linnet, Little Owl, plus passage migrants. *All year:* Peregrine, Raven, Chough.
Other notable fauna: Largest grey seal colony in south-west Britain, red deer, harbour porpoise.
Contact: The Warden, 07836 535 733; e-mail:ramsey. island@rspb.org.uk; www.rspb.org.uk/ramseyisland

7. SKOKHOLM NNR

The Wildlife Trust of South and West Wales.
Location: Sat nav: SA62 3BJ (Marloes). SM 735 050.

Island lying S of Skomer. Boats embark from Martin's Haven.

Access: 3 night, 4 night or weekly stays available. Apr-Sep, tel 01239 621 600 for details and booking. Bookings opened each autumn for the following season.

Facilities: Recently given Bird Observatory status and welcomes visting ringers. Upgraded self-catering accommodation for up to 20 people. Small shop selling basic foodstuffs.

Public transport: None.

Habitats: Cliffs, bays and inlets.

Key birds: *Spring:* Manx Shearwaters arrive at end of March. *Summer:* Internationally important colonies of Razorbill, Puffin, Guillemot, Storm Petrel, Lesser Black-backed Gull. Migrants inc. rare species.

Other notable fauna: Grey seals, harbour porpoise, occasional common, bottlenose and Risso's dolphins, nationally rare moths.

Contact: 01239 621 600; www.welshwildlife.org
e-mail: islands@welshwildlife.org
Blog: skokholm.blogspot.co.uk

8. SKOMER

The Wildlife Trust of South and West Wales.

Location: Sat nav: SA62 3BJ (Marloes). SM 725 095. Fifteen miles from Haverfordwest. Take B4327 turn-off for Marloes, embarkation point at Martin's Haven, two miles past village. National Trust car park at Martin's Haven.

Access: Open between April 1 and Sep 30. Not suitable for infirm (steep landing steps and rough ground). Boats sail from 10am, 11am and noon every day except Mon (Bank Holidays excluded). Check Twitter @skomer_boatinfo or website for more details. Island landing fees (for non-WTSWW members) payable at Lockley Lodge visitor centre.

Facilities: Information centre, toilets, two hides, booklets, guides, nature trails. Visitors need to take water/food.

Public transport: None.

Habitats: Maritime cliff, bluebells, red campion, freshwater ponds.

Key birds: Largest colony of Manx Shearwater in the world (overnight). Puffin, Guillemot, Razorbill (Apr-end Jul). Kittiwake (until end Aug), Fulmar, Short-eared Owl, Chough, Peregrine, Buzzard (all year), migrants (including rare species).

Contact: Reserve Warden, 07971 114 302;
e-mail: skomer.warden@welshwildlife.org
www.welshwildlife.org

9. WELSH WILDLIFE CENTRE

The Wildlife Trust of South and West Wales.

Location: Sat nav: SA43 2TB. SN 188 451. Centre based in Teifi Marshes Nature Reserve, Cilgerran, two miles SE of Cardigan. River Teifi is N boundary. Signposted from A478 Cardigan to Fishguard road.

Access: Nature reserve open all year. Check website for visitor centre opening hours. Free parking for WTSWW members, £3 non-members. Dogs on leads welcome. Disabled access to visitor centre, paths, four hides.

Facilities: Visitor centre, restaurant, network of four nature trails and seven hides. Binoculars for hire.

Public transport: Train station, Haverfordwest (23 miles). Bus station in Cardigan. Access on foot from Cardigan centre, ten mins.

Habitats: Wetlands, marsh, swamp, reedbed, open water, creek (tidal), river, saltmarsh, woodland.

Key birds: Extensive flooding in winter attracts large numbers of wildfowl, notably Teal, Wigeon and Mallard. Other winter regulars are Water Rail, Curlew, Snipe, Lapwing and Peregrine. Breeding birds include Cetti's Warbler, Kingfisher, Greater Spotted Woodpecker, gulls, Sand Martin, Redstart. Occasional Bittern and Red Kite.

Other notable flora and fauna: Otter, water shrew, sika and red deer, good range of dragonflies.

Contact: Welsh Wildlife Centre, 01239 621 600;
e-mail: info@welshwildlife.org;

10. YNYS-HIR

RSPB Wales.

Location: Sat nav: SY20 8TA. SN 682 961. Car park is one mile from Eglwys-fach village, off A487, six miles SW of Machynlleth.

Access: Entrance charge for non-RSPB members. Open every day (9am-9pm or dusk if earlier) except Dec 25. Visitor centre open daily Apr-Oct (10am-5pm), Wed-Sun Nov-Mar (10am-4pm). Coaches welcome but please call for parking information. No dogs allowed.

Facilities: Visitor centre and toilets. Two main circular trails (not suitable for wheelchairs), seven hides, two viewpoints, drinks machine.

Public transport: Bus service to Eglwys-fach from either Machynlleth or Aberystwyth, tel. 01970 617 951. Rail service to Machynlleth.

Habitats: Estuary, freshwater pools, woodland and wet grassland.

Key birds: Large numbers of wintering waders, wildfowl and birds of prey on the estuary are replaced with breeding woodland birds in spring and summer. *All year:* Red Kite, Buzzard, Little Egret, Lapwing, Teal. *Spring:* Wood Warbler, Redstart, Pied Flycatcher, nine species of warbler. *Winter:* Greenland White-fronted Goose, Barnacle Goose, Wigeon, Hen Harrier.

Other notable fauna: Sixteen species of dragonfly and damselfly include small red damselfly and golden-ringed dragonfly. Butterflies include dark green fritillary, brimstone and speckled wood. Otters (rarely seen) and brown hares are resident.

Contact: RSPB Ynys-Hir Reserve, 01654 700 222;
e-mail: ynyshir@rspb.org.uk

DIRECTORY OF ARTISTS, PHOTOGRAPHERS AND LECTURERS

Hilary Cromack

With dramatic scenery like this, Scotland and its birds remain popular topics for club talks as you will see from the Lecturers' Directory.

Wildlife Art Galleries	206
Wildlife Artists	206
Photographers	209
Lecturers	211

DIRECTORY OF WILDLIFE ART GALLERIES

BIRDSCAPES GALLERY
Manor Farm Barns, Glandford, Holt, Norfolk NR25 7JP; 01263 741 742; e-mail:art@birdscapes.co.uk; www.birdscapesgallery.co.uk
Opening times: All year, 11am to 5pm each day, but may be closed for part of the day before a new exhibition.

CHENG KIM LOKE GALLERY, SLIMBRIDGE
Wildfowl & Wetland Trust, Slimbridge, Gloucestershire GL2 7BT; 01453 891 900; e-mail: info.slimbridge@wwt.org.uk; www.wwt.org.uk
Opening times: All year, except Dec 25, 9.30am to 5pm (last admission at 4pm). Admission charge for non-WWT members.

GORDALE (NATIONAL EXHIBITION OF WILDLIFE ART)
Gordale Garden and Home Centre, Chester High Road, Burton, South Wirral, Cheshire CH64 8TF; 01513 362 116; e-mail: admin@gordale.co.uk; www.gordale.co.uk
Opening times: Stages the National Exhibition of Wildlife Art for two weeks each July. 9am to 5.30pm each day. Free admission.

HOUSE OF BRUAR
By Blair Atholl, Perthshire PH18 5TW; 0345 136 0111; e-mail: mailorder@houseofbruar.com; www.houseofbruar.com
Opening times: All year except Dec 25 and Jan 1. 9.30am to 6pm (May to Nov); 10am to 5pm rest of year. Free admission.

MALL GALLERIES
The Mall, London SW1; 0207 930 6844; e-mail: info@mallgalleries.com; www.mallgalleries.org.uk
Opening times: Stages Britsih Wildlife Photography show in September and Society of Wildlife Artists' annual exhibition in Oct/Nov (10am to 5pm). Admission charge.

NATURE IN ART
Wallsworth Hall, Twigworth, Gloucester GL2 9PA; 01452 731 422; e-mail: enquiries@nature-in-art.org.uk; www.nature-in-art.org.uk
Opening times: Closed Mondays (except Bank Holidays) and between Dec 24 and 26. Otherwise 10am to 5pm. Admission charge.

PINKFOOT GALLERY
High Street, Cley-next-the-Sea, Norfolk NR25 7RB; 01263 740 947; e-mail: info@pinkfootgallery.co.uk; www.pinkfootgallery.co.uk
Opening times: All year, 10am to 5pm (Mon to Sat), 11am to 4pm (Sun). Free admission.

ROOKESBURY MANOR
Rookesbury Park School, Wickham, Hampshire PO17 6HT.
Opening times: Stages the annual two-day Marwell International Wildlife Art Society annual exhibition at the end of August each year (10am to 5pm). Free admission, but ticket required for private viewing.

WATERSTON HOUSE
Donald Watson Gallery, SOC HQ, Waterston House, Aberlady, East Lothian EH32 0PY; 01875 871 330; e-mail: mail@the-soc.org.uk; www.the-soc.org.uk
Opening times: All year, 10am to 4pm (weekdays) and 12pm to 6pm (weekends). Free entry.

THE WILDLIFE ART GALLERY
98-99 High St, Lavenham, Sudbury, Suffolk CO10 9PZ; 01787 248 562; e-mail: info@wildlifeartgallery.com; www.wildlifeartgallery.com
Opening times: All year 10am to 4.30pm (Mon to sat), 11.30am to 3.30pm (Sun).

DIRECTORY OF WILDLIFE ARTISTS

AKROYD, Carry
4 Luddington-in-the-Brook, Peterborough PE8 5QU; e-mail: carry@carryakroyd.co.uk; www.carryakroyd.co.uk

ALLEN, Richard
34 Parkwood Avenue, Wivenhoe, Essex, CO7 9AN; 01206 826 753; e-mail: richard@richardallen31.wanadoo.co.uk; www.richardallenillustrator.com

ANGUS, Max
e-mail: max@maxangus.co.uk; www.maxangus.co.uk

ATKINSON, Kim
Ty'n Gamdda, Uwchmynydd, Aberdaron, Pwllheli, Gwynedd LL53 8DA.

BARRETT, Priscilla
Jack of Clubs, Lode, Cambridge, CB5 9HE.

BARTLETT, Paul
Kirkton Barns Cottages, Tayport, Fife DD6 9PD; e-mail: pauljbartlett@hotmail.com; www.naturalselectiongallery.co.uk

BENNETT, David
16 Pearl Street, Starbeck, Harrogate, N. Yorkshire, HGJ 4QW.

BINDER, Adam
Adam Binder Sculptures, Marston Hill Farm, Meysey Hampton, Cirencester, Glos, GL7 5LG

DIRECTORY OF WILDLIFE ARTISTS

BROWN, Diana
Shannel Ballogie, Aboyne, Aberdeenshire, AB34 5DR.

BURN, Hilary
Huish Cleeve Cottage, Huish Champflower, Taunton, Somerset, TA4 2HA; e-mail: hilaryburn@fireflyuk.net

BURTON, P.K.J.
High Kelton, Doctors Commons Road, Berkhampstead, Herts HB4 3DH.

BUSBY, John
Easter Haining, Ormiston Hall, Tranent EH35 5NJ; e-mail: johnbusby.artist@btinternet.com

CALE, Steve
10 Fairview Drive, Colkirk, Norfolk NR21 7NT. 01328 862 265; e-mail: steveshrike@aol.com; www.steve-cale-artist.co.uk

DALRYMPLE, Neil
Unit 9, Ruthin Craft Centre, Clwyd LLl5 lBT; www.neildalrymple.com

DALY, Dave
www.davedalyartist.com

DAVIS, John
6 Redmoor, Birdham, West Sussex PO20 7HS; e-mail: johndavis.wildlife@tiscali.co.uk

DEMAIN, Michael
175 Richmond Road, Accrington, BB5 0JB; 01254 237 378; e-mail: mdemainwildart@aol.com; www.michaeldemainwildlifeart.co.uk

EDE, Basil
Mark Cross House, Ripe, Nr Lewes, East Sussex BN8 6AN.

EDWARDS, Brin
Maple Cottage, 59 Partridge Row, Assington, Suffolk CO10 5LP. 01787 211 162; e-mail: studio@brin-edwards.com; www.brin-edwards.com

EDWARDS, Victoria
403 London Road, Ditton, Aylesford, Kent ME20 6DB; e-mail: vedwards74@hotmail.co.uk

ELLIS, Carl
Meadow View, Glebefields, Woodseaves, Staffordshire ST20 0LA; e-mail: carlellisartist@btinternet.com; www.carlellisfishart.com

GARNER, Jackie FRSA
The Old Cider House Studio, Humphries End, Randwick, Stroud, Glos GL6 6EW; 01453 847 420; (M) 07800 804 847; e-mail: artist@jackiegarner.co.uk; www.jackiegarner.co.uk

GILLMOR, Robert
North Light, Hilltop, Cley-next-the-Sea, Holt, Norfolk NR25 7SE.

GREENHALF, Robert
Romney House, Saltbarn Lane, Playden Rye, East Sussex TN31 7PH; www.robertgreenhalf.co.uk

GRIFFITHS, Ian
Griff's Wildlife Studio, Creftow, 6 Church Street, Helston, Cornwall TR13 8TG; 07971 678 464; e-mail: mail@artbygriff.com; www.artbygriff.com

GUDGEON, Simon
Gill's Hole Farm, Redlynch, Salisbury, Wiltshire SP5 2JX; e-mail: Simon@gudgeon.demon.co.uk; www.simongudgeon.com

HAMPTON, Michael
13 Sandy Way, Shirley, Croydon, Surrey CR0 8QT; www.michael-hampton.com

HASLEN, Andrew
c/o Wildlife Art Gallery, 97 High Street, Lavenham, Suffolk CO10 9PZ; www.wildlifeartgallery.o.uk

HASTE, Kendra
c/o Patrick Davies Contemporary Art; e-mail: question@patrickdaviesca.com; www.kendrahaste.co.uk

HODGES, Gary
Church Mill House, Chirton, Devizes, Wiltshire SN10 3Q; www.garyhodges-wildlife-art.com; e-mail: gary@garyhodges-wildlife-art.com

JOHNSON, Rosalie
18 Clevedon Road, Richmond Bridge, East Twickenham, Middlesex TW1 2HU; www.rosaliejohnsonsculptures.co.uk

KOSTER, David
5 East Cliff Gardens, Folkestone, Kent CTl9 6AR.

LEAHY, Ernest
32 Ben Austins, Redbourn; Herts AL3 7DR. www.flickr.com/photos/ernsbirdart

LOCKWOOD, Rachel
E-mail: rachel@rachellockwoodartist.com; www.rachellockwoodartist.co.uk/

MACKMAN, Nick
E-mail: nick@clayanimalsculptures.co.uk; www.clayanimalsculptures.co.uk

MEAD, Harriet
End Cottage, 24 Westgate Street, Hilborough, Thetford, Norfolk IP26 5BN; e-mail: harrietmead.art@gmail.com; www.harrietmead.co.uk

MICHEL, Sally
30 Woodland Way, Bidborough, Tunbridge Wells, Kent TN4 OUY.

DIRECTORY OF WILDLIFE ARTISTS

MILLER, David
Nyth-Gwdi-Hw, New Mill, St Clears, Carmarthenshire
SA33 4HY; 01994 453 545; (M)07900 825 404;
e-mail: david@davidmillerart.co.uk;
www.davidmillerart.co.uk

MOGER, Jill
The Studio, 75 Millfield Lane, Nether, Poppleton, York
Y026 6NA; e-mail: jill.moger@hotmail.com;
www.jillmogersculptures.co.uk

NEIL, William
Rannacham, Askernish, South Uist, Western Isles H58
5SY; www.william-neill.co.uk

PAIGE, John
The Manor House, King's Cliffe, Peterborough PE8
6XB; e-mail: paiges@oldbrewerystudios.co.uk;
www.oldbrewerystudios.co.uk

PARRY, David
Castle Cottage, Lostwithiel, Cornwall PL22 0JN.

PARTINGTON, Peter
Kettlebaston Hall, Kettlebaston, Nr Ipswich, Suffolk
1P7 7QR; www.peter-partington.fsnet.co.uk

PEARSON, Bruce
www.brucepearson.net

PHILLIPS, Antonia
www.antoniaphillips.co.uk

POLLARD, Nik
e-mail: info@nikpollard.co.uk; www.nikpollard.co.uk

POOLE, Greg
e-mail: greg@gregpoole.co.uk; www.gregpoole.co.uk

POWELL, Dan and Rosie
4 Forth Close, Stubbington, Hants PO14 3SZ; 01329
668 465; e-mail: dan.powell@care4free.net
www.powellwildlifeart.com

PROUD, Alastair
Plas Bach, Newchurch, Carmarthen, Dyfed SA33 6EJ;
www.alastairproud.co.uk

REANEY, John
1 Buxton Road, Brighton, East Sussex BNJ 5DE.

REES, Darren
New East Frew, Thornhill, Stirling FK8 3QX; e-mail:
darrenreesart@btinternet.com;
www.darrenrees.com

ROSE, Chris
Whitelee Cottages, Newton St Boswells, Melrose,
Roxburghire TD6 0SH;
e-mail: chris@chrisrose-artist.co.uk;
www.chrisrose-artist.co.uk

SCOTT, Dafila
White Roses, The Hythe, Reach, Cambridgeshire CB5

0JQ; e-mail: dafilascott@yahoo.co.uk;
www.dafilascott.co.uk

SHACKLETON, Keith
39 Holmead Walk, Poundbury, Dorchester, Dorset DT1
3GE.

STOCK, Andrew
Wyncot, Frog Lane, Cuddington, Bucks HP18 0AX.
Facebook page: AndrewNStock@AOL.com;
www.andrewstock.co.uk

SUTTON, Barry
E-mail: barry.sutton@talktalk.net;
www.barrysutton.co.uk

SYKES, Thelma
Blue Neb Studios, 18 Newcroft, Saughall, Chester CH1
6EL. 01244 880 209;
e-mail: thelmasykes@tiscali.co.uk

THRELFALL, John
Saltflats Cottage, Rockcliffe, Dalbeattie, DG5 4QQ.
01556 630 262; e-mail; john@johnthrelfall.co.uk
www.johnthrelfall.co.uk

TRATT, Richard
10 Sharpley Close, Fordingbridge, Hants SP6 1LG;
www.richardtratt.co.uk

TYSON, Esther
6 Rathborne Croft, Parwich, Ashbourne, Derbyshire
DE6 1QH; e-mail: esther.tyson@network.rca.ac.uk

TURVEY, Simon
2 York Rise, Orpington, Kent BR6 8PR.

UNDERWOOD, Matthew
Eagle Tap, West Street, Kings Cliffe, PE8 6XB;
e-mail: matt@mattunderwood.info;
www.mattunderwood.info

WALLACE, D.I.M.
Mount Pleasant Farm, Main Road, Anslow, Burton-on-
Trent, East Staffordshire DE13 9QU.

WARREN, Michael
The Laurels, The Green, Winthorpe, Nottinghamshire
NG24 2NR; e-mail: mike.warren@tiscali.co.uk;
www.mikewarren.co.uk

WHITE, Vicky
e-mail: mail@vicky-white.co.uk;
www.vicky-white.co.uk

WOOTTON, Tim
Evie, Orkney; e-mail: tim.wootton@tiscali.co.uk;
http://tim-wootton.blogspot.co.uk

WOODHEAD, Darren
2 Ivory Court, Langriggs, Haddington, East Lothian
EH41 4BY; e-mail: darren.woodhead1@virgin.net;
www.darrenwoodheadartist.co.uk

DIRECTORY OF WILDLIFE PHOTOGRAPHERS

ALMOND, Jim
Bird photographer with additional interest in Butterflies and Odonata
Subjects: All UK birds, special interest in wild Peregrines. See website for main interests, gallery and portfolio.
Products and services: Images for publication, lectures and workshops / individual tuition available. Vast library of images. Available for commissions, lectures / tours. Competitive terms for larger projects.
Address: 5 Coolock Close, St Peters Park, Shrewsbury SY3 9QD; 07940 678 719;
e-mail: almond.jim@virgin.net
Website: http://shropshirebirder.co.uk/

BASTON, Bill
Photographer, lecturer.
Subjects: East Anglian rarities and common birds, Mediterranean birds and landscapes, UK wildlife and landscapes, Northern Greece & Western Turkey, Spain, Goa, General wildlife photography, The Gambia, Northern India (birds and tigers), Costa Rica, North East India and the Himalayan foothills, Western Australia, Morocco, Wildlife of Sri Lanka.
Products and services: Prints, slides, digital, mounted/ unmounted.
Address: 86 George Street, Hadleigh, Ipswich, IP7 5BU; 01473 827 062; www.billbaston.com
e-mail: billbaston@btinternet.com

BELL, Graham
Professional ornithologist, photographer, author, cruise lecturer worldwide.
Subjects: Birds, animals, flowers, landscapes, all seven continents, from Arctic to Antarctic.
Products and services: Original slides for sale, £2 each. Lecture: 'Taking Better Photos'.
Address: Ros View, South Yearle, Wooler, Northumberland, NE71 6RB; 01668 281310.
e-mail: seabirdsdgb@hotmail.com

BROOKS, Richard
Wildlife photographer, writer, lecturer, birding guide.
Subjects: Owls (Barn especially), raptors, Kingfisher and a variety of European birds (Lemnos and Lesvos especially) and landscapes.
Products and services: Guided birding and wildlife photography in Norfolk, by arrangement. Mounted and unmounted computer prints (6x4, A3+ size), framed pictures, A5 greetings cards, surplus slides for sale. Norfolk bird calendar available (see website).
Address: 24 Croxton Hamlet, Fulmodeston, Fakenham, Norfolk, NR21 0NP; 01328 878 614.
e-mail: email@richard-brooks.co.uk
(or r.brooks662@btinternet.com)
www.richard-brooks.co.uk

BROADBENT, David
Professional photographer.
Subjects: UK birds and wild places.
Products and services: All new website features a fully searchable picture library of UK wildlife and landscapes to the editorial market, lectures and photo training days, print sales and gallery art prints.
Address: Based in the Forest of Dean. 07771 664 973.
e-mail: info@davidbroadbent.com
www.davidbroadbent.com

BUCKINGHAM, John
Worldwide bird and wildlife photographer.
Subjects: Huge range of birds, botany and wildlife from UK, Europe, Africa, Americas, Australia, Asia and worldwide.
Products and services: Digital images available for publication and purchase plus original slides for lectures and personal use.
Address: 3 Cardinal Close, Tonbridge, Kent, TN9 2EN; (Tel/fax) 01732 354 970.
e-mail: john.birdtalk@btinternet.com

GALVIN, Chris
A birding photographer with passion for birds for more than 30 years.
Subjects: Birds.
Products and services: Images for publication, prints, mounted prints, commissions considered.
Address: 17 Henley Road, Allerton, Liverpool, Merseyside L18 2DN; 07802 428 385 or 0151 729 0123.
e-mail: chris@chrisgalvinphoto.com
www.chrisgalvinphoto.com

GROVE, Ashley
Professional photographer, tour leader, lecturer and runs photography workshops. References on request if required.
Tours: Ashley arranges and leads very reasonably priced tours for wildlife photographers and birdwatchers. He has led tours to The Gambia since 2011 and other destinations are opening up during 2014/15, including a challenging two week tour to Trinidad & Tobago to photograph Hummingbirds and many other resident beauties. Visit Ashley's website for more information on the tours and to see a selection of images he has gathered on his trips.
Address: 16, Lint Meadow, Wythall, Worcestershire B47 5PH; 07704 189 835; e-mail: birdergrove@gmail.com
www.ashleygrovewildimages.co.uk

JAMES HAMILTON-BIRD
Photographer. lecturer and former RSPB local Group leader. Organiser of African photo safari trips to Kenya, Tanzania and Botswana. Plus (in association with the South African company; www.epic-enabled.com) the Kruger for disabled travellers in specially adapted vehicles, (contact James or Epic direct).
Subjects: 12 plus slide talks and digital presentations on wildlife and worldwide travel, having spent 23 years living abroad.
Products for sale: Prints, postcards and mouse mats.
Address: 6 Valentine Gardens, Kimbolton, Huntingdon, Cambridgeshire PE28 0HX; 01480 700 833 (home); (M)07941 633 355; http://birdseyeviewphotos.weebly. com; e-mail: birdseyeviewphotos@yahoo.co.uk
www.flickr.com/photos/birdseyeviewphotos

DIRECTORY OF WILDLIFE PHOTOGRAPHERS

LANE, Mike
Wildlife photographer and lecturer.
Subjects: Birds and wildlife from around the world, also landscapes and the environment.
Products and services: Website with instantly downloadable online pictures. Talks and workshops.
Address: 36 Berkeley Road, Shirley, Solihull, West Midlands B90 2HS; 0121 744 7988; (M)07766 418 013; e-mail: mikelane@nature-photography.co.uk
www.nature-photography.co.uk

LENTON, Graham
PhD Ornithology/Ecology. Former lecturer at Oxford University and Oxford Brookes University. Lifetime photographer of wildlife (LRPS), publications of articles and photographs of birds and wildlife.
Subjects: Worldwide birds, mammals of Africa, wildlife, worldwide travel.
Products and services: Photos available for sale or reproduction.
Address: The Old School, 25A Standlake Road, Ducklington, Witney, Oxon OX29 7UR; 01993 899 033.
e-mail: grahamlenton@btopenworld.com
www.gml-art.co.uk

LINGARD, David
Wildlife photographer, retired from RAF, now UK delegate to LIPU (BirdLife in Italy).
Subjects: Birds and views of places visited around the world.
Products and services: 35mm transparencies (last Century) but now, exclusively digital images.
Address: Fernwood, Doddington Road, Whisby, Lincs LN6 9BX; 01522 689 030; e-mail: mail@lipu-uk.org
www.lipu-uk.org

MAGENNIS, Steve
Steve Magennis Wildlife Photography, wildlife and working dog photographer, lecturer and workshop leader, British Wildlife Photography Awards 2012 highly commended image, Leica Fieldsports Photographer of the Year 2014
Subjects: British wildlife, bird life and landscapes.
Products and services: Commissioned photography, image library, canvases, framed and mounted prints, mounted prints (various sizes), greetings cards (cards can be personalised with personal or company details), photo keyrings plus other products. Photographic workshops, half-day, full-day and holidays.
Address: 3 Chepstow Close,St James, Northampton, Northants, NN5 7EB; 01604 467 848; (M)07803 619 272; e-mail: photos@stevemagennis.co.uk
www.facebook.com/SteveMagennisWildlifePhotography

NEWTON, Ian
Photographer (ARPS) and lecturer, former Chairman York Ornithological Club.
Subjects: Mainly birds and other wildlife of North, Central and South America, Europe and UK.
Products and services: Prints, canvas & board mounted images etc.
Address: 5 Fairfields Drive, Skelton, York YO30 1YP ; 01904 471 446; (M)07976 849 832;
e-mail: iannewton@acsemail.co.uk
www.iannewtonphotography.com

PARKER, Allan and Susan ARPS
Professional photographers (ASPphoto - Images of Nature) lecturers and tutors.
Subjects: Birds plus other flora and fauna from the UK, Spain, Lesvos, Cyprus, Florida and Texas.
Products and services: 35mm and digital images, mounted digital images, greetings cards and digital images on CD/DVD for reproduction (high quality scans up to A3+).
Address: Windhover Barn, 51b Kiveton Lane, Todwick, Sheffield, South Yorkshire, S26 1HJ; 01909 770 238.
e-mail: aspphoto@btinternet.com

READ, Mike
Photographer (wildlife and landscapes), tour leader, writer.
Subjects: Birds, mammals, plants, landscapes, and some insects. UK, France, USA, Ecuador (including Galapagos) plus many more. Behaviour, action, portraits, artistic pictures available for publication. More than 100,000 images in stock.
Products and services: Extensive stock photo library. Canvas and giclee prints, greetings cards, books.
Address: Claremont, Redwood Close, Ringwood, Hampshire, BH24 1PR; 01425 475 008.
e-mail: mike@mikeread.co.uk
www.mikeread.co.uk

SMART, Oliver
Photographer, lecturer and ornithologist.
Subjects: All wildlife subjects, UK based, also Alaska, Antarctica, Canada, Cuba, Ethiopia, Europe, Falkland Islands, Madagascar, New Zealand, Patagonia, Seychelles and South Georgia.
Products and services: Acrylic prints, aluminium prints, aluminescent prints, bean bags, canvas prints, desk calendars, digital image library, digital slideshow lectures, greeting cards, mounted prints (to A2 size), photographic tours and workshops and puzzles.
Address: 78 Aspen Park Road, Weston-Super-Mare, Somerset BS22 8ER; (M)07802 417 810.
e-mail: oliver@smartimages.co.uk
www.smartimages.co.uk

TYLER, John
Subjects: Plants, fungi, insects and other invertebrates.
Products and services: Images for sale.
Address: 5 Woodfield, Lacey Green, Buckinghamshire, HP3 0QQ; 07814 392 335.
e-mail: johnclarketyler@gmail.com
www.johntyler.co.uk

WARD, Chris
Lecturer, N Bucks RSPB local group leader.
Subjects: Primarily birds (and some other wildlife) and landscapes from UK and worldwide (Spain, Mallorca, Romania, Cyprus, Oman, Americas, Africa).
Products and services: Digital images and prints on request.
Address: 41 William Smith Close, Woolstone, Milton Keynes, MK15 0AN; 01908 669 448.
e-mail: cwphotography@hotmail.com
www.cwardphotography.co.uk

DIRECTORY OF LECTURERS

ALMOND, Jim
Photographer and very active birder. Experienced lecturer.
Subjects: See website for full descriptive details and titles. Wild Peregrines; Birding in Shropshire/ Venus Pool; Out and About in the UK (year listing); North Norfolk; Bird and Nature Photography; Bird identification plus other wildlife including butterflies and dragonflies. All talks are digitally presented in an entertaining style with audio-visual finale. I can cater for all levels of interest.
Fees: £80 for standard lecture plus fuel at 30p per mile. **Limits:** None. **Time limitations:** None
Address: 5 Coolock Close, St Peters Park, Shrewsbury SY3 9QD; 07940 678 719.
e-mail: almond.jim@virgin.net
Website: http://shropshirebirder.co.uk/

BASTON, Bill
Photographer, lecturer.
Subjects: East Anglian rarities and common birds, Mediterranean birds and landscapes, Northern Greece & Western Turkey, Spain, Goa, General wildlife photography, The Gambia, Northern India (birds and tigers), Costa Rica, North East India and the Himalayan foothills, Western Australia, Morocco, Wildlife of Sri Lanka.
Fees: Negotiable. **Limits:** Preferably within East Anglia.
Address: 86 George Street, Hadleigh, Ipswich, IP7 5BU; 01473 827 062.
e-mail: billbaston@btinternet.com
www.billbaston.com

BELL, Graham
Cruise lecturer worldwide, photographer, author, former BBRC member.
Subjects: Arctic, Antarctic, Siberia, Australia,Iceland, Seychelles, UK-identification, behaviour, seabirds, garden birds, entertaining bird sound imitations, birds in myth and fact, bird names, taking better photos, etc.
Fees: £20 plus travel and B&B if required. **Limits:** None. **Time limitations:** None.
Address: Ros View, South Yearle, Wooler, Northumberland, NE71 6RB; 01668 281310.
e-mail: seabirdsdgb@hotmail.com

BOND, Terry
Ex-company chairman, international consultant, bank director. Conference speaker worldwide, photographer, group field leader, lecturer on birds for more than 30 years.
Subjects: Six talks - including Scilly Isles, Southern Europe, North America, Scandinavia, 'Birdwatching Identification - a New Approach' (an audience participation evening).
Fees: By arrangement (usually only expenses). **Limits:** Most of UK. **Time limitations:** Evenings.
Address: 3 Lapwing Crescent, Chippenham, Wiltshire, SN14 6YF; 01249 462 674.
e-mail: terryebond@btopenworld.com

BOWDEN, Paul
Birdwatcher and nature photographer (Video, HD-Video and DSLR photos of birds and other wildlife) for 30+ years (serious amateur). Founder member and current Chairman of Glamorgan Wildlife Photographic Club (see website). Member of local bird and nature clubs, RSPB and WWT. I provide my own HD Projector, HD Laptop, amplifier and speakers. I can also bring a screen if necessary.
Subjects: Birds of Europe (Austria, Bulgaria, Estonia, Finland, Germany, Greece, Hungary, Italy, Portugal, Spain, Sweden & UK), Egypt, Libya, Morocco, Oman, Azerbaijan, India, Hong Kong, Japan, Australia, Panama, USA (9 States: AZ, CA, FL, HI, IL, MO, OR, TX, WA) and Canada. Also Butterflies and Dragonflies of UK, Europe and Overseas. Presentations as Video, HD Video and/or Powerpoint.
Fees: Lecture fee of £55 plus reasonable travelling expenses (plus overnight accommodation for longer trips). **Limits:** None, but longer trips may require overnight stay. **Time limitations:** None. Lecture anytime by arrangement.
Address: 4 Patmore Close, Gwaelod-y-Garth, Cardiff, CF15 9SU; 029 2081 3044; (M)077 7166 4819; e-mail: bowden_pe@hotmail.com

BROADBENT, David
Photographer.
Subjects: UK birds and wild places. In praise of natural places.
Fees: £45 locally. **Limits:** 30mls without travel costs, anywhere otherwise.
Time limitations: None.
Address: Based in the Forest of Dean. 07771 664 973; e-mail: info@davidbroadbent.com
www.davidbroadbent.com

BROOKS, Richard
Wildlife photographer, writer, lecturer, birding guide.
Subjects: Over a dozen talks, including Lemnos, Lesvos, Evros Delta, Kerkini, Spain, Israel, Canaries, Oman, plus E.Anglia, Wales, Scotland and Western Isles (Uist, Mull and Islay).
Fees: £80 plus petrol. **Limits:** None if accom provided.
Time limitations: None.
Address: 24 Croxton Hamlet, Fulmodeston, Fakenham, Norfolk, NR21 0NP; 01328 878 632.
e-mail: email@richard-brooks.co.uk
(or r.brooks662@btinternet.com)
www.richard-brooks.co.uk

BUCKINGHAM, John
Long-standing and popular lecturer, photographer, tour leader.
Subjects: 60+ titles covering birds, wildlife, botany, ecology and habitats in UK, Europe, Africa, Australia, Indian sub-continent, North-South and Central America including favourites such as 'How Birds Work', 'The Natural History of Birds' and 'Wonders of Bird Migration'.
Fees: £90 plus expenses. **Limits:** None.
Time limitations: None.

DIRECTORY OF LECTURERS

Address: 3 Cardinal Close, Tonbridge, Kent, TN9 2EN; (Tel/fax) 01732 354 970.
e-mail: john.birdtalk@btinternet.com

CARRIER, Michael
Lifelong interest in natural history.
Subjects: 1) 'Birds in Cumbria', 2) 'The Solway and its Birds' and 3)'The Isle of May', 4)'A look at Bird Migration', 5)'A Lifetime of Birds', 6)'Some Remarkable Islands.
Fees: £20. **Limits:** None but rail connection helpful. **Time limitations:** Sept-March inclusive, afternoons or evenings.
Address: Lismore Cottage, 1 Front Street, Armathwaite, Carlisle, Cumbria, CA4 9PB; 01697 472 218; e-mail: m.carrier333@gmail.com

CLEAVE, Andrew MBE
Wildlife photographer, author, lecturer and tour leader.
Subjects: More than 30 talks (including India, Galapagos, Iceland, Mediterranean birds and wildlife, Lundy, Shetland, Ancient Woodlands, Dormice and Seashore). Full list available.
Fees: £70 plus petrol. **Limits:** Approx. 60 mls without o.n accom. **Time limitations:** Afternoons and evenings, not school holidays.
Address: 31 Petersfield Close, Chineham, Basingstoke, Hampshire, RG24 8WP; 01256 320 050.
e-mail: andrew@bramleyfrith.co.uk

CONWAY, Marcus
Scottish Nature Photographer of the Year, Marcus Conway can share his experience and images from a range of Scottish locations. With a degree in zoology and over 10,000 photography hours Marcus delights audiences with his laid back style and unique photography that captures the essence of wild Scotland.
Subjects: Inspiring and educational media covering Mull, Skye, The Outer Hebrides, Islay, Shetland, Ardnamurchan and his home base in the Highlands.
Fees: £45 plus reasonable expenses, No fee for charitable donation. **Limits:** For discussion! **Time limitations:** No restrictions.
Address: Toll House, Ardersier, Inverness, IV2 7SX; 07957 123 274; e-mail: info@ebirder.net
www.ebirder.net

COUZENS, Dominic
Full-time birdwatcher, tour leader (UK and overseas), writer and lecturer.
Subjects: The Secret Lives of Garden Birds', 'Birds Behaving Badly — the trials and tribulations of birds through the year', 'Have Wings Will Travel' — the marvel of bird migration, 'Vive la Difference' — a comparison of British birds with those across the Channel, 'My Family and 50 Other Animals' — a year spent trying to show 2 young children 50 species of mammals in Britain, 'Birding a Local Patch', Mammal Watching in Britain, Puffins Near and Far, Encounters with Remarkable Birds, Europe's Top 10 Birding Sites.
Fees: £100 plus travel. **Limits:** London and south.

Time limitations: None.
Address: 3 Clifton Gardens, Ferndown, Dorset, BH22 9BE; (Tel/fax) 01202 874 330.
e-mail: dominic.couzens@btinternet.com
www.birdwords.co.uk

CROMACK, David
Professional journalist and publisher, currently President of Peterborough Bird Club.
Subjects: 1) Wild West Birding (Arizona and California); 2) World Class Bird Images (International Wildbird Photographer competitions); 3) More World Class Bird Images; 4) Asia's Teardrop - Birding in Sri Lanka; 5) Bird Artists of the Modern Era. Leaflet available on request. In preparation, 'America's Serengeti — wildlife of Yellowstone'; 'Return to the Splendid Isle (Sri Lanka).
Fees: £80 plus travel expenses (30p per mile). **Limits:** 150 miles from Peterborough. **Times:** All requests considered.
Address: 55 Thorpe Park Road, Peterborough PE3 6LJ. 01733 566 815; e-mail: d.cromack@btinternet.com

COLLINS, Chris
Wildwings tour leader, Neotropical Bird Club council member & treasurer, experienced lecturer and semi-professional wildlife photographer.
Subjects: In search of the Spoon-billed Sandpiper/ Birds of the Russian Far East; Finding a new species: the 'New Caledonian Storm-petrel', Pacific Odyssey: New Zealand to Japan; Birds of Antarctica and the Southern Ocean Islands; Birds of Guyana; South America: The Bird Continent; Amazing Birds; Around the World in 80 minutes.
Fees: £100 + travel expenses. **Limits:** Four hours from Surrey/London or overnight accommodation.
Time limitations: None – lecture dates/times by prior agreement.
Address: 9 Pound Close, Long Ditton, Surbiton, Surrey KT6 5JW. 020 8398 1742;
e-mail: chris@birdsandwildlife.com
www.birdsandwildlife.com/lectures

DAVIES, Alan & MILLER, Ruth
Alan and Ruth both worked for the RSPB before giving up their jobs to travel the world, setting a new birding world record for the most bird species recorded in a single year: 4,341 species. They now run The Biggest Twitch, their own birdwatching tour and talks company. They are based in North Wales but run tours throughout the UK and beyond.
Subjects: The Biggest Twitch, around the world in 4,000 birds — the entertaining warts-and-all story of their big birding year; Also a range of illustrated talks each covering birding in a different region including the UK, Europe, South America, North America, Ethiopia, Southern Africa, Australia, and India. We are continuously adding to our range of talks.
Fees: £70 for the talk plus the cost of fuel used on the return journey. **Limits:** None, though overnight accommodation needed for talks too far from North Wales to return the same evening.
Time limitations: Very flexible all year, please e-mail

DIRECTORY OF LECTURERS

to check availability.
Address: 12 Ormeside Court, 19 Church Walks, Llandudno Ll30 2HG; 01492 872 407; e-mail: info@birdwatchingtrips.co.uk www.birdwatchingtrips.co.uk

ELSOM, Stuart ACIEEM LRPS
Tour leader, professional ecologist and wildlife photographer with Royal Photographic Society distinction.
Subjects: Currently offers around a dozen talks covering a wide range of birding destinations across six continents.
Fees: £70 and 40p per mile travel expenses.
Limits: Willing to travel up to 100 miles.
Time limitations: Daytime and evening. Travelling for approx 5 months per year normally with several weeks in between, so reasonable notice (6+ months) required when booking talks.
Address: 117 Andrew Road, St.Neots, Cambs, PE19 2PP; e-mail: stuartelsom@btinternet.com (please note a delayed e-mail response could be due to tour-leading commitments, definitely not due to lack of interest) www.stuartelsom.co.uk Facebook: www.facebook.com/stu.elsom Flickr: https://www.flickr.com/photos/126819682@N04/sets/

EYRE, John
Author, photographer, ornithological consultant and ex-chairman Hampshire Ornithological Society.
Subjects: Many talks covering birding around the world (Europe, Africa, Asia, Australasia and the Americas), plus special Hampshire subjects. Examples include: 'New Zealand — Seabird Feast, Land Bird Famine', California Birds — Sea, Sage and Spotted Owls', 'Birds of Wallacea — Where Continents Collide', 'Gilbert White's Birds' and 'The Secret Lives of Heathland Birds'. Several others, so please call or e-mail to discuss options.
Fees: £75 plus travel. **Limits:** Any location negotiable. **Time limitations:** None.
Address: 3 Dunmow Hill, Fleet, Hampshire, GU51 3AN; 01252 677 850; e-mail: John.Eyre@ntlworld.com

FORGHAM, Jonathan
Primary school teacher for 30 years, now running science enhancement company and professional bird guide. Has given over 70 illustrated talks to bird groups in last three years in south east of England and occasionally, further afield. Visited most of Europe and parts of Asia and Australia, too. Life-long birder and all round naturalist, recording all aspects of nature within the parish of Little Hadham, East Hertfordshire. References available, all excellent. See website for recent bookings.
Subjects: The Birds of the North Norfolk Coastal Footpath; The Birds of The Camargue; The Birds of The Algarve and Baixa Alentejo; The Birds of southern Sri Lanka; The Bird Reserves of Kent; The Whole Natural History of an East Hertfordshire Parish (will provide own laptop, cables, and projector).
Fees: £80 in total for 150 mile round trip. £100 in total for in excess of 150 mile round trip. In excess

of 200 mile round trip, fee negotiable. **Limits:** Live in Herts so easy access to motorways, no restrictions under around 200 mile round trip. **Time limitations:** Available evenings, daytime too (if early booking).
Address: 6, Chapel Lane, Little Hadham, Ware, Herts SG11 2AA; 01279 776 112 (evenings) 07805 571 551 (day and texts); e-mail: jforgham@hotmail.com; http://littlehadhambirding.blogspot.co.uk

GALLOP, Brian
Speaker, photographer, tour leader.
Subjects: 35 talks covering UK, Africa, India, Galapagos, South America and Europe (All natural history subjects). Made-to-measure talks available on request. 24hr emergency service.
Fees: £50 plus travel expenses. **Limits:** None but overnight accomodation if over 100 mls.
Time limitations: None.
Address: 13 Orchard Drive, Tonbridge, Kent, TN10 4LT; 01732 361 892; e-mail: brian_gallop@hotmail.co.uk

GALVIN, Chris
A birding photographer with passion for birds for more than 30 years.
Subjects: Northwest Year', 'Around the World in 80 Birds', 'Bee-eaters & Kingfishers: an intro to the Birds of Goa', 'Birding by Camera', 'Birding on the Doorstep', 'Just Add Water'.
Fees: £80 to £140 depending on distance travelled.
Limits: 125 miles radius from home.
Address: 17 Henley Road, Allerton, Liverpool, Merseyside L18 2DN; 07802 428 385 or 0151 729 0123; e-mail: chris@chrisgalvinphoto.com www.chrisgalvinphoto.com

GARNER, Jackie, FRSA
Professional wildlife artist, author & illustrator of *The Wildlife Artist's Handbook*.
Subjects: Birds/Nature in Art, Focus on the Falklands, Wildlife of Ancient Egypt, Wildlife Artist's World, The Making of a Wildlife Art Book.
Fees: £100 + expenses.
Distance limits: None. **Time limits:** None.
Address: The Old Cider House Studio, Humphries End, Randwick, Stroud, Glos GL6 6EW; 01453 847 420; (M)07800 804 847; e-mail: artist@jackiegarner.co.uk www.jackiegarner.co.uk

GARTSHORE, Neil
23-years working in nature conservation (National Trust, South Africa, RSPB) now a freelance contractor, writer, lecturer, tour guide and natural history book seller.
Subjects: Various talks including South Africa; Sub-Antarctic Prince Edward Islands; Japan; Farne Islands; Heathlands; and Poole Harbour.
Fees: Negotiable. **Limits:** Anything considered.
Time limitations: Flexible.
Address: Moor Edge, 2 Bere Road, Wareham, Dorset BH20 4DD; 01929 552 560; e-mail: neilgartshore@btinternet.com

213

DIRECTORY OF LECTURERS

GLENN, Neil
Author of *Best Birdwatching Sites in Norfolk*; regular contributor to *Bird Watching* magazine; bird tour leader for Avian Adventures. UK Rep for South Texas Nature and also a Patron for Birding For All.
Subjects: Wildlife of the Lower Rio Grande Valley, Texas. Birding the Arctic Circle. Moroccan Spice: From The Sahara to The Atlas Mountains. More to follow!
Fees: Negotiable. **Limits:** None.
Time limitations: Any day.
Address: 13 Gladstone Avenue, Gotham, Nottingham NG11 0HN; 0115 983 0946.
e-mail: n.glenn@ntlworld.com

GROVE, Ashley
Professional photographer, with a specialism in wildlife images. A list of available lectures is below. References on request if required.
Subjects: 1)'Shetland to Scilly; Birds of the British Isles', 2) 'Jewels of the Gambia, Kingfishers, Bee-eaters & Rollers', 3) 'Great British Birds', 4) 'Lammergeiers of the Spanish Pyrenees'. 5) 'Trinidad & Tobago, Home of the Hummingbird' 6) 'A Beginners Guide to Birdwatching'. More talks under construction.
Fees: £80 plus 25p per mile expenses (this may be negotiable if you are able to recommend a nearby group to speak to on an adjacent evening). **Limits:** None within reason. **Time limitations:** None.
Address: 16, Lint Meadow, Wythall, Worcestershire B47 5PH; 07704 189 835;
e-mail: birdergrove@gmail.com
www.ashleygrovewildimages.co.uk/lectures.php

HAMILTON-BIRD, James
Photographer, lecturer and former RSPB local group leader. Organiser of African Photo safari trips to Kenya, Tanzania and Botswana. Plus (in association with the South African company; www.epic-enabled. com) the Kruger for disabled travellers in specially adapted vehicles, (contact James or Epic direct).
Subjects: 12 plus slide talks and digital presentations on wildlife and worldwide travel, having spent 23 years living abroad.
Fees: £80 within a 50 mile round trip from home, inclusive of fuel. Over 50 miles by arrangement.
Limits: Nowhere too far. **Times:** Any time to suit.
Address: 6 Valentine Gardens, Kimbolton, Huntingdon, Cambridgeshire PE28 0HX; 01480 700 833 (home); (M)07941 633 355;
e-mail: birdseyeviewphotos@yahoo.co.uk
http://birdseyeviewphotos.weebly.com
www.flickr.com/photos/birdseyeviewphotos

LANE, Mike
Wildlife photographer and lecturer.
Subjects: Many talks from the UK and abroad.
Fees: Negotiable. **Limits:** None.
Time limitations: None.
Address: 36 Berkeley Road, Shirley, Solihull, West Midlands B90 2HS; 0121 744 7988; (M)07766 418 013;
e-mail: mikelane@nature-photography.co.uk
www.nature-photography.co.uk

LENTON, Graham
PhD Ornithology/Ecology. Former lecturer at Oxford University and Oxford Brookes University. Lifetime photographer of wildlife (LRPS), has published articles and photographs of birds and wildlife.
Subjects: Barn Owls of Malaysia and rat control; Birds of the Seychelles; Wildlife and birds of Antarctica; Birds of New Zealand; Birds of Namibia; Two Islands (Handa & The Farnes); An Arctic Journey; Svalbard; Gorilla in my midst – a Ugandan Odyssey; Barn Owls – past, present and their future; Wildlife of Madagascar – a genetic melting pot; Springtime in Finland; Alaska – the last frontier.
Fees: £65. **Limits:** Preferably within 60mls.
Time limitations: One hour to 90 minute talks.
Address: The Old School, 25A Standlake Road, Ducklington, Witney, Oxon OX29 7UR; 01993 899 033;
e-mail: grahamlenton@btopenworld.com
www.gml-art.co.uk

LINGARD, David
Photographer, retired from RAF, now UK delegate to LIPU (BirdLife in Italy).
Subjects: Choice of talks on birding but primarily on Birdwatching in Italy and the work of LIPU.
Fees: Donation to LIPU, plus petrol costs.
Limits: None. **Time limitations:** None.
Address: Fernwood, Doddington Road, Whisby, Lincs LN6 9BX; 01522 689 030;
e-mail: mail@lipu-uk.org
www.lipu-uk.org

LOVELL, Stephen
Naturalist, RSPB lecturer, photographer, adult education teacher.
Subjects: Talks available on several European destinations including Lesvos, Majorca, Extremadura and Britain .Other talks available on a wide variety of destinations to include Costa Rica, Trinidad and Tobago, Nepal, Sri Lanka, Southern India, New Zealand, Australia, Tanzania and St Lucia. I also have a wide variety of talks on the topic to encourage Wildlife into our Gardens and generic ornithological topics such as migration etc.
Fees: £50 to £90 plus travel or overnight accommodation. **Limits:** 130 miles from Lincoln.
Time limitations: None.
Address: 6 Abingdon Close, Doddington Park, Lincoln LN6 3UH; 01522 689 456; (M)07957 618 684.
e-mail: stephenlovell58@btinternet.com
www.stevelovellgreenspaces.co.uk

MAGENNIS, Steve
Steve Magennis Wildlife Photography, wildlife and working dog photographer, lecturer and workshop leader, British Wildlife Photography Awards 2012 highly commended image, Leica Fieldsports Photographer of the Year 2014
Subjects: All talks are audio visual and subjects include wildlife photography, bird life and related subjects (contact me for more details).
Fees: £95 plus travel @ 40p per mile. **Limits:** Up to

150 miles. **Time limitations:** Available all year round, day or evening.
Address: 3 Chepstow Close, St James, Northampton, Northants, NN5 7EB; 01604 467 848; (M)07803 619 272; www.facebook.com/SteveMagennisWildlifePhotography
e-mail: photos@stevemagennis.co.uk

MAYER, Edward
Founder of London's Swifts and Swift Conservation, formerly Head of Gallery Management at the Tate Gallery.
Subjects: Swifts, Their lives and their Conservation; Biodiversity Strategies and Techniques for the Built Environment; Presentations and training for enthusiasts, ornithologists, architects, developers, town planners and biodiversity officers.
Fees: From £70 depending on type and length of talk, or collection/donation, plus travel expenses. **Limits:** UK/Europe.
Address: 28 Yale Court, Honeybourne Road, London NW6 1JG; 020 7794 2098.
e-mail: mail@swift-conservation.org
www.swift-conservation.org

MILES, John
Former warden for RSPB Geltsdale in Cumbria, tour guide, consultant and author of *Best Birdwatching Sites: The Solway, Hadrian's Birds, Exploring Lakeland Wildlife, Pharoah's Birds, Hadrian's Wildlife* and magazine articles. Series of children's books.
Subjects: 1) 'The Solway' covers birding throughout the whole of Cumbria and Dumfries & Galloway; 2) 'Hadrian's Wildlife' examines the habitats along Hadrian's Wall from Cumbria to Tyne & Wear and the history of birds back to Roman time. 3) 'Death on the Nile' looks at the history of birds from Ancient Egypt to present time birds while cruising the Nile.
Fees: Prices on request. **Limits:** Anywhere in UK.
Time limitations: Evenings best.
Address: Jockey Shield, Castle Carrock, Carlisle, Cumbria CA4 9NF; 01228 670 205;
e-mail: jmiles3@toucansurf.com

NEWTON, Ian
Photographer (ARPS) and lecturer, former Chairman York Ornithological Club.
Subjects: 14 talks, all digital, mainly birds and other wildlife of North, Central and South America, Europe and UK.
Fees: £60 plus petrol. **Limits:** None.
Time limitations: None.
Address: 5 Fairfields Drive, Skelton, York YO30 1YP; 01904 471 446; (M)07976 849 832;
e-mail: iannewton@acsemail.co.uk
www.iannewtonphotography.com

OFFORD, Keith
Photographer, writer, tour leader, conservationist.
Subjects: 16 talks covering raptors, flight, uplands, gardens, migration, woodland wildlife, Australia, Southern USA, Gambia, Spain, Iceland, Costa Rica, Namibia, Western Cape.
Fees: £100 plus travel. **Limits:** None.
Time limitations: Sept to April.
Address: Yew Tree Farmhouse, Craignant, Selattyn, Nr Oswestry, Shropshire, SY10 7NP; 01691 718 740;
e-mail: keith.offord@virgin.net
www.keithofford.co.uk

PARKER, Allan and Susan ARPS
Professional photographers, (ASPphoto – Images of Nature), lecturers and tutors.
Subjects: 16 plus slide and digital talks on birds and natural history, natural history photography - countries include UK, USA (Texas, Florida), Spain, Greece, Cyprus.
Fees: On application. **Limits:** Any distance with o.n accom or up to 120 mls without.
Time limitations: None.
Address: Windhover Barn, 51b Kiveton Lane, Todwick, Sheffield, South Yorkshire, S26 1HJ; 01909 770 238;
e-mail: aspphoto@btinternet.com

PICKERING, Pollyanna
Wildlife Artist, conservationist.
Subjects: 12 talks available on a variety of subjects, from running a wildlife sanctuary in Derbyshire to travelling into remote areas to paint endangered species in their natural habitat. Details of individual talks on request.
Fees: £150 plus travelling expenses. **Limits:** None.
Time limitations: Evening talks only.
Address: Brookvale House, Oaker, Matlock, Derbyshire DE4 2JJ; 01629 55 851.
e-mail: annalouise@talktalk.net
www.pollyannapickering.co.uk

READ, Mike
Photographer, tour leader, writer.
Subjects: 12 talks featuring British and foreign subjects (list available on receipt of sae or see website).
Fees: £70 plus travel. **Limits:** 100 mls from Ringwood.
Time limitations: Talks available 1st Sept to 31st March each winter.
Address: Claremont, Redwood Close, Ringwood, Hampshire, BH24 1PR; 01425 475 008.
e-mail: mike@mikeread.co.uk
www.mikeread.co.uk

REDMAN, Nigel
Tour leader, publisher and author.
Subjects: Mostly birds, including Ethiopia, Somaliland, Kenya, Morocco, Russia (and former Soviet Union), the Caucasus, and Antarctica.
Fees: Negotiable. **Limits:** None (but overnight accommodation may be required).
Time limitations: None.
Address: Hollyhocks, Edgefield Road, Briston, Norfolk NR24 2HX; 01263 862 866; 07734 886 515.
e-mail: nigel.redman@bloomsbury.com

ROTHERHAM, Prof Ian

Former local authority ecologist, environmental campaigner, researcher, lecturer, writer and broadcaster.
Subjects: Numerous illustrated talks on all aspects of conservation: the 'Lost Fens', 'Wild woods and woodland heritage', 'Wildlife and history of moors, heaths and bogs',' Urban wildlife', 'Gardening for Wildlife', 'Alien and invasive species', 'Wild Peak District', 'Eco-history', 'Wilding Nature' and more.
Fees: £85, plus petrol 50p per mile. **Limits:** Prepared to travel if expenses are covered. **Time limitations:** Any time by arrangement.
Address: 42 School Lane, Norton, Sheffield, S8 8BL; 7751 089 499; e-mail: i.d.rotherham@shu.ac.uk
www.ukeconet.org
Blog: http://ianswalkonthewildside.wordpress.com/

SCOTT, Ann

Retired. Formerly Senior Wildlife Adviser for RSPB, lecturer and teacher of ornithology.
Subjects: Various talks on UK and abroad (please ask for list), plus a new talk entitled; 'Pineapple Peril' tells the story of the purchase of the Kirosa Scott Forest in Kenya, which has been bought through an appeal in memory of her husband Bob. Details of the appeal and its aims can be found at www.justgiving.com/ann-scott/.
Fees: £50 plus expenses (negotiable).
Limits: Normally 2 hours drive from Huntingdon but willing to discuss. **Time limitations:** Any month from Mid-March to Mid-November.
Address: 17, Springfield Close, Buckden, Huntingdon, Cambs. PE19 5UR; 01480 811 848.
e-mail: abscott@buckdencambs.co.uk

SMART, Oliver

Photographer, lecturer and ornithologist.
Subjects: 1) 'A Voyage to the South Atlantic'; 2) 'The Science & Beauty of Birds'; 3) 'Exploring Ethiopia'; 4) 'Butterfly Britain'; 5) 'From 60 Degrees North'; 6) 'Cameras and Creatures, from Cumbria to Canada'; 7) 'Cuba: A Flicker of Interest'; 8) 'Birds of Lesvos'; 9) 'RAW Nature: Images Uncovered'; 10) 'Grizzly Bears of Alaska'.
Fees: £80 plus 25p per mile plus £10 per hour above two hours total travel time. **Limits:** None and can also provide own accommodation.
Time limitations: None.
Address: 78 Aspen Park Road, Weston-Super-Mare, Somerset BS22 8ER; (M)07802 417 810.
e-mail: oliver@smartimages.co.uk
www.smartimages.co.uk

STAMFORD, Alan

Former leader of Blackpool Local RSPB Group, staff member at Leighton Moss RSPB Reserve and former leader of local Wildlife Explorers group.
Subjects: Birding Around Britain; Birds of the Fylde; Leighton Moss RSPB Reserve; Garden Birds; The Lake District and it's Birdlife; and Malhamdale.

Fees: £30 plus mileage 20p per mile. **Limits:** Within 100 miles. **Time limitations:** Any evenings plus daytime except weekends.
Address: 6 Kensington Road, Cleveleys, Lancs. FY5 1ER; e-mail: alanstamford140@msn.com

TODD, Ralph

Lecturer & photographer, former tour leader and course tutor.
Subjects: Galapagos - The Enchanted Isles'; 'On the Trail of the Crane – parts 1 and 2'; 'Polar Odyssey'; 'Operation Osprey'; 'Natural Wonders and Wildlife of Iceland'; 'Man & Birds-Travels through time'; 'Where Yeehaa meets Ole'; Birds in the Land of Disney; Antarctic Adventure; Springtime in Lesvos.
Fees: £75 plus expenses. **Limits:** None.
Time limitations: Anytime — also short notice.
Address: 9 Horsham Road, Bexleyheath, Kent, DA6 7HU; 01322 528 335.
e-mail: rbtodd@btinternet.com

TYLER, John

Wildlife walks and talks.
Subjects: The World of Insects; The World of Plants; The World of Fungi; The Seasons; Animal Architecture; The Glow-worm; The Changing Wildlife of the Chilterns; The Ridgeway: Europe's oldest road?
Fees: £60 plus 50p per mile. **Limits:** 25 mile radius from Princes Risborough, Bucks.
Time limitations: None.
Address: 5 Woodfield, Lacey Green, Buckinghamshire, HP27 0QQ; 07814 392 335.
e-mail: johnclarketyler@gmail.com
www.johntyler.co.uk

WARD, Chris

Photographer, N Bucks RSPB local group leader.
Subjects: 20+ talks on UK and worldwide topics (Spain, Mallorca, Romania, Cyprus, Oman, Americas, Africa) — primarily birds, some other wildlife.
Fees: £50 plus petrol @30p/mile. **Limits:** 120 miles.
Time limitations: None. Short notice possible.
Address: 41 William Smith Close, Woolstone, Milton Keynes, MK15 0AN; 01908 669 448.
e-mail: cwphotography@hotmail.com
www.cwardphotography.co.uk

WREN, Graham J. ARPS

Wildlife photographer, lecturer, tour guide.
Subjects: 25 talks featuring birds — UK 'Breeding Birds of Southern Britain' and 'Northern Britain', including habitats, also Scandinavia. Nest-boxes (new), the environment, wildlife of Kenya. Detailed information package supplied on request.
Fees: £50-80 plus petrol. **Limits:** None. **Time limitations:** None.
Address: The Kiln House, Great Doward, Whitchurch, Ross-on-Wye, Herefordshire, HR9 6DU; 01600 890 488.
e-mail: susanjhampshire@aol.com

BTO SPEAKERS

This directory has been compiled to help Bird Clubs and similar organisations in finding speakers for their indoor meetings. Each entry consists of an individual speaker, a list of talks/ lectures available, details of fees and expenses required and travel distance limitations. If you are interested in any of the speakers, please contact Ieuan Evans (ieuan.evans@bto.org) or Ellen Walford (ellen.walford@bto.org) directly. Alternatively, contact BTO: 01842 750 050. Members of the BTO/ Bird Clubs Partnership have a 25% discount.

Appleton, Graham (Director of Communications)
Subjects: Atlas 2007 – 11; Flyway to Iceland; Time to Fly – Bird Migration; Tracking African Migrants
Fees: £40 Negotiable. Distance: Dependent on expenses.

Austin, Dr Graham (Senior Research Ecologist, Wetland & Marine Research)
Subjects: Wetland Bird Survey.
Fees: £40. Distance: Travel by agreement.

Baillie, Dr Stephen (Science Director Modelling & Demography)
Subjects: BirdTrack; Population Monitoring.
Fees: £40. Distance: Travel by agreement.

Baker, Jeff (Head of Marketing)
Subjects: Little Brown Jobs – Warblers & How to Identify Them; The Work of the BTO; Garden Birds & Feeding.
Fees: £40. Distance: Dependent on expenses.

Balmer, Dawn (Atlas Co-ordinator)
Subjects: Bird Atlas 2007 - 11.
Fees: £40. Distance: 100 mile radius of Thetford.

Barimore, Carl (Nest Records Organiser)
Subjects: Nest Records Scheme.
Fees: £40. Distance: By agreement.

Blackburn, Jez (Licensing and Sales Manager)
Subjects: Demography Team Bird Moult (suitable for ringers); Ringing for Conservation; Sule Skerry Seabirds. Fees: £40 (£70 for private talks). Distance: East Anglia.

Bray, James (Fieldwork & Training Coordinator BTO Scotland)
Subjects: The Work of BTO Scotland; BTO Atlas 2007-11; BBS, Birdtrack & other BTO surveys in Scotland; Garden BirdWatch.
Fees: £40. Distance: By agreement.

Clark, Jacquie (Head of Demography Team & Head of Ringing Scheme)
Subjects: Waders & Severe Weather; Ringing for Conservation; Why Ring Birds?
Fees: £40. Distance: 100 mile radius of Thetford.

Clark, Dr Nigel (Head of Projects Development Department)
Subjects: Waders, Man & Estuaries; What hope for the Spoon-billed Sandpiper?
Fees: £40. Distance: 100 mile radius of Thetford.

Conway, Greg (Research Ecologist, Land-use Research)
Subjects: Nightjars; Woodlarks; Dartford Warblers; Wintering Warblers in the UK; Firecrests.
Fees: £40. Distance: 100 mile radius of Thetford.

Dadam, Dr Daria (Reseach Ecologist Demography)
Subjects: Bird Disease.
Fees: Negotiable. Distance: By agreement.

Fuller, Prof Rob (Director of Science)
Subjects: Changing Times for Woodland Birds.
Fees: £40. Distance: Anywhere.

Gillings, Dr Simon (Senior Research Ecologist Land Use Research)
Subjects: Atlas 2007 – 11; Winter Golden Plovers & Lapwings; Waders; Knot Migration; Winter Farmland Birds. Fees: £40. Distance: Negotiable.

Gough, Su (Editor, *BTO News* & Training Officer)
Subjects: The Work of the BTO; Urban Birds. Private talks: Wildlife of Canada; Wildlife of Southwestern USA; Wildlife of European Mountains; Wildlife of Texas; Wildlife of the Middle East.
Fees: £40. Distance: Negotiable.

Henderson, Dr Ian (Senior Research Ecologist International Research)
Subjects: Arable Farming and Birds.
Fees: £40. Distance: By agreement.

Johnson, Dr Alison (Ecological Statistician, Population Ecology & Modelling)
Subjects: Climate Change and Birds.
Fees: £40. Distance: East Anglia

Lack, Dr Peter (Information Services Manager)
Private talks: Palearctic Migrants in Africa; On Foot in Rwanda and Zambia; Ecology in East African Savannahs; General Natural History of Eastern Africa.
Fees: Negotiable. Distance: 60 miles of Bury St Edmunds.

Marchant, John (Projects Co-ordinator Monitoring)
Subjects: Monitoring Heronries: Nine Decades of Monitoring; Waterways Bird & Breeding Bird Surveys.
Fees: £40. Distance: By agreement.

Moran, Nick (BirdTrack Organiser)
Subjects: Mapping migration with BirdTrack; Hard weather effects on birds; Birds and birding in Arabia (private talk).
Fees: £40. Distance: By agreement.

Musgrove, Dr Andy (Head of Monitoring)
Subjects: The Wetland Bird Survey; Little Egrets in the UK. Fees: £40. Distance: By agreement.

Newson, Dr Stuart (Senior Research Ecologist' Population Ecology & Modelling)
Subjects: Tree nesting Cormorants.
Fees: £40. Distance: By agreement.

217

BTO SPEAKERS

Noble, Dr David (Principal Ecologist, Monitoring)
Subjects: Developing Bird Indicators; Population Trends. Fees: £40. Distance: By agreement.

Pearce-Higgins, Dr James (Principal Ecologist, Climate Change)
Subjects: Birds and climate change; Upland birds; A year in the life of a Golden Plover.
Fees: £40. Distance: By agreement.

Risely, Kate (Breeding Bird Survey National Organiser)
Subjects: BTO/JNCC/RSPB Breeding Birds Survey.
Fees: £40. Distance: By agreement.

Robinson, Dr Rob (Principal Ecologist, Modelling & Demography)
Subjects: Farming & Birds; Conservation Value of Ringing. Fees: £40. Distance: By agreement.

Ross-Smith, Dr Viola (Research Ecologist, Wetland & Marine)
Subjects: Gulls, seabirds, tracking studies.
Fees: £40. Distance: By agreement.

Simm, Clare (GBW Development Officer)
Subjects: Are Gardens Good for Birds or Birdwatchers?
Fees: £40. Distance: 50 mile radius of Thetford.

Siriwardena, Dr Gavin (Head of Land-Use Research)
Subjects: Research Farmland Birds (General); Marsh & Willow Tits; Quantifying Migratory Strategies; Winter Feeding of Farmland Birds.
Fees: £40. Distance: Negotiable.

Stancliffe, Paul (Press Officer)
Subjects: Atlas 2007-11; Homes to Let – Nestboxes; Birds, Birders and the Work of the BTO; Tracking African Migrants
Fees: £40. Distance: Negotiable.

Toms, Mike (Head of Garden Ecology Team)
Subjects: Are Gardens Good for Birds or Birdwatchers?
Fees: £40. Distance: 50 mile radius of Thetford.

Wernham, Dr Chris (Senior Research Ecologist BTO Scotland)
Subjects: The Work of BTO Scotland; Breeding Bird Survey in Scotland; BirdTrack in Scotland.
Fees: £40. Distance: Travel Scotland and NE England.

Wright, Dr Lucy (Research Ecologist, Wetland and Marine Research)
Subjects: Non-native Waterbirds in Eurasia & Africa.
Fees: £40. Distance: By agreement.

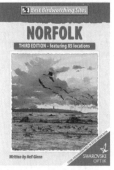
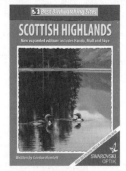

TRADE DIRECTORY

David Cromack

Sri Lanka is an attractive and affordable destination for UK birders and mammal watchers and many of the tour companies listed in our Trade Directory offer escorted tours to the 'Splendid Isle". Green Bee-eater is just one species you'll see.

Bird garden suppliers	220	Holiday companies	222
Bird and wildlife publications	220	Optical dealers	225
Book publishers	221	Optical importers and manufacturers	226
Book sellers	221	Optical repairs and servicing	227
Clothing suppliers	222	Technology products	228
Equipment suppliers	222		

TRADE DIRECTORY

TRADE DIRECTORY

OVER the next few pages you'll find a comprehensive guide to UK-based companies offering products or services of particular interest to active birdwatchers and wildlife enthusiasts. Our goal is to make this directory as up-to-date and comprehensive as possible, so if we've overlooked any companies that you feel should be included in future editions, please e-mail: d.cromack@btinternet.com with the relevant details.

BIRD GARDEN SUPPLIERS

ARK WILDLIFE LTD
Dog Kennel Farm, Charlton Road, Nr Hitchin, Herts SG5 2AB; 01462 420 000;
e-mail: office@arkwildlife.co.uk;
www.arkwildlife.co.uk

BAMFORDS TOP FLIGHT
Globe Mill, Midge Hall, Leyland, Lancashire PR26 6TN; 01772 456 300;
e-mail: sales@bamfords.co.uk;
www.bamfords.co.uk

BRINVALE BIRD FOODS
Brinvale Farm, Broughton Lane, Long Clawson, Melton Mowbray, Leics LE14 4NB; 01664 823 230; www.brinvale.com

CJ WILDBIRD FOODS LTD
The Rea, Upton Magna, Shrewsbury, Shropshire SY4 4UR; 0800 731 2820;
e-mail: sales@birdfood.co.uk;
www.birdfood.co.uk

EYEBROOK WILD BIRD FEEDS
Rectory Farm, Great E aston, LE16 8SN; 01536 770 771; e-mail: rectoryfarm@ eyebrookwildbirdfeeds.co.uk;
www.eyebrookwildbirdfeeds.co.uk

GARDENATURE
Manor Farm Business Centre, Manor Lane, Stutton, Ipswich, Suffolk IP9 2TD: 01473 563 000; www.gardenature.co.uk

JACOBI JAYNE & CO
Wealden Forest Park, Herne Common, Canterbury, Kent CT6 7LQ: 0800 072 0130; e-mail: enquiries@jacobijayne.com;
www.livingwithbirds.com

KENNEDY WILD BIRD FOODS LTD:
74 Station Road, Deeping St James, Peterborough PE6 8RQ; 01778 342 665;
e-mail: info@wildbirdfood.uk.com;
www.wildbirdfood.uk.com

NATURE CAMERAS
3b Bonegate Road, Brighouse, West Yorks HD6 1TQ; 01484 720 220;
e-mail: enquiries@naturecameras.co.uk;
www.naturecameras.co.uk

THE NESTBOX COMPANY
Eastcote House, Barston Lane, Eastcote, Solihull B92 0HS; 01675 442 299;
e-mail: sales@nestbox.co.uk;
www.nestbox.co.uk

THE OWL BOX
Tyddyn Waen, Llangaffo, Isle of Anglesey LL60 6LP; 01248 421 091;
e-mail: robin@the owlbox.co.uk;
www.theowlbox.co.uk

SOAR MILL SEED
Globe Mill, 17 Midge Hall Lane, Midge Hall, Leyland, Lancs PR26 6TN. 01772 456 317;
e-mail: soarmillseeds.co.uk

VINE HOUSE FARM BIRD FOODS
Vine House Farm, Deeping St Nicholas, Spalding, Lincs PE11 3DG. 01775 630 208;
e-mail: birdseed@vinehousefarm.co.uk;
www.vinehousefarm.co.uk

WALTER HARRISON & SONS
The Crescent, Radcliffe-on-Trent, Nottingham NG12 2GS; 01159 332 901;
www.walterharrisons.com

BIRD AND WILDLIFE PUBLICATIONS

ATROPOS
36 Tinker Lane, Metham, Holmfirth, West Yorks HD9 4EX; 01326 290 287;
e-mail: editor@atropos.info; www.atropos.info

BBC WILDLIFE
Immediate Publishing, 4th Floor, Tower House, Fairfax Street, Bristol BS1 3BN; 01173 147 366;
e-mail: wildlifemagazine@immediate.co.uk;
www.discoverwildlife.com

BOOK PUBLISHERS AND BOOK SELLERS

BIRDWATCH
The Chocolate Factory, 5 Clarendon Road, London N22 6XJ; 0208 881 0550; e-mail: editorial@birdwatch.co.uk; www.birdwatch.co.uk

BIRD WATCHING
Bauer Media, Media House, Lynch Wood, Peterborough PE2 6EA; 01733 468 536; e-mail: birdwatching@bauermedia.co.uk; www.birdwatching.co.uk

BRITISH BIRDS
4 Harlequin Gardens, St Leonards-on-Sea, East Sussex TN37 7PF; 01424 755 155; e-mail: subscriptions@britishbirds.co.uk; www.britishbirds.co.uk

BRITISH WILDLIFE PUBLISHING
Kemp House, Chawley Park, Cumnor Hill, Oxford OX2 9PH; 01865 811 316; e-mail: enquiries@britishwildlife.com; www.britishwildlife.com

BOOK PUBLISHERS

BLOOMSBURY PUBLISHING
(incorporating Christopher Helm, T & AD Poyser and New Holland)
50 Bedford Square, London WC1B 3DP; 0207 631 5600; e-mail: nigel.redman@bloomsbury.com; www.bloomsbury.com/naturalhistory

BRADT TRAVEL GUIDES LTD
1st Floor IDC House, The Vale, Chalfont St Peters, Bucks SL9 9RZ; 01753 893 444; e-mail: info@bradtguides.com; www.bradtguides.com

BUCKINGHAM PRESS LTD
55 Thorpe Park Road, Peterborough PE3 6LJ; 01733 561 739; e-mail: admin@buckinghampress.co.uk; www.buckinghampress.co.uk

COXTON PUBLICATIONS LTD
September House, 3 Home Farm, Saunders Lane, Walkington, Beverley HU17 8TX; 01482 881 833.

HARPER COLLINS PUBLISHERS
77-85 Fulham Palace road, Hammersmith, London W6 8JB; 0208 741 7070; e-mail: julia.koppitz@harpercollins.co.uk; www.harpercollins.co.uk

THE LANGFORD PRESS
10 New Rd, Langtoft, Peterborough, Cambs PE6 9LE; 01778 341 132; e-mail: sales@langford-press.co.uk; www.langford-press.co.uk

PRINCETON/WILDGUIDES LTD
Princeton University Press, c/o John Wiley & Sons, New Era Estate, Oldlands Way, Bognor Regis, West Sussex PO22 9NQ; 0800 243 407; e-mail: cs-books@wiley.com; www.press.princeton.edu/wildguides

THE SOUND APPROACH
12 Market Street, Poole, Dorset BH15 1NF; 01202 641 004; e-mail: info@soundapproach.co.uk; www.soundapproach.co.uk

BOOK SELLERS

CALLUNA BOOKS
Moor Edge, 2 Bere Road, Wareham, Dorset BH20 4DD; 01929 552 560; e-mail: enquiries@callunabooks.co.uk; www.callunabooks.co.uk

GARRICK BOOKS
01616 125 236; e-mail: cupajo@hotmail.co.uk

SUE LOWELL NATURAL HISTORY & TRAVEL BOOKS:
101 Cambridge Gardens, Ladbroke Grove, London W10 6JE; 0208 960 4382; e-mail: sue4382@aol.com

KEN MULLIN BOOKS
9 Seafield Road, New Ferry, Wirral, Merseyside CH62 1EQ; 07866 479 010; e-mail: kendonago@hotmail.com

NHBS (Natural History Book Service)
2-3 Wills Road, Totnes, Devonn TQ9 5XN; 01803 865 913; e-mail: customer.service@nhbs.co.uk; www.nhbs.co.uk

PANDION BOOKS
10 Carr Close, Rainton, Thirsk, North Yorkshire YO7 3QE; 01237 459 731; e-mail: pandionbks@aol.com

PICTURE BOOK
6 Stanley Street, Leek, Staffs ST13 5HG; 01538 399 033; e-mail: info@leekbooks.co.uk; www.leekbooks.co.uk

SECOND NATURE
Knapton Bookbarn, Back Lane, Knapton, York, YO26 6QJ; 01904 339 493;

e-mail: secondnatureYork@aol.com;
http://Secondnaturebooks.com

SUBBUTEO NATURAL HISTORY BOOKS
The Rea, Upton Magna, Shrewsbury, Shropshire
SY4 4UR; 01743 709 420;
e-mail: info@wildlifebooks.com;
www.wildlifebooks.com

WILDSIDE BOOKS
29 Kings Avenue, Eastbourne, East Sussex BN21
2PE; 01323 416 211;
e-mail: wildsidebooks@hotmail.com

WILD SOUNDS & BOOKS
Cross Street, Salthouse, Norfolk NR25 7XH;
e-mail: sales@wildsounds.com;
www.wildsounds.com

CLOTHING SUPPLIERS

COUNTRY INNOVATION
1 Broad Street, Congresbury, North Somerset
BS49 5DG; 01934 877 333;
e-mail: sales@countryinnovation.com;
www.countryinnovation.com

OUTDOOR SCENE
78 High Street, Oakham, Rutland LE15 6AS;
01572 770 798; www.outdoorscene.com

PARAMO DIRECTIONAL CLOTHING SYSTEMS LTD:
Unit F, Durgates Industrial Estate, Wadhurst,
East Sussex TN5 6DF; 01892 786 444; e-mail:
info@paramo.co.uk; www.paramo.co.uk

ROHAN
30 Maryland Road, Tongwell, Milton Keynes,
Bucks MK15 8HN; 0800 840 1411; e-mail:
post@rohan.co.uk; www.rohan.co.uk

ROYAL ROBBINS
16 Mill Street, Oakham, Rutland LE15 6EA:
01572 771 133; www.royalrobbins.co.uk

TILLEY ENDURABLES
6 Tresprison Court, Helston, Cornwall TR13
0QD; 01326 574 402; www.tilley.com/uk
e-mail: info@tilley-uk.com;

EQUIPMENT SUPPLIERS

LOWEPRO
DayMen International Limited, Merryhills

Enterprise Park, Park Lane, Wolverhampton
WV10 9TJ; 01902 864 646; www.lowepro.com

(THE) BIRDERS STORE
7 King Charles Place, St Johns, Worcester WR2
5AJ; 01905 312 877; e-mail: sales@birders-
store.co.uk; www.birders-store.co.uk

(THE) ONE STOP NATURE SHOP
Dalegate Market, Burnham Deepdale, Norfolk
PE31 8FB; 01485 211 223;
e-mail: sales@onestopnature.co.uk;
www.onestopnature.co.uk

OUTDOOR PHOTOGRAPHY GEAR:
73 Manchester Road, Warrington, Cheshire
WA1 4AE; 01925 555 727; e-mail: sales@
outdoorphotographygear.co.uk;
www.outdoorphotographygear.co.uk

SCOPAC
21 Bernard Road, Cromer, Norfolk NR27 9AW;
01263 511 587; www.scopac.co.uk

WILDLIFE WATCHING SUPPLIES
Tiverton Way, Tiverton Business Park, Tiverton,
Devon EX16 6TG; 01884 254 191; e-mail:
enquiries@wildlifewatchingsupplies.co.uk;
www.wildlifewatchingsupplies.co.uk

HOLIDAY COMPANIES

AIGAS FIELD CENTRE
Beauly, Inverness-shire IV4 7AD; 01463 782
443; e-mail: info@aigas.co.uk;
www.aigas.co.uk

ARCTIC & ANTARCTIC BOUND
Travel House, 133 Gravel Lane, Wilmslow,
Cheshire SK9 6EG; 0800 988 5578;
e-mail: simon@antarcticabound.com;
www.arcticbound.com

ART SAFARI
Harbourmaster's Office, Ferry Quay,
Woodbridge, Suffolk IP12 1BW; 01394 382 235;
e-mail: info@artsafari.co.uk;
www. artsafari.co.uk

AVIAN ADVENTURES
49 Sandy Road, Norton, Stourbridge, Worcs
DY8 3AJ; 01384 372 013;
e-mail: avianadventures@btinternet.com;
www.avianadventures.co.uk

HOLIDAY COMPANIES

BIRDWATCHING TRIPS WITH THE BIGGEST TWITCH
Alan Davies, 12 Ormeside Court, 19 Church Walks, Llandudno LL30 2HG; 01492 872 407; e-mail: info@birdwatchingtrips.co.uk; www.birdwatchingtrips.co.uk

BIRDFINDERS
Westbank, Cheselbourne, Dorset DT2 7NW; 01258 839 066; e-mail: birdfinders@aol.co.uk; www.birdfinders.co.uk

BIRD HOLIDAYS LTD
10 Ivegate, Yeadon, Leeds LS19 7RE; 01133 910 510; e-mail: info@birdholidays.co.uk; www.birdholidays.co.uk

(THE) BIRD ID COMPANY
Marcus Nash, Church Farm House, Church Lane, Hindolveston, Norfolk NR20 5BT; 01263 861 892; e-mail: info@birdtour.co.uk; www.birdtour.co.uk

BIRDWATCHING BREAKS
Cygnus House, Gordon's Mill, Balblair, Ross-shire IV7 8LQ; 01381 610 495; e-mail: enquiries@birdwatchingbreaks.com; www.birdwatchingbreaks.com

BIRD WATCHING & WILDLIFE CLUB
Grant Arms Hotel, 25 The Square, Grantown-on-Spey, Highlands PH26 3HF; 01479 872 526; e-mail: bookings@bwwc.co.uk; www.bwwc.co.uk

BIRDQUEST LTD
Two Jays, Kemple End, Stonyhurst, Clitheroe, Lancashire BB7 9QY; 01254 826 317; e-mail: birders@birdquest-tours.com; www.birdquest-tours.com

BRITISH-BULGARIAN FRIENDSHIP SOCIETY:
Balkania Travel Ltd, Avanta Harrow, 79 College Road, Harrow, Middx HA1 1BD; 0207 536 9400; e-mail: ognian@balkaniatravel.com; www.bbfs.org.uk

BUTEO WILDLIFE
14 Coolgardie Avenue, London E4 9HP; 07527 454 683; info@buteowildlife.co.uk; www.buteowildlife.co.uk

CAMBRIAN BIRD HOLIDAYS
Rhydlewis, Llandysul, Ceredigion, SA44 5SP; 01239 851 758; e-mail: info@cambrianbirdholidays.co.uk; www.cambrianbirdholidays.co.uk

CLASSIC JOURNEYS
33 Metro Avenue, Newton, Alfreton, Derbyshire DE55 5UF; 01773 873 497; e-mail: info@classicjourneys.co.uk; www.classicjourneys.co.uk

EXPERIENCE NATURE
16 Lint meadow, Wythall, Worcestershire B47 5PH; 07704 189 835; e-mail birdergrove@gmail.com www.ashleygrovewildimages.co.uk

GLENLOY WILDLIFE
Glenloy Lodge Guest House, Banavie, Nr Fort William, Highlands PH33 7PD; 01397 712 700; e-mail: info@glenloylodge.co.uk; www.glenloy-wildlife.co.uk

GREENTOURS LTD
Leigh Cottage, Gauledge Lane, Longnor, Buxton, Derbyshire, SK17 0PA; 01298 83563: e-mail: enquiries@greentours.co.uk; www.greentours.co.uk

HEATHERLEA LTD
The Mountview Hotel, Nethy Bridge, Inverness-shire PH25 3EB; 01479 821 248; e-mail: info@heatherlea.co.uk; www.heatherlea.co.uk

IBERIAN WILDLIFE TOURS
John Muddeman, Calle Alcocer 1 1-C, Fresnedillas de la Oliva, 28214 Madrid, Spain; (0034) 649 608 747; e-mail: john@iberianwildlife.com; www.iberianwildlife.com

JULIAN SYKES WILDLIFE HOLIDAYS
Avinguda Font d'en Carros, 16, Oliva 46780, Valencia, Spain: (0034) 687 567 286: e-mail: info@juliansykeswildlife.com; www.juliansykeswildlife.com

LIMOSA HOLIDAYS
West End Farmhouse, Chapelfield, Stalham, Norfolk NR12 9EJ: 01692 580 623; e-mail: enquiries@limosaholidays.co.uk; www.limosaholidays.co.uk

NATURETREK
Cheriton Mill, Hampshire SO24 0NG; 01962 733 051; e-mail: info@naturetrek.co.uk; www.naturetrek.co.uk

NATURES IMAGES
4 Deer Park Drive, Newport, Shropshire TF10 7HB; 01952 411 436; www.natures-images.co.uk

HOLIDAY COMPANIES

NORTH WEST BIRDS
Mike Robinson, Barn Close, Beetham, Cumbria
LA7 7AL; 01539 563 191;
e-mail: mike@newbirds.co.uk;
www.nwbirds.co.uk

NORTHERN FRANCE WILDLIFE TOURS
Roy Croucher, Place de 'Eglise, 53700 Averton,
France; (0033) 243 006 969;
e-mail: nfwt@online.fr; www.nfwt.online.fr

ORCADIAN WILDLIFE
Gerraquoy St. Margaret's Hope, South
Ronaldsay, Orkney KW17 2TH; 01856 831 240;
www.orcadianwildlife.co.uk

ORIOLE BIRDING
8 Newcastle Hill, Brigend, Glamorgan CF31
4EY; e-mail: info@oriolebirding.com;
www.oriolebirding.com

ORNITHOLIDAYS
29 Straight Mile, Romsey, Hampshire S51 9BB;
01794 519 445; www.ornitholidays.co.uk
e-mail: info@ornitholidays.co.uk;

ROMNEY MARSH BIRDWATCHING BREAKS:
Paul Trodd, Plovers, 1 Toby Road, Lydd-on-Sea,
Romney Marsh, Kent TN29 9PG; 01797 366 935;
e-mail: troddy@plovers.co.uk;
www.plovers.co.uk

SARUS BIRD TOURS
12 Walton Drive, Bury, Lancashire BL9 5JU;
01617 617 279; www.sarusbirdtours.co.uk

SHETLAND NATURE
Rohan, Baltasound, Unst, Shetland Islands
ZE2 9DS; 01957 710 000; e-mail: info@
shetlandnature.net; www.shetlandnature.net

SHETLAND WILDLIFE
Longhill, Maywick, Shetland ZE2 9JF; 01950
422 483; e-mail: info@shetlandwildlife.co.uk;
www.shetlandwildlife.co.uk

SPAINBIRDS NATURE TOURS
Santi Villa C/Nogal, 7 -1B Guadalix de la
Sierra, 28794 Madrid, Spain; (0034) 687 83 77
19; e-mail: info@spainbirds.com;
www.spainbirds.com

SPEYSIDE WILDLIFE
Wester Camerorie, Ballieward, Grantown-on-
Spey, Highlands PH26 3PR: 01479 812 498:
e-mail: enquiries@speysidewildlife.co.uk:
www.speysidewildlife.co.uk

SUNBIRD
26B The Market Square, Potton, Sandy, Beds
SG19 2NP; 01767 262 522; e-mail: sunbird@
sunbirdtours.co.uk; www.sunbirdtours.co.uk

THINK GALAPAGOS
Rachel Dex, Millcote, Mill Lane, Bishop Burton,
HU178QT; 01964 775 055; e-mail: info@
thinkgalapagos.com; www.thinkgalapagos

(THE) TRAVELLING NATURALIST
PO Box 3141, Dorchester, Dorset DT1 2XD;
01305 267 994; e-mail: info@naturalist.co.uk;
www.naturalist.co.uk

WILD ABOUT TRAVEL
25 Sapley Road, Hartford, Huntingdon, Cambs
PE29 1YG; 01480 370 593;
e-mail: jo@wildabouttravel.co.uk;
www.wildabouttravel.co.uk

WILD INSIGHTS
Yew Tree Farmhouse, Craignant, Selattyn,
Oswestry, Salop SY10 7NP; 01691 718 740;
e-mail: keithofford@virgin.net;
www.wildinsights.co.uk

WILDLIFE TRAVEL
The Manor House, Broad Street, Great
Cambourne, Cambridge CB23 6DH; 01954 713
575; e-mail: wildlifetravel@wildlifebcn.org;
www.wildlife-travel.co.uk

WILDLIFE WORLDWIDE
Capitol House, 12-13 Bridge Street,
Winchester, Hampshire SO23 0HL; 0845 130
6982; e-mail: sales@wildlifeworldwide.com;
www.wildlifeworldwide.com

WILDWINGS
Davis House, Lodge Causeway, Bristol, BS16
3JB: 01179 658 333;
e-mail: wildinfo@wildwings.co.uk;
www.wildwings.co.uk

WISE BIRDING HOLIDAYS
3 Moormead, Budleigh Salterton, Devon
EX9 6QA; 07973 483 227; e-mail: chris@
wisebirding.co.uk; www.wisebirding.co.uk

YORKSHIRE COAST NATURE
5 Coastguard Cottages, Lighthouse Road,
Flamborough YO15 1AW; 01262 851 999;
e-mail: info@yorkshirecoastnature.co.uk;
www.yorkshirecoastnature.co.uk

OPTICAL DEALERS

OPTICAL DEALERS

H.A.BAKER (LEWES) LTD:
44 High Street, Lewes, Sussex BN7 2DD; 01273 476 479.

BASS & BLIGH
6 Beulah Street, Harrogate, North Yorks HG1 1QQ; 01423 538 138; www.bassandbligh.com

BIRDNET OPTICS LTD
5 Trenchard Drive, Buxton, Derbyshire SK17 9JY; 01298 71 844;
e-mail: paulflint@birdnet.co.uk;
www.birdnet.co.uk

CLEY SPY
Manor Farm Barns, Glandford, Holt, Norfolk NR25 7JP; 01263 740 088; www.cleyspy.co.uk

CLIFTON CAMERAS
28 Parsonage Street, Dursley, Gloucestershire GL11 4AA; 01453 548 128;
e-mail: sales@cliftoncameras.co.uk;
www.cliftoncameras.co.uk

FOCALPOINT OPTICS
Marbury House Farm, Bentleys farm Lane, Higher Whitley, Warrington WA4 4QW; 01925 730 399: www.fpoint.co.uk

FOCUS OPTICS
Church Lane, Corley, Coventry CV7 8BA: 01676 540 501; e-mail: enquiries@focusoptics.eu; www.focusoptics.eu

A.R.HAWKINS
9 Marefair, Northampton NN1 1SR; 01604 639 674; e-mail: arhawkins@sky.com

IN FOCUS
Gloucestershire: The Wildfowl and Wetlands Trust, Slimbridge, Gloucestershire GL2 7BT. 01453 890 978.

Hertfordshire: Willows Farm Village, Coursers Road, London Colney, Hertfordshire AL2 1BB. 01727 827 799.

Lancashire: The Wildfowl and Wetlands Trust, Martin Mere, Burscough, Ormskirk, Lancashire L40 0TA. 01704 897 020.

London, South West: The Wildfowl and Wetlands Trust, London Wetland Centre, Queen Elizabeth's Walk, Barnes, London SW13 9WT. 020 8409 4433.

Norfolk: Main Street, Titchwell, Nr. King's Lynn, Norfolk PE31 8BB 01485 210 101.

Rutland: Anglian Water Birdwatching Centre, Egleton Reserve, Rutland Water, Rutland LE15 8BT. 01572 770 656.

Yorkshire: Westleigh House Office Estate, Wakefield Road, Denby Dale, West Yorkshire HD8 8QJ. 01484 864 729.

KAY OPTICAL (1962)
89B London Road, Morden, Surrey SM4 5HP: 02086 488 822; e-mail: info@kayoptical.co.uk; www.kayoptical.co.uk

LONDON CAMERA EXCHANGE
Bath: 13 Cheap Street, Bath, Avon, BA1 1NB; 01225 462 234.

Bristol: 53 The Horsefair, Bristol BS1 3JP; 01179 276 185.

Cheltenham: 10-12 The Promenade, Cheltenham, GL50 1LR; 01242 519 851.

Chester: 9 Bridge Street Row, CH1 1NW; 01244 326 531.

Chesterfield: 1A South Street, Chesterfield, Derbyshire, S40 1QZ; 01246 211 891.

Chew Valley: Lakeside Optics, Chew Valley Tea Shop, near Bristol; 01275 332 042.

Colchester: 12 Led Lane, Colchester, Essex CO1 1LS; 01206 573 444.

Derby: 17 Sadler Gate, Derby, Derbyshire, DE1 3NH; 01332 348 644.

Exeter: 174 Fore Street, Exeter, Devon, EX4 3AX; 01392 279 024/438 167.

Fareham: 135 West Street, Fareham, Hampshire, PO16 0DU; 01329 236 441.

Gloucester: 12 Southgate Street, Gloucester, GL1 2DH: 01452 304 513.

Guildford: 8/9 Tunsgate, Guildford, Surrey, GU1 2DH; 01483 504 040.

Leamington: 4c Lunn Poly House, Clarendon Avenue, Royal Leamington Spa CV32 5PP; 01926 886 166.

Lincoln: 6 Silver Street, Lincoln, LN2 1DY; 01522 514 131.

Lincoln: 155 High Street, Lincoln, LN5 7AA; 01522 528 577.

London, Strand: 98 The Strand, London, WC2R 0AG; 020 7379 0200.

OPTICAL DEALERS, IMPORTERS AND MANUFACTURERS

Manchester: 37 Parker Street, Picadilly, M1 4AJ; 0161 236 5819.

Norwich: 12 Timber Hill, Norwich, Norfolk NR1 3LB; 01603 612 537.

Nottingham: 7 Pelham Street, Nottingham, NG1 2EH; 0115 941 7486.

Plymouth: 10 Frankfort Gate, Plymouth, Devon, PL1 1QD; 01752 668 894.

Portsmouth: 40 Kingswell Path, Cascados, Portsmouth, PO1 4RR; 023 9283 9933.

Reading: 7 Station Road, Reading, Berkshire, RG1 1LG; 0118 959 2149.

Salisbury: 6 Queen Street, Salisbury, Wiltshire, SP1 1EY; 01722 335 436.

Southampton: 10 High Street, Southampton, Hampshire, SO14 2DH; 02380 221 597.

Southampton: 11 Civic Centre Road, Southampton SO14 7FJ; 02380 331 720.

Taunton: 6 North Street, Taunton, Somerset, TA1 1LH; 01823 259 955.

Winchester: 15 The Square, Winchester, Hampshire, SO23 9ES; 01962 866 203.

Worcester: 8 Pump Street, Worcester WR1 2QT; 01905 22314.

PARK CAMERAS
53-54 Rathbone Place, London W1T 1JR; 01444 2307 099; www.parkcameras.com

SHERWOODS
The Arden Centre, Little Alne, Wootton Wawen, Henley-in-Arden, Warwickshire B95 6HW; 01527 857 500; e-mail: sales@sherwood-photo.comwww.binocularhouse.com

SOUTH WEST OPTICS
22a River Street, Truro, Cornwall TR1 2SJ; 01872 263 444; e-mail: steve@swoptics.com; www.swoptics.co.uk

UTTINGS
PO Box 672 Norwich, Norfolk NR3 2ZR; 01603 619 811; www.uttings.co.uk

WEX (WAREHOUSE EXPRESS)
Unit B, Frenbury Estate, Drayton High Road, Norwich, Norfolk NR6 5DP; 01603 481 933; e-mail: showroom@wex.co.uk; www.wexphotographic.com

WILKINSON CAMERAS
e-mail: sales@wilkinson.co.uk
www.wilkinson.co.uk

Blackburn: 42 Northgate, Blackburn, Lancs BB2 1JL: 01254 581 272.

Burnley: 95 James Street, Burnley, Lancs BB11 1PY; 01282 424 524.

Bury: 61 The Rock, Bury, Greater Manchester BL9 0NB; 01617 643 402.

Carlisle: 13 Grapes Lane, Carlisle, Cumbria CA3 8NQ; 01228 538 583.

Kendal: 19A The Westmorland Centre, Kendal, Cumbria LA9 4AB; 01539 735 055.

Lancaster: 6 James Street, Lancaster, Lancs LA1 1UP; 01524 380 510.

Liverpool: 51 Lord Street, Liverpool L2 6PB; 0151 255 0345.

Preston: 27 Friargate, Preston, Lancs PR1 2NQ; 01772 556 250.

Southport: 38 Eastbank Street, Southport, Merseyside, PR8 1ET. 01704 534 534.

Warrington: 10 The Mall, The Golden Square, Warrington WA1 1QE. 01925 638 290.

OPTICAL IMPORTERS AND MANUFACTURERS

ACE OPTICS
16 Green Street, Bath BA1 2JZ: 01225 466 364; e-mail: optics@acecameras.co.uk; www.aceoptics.co.uk

ALPHA OPTICAL DISTRIBUTION LTD (importers of Kite optics)
54 Meadow Way, Theale, Berks RG7 4AX; 07725 081 436; e-mail: info@kite-optics.co.uk; www.kite-optics.co.uk

BUSHNELL PERFORMANCE OPTICS UK LTD
Unit C83 Barwell, Chessington, Surrey KT9 2NY; 0208 391 4700; e-mail: info@bushnell-uk.co.uk; http://bushnell.eu/uk/

CANON UK LTD
130 Centennial Park, Elstree, Herts WD6 3SE; 0208 731 4132; www.canon.co.uk

CARL ZEISS LTD
509 Coldhams Lane, Cambridge CB1 3JS: 01223 401 525; e-mail: Christine.karn@zeiss.co.uk; www.zeiss.co.uk/sportsoptics

HAWKE SPORTS OPTICS:
Deben Group Industries, Avocet House, Wilford

OPTICAL IMPORTERS, MANUFACTURERS AND REPAIRS

Bridge Road, Melton, Woodbridge, Suffolk IP12 1RB; 01394 387 762; www.hawkeoptics.com e-mail: sales@deben.com;

DAVID HINDS LTD (importers of Celestron optics):
Unit R, Cherrycourt Way, Leighton Buzzard, Bedfordshire LU7 4UH; www.celestron.uk.com

INTRO 2020 (importers of Steiner binoculars, Velbon and Slik tripods and more)
Unit 1, Priors Way, Maidenhead, Berkshire SL6 2HP; 01628 674 411; www.intro2020.co.uk e-mail: sales@intro2020.co.uk;

KOWA OPTIMED EUROPE LTD
Sandhurst House, 297 Yorktown Road, Sandhurst, Berkshire GU47 0QA; 01276 937 021; www.kowaproducts.com

LEICA CAMERA LTD
27 Bruton Place, Mayfair, London W1J 6NQ; 01207 629 1351; e-mail: welcome@leica-storemayfair.co.uk; www.leica-camera.co.uk

MANFROTTO DISTRIBUTION (Manfrotto and Gitzo Tripods)
Resolution Rd, Ashby-de-la-Zouch, Leicestershire LE65 1DW: 01530 566 090; www.manfrottodistribution.co.uk

MARCHWOOD UK (Meopta, Forest and Bresser Optics)
406/Cannock Chase Enterprise Centre, Cannock WS12 0QU; 01543 424 255; e-mail: sales@marchwooduk.co.uk; www.marchwooduk.co.uk

MONK OPTICS LTD (Fujinon Binoculars)
Wye Valley Observatory, The Old School, Brockweir, Chepstow NP16 7NW; 01291 689 858; e-mail: msales@monkoptics.co.uk; www.monkoptics.co.uk

NEWPRO UK LTD (Vortex Optics, PhoneSkope Cases)
3 Radcot Estate, Park Rd, Faringdon, Oxfordshire SN7 7BP; 01367 242 411; sales@newprouk.co.uk; www.newprouk.co.uk

NIKON UK LTD:
380 Richmond Road, Kingston-upon-Thames, Surrey KT2 5PR; 0330 123 0923; www.nikon.co.uk/en_GB/

OPTICAL VISION LTD (Barr & Stoud and Acuter optics)
Unit 3, Woolpit Business Park, Woolpit, Bury

St Edmunds, Suffolk IP30 9UP; e-mail: info@opticalvision.co.uk; www.opticalvision.co.uk

OPTICRON
Unit 21, Titan Court, Laporte way, Luton, Befordshire LU4 8EF; 01582 726 522; e-mail: sales@opticron.co.uk; www.opticron.co.uk

SWAROVSKI OPTIK
Unit 11, Tarbot House, Perrywood Business Park, Salfords, Surrey RH1 5JQ; 01737 856 812; e-mail: info@swarovski.com; www.swarovski.com

VANGUARD WORLD UK LTD
Unit 73, Basepoint Business Centre, Enterprise Close, Aviation Business Park, Christchurch, Bournemouth BH23 6NX; 01202 651 281; e-mail: info@vanguardworld.co.uk; www.vanguardworld.co.uk

VIKING OPTICAL LTD (Viking and RSPB Optics):
Blyth Road, Halesworth, Suffolk IP19 8EN; 01986 875 315; e-mail: viking@viking optical.co.uk; www.vikingoptical.co.uk

OPTICAL REPAIRS AND SERVICING

ACTION OPTICS
16 Butts Ash Gardens, Hythe, Southampton S45 3BL; 02380 842 801; e-mail: richardjbiggs@btinternet.com; www.actionoptics.co.uk

FIXATION UK LTD (Nikon/Canon repairs & servicing)
250 Kennington Lane, Lambeth, London SE11 5RD; 0207 582 3294; e-mail: admin@fixationuk.com; www.fixationuk.com

OPTREP OPTICAL REPAIRS
16 Wheatfield Road, Selsey, West Sussex PO20 0NY; 01243 601 365; www.opticalrepairs.com

VIKING SERVICE DIVISION
93 Hope Street, Glasgow G2 6LD; 01412 487 179; e-mail: service@vikingoptical.co.uk

TECHNOLOGY PRODUCTS

BIRD IMAGES (DVDS)
Paul Doherty, 28 Carousel Walk, Sherburn-in-Elmet, North Yorkshire LS25 6LP: 01977 684 666; e-mail: paul@birdvideodvd.com; www.birdvideodvd.com

TECHNOLOGY PRODUCTS

BIRDGUIDES LTD
Warners Group Publications PLC, The Chocolate Factory, 5 Clarendon Road, London N22 6XJ; 0208 826 0934; e-mail: contact@birdguides.com; www.birdguides.com

BLUEBIRD TECHNOLOGY
1 Turnbridge Court, Cambridge CB24 4GH; 0845 094 6012; e-mail: mail@bluebirdtechnology.com; www.bluebirdtechnology.com

EASYBIRDER DVDS
Dave Gosney, Valley View Cottage, 15 Low Road, Sheffield S6 5FY; 01142 853 712; e-mail: dave@easybirder.co.uk; www.easybirder.co.uk

ISABELLINE FILMS
Steve Evans, 9 Milverton Close, Halesowen, West Midlands B63 3QL; e-mail: info@isabelline.co.uk; www.isabelline.co.uk

WILD SOUNDS (DVD, CD-Rom, recording equipment)
Cross Street, Salthouse, Norfolk NR25 7XH; e-mail: sales@wildsounds.com; www.wildsounds.com

COUNTY DIRECTORY

David Cromack

Joining your local bird club or RSPB members group is a great way to discover more about the best birdwatching locations in your area. In the County Directory you'll find contact information for hundreds of groups.

England	230	Channel Islands	284
Isle of Man	270	Northern Ireland	285
Scotland	271	Republic of Ireland	286
Wales	279		

ENGLAND

THE INFORMATION in the directory has been obtained either from the persons listed or from the appropriate national or other bodies. In some cases, where it has not proved possible to verify the details directly, alternative responsible sources have been relied upon. When no satisfactory record was available, previously included entries have sometimes had to be deleted. Readers are requested to advise the editor of any errors or omissions.

AVON

See Somerset.

BEDFORDSHIRE

Bird Atlas/Avifauna
An Atlas of the Breeding Birds of Bedfordshire 1988-92 by R A Dazley and P Trodd (Bedfordshire Natural History Society, 1994).

Bird Recorders
Steve Blain, 9 Devon Drive, Biggleswade, Bedfordshire SG18 0FJ. 07979 606 300;
e-mail: recorder@bedsbirdclub.org.uk

Bird Report
BEDFORDSHIRE BIRD REPORT (1946-), from Mary Sheridan, 28 Chestnut Hill, Linslade, Leighton Buzzard, Beds LU7 2TR. 01525 378 245;
e-mail: membership@bnhs.org.uk

BTO Regional Representative
Roger Hicks, 01462 816 028;
e-mail: rogerkhicks@hotmail.com

Club

 BEDFORDSHIRE BIRD CLUB. (1992; 300). Miss Sheila Alliez, Flat 61 Adamson Court, Adamson Walk, Kempston, Bedford MK42 8QZ; e -mail:sjalliez12@btinternet.com
www.bedsbirdclub.org.uk
Meetings: 8.00pm, last Tuesday of the month (Sep-Mar), Maulden Village Hall, Maulden, Beds.

Ringing Groups
IVEL RG. Graham Buss, 11 Northall Close, Eaton Bray, Dunstable LU6 2EB. 01525 221 023;
e-mail: g1j2buss@yahoo.co.uk

RSPB. WB Kirby, The Lodge, Sandy,BedfordshireSG19 2DL.01767 680551;
e-mail: will.kirby@rspb.org.uk

RSPB Local Groups
BEDFORDSHIRE. Mr R I Bashford, 6 Brook Road, Eaton Ford, St Neots, Cambridgeshire PE19 7AX.
E-mail: richard.bashford@rspb.org.uk

BEDFORD. (1970; 80). Ray Wright, Melchbourne End Cottage, 5 Melchbourne Road, Knotting, Beds MK44 1AF. 01234 783 484;
e-mail: ray.wright27@yahoo.com
www.rspb.org.uk/groups/bedford/
Meetings: 7.30pm, 3rd Thursday of the month, A.R.A. Manton Lane, Bedford.

LUTON AND SOUTH BEDFORDSHIRE. (1973; 120+). Allyn Hill. 01582 666 297;
e-mail: cah_halfmoon@yahoo.com
www.rspb.org.uk/groups/luton
Meetings: 7.45pm, 2nd Wednesday of the month, Houghton Regis Social Centre, Parkside Drive, Houghton Regis, LU5 5QN.

Wildlife Trust
See Cambridgeshire.

BERKSHIRE

BirdAtlas/Avifauna
The Birds of Berkshire 2nd Edition by Neil Bucknell, Brian Clews, Renton Righelato and Chris Robinson (Berkshire Atlas Group/Berkshire Ornithological Club 2013).

Bird Recorder
RECORDER (Records Committee and rarity records). Chris DR Heard, 3 Waterside Lodge, Ray Mead Road, Maidenhead, Berkshire SL6 8NP. 01628 633 828; e-mail: bse240@yahoo.com

Bird Reports
BERKSHIRE BIRD BULLETIN (Monthly, 1986-), from Brian Clews, 118 Broomhill, Cookham, Berks SL6 9LQ. 01628 526 091;
e-mail: brian.clews@btconnect.com

THE BIRDS OF BERKSHIRE (1974-), from Mike Turton, 7, Fawcett Crescent, Woodley, Reading RG5 3HX. 07815 644 385;
e-mail: mike.turton@berksoc.org.uk
www.berksoc.org.uk

BIRDS OF THE THEALE AREA (1988-), from Secretary, Theale Area Bird Conservation Group.

NEWBURY DISTRICT BIRD REPORT (1959-) - covering West Berkshire (approx 12 miles from centre of Newbury), plus parts of north Hants, south Oxon, from Secretary, Newbury District Ornithological Club.

ENGLAND

BTO Regional Representatives
Ken and Sarah White. 01635 268 442; e-mail:
btoberks.ken.sarah@googlemail.com

Clubs
BERKSHIRE BIRD BULLETIN GROUP. (1986; 100).
Berkshire Bird Bulletin Group, PO Box 680,
Maidenhead, Berks SL6 9ST. 01628 526 091;
e-mail: brian.clews@btconnect.com

NEWBURY DISTRICT ORNITHOLOGICAL CLUB.
(1959; 110). John Wilding (Webmaster);
e-mail: jls4015-NDOC@yahoo.co.uk
www.ndoc.org.uk
Meetings: Indoor lectures from October to March
and regular bird watching days around Newbury,
throughout the summer and winter. Please see
website for details.

BERKSHIRE ORNITHOLOGICAL CLUB. (1947; 320).
Mike Turton, 7, Fawcett Crescent, Woodley,
Reading RG5 3HX. 07815 644 385;
e-mail: mike.turton@berksoc.org.uk
www.berksoc.org.uk
Meetings: 8pm, alternate Wednesdays (Oct-Mar).
University of Reading.

THEALE AREA BIRD CONSERVATION
GROUP. (1988; 75). Catherine
McEwan, Secretary. 01189 415
792; e-mail: tabcgsec@yahoo.com
www.freewebs.com/tabcg/index.
htm
Meetings: 8pm, 1st Tuesday of the
month, Englefield Social Club.

Ringing Groups
NEWBURY RG. D Long, 6 St Marks Close,
Thatcham, Berks RG19 3SZ.
E-mail: duncanflong@aol.com
www.newburyrg.co.uk

RUNNYMEDE RG. D G Harris, 22 Blossom Waye,
Hounslow, TW5 9HD.
E-mail: daveharris@tinyonline.co.uk
www.rmxrg.org.uk

RSPB Local Groups
EAST BERKSHIRE. (1974; 200). Michael Huddy ,
01844 690 571; e-mail: mmikehuddy@aol.com
www.eastberksrspb.org.uk
Meetings: 7.30pm, Thursdays (Sept-April),
Methodist Church Hall, King Street, Maidenhead,
SL6 1EA

READING. (1986; 130). Carl Feltham. 0118 941
1713; e-mail: carl.feltham@virginmedia.com
www.reading-rspb.org.uk;
www.facebook.com/readingrspb
Meetings:8.00 pm, 2nd Tuesday of the month
(Sep-Jun), Pangbourne Village Hall, Pangbourne.

WOKINGHAM & BRACKNELL. (1979; 200). Les
Blundell,. 01344 861 964;
e-mail: lesrblundell@gmail.com
www.rspb.org.uk/groups/wokinghamandbracknell
Meetings: 7.45pm, 2nd Tuesday of the month
(Sep-Jun), Finchampstead Memorial Hall,
Wokingham, RG40 4JU.

Wetland Bird Survey Organisers
BERKSHIRE. Mr & Mrs White, c/o WeBS Office;
e-mail: white.zoothera@gmail.com

Wildlife Hospital
LIFELINE. Wendy Hermon, Treatment Centre Co-
ordinator, Swan Treatment Centre, Cuckoo Weir
Island, South Meadow Lane, Eton, Windsor, Berks
SL4 6SS. 01753 859 397 (fax) 01753 622 709;
e-mail: wendyhermon@swanlifeline.org.uk
www.swanlifeline.org.uk Registered charity.
Thames Valley 24-hour swan rescue and treatment
service. Veterinary support and hospital unit.
Operates membership scheme.

Wildlife Trust
Director, See Oxfordshire,

BUCKINGHAMSHIRE

Bird Recorder
Andy Harding, 93 Deanshanger Lane, Old
Stratford, Milton Keynes MK19 6AX. 01908 565
896; e-mail: andyh444@sky.com

Bird Reports
*AMERSHAM BIRDWATCHING CLUB ANNUAL REPORT
(1975-)*, from Secretary.

BUCKINGHAMSHIRE BIRD REPORT (1980-) - from
Rob Andrews, 28 Icknield Green, Tring, Herts HP23
5HH; e-mail: secretary@bucksbirdclub.co.uk

NORTH BUCKS BIRD REPORT (12 pa), from Simon
Nichols; e-mail: si.nichols@yahoo.com

BTO Regional Representative
Roger Warren. 01491 638 691;
e-mail: rcwarren@btinternet.com

Club
BUCKINGHAMSHIRE BIRD CLUB. (1981; 340).
Jackie Newcombe, 07414 725 540;
e-mail: Secretary@bucksbirdclub.co.uk
www.bucksbirdclub.co.uk

RSPB Local Groups
See also Herts: Chorleywood.

AYLESBURY. (1981; 220). Brian Fisher. 01844 215
924; e-mail: brian.fisher45@yahoo.co.uk
www.rspb.org.uk/groups/aylesbury
Meetings: Prebendal Farm Community Centre,
Fowler Road, Aylesbury HP19 7QW.

ENGLAND

NORTH BUCKINGHAMSHIRE. (1975; 570). Chris Ward, 41 William Smith Close, Woolstone, Milton Keynes MK15 0AN. 01908 669 448; e-mail: northbucksrspb@hotmail.com www.rspb.org.uk/groups/northbucks
Meetings: 7.45pm, 2nd Thursday of the month, Cruck Barn, City Discovery Centre, Bradwell Abbey, MK13 9AP.

Wetland Bird Survey Organiser
BUCKINGHAMSHIRE. Mr R S Warren, c/o WeBS Office, BTO, The Nunnery, Thetford, Norfolk IP24 2PU. 01491 638 691; e-mail: rcwarren@btinternet.com

Wildlife Hospitals
WILDLIFE HOSPITAL TRUST. St Tiggywinkles, Aston Road, Haddenham, Aylesbury, Bucks HP17 8AF. 01844 292 292 (24hr helpline); e-mail: mail@sttiggywinkles.org.uk www.sttiggywinkles.org.uk
Registered charity. All British species. Veterinary referrals and helpline for vets and others on wild bird treatments. Full veterinary unit and staff. Pub: Bright Eyes (free to members - sae).

Wildlife Trust
Director, See Oxfordshire,

CAMBRIDGESHIRE

BirdAtlas/Avifauna
An Atlas of the Breeding Birds of Cambridgeshire (VC 29) P M M Bircham et al (Cambridge Bird Club, 1994).

The Birds of Cambridgeshire: checklist 2000 (Cambridge Bird Club).

Bird Recorder
CAMBRIDGESHIRE. Louise Bacon, e-mail: recorder@cambridgebirdclub.org.uk www.cambridgeshirebirdclub.org.uk

Bird Report
CAMBRIDGESHIRE BIRD REPORT (1925-), from Bruce Martin, 178 Nuns Way, Cambridge, CB4 2NS. (H)01223 700 656; e-mail: bruce.s.martin@btinternet.com

BTO Regional Representatives
CAMBRIDGESHIRE. Mark Welch; e-mail: mdw@nhm.ac.uk

HUNTINGDON & PETERBOROUGH. Derek Langslow. 01733 232 153; e-mail: derek.langslow@btinternet.com

Clubs
CAMBRIDGESHIRE BIRD CLUB. (1925; 350). Michael Holdsworth, 4a Cavendish Avenue, Cambridge, Cambs CB1 7US.

E-mail: secretary@ cambridgebirdclub.org.uk www.cambridgebirdclub.org.uk
Meetings: 2nd Friday of the month, St John's Church Hall, Hills Road, Cambridge/ Cottenham Village College.

PETERBOROUGH BIRD CLUB. (1999; 210). Keith Stapleford (Secretary). 01733 555 793; e-mail: keith.stapleford@talktalk.net www.peterboroughbirdclub.co.uk
Meetings: 7.30pm, last Tuesday of the month (Sep-Nov, Jan-Apr), PO Social Club, Bourges Boulevard, Peterborough PE1 2AU. Regular outdoor meetings throughout most of year (check website for details).

Ringing Group
WICKEN FEN RG. Dr C J R Thorne, 17 The Footpath, Coton, Cambs CB23 7PX. 01954 210 566; e-mail: cjrt@cam.ac.uk

RSPB Local Groups
CAMBRIDGE. (1977; 100). Melvyn Smith. 01954 202 354; e-mail: mel_brensmith@hotmail.co.uk www.RSPB.org.uk/groups/cambridge
Meetings: 7.30pm, 3rd Wednesday of every month Jan-May and Sept-Dec. The Wilkinson Room, St John's the Evangelist, Hills Road, Cambridge, CB2 8RN.

HUNTINGDONSHIRE. (1982; 150). Ursula Bulpitt. 01487 814 414; e-mail: ujbulpitt@btinternet.com www.rspb.org.uk/groups/huntingdonshire
Meetings: 7.30pm, last Wednesday of the month (Sep-Apr), Free Church, St Ives.

Wetland Bird Survey Organisers
CAMBRIDGESHIRE (including Huntingdonshire). Bruce Martin, 178 Nuns Way, Cambridge, CambsCB4 2NS. 01223 700 656; 07977 381 625; e-mail: bruce.s.martin@ntlworld.com

NENE WASHES. Mr C E F Kitchin, RSPB Nene Washes Nature Reserve, 21a East Delph, Whittlesey, Cambridgeshire PE7 1RH. 01733 205 140; 07711 157 859; e-mail: Charlie.kitchin@rspb.org.uk

OUSE WASHES. Mr P Harrington, Ouse Washes RSPB Reserve, Welches Dam, Manea, March PE15 0NF.01354 680 212; e-mail: paul.harrington@rspb.org.uk

SOUTH LINCOLNSHIRE/PETERBOROUGH (inland). Mr R Titman, 28 Eastgate, Deeping St James, Peterborough PE6 8HJ. 01733 583 254; 01778 380 695; e-mail: bob.titman@gmail.com

Wildlife Trust
THE WILDLIFE TRUST FOR BEDFORDSHIRE,

CAMBRIDGESHIRE, NORTHAMPTONSHIRE AND PETERBOROUGH. (1990; 36,000). The Manor House, Broad Street, Great Cambourne, Cambridgeshire CB23 6DH. 01954 713 500; e-mail: cambridgeshire@wildlifebcnp.org www.wildlifebcnp.org

CHESHIRE

BirdAtlas/Avifauna
Birds in Cheshire and Wirral - A Breeding and Wintering Atlas 2004-2007 by Professor David Norman, Liverpool University Press, Autumn 2008.

The Birds of Sandbach Flashes 1935-1999 by Andrew Goodwin and Colin Lythgoe (The Printing House, Crewe, 2000).

Bird Recorder (inc Wirral)
CHESHIRE & WIRRAL. Hugh Pulsford, 6 Buttermere Drive, Great Warford, Alderley Edge, Cheshire SK9 7WA. 01565 880 171; e-mail: countyrec@cawos.org

Bird Report
CHESHIRE & WIRRAL BIRD REPORT (1969-), from David Cogger, 113 Nantwich Road, Middlewich, Cheshire CW10 9HD. www.cawos.org

BTO Regional Representatives
MID CHESHIRE. Paul Miller. 01928 787 535; e-mail: paulandhilarymiller@o2.co.uk

NORTH, EAST & SOUTH CHESHIRE. Mark Eddowes, 59 Westfield Drive, Knutsford, Cheshire WA16 0BH. 01298 214 144; e-mail: mark@eddowesaviationsafety.com

Clubs
CHESHIRE & WIRRAL ORNITHOLOGICAL SOCIETY. (2012; 311). Dr Ted Lock (Secretary); e-mail: info@cawos.org www.cawos.org **Meetings:** 7.45pm, 1st Friday of the month, St Vincent's Church Hall, Tatton Street, Knutsford.

CHESTER & DISTRICT ORNITHOLOGICAL SOCIETY. (1967; 50). David King, 13 Bennett Close, Willaston, South Wirral CH64 2XF. 0151 327 7212. **Meetings:** 7.30pm, 1st Thursday of the month (Oct-Mar), Caldy Valley Community Centre.

KNUTSFORD ORNITHOLOGICAL SOCIETY. (1974; 55). Derek A Pike (Secretary). 01565 653 811; e-mail: tony@mobberley.eu www.10X50.com **Meetings:** 7.30pm, 4th Friday of the month (not Dec), Jubilee Hall, Stanley Road, Knutsford.

LANCASHIRE & CHESHIRE FAUNA SOCIETY. (1914; 140). Dave Bickerton, 64 Petre Crescent, Rishton, Blackburn, Lancs BB1 4RB. 01254 886 257; e-mail: bickertond@aol.com www.lacfs.org.uk

MID-CHESHIRE ORNITHOLOGICAL SOCIETY. (1963; 80). John Drake, 17 Wisenholme Close, Beechwood West, Runcorn, Cheshire WA7 2RU. 01928 561 133; e-mail: contact@ midcheshireos.co.uk www.midcheshireos.co.uk **Meetings:** 7:30pm, 2nd Friday of the month (Oct-Mar), Cuddington and Sandiway Village Hall.

SOUTH EAST CHESHIRE ORNITHOLOGICAL SOCIETY. (1964; 140). Derek Owen (Chairman); e-mail: derek_owen07@tiscali.co.uk www.secos.org.uk **Meetings:** 2nd Friday (Sept-Apr), 7.30pm, Ettiley Heath Church Community Centre, Sandbach.

WILMSLOW GUILD BIRDWATCHING GROUP. (1965; 67). http://wgbwcopy.wikidot.com/wgbg **Meetings:** 7.30pm last Friday of the month, Wilmslow Guild, Bourne St, Wilmslow.

Ringing Groups
CHESHIRE SWAN RINGING GROUP. David Cookson. 01270 567 526; e-mail: Cheshireswans@aol.com http://cheshireswanstudygroup.wordpress. com (blog for Swan news, weather records, bird reports and photos).

MERSEYSIDE RG. Bob Harris, 3 Mossleigh, Whixalll, Whitchurch, Shropshire SY13 2SA. 0151 706 4397; e-mail: harris@liv.ac.uk

SOUTH MANCHESTER RG. Mr N.B. Powell; e-mail: neville.powell@tiscali.co.uk

RSPB Local Groups
CHESTER. (1988; 220). Norman Sadler. 01244 335 670; e-mail: chester1RSPB@btinternet.com www.rspb.org.uk/groups/chester **Meetings:** 7.30pm, 3rd Wednesday of the month (Sep-Apr), St Mary's Centre, Chester.

MACCLESFIELD. (1979; 250). Daryll Bailey, Group Secretary. 01625 430 311; e-mail: secretary@macclesfieldrspb.org.uk www.macclesfieldrspb.org.uk **Meetings:** 7.45pm, 2nd Tuesday of the month (Sept-May), Macclesfield Methodist Church, Westminster Road, Macclesfield SK10 1BX.

NORTH CHESHIRE. (1976; 80). Paul Grimmett. 01925 268 770; e-mail: paulwtwitcher@hotmail.com www.rspb.org.uk/groups/north_cheshire **Meetings:** 7.45pm, 3rd Friday (Jan-April and Sept-Nov), Appleton Parish Hall, Dudlow Green Road, Appleton, Warrington.

Wetland Bird Survey Organisers
CHESHIRE NORTH. Mr K Brides, c/o WeBS Office,

BTO, The Nunnery, Thetford, Norfolk IP24 2PU. 07966 95 494; e-mail: kane.brides@wwt.org.uk

CHESHIRE SOUTH. Mr D.A. Cookson, 70 Rope Lane, Rope, CreweCheshire CW2 6RD. 01270 567 526; 07976 725 031; e-mail: cheshireswans@aol.com

Wildlife Hospitals
RSPCA STAPELEY GRANGE WILDLIFE CENTRE. London Road, Stapeley, Nantwich, Cheshire, CW5 7JW. 0300 123 0722. All wild birds. Oiled bird wash facilities and pools. Veterinary support.

Wildlife Trust
CHESHIRE WILDLIFE TRUST. (1962; 13,100). Bickley Hall Farm, Bickley, Malpas, Cheshire SY14 8EF. 01948 820 728;
e-mail: info@cheshirewt.org.uk
www.cheshirewildlifetrust.org.uk

CLEVLAND & CO. DURHAM

Bird Atlas/Avifauna
The Breeding Birds of Cleveland. Teesmouth Bird Club, 2008.

A Summer Atlas of Breeding Birds of County Durham by Stephen Westerberg/Kieth Bowey. (Durham Bird Club, 2000).

Bird RecorderS
CLEVELAND. Tom Francis.
E-mail: mot.francis@ntlworld.com

DURHAM. Mark Newsome, 69 Cedar Drive, Jarrow, NE32 4BF. 07834 978 255;
e-mail: mvnewsome@hotmail.com

Bird Report
CLEVELAND BIRD REPORT (1974-), from Mr J Fletcher, 43 Glaisdale Avenue, Middlesbrough TS5 7PF. 01642 818 825.

BIRDS IN DURHAM (1971-), from D Sowerbutts, 9 Prebends Fields, Gilesgate, Durham DH1 1HH. (H)0191 386 7201; e-mail: d16lst@tiscali.co.uk

BTO Regional Representatives
CLEVELAND. Vic Fairbrother, 8, Whitby Avenue, Guisborough, Cleveland TS14 7AP. 01287 633 744; e-mail: vic.fairbrother@ntlworld.com

DURHAM. David L Sowerbutts, 9 Prebends Field, Gilesgate Moor, Durham DH1 1HH. 0191 386 7201; e-mail: david.sowerbutts@dunelm.org.uk

Clubs
DURHAM BIRD CLUB. (1975; 320). Paul Anderson, Chairman, 2 Hawsker Close, Tunstall Village, Sunderland SR3 2YD. 0191 523 6236;
e-mail: paulandcath29@aol.com
www.durhambirdclub.org

Meetings: Monthly indoor meetings (Sept-Apr), Durham Wildlife Trust HQ at Rainton Meadows, Houghton le Spring.

TEESMOUTH BIRD CLUB. (1960; 425). Chris Sharp (Hon Sec.), 45 Endeavour Close, Seaton Carew, Hartlepool TS25 1EY. 01429 865 163.
www.teesmouthbc.com
Meetings: 7.30pm, 1st Monday of the month (Sep-Apr), Stockton Library, Church Road, Stockton.

Ringing Groups
TEES RG. E Wood, Southfields, 16 Marton Moor Road, Nunthorpe, Middlesbrough, Cleveland TS7 0BH. 01642 323 563.

SOUTH CLEVELAND RG. W Norman, Ruthwell, Beck Hole Road, Goathland, Whitby, North Yorkshire YO22 5NA. 01947 896 665;
e-mail: wilfgros@btinternet.com

Ringing Group
DURHAM DALES RG. J R Hawes, Fairways, 5 Raby Terrace, Willington, Crook, Durham DL15 0HR.

RSPB Local Groups
CLEVELAND. (1974; 150). Terry Reeve. 01642 512 693; e-mail: ClevelandRSPB@googlemail.com
www.rspb.org.uk/groups/cleveland
Meetings: 7.00 for 7.30pm, 2nd Monday of each month (Sep-Apr), The Jack Hatfield Sports Club, Rockingham Court, Middlesbrough, TS5 7BN.

DARLINGTON. (2005). Clifford Evans. 01325 466 471; e-mail: cgevans1@virginmedia.com
www.communigate.co.uk/ne/darlingtonrspbgroup/index.phtml
Meetings: 1st Thursday of the month (Sept-July), Cockerton Methodist Church, Cockerton Green, Darlington.

DURHAM. (1974; 125). Richard Cowen. 0191 377 2061; e-mail: richard.cowen313@gmail.com
www.durham-rspb.org.uk
Meetings: 7.30pm, 2nd Tuesday of the month (Oct-Mar), Room CG83, adjacent to Scarborough Lecture Theatre, University Science Site, Stockton Road entrance.

Wetland Bird Survey Organisers
CLEVELAND (excl. Tees Estuary). Mr C Sharp, 45 Endeavour Close, Seaton Carew, Hartlepool TS25 1EY. 01429 865 163;
e-mail: chrisandlucia@ntlworld.com

TEES ESTUARY. Mike Leakey, c/o EDF Energy, Tees Road, Hartlepool, Cleveland TS25 2BZ;
e-mail: mike.leakey@naturalengland.org.uk

ENGLAND

Wildlife Trusts

DURHAM WILDLIFE TRUST. (1971; 4,000). Rainton Meadows, Chilton Moor, Houghton-le-Spring, Tyne & Wear, DH4 6PU. 0191 584 3112 (fax) 0191 584 3934; e-mail: mail@durhamwt.co.uk www.durhamwt.co.uk

TEES VALLEY WILDLIFE TRUST. (1979; 5,000). Margrove Heritage Centre, Margrove Park, Boosbeck, Saltburn-by-the-Sea, TS12 3BZ. 01287 636 382 (fax) 01287 636 383; e-mail: info@teeswildlife.org www.teeswildlife.org

CORNWALL

Bird Recorders
CORNWALL. Dave Parker; e-mail: recorder@cbwps.org.uk

ISLES OF SCILLY. Will Wagstaff, 42 Sally Port, St Mary's, Isles of Scilly TR21 0JE. 01720 422 212; e-mail: will@islandwildlifetours.co.uk www.carnithen.co.uk

Bird Atlas/Avifauna
The Essential Guide to Birds of The Isles of Scilly 2007 by RL Flood, N Hudson and B Thomas, published by authors.

Bird Reports
BIRDS IN CORNWALL (1931-), from the Secretary; e-mail: secretary@cbwps.org.uk www.cbwps.org.uk

ISLES OF SCILLY BIRD REPORT and NATURAL HISTORY REVIEW 2000 (1969-), from see website;. www.scilly-birding.co.uk

BTO Regional Representatives
CORNWALL. Peter Kent, 01822 833 782; e-mail: peter.kent@tesco.net

ISLES OF SCILLY. Will Wagstaff, 42 Sally Port, St Mary's, Isles of Scilly TR21 0JE. 01720 422 212; e-mail: will@islandwildlifetours.co.uk

Clubs
CORNWALL BIRDWATCHING & PRESERVATION SOCIETY. (1931;1105). Cait Hutchings, 24 Kernick Road, Penryn, Cornwall TR10 8NT. 01326 375 593; (M)07896 353 601; e-mail: secretary@cbwps.org.uk www.cbwps.org.uk

CORNWALL WILDLIFE TRUST PHOTOGRAPHIC GROUP. (40). David Chapman, 41 Bosence Road, Townshend, Nr Hayle, Cornwall TR27 6AL. 01736 850 287; e-mail: david@davidchapman.org.uk www.davidchapman.org.uk/

Meetings: Mixture of indoor and outdoor meetings, please phone for details.

ISLES OF SCILLY BIRD GROUP. (2000; 510). Membership Secretary, 32 Sallyport, St Mary's, Isles of Scilly TR21 0JE; e-mail: isbgmembership@btinternet.com www.scilly-birding.co.uk

Ringing Group
SCILLONIA SEABIRD GROUP. Peter Robinson, Secretary, 19 Pine Park Road, Honiton, Devon EX14 2HR. (Tel/fax) 01404 549 873 (M)07768 538 132; e-mail: pjrobinson2@aol.com www.birdexpertuk.com

RSPB Local Group
CORNWALL. (1972; 420). Roger Hooper. 01209 820 610; e-mail: rogerwhooper@btinternet.com www.rspb.org.uk/groups/cornwall
Meetings: Indoor meetings (Oct-Apr), outdoor throughout the year.

Wetland Bird Survey Organisers
CORNWALL (excl. Tamar Complex). Mr P Roseveare, c/o WeBS Office, BTO, The Nunnery, Thetford, Norfolk IP24 2PU. 07955 216 836; e-mail: pete@theroseveares.adsl24.co.uk

TAMAR COMPLEX. Gladys Grant, 18 Orchard Crescent, Oreston, Plymouth, Devon PL9 7NF. E-mail: gladysgrant@talktalk.net

Wildlife Hospital
MOUSEHOLE WILD BIRD HOSPITAL & SANCTUARY ASSOCIATION LTD. Raginnis Hill, Mousehole, Penzance, Cornwall, TR19 6SR. 01736 731386. All species. No ringing.

Wildlife Trusts
CORNWALL WILDLIFE TRUST. (1962; 14,000). Five Acres, Allet, Truro, Cornwall, TR4 9DJ. 01872 273 939 (fax) 01872 225476; e-mail: info@cornwallwildlifetrust.org.uk www.cornwallwildlifetrust.org.uk

THE ISLES OF SCILLY WILDLIFE TRUST. (1984: 324) Trenoweth,St Marys, Isles of Scilly TR21 0NS. 01720 422 153; e-mail: enquiries@ios-wildlifetrust.org.uk www.ios-wildlifetrust.org.uk

CUMBRIA

BirdAtlas/Avifauna
The Breeding Birds of Cumbria by Stott, Callion, Kinley, Raven and Roberts (Cumbria Bird Club, 2002).

Bird Recorders
CUMBRIA. Stephen Westerberg, 8 Beckside Gardens, Brampton, Cumbria CA8 1US. 01697 742

ENGLAND

652; e-mail: swesterberg@btintnernet.com

NORTH EAST. Chris Hind, 01697 746 379;
E-mail: chris.m.hind@gmail.com

NORTH WEST. Derek McAlone
e-mail: derek@derekmcalone3.wanadoo.co.uk

SOUTH CUMBRIA (South Lakeland & Furness).
Ronnie Irving, 24 Birchwood Close, Vicarage Park,
Kendal, Cumbria LA9 5BJ.
E-mail: ronnie@fenella.fslife.co.uk

Bird Reports
BIRDS AND WILDLIFE IN CUMBRIA, from Dave
Piercy, Secretary, Derwent Water Independent
Hostel, Borrowdale, Keswick CA12 5UR. 01768 777
909; e-mail: daveandkathypiercy@tiscali.co.uk
www.cumbriabirdclub.org.uk

WALNEY BIRD OBSERVATORY REPORT, from
Warden, see Reserves.

BTO Regional Representative
CUMBRIA. Colin Gay, 01229 773 820;
e-mail: colinathodbarrow@btinternet.com

Clubs
ARNSIDE & DISTRICT NATURAL HISTORY SOCIETY.
(1967; 221). Jennifer Rae, 01524 736 211.
http://www.arnsidesilverdaleaonb.org.uk/AONB/
Support/Local-societies-and-groups/Arnside-
Natural-History-Society.html
Meetings: 7.30pm, 2nd Tuesday of the month
(Sept-Apr). WI Hall, Arnside. (Also summer walks).

CUMBRIA BIRD CLUB. (1989; 330). Dave Piercy,
Secretary, Derwent water Youth Hostel,
Borrowdale, Keswick CA12 5UR. 01768 777 246;
e-mail: daveandkathypiercy@tiscali.co.uk
www.cumbriabirdclub.org.uk
Meetings: Various evenings and venues (Oct-Mar)
check on website for further details.

Ringing Groups
EDEN RG. G Longrigg, 1 Spring Cottage, Heights,
Appleby-in-Westmorland, Cumbria CA16 6EP.

MORECAMBE BAY WADER RG. J Sheldon, 140
Oxford Street, Barrow-in-Furness, Cumbria LA14
5PJ.

WALNEY BIRD OBSERVATORY. K Parkes, 176
Harrogate Street, Barrow-in-Furness, Cumbria
LA14 5NA. 01229 824 219.

RSPB Local Groups
CARLISLE. (1974; 400). Richard Dixon. 01697 473
544; e-mail: sunzeco@hotmail.co.uk
www.rspb.org.uk/groups/carlisle
Meetings: 7.30pm, Wednesday monthly (Sep-
Mar), Tithe Barn, (Behind Marks And Spencer's),
West Walls, Carlisle, Cumbria, CA3.

SOUTH LAKELAND. (1973; 260). Richard Evans, 33
Castle Green Lane, Kendal LA9 6BB. 01539 722
221; e-mail:
RSPBsouthlakelandlocalgroup@gmail.com
www.rspb.org.uk/groups/southlakeland/
www.facebook.com/RSPBSouthLakeland?ref=hl
Meetings: Evening meetings at 7:30pm in Kendal
(LA9 4BH), Ulverston (LA12 7LZ), Ambleside (LA22
9DH) or Arnside (LA5 0DP), check website for
details.

WEST CUMBRIA. (1986; 270). Marjorie Hutchin.
01900 825 231;
e-mail: majorie.hutchin@btinternet.com
www.rspb.org.uk/groups/westcumbria
Meetings: 7.30pm, 1st Tuesday (Sept-Apr), United
Reformed Church, Main St, Cockermouth

Wetland Bird Survey Organisers
CUMBRIA (excl. estuaries). Mr D Shackleton, 8
Burnbanks, Bampton, Penrith, Cumbria CA10 2RW.
01931 713 693;
e-mail: d.shackleton@btinternet.com

DUDDON ESTUARY. Mr C Gay, 8 Victoria Street,
Millom, Cumbria LA18 5AS. 01229 773 820; 07896
520 5351;
e-mail: colinathodbarrow@btinternet.com

IRT/MITE/ESK ESTUARY. Mr P Jones, c/o WeBS
Office, BTO, The Nunnery, Thetford, Norfolk IP24
2PU. 01842 750 050; e-mail: webs@bto.org

SOLWAY ESTUARY INNER SOUTH. Mr N Holton,
North Plain Farm, Bowness on Solway, Carlisle,
Cumbria CA7 5AG;
e-mail: norman.holton@rspb.org.uk

SOLWAY ESTUARY NORTH. Mr A C Riches, c/o WeBS
Office, BTO, The Nunnery, Thetford, Norfolk IP24
2PU. 01683 300 393; 07792 142 446;
e-mail: slioch69@aol.com

Wildlife Trust
CUMBRIA WILDLIFE TRUST. (1962; 15,000).
Plumgarths, Crook Road, Kendal, Cumbria LA8
8LX. 01539 816 300 (fax) 01539 816 301;
e-mail: mail@cumbriawildlifetrust.org.uk
www.cumbriawildlifetrust.org.uk

DERBYSHIRE

The Birds of Derbyshire (2014),
ed. RA Frost and Steve Shaw,
Liverpool University Press. £45
(plus postage). Order from:
e-mail:
janet.mcdermott@liv.ac.uk;
0151 795 2149.

ENGLAND

Bird Recorders
1. JOINT RECORDER. Roy A Frost, 66 St Lawrence Road, North Wingfield, Chesterfield, Derbyshire S42 5LL. 01246 850 037; e-mail: frostra66@btinternet.com

2. Records Committee & rarity records. Rodney W Key/Richard James. 01332 678 571; e-mail: r_key@sky.com

3. JOINT RECORDER AND EDITOR (of *Derbyshire Bird Report*). Tony Garton, 13 Field Close, Burton-upon-Trent, Staffordshire DE13 0NS. 01283 544 870; e-mail: tonygarton13@sky.com

Bird Reports
CARSINGTON BIRD CLUB ANNUAL REPORT, from The Secretary.

DERBYSHIRE BIRD REPORT (1954- 2012). 2013 will be published Nov 2014, from Bryan Barnacle, Mays, Malthouse Lane, Froggatt, Hope Valley, Derbyshire S32 3ZA. 01433 630 726; e-mail: barney@mays1.demon.co.uk

OGSTON BIRD CLUB REPORT (1970-), records now published online; www.ogstonbirdclub.co.uk

BTO Regional Representative
NORTH & SOUTH DERBYSHIRE. Dave Budworth, 121 Wood Lane, Newhall, Swadlincote, Derbys DE11 0LX. 01283 215 188; e-mail: dbud01@aol.com

Clubs
BAKEWELL BIRD STUDY GROUP. (1987; 80). Mike Nelms (Secretary), 01629 57918; e-mail: mikenelms23@tiscali.co.uk www.bakewellbirdstudygroup.co.uk
Meetings: 7.30pm, 2nd Monday of the month (Sep-May), Friends Meeting House, Bakewell.

BUXTON FIELD CLUB. (1946; 50). Rosemary Furness. 01246 582 213; e-mail: rosemary.furness@virgin.net
Meetings: Winter: Saturday 7:30pm fortnightly (usually), Methodist Church Hall, Buxton. Summer: Saturday afternoon walks, usually fortnightly, commencing 2pm, venues vary - please email me for a programme.

CARSINGTON BIRD CLUB. (1992; 257). Peter Gibbon (Chairman), www.carsingtonbirdclub.co.uk See website for email contact.
Meetings: 7.30pm, 3rd Tuesday of the month (Sep-Mar), the Henmore Room, Carsington Water's main centre.

DERBYSHIRE ORNITHOLOGICAL SOCIETY. (1954; 550). Steve Shaw, 84 Moorland View Road, Walton, Chesterfield, Derbys S40 3DF. 01246 236 090; e-mail: steveshaw84mvr@btinternet.com www.derbyshireOS.org.uk
Meetings: 7.30pm, last Friday of the winter months, various venues.

OGSTON BIRD CLUB. (1969; 1,126). Peter Birley, 35 Rosemary Drive, Alvaston, Derby DE24 0TA. 01332 753 078; e-mail: peter.birley@sky.com www.ogstonbirdclub.co.uk

Ringing Groups
SORBY-BRECK RG. Dr Geoff P Mawson, Moonpenny Farm, Farwater Lane, Dronfield, Sheffield S18 1RA. E-mail: moonpenny@talktalk.net www.sorbybreckringinggroup.co.uk

SOUDER RG. Dave Budworth, 121 Wood Lane, Newhall, Swadlincote, Derbys DE11 0LX. E-mail: dbud01@aol.com

RSPB Local Groups
CHESTERFIELD. (1987; 274). Alan Goddard. 01246 230 244; (M)07764 895 657; e-mail: alangoddard@icloud.com www.rspb.org.uk/groups/chesterfield
Meetings: 7.15pm, usually 3rd Monday of the month, Winding Wheel, New Exhibition Centre, 13 Holywell Street, Chesterfield.

DERBY LOCAL GROUP. (1973; 300). Ray Worthy, 01332 232 748; e-mail: derbyrspblocalgroup@hotmail.co.uk www.rspb.org.uk/groups/derby
Meetings: 7.30pm, 2nd Wednesday of the month (Sep-Apr), Broughton Suite, Grange Banqueting Suite, 457 Burton Road, Littleover, Derby DE23 6XX.

HIGH PEAK. (1974; 110). Richard Stephenson. 0161 427 4187; e-mail: stephenson3rj@gmail.com www.rspb.org.uk/groups/highpeak
Meetings: 7.30pm, 3rd Monday of the month (Sep-May), Marple Senior Citizens Hall, Memorial Park, Marple, STOCKPORT SK6 6BA.

Wetland Bird Survey Organiser
DERBYSHIRE. Mr P J Gibbon, 25 Church Street, Holloway. Derbyshire DE4 5AY. 01629 534 173; e-mail: peter.gibbon@w3z.co.uk

Wildlife Trust
DERBYSHIRE WILDLIFE TRUST. (1962; 14,000). East Mill, Bridge Foot, Belper, Derbyshire DE56 1XH. 01773 881 188; e-mail: enquiries@derbyshirewt.co.uk www.derbyshirewildlifetrust.org.uk

DEVON

BirdAtlas/Avifauna
BIRDS of DEVON by Michael Tyler (Devon

ENGLAND

Birdwatching & Preservation Society, 2010).
Tetrad Atlas of Breeding Birds of Devon by H
P Sitters (Devon Birdwatching & Preservation
Society, 1988).

The Birds of Lundy by Tim Davis and Tim Jones
2007. Available from R M Young (Bookseller) on
01769 573 350 (see www.birdsoflundy.org.uk for
further details).

Bird Recorder
Steve Waite, 46 Primrose Way, Seaton, Devon
EX12 2XQ. 01297 792 339;
e-mail: recorder@devonbirds.org
www.devonbirds.org/

Bird Reports
DEVON BIRDS (1971), from Mike Daniels, 1 Babbs
Cottage, Plymouth Hill, Princetown, Devon PL20
6QJ. 01822 890 899;
e-mail: nellmegfly@gmail.com
www.devonbirds.org

LUNDY FIELD SOCIETY ANNUAL REPORT (1946-). £3
each inc postage, check website for availability,
from Frances Stuart, 3 Lower Linden Road,
Clevedon, North Somerset BS21 7SU.
E-mail: lfssec@hotmail.co.uk

BTO Regional Representative
Stella Beavan;
e-mail: stella@treedown.eclipse.co.uk

Clubs
DEVON BIRDS. (1928; 1200). Mr Mike Daniels, 1
Babbs Cottage, Princetown, Yelverton, Devon
PL20 6QJ. 01822 890 899;
e-mail: nellmegfly@gmail.com
www.devonbirds.org
Branches
East Devon: Jonathan Ruscoe, 01404 822 689;
e-mail: ruscoe@talktalk.net

Mid Devon: Annabelle Strickland, 07557 736 456;
e-mail: jastrickland@talktalk.net

Plymouth: Liz Harris, 01752 789 594;
e-mail: libbymharris@yahoo.co.uk
Meetings: Held at Spugeon Hall, Mutley Baptist
Church, Mutley Plain, Plymouth PL4 6LB at
7.30pm. Refreshments provided. Everyone
welcome.

South Devon: Martin Lees, 01803 852 067.
Meetings: Held at Court Farm Inn,
Abbotskerswell, TQ12 5PG commencing at
7.30pm in the upstairs room. Everyone welcome,
you could have a drink or even a meal first.
Admission: £1.50.

Taw & Torridge: Vicky Hassell, Barnside, Buckland
Brewer, Bideford, Devon EX39 5NF. 01237 452 167;

e-mail: v.hassell@googlemail.com
Meetings: Held at The Castle Centre, Barnstaple
on the second Tuesday during the winter months,
commencing at 7.30pm. Admission: £3.00
including refreshments. Everyone welcome.

KINGSBRIDGE & DISTRICT NATURAL HISTORY
SOCIETY. (1989; 130). Mick Loates, Chairman.
www.knhs.org.uk
Meeting: 7.30pm 4th Monday of Sept-Apr, West
Charleton Village Hall.

LUNDY FIELD SOCIETY. (1946; 450). Mr Michael
Williams, 5 School Place, Oxford,
Oxon OX1 4RG. E-mail: secretary@
lundy.org.uk
www.lundy.org.uk
Meeting: AGM 2nd Saturday of March
in Crediton.

TOPSHAM BIRDWATCHING & NATURALISTS'
SOCIETY. (1969; 140). Keith Chester (Membership
Secretary). 01392 877 817;
e-mail: tbns@talktalk.net
http://topshambns.blogspot.com
Meetings: 7.30pm, 2nd Friday of the month (Sep-
May), Matthews Hall, Topsham.

Ringing Groups
AXE ESTUARY RINGING GROUP. Mike Tyler, The
Acorn, Shute Road, Kilmington, Axminster EX13
7ST. 01297 349 58;
e-mail: mwtyler2@googlemail.com
axeestuaryringinggroup.blogspot.co.uk

DEVON & CORNWALL WADER RG. R C Swinfen,
72 Dunraven Drive, Derriford, Plymouth PL6 6AT.
01752 704 184.

LUNDY FIELD SOCIETY. A M Taylor, 26 High Street,
Spetisbury, Blandford, Dorset DT11 9DJ. 01258
857336; e-mail: ammataylor@yahoo.co.uk

SLAPTON BIRD OBSERVATORY. R C Swinfen, 72
Dunraven Drive, Derriford, Plymouth PL6 6AT.
01752 704 184.

RSPB Local Groups
EXETER & DISTRICT. (1974; 400). Roger Tucker.
01392 860 518;
e-mail: r.345tucker@btinternet.com
www.exeter-rspb.org.uk
Meetings: 7.30 pm, Second Tuesday each month,
(Sep-Apr), Southernhay United Reformed Church
Rooms, Dix's Field, EXETER

PLYMOUTH. (1974; 600). Mrs Eileen Willey, 11
Beverstone Way, Roborough, Plymouth PL6 7DY.
01752 208 996; e-mail: edward.willey@sky.com
Meetings: Trinity United Reform Church, Tor
Lane, Plymouth PL3 5NY.

TORBAY AND SOUTH DEVON TEAM. John Allan.
01626 821 344; e-mail: john@morsey.f2s.com
www.rspb.org.uk/groups/torbayandsouthdevon

Wetland Bird Survey Organisers
DEVON (Excl. Tamar). Dr P J Reay, Crooked Fir,
Moorland Park, South Brent, Devon TQ10 9AS.
01364 73293; e-mail:
peter.p.j.reay@btinternet.com

TAMAR COMPLEX. Gladys Grant, 18 Orchard
Crescent, Oreston, Plymouth PL9 7NF.
E-mail: gladysgrant@talktalk.net

Wildlife Trust
DEVON WILDLIFE TRUST. (1962; 33,000).
Cricklepit, Commercial Road, Exeter, EX2 4AB.
01392 279 244 (fax) 01392 433 221;
e-mail: contactus@devonwildlifetrust.org
www.devonwildlifetrust.org

DORSET

BirdAtlas/Avifauna
Dorset Breeding Bird Atlas (working title). In
preparation.

The Birds of Dorset by Dr George Green
(Christopher Helm 2004)

Bird Recorder
Kevin Lane. E-mail: kevin@broadstoneheath.co.uk

Bird Reports
DORSET BIRDS (1977-), from Neil
Gartshore, Moor Edge, 2 Bere
Road, Wareham, Dorset BH20
4DD. 01929 552 560; e-mail:
enquiries@callunabooks.co.uk

*THE BIRDS OF CHRISTCHURCH
HARBOUR (1956-)*, from Ian Southworth, 1
Bodowen Road, Burton, Christchurch, Dorset BH23
7JL. E-mail: ianbirder@aol.com

PORTLAND BIRD OBSERVATORY REPORT, from
Warden, see Reserves,

BTO Regional Representative
DORSET. Ieuan Evans (temporary). 01842 750 050;
e-mail: ieuan.evans@bto.org

Clubs
CHRISTCHURCH HARBOUR ORNITHOLOGICAL
GROUP. (1956; 290). Mr I.Southworth, Membership
Secretary. 01202 478 093; www.chog.org.uk
e-mail: ianbirder@aol.com

DORSET BIRD CLUB. (1987; 525). Mrs Diana Dyer,
The Cedars, 3 Osmay Road, Swanage, Dorset BH19
2JQ. 01929 421 402;
e-mail: membership@dorsetbirds.org.uk
www.dorsetbirds.org.uk

DORSET NATURAL HISTORY & ARCHAEOLOGICAL
SOCIETY. (1845; 2188). Dorset County Museum,
High West Street, Dorchester, Dorset DT1 1XA.
01305 262 735;
e-mail: secretary@dorsetcountymuseum.org
www.dorsetcountymuseum.org

Ringing Groups
CHRISTCHURCH HARBOUR RS. E C Brett, 3
Whitfield Park, St Ives, Ringwood, Hants BH24
2DX. E-mail: ed_brett@lineone.net

PORTLAND BIRD OBSERVATORY. Martin Cade, Old
Lower Light, Portland Bill, Dorset DT5 2JT. 01305
820553; e-mail: obs@btinternet.com
www.portlandbirdobs.org.uk
STOUR RG. R Gifford, 62 Beacon Park Road,
Upton, Poole, Dorset BH16 5PE.

RSPB Local Groups
BLACKMOOR VALE. (1981; 130). Alison Rymell.
0782 574 7546; e-mail: rspb.bv@gmail.com
www.rspb.org.uk/groups/blackmoorvale
Meetings: 7.30pm, 3rd Friday in the month,
Gillingham Primary School.

EAST DORSET. (1974; 435). Hugh Clark. 01425 475
487; e-mail: hugh.clark@hotmail.co.uk
www.rspb.org.uk/groups/eastdorset
Meetings: 7.30pm, 2nd Wednesday of the month,
St Mark's Church Hall, Talbot Village, Wallisdown,
Bournemouth.

POOLE. (1982; 305). Pam Hunt, 01929 553 338;
e-mail: pam.hunt@talktalk.net
www.rspb.org.uk/groups/poole
Meetings: 7.30pm, Upton Community Centre,
Poole Road, Upton.

SOUTH DORSET. (1976; 422). Andrew Parsons.
013058 772 678;
e-mail: andrew_parsons_141@yahoo.co.uk
www.rspb.org.uk/groups/southdorset
Meetings: 3rd Thursday of each month (Sep-
April), St. Georges Church Hall, Fordington,
DORCHESTER, Dorset, DT1 1LB.

Wetland Bird Survey Organisers
DORSET (excl estuaries). Mr J M Jones, Blackbird
Cottage, 14 Church Lane, Sutton Waldron, Nr
Blandford, Dorset DT11 8PA. 01747 811 490;
e-mail: blackbirdcott@tiscali.co.uk

POOLE HARBOUR. Mr P Morton, c/o WeBS Office,
BTO, The Nunnery, Thetford, Norfolk IP24 2PU;
e-mail: paulolua@yahoo.co.uk

THE FLEET & PORTLAND HARBOUR. Mr S Groves,
7 Grove Lane, Abbotsbury, Weymouth, Dorset DT3
4JH. 01305 871 684; 07531 939 081;
e-mail: cygnusolor@yahoo.co.uk

ENGLAND

RADIPOLE & LODMOOR. Mr T Branston, RSPB, Ryan House, Sandford Lane, Wareham, Dorset BH20 4DY; e-mail: toby.branston@rspb.org.uk

Wildlife Hospital
SWAN RESCUE SANCTUARY. Ken and Judy Merriman, The Wigeon, Crooked Withies, Holt, Wimborne, Dorset BH21 7LB. 01202 828 166.www. swan.jowebdesign.co.uk 24 hr rescue service for swans. Large sanctuary of 40 ponds and lakes. Hospital and intensive care. Veterinary support. Free advice and help line. Three fully equipped rescue ambulances. Rescue water craft for all emergencies. Viewing by appointment only.

Wildlife Trust
DORSET WILDLIFE TRUST. (1961; 25,000). Brooklands Farm, Forston, Dorchester, Dorset, DT2 7AA. 01305 264 620 (fax) 01305 251 120; e-mail: enquiries@dorsetwildlifetrust.org.uk www.dorsetwildlife.org.uk

DURHAM

See Cleveland and Co. Durham.

ESSEX

Bird Atlas/Avifauna
The Birds of Essex (Helm, 2007) by Simon Wood (A&C Black, August 2007).

The Breeding Birds of Essex by M K Dennis (Essex Birdwatching Society, 1996).

Bird Recorder
RECORDER. Les Steward, 6 Creek View, Basildon, Essex SS16 4RU. 01268 551 464, e-mail: les.steward@btinternet.com

Bird Report
ESSEX BIRD REPORT (inc Bradwell Bird Obs records) (1950-), from Peter Dwyer, Sales Officer, 48 Churchill Avenue, Halstead, Essex CO9 2BE. 01787 476 524; e-mail: petedwyer@ petedwyer.plus.com

BTO Regional Representatives
NORTH-EAST & SOUTH. Positions vacant. 01842 750 050.E-mail: info@bto.org

NORTH-WEST. Graham Smith. 01277 354 034; e-mail: silaum.silaus@tiscali.co.uk

Club
ESSEX BIRDWATCHING SOCIETY. (1949; 700). John and Louise Sykes, Joint General Secretary, 14 Acres End, Chelmsford, Essex CM1 2XR. 01245 355 132; e-mail: john.sykes@btinternet.com www.ebws.org.uk

Meetings: 1st Friday of the month (Oct-Mar), Friends' Meeting House, Rainsford Road, Chelmsford.

Ringing Groups
ABBERTON RG. C P Harris, Wyandotte, Seamer Road, Southminster, Essex CM0 7BX.

BRADWELL BIRD OBSERVATORY. C P Harris, Wyandotte, Seamer Road, Southminster, Essex CM0 7BX.

RSPB Local Groups
CHELMSFORD AND CENTRAL ESSEX. (1976; 1200). Viv Connett. 07985 796 657; e-mail: vivconnett@mail.com www.rspb.org.uk/groups/chelmsford **Meetings:** 8pm, Thursdays, eight times a year. The Cramphorn Theatre, Chelmsford.

COLCHESTER. (1981; 220). Mr Ron Firmin, 17 Edward Paxman Gardens, Colchester, Essex CO1 2NT. 07714 210 746; e-mail: ron.firmin@btinternet.com www.rspb.org.uk/groups/colchester **Meetings:** 7.45pm, 2nd Thursday of the month (Sep-Apr), Shrub End Community Hall, Shrub End Road, Colchester. Regular coach and car trips to local birding sites and those further afield.

SOUTH EAST ESSEX. (1983; 200). Graham Mee, 34 Park View Drive, Leigh on Sea, Essex SS9 4TU. 01702 525 152; e-mail: grahamm@southendrspb.co.uk www.southeastrspb.org.uk **Meetings:** 7.30pm, usually 1st Tuesday of the month (Sep-May), Belfairs School Hall, School Way, Leigh-on-Sea SS9 4HX.

Wetland Bird Survey Organisers
CROUCH/ROACH ESTUARY and SOUTH DENGIE. Canon P Mason, 8 Canuden Road, Chelmsford, Essex CM1 2SX. 01245 351 465; e-mail: Petermason32@waitrose.com

HAMFORD WATER. Mr J Novorol, The Brents, Harwich Road, Great Oakley, Harwich, Essex CO12 5AD. 01255 880 552; e-mail: webs@bto.org

LEE VALLEY. Ms D Richardson, c/o LVRPA, Myddelton House, Bulls Cross, Enfield, Middlesex EN2 9HG; e-mail: drichardson@leevalleypark.org.uk

NORTH BLACKWATER. Mr J Thorogood, 18 Smallwood Road, Colchester, Essex CO2 9HA. 01206 768 771.E-mail: webs@bto.org

SOUTH BLACKWATER AND NORTH DENGIE. Mr A G Harbott, 5 Allnutts Road, Epping, Essex CM16 7BD. 01992 575 213; e-mail: anthonyharbott@talktalk.net

STOUR ESTUARY. Mr R Vonk, RSPB, Unit 1 Brantham Mill, Bergholt Road, Brantham, Manningtree, Essex CO11 1QT. 01206 391 153; 07711 129 149; e-mail: rick.vonk@rspb.org.uk

THAMES ESTUARY - Foulness. Dr C Lewis, c/o WeBS Office, BTO, The Nunnery, Thetford, Norfolk IP24 2PU; e-mail: cpm.lewis@gmail.com

Wildlife Trust
ESSEX WILDLIFE TRUST. (1959; 36,000). The Joan Elliot Visitor Centre, Abbots Hall Farm, Great Wigborough, Colchester, CO5 7RZ. 01621 862 960 (fax) 01621 862 990;
e-mail: admin@essexwt.org.uk
www.essexwt.org.uk

GLOUCESTERSHIRE

Bird Atlas/Avifauna
Atlas of Breeding Birds of the North Cotswolds. (North Cotswold Ornithological Society, 1990)

The Birds of Gloucestershire. Gordon Kirk and John Phillips (Liverpool University Press) 2013.

Birds of The Cotswolds (Liverpool University Press 2009).

Bird Recorder
GLOUCESTERSHIRE EXCLUDING S.GLOS (AVON). Richard Baatsen. E-mail: baatsen@surfbirder.com

Bird Reports
CHELTENHAM BIRD CLUB BIRD REPORT (1998-2001) - no longer published, from Secretary.

GLOUCESTERSHIRE BIRD REPORT (1953-). £8 from Mike Sutcliffe, 18 Carlton Street, Cheltenham, Glos GL52 6AQ. www.glosnats.org

NORTH COTSWOLD ORNITHOLOGICAL SOCIETY ANNUAL REPORT £3.50,
from Dave Piercy, 60 King William Drive, Charlton Park, Cheltenham, Glos. GL53 7RP;
e-mail: info@ncosbirds.org.uk
www.ncosbirds.org.uk

BTO Regional Representative
Gordon Kirk. 01452 741 724;
e-mail: gordonkirk@aol.com

Clubs
CHELTENHAM BIRD CLUB. (1976; 100). Membership Secretary. 01451 850 385.
www.cheltenhambirdclub.org.uk
Meetings: 7.15pm, Mondays (Oct-Mar), Bournside School, Warden Hill Road, Cheltenham.

DURSLEY BIRDWATCHING & PRESERVATION SOCIETY. (1953; 240). The Secretary, Ruth Mitchell, 17 Woodland Avenue, Dursley, Glos GL11 4EW; e-mail: dbwps@yahoo.com

http://dursleybirdwatchers.btck.co.uk/
Meetings: 7.45pm, 2nd and 4th Monday (Sept-Mar), Dursley Community Centre.

GLOUCESTERSHIRE NATURALISTS' SOCIETY. (1948; 500). Mike Smart, 143 Cheltenham Road, Gloucester, GL2 0JH. 01452 421 131;
www.glosnats.org
e-mail: smartmike@btinternet.com
Meetings: 7.30pm, 2nd Friday of the month (Oct-April), Watermoor Church Hall, Cirencester GL7 1JR.

NORTH COTSWOLD ORNITHOLOGICAL SOCIETY. (1982; 70). A Lewis, 41 Roman Way, Bourton-on-the-Water, Cheltenham, Glos GL54 2EW;
e-mail: info@ncosbirds.org.uk
www.ncosbirds.org.uk
Meetings: Monthly field meetings, usually Sunday 9.30pm. This is a small surveying and recording group based in Cheltenham and the Cotswolds.

Ringing Groups
COTSWOLD WATER PARK RG. John Wells, 25 Pipers Grove, Highnam, Glos GL2 8NJ.
E-mail: john.wells2@btinternet.com

SEVERN ESTUARY GULL GROUP. M E Durham, 6 Glebe Close, Frampton-on-Severn, Glos GL2 7EL. 01452 741 312.

RSPB Local Group
GLOUCESTERSHIRE. (1972; 600). David Cramp, 2 Ellenor Drive, Alderton, Tewkesbury GL20 8NZ. 01242 620 281; e-mail: djcramp@btinternet.com
www.rspb.org.uk/groups/gloucestershire
Meetings: 7.30pm, 3rd Tuesday of the month, Gala Club, Longford, Gloucester GL2 9EB.

Wildlife Hospital
VALE WILDLIFE RESCUE - WILDLIFE HOSPITAL + REHABILITATION CENTRE. Any staff member, Station Road, Beckford, Tewkesbury, Glos GL20 7AN. 01386 882 288;
e-mail: info@valewildlife.org.uk
www.valewildlife.org.uk All wild birds. Intensive care. Registered charity. Veterinary support.

Wetland Bird Survey Organisers
GLOUCESTERSHIRE. Mr M Smart, 143 Cheltenham Road, Gloucester, Glos GL2 0JH. 01452 421 131. 07816 140 513;
e-mail: smartmike@btinternet.com

COTSWOLD WATER PARK. Mr G O Harris, 10 The Paddock, Market Lavington, Devizes, Wiltshire SN10 4BP. 07868 427 916;
e-mail: gharris_doh@hotmail.com

ENGLAND

Wildlife Trust
GLOUCESTERSHIRE WILDLIFE TRUST. (1961; 27,500). Conservation Centre, Robinswood Hill Country Park, Reservoir Road, Gloucester, GL4 6SX. 01452 383 333;
e-mail: info@gloucestershirewildlifetrust.co.uk
www.gloucestershirewildlifetrust.co.uk

HAMPSHIRE

Bird Atlas/Avifauna
Birds of Hampshire by J M Clark and J A Eyre (Hampshire Ornithological Society, 1993).

Bird Recorder
RECORDER. Keith Betton, 8 Dukes Close, Folly Hill, Farnham, Surrey GU9 0DR. 01252 724 068; e-mail: keithbetton@hotmail.com

Bird Report
HAMPSHIRE BIRD REPORT (1955-). 2012 now available. 2013 edition expected before the end of 2014, from Mr Bryan Coates, 8 Gardner Way, Chandler's Ford, Eastleigh,, Hants SO53 1JL. 023 80 252 960; e-mail: sandyandbryan@tiscali.co.uk
www.hos.org.uk

BTO Regional Representative
Glynne C Evans, Waverley, Station Road, Chilbolton, Stockbridge, Hants SO20 6AL. 01264 860 697; e-mail: hantsbto@hotmail.com

Club
HAMPSHIRE ORNITHOLOGICAL SOCIETY. (1979; 1,500). John Shillitoe, Honarary Secretary, Westerly, Hundred Acres Road, Wickham, Hampshire PO17 6HY. 01329 833 086; www.hos.org.uk
e-mail: john@shillitoe.
freeserve.co.uk

Ringing Groups
FARLINGTON RG. D A Bell, 38 Holly Grove, Fareham, Hants PO16 7UP.

ITCHEN RG. W F Simcox, 10 Holdaway Close, Kingsworthy, Winchester SO23 7QH.
E-mail: wilfsimcox@gmx.com

RSPB Local Groups
BASINGSTOKE. (1979; 62). Peter Hutchins, 35 Woodlands, Overton, Whitchurch RG25 3HN. 01256 770 831; (M)07895 388 378;
e-mail: fieldfare@jaybry.gotadsl.co.uk
www.rspb.org.uk/groups/basingstoke
Meetings: 7.30pm 3rd Wednesday of the month (Sept-May), The Barn, Church Cottage, St Michael's Church, Church Square, Basingstoke.

NEW FOREST. Les Easom. 02380 328 085; e-mail: lesweasom@gmail.com

www.rspb.org.uk/groups/newforest
Meetings: 7.30pm 2nd Wednesday of the month (Sept-June) Lyndhurst Community Centre, High Street, Lyndhurst SO43 7NY.

NORTH EAST HAMPSHIRE. (1976; 215). Sue Radbourne. 0127 629 434;
e-mail: Mailto@northeasthantsRSPB.org.uk
www.northeasthantsrspb.org.uk
Meetings: See website.

PORTSMOUTH. (1974; 210). Gordon Humby, 19 Charlesworth Gardens, Waterlooville, Hants PO7 6AU. 02392 353 949;
e-mail: PortsmouthRSPB@gmail.com
www.rspb.org.uk/groups/portsmouth
Meetings: 7.30pm, 4th Saturday of every month. St Andrews Church Hall, Havant Road, Farlington, Portsmouth, PO6 1AA

WINCHESTER & DISTRICT LOCAL GROUP. (1974; 100). Pam Symes, 29A Maytree Close, Badger Farm, Winchester SO22 4JE. 01962 851 821;
e-mail: psymes033@gmail.com
www.rspb.org.uk/groups/winchester
Meetings: 7.45pm, 1st Wednesday of the month (not Jan or Aug), Shawford Parish Hall, Pearson Lane, Shawford.

Wetland Bird Survey Organisers
AVON VALLEY. John Clark, 4 Cygnet Court, Old Cove Road, Fleet, Hants GU51 2RL; e-mail: johnclark50@sky.com

HAMPSHIRE (estuaries/coastal). Mr J R D Shillitoe, c/o WeBS Office, BTO, The Nunnery, Thetford, Norfolk IP24 2PU;
e-mail: john@shillitoe.freeserve.co.uk

HAMPSHIRE (Inland - excluding Avon Valley). Mr K Wills, 51 Peabody Road, Farnborough, Hampshire GU14 6EB; e-mail: kwills57@btinternet.com

ISLE OF WIGHT. Mr J R Baldwin, 21 Hillcrest Road, Rookley, Ventnor, Isle of Wight PO38 3PB. 01983 202 223; 0779 342 1938;
e-mail: jimr.baldwin@tiscali.co.uk

Wildlife Hospital
HAWK CONSERVANCY TRUST. Visitor Centre, Weyhill, Andover, Hampshire SP11 8DY. 01264 773 850; e-mail: info@hawkconservancy.org
www.hawk-conservancy.org/ The Hawk Conservancy Trust is an important centre for receiving injured birds of prey and has one of the only specialist bird of prey hospitals in the UK.

Wildlife Trust
HAMPSHIRE & ISLE OF WIGHT WILDLIFE TRUST. (1960; 27,000). Beechcroft House, Vicarage Lane, Curdridge, Hampshire SO32 2DP. 01489 774 400 (fax) 01489 774 401;

e-mail: feedback@hiwwt.org.uk
www.hiwwt.org.uk

HEREFORDSHIRE

Bird Recorder
Mick Colquhourn;
e-mail: mcc@mcolquhoun.plus.com

Bird Reports
THE BIRDS OF HEREFORDSHIRE (2008 -), from
Mr WJ Marler, Cherry Tree House, Walford,
Leintwardine, Craven Arms, Shropshire SY7 0JT.

HEREFORDSHIRE ORNITHOLOGICAL CLUB ANNUAL
REPORT, from Mr J Wilkinson, Coughton Forge,
Coughton, Ross-on-Wye HR9 5SF. 01989 763 182;
e-mail: m.jim.wilkinson@googlemail.com

BTO Regional Representative
Chris Robinson, Rock Cottage, Newton St.
Margarets, HerefordHR2 0QW. 01981 510 360;
e-mail: herefordbtorep@btinternet.com

Club
HEREFORDSHIRE ORNITHOLOGICAL CLUB. (1950;
416). TM Weale, Foxholes, Bringsty Common,
Worcester WR6 5UN. 01886 821 368;
e-mail: tom@tomweale.plus.com
www.herefordshirebirds.org
Meetings: 7.30pm, 2nd Thursday of the month
(Autumn/winter), Holmer Parish Centre, Holmer,
Hereford.

Ringing Group
LLANCILLO RG. Dr G R Geen, 2 Mundford Farm,
Cranwich Road, Mundford, Thetford, Norfolk
IP26 5JJ. 07919 880 281; e-mail: grahamgeen@
btinternet.com

Wetland Bird Survey Organiser
HEREFORDSHIRE. Mr C M Robinson, Rock Cottage,
Newton St Margarets, Hereford HR2 0QW. 01981
510 360; 07717 831 577;
e-mail: herefordbtorep@btinternet.com

Wildlife Trust
HEREFORDSHIRE NATURE TRUST. (1962; 2,535).
Lower House Farm, Ledbury Road, Tupsley,
Hereford, HR1 1UT. 01432 356 872 (fax) 01432
275 489;
e-mail: enquiries@herefordshirewt.co.uk
www.herefordshirewt.org

HERTFORDSHIRE

Bird Atlas/Avifauna
Birds at Tring Reservoirs by R Young et al
(Hertfordshire Natural History Society, 1996).

Mammals, Amphibians and Reptiles of

Hertfordshire by Hertfordshire NHS in association
with Training Publications Ltd, 3 Finway Court,
Whippendell Road, Watford WD18 7EN, (2001).

The Breeding Birds of Hertfordshire by K W Smith
et al (Herts NHS, 1993). Purchase from HNHS at
£5 plus postage.
E-mail: herts.naturalhistorysociety@aol.com

Bird Recorder
Ken Smith, 24 Mandeville Rise, Welwyn Garden
City, Herts AL8 7JU. 01707 330 405;
e-mail: birdrecorder@hnhs.org
www.hnhs.org/birds

Bird Report
HERTFORDSHIRE BIRD REPORT
2012 (from 1878-2012), from Linda
Smith, 24 Mandeville Rise, Welwyn
Garden City, Herts AL8 7JU. 01707
330 405;
e-mail: secretary@hnhs.org
www.hnhs.org

BTO Regional Representative
Chris Dee, 26 Broadleaf Avenue, Thorley Park,
Bishop's Stortford, Herts CM23 4JY. 01279 755
637; e-mail: hertsbto@hotmail.com
website: http://hertsbto.blogspot.com

Clubs
FRIENDS OF TRING RESERVOIRS. (1993; 400).
Membership Secretary, PO Box 1083, Tring HP23
5WU. 01442 822 471; www.fotr.org.uk
e-mail: keith@fotr.org.uk
Meetings: See website.

HERTFORDSHIRE BIRD CLUB. (1971; 420) Part
of Hertfordshire Natural History Society. Linda
Smith, 24 Mandeville Rise, Welwyn Garden City,
Herts AL8 7JU. 01707 330 405;
e-mail: secretary@hnhs.org
www.hnhs.org/birds

HERTFORDSHIRE NATURAL HISTORY SOCIETY.
(1875; 420) Linda Smith, 24 Mandeville Rise,
Welwyn Garden City, Herts AL8 7JU. 01707 330
405; e-mail: secretary@hnhs.org
www.hertsbirdclub.org.uk
Meetings: Saturday afternoon in Mar and Oct/Nov
(date varies) at Woolmer Green Hall, SG3 6XA.

Ringing Groups
MAPLE CROSS RG. P Delaloye.
E-mail: pdelaloye@tiscali.co.uk

RYE MEADS RG. Chris Dee, 26 Broadleaf Avenue,
Thorley Park, Bishop's Stortford, Herts CM23 4JY.
H:01279 755 637;
e-mail: ringingsecretary@rmrg.org.uk
www.rmrg.org.uk

ENGLAND

RSPB Local Groups
CHORLEYWOOD & DISTRICT. (1977; 142). Carol Smith, 24 Beacon Way, Rickmansworth, Herts WD3 7PE. 01923 897 885;
e-mail: carolsmithuk@hotmail.com
www.rspb.org.uk/groups/chorleywood
Meetings: 8pm, 3rd Thursday of the month (Sept-Nov, Jan-May), 2nd Thursday (Dec), Russell School, Brushwood Drive, Chorleywood.

HARPENDEN. (1974; 1000). Geoff Horn, 41 Ridgewood Drive, Harpenden, Herts AL5 3LJ. 01582 765 443; e-mail: geoffrhorn@yahoo.co.uk
www.rspb.org.uk/groups/harpenden
Meetings: 8pm, 2nd Thursday of the month (Sept-June), All Saint's Church Hall, Station Road, Harpenden.

HEMEL HEMPSTEAD. (1972; 150). Ian Wilson, 15 Seymour Crescent, Hemel Hempstead, Herts HP2 5DS. 01442 265 022;
e-mail: ian.aeronautics@gmail.com
www.hemelrspb.org.uk
Meetings: 8pm, 1st Monday of the month (Sep-Jun),The Cavendish School, Warners End, Hemel Hempstead.

HITCHIN & LETCHWORTH. (1972; 102). Dr Martin Johnson, 1 Cartwright Road, Royston, Herts SG8 9ET. 01763 249 459;
e-mail: martinrjspc@hotmail.com
www.rspb.org.uk/groups/hitchinandletchworth
Meetings: 7.30pm, 1st Friday of the month, The Settlement, Nevells Road, Letchworth SG6 4UB.

POTTERS BAR & BARNET. (1977; 1400). Lesley Causton, 57 Lakeside Crescent, East Barnet, Herts EN4 8QH. 0208 440 2038;
e-mail: lesleycauston@talktalk.net
www.pottersbar-rspb.org.uk
Meetings: 2.00pm, 2nd Wednesday of the month, St Johns URC Hall, Mowbray Road, Barnet. Evening meetings, 3rd Friday of the month (not Jul, Aug or Dec) 7.45pm, Potters Bar United Reform Church, Tilbury Hall, Darkes Lane, Potters Bar, EN6 1BZ.

ST ALBANS. (1979; 1550 in catchment area). Julie Wakefield, 01727 683 509;
e-mail: st-albans-rspb@hotmail.co.uk
www.rspb.org.uk/groups/stalbans
Meetings: 7.30pm, 2nd Tuesday of the month (Sep-May), St Saviours Church Hall, Sandpit Lane, St Albans.

SOUTH EAST HERTS. (1971; 2,400 in catchment area). Terry Smith, 31 Marle Gardens, Waltham Abbey, Essex EN9 2DZ. 01992 715634;
e-mail: se_herts_rspb@yahoo.co.uk
www.rspb.org.uk/groups/southeasthertfordshire
Meetings: 7.30pm, usually last Tuesday of the month (Sept-June), URC Church Hall, Mill Lane, Broxbourne EN10 7BQ.

STEVENAGE. (1982; 1300 in the catchment area). Mrs Ann Collis, 16 Stevenage Road, Walkern, Herts 01483 861 547;
e-mail: p.collis672@btinternet.com
www.rspb.org.uk/groups/stevenage
Meetings: 7.30pm, 3rd Tuesday of the month, Friends Meeting House, Cuttys Lane, Stevenage.

WATFORD. (1974; 590). Janet Reynolds. 01923 249 647; e-mail: janet.reynolds@whht.nhs.uk
www.rspb.org.uk/groups/watford
Meetings: 7.30pm, 2nd Wednesday of the month (Sep-Jun), Stanborough Centre, St Albans Rd, Watford.

Wetland Bird Survey Organiser
HERTFORDSHIRE (excl. Lee Valley). Mr J H Terry, 46 Manor Way, Borehamwood, Herts WD6 1QY. 0208 9051 461;
e-mail: jimjoypaddy@virginmedia.com

LEE VALLEY. Ms D Richardson, c/o LVRPA, Myddelton House, Bulls Cross, Enfield, Middlesex EN2 9HG; e-mail:
drichardson@leevalleypark.org.uk

Wildlife Trust
HERTS & MIDDLESEX WILDLIFE TRUST. (1964; 18,500). Grebe House, St Michael's Street, St Albans, Herts, AL3 4SN. 01727 858 901 (fax) 01727 854 542; e-mail: info@hmwt.org
www.wildlifetrust.org.uk/herts/

ISLE OF WIGHT

Bird Recorder
Robin Attrill, 17 Waterhouse Moor, Harlow, Essex CM18 6BA. 01279 423 467;
e-mail: robin@rpattrill.freeserve.co.uk

Bird Reports
ISLE OF WIGHT BIRD REPORT (1986-) (Pre-1986 not available), £7.50, from Mr DJ Hunnybun, 40 Churchill Road, Cowes, Isle of Wight PO31 8HH. 01983 292 880;
e-mail: davehunnybun@hotmail.com

BTO Regional Representative
James C Gloyn, 3 School Close, Newchurch, Isle of Wight PO36 0NL. 01983 865 567;
e-mail: gloynjc@yahoo.com

Clubs
ISLE OF WIGHT NATURAL HISTORY & ARCHAEOLOGICAL SOCIETY. (1919; 500). The Secretary, Unit 16, Prospect Business Centre, Prospect Business Centre, West Cowes,

Isle of Wight PO31 7HD.
E-mail: society@iwnhas.org
www.iwnhas.org

ISLE OF WIGHT ORNITHOLOGICAL GROUP. (1986; 155). Mr DJ Hunnybun, 40 Churchill Road, Cowes, Isle of Wight PO31 8HH. 01983 292 880; e-mail: davehunnybun@hotmail.com http://iowbirds.awardspace.com/IWOG.htm

RSPB Local Group
Wildlife Trust
Director, See Hampshire,

KENT

Bird Atlas/Avifauna
Birding in Kent by D W Taylor et al 1996. Pica Press.

Bird Recorder
Barry Wright, 6 Hatton Close, Northfleet, Kent DA11 8SD. 01474 320 918 (M)07789 710 555; e-mail: umbrellabirds66@gmail.com

Bird Reports
DUNGENESS BIRD OBSERVATORY REPORT (1989-), from Warden, see Reserves.

KENT BIRD REPORT (1952-), from Chris Roome, Rowland House, Station Road, Staplehurst, Kent TN12 0PY. 01580 891 686; e-mail: chris.roome@zulogic.co.uk

SANDWICH BAY BIRD OBSERVATORY REPORT, from Warden, see Reserves,

BTO Regional Representatives
Geoff Orton, 07788 102 238; e-mail: geofforton@hotmail.com

Club

KENT ORNITHOLOGICAL SOCIETY. (1952; 650). Mr Martin Coath, 14A Mount Harry Road, Sevenoaks, Kent TN13 3JH. 01732 460 710; www.kentos.org.uk e-mail: crag_martin2000@yahoo.co.uk **Meetings:** Indoor: October-April at various venues; the AGM in April is at Grove Green community Hall, Grovewood Drive, Maidstone ME14 5TQ. See website for details.

Ringing Groups
DARTFORD RG. R Taylor.
E-mail: dreolin@btopenworld.com

DUNGENESS BIRD OBSERVATORY. David Walker, Dungeness Bird Observatory, Dungeness, Romney Marsh, Kent TN29 9NA. 01797 321 309; e-mail: dungeness.obs@tinyonline.co.uk www.dungenessbirdobs.org.uk

RECULVER RG. Chris Hindle, 42 Glenbervie Drive, Herne Bay, Kent CT6 6QL. 01227 373 070; e-mail: christopherhindle@hotmail.com

SANDWICH BAY BIRD OBSERVATORY. Mr KB Ellis, 6 Alderney Gardens, St Peters, Broadstairs, Kent CT10 2TN. 01304 617 341; e-mail: keithjulie@talktalk.net

SWALE WADER GROUP. Rod Smith, 67 York Avenue, Chatham, Kent ME5 9ES. 01634 865 836. www.swalewaders.co.uk

RSPB Local Groups
CANTERBURY. (1973; 216). Wendy Kennett. 01227 477 113; e-mail: wendyjkennett@gmail.com www.rspb.org.uk/groups/canterbury
Meetings: 8.00pm, 2nd Tuesday of the month (Sept-Apr), Chaucer Social Club, Off Chaucer Drive, Canterbury, CT1 1YW.

GRAVESEND. (1977; 250). Paul Yetman. 01474 332 417; e-mail: Groupleader@RSPBgravesend.org.uk www.rspbgravesend.org.uk
Meetings: 7.45pm, 2nd Wednesday of the month (Sep-May), St Botolph's Hall, Northfleet, Gravesend DA11 9EX. 2.00pm 4th Tuesday of the month (Nov, Jan-Mar), Kent Room, Woodville Halls, Gravesend DA12 1AU.
Full details of our indoor and outdoor programme, news and announcements can be found on website and also on Facebook at www.facebook.com/rspbgravesend

MAIDSTONE. (1973; 250). Adrian Tear; e-mail: leader2@maidstone.localrspb.org.uk
Meetings: 7.30pm, 3rd Thursday of the month, Grove Green Community Hall, Penhurst Close, Grove Green, opposite Tesco's.

MEDWAY. (1974; 230). Marie Tilley. 01634 387 431; e-mail: medwayRSPB.leader@btinternet.com www.medway-rspb.pwp.blueyonder.co.uk
Meetings: 7.45pm 3rd Tuesday of the month (except Aug), Parkwood Community Centre, Parkwood Green, Gillingham ME8 9PN

SEVENOAKS. (1974; 265). Anne Chapman. 01732 456 459; e-mail: anneanddave.chapman@virgin.net www.rspb.org.uk/groups/sevenoaks
Meetings: 7.45pm 1st Thursday of the month, Otford Memorial Hall.

THANET. (1975; 53). Brian Short, 07721 452 294; e-mail: brian@brianshort.co.uk www.rspb.org.uk/groups/thanet
Meetings: 7.30pm last Tuesday of the month (Jan-Nov), Portland Centre, St Peters, Broadstairs.

TONBRIDGE. (1975; 100 reg attendees/1700 in catchment). Martin Ellis. 01892 521 413;

e-mail: martin@ellismp.plus.com
www.rspb.org.uk/groups/tonbridge
Meetings: 7.45pm 3rd Wednesday of the month
(Sept-Apr), St Philips Church, Salisbury Road TN10
4PA. These meetings are followed by field trips on
the Sat and Wed, which also run in May and June.

Wetland Bird Survey Organisers
DUNGENESS AREA. David Walker, Dungeness
Bird Observatory, 11 RNSSS, Dungeness, Romney
Marsh, Kent TN29 9NA. 01797 321 309;
e-mail: dungenessobs@vfast.co.uk
www.dungenessbirdobs.org.uk

NORTH KENT ESTUARIES. Mr G R Orton, c/o WeBS
Office, BTO, The Nunnery, Thetford, Norfolk IP24
2PU. 07788 102 238;
e-mail: geofforton@hotmail.com

PEGWELL BAY. Mr P W J Findley, 62 Elizabeth
Carter Avenue, Deal, Kent CT14 9NT;
e-mail: pwjfindley@hotmail.com

Wildlife Hospital
RAPTOR CENTRE. Eddie Hare, Ivy Cottage,
Groombridge Place, Groombridge, Tunbridge
Wells, Kent TN3 9QG. 01892 861 175;
e-mail: raptorcentre@btconnect.com
www.raptorcentre.co.uk
Birds of prey. Veterinary support. 24hr rescue
service for sick and injured birds of prey that
covers the South-East.

Wildlife Trust
KENT WILDLIFE TRUST. (1958; 10500). Tyland
Barn, Sandling, Maidstone, Kent, ME14 3BD. 01622
662 012 (fax) 01622 671 390;
e-mail: info@kentwildlife.org.uk
www.kentwildlifetrust.org.uk

LANCASHIRE

Bird Atlas/Avifauna
*An Atlas of Breeding Birds of Lancaster and
District* by Ken Harrison (Lancaster & District
Birdwatching Society, 1995).

 *Birds of Lancashire and North
Merseyside* by White, McCarthy
and Jones (Hobby Publications
2008).

*Breeding Birds of Lancashire and North
Merseyside* (2001), sponsored by North West
Water. Contact: Bob Pyefinch, 12 Bannistre Court,
Tarleton, Preston PR4 6HA.

Bird Recorder
(See also Manchester).
Inc North Merseyside. Steve White, 102 Minster
Court, Crown Street, Liverpool L7 3QD. 0151 707
2744; e-mail: stevewhite102@btinternet.com

Bird Reports
BIRDS OF LANCASTER & DISTRICT (1959-2012),
(£8.00) from Peter Cook (Secretary, LDBWS), 21
Threshfield Avenue, Heysham, Lancashire LA3
2DU; 01524 851 454;
e-mail: peter.cook33@btinternet.com
www.lancasterbirdwatching.org.uk

*EAST LANCASHIRE ORNITHOLOGISTS' CLUB BIRD
REPORT (1982-),* Members £2.50, Non-members
£5.50, from Tony Cooper, 28 Peel Park Ave,
Clitheroe BB7 1ET.
www.eastlancashireornithologists.org.uk

*CHORLEY AND DISTRICT NATURAL HISTORY
SOCIETY ANNUAL REPORT (1979 -),* published on
website; www.chorleynats.org.uk

*BLACKBURN & DISTRICT BIRD CLUB ANNUAL
REPORT (1992-),* from Doreen Bonner, 6 Winston
Road, Blackburn, BB1 8BJ. 01254 261 480;
e-mail: webmaster@blackburnbirdclub.co.uk
www.blackburnbirdclub.co.uk

FYLDE BIRD REPORT (1983-), from Paul Ellis, 18
Staining Rise, Blackpool, FY3 0BU. 01253 891281;
e-mail: paul.ellis24@btopenworld.com or
news@fyldebirdclub.org www.fyldebirdclub.org

LANCASHIRE BIRD REPORT (1914-), from Dave
Bickerton, 64 Petre Crescent, Rishton, Blackburn,
Lancs BB1 4RB. 01254 886 257;
e-mail: bickertond@aol.com

*ROSSENDALE ORNITHOLOGISTS' CLUB BIRD
REPORT (1977-).*from Ian Brady. 01706 222 120;
http://roc.wikispaces.com

BTO Regional Representatives
EAST. Tony Cooper, 28 Peel Park Avenue,
Clitheroe, Lancs BB7 1ET. 01200 424 577;
e-mail: anthony.cooper34@btinternet.com

NORTH & WEST. Jean Roberts. 01524 770 295;
e-mail: JeanRbrts6@aol.com

SOUTH. Stuart Piner, 25 Salford Road, Galgate,
Lancaster, Lancs LA2 0LW. 07976 201 755;
e-mail: stuartpiner@hotmail.com

Clubs
BLACKBURN & DISTRICT BIRD CLUB. (1991; 100).
Jim Bonner, 6 Winston Road, Blackburn, BB1 8BJ.
01254 261 480;
e-mail: webmaster@blackburnbirdclub.co.uk
www.blackburnbirdclub.co.uk

ENGLAND

Meetings: Normally 7.30pm, 1st Monday of the month, (Sept-Apr), St Silas's Church Hall, Preston New Road. Check website for all indoor and outdoor meetings.

CHORLEY & DISTRICT NATURAL HISTORY SOCIETY. (1979; 170). Phil Kirk, Millend, Dawbers Lane, Euxton, Chorley, Lancs PR7 6EB. 01257 266 783; e-mail: secretary@chorleynats.org.uk
www.chorleynats.org.uk
Meetings: 7.30pm, 3rd Thursday of the month (Sept-Apr), St Mary's Parish Centre, Chorley

EAST LANCASHIRE ORNITHOLOGISTS' CLUB. Year formed and number of members: (1955; 43). David Chew. 01282 695 649; e-mail: via the website.
www.eastlancsornithologists.org.uk
Meetings: 7.30pm, Tuesdays (Sep-Jun), St Anne's Church Hall, Wheatley Lane Rd, Fence BB12 9ED, see website for details.

FYLDE BIRD CLUB. (1982; 150). Paul Ellis, 18 Staining Rise, Blackpool, FY3 0BU. 01253 891 281; www.fyldebirdclub.org
e-mail: paul.ellis24@btopenworld.com
Meetings: 7.45pm, 4th Tuesday of the month, River Wyre Hotel, Breck Road, Poulton le Fylde.

FYLDE NATURALISTS' SOCIETY. (1946; 140). Julie Clarke, 7 Cedar Avenue, Poulton-le-Fylde, Blackpool FY6 8DQ. 01253 883 785; e-mail: secretary@fyldenaturalists.co.uk
www.fyldenaturalists.co.uk
Meetings: 7.30pm, fortnightly (Sep-Mar), Fylde Coast Alive, Church Hall, Raikes Parade, Blackpool unless otherwise stated in the Programme.

LANCASHIRE & CHESHIRE FAUNA SOCIETY. (1914; 150). Dave Bickerton, 64 Petre Crescent, Rishton, Lancs BB1 4RB. 01254 886 257; e-mail: bickertond@aol.com
www.lacfs.org.uk

LANCASTER & DISTRICT BIRD WATCHING SOCIETY. (1959; 200). Peter Cook (Secretary), 21 Threshfield Avenue, Heysham, Morecambe, Lancs LA3 2DU. 01524 851 454 / (M) 07880 541 798; e-mail: peter.cook33@btinternet.com
www.lancasterbirdwatching.org.uk
Meetings: 7.30pm, last Monday of the month (Sep-Nov, Jan-Mar) For details and venues see website.

PRESTON BIRD WATCHING & NATURAL HISTORY SOCIETY. (1876 as the Preston Scientific Society; 140). Peter Lewenz, Secretary. 01772 611 509; e-mail: prestonwildlife@gmail.com
www.prestonsociety.co.uk

Meetings: Check website for details.

ROSSENDALE ORNITHOLOGISTS' CLUB. (1976; 35). Ian Brady. 01706 222 120; http://roc.wikispaces.com
Meetings: 7.30pm, 3rd Monday of the month, Weavers Cottage, Bacup Road, Rawtenstall.

Ringing Groups
FYLDE RG. G Barnes, 17 Lomond Avenue, Marton, Blackpool FY3 9QL.

NORTH LANCS RG. John Wilson BEM, 40 Church Hill Avenue, Warton, Carnforth, Lancs LA5 9NU. E-mail: johnwilson711@btinternet.com

SOUTH WEST LANCASHIRE RG. I H Wolfenden, 35 Hartdale Road, Thornton, Liverpool, Merseyside L23 1TA. 01519 311 232.

RSPB Local Group
LANCASTER. (1972; 176). Michael Gardner. 01524 65 211; e-mail: RSPBlancaster@gmail.com
www.rspb.org.uk/localgroups/lancaster
Meetings: See website.

Wetland Bird Survey Organisers
MORECAMBE BAY NORTH. Mr C Hartley, Undercragg, Charney Well Lane, Grange-over-Sands, Cumbria LA11 6DB. 01539 536 824; e-mail: clive.hartley304@btinternet.com

MORECAMBE BAY SOUTH. Mrs J Roberts, 3 Claughton Terrace, Claughton, Lancaster LA2 9JZ. 01524 770 295; 07815 979 856; e-mail: Jeanrbrts6@aol.com

NORTH LANCASHIRE (Inland). Mr P J Marsh, Leck View Cottage, Ashleys Farm, High Tatham, Lancaster LA2 8PH. 07989 866 487; e-mail: pmrsh123@aol.com

RIBBLE ESTUARY. Mr K Abram, 25 Schwarzman Drive, Banks, Southport Merseyside PR9 8BG; e-mail: k.abram@btinternet.com

RIVER LUNE. Mrs J Roberts, 3 Claughton Terrace, Claughton, Lancaster LA2 9JZ. 01524 770 295; 07815 979 856; e-mail: Jeanrbrts6@aol.com

WEST LANCASHIRE (INLAND)Mr T Clare, c/o WeBS Office, BTO, The Nunnery, Thetford, Norfolk IP24 2PU; e-mail: Tom.Clare@www.org.uk

Wildlife Trust
THE WILDLIFE TRUST FOR LANCASHIRE, MANCHESTER AND NORTH MERSEYSIDE. (1962; 18,000). Communications Officer, The Barn, Berkeley Drive, Bamber Bridge, Preston PR5 6BY. 01772 324 129; e-mail: info@lancswt.org.uk
www.lancswt.org.uk

ENGLAND

LEICESTERSHIRE & RUTLAND

The Birds of Leicestershire and Rutland by Rob Fray et al. (2009, Helm County Avifauna).

Bird Recorder
Steve Lister, 6 Albert Promenade, Loughborough,, Leicestershire LE11 1RE. 01509 829 495; e-mail: stevelister@surfbirder.com

Bird Reports
LEICESTERSHIRE & RUTLAND BIRD REPORT (1941-), from Mrs S Graham, 5 Lychgate Close, Cropston, Leicestershire LE7 7HU. 0116 236 6474; e-mail: JSGraham83@aol.com
www.lros.org.uk

RUTLAND NAT HIST SOC ANNUAL REPORT (1965-), from the Secretary. 01572 747 302.

BTO Regional Representative
LEICESTER & RUTLAND. David Wright, 01530 231 102; e-mail: davewrightbto@gmail.com

Clubs
BIRSTALL BIRDWATCHING CLUB. (1976; 50). Mr KJ Goodrich, 6 Riversdale Close, Birstall, Leicester LE4 4EH. 0116 267 4813; e-mail: kjgood1532@aol.com
www.leicestershirevillages.com/rothley/birdwatchingclub.html
Meetings: 7.30pm, 2nd Tuesday of the month (Oct-Apr), The Rothley Centre, Mountsorrel Lane, Rothley, Leics LE7 7PR.

LEICESTERSHIRE & RUTLAND ORNITHOLOGICAL SOCIETY. (1941; 580). Jennifer Thompson, 36 Burnside Road, Leicester, LE12 6QD. 0116 233 0320; www.lros.org.uk
e-mail: jennythompson1301@gmail.com
Meetings: 7.30pm, 1st Friday of the month (Oct-May), Oadby Methodist Church, off Central Car Park, alternating with The Rothley Centre, Mountsorrel Lane, Rothley. Additional meeting at Rutland Water Birdwatching Cntr.

SOUTH LEICESTER BIRDWATCHERS. (2006; 60). Marion Turner. 01455 282 854; (M)07852 782 002; e-mail: graham.turner@btinternet.com
Meetings: 7.15 pm, 2nd Wednesday of the month (Sep-Jun), All Saints Parish Centre, Wigston Road, Blaby, Leicester, LE8 4FA. New members welcome.

RUTLAND NATURAL HISTORY SOCIETY. (1964; 256). Mrs L Worrall, 6 Redland Close, Barrowden, Oakham, Rutland LE15 8ES. 01572 747 302;

e-mail: rnhscontact@btinternet.com
www.rnhs.org.uk
Meetings: 7.30pm, 1st Tuesday of the month (Oct-Apr), Voluntary Action Rutland, Lands End Way, Oakham LE15 6RB.

Ringing Groups
RUTLAND WATER RG. Tim Appleton, Reserve Manager, Egleton, Oakham, Rutland LE15 8BT; e-mail: awbc@rutland water.org.uk

STANFORD RG. John Cranfield, 41 Main Street, Fleckney, Leicester LE8 8AP. 0116 240 4385; e-mail: JacanaJohn@talktalk.net
www.stanfordrg.org.uk

RSPB Local Groups
LEICESTER. (1969; 1600 in catchment area). Graham Heninghem, 01455 616 098; e-mail: graham.heninghem@hotmail.co.uk
www.rspb.org.uk/groups/leicester
Meetings: 7.30pm, 3rd Friday of the month (Sep-May), Trinity Methodist Hall, Harborough Road, Oadby, Leicester, LE2 4LA

LOUGHBOROUGH. (1970; 300). Peter Farnworth. 01295 253 330; e-mail: Lboro.RSPB@virgin.net
www.rspb.org.uk/groups/loughborough
Meetings: Monthly Friday nights, Loughborough University.

Wetland Bird Survey Organisers
LEICESTERSHIRE & RUTLAND (excl Rutland Water). Mr B Moore,13 Swinford Avenue, Glon Parva, Leics LE2 9RW;
e-mail: b_moore@ntlworld.com

RUTLAND WATER. Reserve Manager, Rutland Water Nature Reserve, Egleton, Oakham, Rutland LE15 8BT. 01572 770 651;
e-mail: tim@rutlandwater.org.uk

Wildlife Trust
LEICESTERSHIRE & RUTLAND WILDLIFE TRUST. (1956; 14,000). Brocks Hill Environment Centre, Washbrook Lane, Oadby, Leicestershire LE2 5JJ. 0116 272 0444 (fax) 0116 272 0404;
e-mail: info@lrwt.org.uk
www.lrwt.org.uk

LINCOLNSHIRE

Bird Recorders
John Clarkson.
E-mail: recorder_north@lincsbirdclub.co.uk

John Badley.
E-mail: recorder_south@lincsbirdclub.co.uk

Bird Reports
LINCOLNSHIRE BIRD REPORT (1979-), 2011 report,

£15 + £2 p&p, from Bill Sterling, Newlyn, 5 Carlton Avenue, Healing, NE Lincs DN41 7PW. E-mail: wbsterling@hotmail.com

SCUNTHORPE & NORTH WEST LINCOLNSHIRE BIRD REPORT (1973-), from Secretary, Scunthorpe Museum Society, Ornithological Section, (Day)01724 402 871 (Eve)01724 734 261.

BTO Regional Representatives
EAST. Philip Espin. 01507 605 448; e-mail: pmjespin@gmail.com

NORTH. Chris Gunn. 01777 707 888; e-mail: donandchris@hotmail.co.uk

SOUTH. Hugh Dorrington. 01778 440 716; e-mail: hdorrington@btconnect.com

WEST. Peter Overton, 01400 273 323; e-mail: bto@hilltopfarmholidays.co.uk

Club
LINCOLNSHIRE BIRD CLUB. (1979; 304). Robert Carr, 35 St Leonard's Close, Woodhall Spa, Lincs LN10 6SX. E-mail: secretary@lincsbirdclub.co.uk www.lincsbirdclub.co.uk
Meetings: Local groups hold winter evening meetings (contact Secretary for details). AGM in March with a guest speaker.

LINCOLNSHIRE NATURALISTS' UNION. Lincolnshire Naturalists' Union, c/o Lincolnshire Wildlife Trust, Banovallum House, Manor House Street, Horncastle, Lincs LN9 5HF.
Website: http://lnu.org/
Meetings: Saturdays at the Whisby Education Centre, Whisby Nature Park, Moor Lane, Thorpe on the Hill, Lincoln and start at 2pm.

Ringing Groups
GIBRALTAR POINT BIRD OBSERVATORY. Mr M.R. Briggs; e-mail: mbriggs@gibobs.fsworld.co.uk

MID LINCOLNSHIRE RG. J Mawer, 2 The Chestnuts, Owmby Road, Searby, Lincolnshire DN38 6EH. 01652 628 583.

WASH WADER RG. P L Ireland, 27 Hainfield Drive, Solihull, W Midlands B91 2PL. 0121 704 1168; e-mail: enquiries@wwrg.org.uk

RSPB Local Groups
GRIMSBY AND CLEETHORPES. (1986; 2200 in catchment area). Terry Whalin. 01472 211 115; e-mail: terence@terencewhalin.wanadoo.co.uk www.rspb.org.uk/groups/grimsby
Meetings: 7.30pm, 1st Monday of the month (Sept-May), Corpus Christi Church Hall, Grimsby Road, Cleethorpes, DN35 7LJ.

LINCOLN. (1974; 250). Peter Skelson, 26 Parksgate Avenue, Lincoln, LN6 7HP. 01522 695747; e-mail: peter.skelson@lincolnrspb.org.uk www.lincolnrspb.org.uk
Meetings: 7.30pm, 2nd Thursday of the month (not Jun-Aug), The Robert Hardy Centre, Bishop Grosseteste University, Longdales Road, Lincoln.

SOUTH LINCOLNSHIRE. (1987; 350). Adrian Slater. 01205 360 858; www.southlincsrspb.org.uk e-mail: SouthlincsRSPB@btinternet.com
Meetings: Contact group.

Wetland Bird Survey Organisers
HUMBER ESTUARY - Inner South. Mr K Parker, 22 Hayton Close, Winterton, Scunthorpe, Lincolnshire DN15 9QR; e-mail: keith.parker@tatasteel.com

HUMBER ESTUARY -Mid South. Mr R Barnard, RSPB Northern England, Westleigh Mews, Wakefield Road, Denby Dale, Huddersfield HD8 8QD. 01484 868 425; e-mail: richard.barnard@rspb.org.uk

HUMBER ESTUARY -North. Mr N Cutts, c/o WeBS Office, BTO, The Nunnery, Thetford, Norfolk IP24 2PU. 01842 750 050; e-mail: webs@bto.org.uk

HUMBER ESTUARY - Outer South. Mr J R Walker MBE, 3 Coastguard Cottage, Churchill Lane, Theddlethorpe, Mablethorpe, Lincs LN12 1PQ. 01507 338 038; e-mail: webs@bto.org

NORTH LINCOLNSHIREMs C Gunn, c/o WeBS Office, BTO, The Nunnery, Thetford, Norfolk IP24 2PU. 01777 707 888; e-mail: donandchris@hotmail.co.uk

SOUTH LINCOLNSHIRE/PETERBOROUGH (inland). Mr R Titman, 28 Eastgate, Deeping St James, Peterborough PE6 8HJ. 01733 583 254; 01778 380 695; e-mail: bob.titman@gmail.com

Wildlife Trust
LINCOLNSHIRE WILDLIFE TRUST. (1948; 26,000). Banovallum House, Manor House Street, Horncastle, Lincs, LN9 5HF. 01507 526 667 (fax) 01507 525 732; e-mail: info@lincstrust.co.uk www.lincstrust.org.uk

LONDON, GREATER

Bird Atlas/Avifauna
The Breeding Birds Illustrated magazine of the London Area, 2002. ISBN 0901009 121 ed Jan Hewlett(London Natural History Society).

Two Centuries of Croydon's Birds by John Birkett (RSPB Croydon Local Group 2007). £10 plus p&p.

Bird Recorder see also Surrey
Andrew Self, 16 Harp Island Close, Neasden,

London NW10 0DF. 07443 221 382;
e-mail: a-self@sky.com
http://londonbirders.wikia.com

Bird Report
CROYDON BIRD SURVEY (1995), from Secretary,
Croydon RSPB Group, 020 8640 4578;
e-mail: johndavis.wine@care4free.net
www.croydon-rspb.org.uk

LONDON BIRD REPORT (20-mile radius of St
Paul's Cath) (1936-), from Catherine Schmitt,
Publications Sales, London Natural History
Society, 4 Falkland Avenue, London N3 1QR. 020
8346 4359.

BTO Regional Representatives
LONDON, NORTH. Ian Woodward, 245 Larkshall
Road, Chingford, London E4 9HY. 07947 321 889;
e-mail: ianw_bto_nlon@hotmail.co.uk

LONDON, SOUTH. Richard Arnold. 0208 224 1135;
e-mail: bto@thomsonecology.com

Clubs
THE LONDON BIRD CLUB (formerly the
Ornithological Section of the London Natural
History Society). (1858; 1000). Mrs Angela Linnell,
20 Eleven Acre Rise, Loughton, Essex IG10 1AN.
020 8508 2932; www.lnhs.org.uk
e-mail: angela.linnell@phonecoop.coop
Meetings: See website.

MARYLEBONE BIRDWATCHING SOCIETY. (1981;
114). Marion Hill, 20 Howitt Close, Howitt Road,
London NW3 4LX. E-mail:
birdsmbs@yahoo.com
www.birdsmbs.org.uk;
www.facebook.com/
birdsmbs; www.flickr.com/
photos/mbsbirds
Meeting: 3rd Friday of month
(Sept-May), 7.15pm Gospel
Oak Methodist Church,
Lisburne Road, London NW3
2NT. Weekly Tuesday walks
on Hampstead Heath. Programme of Local and
Coach Outings to reserves in and around London
and the South East.

Ringing Groups
LONDON GULL STUDY GROUP - (SE including
Hampshire, Surrey, Sussex, Berkshire and
Oxfordshire). This group is no longer active
but still receiving sightings/recoveries of
ringed birds. (Also includes Hampshire, Surrey,
Sussex, Berkshire and Oxfordshire). No longer in
operation but able to give information on gulls.
Mark Fletcher, 24 The Gowans, Sutton-on-the-
Forest, York YO61 1DJ.
E-mail: m.fletcher48@btinternet.com

RUNNYMEDE RG. D G Harris, 22 Blossom Waye,
Hounslow, TW5 9HD.
E-mail: daveharris@tinyonline.co.uk
http://rmxrg.org.uk

RSPB Local Groups
BEXLEY. Stuart Banks, 157 Garland Road,
Plumstead, London SE18 2PP. 0208 854 7251;
e-mail: stuartbans@hotmail.co.uk
www.rspb.org.uk/groups/bexley/
Meetings: 7.30pm, 2nd Friday of the month,
Hurstmere School Hall, Hurst Road, Sidcup.

BROMLEY. (1972; 285). Des Garrahan, 0207 808
1240; e-mail: Cnrobinson@btinternet.com
www.rspb.org.uk/groups/bromley
Meetings: 2nd Wednesday of the month (Sep-
Jun), 4th floor, Central Library Building, Bromley
High Street.

CENTRAL LONDON. (1974; 250). Graeme
Hutchinson. 020 7738 7232;
e-mail: Graemehutchinson@hotmail.com
www.rspb.org.uk/groups/centrallondon
Meetings: (Indoor) 2nd Thursday of the month
(Sep-May), St Columba's Church Hall, Pont St,
London SW1. See website for details of field
meetings.

CROYDON. (1973; 4000 in catchment area). John
Davis, 9 Cricket Green, Mitcham, CR4 4LB. 020
8640 4578; e-mail: johndavis.wine@care4free.net
www.croydon-rspb.org.uk
Meetings: 2nd Monday of each month at 2pm-
4pm and again at 8pm-10pm at Whitgift Sports
Club, The Clubhouse, Croham Manor Road, South
Croydon, Surrey, CR2 7BG.

ENFIELD. (1971; 2700). Norman G Hudson, 125
Morley Hill, Enfield, Middx EN2 0BQ. 020 8363
1431 (daytime); e-mail: dorandnor@tiscali.co.uk
www.rspb.org.uk/groups/enfield
Meetings: 8pm, 1st Thursday of the month, St
Andrews Hall, Enfield Town.

HAVERING. (1972; 270). Martin Runchman. 01767
690 093; e-mail: RSPB.havering@gmail.com
www.rspb.org.uk/groups/havering/
Meetings: 8pm, 2nd Friday of the month,
Hornchurch Library, North Street, Hornchurch.

NORTH EAST LONDON. David Littlejohns. 0208 989
4746; e-mail: NelondonRSPB@yahoo.co.uk
www.rspb.org.uk/groups/northeastlondon
Meetings: 7.30pm, 2nd Tuesday of every month,
St Mary's Church - Gwinnell Room, 207 High Road,
South Woodford, LONDON, E18 2PA.

NW LONDON RSPB GROUP. (1983; 2000 in
catchment area). Bob Husband, The Firs, 49
Carson Road, Cockfosters, Barnet, Herts EN4 9EN.
020 8441 8742;

e-mail: bobhusband@hotmail.co.uk
www.rspb.org.uk/groups/nwlondon. A full
programme of events can be downloaded from
the site.
Meetings: 8pm, Usually last Tuesday of the
month, (Sep-Mar), Wilberforce Centre, St Paul's
Church, The Ridgeway, Mill Hill, London, NW7
1QU.

PINNER & DISTRICT. (1972; 300). Ian Jackson, 5
Oakfield Avenue, Kenton, Harrow, Middx HA3 8TH.
020 8907 3513; e-mail: imnme@btinternet.com
www.rspb.org.uk/groups/pinner/
Meetings: 8pm, 2nd Thursday of the month (Sept-
May), Church Hall, St John The Baptist Parish
Church, Pinner HA5 3AS.

RICHMOND & TWICKENHAM. (1979; 215). Roger
Theobald. 0208 977 6343;
e-mail: RichmondRSPB@yahoo.co.uk
www.rspb.org.uk/groups/richmond
Meetings: 8.00pm, 1st Wednesday of the month
and 2pm 2nd Tuesday of the month, both
meetings held York House, Twickenham.

Wetland Bird Survey Organisers
GREATER LONDON (excl. Thames Estuary), Miss H
Baker, 60 Townfield, Rickmansworth, HertsWD3
7DD. 01923 772 441.
E-mail: helen.baker60@tiscali.co.uk

LEE VALLEY. Ms D Richardson, c/o LVRPA,
Myddelton House, Bulls Cross, Enfield, Middlesex
EN2 9HG;
e-mail: drichardson@leevalleypark.org.uk

Wildlife Trust
LONDON WILDLIFE TRUST. (1981; 7500). Skyline
House, 200 Union Street, London, SE1 0LX. 0207
261 0447 (fax) 0207 633 0811;
e-mail: enquiries@wildlondon.org.uk
www.wildlondon.org.uk

MANCHESTER, GREATER

Bird Atlas/Avifauna
Breeding Birds in Greater Manchester by Philip
Holland et al (1984).

Bird Recorder
RECORDER. Ian McKerchar, 42 Green Ave, Astley,
Manchester M29 7EH. 01942 701 758;
e-mail: ianmckerchar1@gmail.com
www.manchesterbirding.com

Bird Reports
BIRDS IN GREATER MANCHESTER
£7 (+ £1.50 P&P) from the Recorder (see above).

*LEIGH ORNITHOLOGICAL SOCIETY BIRD REPORT
(1971-)*, from Mr D Shallcross, 28 Surrey Avenue,
Leigh, Lancs WN7 2NN. www.leighos.org.uk

E-mail: leighos.chairman@gmail.com
L.O.S. Young Birders: www.losybc.blogspot.co.uk/

BTO Regional Representative
MANCHESTER. Position vacant.

Clubs
ALTRINGHAM AND DISTRICT NATURAL HISTORY
SOCIETY. Claire Joures (Secretary). 0161 928
4513.
Meetings: 7:30pm, Tuesdays, Hale Methodist
Church Hall, Oak Road, off Hale Road, Hale. 50p
charge includes refreshments.

GREATER MANCHESTER BIRD RECORDING GROUP.
(2002; 61). Ian McKerchar.
E-mail: ianmckerchar1@gmail.com

LEIGH ORNITHOLOGICAL SOCIETY. (1971; 98). Mr
D Shallcross, 28 Surrey Avenue, Leigh, Lancs WN7
2NN. E-mail: leighos.chairman@gmail.com
www.leighos.org.uk
L.O.S. Young Birders: www.
losybc.blogspot.co.uk/
Meetings: 7.15pm, Fridays,
Leigh Library (check website
for details).

ROCHDALE FIELD NATURALISTS' SOCIETY. (1970;
90). Mrs D Francis, 20 Hillside Avenue, Shaw,
Oldham OL2 8HR. 01706 843 685; e-mail:
secretary@rochdalefieldnaturalistssociety.co.uk
www.rochdalefieldnaturalistssociety.co.uk
Meetings: 7.30pm (Sept-Apr) at Cutgate Baptist
Church, Edenfield Rd, Rochdale. Yearly syllabus
(out after AGM in Sept) states dates of lectures
and outings.

STOCKPORT BIRDWATCHING SOCIETY. (1972; 80).
Dave Evans, 36 Tatton Road South, Stockport,
Cheshire SK4 4LU. 0161 432 9513; (M)07790 377
396; e-mail: windhover1972@yahoo.co.uk
Meetings: 7.30pm, last Wednesday of the month
(Sep-Apr), The Heatons Sports Club, Heaton Moor
Stockport.

Ringing Groups
LEIGH RG. A J Gramauskas, 21 Elliot Avenue,
Golborne, Warrington WA3 3DU. 0151 929 215.

SOUTH MANCHESTER RG. Mr N.B. Powell.
E-mail: neville.powell@tiscali.co.uk

RSPB Local Groups
BOLTON. (1978; 320). Holly Page. 07508 730 823;
e-mail: holly.page26@gmail.com
www.rspb.org.uk/groups/bolton/
Meetings: 7.30pm, Thursdays (dates vary),Canon
Slade School, Bradshaw Brow, BOLTON, BL2 3BP.

STOCKPORT LOCAL GROUP. (1979; 120). Jane
Skelhorn, 23 Bodmin Road, Sale Cheshire M33
5JH. 0161 282 8758;

COUNTY DIRECTORY

e-mail: StockportRSPB@googlemail.com
www.rspb.org.uk/groups/stockport
Meetings: 7.30pm, 2nd Monday of the month
(Sep-Apr), Stockport College of Technology, Peter
Barkworth Theatre, (Dec lecture in Theatre B).

WIGAN. (1973; 80). Neil Martin. 01695 624 860;
e-mail: neimaz07@yahoo.co.uk
www.rspb.org.uk/groups/wigan
Meetings: 7.45pm. St Anne's Parish Hall, Church
Lane, Shevington, Wigan, Lancashire, WN6 8BD.

Wetland Bird Survey Organiser
GREATER MANCHESTER. Mr J Dunning, c/o WeBS
Office, BTO, The Nunnery, Thetford, Norfolk IP24
2PU. 07984 237 822;
e-mail: jamiedunning8@googlemail.com

Wildlife Trust
Communications Officer, See Lancashire,

MERSEYSIDE & WIRRAL

Bird Atlas see Cheshire

Bird Recorders see Cheshire; Lancashire

Bird Reports see also Cheshire
HILBRE BIRD OBSERVATORY REPORT, from Warden,
see Reserves,

BTO Regional Representatives
MERSEYSIDE RR and RDO. Bob Harris, 3 Mossleigh,
Whixalll, Whitchurch, Shropshire SY13 2SA. 01948
880 112; e-mail: harris@liv.ac.uk

WIRRAL. Paul Miller. 01928 787 535;
e-mail: paulandhilarymiller@o2.co.uk

Clubs
MERSEYSIDE NATURALISTS'
ASSOCIATION. (1938; 150). David
Bryant, Chairman, 13, Strafford
Drive, Bootle, Merseyside L20 9JN.
0151 523 5240;
e-mail: chairman@mnapage.info
www.mnapage.info
Meetings: 2-4pm, Saturday
afternoons (Feb, Oct and Nov),
Bootle Cricket Club, check website
for details. 7-8 coach outings per year.

WIRRAL BIRD CLUB. (1977; 150). The Secretary.
E-mail: wirralbirdclub@gmail.com
www.wirralbirdclub.com
Meetings: 8pm, 4th Thursday of the month,
(Sept-Nov and Jan-Jul), Kingsmead School Hall,
Bertram Drive, Hoylake.

Ringing Groups
MERSEYSIDE RG. Bob Harris, 3 Mossleigh, Whixalll,
Whitchurch, Shropshire SY13 2SA. 0151 706 4397;
e-mail: harris@liv.ac.uk

SOUTH WEST LANCASHIRE RG. I H Wolfenden, 35
Hartdale Road, Thornton, Liverpool, Merseyside
L23 1TA. 01519 311 232.

RSPB Local Groups
LIVERPOOL. (1972; 180). Chris Tynan, 10 Barker
Close, Huyton, Liverpool L36 0XU. 0151 480 7938
(M)07831 352 870; e-mail: christtynan@aol.com
www.rspb.org.uk/groups/Liverpool/; twitter@
RSPBLiverpool
Meetings: Indoor meetings, 7 for 7.30pm, 3rd
Monday of the month (Sep-Apr), Mossley Hill
Parish Church, Junc. Rose Lane and Elmswood Rd.
Outdoor meetings visiting sites acress the north
west.

SOUTHPORT. (1974; 240). Kathryn Hall. 07802 426
376; e-mail: southportRSPB@btinternet.com
www.rspb.org.uk/groups/southport
Meetings: 7.45pm, 3rd Friday of the month, Lord
Street West Church Hall, Duke Street, Southport.

WIRRAL. (1982; 120). Jeremy Bradshaw. 0151 632
2364; e-mail: Info@wirralRSPB.org.uk
www.rspb.org.uk/groups/wirral
Meetings: 7.30pm, 1st Thursday of the month,
Bromborough Civic Centre, 2 Bromborough Village
Road, Wirral.

Wetland Bird Survey Organiser
ALT ESTUARY. Steve White, c/o WeBS Office,
Thetford, Norfolk IP24 2PU;
e-mail: stevewhite102@btinterncom

DEE ESTUARY. Mr C E Wells, The Cottage, 1 Well
Lane, Ness, Neston, Wirral, Cheshire CH64 4AW;
e-mail: colin.wells@rspb.org.uk

MERSEY ESTUARY. Mr D J Smith, 71 Richmond
Avenue, Grappenhall, Warrington, Cheshire WA4
2NX. 01925 542 745; 01925 602 397;
e-mail: dermot.smith71@googlemail.com

Wildlife Trust
See Lancashire.

NORFOLK

Bird Atlas/Avifauna
The Birds of Norfolk by Moss Taylor, Michael
Seago, Peter Allard & Don Dorling (Pica Press,
1999).

Bird Recorder
JOINT COUNTY RECORDERS. Dave and Jacquie
Bridges, 27 Swann Close, Hempstead Road, Holt,
Norfolk NR25 6DP. 01263 713 249;
e-mail: dnjnorfolkrec@btinternet.com

Bird Reports
CLEY BIRD CLUB 10-KM SQUARE BIRD REPORT
(1987-), from Peter Gooden, 45 Charles Road,

Holt, Norfolk NR25 6DA. 01263 712368.

NAR VALLEY ORNITHOLOGICAL SOCIETY ANNUAL REPORT (1976-), from The Chairman, Ian Black. www.narvos.org.uk

NORFOLK BIRD & MAMMAL REPORT (1953-), from DL Paull, 8 Lindford Drive, Eaton, Norwich NR4 6LT. E-mail: info@nnns.org.uk www.NNNS.org.uk

NORFOLK ORNITHOLOGISTS' ASSOCN ANNUAL REPORT (1961-), from Holme Bird Observatory, 01485 525 406, or NOA, Broadwater Road, Holme Next the Sea, Hunstanton, Norfolk, PE36 6LQ. E-mail: info@noa.org.uk

WENSUM VALLEY BIRDWATCHING SOCIETY (2003-), from E-mail: admin@wvbs.co.uk www.wvbs.co.uk

BTO Regional Representatives
NORTH-EAST. Chris Hudson, Cornerstones, 5 Ringland Road, Taverham, Norwich NR8 6TG. 01603 868 805 (M)07771 635 844; e-mail: Chris697@btinternet.com

NORTH-WEST. Bob Osborne. 01553 670 430; e-mail: rtoclass40@yahoo.co.uk

SOUTH-EAST. Rachel Warren. 01603 593 912; e-mail: campephilus@btinternet.com

SOUTH-WEST. Vince Matthews, Rose's Cottage, The Green, Merton, Thetford, Norfolk IP25 6QU. 01953 884 125; e-mail: norfolksouthwest@tiscali.co.uk

Clubs
CLEY BIRD CLUB. (1986; 500). John Dicks, Chairman, Cherry Tree House, Cherry Tree Road, Plumstead, Norfolk NR11 7LQ. 01263 577 354; e-mail: cleybcnewsletter@gmail.com www.cleybirdclub.org.uk/
Meetings: 8.00pm, Wednesdays, monthly (Dec-Feb), White Horse Hotel, Blakeney.

GREAT YARMOUTH BIRD CLUB. (1989; 30). Andrew Grieve (Webmaster); e-mail: ag1947@hotmail.co.uk www.gybc.org.uk
Meetings: 7.30pm, 4th Monday of the month, Rumbold Arms, Southtown Road.

NAR VALLEY ORNITHOLOGICAL SOCIETY. (1976; 125). Ian Black, Three Chimneys, Tumbler Hill, Swaffham, Norfolk PE37 7JG. 01760 724 092; e-mail: ian_a_black@hotmail.com www.narvos.org.uk e-group: narvalleyornithologicalsociety@

yahoogroups.com; subscribe at: narvalleyornithologicalsociety-subscribe@ yahoogroups.com
Meetings: 7.30pm, last Tuesday of the month (Jul-Nov and Jan-May), Barn Theatre, Convent of The Sacred Heart, Mangate Street, Swaffham, PE37 7QW.

NORFOLK & NORWICH NATURALISTS' SOCIETY. (1869; 630). The Secretary, 22 Springfield Close, Weybourne, Holt, NR25 7IB. www.NNNS.org.uk
Meetings: 7.30pm, 3rd Tuesday of the month (Oct-Mar), St Andrew's Church Hall, Church Lane, Norwich

NORFOLK ORNITHOLOGISTS' ASSOCIATION. (1962; 1500). Sophie Barker, Broadwater Road, Holme-next-Sea, Hunstanton, Norfolk PE36 6LQ. 01485 525 406; e-mail: info@noa.org.uk www.noa.org.uk

WENSUM VALLEY BIRDWATCHING SOCIETY. (2003; 125). Lin Pateman (Secretary); e-mail: wvbs.secretary@gmail.com www.wvbs.co.uk
Meetings: 7.30pm, 3rd Thursday of the month, Weston Longville village hall.

Ringing Groups
BTO NUNNERY RG. Kate Risely, c/o BTO, The Nunnery, Thetford, Norfolk IP24 2PU. E-mail: kate.risely@bto.org

HOLME BIRD OBSERVATORY. Miss SA Barker. E-mail: info@noa.org.uk

NORTH NORFOLK FARMLAND STUDY & RINGING GROUP. Keith Herber, Laleham, 60 Dale End, Brancaster Staithe, Kings Lynn PE31 8DA. 07785 920 044; e-mail: keith.herber@btinternet.com

NORTH WEST NORFOLK RG. Mr J L Middleton, 8 Back Lane, Burnham Market, Norfolk PE31 8EY. E-mail: johnmiddleton@bmarket.freeserve.co.uk

SHERINGHAM RG. D Sadler, 26 Abbey Road, Sheringham, Norfolk NR26 8NN. 01263 821 904.

WASH WADER RG. P L Ireland, 27 Hainfield Drive, Solihull, W Midlands B91 2PL. 0121 704 1168; e-mail: pli@blueyonder.co.uk

RSPB Local Groups
NORWICH. (1971; 230). David Porter. 01603 745 310; e-mail: RSPBnorwichgroup@virginmedia.com www.rspb.org.uk/groups/norwich
Meetings: 7.30pm, 2nd Monday of the month (except Jul & Aug), Hellesdon Community Centre, Middletons Lane, Hellesdon, Norwich (entrance of Woodview Road).

ENGLAND

Wetland Bird Survey Organisers
BREYDON WATER. Jim Rowe, c/o WeBS Office
BTO, The Nunnery, Thetford, Norfolk IP24 2PU.
01842 750050; e-mail: webs@bto.org

NORTH NORFOLK COAST. Mr M Rooney, The Old
Bakery, High Street, Docking, Norfolk PE31 8NH.
E-mail: michael.rooney@naturalengland.org.uk

NORFOLK (excl. estuaries). Tim Strudwick, RSPB
Strumpshaw Fen, Staithe Cottage, Low Road,
Strumpshaw, Norfolk NR13 4HS;
e-mail: tim.strudwick@rspb.org.uk

THE WASH. Mr J Scott, RSPB Snettisham Site
Manager, Barn A, Home Farm Barns, Snettisham,
Kings Lynn PE31 7PD. 01485 545 261;
e-mail: jim.scott@rspb.org.uk

Wildlife Trust
NORFOLK WILDLIFE TRUST. (1926; 35,000). Bewick
House, 22 Thorpe Road, Norwich, Norfolk NR1
1RY. 01603 625 540 (fax) 01603 598 300;
e-mail: info@norfolkwildlifetrust.org.uk
www.norfolkwildlifetrust.org.uk

NORTHAMPTONSHIRE

Bird Recorder
Mike Alibone, 25 Harrier Park, East Hunsbury,
Northampton, Northants NN4 0QG.
E-mail: northantsbirds@ntlworld.com

Bird Report
Northamptonshire Bird Report 2012.
£7.00 + £1.20 p&p. Cheques payable to
'Northamptonshire Bird Report', from R W
Bullock, 81 Cavendish Drive, Northampton NN3
3HL. http://northamptonshirebirdclub.ning.com

BTO Regional Representative
Barrie Galpin. 01780 444 351;
e-mail: barrie.galpin@zen.co.uk

Club
NORTHAMPTONSHIRE BIRD CLUB. (1973; 100).
01604 880 009; https://sites.google.com/site/
northantsbirdclub/home
Meetings: 7.30pm, 1st Wednesday of the month.
Anglian Water's Holcot Fishing Lodge (on the edge
of Holcot village on the Brixworth road), Pitsford
Reservoir, Northants.

Ringing Groups
NORTHANTS RG. D M Francis, 2 Brittons Drive,
Billing Lane, Northampton NN3 5DP.

STANFORD RG. John Cranfield, 41 Main Street,
Fleckney, Leicester LE8 8AP. 0116 240 4385;
e-mail: JacanaJohn@talktalk.net

RSPB Local Groups
MID NENE. (1975; 280). Ian Wrisdale.
www.rspb.org.uk/groups/midnene
Meetings: 7.30pm, 2nd or 3rd Thursday of the
month (Sep-Apr), The Saxon Hall, Thorpe Street/
Brook Street, Raunds.

Wildlife Trust
Director, See Cambridgeshire,

NORTHUMBERLAND

Bird Atlas/Avifauna
The Atlas of Breeding Birds in Northumbria
edited by J C Day et al (Northumberland and
Tyneside Bird Club, 1995).

Bird Recorder
Tim Dean, 2 Knocklaw Park, Rothbury,
Northumberland NE65 7PW. 01669 621 460
(M)07766 263 167;
e-mail: t.r.dean@btinternet.com

Bird Reports
BIRDS IN NORTHUMBRIA (1970-), from Trevor
Blake, 6 Glenside, Ellington, Morpeth,
Northumberland NE61 5LS. 01670 862 635;
e-mail: trevor.1958@live.co.uk

BIRDS ON THE FARNE ISLANDS (1971-), from
Secretary, Natural History Society of Northumbria,
Great North Museum, Hancock, Barras Bridge,
Newcastle upon Tyne NE2 4PT. 0191 208 2790;
e-mail: nhsn@ncl.ac.uk
www.nhsn.ncl.ac.uk

**BTO Regional Representative & Regional
Development Officer**
RR. Tom Cadwallender, 22 South View, Lesbury,
Alnwick, Northumberland NE66 3PZ. 01665 830
884; e-mail:
tomandmurielcadwallender@hotmail.com

RDO. Muriel Cadwallender, 22 South
View, Lesbury, Alnwick, Northumberland
NE66 3PZ. 01665 830 884; e-mail:
tomandmurielcadwallender@hotmail.com

Clubs
NORTH NORTHUMBERLAND BIRD CLUB. (1984;
210). Richard Narraway. 01668 214 759; e-mail:
ringouzel@northnorthumberlandbirdclub.co.uk
www.northnorthumberlandbirdclub.co.uk
Meetings: 7.30pm, 3rd Friday of the month(Sept),
2nd Friday (Oct-Jun), Bamburgh Pavilion (below
castle).

NORTHUMBERLAND &
TYNESIDE BIRD CLUB.
(1958; 270). Andrew Brunt
(Secretary). 01670 788 352;

ENGLAND

e-mail: ntbcorg@gmail.com
www.ntbc.org.uk
Meetings: 7.00pm, 2nd Thursday of the month (Sep-Apr), Newcastle Falcons Rugby Club, Brunton Road, Kenton Bank Foot, Newcastle upon Tyne NE13 8AF.

NATURAL HISTORY SOCIETY OF NORTHUMBRIA. (1829; about 1200). James Littlewood, Natural History Society of Northumbria, Great North Museum: Hancock, Barras Bridge, Newcastle upon Tyne NE2 4PT. 0191 208 2790;
e-mail: nhsn@ncl.ac.uk www.nhsn.ncl.ac.uk
Meetings: Weekly indoor and outdoor meetings throughout the year, details can be found at www.nhsn.ncl.ac.uk

Ringing Groups
NORTHUMBRIA RG. Secretary. B Galloway, 34 West Meadows, Stamfordham Road, Westerhope, Newcastle upon Tyne NE5 1LS. 0191 286 4850.

Wetland Bird Survey Organisers
LINDISFARNE. Mr A Craggs, Natural England, Lindisfarne National Nature Reserve, Beal StationBeal, Berwick Upon Tweed TD15 2SP. 01289 381 470;
e-mail: andrew.craggs@naturalengland.org.uk

NORTHUMBERLAND COAST. Mr D M Turner, 9 Haswell Gardens, North Shields, Tyne & Wear NE3 2DY. 01912 576 680;
e-mail: Dan.M.Turner@btopenworld.com

NORTHUMBERLAND (Inland). Steve Holliday, 2 Larriston Place, Cramlington, Northumberland NE23 8ER; e-mail: steveholliday@hotmail.co.uk

Wildlife Hospital
BERWICK SWAN & WILDLIFE TRUST. The Honorary Secretary, Windmill Way East, Ramparts Business Park, Berwick-upon-Tweed TD15 1TU. 01289 302 882; e-mail: swan-trust@hotmail.co.uk www.swan-trust.org Registered charity. All categories of wildlife. Pools for swans and other waterfowl. Veterinary support.

Wildlife Trust
NORTHUMBERLAND WILDLIFE TRUST. (1962; 13,000). The Garden House, St Nicholas Park, Jubilee Road, Gosforth, Newcastle upon Tyne, NE3 3XT. 0191 284 6884; e-mail: mail@northwt.org.uk www.nwt.org.uk

NOTTINGHAMSHIRE

Bird Recorder
Andy Hall. E-mail: andy.h11@ntlworld.com

Bird Reports
LOUND BIRD REPORT (1990-) latest 2007 report £4, from Gary Hobson, 18 Barnes Avenue,

Wrenthorpe, Wakefield WF1 2BH. 01924 384 419; e-mail: gary.lbc1@tiscali.co.uk

BIRDS OF NOTTINGHAMSHIRE (1943-) - £9 for 2012, £3 for previous issues, depending on scarcity. Plus p&p, from Ms Jenny Swindells, 21 Chaworth Road, West Bridgford, Nottingham NG2 7AE. 0115 9812 432;
e-mail: j.swindells@btinternet.com
www.nottsbirders.net; Twitter: @NottsBirders

NETHERFIELD WILDLIFE GROUP ANNUAL REPORT (1990-). £5 inc postage, from Mr N Matthews, 4 Shelburne Close, Heronridge, Nottingham NG5 9LL. www.netherfieldwildlife.org.uk

BTO Regional Representative
Mrs Lynda Milner, 6 Kirton Park, Kirton, Newark, Notts NG22 9LR. 01623 862 025;
e-mail: milner.lynda@googlemail.com

Clubs
LOUND BIRD CLUB. (1991; 90). Mike B. Vickers (New Member Contact), 01777 818 291;
e-mail: avesinsight@yahoo.co.uk
www.loundbirdclub.com
Meetings: Various walks and talks throughout the year, see website for details.

NETHERFIELD WILDLIFE GROUP. (1999; 130). Philip Burnham, 57 Tilford Road, Newstead Village, Nottingham NG15 0BU. 01623 401 980 (M)07964 037 657; e-mail: philb50@fastmail.fm
www.netherfieldwildlife.org.uk

NOTTINGHAMSHIRE BIRDWATCHERS. (1935; 320). Ms Jenny Swindells, 21 Chaworth Road, West Bridgford, Nottingham NG2 7AE. 0115 9812 432; e-mail: j.swindells@btinternet.com
www.nottsbirders.net;
Twitter: @NottsBirders
Meetings and events: Please see website for details.

WOLLATON NATURAL HISTORY SOCIETY. (1976; 86). Graham Birkett, 07528 753 470;
e-mail: graham.birkett@ntlworld.com
www.spanglefish.com/wollatonnaturalhistory/
Meetings: 7.30pm, 3rd Wednesday of the month, St Leonards Community Centre, Wollaton Village, HG8 2ND.

Ringing Groups
BIRKLANDS RG. A Ashley, 39 Winkburn Road, Mansfield, Notts NG19 6SJ. 07794 179 494;
e-mail: alowe@nottswt.co.uk

NORTH NOTTS RG. Adrian Blackburn, Willows End, 27 Palmer Road, Retford, Notts DN22 6SS. 01777

COUNTY DIRECTORY

255

706 516 (M)07718 766 873;
e-mail: adrian.blackburn@sky.com

SOUTH NOTTINGHAMSHIRE RG. K J Hemsley, 8
Grange Farm Close, Toton, Beeston, Notts NG9
6EB; e-mail: k.hemsley@ntlworld.com

Integrated Population Monitoring Group
TRESWELL WOOD INTEGRATED POPULATION
MONITORING GROUP. Chris du Feu, 66 High Street,
Beckingham, Notts DN10 4PF.
E-mail: chris@chrisdufeu.force9.co.uk

RSPB Local Groups
MANSFIELD LOCAL GROUP. (1986; 200). John
Barlow, 240 Southwell Road West, Mansfield,
Notts NG18 4LB. 01623 626 647;
e-mail: Terri-Cumberland@supanet.com
www.rspb.org.uk/groups/mansfield
Meetings: 7pm, 1st Wednesday of the month
(Sep-Jun), Bridge St Methodist Church, Rock
Valley, Mansfield.

NOTTINGHAM. (1974; 300). Doreen Markam, 3
Mirberry Mews, Sherwin Road, Nottingham, NG7
2FR. 0115 978 2741;
e-mail: dmarkam@mindspring.com
www.notts-rspb.org.uk
Meetings: 7.30pm, 1st Wed of month (Sept -
May). Nottingham Mechanics, North Sherwood St.
Nottingham, NG1 4EZ.

Wetland Bird Survey Organiser
Professor D Parkin, 151 Nottingham Road, Trowell,
Nottingham NG9 3PN. 0115 932 0090 (evenings
are prefered for telephone contact);
e-mail: bluethroat@btinternet.com

Wildlife Trust
NOTTINGHAMSHIRE WILDLIFE TRUST. (1963;
4,300). The Old Ragged School, Brook Street,
Nottingham, NG1 1EA. 0115 958 8242 (fax) 0115
924 3175; e-mail: info@nottswt.co.uk
www.nottinghamshirewildlife.org.uk

OXFORDSHIRE

Bird Atlas/Avifauna
Birds of Oxfordshire by J W Brucker et al (Oxford,
Pisces, 1992).

The New Birds of the Banbury Area by T G
Easterbrook (Banbury Ornithological Society,
1995).

Bird Recorder
Ian Lewington, 119 Brasenose Road, Didcot, Oxon
OX11 7BP. 01235 819 792;
e-mail: lewbirder@btinternet.com

Bird Reports
BIRDS OF OXFORDSHIRE (1921-), £7.50, from Roy

Overall, 30 Hunsdon Road, Iffley Oxford OX4 4JE.
www.ooos.org.uk

*BANBURY ORNITHOLOGICAL SOCIETY ANNUAL
REPORT (1952-)*. £5 each including postage,
from MJ Lewis, Old Mill Cottage, Avon Dassett,
Southam, Warwickshire CV47 2AE. 01295 690 643;
e-mail: mikelewisad@hotmail.com

BTO Regional Representatives
NORTH. Frances Buckel, Witts End, Radbones Hill,
Over Norton, Chipping Norton, Oxon OX7 5RA.
01608 644 425;
e-mail: fran.buckel@btinternet.com

SOUTH. Mr John Melling, 17 Lime Grove,
Southmoor, Nr Abingdon, Oxon OX13 5DN. 01865
820 867; e-mail: bto-rep@oos.org.uk

Clubs
BANBURY ORNITHOLOGICAL SOCIETY (includes
parts of Northamptonshire, Oxfordshire and
Warwickshire). (1952; 100). Frances Buckel,
Witts End, Radbones Hill, Over Norton, Chipping
Norton, Oxon OX7 5RA. 01608 644 425;
e-mail: fran.buckel@btinternet.com
www.banburyornithologicalsociety.org.uk
Meetings: 7.30pm, 2nd Monday of the month,The
Banbury Cricket Club, White Post Road, Bodicote
OX15 4BN.

OXFORD ORNITHOLOGICAL SOCIETY. (1921; 330).
Barry Hudson, 07833 350 288;
e-mail: secretary@oos.org.uk
www.oos.org.uk
Meetings: 7.45pm, various
dates, Stratfield Brake,
Kidlington.

Ringing Group
EDWARD GREY INSTITUTE. Dr
A G Gosler, c/o Edward Grey
Institute, Department of Zoology, South Parks
Road, Oxford OX1 3PS. 01865 271 158;
e-mail: andrew.gosler@zoo.ox.ac.uk

RSPB Local Groups
OXFORD. (1977; 100). Roy Grant, 23 St
Christopher's Place, Cowley, Oxford OX4 2HS.
01865 774 659; e-mail: roy.otters@hotmail.co.uk
www.rspb-oxford.org.uk
Meetings: 7.45pm, normally 1st Thursday of the
month (Sept-May), Sandhills Primary School,
Terret Avenue, Headington, Oxford (opposite
Thornhill park and ride).

VALE OF WHITE HORSE. (1977; 330). Steve Bastow.
07900 213 698; www.rspb-vwh.org.uk
e-mail: stevebastow@btinternet.com
Meetings: 7.45pm, 3rd Monday of the month
(Sep-May). Civic Hall, Britwell Road, DIDCOT,
Oxfordshire, OX11 7HN.

ENGLAND

Wetland Bird Survey Organiser
OXFORDSHIRE (North). Mrs S Bletchly, 11 Orchard Grove, Bloxham, Banbury, Oxfordshire OX15 4NZ. 01295 721 048;
e-mail: sandra.banornsoc@btinternet.com

OXFORDSHIRE (South). c/o WeBS Office BTO, The Nunnery, Thetford, Norfolk IP24 2PU;
e-mail: webs@bto.org

Wildlife Trust
BBOWT. (1959; 24,000). The Lodge, 1 Armstrong Road, Littlemore, Oxford, OX4 4XT. 01865 775 476 (fax) 01865 711 301; e-mail: info@bbowt.org.uk
www.bbowt.org.uk

SHROPSHIRE

Bird Atlas/Avifauna
Atlas of the Breeding Birds of Shropshire (Shropshire Ornithological Society, 1995).

Bird Recorder
Geoff Holmes, 22 Tenbury Drive, Telford Estate, Shrewsbury SY2 5YF. 01743 364 621;
e-mail: geoff.holmes.4@btinternet.com

Bird Report
SHROPSHIRE BIRD REPORT (1956-) Annual, from Helen Griffiths (Hon Secretary), 104 Noel Hill Road, Cross Houses, Shrewsbury SY5 6LD. 01743 761 507;
e-mail: helen.griffiths@naturalengland.org.uk
www.shropshirebirds.com

BTO Regional Representative
Allan Dawes. 01691 654 245;
e-mail: allandawes@btinternet.com

Club
SHROPSHIRE ORNITHOLOGICAL SOCIETY. (1955; 800). Helen Griffiths, 104 Noel Hill Road, Cross Houses, Shrewsbury SY5 6LD. 01743 761 507; e-mail:
hjgriffiths104@btinternet.com
www.shropshirebirds.com
Meetings: 7.15pm, 1st Thursday of month (Oct-Apr), Shirehall, Shrewsbury.

Ringing Group
SHROPSHIRE RG. Bob Harris, 3 Mossleigh, Whixalll, Whitchurch, Shropshire SY13 2SA. 0151 706 4397; e-mail: harris@liv.ac.uk

RSPB Local Group
SHROPSHIRE. (1991; 108). Anne Trigg. 01295 253 330 (RSPB Midlands Regional Office);
e-mail: RSPBshrewsbury@yahoo.co.uk
www.rspb.org.uk/groups/shropshire
Meetings: 7.15 pm, usually third Tuesday of the month (Sept – April), but see website for dates. Bayston Hill Memorial Hall, Lyth Hill Road, Shrewsbury, SY3 0DR. Also field trips year round. See website for details of activities.

SOUTH SHROPSHIRE Sub Group - CRAVEN ARMS. (2004; c100). Alvin Botting. 01547 540 176;
e-mail: Christinelbateman@yahoo.com
www.rspbsouthshropshire.co.uk
Meetings: 7.30pm, 2nd Tuesday of the month (Sep-Apr), Culmington Village Hall, Culmington, Ludlow SY8 2DA.

Wetland Bird Survey Organiser
SHROPSHIRE. Mr M F Wallace, 75 Larkhill Road, Copthorne, Shrewsbury, Shropshire SY3 8XJ. 01743 369 035; e-mail: michaelwallace47@gmail.com

Wildlife Trust
SHROPSHIRE WILDLIFE TRUST. (1962; 10,000). 193 Abbey Foregate, Shrewsbury, Shropshire SY2 6AH. 01743 284 280 (fax) 01743 284281;
e-mail: enquiries@shropshirewildlifetrust.org.uk
www.shropshirewildlifetrust.org.uk

SOMERSET & BRISTOL

Bird Atlas/Avifauna
Somerset Atlas of Breeding and Wintering Birds 2007-2012 by David Ballance, Rob Grimmond, Stephen Moss, Julian Thomas & Eve Tigwell from Somerset Ornithological Society, c/o Motcombe House, Combe Wood Lane, Combe St. Nicholas, Chard, Somerset TA20 3NH, 01460 261 234,
e-mail: rob.grimmond@somersetbirds.net

The Birds of Exmoor and the Quantocks by DK Ballance and BD Gibbs.

History of the Birds of Somerset by D.K. Ballance. Both titles from Isabelline Books (Michael Whetman), 6 Bellevue, Enys, Penryn, Cornwall TR10 9LB; 01326 373 602, email mikann@ beakbook.demon.co.uk. Contact for prices.

Avon Atlas 2007-11, by R.L. Bland & M. Dadds. From first author at 18a Knoll Hill, Bristol BS9 1RA, 0117 968 1061.

Bird Recorders
Brian D Gibbs, 23 Lyngford Road, Taunton, Somerset TA2 7EE. 01823 274 887;
e-mail: brian.gibbs@virgin.net
www.somersetbirds.net

BRISTOL, S GLOUCESTERSHIRE, BATH AND NE SOMERSET, NORTH SOMERSET. John Martin, 34 Cranmoor Green, Pilning, Bristol BS35 4QF. 01454 633 040; (M)07767 867 341;
e-mail: avonbirdrecorder@googlemail.com
www.boc-bristol.org.uk

ENGLAND

Bird Reports
AVON BIRD REPORT (1977-), £9 plus postage, from Harvey Rose; e-mail: h.e.rose@bris.ac.uk

EXMOOR NATURALIST (1974-), from Secretary, Exmoor Natural History Society.E-mail: carol. enhs@virgin.net

SOMERSET BIRDS (1912-) £7.50 inc p&p, from Somerset Ornithological Society, c/o Flat 2, Dunboyne, Bratton Lane, Minehead, Somerset TA24 8SQ. 01643 706 820.

BTO Regional Representatives
AVON. Gordon Youdale, 36 Quedgeley, Yate, Bristol PS37 4JJ. 01454 881 690; e-mail: gordon.youdale@blueyonder.co.uk

SOMERSET. Eve Tigwell, Hawthorne Cottage, 3 Friggle Street, Frome, Somerset BA11 5LP. 01373 451 630; e-mail: eve.tigwell@zen.co.uk

Clubs
BRISTOL NATURALISTS' SOCIETY (Ornithological Section). (1862; 550). Hon. Secretary, Mike Johnson (President Ornithology Section), 0117 953 2545. See website for email contact.
http://bns.myspecies.info/
Meetings: 7.30pm, 2nd Wednesday in the month (check for dates, Oct-Mar), Westmorland Hall, Westmorland Road, Bristol

BRISTOL ORNITHOLOGICAL CLUB. (1966; 660). Mrs Judy Copeland, 19 St George's Hill, Easton-in-Gordano, North Somerset BS20 0PS. 01275 373 554; e-mail: judy.copeland@tiscali.co.uk
www.bristolornithologicalclub.co.uk
Meetings: 7.30pm, 3rd Thursday of the month, Newman Hall, Grange Court Road, Westbury-on-Trym.

CAM VALLEY WILDLIFE GROUP. (1994: 356). The Secretary; e-mail: enquiries@cvwg.org.uk
www.somersetmade.co.uk/cvwg/

EXMOOR NATURAL HISTORY SOCIETY. (1974; 480). The Secretary, 01643 707 624; e-mail: carol.enhs@talktalk.net
www.enhs.org.uk
Meetings: 7.30pm, 1st Wednesday of the month (Oct-Mar), Methodist Church Hall, The Avenue, Minehead.

SOMERSET ORNITHOLOGICAL SOCIETY. (1974; 475). Mr JA Hazell, Membership Secretary, 9 Hooper Road, Street, Somerset BA16 0NP. 01458 443 780; e-mail: jeff.hazell@somersetbirds.net
www.somersetbirds.net
Meetings: Indoor meetings, with guest speaker, various Thursdays Oct to Apr; and Field meetings,

with leader, on 10 to 12 dates throughout the year.

Ringing Groups
GORDANO VALLEY RG. Lyndon Roberts, 20 Glebe Road, Long Ashton, Bristol BS41 9LH. 01275 392722; e-mail: mail@lyndonroberts.com

RSPCA. Mr K Leighton.
E-mail: kev.leighton@O2.co.uk

STEEP HOLM RS. A J Parsons, Barnfield, Tower Hill Road, Crewkerne, Somerset TA18 8BJ. 01460 73640.

RSPB Local Groups
BATH AND DISTRICT. (1969; 260). Jean Melksham. 01225 404 985;
e-mail: jeanmelksham@blueyonder.co.uk
www.rspb.org.uk/groups/bath
Meetings: 7.30pm, 3rd Wednesday of the month (Sep-Apr), Bath Society Meeting Room, Green Park Road, BATH BA1 2DR.

SOUTH SOMERSET. (1979; 300). Denise Chamings, Daniels Farm, Lower Stratton, South Petherton, Somerset TA13 5LP. 01460 240 740;
e-mail: denise.chamings@talktalk.net
www.rspb.org.uk/groups/southsomerset
Meetings: 7.30pm, 3rd Thursday of the month (Sep-May), The Millennium Hall, Seavington St. Mary, Ilminster, TA19 0QH.

TAUNTON. (1975; 148). Eric Luxton. 01823 283 033; e-mail: eric.luxton@btinternet.com
www.rspb.org.uk/groups/taunton
Meetings: 7.30pm, last Friday of the month, Trull Memorial Hall, Church Road, Trull, TAUNTON TA3 7JZ.

WESTON-SUPER-MARE (N SOMERSET). (1976; 215). Tony West. 01934 622 793;
e-mail: tony.west34@yahoo.com
www.rspb.org.uk/groups/westonsupermare
Meetings: 7.45pm, 1st Thursday of the month (Sep-Apr), St Pauls Church Hall, Walliscote Road, Weston-Super-Mare.

Wetland Bird Survey Organisers
AVON (other sites). Mr R Higgins, 28 Egerton Road, Bishopston, Bristol BS7 8HL. 0117 944 1034; e-mail: rupert@wessexeco.fsnet.co.uk

SEVERN ESTUARY - SOUTHERN COAST. Dr H E Rose, Arncliffe, Walton Bay, Clevedon. 0127 587 3407; e-mail: H.E.Rose@bristol.ac.uk

SOMERSET (other sites). Ms E M Tigwell, c/o WeBS Office, BTO, The Nunnery, Thetford, Norfolk IP27 0AB. 01373 451 630;
e-mail: eve.tigwell@zen.co.uk

ENGLAND

SOMERSET LEVELS. Steve Meen, RSPB West Sedgemoor, Dewlands Farm, Redhill, Curry Rivel, Langport Somerset TA10 0PH. 01458 252 805; 01458 252 820; e-mail: steve.meen@rspb.org.uk

Wildlife Trusts
AVON WILDLIFE TRUST. (1980; 17,000). 32 Jacobs Wells Road, Bristol, BS8 1DR. 0117 917 7270 (fax) 0117 929 7273; e-mail: mail@avonwildlifetrust.org.uk www.avonwildlifetrust.org.uk

SOMERSET WILDLIFE TRUST. (1964; 21,000). 34 Wellington Road, Taunton, Somerset TA1 5AW, 01823 652 400, fax 01823 652 411; e-mail: enquiries@somersetwildlife.org www.somersetwildlife.org

STAFFORDSHIRE

Bird Recorder
Nick Pomiankowski, 22 The Villas, West End, Stoke ST4 5AQ. 01782 849 682; e-mail: staffs-recorder@westmidlandbirdclub.com

Bird Report See West Midlands

BTO Regional Representative
NORTH EAST, SOUTH & CENTRAL & WEST. Scott Petrek; e-mail: scott.petrek@gmail.com

Clubs
WEST MIDLAND BIRD CLUB (STAFFORD BRANCH). David Dooc (Branch Chairman). E-mail: staff.chair@outlook.com www.westmidlandbirdclub.com/ stafford
Meetings: 7.30pm, 2nd Friday of the month (Oct-Mar), at Perkins Engines Sports & Social Club, Tix Road, Stafford.

WEST MIDLAND BIRD CLUB (TAMWORTH BRANCH). (1992). Tamworth Branch contact, 0182 754 557 or 0182 789 5718; e-mail: tamworth@ westmidlandbirdclub.org.uk http://westmidlandbirdclub.org.uk/www02/ tamworth-branch.html
Meetings: 7.30pm, 3rd Friday of the month (Sep-Apr),The Carnegie Centre, Corporation Street, Tamworth B79 7DN.

RSPB Local Groups
BURTON-ON-TRENT AND SOUTH DERBYSHIRE. (1973; 50). Dave Lummis, 121 Wilmot Road, Swadlincote, Derbys DE11 9BN. 01283 219 902; e-mail: david.lummis@btinternet.com www.basd-rspb.co.uk
Meetings: 7.30pm 1st Wednesday of the month, All Saint's Church, Branston Road, Burton.

LICHFIELD & DISTRICT. (1977; 1150). Bob Russon, 108 Walsall Road, Lichfield, Staffs WS13 8AF. 01543 252 547; e-mail: LichfieldRSPB@hotmail.co.uk www.rspb.org.uk/groups/lichfield
Meetings: 7.30pm, 2nd Tuesday of the month (Jan-May, Sept-Dec), St Mary's Centre, Lichfield. NORTH STAFFS. (1982; 208). John Booth. 01782 262 082; e-mail: j.booth6@aol.co.uk www.rspb.org.uk/groups/northstaffordshire
Meetings: 7.30pm, normally 3rd Wednesday of the month, North Staffs Conference Centre (Medical Institute).

SOUTH WEST STAFFORDSHIRE. (1972; 165). Mrs Theresa Dorrance, 39 Wilkes Road, Codsall, Wolverhampton WV8 1RZ. 01902 847 041; e-mail: stevedorrance@googlemail.com ww.rspb.org.uk/groups/southweststaffs
Meetings: 8.00pm, 2nd Tuesday of the month (Sep-May), Codsall Village Hall.

Wetland Bird Survey Organisers
STAFFORDSHIRE. Mr S Turner, c/o WeBS Office, BTO, The Nunnery, Thetford, Norfolk IP24 2PU; e-mail: sjturner76@btinternet.com

Wildlife Hospitals
BRITISH WILDLIFE RESCUE CENTRE. Dawn Blacker, Amerton Working Farm, Stowe-by-Chartley, Stafford ST18 0LA. 01889 271 308; e-mail: admin@thebwrc.com www.britishwildliferescue.co.uk On A518 Stafford/Uttoxeter road. All species, including imprints and permanently injured. Hospital, large aviaries and caging. Open to the public every day. Veterinary support.

GENTLESHAW BIRD OF PREY AND WILDLIFE CENTRE. Jenny Smith, Gentleshaw Wildlife Centre, Fletcher's Country Garden Centre, Stone Road, Eccleshall, Staffs ST21 6JY. 01785 850 379; e-mail: info@gentleshawwildlife.co.uk www.gentleshawwildlife.co.uk Registered charity. All birds of prey (inc. owls). Hospital cages and aviaries; release sites. Veterinary support. Also

Wildlife Trust
STAFFORDSHIRE WILDLIFE TRUST. (1969; 14,000). The Wolseley Centre, Wolseley Bridge, Stafford, ST17 0WT. 01889 880 100 (fax) 01889 880 101; e-mail: info@staffs-wildlife.org.uk www.staffs-wildlife.org.uk

SUFFOLK

Bird Atlas/Avifauna
Birds of Suffolk by S H Piotrowski (February 2003) Quatermelon.

ENGLAND

Bird Recorders

NORTH EAST. Andrew Green,
E-mail: andrew@waveney1.fsnet.co.uk

SOUTH EAST (inc. coastal region from Slaughden Quay southwards). Scott Mayson.
E-mail: smsuffolkbirder@gmail.com

WEST (whole of Suffolk W of Stowmarket, inc. Breckland). Colin Jakes, 7 Maltward Avenue, Bury St Edmunds, Suffolk IP33 3XN. 01284 702 215; e-mail: colin@jakes.myzen.co.uk

Bird Report

SUFFOLK BIRDS (inc Landguard Bird Observatory Report) (1950-), from Ipswich Museum, High Street, Ipswich, Suffolk

BTO Regional Representative

Mick T Wright, 15 Avondale Road, Ipswich, IP3 9JT. 01473 721 486; e-mail: kupe1515@sky.com

Clubs

SUFFOLK ORNITHOLOGISTS' GROUP. (1973; 650). Phil Whittaker, Oak Barn, Pipps Ford, Needham Market, Ipswich, Suffolk IP6 8LJ. 01449 76 0353; e-mail: oakbarn@hotmail.com www.sogonline.org.uk
Meetings: Last Thursday of the month (Jan-Apr, Sep-Nov), London Road Holiday Inn (IP2 0UA) on the SW side of Ipswich near the A14/A12 Copdock roundabout.

Ringing Groups

DINGLE BIRD CLUB. Dr D Pearson, 4 Lupin Close, Reydon, Southwold, Suffolk IP18 6NW. 01502 722348.

LACKFORD RG. Dr Peter Lack, 11 Holden Road, Lackford, Bury St Edmunds, Suffolk IP28 6HZ. E-mail: bee.eaters@btinternet.com

LANDGUARD RG. Landguard Ringing Group, Landguard Bird Observatory, View Point Road, Felixstowe, Suffolk, IP11 3TW. 01394 673782; e-mail: landguardbo@yahoo.co.uk www.lbo.co.uk

LITTLE OUSE RG (formerly MARKET WESTON RG). Dr R H W Langston, Walnut Tree Farm, Thorpe Street, Hinderclay, Diss, Norfolk IP22 1HT. E-mail: rlangston@wntfarm.demon.co.uk

RSPB Local Groups

IPSWICH. (1975; 230). Mr Chris Courtney. 01473 423 213; e-mail: chrisc.courtney@yahoo.co.uk www.rspb.org.uk/groups/ipswich
Meetings: 7.30pm, 2nd Thursday of the month (Sep-Apr), Sidegate Lane Primary School, Sidegate Lane, Ipswich.

LOWESTOFT & DISTRICT. (1976; 88). Julie Martin, 19 The Boundaries, Geldeston Road, Gillingham, Beccles, Suffolk NR34 0HT. 01502 715 940; e-mail: swottouk@yahoo.co.uk www.rspb.org.uk/groups/lowestoft
Meetings: 7.15pm 1st Friday in the month, St Marks Church Centre, Oulton Broad.

WOODBRIDGE. (1987; 322). Malcolm Key, Riverside, Parham, Suffolk IP13 9LZ. 01728 723 155; e-mail: malcolm.key@btopenworld.com
Meetings: 7.30pm, 1st Thursday of the month (Oct-May), Woodbridge Community Hall.

Wetland Bird Survey Organisers

ALDE COMPLEX. Mr I Castle, 5 Chapelfield, Orford, Woodbridge, Suffolk IP12 2HW. 01394 450 188; e-mail: ian@castle-hamlett.co.uk

ALTON WATER. Mr J A Glazebrook, c/o WeBS Office; e-mail: johnglazebrook@btopenworld.com

BLYTH ESTUARY (Suffolk). Mr A Burrows, c/o WeBS Office, BTO, The Nunnery, Thetford, Norfolk IP24 2PU. 01842 750 050; e-mail: webs@bto.org

ORWELL ESTUARY. Mick T Wright, 15 Avondale Road, Ipswich, Suffolk IP3 9JT. 01473 721 486; 07540 880 095; e-mail: kupe1515@sky.com

DEBEN ESTUARY. Mr NJ Mason, The Decoy, 8 Mallard Way, Hollesley, Nr Woodbridge, Ipswich IP12 3QU. 07876 086 039; 01394 411 150; e-mail: nick.mason4@btinternet.com

STOUR ESTUARY. Mr R Vonk, RSPB, Unit 1 Brantham Mill, Bergholt Road, Brantham, Manningtree, Essex CO11 1QT. 01206 391 153; 07711 129 149; e-mail: rick.vonk@rspb.org.uk

SUFFOLK (other sites). Alan Miller, Suffolk Wildlife Trust, Moonrakers, Back Lane, Wenhaston, Halesworth, Suffolk, IP19 9DY. 01502 478 788; 00776 741 1778; e-mail: alan.miller@suffolkwildlifetrust.org

Wildlife Trust

SUFFOLK WILDLIFE TRUST. (1961; 25,000). Brooke House, The Green, Ashbocking, Ipswich, IP6 9JY. 01473 890 089 (fax) 01473 890 165; e-mail: info@suffolkwildlifetrust.org www.suffolkwildlifetrust.org

SURREY

Bird Atlas/Avifauna

Birds of Surrey by Jeffery Wheatley (Surrey Bird Club 2007).

Bird Recorder (inc London S of Thames & E to Surrey Docks)

SURREY (includes Greater London south of the Thames and east to the Surrey Docks, excludes

ENGLAND

Spellthorne). Eric Soden, Ceres, Moushill Lane, Milford, Surrey GU8 5BQ. 01483 429 799; e-mail: eric.soden@talktalk.net

Bird Report
SURBITON AND DISTRICT BIRD WATCHING SOCIETY (1972-), 2012 edition £5 including postage, From Thelma Caine, 21 More Lane, Esher, Surrey KT10 8AJ. E-mail: sdbws@encief.co.uk www.encief.co.uk/sdbws

SURREY BIRD REPORT (1952-), from J Gates, 5 Hillside Road, Weybourne, Farnham, Surrey GU9 9DW. 01252 315 047; e-mail: jeremygates@live.com

BTO Regional Representative
Penny Williams, Bournbrook House, Sandpit Hall Lane, Chobham Surrey GU24 8HA. 01276 857 736; e-mail: bto@waxwing.plus.com

Clubs
SURBITON & DISTRICT BIRDWATCHING SOCIETY. (1954; 140). Gary Caine, Membership Secretary. 01372 468 432; e-mail: gary.caine@royalmail.co.uk www.encief.co.uk/sdbws
Meetings: 8pm, 3rd Tuesday of each month (except August), Surbiton Library Annex.

SURREY BIRD CLUB. (1957; 340). Penny Williams, Bournbrook House, Sandpit Hall Lane, Chobham Surrey GU24 8HA. 01276 857 736; e-mail: birdclub@ waxwing.plus.com www.surreybirdclub.org.uk
Meetings: See website for full details. Field meetings every month.

Ringing Groups
HERSHAM RG. A J Beasley, 29 Selbourne Avenue, New Haw, Weybridge, Surrey KT15 3RB. E-mail: abeasley00@hotmail.com

RUNNYMEDE RG. D G Harris, 22 Blossom Waye, Hounslow, TW5 9HD. E-mail: daveharris@tinyonline.co.uk http://rmxrg.org.uk

RSPB Local Groups
DORKING & DISTRICT. (1982; 230). John Burge, Broughton Norrels Drive, East Horsley, Leatherhead KT24 5DR. 01483 283 803; e-mail: burgejs@gmail.com www.rspb.org.uk/groups/dorkinganddistrict
Meetings: 8.00pm, Fridays once a month (Sep-Apr), Christian Centre, next to St Martin's Church, Dorking.

EAST SURREY. (1984; 2800 plus in catchment area). John Lawrence, 123 Chaldon Way,

Coulsdon, Surrey CR5 1DN. 01737 553 316 (evenings); e-mail: jfjlawrence@gmail.com www.eastsurreyrspb.co.uk
Meetings: 8.00pm, 2nd Wednesday of the month (except August), White Hart Barn, Godstone, RH9 8DT.

EPSOM & EWELL. (1974; 102). Timothy Tomkins, 48 Derek Avenue, West Ewell, Epsom, Surrey KT19 9HR. 020 8391 0116; e-mail: timothy.tomkins@yahoo.co.uk www.rspb.org.uk/groups/epsom
Meetings: 7.45pm, 2nd Friday of the month, All Saints Church Hall, Fulford Road, West Ewell.

GUILDFORD AND DISTRICT. (1974; 550). Michael Grimshaw. 01372 467 074; e-mail: michaelgrimshaw@btinternet.com www.rspb.org.uk/groups/guildford
Meetings: 2.15pm 2nd Thursday and 7.45pm 4th Wednesday (Oct-Apr), Onslow Village Hall, Guildford.

NORTH WEST SURREY. (1973; 150). Dave Braddock, 20 Meadway Drive, New Haw, Surrey KT15 2DT. 01932 858 692; e-mail: dave.braddock@btinternet.com www.rspb.org.uk/groups/nwsurrey
Meetings: 7.45pm, 4th Wednesday of the month (not Dec, Jul, Aug), St James Parish Church Hall, Church Street, Weybridge, Surrey KT13 8DE.

Wetland Bird Survey Organiser
SURREY (includes Greater London south of the Thames and east to the Surrey Docks, excludes Spellthorne). Mrs P Williams, Bournbrook House, Sandpit Hall Road, Chobham, Surrey GU24 8HA. E-mail: penny@waxwing.plus.com

Wildlife Hospitals
THE SWAN SANCTUARY. See National Directory.

THE WILDLIFE AID FOUNDATION. Randalls Farm House, Randalls Road, Leatherhead, Surrey, KT22 0AL. 24-hr Wildlife Help & Enquiries line: 09061 800 132 (50p/min), (fax) 01372 375 183; e-mail: lou@wildlifeaid.org.uk www.wildlifeaid.org.uk Registered charity. Wildlife hospital and rehabilitation centre helping all native British species. Special housing for birds of prey. Membership scheme and fund raising activities. Veterinary support.

Wildlife Trust
SURREY WILDLIFE TRUST. (1959; 25,700). School Lane, Pirbright, Woking, Surrey, GU24 0JN. 01483 795 440 (fax) 01483 486 505; e-mail: info@surreywt.org.uk www.surreywildlifetrust.org

ENGLAND

SUSSEX

Bird Atlas/Avifauna
The Birds of Selsey Bill and the Selsey Peninsular (a checklist to year 2000) From: Mr O Mitchell,

21 Trundle View Close, Barnham, Bognor Regis, PO22 0JZ.

Birds of Sussex ed by Paul James (Sussex Ornithological Society, 1996).

Fifty Years of Birdwatching, a celebration of the acheivements of the Shoreham District OS from 1953 onwards. £5 + P&P at current rates. Mrs Sue Miles, SDOS Hon.Secretary, 24 Chancellors Park, Hassocks, West Sussex BN6 8EZ.
e-mail: secretary@sdos.org or through website www.sdos.org

Henfield Birdwatcher Reports 2000 and 2005 ed Mike Russell et al, Henfield Birdwatch

Bird Recorder
Mr David Howey, 2 Portobello Cottages, South Coast Road, Telscombe Cliffs, East Sussex BN10 7BD. 01273 300906; e-mail: recorder@sos.org.uk www.sos.org.uk

Bird Reports
BIRDS OF RYE HARBOUR NR ANNUAL REPORT (1977- no longer printed, but available on www. WildRye.info), from Dr Barry Yates, see Clubs.

PAGHAM HARBOUR LOCAL NATURE RESERVE ANNUAL REPORT, from Warden, see Reserves,

SHOREHAM DISTRICT ORNITHOLOGICAL SOCIETY ANNUAL REPORT (1952-) - from Brian Reeve, The Old Rectory, Coombes, Lancing, West Sussex BN15 0RS; www.sdos.org

SUSSEX BIRD REPORT (1963-), from J E Trowell, Lorrimer, Main Road, Icklesham, Winchelsea, E Sussex TN36 4BS. E-mail: membership@sos.org.uk www.sos.org.uk

BTO Regional Representative
Dr Helen Crabtree. 01444 441 687; e-mail: hcrabtree@gmail.com

Clubs
FRIENDS OF RYE HARBOUR NATURE RESERVE. (1973; 1900). Friends of Rye Harbour, Lime Kiln Cottage, Rye Harbour Road, Rye, E Sussex TN31 7TU. 01797 227 784;
www.wildrye.info/reserve/friends/
Meetings: Monthly talks in winter, monthly walks all year.

HENFIELD BIRDWATCH. (1999; 135). Mike Russell. 01273 494311;

e-mail: mikerussell@sussexwt.org.uk
http://henfieldbirdwatch.co.uk/

SHOREHAM DISTRICT ORNITHOLOGICAL SOCIETY. (1953; 200). SDOS Honorary Secretary, 24 Chancellors Park, Hassocks, West Sussex, BN6 8EZ or Membership Secretary (by email).
E-mail: membership@sdos.org
www.sdos.org
Meetings: 7.30pm, 2nd Tuesday of the month (Oct-Apr), St Peter's Church Hall, Shoreham-by-Sea. (7 indoor meetings, 18+ field outings).

SUSSEX ORNITHOLOGICAL SOCIETY. (1962; 1800). Val Bentley, Lanacre, Blackgate Lane, Henfield, West Sussex BN5 9HA. 01273 494 723; e-mail: secretary@sos.org.uk www.sos.org.uk
Meetings: Annual conference in January (Haywards Heath), AGM in April, field outings throughout year.

Ringing Groups
BEACHY HEAD RS. R D M Edgar, 32 Hartfield Road, Seaford, E Sussex BN25 4PW.

CUCKMERE RG. Tim Parmenter, 18 Chapel Road, Plumpton Green, East Sussex BN7 3DD. 01273 891 881.

RYE BAY RG. P Jones, Elms Farm, Pett Lane, Icklesham, Winchelsea, E Sussex TN36 4AH. 01797 226 374;
e-mail: philjones@beamingbroadband.com

STEYNING RINGING GROUP. B R Clay, Meghana, Honeysuckle Lane, High Salvington, Worthing, West Sussex BN13 3BT.
E-mail: brian.clay@ntlworld.com

RSPB Local Groups
BRIGHTON & DISTRICT. (1974; 260). Mark Weston. 07802 293 417; e-mail: mark.weston@rspb.org.uk www.rspb.org.uk/groups/brighton
Meetings: 7.30pm, 4th Thursday of the month, Brighton and Hove Sixth Form College, BHASVIC Sports Hall Café, 205, Dyke Road, HOVE, East Sussex, BN3 6EG Anyone is welcome, non-members should phone first as dates can vary.

CHICHESTER & SW SUSSEX. (1979; 245). Kerry Jackson. 01243 265 783;
e-mail: chichesterrspb@gmail.com
www.rspb.org.uk/groups/chichester
Meetings: 7.30, 4th Thursday of month Sept to May (ex Dec), The Masonic Hall, 7 South Pallant, Chichester PO19 1SY. Three monthly walks all year.

CRAWLEY & HORSHAM. (1978; 148). Andrea Saxton, 104 Heath Way, Horsham, W Sussex RH12 5XS. 01403 242 218;
e-mail: Andrea.saxton@sky.com
www.rspb.org.uk/groups/crawley
Meetings: 8.00pm, 3rd Wednesday of the month (Sept-Apr), The Friary Hall, Crawley.

EAST GRINSTEAD. (1998; 185). Nick Walker, 14 York Avenue, East Grinstead, W Sussex RH19 4TL. 01342 315 825;
e-mail: nickwalker55@btinternet.com
www.rspb.org.uk/groups/egrinstead
Meetings: 8.00pm, last Wednesday of the month, East Court, College Lane, EAST GRINSTEAD, West Sussex, RH19 3LT

EASTBOURNE & DISTRICT. (1993; 320). David Jode. 01323 422 368 (daytime);
e-mail: david@parkmove.com
www.rspb.org.uk/groups/eastbourne
Meetings: 2.15 pm and 7.30 pm,1st Wednesday of the month (Sep-Jun), St. Wilfrid's Church Hall, Eastbourne Road, Pevensey Bay.

HASTINGS & ST LEONARDS. (1983; 65). Richard Prebble. 01424 751 790;
e-mail: Lynn.jenkins98@gmail.com
www.rspb.org.uk/groups/hastings
Meetings: 7.30pm, 3rd Friday of the month, Taplin Centre, Upper Maze Hill.

Wetland Bird Survey Organisers
CHICHESTER HARBOUR. Mr E Rowsell, Field House, Bury Gate, Bury, Pulborough, West Sussex RH20 1NN. 01798 839 230; 07843 380 202;
e-mail: edrowsell@gmail.com

OTHER SITES. Mr H R Bown, 49 Long Beach View, Sovereign Harbour North, Eastbourne, East Sussex BN23 5NB. 01323 479 569;
e-mail: hr.bown@btinternet.com

Wildlife Hospital
BRENT LODGE BIRD & WILDLIFE TRUST. Penny Cooper, Brent Lodge, Cow Lane, Sidlesham, Chichester, West Sussex PO20 7LN. 01243 641 672 (emergency number).
www.brentlodge.org All species of wild birds and small mammals. Full surgical and medical facilities (inc. X-ray) in conjunction with veterinary support. Purpose-built oiled bird washing unit. Veterinary support.

Wildlife Trust
SUSSEX WILDLIFE TRUST. (1961; 33,000). Woods Mill, Shoreham Road, Henfield, W Sussex, BN5 9SD. 01273 492 630;
e-mail: enquiries@sussexwt.org.uk
www.sussexwildlifetrust.org.uk

TYNE & WEAR

Bird Recorders/Bird Reports
See Cleveland & Co. Durham; Northumberland.

Clubs
NATURAL HISTORY SOCIETY OF NORTHUMBRIA. (1829; about 1200). James Littlewood, Natural History Society of Northumbria, Great North Museum: Hancock, Barras Bridge, Newcastle upon Tyne NE2 4PT. 0191 208 2790;
e-mail: nhsn@ncl.ac.uk
www.nhsn.ncl.ac.uk
Meetings: Weekly indoor and outdoor meetings throughout the year, details can be found at www.nhsn.ncl.ac.uk

NORTHUMBERLAND & TYNESIDE BIRD CLUB. (1958; 250). Andrew Brunt (Secretary). 01670 788 352;
e-mail: ntbcorg@gmail.com
www.ntbc.org.uk
Meetings: 7.00pm, 2nd Thursday of the month (Sep-Apr), Newcastle Falcons Rugby Club, Brunton Road, Kenton Bank Foot, Newcastle upon Tyne NE13 8AF.

RSPB Local Group
NEWCASTLE UPON TYNE. (1969; 250). Marie Ollerenshaw. 0191 2854 395; e-mail: NewcastleRSPBgroup@gmail.com
www.rspb.org.uk/groups/newcastle
Meetings: 7pm, (Mar, Jun, Sep, Nov), St James Urc, Northumberland Road, Newcastle upon Tyne, Tyne & Wear, NE1 8JF

WARWICKSHIRE

Bird Recorder
Steven Haynes; e-mail: warks-recorder@westmidlandbirdclub.com

Bird Report See West Midlands.

BTO Regional Representatives
WARWICKSHIRE. Mark Smith. 01926 735 398;
e-mail: mark.smith36@ntlworld.com
www.wildwarwickshire.co.uk (This website is an independant site from the BTO and covers wildlife inc. birds in Warwickshire).

Clubs
NUNEATON & DISTRICT BIRDWATCHERS' CLUB. (1950; 31). The Secretary, e-mail: via the website; http://ndbwc.webs.com/
Meetings: 7.30pm, 3rd Thursday of the month (Sep-Jun), Hatters Space Community Centre, Upper Abbey Street, Nuneaton.

ENGLAND

Ringing Groups
ARDEN RG. Roger J Juckes, 24 Croft Lane, Temple Grafton, Alcester, Warks B49 6PA. 01789 778 748.

BRANDON RG. David Stone, Overbury, Wolverton, Stratford-on-Avon, Warks CV37 0HG. 01789 731488.

RSPB Local Group
See West Midlands.

Wetland Bird Survey Organiser
Mr M Griffiths, 422 Tilehouse Lane, Tidbury Green, Solihull, West Midlands B90 1PX. 01564 826 685; 07837 138 815; e-mail: matt_avesmaster@hotmail.com

Wildlife Trust
WARWICKSHIRE WILDLIFE TRUST. (1970; 13,000). Brandon Marsh Nature Centre, Brandon Lane, Coventry, CV3 3GW. 024 7630 2912 (fax) 024 7663 9556; e-mail: enquiries@wkwt.org.uk www.warwickshire-wildlife-trust.org.uk

WEST MIDLANDS

Bird Atlas/Avifauna
The New Birds of the West Midlands edited by Graham and Janet Harrison (West Midland Bird Club, 2005). Available from 147 Worlds End Lane, Quinton, Birmingham B32 1JX.

Bird Recorder
Kevin Clements, 26 Hambrook Close, Dunstall Park, Wolverhampton, West Midlands WV6 0XA. 01902 568 997; e-mail: west-mids-recorder@ westmidlandbirdclub.com

Bird Reports
THE BIRDS OF SMESTOW VALLEY AND DUNSTALL PARK (1988-), from the Secretary, Smestow Valley Bird Group.

WEST MIDLAND BIRD REPORT (inc Staffs, Warks, Worcs and W Midlands) (1934-), from Barbara Oakley, 147 Worlds End, Quinton, Birmingham B32 1JX. E-mail: secretary@westmidlandbirdclub.com - www.westmidlandbirdclub.com

BTO Regional Representative
BIRMINGHAM & WEST MIDLANDS. Steve Davies. 01562 885 789; e-mail: stevedaviesbtorep@ hotmail.co.uk

Clubs
WEST MIDLAND BIRD CLUB - serving Ornithologists in Staffs, Warks, Worcs and the West Midlands County. (1929; 2000). Mark Rickus, 27 Ringmere Avenue, Castle Bromwich, Birmingham B36 9AT. 0121 749 5348; e-mail: secretary@westmidlandbirdclub.com - www. westmidlandbirdclub.com

Meetings: Check website for details of the different branches and their events.

WEST MIDLAND BIRD CLUB (BIRMINGHAM BRANCH). (1995; 800). Ray Davies. 0121 682 4375; e-mail: ray.davies@westmidlandbirdclub.com www.westmidlandbirdclub.com/birmingham

WEST MIDLAND BIRD CLUB (SOLIHULL BRANCH). (1973). Humphrey Miller, 29 Dorchester Court, Dorchester Road, Solihull B91 1LL. 0212 705 85070; e-mail: solihull@westmidlandbirdclub www.westmidlandbirdclub.com/solihull
Meetings: 7.30 pm, Fridays (usually 1st of month), Guild House, 1715 High Street, Knowle, Solihull, West Midlands B93 0LN.

Ringing Group
MERCIAN RG (Sutton Coldfield). Mr DJ Clifton, 59 Daisybank Crescent, Walsall, WS5 3BH. 01922 628 572.

RSPB Local Groups
BIRMINGHAM. (1975; 50). Sandra Bourne, 0121 382 7154 (Paul Hobbs); e-mail: BhamlocalRSPB@gmail.com www.rspb.org.uk/groups/Birmingham
Meetings: 7.30pm, 3rd Thursday of month (2nd Thursday in December), The Nautical Club, 5 Bishopsgate Street, Birmingham B15 1ET.

COVENTRY AND WARWICKSHIRE. (1969; 120). Peter Worthy. 01926 497 967; e-mail: pete@cpworthy.plus.com www.rspb.org.uk/groups/ coventryandwarwickshire
Meetings: 7:30pm, 3rd Friday of the month(Sep-April unless otherwise stated), Baginton Village Hall.

SOLIHULL. (1983; 2600). John Roberts, 115 Dovehouse Lane, Solihull, West Midlands B91 2EQ. 0121 707 3101; e-mail: johnbirder@care4free.net www.rspb.org.uk/groups/solihull
Meetings: 7.30pm, usually 2nd Tuesday of the month (Sep-Apr), Oliver Bird Hall, Church Hill Road, Solihull.

STOURBRIDGE. (1978; 150). David Ackland. 01384 293 090; e-mail: davidackland@blueyonder.co.uk www.rspb.org.uk/groups/stourbridge
Meetings: 2nd Wednesday of the month (Sep-May), Wollaston Suite, Stourbridge Town Hall, Crown Centre, STOURBRIDGE, West Midlands, DY8 1YE

SUTTON COLDFIELD. (1986; 250). Martin Fisher. 01295 253 330; e-mail: Anna.keen@RSPB.org.uk www.rspb.org.uk/groups/suttoncoldfield
Meetings: 7.30pm, 1st Monday of the month, Bishop Vesey's Grammer School.

ENGLAND

WALSALL. (1970). Mike Pittaway, 2 Kedleston Close, Bloxwich, Walsall WS3 3TW. 01922 710 568; e-mail: michaelp@kedclose.freeserve.co.uk www.rspb-walsall.org.uk
Meetings: 7.30pm, 3rd Wednesday of the month, St Marys School, Jesson Road, Walsall.

WOLVERHAMPTON. (1974; 100). Barry Proffitt. 01902 751 835; e-mail: RSPBwolverhampton@hotmail.co.uk www.rspb.org.uk/groups/wolverhampton
Meetings: 7.30pm, 2nd Wednesday of the month (Sept-Apr), The Newman Centre, Haywood Drive, Tettenhall, Wolverhampton WV6 8RF. This venue may change so please contact for details. Also monthly field-trips (Sep-Jun).

Wetland Bird Survey Organiser
Mr N R Lewis, 99 Lyttelton Road, Stechford, Birmingham, West Midlands B33 8BN. 0121 783 0874; e-mail: nick.r.lewis@virginmedia.com

Wildlife Trust
THE WILDLIFE TRUST FOR BIRMINGHAM AND THE BLACK COUNTRY. (1980; 10,000). Paula Reilly (Administrator) or Joe Peacock (Communications Officer), 16 Greenfield Crescent, Edgbaston, Birmingham, B15 3AU. 0121 454 1199 (fax) 0121 454 6556; e-mail: info@bbcwildlife.org.uk www.bbcwildlife.org.uk

WILTSHIRE

Bird Atlas/Avifauna
Birds of Wiltshire by James Ferguson-Lees 2007, Wiltshire Ornithological Society

Bird Recorder
Rob Turner, 14 Ethendun, Bratton, Westbury, Wilts BA13 4RX. 01380 830 862; e-mail: recorder@wiltshirebirds.co.uk

Bird Report
HOBBY (journal of the Wiltshire OS) (1975-), from John Osborne, 4 Fairdown Avenue, Westbury, Wiltshire BA13 3HS. 01373 8645 98; e-mail: josb@talktalk.net www.wiltshirebirds.co.uk

BTO Regional Representatives
NORTH & SOUTH. Bill Quantrill. 01225 866 245; e-mail: william.quantrill@btinternet.com

Clubs
SALISBURY & DISTRICT NATURAL HISTORY SOCIETY. (1952; 146). Rosemary Nichols, Chairman, e-mail: via the website. www.salisburynaturalhistory.com
Meetings: 7.30pm, 3rd Thursday of the month (Sept-Apr), The

Meeting Room, Salisbury Baptist Church, Brown Street, Salisbury.

WILTSHIRE ORNITHOLOGICAL SOCIETY. (1974; 500). Main contact point is website - www.wiltshirebirds.co.uk
Phil Deacon, 12 Rawston Close, Nythe, Swindon, Wilts SN3 3PW. 01793 528 930; e-mail: phil.deacon@ntlworld.com www.wiltshirebirds.co.uk
Meetings: See website for details.

Ringing Group
COTSWOLD WATER PARK RG. John Wells, 25 Pipers Grove, Highnam, Glos GL2 8NJ. E-mail: john.wells2@btinternet.com
WEST WILTSHIRE RG. Mr M.J. Hamzij, 13 Halfway Close, Trowbridge, Wilts BA14 7HQ. E-mail: m.hamzij@btinternet.com

RSPB Local Groups
SOUTH WILTSHIRE. (1986; 630). Tony Goddard, 3 Forestry Houses, Livery Road, Farley, Salisbury SP5 1AG. 01722 712 713; e-mail: goddard543@hotmail.com www.rspb.org.uk/groups/southwiltshire
Meetings: 7.30pm, Tuesday evenings (monthly), Salisbury Arts Centre, Salisbury.

Wetland Birds Survey Organiser
COTSWOLD WATER PARK. Mr G O Harris, 10 The Paddock, Market Lavington, Devizes, Wiltshire SN10 4BP. 07868 427 916; e-mail: gharris_doh@hotmail.com

WILTSHIRE. Mr W Quantrill, c/o WeBS Office, BTO, The Nunnery, Thetford, Norfolk IP24 2PU. 01842 750 050; webs@bto.org

Wildlife Trust
WILTSHIRE WILDLIFE TRUST. (1962; 18,500). Elm Tree Court, Long Street, Devizes, Wilts, SN10 1NJ. 01380 725 670; e-mail: info@wiltshirewildlife.org www.wiltshirewildlife.org

WORCESTERSHIRE

Bird Recorder
Steven Payne, 6 Norbury Close, Redditch B98 8RP. 01527 60169; e-mail: worcs-recorder@westmidlandbirdclub.com www.westmidlandbirdclub.com

Bird Report See West Midlands.

BTO Regional Representative
G Harry Green MBE, Windy Ridge, Pershore Road, Little Comberton, Pershore, Worcs WR10 3EW. 01386 710 377; e-mail: zen130501@zen.co.uk

Ringing Group
WYCHAVON RG. J R Hodson, 15 High Green,

ENGLAND

Severn Stoke, Worcester WR8 9JS. 01905 371 333; e-mail: hodson77@btinternet.com

Club
WEST MIDLAND BIRD CLUB (KIDDERMINSTER BRANCH). Brian Rickett, 1 Russell Road, Kidderminster DY10 3HT. 01562 824 615; e-mail: kidderminster@westmidlandbirdclub.com www.westmidlandbirdclub.com
Meetings: 7.30pm, 4th Wednesday of the month (Sep-Apr), St Oswalds Church Centre, Broadwaters, Kidderminster.

RSPB Local Group
WORCESTER & MALVERN. (1980; 300). Frances Evans, 120 Bath Road, Worcester WR5 3EP. 01905 359 132; e-mail: francesevans@gmail.com www.rspb.org.uk/groups/worcester
Meetings: 7.30pm, 2nd Wednesday in month (Sept-May), Powick Village Hall.

Wetland Birds Survey Organiser
WORCESTERSHIRE. Mr A Warr, 14 Bromsgrove Street, Barbourne, Worcester WR3 8AR. 01905 28 28; e-mail: andrew.warr3@btopenworld.com

Wildlife Hospital
VALE WILDLIFE RESCUE - WILDLIFE HOSPITAL + REHABILITATION CENTRE. Any staff member, Station Road, Beckford, Tewkesbury, Glos GL20 7AN. 01386 882 288; e-mail: info@valewildlife.org.uk www.valewildlife.org.uk All wild birds. Intensive care. Registered charity. Veterinary support.

Wildlife Trust
WORCESTERSHIRE WILDLIFE TRUST. (1968; 9,000). Lower Smite Farm, Smite Hill, Hindlip, Worcester, WR3 8SZ. 01905 754 919 (fax) 01905 755 868; e-mail: enquiries@ worcestershirewildlifetrust.org www.worcswildlifetrust.co.uk

YORKSHIRE

Bird Atlas/Avifauna
Atlas of Breeding Birds in the Leeds Area 1987-1991 by Richard Fuller et al (Leeds Birdwatchers' Club, 1994).

The Birds of Halifax, by Nick Dawtrey (only 20 left), 14 Moorend Gardens, Pellon, Halifax, W Yorks, HX2 0SD.

The Birds of Yorkshire by John Mather (Croom Helm, 1986).

*An Atlas of the Breeding Birds of the Huddersfield Area, 1987-1992.*by Brian Armitage et al (2000) - very few copies left.

Birds of Barnsley by Nick Addey (Pub by author, 114 Everill Gate Lane, Broomhill, Barnsley S73 0YJ, 1998).

Birds of The Huddersfield Area by Paul and Betty Bray (Huddersfield Birdwatchers Club 2008).

Breeding Bird Atlas for Barnsley in preparation.

County Bird Recorders
YORKSHIRE. Craig Thomas, Sunnybank, Church Lane, Flamborough YO15 1PG. 01262 851 677; e-mail: craigcthomas@yahoo.co.uk

EAST YORKSHIRE AND EDITOR. Geoff Dobbs, 1 Priory Road, Beverley, East Yorkshire HU17 0EG. 07778 559 763; e-mail: geoffdobbs@aol.com

NORTH YORKSHIRE. Ian Court, 2 Burley Mews, Steeton, Keighley BT20 6TX. 01535 658 582; e-mail: ian.court@mypostoffice.co.uk

SOUTH YORKSHIRE. Martin Wells, 715 Manchester Road, Stocksbridge, Sheffield S36 1DQ. 0114 288 4211; e-mail: martinwells@barnsleybsg.plus.com

WEST YORKSHIRE. Covering all bird study groups and South and West Yorkshire and three reserves - Fairburn Ings, Old Moor (both RSPB) and Potteric Carr (Yorkshire Wildlife Trust), Craig Thomas (see above).01262 851 677; e-mail: craigcthomas@yahoo.co.uk

Jill Warwick (Secretary), 01765 602 832; e-mail: jill@swland.co.uk

Bird Reports
BARNSLEY & DISTRICT BIRD STUDY GROUP REPORT (1971-), from Waxwing Books, Sunnybank Cottage, Ruston Parva, Driffield YO25 4DG.

*YORK ORNITHOLOGICAL CLUB REPORT.*The 2013 report is due to be published in December 2014. Latest report and some back numbers can be ordered and paid for through the club website from, from Jane Chapman, 12 Moorland Road, York YO10 4HF, 01904 633 558; e-mail: secretary@yorkbirding.org.uk www.yorkbirding.org.uk

YORKSHIRE BIRD REPORT, published by the Yorkshire Naturalists' Union (1940-). 2011 edition £14 including postage, from Jill Warwick, Sharow Grange, Sharow, Ripon HG4 5BN. 01765 602 832; e-mail: jill@swland.co.uk

BRADFORD NATURALISTS' SOCIETY ANNUAL REPORT, from Mr I Hogg, 23 St Matthews Road, Bankfoot, Bradford BD5 9AB. 01274 727 902.

BRADFORD ORNITHOLOGICAL GROUP REPORT (1987-) - after the 2008 issue, this report will only be available to paid up members of the group, from Jenny Barker, 3 Chapel Fold, Slack Lane,

ENGLAND

Oakworth, Keighley BD22 0RQ.
DONCASTER BIRD REPORT (1955-), from Mr M Roberts, 8 Sandbeck court, Rossington, Doncaster DN11 0FN. 01302 326 265.

 *FILEY BRIGG BIRD REPORT (1976-)*, Send a cheque payable to FBOG for £6.00 + £1.50 p&p to: Janet Robinson, 31 Wharfedale, Filey, YO14 0DG. 01723 513 991; e-mail: ianrobinson@yorkshire.net www.fbog.co.uk

HARROGATE & DISTRICT NATURALISTS' SOCIETY BIRD REPORT (1996-) 2012 edition £6 including postage, from Jill Warwick, Sharow Grange, Sharow, Ripon HG4 5BN. 01765 602 832; e-mail: jill@swland.co.uk

HULL VALLEY WILDLIFE GROUP REPORT (2000-) covering Hull Valley. from www.hullvalleywildlifegroup.co.uk

BIRDS IN HUDDERSFIELD (1966-), from Mr M Wainman, 2 Bankfield Avenue, Taylor Hill, Huddersfield HD4 7QY. 01484 305 054; e-mail: m.wainman@ntlworld.com

BIRDS OF ROTHERHAM (1975-) - cost £2.50 inc p&p, cheque payable to R.D.O.S, from The Secretary, Rotherham & District Bird Club. E-mail: rdos@hotmail.co.uk www.rotherhambirds.co.uk

BIRDS IN THE SHEFFIELD AREA (1973-), from Martin Hodgson, 142 Hangingwater Road, Sheffield S11 7ET. £9. www.sbsg.org

LEIGH ORNITHOLOGIAL SOCIETY REPORT Available to download, donations welcomed; www.leighos.org.uk

SORBY RECORD (1962-), from Ken Dorning, Sorby NHSoc, c/o Room C12i, Dainton Building, Brook Hill, Sheffield S3 7HF.

SPURN BIRD OBSERVATORY ANNUAL REPORT, from Warden, see Reserves.

SWILLINGTON INGS BIRD GROUP - ANNUAL REPORT AND TWENTY YEAR REVIEW - 2008, from Chris Robinson, 43 Northfield Road, Sprotbrough, Doncaster DN5 8AY. 07534 271 254; e-mail: GBFShrike@hotmail.com http://sibg1.wordpress.com

THE BIRDS OF SK58 (1993-), from Secretary, SK58 Birders. E-mail: recorder@sk58birders.com www.sk58birders.com

WINTERSETT AREA ANNUAL REPORT (1988-), from

Steve Denny, 13 Rutland Drive, Crofton, Wakefield WF4 1SA. 01924 864 487.

BTO Regional Representatives & Regional Development Officers
NORTH-EAST. Mick Carroll, 10 Crofts Avenue, Pickering, North Yorkshire YO18 7HP. 01751 476 550; e-mail: mickcarroll47@btinternet.com

NORTH-WEST. Gerald Light. 01756 753 720; e-mail: gerald@uwlig.plus.com

SOUTH-EAST AND SOUTH-WEST. Position vacant. 01842 750 050; e-mail: info@bto.org

EAST. Geoff Dobbs, 1 Priory Road, Beverley, East Yorkshire HU17 0EG. 07778 559 763; e-mail: geoffdobbs@aol.com

BRADFORD RR & RDO. Mike L Denton, 77 Hawthorne Terrace, Crosland Moor, Huddersfield HD4 5RP. 01484 646 990; e-mail: michael@atheta.plus.com

YORKSHIRE (HARROGATE). Mike Brown, 48 Pannal Ash Drive, Harrogate, N Yorks HG2 0HU. 01423 567 382; e-mail: mikebtorep@gmail.com

HULL. Geoff Dobbs, 1 Priory Road, Beverley, East Yorkshire HU17 0EG. 07778 559 763; e-mail: geoffdobbs@aol.com

LEEDS & WAKEFIELD. Position vacant.

RICHMOND. John Edwards, 7 Church Garth, Great Smeaton, Northallerton, N Yorks DL6 2HW. 01609 881 476; e-mail: john@jhedwards.plus.com

YORK. Rob Chapman, 12 Moorland Road, York, YO10 4HF. 01904 633 558; e-mail: robert.chapman@tinyworld.co.uk

Clubs
BRADFORD ORNITHOLOGICAL GROUP. (1987; 160). Shaun Radcliffe, Chairman. 01274 770 960; e-mail: shaun. radcliffe@btinternet.com www.bradfordbirding.org **Meetings:** 1st Tuesday of the month - United Reformed Church, Victoria Road, Saltaire. See website for details.

FILEY BRIGG ORNITHOLOGICAL GROUP. (1977; 100). Dr Sue Hull (Secretary). 01723 515 042; e-mail: secretary@fbog.co.uk www.fbog.co.uk
HARROGATE & DISTRICT NATURALISTS' SOCIETY. (1947; 230). Mrs S Coldwell, General Secretary, 4 Abbots Way, Knaresborough, North Yorkshire HG5 8EU. E-mail: gen.sechdns@yahoo.co.uk www.hdns.org.uk

ENGLAND

Meetings: 7.30pm, St. Roberts Centre, 2/3 Robert Street, Harrogate. The programme of meetings is sent out to members in April.

HUDDERSFIELD BIRDWATCHERS' CLUB. (1966; 90). Chris Abell, 57 Butterley Lane, New Mill, Holmfirth HD9 7EZ. 01484 681 499; e-mail: cdabell@gmail.com
www.huddersfieldbirdwatchersclub.co.uk
Meetings: 7.30pm, Tuesday's fortnightly (Sep-May), The Old Court Room, Town Hall, Ramsden St, Huddersfield HD1 2TA.

HULL VALLEY WILDLIFE GROUP. (1997; 175). Barry Warrington (Treasurer and Membership Secretary): e-mail: wildlife_barrywarrington@yahoo.co.uk
http://hullvalleywildlifegroup.blogspot.co.uk/

ROTHERHAM & DISTRICT ORNITHOLOGICAL SOCIETY. (1974; 80). The Secretary, RDOS, c/o Galaxy Four, 493 Glossop Road, Sheffield S10 2QE; e-mail: via the website — www.rotherhambirds.co.uk
Meetings: 7.30pm, 2nd Friday of the month, 7-30pm in Herringthorpe United Reform Church Hall, Wickersley Road, Rotherham S60 4JN.

SCARBOROUGH BIRDERS. (1993; 49). Steve Wignill, Flat 3, 101 Castle Road, Scarborough, North Yorkshire YO11 1HX. 07859 435 592; e-mail: steve.wignill@scarboroughbirding.co.uk
www.scarboroughbirding.co.uk
Meetings: 3rd Thursday of the month (Sep-Nov) and (Jan-Apr). Check website for details.

SHEFFIELD BIRD STUDY GROUP. (1972; 227). Richard Hill, Honorary Secretary, 22 Ansell Road, Sheffield, South Yorkshire S11 7PE. www.sbsg.org
E-mail: Secretary@sbsg.org
Meetings: 7.15pm, 2nd Wednesday of the month (Sep-May), Lecture Theatre 5, Sheffield University Arts Tower.

SK58 BIRDERS. (1993; 66). Brian Chambers (Secretary), 01909 770 816; e-mail: brianchambers101940@hotmail.com
www.sk58birders.com
Chair: Mick Clay, 2 High St, S.Anston, Sheffield. 01909 566 000.
Meetings: 7.30pm, last Wednesday of the month (Sep-Nov and Jan-Jun), Anston Parish Hall,15A Ryton Road, North Anston, Sheffield S25 4DL.

SORBY NHS (ORNITHOLOGICAL SECTION). (1918; 400). The Secretary, c/o 159 Bell Hagg Road, Sheffield S6 5DA; e-mail: secretary@sorby.org.uk
www.sorby.org.uk
Meetings: Indoor and field meetings held regularly as advertised on the website and in the newsletter.

SWILLINGTON INGS BIRD GROUP. (1989; 180). Martin Robinson (Secretary); e-mail: via comments box on website.
http://sibg1.wordpress.com
Meetings: 7.30pm, Two Pointers, 69 Church Street, Woodlesford, LS26 8RE. (Dates may vary so check website).

WAKEFIELD NATURALISTS' SOCIETY. (1851; 32). The Secretary; e-mail: via website.
http://wakefieldnaturalists.org/?tag=wakefield-naturalists-society
Meetings: 7.30pm, 2nd Tuesday of the month (Sep-Apr), Friends Meeting House, Thornhill Street, Wakefield.

YORK ORNITHOLOGICAL CLUB. (1967; 80). Jane Chapman, 12 Moorland Road. York YO10 4HF. 01904 633 558;
e-mail: secretary@yorkbirding.org.uk
www.yorkbirding.org.uk
Meetings: 7.30pm, 1st Tuesday of the month, St Olaves Church Hall, Marygate Lane, Marygate, YORK YO30 7BJ.

YORKSHIRE NATURALISTS' UNION (Bird Section). (1875; 500). The Secretary; e-mail: via the website. www.ynu.org.uk

Ringing Groups
BARNSLEY RG. M C Wells, 715 Manchester Road, Stocksbridge, Sheffield S36 1DQ. 0114 288 4211; e-mail: barnsleybsg.plus.com

DONCASTER RG. D Hazard, 41 Jossey Lane, Scawthorpe, Doncaster, S Yorks DN5 9DB. 01302 788 044; e-mail: dave.hazard@tiscali.co.uk

EAST DALES RG. P. Bone.
E-mail: philsarab@aol.co.uk

EAST YORKS RG. Peter J Dunn, 43 West Garth Gardens, Cayton, Scarborough, N Yorks YO11 3SF. 01723 583149; e-mail: pjd@fbog.co.uk
www.eyrg.co.uk

SORBY-BRECK RG. Geoff P Mawson, Moonpenny Farm, Farwater Lane, Dronfield, Sheffield S18 1RA. E-mail: moonpenny@talktalk.net

SPURN BIRD OBSERVATORY. Paul Collins, Kew Villa, Seaside Road, Kilnsea, Hull HU12 0UB. 01964 650 479; e-mail: pcnfa@hotmail.com
WINTERSETT RG. P Smith, 16 Templar Street, Wakefield, W Yorks WF1 5HB. 01924 375 082.

RSPB Local Groups
AIREDALE AND BRADFORD. (1972; 3500 in catchment area). Paul Barrett. 01274 582 078;

ENGLAND

e-mail: AbRSPB@blueyonder.co.uk
www.rspb.org.uk/groups/airedaleandbradford
Meetings: 7.30pm, monthly on Fridays, Room 3, Shipley Library.

WAKEFIELD. (1987; 130). Duncan Stokoe. 01924 280 458; e-mail: duncanstokoe@gmail.com
www.rspb.org.uk/groups/wakefield
Meetings: 7.30pm, 4th Thursday of the month (Sep-Apr), Ossett Community Centre, Prospect Road, Ossett, WF5 8AN.

YORK. (1972; 600). Chris Lloyd, 7 School Lane, Upper Poppleton, York YO26 6JS. 01904 794 865; e-mail: rspb.calyork@btinternet.com
www.yorkrspb.org.uk
Meetings: 7.30pm, Tues, Wed or Thurs, Temple Hall, York St John University, Lord Mayors Walk, York.

CRAVEN & PENDLE. (1986; 300). Colin Straker. 01756 751 888;
e-mail: colin.straker@btinternet.com
www.cravenandpendlerspb.org
Meetings: 7.30pm 2nd Thursday of the month (Sep-May), Annexe Hall, Skipton Town Hall.

DONCASTER. (1984; 79). Trevor Bonham, Willowford, Melton Mill Lane, High Melton, Doncaster DN5 7TE. 01709 585 677;
e-mail: trevorbonham@yahoo.co.uk
www.rspbdoncaster.com
Meetings: 7.00pm on the second Wednesday of the month from 10th September 2014, at Castle Park Rugby Club, Armthorpe Road, Doncaster DN2 5QB.

EAST YORKSHIRE. (1986;120). Paul Leyland, 61 Muston Road. 01723 891 507;
e-mail: eastyorksrspb@yahoo.co.uk
www.rspb.org.uk/groups/eastyorkshire
Meetings: 7.30pm, North Bridlington Library, Martongate, Bridlington (check website for details).

HARROGATE DISTRICT. (2005). Bill Sturman. 01423 870 883; e-mail: pam-bill@sturmanw.fsnet.co.uk
www.harrogaterspb.com
Meetings: 7.50pm, 3rd Monday of the month (Oct-Mar). Christ Church Parish Centre, The Stray, Harrogate HG1 4SW.

HUDDERSFIELD & HALIFAX. (1981; 100). David Hemingway, 267 Long Lane, Dalton, Huddersfield HD5 9SH. 01484 301 920;
e-mail: d.hemingway@ntlworld.com
www.rspb.org.uk/groups/huddersfieldandhalifax
Meetings: 7.30pm, Huddersfield Methodist Mission, 3-13 Lord Street, Huddersfield, HD1 1QA.

HULL & DISTRICT. (1983; 334). Betty Hilton. 01482 849 503; e-mail: betty9hilton@gmail.com
www.rspb.org.uk/groups/hull
Meetings: 7.30pm, Tuesdays (Sept-Apr), Christchurch United Reformed Church, South Ella Way, Kirk Ella, Hull. (£2 for Local Group Members and £2.50 for Non Members).

LEEDS. (1974; 560). Ian Willoughby. 0113 258 6555. E-mail: RSPBleeds@googlemail.com
www.rspb.org.uk/groups/leeds
Meetings: 7.30pm, 3rd Wednesday of the month (Sep-Apr), Friends Meeting House, 188 Woodhouse Lane, Leeds, Yorkshire, LS2 9DX.

RICHMONDSHIRE & HAMBLETON. (2005). Grahame Bentley. 01748 824 776;
e-mail: grahame@bentley000.plus.com
www.rspb.org.uk/groups/
richmondshireandhambleton
Meetings: Check website.

SHEFFIELD. (1981; 500). Susan Bradshaw. 0114 239 9072;
e-mail: SheffieldRSPBlocalgroup@talktalk.net
www.rspb-sheffield.org.uk
Meetings: 7.30pm 1st Thursday of the month (Sept-May), Central United Reformed Church, Norfolk St, Sheffield.

Wetland Bird Survey Organisers
EAST YORKSHIRE AND SCARBOROUGH (excl. Humber). Mr J Morgan, 4 Rise Lane, Catwick, Beverley, North Humberside HU17 5PL. 01964 544 947; 07951 075 045;
e-mail: jimmygpz@hotmail.com

HARROGATE AND YORKSHIRE DALES. Mr W G Haines, 3 Rosemount Road, Ealing, London W13 0HJ. 07870 828 978;
e-mail: bill.haines@tiscali.co.uk

LEEDS AREA. Mr P R Morris, 10 The Grove, Alwoodley, Leeds LS17 7BW;
e-mail: pmorris@wyjs.org.uk

WAKEFIELD AREA. c/o WeBS Office, BTO, The Nunnery, Thetford, Norfolk IP24 2PU. 01842 750 050; e-mail: webs@bto.org

Wildlife Hospital
ANIMAL HOUSE WILDLIFE WELFARE. Mr T Buckroyd, 14 Victoria Street, Scarborough, YO12 7SS. 07581 219 803 (please leave a message on the answer machine and callers will be contacted as soon as possible). www.facebook.com/AnimalHouse1059674.
All species of wild birds. Oiled birds given treatment before forwarding to cleaning stations. Incubators, hospital cages, heat pads, release

sites. Birds ringed before release. Prior telephone call requested. Collection if required. Veterinary support. Charity shop at 127 Victoria Road.

Wildlife Trusts
THE WILDLIFE TRUST FOR SHEFFIELD AND ROTHERHAM. (1985; 5,613). 37 Stafford Road, Sheffield, S2 2SF. 0114 263 4335 (fax) 0114 263 4345; e-mail: mail@wildsheffield.com
www.wildsheffield.com

YORKSHIRE WILDLIFE TRUST. (1946; 37,000). 1 St George's Place, Tadcaster Road,YorkYO24 1GN. 01904 659 570 (fax) 01904 613 467; e-mail: info@ywt.org.uk
www.ywt.org.uk

ISLE OF MAN

Bird Atlas/ Avifauna
Manx Bird Atlas. 5-yr BBS and Winter Atlas research completed. (Liverpool University Press, 2007). Contact: Chris Sharpe (see below).

Bird Recorder
Chris Sharpe; e-mail: birdman@manx.net

Bird Reports
MANX BIRD REPORT (1947-), published in *Peregrine.* From Mrs A C Kaye, Cronk Ny Ollee, Glen Chass, Port St Mary, Isle of Man IM9 5PL. 01624 834 015.

CALF OF MAN BIRD OBSERVATORY ANNUAL REPORT, from Secretary, Manx National Heritage, Manx Museum, Douglas, Isle of Man, IM1 3LY.

BTO Regional Representatives
Dr Pat Cullen, 01624 623 308; e-mail:bridgeen@mcb.net

Club
MANX ORNITHOLOGICAL SOCIETY. (1967; 150). Mrs A C Kaye, Cronk Ny Ollee, Glen Chass, Port St Mary, Isle of Man IM9 5PL. 01624 834 015. http://manxbirdlife.im/manx-ornithological-society
Meetings: 1st Tues in month, 7.30pm, Union Mills Hall, IM4 4NP.

Ringing Group
MANX RINGING GROUP. Mr Kevin Scott; e-mail: manxrg@gmail.com
www.manxringer.blogspot.com

Wetland Bird Survey Organiser
Dr Pat Cullen, Troutbeck, Cronkbourne, Braddan, Isle of Man, IM4 4QA. Home: 01624 623 308, Work 01624 676 774; E-mail:bridgeen@mcb.net

Wildlife Trust
MANX WILDLIFE TRUST. (1973; 900). 7-8 Market Place, Peel, Isle of Man IM5 1AB. 01624 844 432; E-mail:enquiries@manxwt.org.uk
www.manxwt.org.uk

SCOTLAND

Bird Report
SCOTTISH BIRD REPORT, now online from www.the-soc.org.uk

Club
See Scottish Ornithologists' Club in National Directory.

ANGUS & DUNDEE

Bird Recorder
ANGUS & DUNDEE. Jon Cook. 01382 738 495; e-mail:1301midget@tiscali.co.uk

Bird Report
ANGUS & DUNDEE BIRD REPORT (1974-), From the County Recorder. 2010 edition sold out, 2011 in preparation. 01382 738 495; e-mail:1301midget@tiscali.co.uk

BTO Regional Representative
ANGUS. Position vacant.

Clubs
ANGUS & DUNDEE BIRD CLUB. (1997; 230). Gus Guthrie. 01575 574 548; e-mail: gusguthrie@btinternet.com http://www.angusbirding.com/html/adbc.html
Meetings: 7.30pm, Tuesdays, Panbride Church Hall, Carnoustie, Angus

SOC TAYSIDE BRANCH. (145). Brian Brocklehurst. 01382 778 348; e-mail: brian.brocklehurst1@btinternet.com www.the-soc.org.uk
Meetings: Methodist Church Halls, 20 Marketgait, Dundee.

Ringing Group
TAY RG. Ms S Millar, Edenvale Cottage, 1 Lydox Cottages, Dairsie, Fife, KY15 4RN; e-mail:shirley@edenecology.co.uk

RSPB Members' Group
DUNDEE. (1972;110). Graham Smith, 01382 532 461; e-mail:grahamnjen@hotmail.com www.RSPB.org.uk/groups/dundee
Meetings: 7.30 pm, monthly on a Wednesday (Sep-Mar), Methodist Church, 20, West Marketgait, DUNDEE. Admission £1.00 for all, including refreshments. outdoor meetings on Sunday leaving Crichton Street, Dundee at 9am.

Wetland Bird Survey Organisers
ANGUS (excl Montrose Basin). c/o WeBS Office, BTO, The Nunnery, Thetford, NorfolkIP24 2PU.

01842 750 050; e-mail:webs@bto.org

MONTROSE BASIN. Miss A Cheshier, Scottish Wildlife Trust, Montrose Basin Wildlife Centre, Rossie Braes, Montrose, Angus DD10 9TA; e-mail:acheshier@swt.org.uk

ARGYLL

Birds of Argyll (Argyll Bird Club 2007, £45 inc postage), available from Bob Furness, The Cnoc, Tarbert, Arrochar, Dunbartonshire G83 7DG. 01301 702 603.

Bird Recorders
ARGYLL. Jim Dickson, 11 Pipers Road, Cairnbaan, Lochgilphead, Argyll PA31 8UF. 01546 603 967; e-mail:meg@jdickson5.plus.com
Also for submission of rare bird records.

Assistant Recorder (non rare bird records). Malcolm Chattwood, 1 The Stances, Kilmichael Glassary, Lochgilphead, Argyll PA31 8QA. 01546 603 389; e-mail:abcrecorder@outlook.com
For submission of all non-rare bird records.

Bird Reports
ARGYLL BIRD REPORT (1984-), £6 including postage, From Dr Bob Furness, The Cnoc, Tarbet, Dunbartonshire G83 7DG.01301 702 603; e-mail:r.furness@bio.gla.ac.uk

ISLE OF MULL BIRD REPORT (2011), £7.15, From Mr Alan Spellman, Maridon, Lochdon, Isle of Mull, Argyll. PA64 6AP. 01680 812 448; e-mail:mullbirds@btinternet.com www.mullbirds.com

MACHRIHANISH SEABIRD OBSERVATORY REPORT (1992-), From the Observatory, see Reserves & Observatories.

BTO Regional Representatives
ARGYLL (MULL, COLL, TIREE AND MORVERN). Arthur Brown, 01688 400 415; e-mail:pamartbrown@btinternet.com or rltt@aol.com

ARGYLL MAINLAND, BUTE AND GIGHA. Position vacant, 01842 750 050; e-mail:info@bto.org

ISLAY, JURA, COLONSAY. John S Armitage. 01496 860 396; e-mail:jsa@ornquest.plus.com www.birdingodyssey.blogspot.com

Clubs
ARGYLL BIRD CLUB. (1983;270). Katie Pendreigh, The Whins, Farry Road, Tayinloan, Argyll PA37 1PT. 01583 441 359. www.argyllbirdclub.org

SCOTLAND

Meetings: All-day Indoor Meetings are held on a Saturday in early March and early November each year, see website for details.

ISLE OF MULL BIRD CLUB. (2001;160), The Club Secretary; e-mail:j.phall142@gmail.com www.mullbirdclub.org.uk
Meetings: 7 for 7.30pm start, 3rd Friday of the month (Oct-Apr), Craignure Village Hall.

Ringing Groups
TRESHNISH ISLES AUK RG. Robin Ward, 15 Church Clost,Great Stukeley,CambridgeshirePE28 4AP.e-mail: robin.ward2@virginmedia.com

HELENSBURGH. (1975; 62). John Clark, 01436 821 178; e-mail: johnclark@jcmc.demon.co.uk www.rspb.org.uk/groups/helensburgh
Meetings: 7.30 pm, 3rd Wednesday of the month (Sep-Apr), The Guide Halls, Lower John Street, Helensburgh.

Wetland Bird Survey Organisers
ARGYLL MAINLAND. Mr P C Daw, Tigh-na-Tulloch, Minard, Inveraray, Argyll PA32 8YQ. 01546 886 260; e-mail:monedula@globalnet.co.uk

MULL. Mr P C Daw, Tigh-na-Tulloch, Minard, Inveraray, Argyll PA32 8YQ. 01546 886 260; e-mail:monedula@globalnet.co.uk

TIREE & COLL. Dr J Bowler, c/o WeBS Office, BTO, The Nunnery, Thetford, Norfolk IP24 2PU. 01879 220 748; e-mail:john.bowler@rspb.org.uk

AYRSHIRE

Bird Recorder
AYRSHIRE. Fraser Simpson, 4 Inchmurrin Drive, Kilmarnock, Ayrshire KA3 2JD; e-mail:recorder@ayrshire-birding.org.uk www.ayrshire-birding.org.uk

Bird Report
AYRSHIRE BIRD REPORT (1976-), From Dr RG Vernon, 29 Knoll Park, Ayr KA7 4RH. 01292 442 195; e-mail: rgv_mcv@tiscali.co.uk

BTO Regional Representative
AYRSHIRE RR. Brian Broadley, 01290 424 241; e-mail:brianbroadley@onegreendoor.com

Club
SOC AYRSHIRE. (1962; 154). Anne Dick. 01292 541 981; e-mail: a_m_dick@btinternet.com www.ayrshire-birding.org.uk www.the-soc.org.uk
Meetings: 7.30pm, Tuesdays monthly, Monkton Community Church, Monkton by Prestwick.

Newsletter *The Stonechat,* produced three times a year.

RSPB Members' Groups
CENTRAL AYRSHIRE LOCAL GROUP. (1978; 85). Ronnie Coombes (Group Leader), 01292 265 891; e-mail: ronnie.coombes@tesco.net www.ayrshire-birding.org.uk
Meetings: 7.40pm. 3rd Monday of the month (Sep-Apr), Newton Wallacetown Church Hall, 60 Main Street, Ayr.

NORTH AYRSHIRE. (1976; 180). John Tedd, 01294 823 434; e-mail:john.tedd@virgin.net www.narspb.org.uk
Meetings: 7.30pm, various Fridays (Sep-Apr), Argyll Centre, Donaldson Avenue, SALTCOATS, Ayrshire, KA21 5AG.

Wetland Bird Survey Organisers
AYRSHIRE. Mr D A Grantc/o WeBS OfficeBTO, The NunneryThetfordNorfolkIP24 2PUe-mail:daveg466@gmail.com

ARRAN. Mr J Cassels, Kilpatrick Kennels, Kilpatrick, Blackwaterfoot, Isle of Arran KA27 8EY. 01770 860316e-mail:james.cassels@virgin.net

Wildlife Hospital
HESSILHEAD WILDLIFE RESCUE CENTRE. Gay & Andy Christie, Gateside, Beith, Ayrshire, KA15 1HT. 01505 502 415; e-mail:info@hessilhead.org.uk www.hessilhead.org.uk
All species. Releasing aviaries. Veterinary support. Visits only on open days please.

THE SCOTTISH BORDERS

Bird Atlas/Avifauna
The Breeding Birds of South-east Scotland, a tetrad atlas 1988-1994 by R D Murray et al. (Scottish Ornithologists' Club, 1998).

Bird Recorder
Ray Murray, 4 Bellfield Crescent, Eddleston, Peebles, EH45 8RQ. 01721 730 677; e-mail:ray1murray@btinternet.com

Bird Report
BORDERS BIRD REPORT (1979-), From Malcolm Ross, Westfield Cottage, Smailholm, Kelso TD5 7PN.01573 460 699; e-mail:eliseandmalcolm@btinternet.com

BTO Regional Representative & Regional Development Officer
Graham Pyatt. 01721 740 319; e-mail:d.g.pyatt@btinternet.com

SCOTLAND

Club
SOC BORDERS BRANCH. (100). Neil Stratton.
01573 450 695;
e-mail:neildstratton@btinternet.com
www.the-soc.org.uk
Meetings:7.30pm, 2nd Monday of the month,
George & Abbotsford Hotel, Melrose.

Ringing Group
BORDERS RG. (1991; 10)Dr T W Dougall, 38
Leamington Terrace, Edinburgh,EH10 4JL. (Office)
0131 344 2600

RSPB Members' Group
BORDERS. (1995; 94). John Marshall, 01896 850
564; e-mail:ncmandjrm@btinternet.com
www.rspb.org.uk/groups/borders
Meetings: 7.30pm, 3rd Wednesday of the month,
The Corn Exchange, Market Square, MELROSE

Wetland Bird Survey Organiser
BORDERS. Mr A T Bramhall, 2 Abbotsferry Road,
Tweedbank, Galashiels, Scottish Borders TD1 3RX;
01896 755 326;
e-mail:andrewtbramhall@gmail.com

CAITHNESS

Bird Recorder
CAITHNESS. Sinclair Manson, 01847 892 379;
e-mail:sinclairmanson@btinternet.com

Bird Report
CAITHNESS BIRD REPORT (1983-97). No longer
published but the 2012 report can now be
downloaded from www.the-soc.org.uk

BTO Regional Representative
CAITHNESS. Donald Omand. 01847 811 403;
e-mail:achreamie@yahoo.co.uk

Club
SOC CAITHNESS BRANCH. (51). Angus McBay.
01847 894 663; e-mail:angmcb@btinternet.com
www.the-soc.org.uk
Meetings: Castlehill Heritage Centre, Harbour
Road, Castletown, Caithness KW14 8TG.

CLYDE

Bird Recorders
CLYDE ISLANDS (ARRAN, BUTE & CUMBRAES).
Bernard Zonfrillo, 28 Brodie Road, Glasgow,G21
3SB. e-mail:b.zonfrillo@bio.gla.ac.uk

CLYDE. Iain P Gibson, 8 Kenmure View, Howwood,
Johnstone, Renfrewshire, PA9 1DR. 01505 705
874; e-mail:iaingibson.soc@btinternet.com

Bird Report
CLYDE BIRDS (1973-2006), download the 2006
report from www.the-soc.org.uk

BTO Regional Representative
LANARK, RENFREW, DUMBARTON. Andy
Winnington. 01475 528 841;
e-mail:andy.winnington@yahoo.com

Club
SOC CLYDE BRANCH. (300). Ian Fulton0141 773
4329; e-mail:SOC.Clyde@btinternet.com
www.the-soc.org.uk
Meetings: Zoology Dept, Graham Kerr Building,
University of Glasgow G12 8QQ.

Ringing Group
CLYDE RG. (1976; 22). I Livingstone, 57 Strathview
Road, Bellshill, Lanarkshire, ML4 2UY. 01698 749
844; e-mail:iainlivcrg@googlemail.com

RSPB Members' Groups
GLASGOW. (1972;141). Alan Hill. 01389 730 696;
e-mail:RSPBglasgowleader@btinternet.com
www.rspb.org.uk/groups/glasgow
Meetings: 7.30pm, monthly on a Thursday (Sep-
Apr), Adelaides, 209 Bath Street, Glasgow G2
4HZ.

HAMILTON. (1976;90). Jim Lynch, 0141 583 1044;
e-mail:birder45a@yahoo.co.uk
www.baronshaugh.co.uk
Meetings: 7.00pm, 3rd Thursday of the month
(Sept-May), Watersports Centre, (Motherwell
entrance), Hamilton Road, Motherwell ML1 3ED.

RENFREWSHIRE. (1986; 200). Margaret Brown,
e-mail:RenfrewRSPB@hotmail.co.uk
www.rspb.org.uk/groups/renfrewshire
Meetings: 1st Friday of the month (Sep-May), The
McMaster Centre, 2a Donaldson Drive, RENFREW

Wetland Bird Survey Organisers
CLYDE ESTUARY. Mr J Clark, Laighfield, Station
Road, Shandon, Helensburgh G84 8NX; 01436 821
178e-mail: johnclark@jcmc.demon.co.uk

GLASGOW/RENFREWSHIRE/LANARKSHIRE/
DUNBARTONSHIRE. Mr J Clark, Laighfield, Station
Road, Shandon, Helensburgh G84 8NX; 01436 821
178e-mail: johnclark@jcmc.demon.co.uk

BUTE. Mr I L Hopkins, 2 Eden Place, 179 High
Street, Rothesay, Isle of Bute PA20 9BS. 01700 504
042; e-mail:ian@hopkins0079.freeserve.co.uk

DUMFRIES & GALLOWAY

Bird Recorder
Paul Collin, Gairland, Old Edinburgh Road,
Minnigaff, Newton Stewart, DG8 6PL. 01671 402
861; e-mail:pncollin@live.co.uk

SCOTLAND

Bird Report
DUMFRIES & GALLOWAY REGION BIRD REPORT
(1985-), £6, from Peter Swan, 3 Castle View,
Castle Douglas, DG7 1BG, 01556 502 144;
e-mail:pandmswan@btinternet.com

BTO Regional Representatives
DUMFRIES. Edmund Fellowes, 01387 262 094;
e-mail:edmundfellowes@aol.com

KIRKCUDBRIGHT RR and Atlas Co-ordinator.
Andrew Bielinski. 01644 430 418 (evening);
e-mail:andrewb@bielinski.fsnet.co.uk

WIGTOWN. Geoff Sheppard. 01776 870 685;
e-mail:geoff.roddens@btinternet.com

Clubs
SOC DUMFRIES BRANCH. (1961; 105). Mrs Pat
Abery. 01556 630 483. www.the-soc.org.uk
Meetings: 7.30pm, 2nd Wednesday of the month
(Sept-Apr), Cumberland St Day Centre, Dumfries
(off Brooms Rd car park).

SOC STEWARTRY BRANCH. (1976; 80). Miss Joan
Howie.01644 430 280. www.the-soc.org.uk
Meetings: 7.30pm, usually 2nd Thursday of the
month (Sep-Apr), Kells School, New Galloway.

SOC WEST GALLOWAY BRANCH. (1975; 50). Geoff
Sheppard. 01776 870 685;
e-mail:geoff.roddens@btinternet.com
www.the-soc.org.uk
Meetings: 7.30pm, 2nd Tuesday of the month
(Oct-Mar), Stranraer Library.

Ringing Group
NORTH SOLWAY RG. Geoff Sheppard, The Roddens,
Leswalt, Stranraer, Wigtownshire, DG9 0QR.
01776 870 685;
e-mail:geoff.roddens@btinternet.com

RSPB Members' Group
GALLOWAY. (1985;150). John Dewhurst, 01566 502
736; e-mail:johnsteph@mkcott.wanadoo.co.uk
www.rspb.org.uk/groups/galloway
Meetings: 7.30pm 3rd Tuesday in the month
(Sep-Apr inc), Castle Douglas Town Hall, St
Andrew Street, Castle Douglas DG7 1DE.

Wetland Bird Survey Organisers
AUCHENCAIRN AND ORCHARDTON BAYS. Mr E
MacAlpine, Auchenshore, Auchencairn, Castle
Douglas, Galloway DG7 1QZ. 01556 640 244;
e-mail:js.eamm@sky.com

FLEET BAY. Mr D M Hawker, Windywalls, Upper
Drumwall, Gatehouse of Fleet, Castle Douglas
DG7 2DE. 01557 814 249; 07748 590 838;
e-mail:hawker398@btinternet.com

LOCH RYAN. Mr P N Collin, Gairland, Old

Edinburgh Road, Minnigaff, Newton Stewart DG8
6PL. 01671 402 861; e-mail:pncollin@live.co.uk

ROUGH FIRTH. Ms J Baxter, c/o WeBS Office, BTO,
The Nunnery, Thetford, Norfolk IP24 2PU. 01842
750 050; e-mail:jbaxter@nts.org.uk

WIGTOWN BAY. Mr P N Collin, Gairland, Old
Edinburgh Road, Minnigaff, Newton Stewart, DG8
6PL. 01671 402 861; e-mail:pncollin@live.co.uk

DUMFRIES AND GALLOWAY (other sites). Mr A
C Riches, c/o WeBS Office, BTO, The Nunnery,
Thetford, Norfolk IP24 2PU. 07792 142 446;
e-mail:slioch69@aol.com

SOLWAY ESTUARY - NORTH. Mr A C Richesc/o
WeBS Office, BTO, The Nunnery, Thetford,
Norfolk IP24 2PU. 01683 300 393; 07792 142 446;
e-mail:slioch69@aol.com

FIFE

Bird Atlas/Avifauna
The Fife Bird Atlas 2003 by Norman Elkins, Jim
Reid, Allan Brown, Derek Robertson & Anne-Marie
Smout. Available from Allan W. Brown (FOAG), 61
Watts Gardens, Cupar, Fife KY15 4UG, Tel. 01334
656804; e-mail: swans@allanwbrown.co.uk

Bird Recorders
FIFE REGION INC OFFSHORE ISLANDS (NORTH
FORTH) - (NOT Isle of May). Mr Malcolm Ware,
80 Castlandhill Road, Rosyth, Fife, KY11 2DH;
e-mail:malcolm.ware12@talktalk.net

ISLE OF MAY BIRD OBSERVATORY. Iain English, 19
Nethan Gate, Hamilton, S Lanarks, ML3 8NH;
e-mail:i.english@talk21.com

Bird Reports
FIFE BIRD REPORT (1988-) (FIFE
& KINROSS BR 1980-87), £10 inc
postage, From Mr Malcolm Ware,
80 Castlandhill Road, Rosyth, Fife,
KY11 2DH; e-mail:
malcolm.ware12@talktalk.net

Fife Bird Report
2010

ISLE OF MAY BIRD OBSERVATORY REPORT (1985-),
From Stuart Rivers, Flat 8 (2F2), 10 Waverley
Park, Edinburgh, EH8 8EU. e-mail:slr.bee-eater@
blueyonder.co.uk

BTO Regional Representative
FIFE & KINROSS. Norman Elkins, 18 Scotstarvit
View, Cupar, Fife, KY15 5DX. 01334 654 348;
e-mail:jandnelkins@btinternet.com

Clubs
FIFE BIRD CLUB. (1985; 200). Keith Ballantyne
(Chairperson); e-mail:chairman@fifebirdclub.org

SCOTLAND

www.fifebirdclub.org
Meetings: 7.30pm, (various evenings), Dean Park Hotel, Chapel Level, Kirkcaldy.

LOTHIANS AND FIFE SWAN & GOOSE STUDY GROUP. (1978; 12)Allan & Lyndesay Brown, 61 Watts Gardens, Cupar, Fife, KY15 4UG.
e-mail:swans@allanwbrown.co.uk

SOC FIFE BRANCH. (1950;170). Alison Creamer. 01334 657 188. www.the-soc.org.uk
Meetings: Supper Room of St Andrews Town Hall (at corner of South Street & Queen's Gardens), KY16 9TA.

Ringing Groups
ISLE OF MAY BIRD OBSERVATORY. David Grieve, 50 Main Street, Symington, Biggar, South Lanarkshire ML12 6LJ. 01899 309 176.

TAY RG. Ms S Millar, Edenvale Cottage, 1 Lydox Cottages, Dairsie, Fife, KY15 4RN;
e-mail:shirley@edenecology.co.uk

Wetland Bird Survey Organisers
FIFE (excluding estuaries). Grey Goose count organiser for Fife, Lothians and Borders. Mr A W Brown, 61 Watts Gardens, Cupar, Fife KY15 4UG. 01334 656 804; 07871 575 131;
e-mail:swans@allanwbrown.co.uk

FORTH ESTUARY (North). Mr A Inglis, 5 Crowhill Road, Dalgety Bay, Fife KY11 5LJ. 01383 822 115;
e-mail:aandjinglis@hotmail.com

TAY & EDEN ESTUARY. Mr N Elkins, 18 Scotstarvit View, Cupar, Fife KY15 5DX. 01334 654 348;
e-mail:jandnelkins@btinternet.com

TAY & EDEN ESTUARY. Mr N Elkins, 18 Scotstarvit View, Cupar, Fife KY15 5DX. 01334 654 348;
e-mail:jandnelkins@btinternet.com

Wildlife Hospital
SCOTTISH SPCA WILD LIFE REHABILITATION CENTRE. Middlebank Farm, Masterton Road, Dunfermline, Fife, KY11 8QN. 01383 412 520 All species. Open to visitors, groups and school parties. Illustrated talk on oiled bird cleaning and other aspects of wildlife rehabilitation available. Veterinary support.

FORTH

Bird Recorder
UPPER FORTH (Does not include parts of Stirling in Loch Lomondside/Clyde Basin). Chris Pendlebury, 3 Sinclair Street, Dunblane, FK5 0AH. 07798 711 134; e-mail:chris@upperforthbirds.co.uk

Bird Report
FORTH AREA BIRD REPORT (1975-) - enlarged report published annually in The Forth Naturalist and Historian, University of Stirling, from Smith Art Gallery and Museum, Dumbarton Road, Stirling.

BTO Regional Representative
CENTRAL RR. Neil Bielby, 56 Ochiltree, Dunblane, Perthshire, FK15 0DF. 01786 823 830;
e-mail:n.bielby@sky.com

Club
SOC CENTRAL SCOTLAND BRANCH. (1968; 101). Neil Bielby. 01786 823 830;
e-mail:n.bielby@sky.com
www.the-soc.org.uk
Meetings: 7.30pm, The Allan Centre, Fountain Road, Bridge of Allan FK9 4AT.

RSPB Members' Group
CENTRAL, FORTH VALLEY. (1995; 111). Tam Craig, 01259 211 550; e-mail:tam_craig@btinternet.com
www.rspb.org.uk/groups/forthvalley
Meetings: 7.30pm, 3rd Thursday of the month (Sept-Apr), Hillpark Community Centre, Morrison Drive, Bannockburn, Stirling.

Wetland Bird Survey Organiser
CENTRAL (excl Forth Estuary). Mr N Bielby, 56 Ochiltree, Dunblane, Perthshire FK15 0DF. 01786 823 830; e-mail:n.bielby@sky.com

HIGHLAND

Bird Atlas/Avifauna
The Birds of Sutherland by Alan Vittery (Colin Baxter Photography Ltd, 1997).

Skye Birds (updated 2009), by Bob McMillan.

Bird Recorder
ROSS-Shire, INVERNESS-SHIRE, SUTHERLAND, BADENOCH & STRATHSPEY, LOCHABER, LOCHALSH and SKYE. Peter Gordon, 2 Criagmore Crescent, Nethy Bridge, Highland PH25 3RA. 01479 821 339;
e-mail:gordon890@btinternet.com

Bird Report
HIGHLAND BIRD REPORT (1991-). £8 + £2 P&P, from Mrs Lynda Graham, 9 Burn Brae Terrace, Westhill, Inverness, IV2 5HD, 01463 791 292. Cheques should be made payable to 'Scottish Ornithologists' Club HBR

BTO Regional Representatives & Regional Development Officers
INVERNESS & SPEYSIDE RR & RDO. Hugh Insley, 1 Drummond Place, Inverness,IV2 4JT. 01463 230 652; e-mail:hugh.insley@btinternet.com

SCOTLAND

RUM, EIGG, CANNA & MUCK RR & RDO. Bob
Swann, 14 St Vincent Road, Tain, Ross-shire, IV19
1JR. 01862 894 329;
e-mail:robert.swann@homecall.co.uk

ROSS-SHIRE RR. Simon Cohen,
E-mail:saraandsimon@hotmail.com
SUTHERLAND. Position vacant.

SKYE. Position vacant.

Clubs
EAST SUTHERLAND BIRD GROUP. (1976; 120).
Tony Mainwood, 13 Ben Bhraggie Drive, Golspie,
Sutherland KW10 6SX. 01408 633 247;
e-mail:tony.mainwood@btinternet.com
Meetings: 7.30pm, Last Monday of the month
(Oct, Nov, Jan, Feb, Mar), Golspie Community
Centre.

SOC HIGHLAND BRANCH. (1955; 151). Kathy
Bonniface. 01808 511 740.
e-mail:kathybonniface@aol.com
www.the-soc.org.uk
Meetings: Culloden Library, Keppoch Road,
Culloden, IV2 7LL.

Ringing Groups
HIGHLAND RG. Bob Swann, 14 St Vincent Road,
Tain, Ross-shire, IV19 1JR.
e-mail:robert.swann@homecall.co.uk

RSPB Members' Group
HIGHLAND. (1987; 214). Doreen Manson. 01997
433 283; e-mail:john@jmanson2.wanadoo.co.uk
www.rspb.org.uk/groups/highland
Meetings: 7.30pm, last Thursday of the month
(Sep-Apr), Fraser Park Bowling Club, MacEwen
Drive, Inverness.

Wetland Bird Survey Organisers
BADENOCH AND STRATHSPEY. Mr K Duncan, c/o
WeBS Office, BTO, The Nunnery, Thetford, Norfolk
IP24 2PU. 01842 750 050;e-mail:webs@bto.org

CAITHNESS. Mr S A M Manson, 7 Duncan Street,
Thurso, Caithness KW14 7HZ. 01847 892 387;
e-mail:sinclairmanson@btinternet.com

LOCHABER. Mr J DyeToad, Hall, Dalnabreac,
Acharacle, Argyll PH36 4JX;
e-mail:john.dye@virgin.net

SKYE & LOCHALSH. Mr R L McMillan, Askival, 11
Elgol, Broadford, Isle of Skye IV49 9BL. 01471 866
305; e-mail:bob@skye-birds.com

LOTHIAN

Bird Atlas/Avifauna
The Breeding Birds of South-east Scotland, a

tetrad atlas 1988-1994 by R D Murray et al.
(Scottish Ornithologists' Club, 1998).

Bird Recorder
Stephen Welch, 25 Douglas Road, Longniddry,
EH32 0LQ; 01875 852 802;(M) 07931 524 963;
e-mail:lothianrecorder@the-soc.org.uk

Bird Report
LOTHIAN BIRD REPORT (1979-),
From Gillian Herbert, 30 Garscube
Terrace, Edinburgh, EH12 6BN;
e-mail:gillianiherbert@
btinternet.com

BTO Regional Representative
Alan Heavisides, 9 Addiston
Crescent, Balerno, Edinburgh, EH14 7DB. 0131
449 3816; e-mail:alanheavisides@yahoo.com

Clubs
EDINBURGH NATURAL HISTORY SOCIETY.
(1869; 200). The Secretary, e-mail:enquiries@
edinburghnaturalhistorysociety.org.uk
www.edinburghnaturalhistorysociety.org.uk
Meetings: 7.30pm, 4th Wednesday of the month
The Guide Hall, 33 Melville Street, Edinburgh.

LOTHIANS AND FIFE SWAN AND GOOSE STUDY
GROUP. (1978; 12). Allan & Lyndesay Brown,
61 Watts Gardens, Cupar, Fife, KY15 4UG.
e-mail:swans@allanwbrown.co.uk

LOTHIAN SOC. (1936; 570). Doreen Main. 01620
844 532; e-mail:doreen.main@yahoo.com
www.the-soc.org.uk
Meetings: 7.30pm, 2nd Tuesday (Sep, Dec, Jan and
Apr), 33 Melville Street, Edinburgh EH3 7JF. Oct and
Mar meetings are at Waterston House, Aberlady.

Ringing Group
LOTHIAN RG. Mr M Cubitt, 12 Burgh Mills Lane,
Linlithgow,West Lothian EH49 7TA.

RSPB Members' Group
EDINBURGH. (1974;480). Rosie Filipiak .
e-mail:rosie.birds1@gmail.com
www.rspb.org.uk/groups/edinburgh/
Meetings: 7.30pm, 3rd Tuesday or Wednesday of
the month (Sep-Apr), Napier University, Lindsay
Steward Lecture Theatre, Craiglockhart Campus,
Edinburgh. Outdoor meetings held year round
(check group website for details).

Wetland Bird Survey Organisers
FORTH ESTUARY (Outer South). Mr D J Priddlec/o
WeBS Office, BTO, The Nunnery, Thetford, Norfolk
IP24 2PU. 01620 827 459;
e-mail:dpriddle@eastlothian.gov.uk

LOTHIAN (excl estuaries). Mr A W Brown, 61 Watts
Gardens, Cupar, Fife KY15 4UG. 01334 656 804;

07871 575 131;
e-mail:swans@allanwbrown.co.uk

TYNINGHAME ESTUARY. Mr B Anderson, c/o Webs OfficeBTO, The Nunnery, Thetford, Norfolk IP24 2PU. 01620 827 318;
e-mail:randerson@eastlothian.gov.uk

MORAY & NAIRN

Bird Atlas/Avifauna
The Birds of Moray and Nairn by Martin Cook (Mercat Press, 1992).

Bird Recorder
NAIRN & MORAY. Martin J H Cook, Rowanbrae, Clochan, Buckie, Banffshire, AB56 5EQ. 01542 850 296; e-mail:martin.cook99@btinternet.com

Bird Reports
BIRDS IN MORAY AND NAIRN (1988-), download from www.birdsinmorayandnairn.org,

MORAY & NAIRN BIRD REPORT (1985-1998), From The Moray & Nairn Recorder, 01542 850 296; e-mail:martin.cook99@btinternet.com

BTO Regional Representative
MORAY & NAIRN. Melvin Morrison.01542 882 940; e-mail:wmmorrison@btinternet.com

Club
SOC MORAY. Martin Cook 01542 850 296; e-mail:martin.cook99@btinternet.com
www.the-soc.org.uk
Meetings: Elgin Museum Hall, 1 High Street, Elgin IV30 1EQ.

Wetland Bird Survey Organisers
LOSSIE ESTUARY. Mr R Proctor, 78 Marleon Field, Silvercrest, Bishopmill, Elgin, IV30 4GE; 07976 456 657e-mail:bobandlouise@proctor8246.fsnet.co.uk

MORAY & NAIRN (Inland). Mr D Law, Hollybrae, South Darkland, Elgin, Moray IV30 8NT. 01463 725 200; 01343 842 007;
e-mail:jdavidlaw@btinternet.com

MORAY BASIN COAST. Mr R.L. Swann, 14 St Vincent Road, Tain , Ross-Shire IV19 1JR.
e-mail:robert.swann@homecall.co.uk

NORTH EAST SCOTLAND

Bird Atlas/Avifauna
The Birds of North East Scotland by S T Buckland, M V Bell & N Picozzi (North East Scotland Bird Club, 1990).

Bird Recorder
NORTH-EAST SCOTLAND. Nick Littlewood, The

James Hutton Institute, Craigiebuckler, Aberdeen AB15 8Q. (H)07748 965 920
e-mail:nesrecorder@yahoo.co.uk

Bird Reports
NORTH-EAST SCOTLAND BIRD REPORT (1974-), From Dave Gill, Drakemyre Croft, Cairnorrie, Methlick, Aberdeenshire, AB41 7JN. 01651 806 252; e-mail:david@gilldavid1.orangehome.co.uk
NORTH SEA BIRD CLUB ANNUAL REPORT, from Andrew Thorpe, Ocean Laboratory and Centre for Ecology, Aberdeen University, Newburgh, Ellon, Aberdeenshire, AB41 6AA01224 274428; e-mail:nsbc@abdn.ac.uk

BTO Regional Representatives
ABERDEEN. Moray Souter. 01358 788 828; e-mail: souter@iolfree.ie

KINCARDINE & DEESIDE. Graham Cooper. 01339 882 706; e-mail:grm.cooper@btinternet.com

Club
SOC NORTH-EAST SCOTLAND BRANCH. (1956; 130). Hugh Addlesee. 01330 829 949; e-mail:grampian.secretary@the-soc.org.uk
www.the-soc.org.uk
Meetings: 7.30pm, usually 1st Monday of the month (Oct-Apr), Sportsmans's Club, 11 Queens Road, Aberdeen AB15 4YL.

Ringing Group
GRAMPIAN RG. R Duncan, 86 Broadfold Drive, Bridge of Don, Aberdeen, AB23 8PP.
e-mail:Raymond@waxwing.fsnet.co.uk

RSPB Members' Group
ABERDEEN & DISTRICT. (1975; 210). Mark Sullivan. 01224 861 446;
e-mail:geolbird_abz@btinternet.com
www.rspb.org.uk/groups/aberdeen
Meetings: 7.30pm, monthly in the winter, Lecture Theatre, Zoology Dept, Tillydrone Av, Aberdeen. Two birding trips monthly throughout the year.

Wetland Bird Survey Organiser
ABERDEENSHIRE. Mr R Minshullc/o Webs OfficeBTO, The Nunnery, Thetford, Norfolk IP24 2PU. 01842 750 050; e-mail: webs@bto.org

ORKNEY

Bird Atlas/Avifauna
The Birds of Orkney by CJ Booth et al (The Orkney Press, 1984).

Bird Recorder
Mr EJ Williams, Fairholm, Finstown, Orkney, KW17 2EQ. e-mail:jim@geniefea.freeserve.co.uk

COUNTY DIRECTORY

SCOTLAND

Bird Report
ORKNEY BIRD REPORT (inc North Ronaldsay Bird
Report) (1974-), From Mr EJ Williams, Fairholm,
Finstown, Orkney, KW17 2EQ.
e-mail:jim@geniefea.freeserve.co.uk

BTO Regional Representative
Colin Corse. 01856 874 484;
e-mail:ccorse@btinternet.com

Club
SOC ORKNEY BRANCH. (1993; 15). Colin Corse.
01856 874 484; e-mail:ccorse@btinternet.com
www.the-soc.org.uk
Meetings: 7.30pm, St Magnus Centre, Kirkwall.

Ringing Groups
NORTH RONALDSAY BIRD OBSERVATORY. Ms A E
Duncan, Twingness, North Ronaldsay, Orkney,
KW17 2BE. e-mail:alison@nrbo.prestel.co.uk
www.nrbo.co.uk

ORKNEY RG. Colin Corse, Garrisdale, Lynn Park,
Kirkwall, Orkney, KW15 1SL. H:01856 874 484;
e-mail:ccorse@btinternet.com

SULE SKERRY RG. Dave Budworth, 121 Wood
Lane, Newhall, Swadlincote, Derbys, DE11 0LX.
01283 215 188.

RSPB Members' Group
ORKNEY. (1985;300 in catchment area). Dick
Matson, 01856 751 426;
e-mail:p.wilson410@btinternet.com
Meetings: Meetings advertised in newsletter and
local press, held at St Magnus Centre, Kirkwall.

Wetland Bird Survey Organiser
ORKNEY. Mr ER Meek, Smyril, Stenness,
Stromness, Orkney KW16 3JX. 01856 851 755;
07879 238 391; e-mail:erandammeek@gmail.com

OUTER HEBRIDES

Bird Recorders
OUTER HEBRIDES AND WESTERN ISLES. Yvonne
Benting (joint recorder).07501 332 803;
e-mail:recorder@outerhebridesbirds.org.uk

OUTER HEBRIDES AND WESTERN ISLES. Ian
Thompson (joint recorder);
e-mail:recorder@outerhebridesbirds.org.uk

Bird Report
OUTER HEBRIDES BIRD REPORT (1989-91 and
1997-2007), From Brian Rabbitts, 6 Carinish,
Isle of North Uist HS6 5HL01876 580 328;
e-mail:rabbitts@hebrides.net

BTO Regional Representatives
BENBECULA & THE UISTS. Yvonne Benting. 07501
332 803; e-mail:uistbto@gmail.com

LEWIS & HARRIS. Chris Reynolds. 01851 672 376;
e-mail:cmreynolds@btinternet.com

Ringing Group
SHIANTS AUK RG. Group Secretary, Jim Lennon,
The Dovecote, Main Street, Flintham, Newark
NG23 5LA. 01636 525 963.

Wetland Bird Survey Organisers
HARRIS & LEWIS. Ms Y Benting, Suthainn,
Askernish, Isle of South Uist, Western Isles HS8
5SY. 07837 253 698; e-mail: uistbto@gmail.com

UISTS AND BENBECULA. Ms Y Benting, Suthainn,
Askernish, Isle of South Uist, Western Isles HS8
5SY. 07837 253 698; e-mail:uistbto@gmail.co

ISLAY, JURA AND COLONSAY. Mr J S Armitage,
Airigh Sgallaidh, Portnahaven, Isle of Islay PA47
7SZ. 01496 860 396;
e-mail:jsa@ornquest.plus.com
www.islaybirder.blogspot.com/

PERTH & KINROSS

Bird Recorder
PERTH & KINROSS. Scott Paterson, 12 Ochil
View, Kinross, KY13 8TN. 01577 864 248,
e-mail:scottpaterson12@yahoo.co.uk

Bird Report
PERTH & KINROSS BIRD REPORT (1974-) -1974
- 2006 available as PDF's. 2006 onwards in
preparation, from The Recorder. 12 Ochil
View, Kinross, KY13 8TN. 01577 864 248,
e-mail:scottpaterson12@yahoo.co.uk

BTO Regional Representative
PERTHSHIRE. Richard Paul. 01882 632 212;
e-mail:richard@rannoch.info

Clubs
PERTHSHIRE SOCIETY OF NATURAL SCIENCE
(Ornithological Section). (1964; 25). Miss Esther
Taylor, 23 Verena Terrace, Perth,PH2 0BZ. 01738
621 986; e-mail:President@psns.org.uk
www.psns.org.uk
Meetings: 7.30pm, Fridays, twice monthly (Oct-
Mar), Perth Museum - check website for details.
Summer outings.

Wetland Bird Survey Organisers
LOCH LEVEN. Mr J Squire, c/o Scottish
Natural Heritage, The Pier, Kinross, KY13 8UF.
e-mail:jeremy.squire@snh.gov.uk

PERTH AND KINROSS (INLAND). Dr M V Bell, 48
Newton Crescent, Dunblane, Perthshire FK15 0DZ;
e-mail:mvbell34@tiscali.co.uk

TAY & EDEN ESTUARY. Mr N Elkins, 18 Scotstarvit

278

View, Cupar, Fife KY15 5DX. 01334 654 348;
e-mail:jandnelkins@btinternet.com

SHETLAND

Bird Recorders
FAIR ISLE. David Parnaby,
e-mail:fibo@btconnect.com

SHETLAND. Rob Fray, Sunnydell, Virkie, Shetland
ZE3 9JS. 01950 461 929;
e-mail:recorder@shetlandbirdclub.co.uk
www.shetlandbirdclub.co.uk

Bird Reports
FAIR ISLE BIRD OBSERVATORY REPORT (1949-),
From Scottish Ornithologists' Club, 21 Regent
Terrace, Edinburgh, EH7 5BT. 0131 556 6042

SHETLAND BIRD REPORT (1969-) £10 inc p&p, no
pre 1973 available, From Rob Fray, Shetland Bird
Club, Sunnydell, Virkie, Shetland ZE3 9JS.
e-mail:recorder@shetlandbirdclub.co.uk
£10 plus P&P.

BTO Regional Representative
Dave Okill. 01595 880 450;
e-mail:david@auroradesign.plus.com

Club
SHETLAND BIRD CLUB. (1973;
200). Helen Moncrieff;
e-mail: secretary@
shetlandbirdclub.co.uk
www.shetlandbirdclub.co.uk/
Meetings: See website for
details.

Ringing Groups
FAIR ISLE BIRD OBSERVATORY. Deryk Shaw, Bird
Observatory, Fair Isle, Shetland, ZE2 9JU.
e-mail:fairisle.birdobs@zetnet.co.uk

SHETLAND RG. Dave Okill, Heilinabretta, Trondra,
Shetland, ZE1 0XL. 01595 880 450

Wetland Bird Survey Organiser
SHETLAND. Mr P V Harvey, Headlands, Virkie,
Shetland ZE3 9JS. 01595 694 688; 07879 444 612;
e-mail:paul@shetlandamenity.org

WALES

Bird Report
WELSH BIRD REPORT. Published in January issue of
Welsh Birds. From Welsh Ornithological Society,
www.birdsinwales.org.uk

BTO Honorary Wales Officer
BTO WALES OFFICER. John Lloyd, Cynghordy Hall,
Cynghordy, Llandovery, Carms SA20 0LN;
e-mail: the_lloyds@dsl.pipex.com

Club
See Welsh Ornithological Society in National
Directory.

EASTERN AREA OF WALES

Bird Atlas/Avifauna
The Birds of Gwent by Venables et al, published
by Helm on behalf of Gwent
Ornithological Society.

The Birds of Radnorshire (2014) by
Peter Jennings.

The Gwent Atlas of Breeding Birds
by Tyler, Lewis, Venables & Walton
(Gwent Ornithological Society,
1987).

Bird Recorders
BRECONSHIRE. Andrew King, Heddfan, Pennorth,

Brecon, Powys LD3 7EX. 01874 658 351;
e-mail: andrew.king53@virgin.net

GWENT. Tom Chinnick;
-mail: countyrecorder@gwentbirds.org.uk

MONTGOMERYSHIRE. Mike Haigh;
e-mail: montbird@gmail.com

RADNORSHIRE (VC43). Pete Jennings, Park View,
Staunton-on-Arrow, Leominster HR6 9HT. 01544
388 905; e-mail: radnorshirebirds@hotmail.com

Bird Reports
BRECONSHIRE BIRDS (1962-), from Brecknock
Wildlife Trust.

BRECONSHIRE BIRDS (1962-), from Brecknock
Wildlife Trust.

GWENT BIRD REPORT (1964-), from Jerry Lewis,
Y Bwthin Gwyn, Coldbrook, Abergavenny,
Monmouthshire NP7 9TD. (H)01873 855 091;
(W)01633 644 856

MONTGOMERYSHIRE BIRD REPORT (1981-82-),
from Montgomeryshire Wildlife Trust.

MONTGOMERYSHIRE BIRD REPORT (1981-82-),
from Montgomeryshire Wildlife Trust.

BTO Regional Representatives
BRECKNOCK. John Lloyd, Cynghordy Hall,

Cynghordy, Llandovery, Carms, SA20 0LN. 01550 750 202; e-mail: the_lloyds@dsl.pipex.com

GWENT. Jerry Lewis, Y Bwthyn Gwyn, Coldbrook, Abergavenny, Monmouthshire NP7 9TD. 01873 855 091; e-mail: jmsl2587@yahoo.co.uk

MONTGOMERY. Jane Kelsall, 01970 872 019; e-mail: janekelsall@phonecoop.coop

RADNOR. Carlton Parry, 01597 824 050; e-mail: cj.parry@tiscali.co.uk

Clubs
THE GWENT ORNITHOLOGICAL SOCIETY. (1964; 420). Trevor Russell; e-mail: secretary@ GwentBirds.org.uk or via website; www.gwentbirds.org.uk
Meetings: 7.30pm, alternate Saturdays (Sept-Apr), Goytre Village Hall.

MONTGOMERYSHIRE WILDLIFE TRUST BIRD GROUP. (1997; 110). A M Puzey, Four Seasons, Arddleen, Llanymynech, Powys SY22 6RU. 01938 590 578. www.montwt.co.uk/bird_group.html
Meetings: 7.30pm, 3rd Wednesday of the month (Jan-Mar) and (Sep-Dec), Welshpool Methodist Hall.

RADNORSHIRE BIRD GROUP. Pete Jennings, Park View, Staunton-on-Arrow, Leominster HR6 9HT. 01544 388 905; e-mail: radnorshirebirds@hotmail.com
Co-ordinates bird recording and surveys in the county through the county recorder

Ringing Groups
GOLDCLIFF RG. Mr Richard M Clarke. e-mail: chykembro2@aol.com

LLANGORSE RG. (1987; 15). Jerry Lewis, Y Bwthyn Gwyn, Coldbrook, Abergavenny, Monmouthshire NP7 9TD. H:01873 855091; W:01633 644856

Wetland Bird Survey Organisers
BRECONSHIRE. Mr V A King, Heddfan, Pennorth, Brecon LD3 7EX. 01874 658 351; e-mail: andrew.king53@virgin.net

GWENT (excl. Severn Estuary). Dr W A Venables, 111 Blackoak Road, Cyncoed, Cardiff CF23 6QW. 01222 874000; 01222 756 697; e-mail: wa.venables@zen.co.uk

MONTGOMERYSHIRE. Ms J Kelsall, c/o WeBS Office, BTO, The Nunnery, Thetford, Norfolk IP24 2PU. 01970 872 019; e-mail:janekelsall@phonecoop.coop

RADNORSHIRE. Mr P P Jennings, Park View, Staunton-on-Arrow, Leominster, HR6 9HT. 01597 811 522; e-mail: ppjennings@hotmail.co.uk

Wildlife Trusts
BRECKNOCK WILDLIFE TRUST. (1963; 650). Lion House, Bethel Square, Brecon, Powys LD3 7AY. 01874 625 708; e-mail: enquiries@brecknockwildlifetrust.org.uk www.brecknockwildlifetrust.org.uk

GWENT WILDLIFE TRUST. (1963; 9,950). Seddon House, Dingestow, Monmouth, NP25 4DY. 01600 740 600; fax 01600 740 299; e-mail: info@gwentwildlife.org www.gwentwildlife.org

MONTGOMERYSHIRE WILDLIFE TRUST. (1982; 1000). 42 Broad Street, Welshpool, Powys, SY21 7RR. 01938 555 654; e-mail: info@montwt.co.uk www.montwt.co.uk

RADNORSHIRE WILDLIFE TRUST. (1987; 878). Warwick House, High Street, Llandrindod Wells, Powys LD1 6AG. 01597 823 298; e-mail:info@rwtwales.org www.radnorshirewildlifetrust.org.uk

NORTHERN AREA OF WALES

Bird Atlas/Avifauna
The Birds of Caernarfonshire by John Barnes (1998, from Lionel Pilling, 51 Brighton Close, Rhyl LL18 3HL).

Bird Recorders
ANGLESEY. Steve Culley, 22 Cae Derwydd, Cemaes Bay, Anglesey, LL67 0LP. 01407 710 542; e-mail: SteCul10@aol.com

CAERNARFONSHIRE. Rhion Pritchard, Pant Afonig, Hafod Lane, Bangor, Gwynedd LL57 4BU. e-mail: rhion678pritchard@btinternet.com

DENBIGHSHIRE & FLINTSHIRE. Ian Spence, 43 Blackbrook, Sychdyn, Mold, Flintshire CH7 6LT. 01352 750118; e-mail: ianspence.cr1@btinternet.com www.cbrg.org.uk

MEIRIONNYDD (Vice County Recorder). Jim Dustow, Warden, Lake Vyrnwy/Llyn Efyrnwy RSPB, Llanwddyn, Oswestry, Shropshire SY10 OLZ; e-mail: Jim.Dustow@rspb.org.uk

Bird Reports
BARDSEY BIRD OBSERVATORY ANNUAL REPORT, from the Warden, see Reserves.

CAMBRIAN BIRD REPORT (sometime Gwynedd Bird Report) (1953-), from Geoff Gibbs. 01248 681 936; e-mail: geoffkate.gibbs@care4free.net www.welshos.org.uk/cambrian/

NORTH-EAST WALES BIRD REPORT (2004-),

formerly *CLWYD BIRD REPORT (2002-2003)*, from Ian M Spence, 43 Blackbrook, Sychdyn, Mold, Flintshire CH7 6LT. 01352 750 118; e-mail: ianspence.cr1@btinternet.com www.cbrg.org.uk

MEIRIONNYDD BIRD REPORT Published in Cambrian Bird Report (above).
WREXHAM BIRDWATCHERS' SOCIETY ANNUAL REPORT (1982-), from The Secretary, Wrexham Birdwatchers' Society.

BTO Regional Representatives
ANGLESEY. Kelvin Jones. 01248 383285; e-mail: kelvin.jones@bto.org

CAERNARFON. Geoff Gibbs. 01248 681 936; e-mail: geoffkate.gibbs@care4free.net

CLWYD EAST. Dr Anne Brenchley, Ty'r Fawnog, 43 Black Brook, Sychdyn, Mold, Flints CH7 6LT. 01352 750 118; e-mail: anne.brenchley1@btinternet.com

CLWYD WEST. Mel ab Owain, 31 Coed Bedw, Abergele, Conwy, LL22 7EH. 01745 826 528; e-mail: melabowain@btinternet.com

MEIRIONNYDD. Rob Morton. 01341 422 426; e-mail: r.morton1@btinternet.com

Clubs
BANGOR BIRD GROUP. (1947; 100). Jane Prosser, 15 Victoria Street, Bangor, Gwynedd LL57 2HD. 01248 364 632.
Meetings: 7.30pm every Wednesday, Semester terms, Brambell Building, University of Bangor.

CAMBRIAN ORNITHOLOGICAL SOCIETY. (1952; 190). Dr D Jones, Hon. President.01248 601 319; e-mail: gareth.jones58@mail.com www.welshos.org.uk/cambrian/
Meetings: 7.30pm, 1st Friday of the month, Pensychnant Centre, Sychnant Pass.

CLWYD BIRD RECORDING GROUP (committee that produces the Bird Report). Giles Pepler, Secretary, e-mail: gilesp64@gmail.com www.cbrg.org.uk

CLWYD ORNITHOLOGICAL SOCIETY. (1956; 45). Angela Ross. 01745 338 493; e-mail: angela.ross@talktalk.net
Meetings: 7.30pm, last Wednesday in the month (Sep-Apr),Rhuddlan Community Centre, Parliament Street, Rhuddlan LL18 5AW.

DEE ESTUARY CONSERVATION GROUP. (1973; 25 grps). Richard Smith, Secretary, e-mail: decg@deeestuary.co.uk www.deeestuary.co.uk/decg.htm

DEESIDE NATURALISTS' SOCIETY. (1973; 1,000). The Secretary, e-mail: secretary@deesidenaturalists.org.uk www.deesidenaturalists.org.uk

WREXHAM BIRDWATCHERS' SOCIETY. (1974; 90). Miss Marian Williams, 10 Lake View, Gresford, Wrexham, Clwyd LL12 8PU. 01978 854 633.
Meetings: 7.30pm, 1st Friday of the month (Sep-Apr), Gresford Memorial Hall, Gresford.

Ringing Groups
BARDSEY BIRD OBSERVATORY. Steven Stansfield, Bardsey Island, off Aberdaron, Pwllheli, Gwynedd LL53 8DE. 07855 264151; e-mail: warden@bbfo.org.uk bbfo.org.uk; bbfo.blogspot.com

CHESHIRE SWAN GROUP. David Cookson, 01270 567 526; E-mail:Cheshireswans@aol.com http://cheshireswanstudygroup.wordpress.com (blog for Swan news, weather records, bird reports and photos).

MERSEYSIDE RG. Bob Harris, 3 Mossleigh, Whixall, Whitchurch, ShropshireSY13 2SA. Work 0151 706 4397; e-mail: harris@liv.ac.uk

SCAN RG. Dr D. Moss. e-mail: dorian@dorianmoss.com

RSPB Local Group
NORTH WALES. (1986; 80). John Beagan, 01492 531 409 (answerphone); e-mail: colwynbooks@waitrose.com www.rspb.org.uk/groups/northwales
Meetings: 7.30pm, 3rd Friday of the month (Sep-Apr), St Davids Church Hall, Penrhyn Bay, LLANDUDNO, Gwynedd, LL30 3EJ.

Wetland Bird Survey Organisers
ANGLESEY (other sites). Ian Sims, RSPB Malltraeth Marsh, Tai'r Gors, Pentre Berw, Gaerwen, Anglesey, LL60 6LB; e-mail: ian.sims@rspb.org.uk

CAERNARFONSHIRE . Rhion Pritchard, Pant Afonig, Hafod Lane, Bangor, Gwynedd LL57 4BU; e-mail: rhion678pritchard@btinternet.com

ARTRO/MAWDDACH/TRAETH BACH/DYSYNNI ESTUARY. Mr J Dustow, Warden, Lake Vyrnwy/ Llyn Efyrnwy RSPB, Llanwddyn, Oswestry, Shropshire SY10 OLZ; e-mail: Jim.Dustow@rspb.org.uk

MEIRIONNYDD (other sites). Mr TG Owen, Crochendy Twrog, Maentwrog, Blaenau Ffestiniog, Gwynedd LL41 3YU. 01766 590 302; e-mail: webs@bto.org

DEE ESTUARY. Mr C E Wells, The Cottage, 1 Well Lane, Ness, Neston, Wirral, Cheshire CH64 4AW; e-mail: colin.wells@rspb.org.uk

WALES

FORYD BAY. Mr S Hugheston-Roberts, c/o WeBS Office, BTO, The Nunnery, Thetford, Norfolk IP24 2PU; e-mail: simon.hr@btinternet.com

Wildlife Trust
NORTH WALES WILDLIFE TRUST. (1963; 6,450). 376 High Street, Bangor, Gwynedd, LL57 1YE. 01248 351 541; fax 01248 353 192; e-mail: nwwt@wildlifetrustswales.org www.northwaleswildlifetrust.org.uk

SOUTHERN AREA OF WALES

Bird Atlas/Avifauna
An Atlas of Breeding Birds in West Glamorgan by David M Hanford et al (Gower Ornithological Society, 1992).

Birds of Glamorgan by Clive Hurford and Peter Lansdown (Published by the authors, c/o National Museum of Wales, Cardiff, 1995)

Bird Recorders
GLAMORGAN (EAST). David RW Gilmore. 7779 176 766; e-mail: d.gilmore2@ntlworld.com

GOWER (WEST GLAMORGAN). Mark Hipkin; e-mail: markhipkin1@gmail.com

Bird Reports
EAST GLAMORGAN BIRD REPORT (title varies 1963-95) 1996-2011. From the Glamorgan Bird Club; http://www.glamorganbirds.org.uk/glamorgan-bird-club.html

GOWER BIRDS (1965-) - covers Swansea, Neath and Port Talbot counties, from Barry Stewart, 36 Pencaecrwn Road, Gorseinon, Swansea SA4 4FU. e-mail: gowerbirdsf@hotmail.co.uk www.glamorganbirds.org.uk

BTO Regional Representatives
EAST GLAMORGAN (former Mid & South Glam). Wayne Morris, 8 Hughes Street, Penygraig, Tonypandy, Rhondda Cynon Taf CF40 1LX. 01443 430 284; e-mail: eastglambto@gmail.com http://eastglambto.wordpress.com

GLAMORGAN (WEST). Alastair Flannagan, 27 Llys Dol, Morriston, Swansea SA6 6LD. 01792 537 439; e-mail: alastair.flannagan@ntlworld.com

Clubs
CARDIFF NATURALISTS' SOCIETY. (1867; 200). Mike Dean (Secretary)029 2075 6869; e-mail: secretary@cardiffnaturalists.org.uk www.cardiffnaturalists.org.uk
Meetings: 7.30pm, various evenings, Lecture Theatre, Room D.106, 1st floor of the UWIC Llandaff Campus, Western Avenue, Cardiff, CF5 2YB.

GLAMORGAN BIRD CLUB. (1990; 300). Graham Powell. 07414 813 853; e-mail: glambirds@gmail.com www.glamorganbirds.org.uk
Meetings: 7.30pm, 2nd Tuesday of winter months, Kenfig Reserve Centre.

GOWER ORNITHOLOGICAL SOCIETY. (1956; 120). Jeremy Douglas-Jones, 14 Alder Way, West Cross, Swansea, SA3 5PD. 01792 551 331; e-mail: jeremy@douglas-jones.biz www.glamorganbirds.org.uk
Meetings: 7.15pm, last Friday of the month (Sep-Mar), The Environment Centre, Pier Street, Swansea.

Ringing Groups
FLAT HOLM RG.

KENFIG RG. Mr D.G. Carrington, Kenfig NNR, Ton Kenfig, Bridgend, CF33 4PT. 01656 743 386; (M) 07779 978 738; e-mail: david.carrington@bridgend.gov.uk kenfignnr.blogspot.com www.bridgendcountryside.com

RSPB Local Groups
CARDIFF & DISTRICT. (1973:). Huw Moody-Jones. 01446 760 757; e-mail: huwmoodyjones@hotmail.com www.RSPB.org.uk/groups/cardiff
Meetings: 7.30pm, various Fridays (Sept-May), Llandaff Parish Hall, Llandaff, Cardiff.

WEST GLAMORGAN. (1985; 346). Maggie Cornelius. 01792 229 244; e-mail: RSPBwglamgrp@googlemail.com www.rspb.org.uk/groups/westglamorgan
Meetings: 7.30pm, Environment Centre, Pier Street, SWANSEA, SA1 1RY

Wetland Bird Survey Organisers
BURY INLET (NORTH). Mr J Lyndon, c/o WeBS Office, BTO, The Nunnery, Thetford, Norfolk IP24 2PU; e-mail: norma.jeffery@virginmedia.com

EAST GLAMORGAN. Mr D Jenkins-Jones, 18 St. Margarets Road, Whitchurch, Cardiff, South Glamorgan CF14 7AA. (Eve)02920 621 394; (M)07828 093 613; e-mail: jenkinsjones@btinternet.com

SEVERN ESTUARY. Dr W A Venables, 111 Blackoak Road, Cyncoed, Cardiff CF23 6QW. 01222 874 000; (eve)01222 756 697;e-mail: wa.venables@zen.co.uk

WEST GLAMORGAN. Mr J Lyndon, c/o WeBS Office, BTO, The Nunnery, Thetford, Norfolk IP24 2PU; e-mail: norma.jeffery@virginmedia.com

WALES

Wildlife Hospital
GOWER BIRD HOSPITAL. Karen Kingsnorth and Simon Allen, Valetta, Sandy Lane, Pennard, Swansea, SA3 2EW. 01792 371 630; e-mail: admin@gowerbirdhospital.org.uk www.gowerbirdhospital.org.ukAll species of wild birds, also hedgehogs and small mammals. Prior phone call essential. Gower Bird Hospital cares for sick, injured and orphaned wild birds and animals with the sole intention of returning them to the wild. Post release radio tracking projects, ringing scheme. Contact us for more information.

Wildlife Trust
WILDLIFE TRUST OF SOUTH AND WEST WALES. (2002; 4,000). Nature Centre, Parc Slip, Fountain Road, Tondu, Bridgend CF32 0EH. 01656 724 100; fax 01656 726 980; e-mail: info@welshwildlife.org www.welshwildlife.org

WESTERN AREA OF WALES

Bird Atlas/Avifauna
Birds of Ceredigion by Hywel Roderick and Peter Davis (2010).

Carmarthenshire Birds 2008/2009, by G. Harper, R. Hunt, J.V. Lloyd, Carmarthenshire Bird Club.

Birds of Pembrokeshire by Jack Donovan and Graham Rees (Dyfed Wildlife Trust, 1994).

Bird Recorders
CARMARTHENSHIRE. Gary Harper; e-mail: gary.harper3@gmail.com

CEREDIGION. Russell Jones, Bron y Gan, Talybont, Ceredigion, SY24 5ER. 07753 774 891; e-mail: russell.jones@rspb.org.uk

PEMBROKESHIRE. Jon Green, Crud Yr Awel, Bowls Road, Blaenporth, Ceredigion SA43 2AR. 01239 811 561; e-mail: jonrg@tiscali.co.uk

Bird Reports
CARMARTHENSHIRE BIRD REPORT (1982-) £6.80 by post or £6.30 online from www.carmarthenshirebirds.co.uk.

CEREDIGION BIRD REPORT (biennial 1982-87; annual 1988-2010) - costs £7 and is available from RSPB Ynys-hir, Teifi Marshes Welsh Wildlife Centre and Ystwyth Bookshop (Aberystwyth). Also available by post (cheques for £8 to include p&p payable to The Wildlife Trust for South and West Wales), from John Davis, Pantllidiart, Tristant, ABERYSTWYTH, SY23 4RQ

PEMBROKESHIRE BIRD REPORT (1981-) - £7, including postage, from Jon Green (County Recorder), Crud Yr Awel, Bowls Road, Blaenporth,

Cardigan SA43 2AR. e-mail: jonrg@tiscali.co.uk

BTO Regional Representatives
CARDIGAN. Moira Convery, 41 Danycoed, Aberystwyth, SY23 2HD. 01970 612 998; e-mail: moira.convery@gmail.com

CARMARTHEN. Terry Wells, 01267 238 836 ; e-mail: bto@twells.me.uk

PEMBROKE. Bob Haycock. 01834 891 667; e-mail: bob.rushmoor1@tiscali.co.uk

Clubs
CARMARTHENSHIRE BIRD CLUB. (2003; 120). Sian Rees-Harper. 01269 831 496; e-mail: via website www.carmarthenshirebirds.co.uk
Meetings: Winter evenings at WWT Penclacwydd (check website for details).

PEMBROKESHIRE BIRD GROUP. (1993; 60). Peter Royle (Secretary). 01646 636 970; e-mail: pdroyle@orlandon.co.uk http://pembrokeshirebirdgroup.blogspot.co.uk/
Meetings: 7.30pm, 1st Monday of the month (Oct-Apr), The Patch Community Centre, Furzy Park, Haverfordwest.

Ringing Group
PEMBROKESHIRE RG. J Hayes, 3 Wades Close, Holyland Road, Pembroke, SA71 4BN. 01646 687 036; e-mail: hayes313@btinternet.com

Wetland Bird Survey Organisers
CARDIGAN (incl Dyfi Estuary). Mr R J Jones, c/o WeBS Office, BTO, The Nunnery, Thetford, Norfolk IP24 2PU; e-mail: russell.jones@rspb.org.uk

CARMARTHENSHIRE. Mr T Wells, 24 Heol Beca, Carmarthen, SA31 3LS. 01792 205 693; e-mail: bto@twells.me.uk

PEMBROKESHIRE. Mrs A N Haycock, c/o WeBS Office, BTO, The Nunnery, Thetford, Norfolk IP24 2PU; e-mail: annie@rushmoorphotos.co.uk

Wildlife Hospital
NEW QUAY BIRD HOSPITAL. Jean Bryant, Penfoel, Cross Inn, Llandysul, Ceredigion, SA44 6NR. 01545 560 462.All species of birds. Fully equipped for cleansing oiled seabirds. Veterinary support.

Wildlife Trust
WILDLIFE TRUST OF SOUTH AND WEST WALES. (2002; 4,000). Nature Centre, Parc Slip, Fountain Road, Tondu, Bridgend CF32 0EH. 01656 724 100; (fax) 01656 726 980; e-mail: info@welshwildlife.org www.welshwildlife.org

CHANNEL ISLANDS

Wetland Bird Survey Organisers
CHANNEL ISLANDS (inland). Glyn Young. 01534 860 000; e-mail:glyn.young@durrell.org

ALDERNEY

Atlas/Avifauna
The Birds of Alderney, by JG Sanders. (The Press at St Anne, 2007).

Bird Recorder
Mark Atkinson; e-mail:atkinson@cwgsy.net

Bird Report
ALDERNEY SOCIETY AND COUNTY ORNITHOLOGICAL REPORT (1992-), from Recorder; e-mail: atkinson@cwgsy.net

BTO Regional Representative
See Guernsey.

Wetland Birds Survey Organiser
Trust Ecologist, Alderney Wildlife Trust Office, 51 Victoria Street, St Anne, Alderney GY9 3TA. 01481 822 935; e-mail:info@alderneywildlife.org

Wildlife Trust
ALDERNEY WILDLIFE TRUST. (2002; 460). Alderney Wildlife Trust Office, 51 Victoria Street, St Anne, Alderney GY9 3TA. 01481 822 935; e-mail:info@alderneywildlife.org www.alderneywildlife.org

GUERNSEY

Bird Atlas/Avifauna
Birds of the Bailiwick: Guernsey, Alderney, Sark and Herm by Duncan Spencer & Paul Hillion, (Jill Vaudin Publishing 2010).

Bird Recorder
Mark Lawlor; e-mail:mplawlor@cwgsy.net

Bird Report
REPORT & TRANSACTIONS OF LA SOCIETE GUERNESIAISE (1882-), from Recorder.

BTO Regional Representative
Philip Alexander. 01481 726 173; e-mail:alybru@cwgsy.net

Clubs
LA SOCIÉTÉ GUERNESIAISE (Ornithological Section). (1882; 1,400). Secretary, La Société Guernesiaise, Candie Gardens, St Peter Port, Port Guernsey GY1 1UG. 01481 725 093; e-mail:societe@cwgsy.net www.societe.org.gg
Meetings: First Thurs of month, 8pm, Candie Gardens lecture theatre, St Peter Port.

RSPB Local Group
GUERNSEY BAILIWICK. (1975; 350+). Donna Francis. 01481 232 632; e-mail:donna@cwgsy.net www.rspbguernsey.co.uk
Meetings: 8pm, La Villette Hotel, St Martins, Guernsey, GY4 6QG.

Wetland Bird Survey Organiser
GUERNSEY COAST. Mary Simmons, Les Maeures, Mont d'Aval, Castel, Guernsey GY5 7UQ. 01481 256 016; e-mail:msim@cwgsy.net

Wildlife Hospital
GUERNSEY. GSPCA ANIMAL SHELTER. Mrs Jayne Le Cras, Les Fiers Moutons, St Andrews, Guernsey, Channel Islands GY6 8UD. 01481 257 261; (emergency number 07781 104 082); e-mail:admin@gspca.org.gg www.gspca.org.gg
All species. Modern cleansing unit for oiled seabirds. 24-hour emergency service. Veterinary support.

JERSEY

Bird Recorder
Tony Paintin, Cavok, 16 Quennevais Gardens, St Brelade, Jersey, Channel Islands, JE3 8FQ. 01534 741 928; e-mail:cavokjersey@hotmail.com

Bird Report
JERSEY BIRD REPORT (1991-), from La Société Jersiaise, 7 Pier Road, St Helier, Jersey JE2 4XW; e-mail:societe@societe-jersiaise.org

BTO Regional Representative
Tony Paintin, Cavok, 16 Quennevais Gardens, St Brelade, Jersey, Channel Islands, JE3 8FQ. 01534 741 928; e-mail:cavokjersey@hotmail.com

Club
SOCIÉTIÉ JERSIAISE (Ornithological Section). (1948; 40). La Société Jersiaise, 7 Pier Road, St Helier, Jersey JE2 4XW. 01534 758 314; e-mail:societe@societe-jersiaise.org www.societe-jersiaise.org
Meetings: 8.00pm, alternate Thursdays throughout the year, Museum in St.Helier.

Wetland Bird Survey Organiser
JERSEY COAST. Roger Noel.
e-mail:rogernoel1@googlemail.com

Wildlife Hospital
JERSEY. JSPCA ANIMALS' SHELTER. The Manager, 89 St Saviour's Road, St Helier, Jersey, JE2 4GJ. 01534 724 331; e-mail:info@jspca.org.je www.jspca.org.je
All species. Expert outside support for owls and raptors. Oiled seabird unit. Veterinary surgeon on site. Educational Centre.

NORTHERN IRELAND

Bird Recorder
George Gordon, 2 Brooklyn Avenue, Bangor, Co Down, BT20 5RB. 028 9145 5763; e-mail: gordon@ballyholme2.freeserve.co.uk

Bird Reports
NORTHERN IRELAND BIRD REPORT, from Secretary, Northern Ireland, Birdwatchers' Association (see National Directory).

IRISH BIRD REPORT, Included in Irish Birds, BirdWatch Ireland in National Directory.

COPELAND BIRD OBSERVATORY REPORT, from the Bookings Secretary: David Galbraith, 028 9338 2539 or 07885 834 398;
e-mail: davidgalbraith903@btinternet.com

BTO Regional Representatives
BTO IRELAND OFFICER. Shane Wolsey. 028 9146 7947; e-mail:shane@swolsey.biz

ANTRIM & BELFAST. Adam McClure. 028 2827 1875; e-mail:a.d.mcclure84@hotmail.co.uk

ARMAGH. Stephen Hewitt;
e-mail: sjameshewitt@hotmail.com

DOWN. Kerry Leonard. 028 9145 2602;
e-mail:kerrysleonard@hotmail.com

FERMANAGH. Michael Stinson. 07890 358 239;
e-mail:mick.stinston@hotmail.com

LONDONDERRY. Charles Stewart, Bravallen, 18 Duncrun Road, Bellarena, Limavady, Co Londonderry BT49 0JD. 028 7775 0468;
e-mail:charles.stewart2@btinternet.com

TYRONE. Michael Stinson. 07890 358 239;
E-mail:mick.stinston@hotmail.com

BTO Garden BirdWatch Ambassador
Pat Flowerday. E-mail: pflowerday@utvinternet.com

Clubs
NORTHERN IRELAND BIRDWATCHERS' ASSOCIATION
See National Directory.

NORTHERN IRELAND ORNITHOLOGISTS' CLUB
See National Directory.

CASTLE ESPIE BIRDWATCHING CLUB (COMBER). (1995; 60). Dot Blakely, 8 Rosemary Park, Bangor, Co Down, BT20 3EX. 028 9145 0784;
e-mail: dotbirdblakely@gmail.com

Ringing Groups
COPELAND BIRD OBSERVATORY. C Chris Acheson;
e-mail: CWA70@hotmail.com

NORTH DOWN RINGING GROUP. Mr D C Clarke. 07774 780 750; e-mail: declan.clarke@homecall.co.uk;

RSPB Local Groups
ANTRIM. (1977; 23). Brenda Campbell. 02893 323 657; e-mail:brendacampbell@supanet.com
www.rspb.org.uk/groups/antrim
Meetings: 8pm, 2nd Monday of the month, College of Agriculture Food & Rural Enterprise, 22 Greenmount Road, Antrim.

BANGOR. (1973; 25). Fulton Somerville;
e-mail: fultonsomerville@yahoo.co.uk
Meetings: Trinity Presbyterian Church Hall, Main Street, Bangor, County Down.

BELFAST. (1970; 130). Derek McLain. 028 9334 1488;
e-mail: d.mclain@btinternet.com
Meetings: Cooke Centenary Church Hall, Park Road, Belfast BT7 2FW.

COLERAINE. (1978; 45). Peter Robinson, 34 Blackthorn Court, Coleraine, Co Londonderry, BT52 2EX. 028 7034 4361; e-mail: robinson493@btinternet.com
Meetings: 7.30pm, third Monday of the month (Sept-Apr), St Patricks Church, Minor Church Hall, Corner of Brook St and Circular Road, Coleraine.

FERMANAGH. (1977; 28). Doreen Brown. 028 6632 2479; e-mail: dbrown498@btinternet.com
Meetings: 8pm, Cathedral Hall, Halls Lane, Enniskillen BT74 7DR.

LARNE. (1974; 35). Jimmy Christie, 314 Coast Road, Ballygally, Co Antrim, BT40 2QZ. 028 2858 3223;
E-mail: candjchristie@btinternet.com
Meetings: 7.30pm, 1st Wednesday of the month, Larne Grammar School.

LISBURN. (1978; 30). Peter Galloway. 028 9266 1982;
E-mail: pgalloway56@o2.co.uk
www.rspblisburn.com
Meetings: 7.30pm, 4th Monday of the month, Friends Meeting House, 4 Magheralave Road, Lisburn.

Wetland Bird Survey Organisers
BANN ESTUARY. Hill Dick. 02870 329 720;
e-mail: webs@bto.org

BELFAST LOUGH. Shane Wolsey, 25 Ballyholme Esplanade, Bangor, County Down, BT20 5LZ. 07831 697 371; e-mail:shane@swolsey.biz

DUNDRUM BAY. Malachy Martin, Murlough NNR, Keel Point, Dundrum, Co. Down BT33 0NQ. 028 4375 1467; e-mail: Malachy.Martin@nationaltrust.org.uk

LARNE LOUGH. Doreen Hilditch;
E-mail: mail18brae@btinternet.com

LOUGH FOYLE. Matthew Tickner. 02890 491 547;
e-mail:matthew.tickner@rspb.org.uk

STRANGFORD LOUGH. Kerry Mackie, WWT Castle Espie; 78 Ballydrain Road, Co Down. 02891 874 146; e-mail: kerry.mackie@wwt.org.uk

Wildlife Hospital
TACT WILDLIFE CENTRE. Mrs Patricia Nevines, 2 Crumlin Road, Crumlin, Co Antrim, BT29 4AD. 028 9442 2900; e-mail: tactwildlife@btinternet.com www.tactwildlifecentre.org.uk All categories of birds treated and rehabilitated; released where

practicable, otherwise given a home. Visitors (inc. school groups and organisations) welcome by prior arrangement. Veterinary support.

Wildlife Trust
ULSTER WILDLIFE TRUST. (1978; 7.500). 3 New Line, Crossgar, Co Down, BT30 9EP. 028 4483 0282 (fax) 028 4483 0888; e-mail: info@ulsterwildlifetrust.org www.ulsterwildlifetrust.org

---

REPUBLIC OF IRELAND

BirdWatch Ireland, Unit 20, Block D, Bullford Business Campus, Kilcoole, Co. Wicklow, Ireland 353 (0)1 281 9878 E-mail: info@ birdwatchireland.ie www.birdwatchireland.ie

BirdWatchIreland

Rarities. Paul Milne, 100 Dublin Road, Sutton, Dublin 13, +353 (0)1 832 5653; e-mail: paul.milne@oceanfree.net

CLARE. John Murphy, e-mail: jemurphy@esatclear.ie

CORK. Mark Shorten, e-mail: mshorten@indigo.ie

DONEGAL. Ralph Sheppard, e-mail: rsheppard@eircom.net

DUBLIN, LOUTH, MEATH AND WICKLOW. Declan Murphy & Dick Coombes, e-mail: dmurphy@birdwatchireland.ie or e-mail: rcoombes@birdwatchireland.ie

GALWAY. Chris Peppiatt, e-mail: chris.peppiatt@iol.ie

KERRY. Michael O'Clery & Jill Crosher, e-mail: moclery@tinet.ie

LIMERICK. Tony Mee, Ballyorgan, Kilfinane, Co. Limerick.

MAYO. Tony Murray, National Parks and Wildlife, Lagduff More, Ballycroy, Westport; e-mail: murraytony@hotmail.com

MID-SHANNON. Stephen Heery, e-mail: sheery@eircom.net

MONAGHAN. Joe Shannon, e-mail: joeshan@eircom.net

WATERFORD. Paul Walsh, 16 Castlepoint, Crosshaven, Co. Cork; e-mail: pmwalsh@waterfordbirds.com

WEXFORD. Tony Murray, Wexford Wildfowl Reserve, North Slob; e-mail: murraytony@hotmail.com

Bird Reports
IRISH BIRD REPORT, contact BirdWatch Ireland in National, Directory).

CAPE CLEAR BIRD OBSERVATORY ANNUAL REPORT, from the observatory.

CORK BIRD REPORT (1963-71; 1976-), Cork Bird Report Editorial Team, Long Strand, Castlefreke, Clonakilty, Co. Cork; e-mail: cbr@corkecology.net

EAST COAST BIRD REPORT (1980-), Contact BirdWatch Ireland.

BirdWatch Ireland Branches
Branches may be contacted in writing via BirdWatch Ireland HQ (see entry in National Directory).

Ringing Groups
CAPE CLEAR B.O, Steve Wing, e-mail: steve.ccbo@gmail.com

GREAT SALTEE RINGING STATION, Mr O J Merne, 20 Cuala Road, Bray, Co Wicklow, Ireland, e-mail: omerne@eircom.net

MUNSTER RG, Mr K.P.C. Collins, Ballygambon, Lisronagh, Clonmel, County Tipperary, e-mail: kcsk@eircom.net

NATIONAL DIRECTORY

David Cromack

Anyone with an interest in waders, both amateur or professional, will find the Wader Study Group a useful resource. This National Directory provides information on scores of organisations serving the UK birding world.

National directory of organisations   288

National research projects   301

NATIONAL ORGANISATIONS

After the title of each organisation you will see (in brackets) the year the group was founded and, where known, the current membership figure.

ARMY ORNITHOLOGICAL SOCIETY (1960; 200)

Open to serving and retired MoD employees who have an interest in birdlife in general and in their local MoD estate. Activities include field meetings, expeditions, assistance with bird surveys and ringing projects, and a long term survey of seabirds on Ascension Island. Annual journal *Adjutant*. **Contact:** Membership Secretary, (email via the website), www.armybirding.com

ASSOCIATION FOR THE PROTECTION OF RURAL SCOTLAND (1926)

Works to protect Scotland's countryside from unnecessary or inappropriate development, recognising the needs of those who live and work there and the necessity of reconciling these with the sometimes competing requirements of recreational use.
Contact: Association for the Protection Rural Scotland, Gladstone's Land, 3rd Floor, 483 Lawnmarket, Edinburgh EH1 2NT. 0131 225 7012; e-mail: info@ruralscotland.org www.ruralscotland.btik.com

ASSOCIATION OF COUNTY RECORDERS AND EDITORS (1993; 120)

The basic aim of ACRE is to promote best practice in the business of producing county bird reports, in the work of Recorders and in problems arising in managing record systems and archives. Organises periodic conferences and publishes *newsACRE*.
Contact: The Secretary; e-mail: countyrec@cawos.org

BARN OWL TRUST (1988)

A registered charity dedicated to conserving the Barn Owl and its environment. It is the main source of Barn Owl information in the UK. It carries out surveys of old buildings, due for development, and advises on Barn Owl mitigation measures. A booklet *Barn Owls on Site*, a guide for developers and planners, published by English Nature is widely used by local authorities and other official bodies. Trust members have erected more than 2,000 nestboxes and is closely involved in habitat creation both on its own land and through farm visits.
Contact: Barn Owl Trust, Waterleat, Ashburton, Devon TQ13 7HU. 01364 653 026; www.barnowltrust.org.uk e-mail: info@barnowltrust.org.uk

BIRDING FOR ALL (formerly The Disabled Birder's Association) (2000; 750)

Birding For All is a registered charity and international movement, which aims to promote access to reserves and other birding places and to a range of services, so that people with different needs can follow the birding obsession as freely as able-bodied people. Membership is currently free and new members are needed to help send a stronger message to those who own and manage nature reserves to improve access when they are planning and improving facilities. DBA also seeks to influence those who provide birdwatching services and equipment. The DBA also runs overseas trips. Chairman, Bo Beolens.
Contact: Birding For All, 18 St Mildreds Road, Cliftonville, Margate CT9 2LT; e-mail: bo@birdingforall.com www.birdingforall.com

BIRD OBSERVATORIES COUNCIL (1970)

Aims to provide a forum for establishing closer links and co-operation between individual observatories and to help co-ordinate the work carried out by them. All accredited bird observatories affiliated to the Council undertake a ringing programme and provide ringing experience to those interested. Most are also provide accommodation for visiting birdwatchers.
Contact: Peter Howlett, 87 Halliard Court, Atlantic Wharf, Cardiff. CF10 4NH. e-mail: info@birdobscouncil.org.uk www.birdobscouncil.org.uk

BIRD STAMP SOCIETY (1986; 170)

Quarterly journal *Flight* contains philatelic and ornithological articles. Lists all new issues and identifies species. Runs a quarterly Postal Auction; number of lots range from 400 to 800 per auction. UK subs £14 per annum from 1st August.
Contact: Bob Wilks, Membership Secretary, 4 Curlew Road, Porthcawl, Mid-Glamorgan CF36 3QA; 01656 785 055; e-mail: bobwilks581@btinternet.com www.birdstampsociety.org

BIRDWATCH IRELAND (1968; 14,000 with a network of 20 branches)

The largest independent conservation orga=nisation in Ireland. Its primary objective is the protection of wild birds and their habitats in Ireland through the efforts of its staff, members and volunteers alike. It carries out extensive research and survey work, operates applied conservation projects and manages a network of reserves nationwide. It publishes *Wings* magazine and an annual journal *Irish Birds*.
Contact: BirdWatch Ireland, Unit 20, Block D, Bullford Business Campus, Kilcoole, Co. Wicklow, Ireland. +353 (0)1 2819 878; Fax: +353 (0)1 281 0997; e-mail: info@birdwatchireland.org www.birdwatchireland.ie

NATIONAL ORGANISATIONS

BRITISH BIRDS RARITIES COMMITTEE (1959, 16)
The Committee adjudicates records of species of rare occurrence in Britain (marked `R' in the Log Charts) and publishes its annual report in B*ritish Birds*. The BBRC also assesses records from the Channel Islands. In the case of rarities trapped for ringing, records should be sent to the Ringing Office of the British Trust for Ornithology, who will in turn forward them to the BBRC.
Contact: Nigel Hudson, Secretary, British Birds Rarities Committee, Carn Ithen, Trench Lane Old Town, St. Mary's, Isles of Scilly TR21 0PA, e-mail: secretary@bbrc.org.uk
www.bbrc.org.uk

BRITISH DECOY WILDFOWL CARVERS ASSOCIATION (1990)
The Association is a non-profitmaking organisation, run by carvers to promote all aspects of their art. Its aims are: to produce three annual *Wingspan* newsletters: to keep the members in touch with the art; to promote regional groups; to generate local interest; to organise competitions and exhibitions; and finally, to care generally for wildfowl carvers' interests. Each September the Association stages the Bakewell Festival of Bird Art in the Peak District, which includes the national carving championships.
Contact: www.bdwca.org.uk

BRITISH DRAGONFLY SOCIETY (1983; 1,500)
The BDS aims to promote the conservation and study

of dragonflies. Members receive two issues of *Dragonfly News* and *BDS Journal* each year. There are countrywide field trips, an annual members' day and training is available on aspects of dragonfly ecology. The BDS has published a booklet, *Dig a Pond for Dragonflies* containing advice on pond creation and maintenance to attract dragonflies. *Managing Habitats for Dragonflies* is aimed at countryside managers.
Contact: Mr H Curry, Hon Secretary, British Dragonfly Society, 23 Bowker Way, Whittlesey, Cambs PE7 1PY. e-mail: secretary@british-dragonflies.org.uk
www.british-dragonflies.org.uk

BRITISH FALCONERS' CLUB (1927; 1,200)
Largest falconry club in Europe, with regional branches. Its aim is to encourage responsible falconers and conserve birds of prey by breeding, holding educational meetings and providing facilities, guidance and advice to those wishing to take up the sport. Publishes *The Falconer* annually and newsletter twice yearly.
Contact: British Falconers' Club, Westfield, Meeting Hill, Worstead, North Walsham, Norfolk NR28 9LS. 01692 404 057; www.britishfalconersclub.co.uk
e-mail: admin@britishfalconersclub.co.uk

BRITISH LIBRARY SOUND ARCHIVE - WILDLIFE SOUNDS (1969).
The most comprehensive collection of bird sound recordings in existence: over 150,000 recordings

of more than 8,000 species of birds worldwide, available for free listening. Copies or sonograms of most recordings can be supplied for private study or research and, subject to copyright clearance, for commercial uses. Contribution of new material and enquiries on all aspects of wildlife sounds and recording techniques are welcome. Publishes *Bioacoustics* journal, CD guides to bird songs and other wildlife, including ambience titles. Comprehensive catalogue available on-line at http://cadensa.bl.uk/uhtbin/cgisirsi/x/x/0/49/
Contact: Cheryl Tipp, Curator, Wildlife Sounds, The British Library Sound Archive, 96 Euston Road, London NW1 2DB. 020 7412 7403; (Fax) 020 7412 7441; e-mail: wildlifesound@bl.uk
www.bl.uk/reshelp/findhelprestype/sound/wildsounds/wildlife.html

BRITISH NATURALISTS ASSOCIATION (1905)
The association was founded to promote the interests of nature lovers and bring them together. It encourages and supports schemes and legislation for the protection of the country`s natural resources. It organises meetings, field weeks, lectures and exhibitions to help popularise the study of nature. BNA publishes two magazines, *Countryside* (bi-annual) and *British Naturalist* (bi-annual).
Contact: General Secretary, BNA, BM 8129, London WC1N 3XX. 0844 892 1817; www.bna-naturalists.org
e-mail: info@bna-naturalists.org

BRITISH ORNITHOLOGISTS' CLUB (1892; 450)
The Club's objects are 'the promotion of scientific discussion between members of the BOU, and others interested in ornithology, and to facilitate the publication of scientific information in connection with ornithology'. The Club maintains a special interest in avian systematics, taxonomy and distribution and publishes the *Bulletin of the British Ornithologists' Club* quarterly, as well as a continuing series of publications. It also holds a number of evening meetings each year (see website for details).
Contact: BOC Office, British Ornithologists' Club, PO Box 417, Peterborough, PE7 3FX. (Tel/Fax) 01733 844 820; e-mail: boc@bou.org.uk
www.boc-online.org

BRITISH ORNITHOLOGISTS' UNION (1858; 1,100)
The BOU is one of the world's oldest and most respected ornithological societies. It aims to promote ornithology within the scientific and birdwatching communities, both in Britain and around the world. This is largely achieved by the publication of its quarterly international journal, Ibis, featuring work at the cutting edge of our understanding of the world's birdlife. It also runs an active programme of meetings, seminars and conferences covering major ornithological topics and issues of the day, the proceedings of which are

published free on the BOU website.
Via social media (see below/website for links) the BOU acts as a global ornithological hub providing details of newly published research articles, conferences, jobs, PhD opportunities and more. Work being undertaken around the world can include research projects that have received financial assistance from the BOU's on-going programme of Small Ornithological Research Grants and Career Development Bursaries (for ornithological students). The BOU also runs the Bird Grants website (www.birdgrants.net) which provides details of funding sources for ornithological research around the world. The BOU's Records Committee maintains the official British List (see below). It has also published a series of country/island group 'checklists' (see website for details)

Contact: Steve Dudley, British Ornithologists' Union, PO Box 417, Peterborough, PE7 3FX. (Tel/Fax) 01733 844 820; e-mail: bou@bou.org.uk www.bou.org.uk and www.ibis.ac.uk

BRITISH ORNITHOLOGISTS' UNION RECORDS COMMITTEE (11)
A standing committee of the British Ornithologists' Union, the BOURC's function is to maintain the British List, the official list of birds recorded in Great Britain. The up-to-date list can be viewed on the BOU website. Where vagrants are involved it is concerned only with those which relate to potential additions to the British List (ie first records). In this it differs from the British Birds Rarities Committee (qv).

It also examines, where necessary, important pre-1950 records, monitors introduced species for possible admission to, or deletion from, the List, and reviews taxonomy and nomenclature relating to the List. BOURC reports are published in Ibis and are also available via the BOU website.

Contact: Steve Dudley, BOURC, PO Box 417, Peterborough, PE7 3FX. (Tel/Fax) 01733 844 820; e-mail: bourc@bou.org www.bou.org.uk

BRITISH TRUST FOR ORNITHOLOGY (1933; 13,200)

A registered charity governed by an elected Council, BTO enjoys the support of a large number of county and local birdwatching clubs and societies through the BTO/Bird Clubs Partnership. Its aims are: 'To promote and encourage the wider understanding, appreciation and conservation of birds through scientific studies using the combined skills and enthusiasm of its members, other birdwatchers and staff.'

Through the fieldwork of its members and other birdwatchers, the BTO is responsible for the majority of the monitoring of British birds, British bird population and their habitats. BTO surveys include the National Ringing Scheme, the Nest Record Scheme, the Breeding Bird Survey (in collaboration with JNCC and RSPB), and the Waterways Breeding Bird Survey, which all contribute to an integrated programme of population monitoring.

The BTO also runs projects on the birds of farmland and woodland, also (in collaboration with WWT, RSPB and JNCC) the Wetland Bird Survey, in particular Low Tide Counts. Garden BirdWatch, now has more than 14,000 participants. The Trust has 140 voluntary regional representatives (see County Directory) who organise fieldworkers for the BTO's programme of national surveys in which members participate. The results of these co-operative efforts are communicated to government departments, local authorities, industry and conservation bodies for effective action.

For details of current activities see National Projects. Members receive *BTO News* six times a year and have the option of subscribing to the thrice-yearly journal, *Bird Study* and twice yearly *Ringing & Migration*. Local meetings are held in conjunction with bird clubs and societies; there are regional and national birdwatchers' conferences, and specialist courses in bird identification and modern censusing techniques. Grants are made for research, and members have the use of a lending and reference library at Thetford and the Alexander Library at the Edward Grey Institute of Field Ornithology (qv)

Contact: British Trust for Ornithology, The Nunnery, Thetford, Norfolk IP24 2PU. 01842 750 050; (Fax) 01842 750 030; e-mail: info@bto.org www.bto.org

BTO SCOTLAND (2000; 989)
BTO Scotland's main functions are to promote the work of the Trust and develop wider coverage for surveys in Scotland, by encouraging greater participation in survey work. It also seeks to develop contract research income within Scotland. BTO Scotland ensures that the Trust's work is not just related to the priorities of the UK as a whole but is also focused on the priorities of Scotland, with a landscape and wildlife so different from the rest of the UK.

Contact: BTO Scotland, British Trust for Ornithology, Biological and Environmental Sciences, University of Stirling, Stirling FK9 4LA. 01786 466 560 (Fax) 01786 466 561; e-mail: scot.info@bto.org www.bto.org

BRITISH WATERFOWL ASSOCIATION
The BWA is an association of enthusiasts interested in keeping, breeding and conserving all types of waterfowl, including wildfowl and domestic ducks and geese. It is a registered charity, without trade affiliations, dedicated to educating the public about waterfowl and the need for conservation as well as to raising the standards of keeping and breeding ducks, geese and swans in captivity. Publishes *Waterfowl* magazine for members three times a year

Contact: BWA Secretary, Kate Elkington
The Old Bakehouse, Ashperton, Ledbury HR8 2SA. 01531 670658; e-mail: info@waterfowl.org.uk www.waterfowl.org.uk

BRITISH WILDLIFE REHABILITATION COUNCIL (1987)
Promoting the care and rehabilitation of wildlife casualties through the exchange of information between people such as rehabilitators, zoologists and veterinary surgeons who are active in this

field. Organises an annual symposium or workshop. Publishes a regular newsletter, *The Rehabilitator*. Supported by many national bodies including the Zoological Society of London, the British Veterinary Zoological Society, the RSPCA, the SSPCA, and the Vincent Wildlife Trust.

Contact: To make a contribution - Janet Peto, BWRC, PO Box 8686, Grantham, Lincolnshire NG31 0AG; e-mail: admin@bwrc.org.uk www.bwrc.org.uk

TCV (formerly British Trust for Conservation Volunteers) (1959)

TCV's mission is to create a more sustainable future by inspiring people and improving places. It aims to enrich the lives of people, through volunteering opportunities, employment, improved health, and life skills development; to improve the biodiversity and local environment of 20,000 places and to support active citizenship in 5,000 community-based groups. TCV currently supports 140,000 volunteers to take practical action to improve their urban and rural environments. Publishes a quarterly magazine, *Roots*, a series of practical handbooks and a wide range of other publications.

Contact: TCV, Sedum House, Mallard Way, Potteric Carr, Doncaster DN4 8DB. 01302 388 883; e-mail: Information@tcv.org.uk www.tcv.org.uk

BUGLIFE – THE INVERTEBRATE CONSERVATION TRUST (2000)

The first organisation in Europe devoted to the conservation of all invertebrates, actively engaged in halting the extinction of Britain's rarest slugs, snails, bees, wasps, ants, spiders, beetles and many more. It works to achieve this through practical conservation projects; promoting the environmental importance of invertebrates and raising awareness about the challenges for their survival; assisting in the development of helpful legislation and policy and encouraging and supporting invertebrate conservation initiatives by other organisations in the UK, Europe and worldwide.

Contact: Buglife (ICT), 1st Floor, 90 Bridge Street, Peterborough PE1 1DY. 01733 201 210; e-mail: info@buglife.org.uk www.buglife.org.uk

CAMPAIGN FOR THE PROTECTION OF RURAL WALES (1928; 2,800)

Its aims are to help the conservation and enhancement of the landscape, environment and amenities of the countryside, towns and villages of rural Wales and to form and educate opinion to ensure the promotion of its objectives. It gives advice and information upon matters affecting protection, conservation and improvement of the visual environment.

Contact: Ty Gwyn, 31 High Street, Welshpool, Powys SY21 7YD. 01938 552 525 or 01938 556 212;

e-mail: info@cprwmail.org.uk www.cprw.org.uk

CENTRE FOR ECOLOGY & HYDROLOGY (CEH)

The work of the CEH, a component body of the Natural Environment Research Council, includes a range of ornithological research, covering population studies, habitat management and work on the effects of pollution. The CEH has a long-term programme to monitor pesticide and pollutant residues in the corpses of predatory birds sent in by birdwatchers, and carries out detailed studies on affected species. The Biological Records Centre (BRC), which is part of the CEH, is responsible for the national biological data bank on plant and animal distributions (except birds).

Contact: Centre for Ecology & Hydrology, Maclean Building, Benson Lane, Crowmarsh Gifford, Wallingford, Oxfordshire OX10 8BB. 01491 692 371. E-mail: enquiries@ceh.ac.uk www.ceh.ac.uk

CONSERVATION FOUNDATION (1982)

Created by David Bellamy and David Shreeve, it provides a means for people in public, private and not-for-profit sectors to collaborate on environmental causes. Over the years its programme has included award schemes, conferences, promotions, special events, field studies, school programmes, media work, seminars and workshops etc. The Conservation Foundation has created and managed environmental award schemes of all kinds including the Ford European Awards, The Trust House Forte Community Chest, The PA Golden Leaf Awards, The Co-op Save Our Species Awards, the Pollution Abatement Technology Awards and many others. For information about how to apply for current award schemes visit the website.

Contact: Conservation Foundation, 1 Kensington Gore, London SW7 2AR. 020 7591 3111; e-mail: info@conservationfoundation.co.uk www.conservationfoundation.co.uk

CLA (Country Land and Business Association) (1907; 36,000).

The CLA is at the heart of rural life and is the voice of the countryside for England and Wales, campaigning on issues which directly affect those who live and work in rural communities. Its members, ranging from some of the largest landowners, with interests in forest, moorland, water and agriculture, to some with little more than a paddock or garden, together manage 50% of the countryside.

Contact: Country Land and Business Association, 18 Belgrave Square, London, SW1X 8PQ. 020 7235 0511; (Fax) 020 7235 4696; e-mail: mail@cla.org.uk www.cla.org.uk

CPRE (Campaign to Protect Rural England) (1926; 60,000)

Patron HM The Queen. CPRE now has 43 county branches and 200 local groups. It highlights threats to the countryside and promotes positive solutions. In-depth research supports active campaigning, and through reasoned argument and lobbying, CPRE seeks to influence public opinion and decision-makers at every level. Membership is open to all.

NATIONAL ORGANISATIONS

Contact: Campaign to Protect Rural England, 5-11 Lavington Street, London SE1 0NZ. 020 7981 2800; (Fax) 020 7981 2899; e-mail: info@cpre.org.uk www.cpre.org.uk

DEPARTMENT OF THE ENVIRONMENT FOR NORTHERN IRELAND

Responsible for the declaration and management of National Nature Reserves, the declaration of Areas of Special Scientific Interest, the administration of Wildlife Refuges, the classification of Special Protection Areas under the EC Birds Directive, the designation of Special Areas of Conservation under the EC Habitats Directive and the designation of Ramsar sites under the Ramsar Convention. It administers the Nature Conservation and Amenity Lands (Northern Ireland) Order 1985, the Wildlife (Northern Ireland) Order 1985, the Game Acts and the Conservation (Natural Habitats, etc) Regulations (NI) 1995 and the Environment (Northern Ireland) Order 2002.

Contact: Environment and Heritage Service, Klondyke Building, Cromac Avenue, Gasworks Business Park, Lower Ormeau Road, Belfast BT7 2JA. 0845 302 0008; (pollution hotline; 0800 807 060); e-mail: nieainfo@doeni.gov.uk www.ehsni.gov.uk

EARTHWATCH INSTITUTE (1971)

Earthwatch developed the innovative idea of engaging the general public into the scientific process by bringing together individual volunteers and scientists on field research projects, thereby providing an alternative means of funding, as well as a dedicated labour force for field scientists. Last year, more than 3,500 volunteers had worked on Earthwatch projects, which have grown to 140 projects in more than 50 countries around the world.

Contact: Earthwatch Institute (Europe), Mayfield House, 256 Banbury Road, Oxford OX2 7DE. 01865 318 838; e-mail: info@earthwatch.org.uk http://eu.earthwatch.org/

EDWARD GREY INSTITUTE OF FIELD ORNITHOLOGY (1938)

The EGI takes its name from Edward Grey, first Viscount Grey of Fallodon, a life-long lover of birds and former Chancellor of the University of Oxford. The Institute now has a permanent research staff of 12-15 research students, five or six senior visitors and post-doctoral research workers. Field research is carried out mainly in Wytham Woods near Oxford and on the island of Skomer in West Wales. In addition there are laboratory facilities and aviary space for experimental work.

The Institute houses the Alexander Library, one of the largest collections of 20th Century material on birds in the world, and which is supported by the British Ornithologists Union which provides much of the material. It also houses the British Falconers Club library. The Library is open to members of the BOU and Oxford Ornithological Society; other bona fide ornithologists may use the library by prior arrangement.

Contact: Claire Harvey, PA to Professor Sheldon, The

EGI, Department of Zoology, South Parks Road, Oxford OX1 3PS; +44(0)1865 271 234; e-mail: claire.harvey@zoo.ox.ac.uk www.zoo.ox.ac.uk/egi/

ENVIRONMENT AGENCY

A non-departmental body which aims to protect and improve the environment and to contribute towards the delivery of sustainable development through the integrated management of air, land and water. Functions include pollution prevention and control, waste minimisation, management of water resources, flood defence, improvement of salmon and freshwater fisheries, conservation of aquatic species, navigation and use of inland and coastal waters for recreation. Sponsored by the Department of the Environment, Transport and the Regions, MAFF and the Welsh Office.

Contact: Environment Agency, National Customer Contact Centre, PO Box 544, Rotherham S60 1BY. General enquiries; 03708 506 506 (Mon-Fri, 8am - 6pm); pollution hotline 0800 807 060; floodline 0345 988 1188 or 0845 988 1188; www.environment-agency.gov.uk e-mail: enquiries@environment-agency.gov.uk

EURING

EURING is the co-ordinating organisation for European bird-ringing schemes. It aims to promote and encourage:

• Scientific and administrative co-operation between national ringing schemes.

• Development and maintenance of high standards in bird ringing.

• Scientific studies of birds, in particular those based on marked individuals.

• The use of data from bird ringing for the management and conservation of birds.

These objectives are achieved mainly through co-operative projects, the organisation of meetings and the collection of data in the EURING Data Bank.

Contact: www.euring.org/

FWAG ASSOCIATION (2011-) (previously FWAG)

The FWAG Association succeeded FWAG in 2011. It represents a coming together of the local Farming & Wildlife Advisory Groups which continue to serve the farming community up and down the country today, according to the original FWAG standards and values which unite farming and forestry with wildlife and landscape conservation.

Contact: FWAG Association e-mail: hello@fwag.org.uk www.fwag.org.uk

Local FWAG Groups:
Cumbria Farm Environment Partnership

01768 892 622; e-mail: hello@cumbriafep.co.uk
www.cumbriafep.co.uk

Farm Conservation Ltd. (Norfolk)
01603 814 869
e-mail: henry@farmconservation.co.uk
www.farmconservation.co.uk

FWAG South East
01233 813186/ 0771 3333 160
e-mail: paul.cobb@fwagadvice.co.uk
www.fwagadvice.co.uk

FWAG East (Cambs, Herts Essex & Beds)
01223 841 507
e-mail: hello@fwageast.org.uk
www.fwageast.org.uk

FWAG South West (including Herefordshire)
01823 355 427
e-mail: admin@fwagsw.org.uk
www.fwagsw.org.uk

Nottinghamshire Farming & Wildlife
01777 870 817/ 07707 220 121
e-mail: lesley.sharpe@nottsfarmingandwildlife.org
www.nottsfarmingandwildlife.org

Suffolk FWAG
01728 748 030
e-mail: tim.schofield@suffolkfwag.co.uk
www.suffolkfwag.co.uk

FIELD STUDIES COUNCIL (1943)
Manages Centres where students from schools,
universities and colleges, as well as individuals of
all ages, can stay to study various aspects of the
environment under expert guidance. Courses include
many for birdwatchers, providing opportunities to
study birdlife on coasts, estuaries, mountains and
islands. Others demonstrate bird ringing. Research
workers and naturalists wishing to use the records
and resources are welcome. There are centres in
England, Scotland, Wales and Northern Ireland — see
website for contacts and courses available.
Contact: Field Studies Council, Preston Montford,
Montford Bridge, Shrewsbury SY4 1HW. 0845 345
4071; 01743 852 100; www.field-studies-council.org
e-mail: enquiries@field-studies-council.org

FIELDFARE TRUST
Fieldfare works with people with disabilities and
countryside managers to improve access to the
countryside for everyone. It provides advice and
training services to countryside management teams,
supported by its research into national standards
for accessibility under the BT Countryside for All
Project. For members of the public, it runs projects
which can enable them to take action locally,
provide information on accessible places to visit
and run events like the Fieldfare Kielder Challenge
which encourages young people to get active in the
countryside.
Contact: Fieldfare Trust, Volunteer House, 69
Crossgate, Cupar, Fife KY15 5AS. 01334 657 708;
e-mail: info@fieldfare.org.uk www.fieldfare.org.uk

FORESTRY COMMISSION OF GREAT BRITAIN (1919)
The government department responsible for the
protection and expansion of Britain's forests and
woodlands, it runs from national offices in England,
Wales and Scotland, working to targets set by
Commissioners and Ministers in each of the three
countries. Its objectives are to protect Britain's
forests and resources, conserve and improve the
biodiversity, landscape and cultural heritage of
forests and woodlands, develop opportunities
for woodland recreation and increase public
understanding and community participation in
forestry.
Contact: *Forestry Commission England*, England
National Office, 620 Bristol Business Park,
Coldharbour Lane, Bristol BS16 1EJ. 0117 906 6000:
e-mail: fe.england@forestry.gsi.gov.uk
www.forestry.gov.uk

Forestry Commission Scotland
231 Corstorphine Road, Edinburgh EH12 7AT. 0300 067
6156; e-mail: fcscotland@forestry.gsi.gov.uk
http://scotland.forestry.gov.uk/

Forestry Commission Wales
Natural Resources Wales, Tŷ Cambria, 29 Newport
Road, Cardiff CF24 0TP. 0300 065 3000:
E-mail: enquiries@naturalresourceswales.gov.uk
www.naturalresourceswales.gov.uk

FRIENDS OF THE EARTH (1971; 100,000)
The largest international network of environmental
groups in the world, represented in 68 countries.
In the UK it has a unique network of campaigning
local groups, working in 200 communities in England,
Wales and Northern Ireland. It is largely funded by
supporters with more than 90% of income coming
from individual donations, the rest from special
fundraising events, grants and trading.
Contact: Friends of the Earth, The Printworks,
1st Floor, 139 Clapham Road, London SW9 0HP.
020 7490 1555; www.foe.co.uk

Friends of the Earth Cymru
33 Castle Arcade Balcony, Cardiff CF10 1BY. 029 2022
9577; e-mail: cymru@foe.co.uk
www.foe.co.uk/cymru

Friends of the Earth Northern Ireland
7 Donegall Street Place, BELFAST BT1 2FN.
028 9023 3488; e-mail: foe-ni@foe.co.uk
www.foe.co.uk/northern_ireland

Friends of the Earth Scotland
Thorn House, 5 Rose Street, Edinburgh EH2 2PR.
0131 243 2700; www. www.foe-scotland.org.uk

GAME AND WILDLIFE CONSERVATION TRUST (1933; 22,000)
A registered charity which researches
the conservation of game and other
wildlife in the British countryside.
More than 60 scientists are engaged
in detailed work on insects,
pesticides, birds (30 species inc.
raptors) mammals (inc. foxes), and

habitats. The results are used to advise government, landowners, farmers and conservationists on practical management techniques which will benefit game species, their habitats, and wildlife. Each June the *Annual Review* lists about 50 papers published in the peer-reviewed scientific press.
Contact: Game & Wildlife Conservation Trust, Burgate Manor, Fordingbridge, Hampshire, SP6 1EF. 01425 652 381; (Fax) 01425 655 848; e-mail: info@gwct.org.uk www.gwct.org.uk

GAY BIRDERS CLUB (1994; 350+)
A voluntary society for lesbian, gay and bisexual birdwatchers, their friends and supporters, over the age of consent, in the UK and worldwide. The club has a network of regional contacts and organises day trips, weekends and longer events at notable birding locations in the UK and abroad; about 200+ events in a year. Members receive a quarterly newsletter Out *Birding* with details of all events. There is a Grand Get-Together every 18 months. Membership £12 waged and £5 unwaged.
Contact: Gay Birders Club, GeeBeeCee, BCM-Mono, London WC1N 3XX. e-mail: contact@gbc-online.org.uk www.gbc-online.org.uk

HAWK AND OWL TRUST (1969)

Hawk
and
Owl
Trust

Registered charity dedicated to the conservation and appreciation of wild birds of prey and their habitats. Publishes a newsletter members' magazine, *Peregrine* and educational materials for all ages. The Trust achieves its major aim of creating and enhancing nesting, roosting and feeding habitats for birds of prey through projects which involve practical research, creative conservation and education, both on its own reserves and in partnership with landowners, farmers and others. Members are invited to take part in fieldwork, population studies, surveys, etc. The Trust manages three main reserves: Sculthorpe Moor in Norfolk; Shapwick Moor on the Somerset Levels; and Fylingdales Moor conservation area in North Yorkshire. Its Sculthorpe reserve near Fakenham, Norfolk and National Conservation and Education Centre at Chiltern Open Air Museum near Chalfont St Giles, Buckinghamshire, offers schools and other groups cross-curricular environmental activities
Contact: Hawk and Owl Trust, PO Box 400, Bishops Lydeard, Taunton TA4 3WH. 0844 984 2824; e-mail: enquiries@hawkandowl.org www.hawkandowl.org

HELPWILDLIFE.CO.UK (2005)
HelpWildlife.co.uk is maintained by a very small team of people involved in British wildlife rehabilitation to fully utilise the internet to help with wildlife issues. The site aims to provide informed, unbiased advice about caring for sick or injured birds and animals. Volunteers trawl the internet for details of those who might be able to help so that assistance can be offered quickly in an emergency. Visitors to the site are invited to provide feedback on the listings published to ensure they are kept as up to date as possible. E-mail: info@helpwildlife.co.uk www.helpwildlife.co.uk

INTERNATIONAL CENTRE FOR BIRDS OF PREY (1967)
The ICBP works for the conservation of birds of prey and their habitats through public education, captive breeding, treatment and rehabilitation of wild injured birds of prey. Education is on-going to visitors and specific groups and parties, from first schools to universities, offering off-site lectures and teaching. The Centre continues its captive breeding aims; to research species; maintain the Collection and provide birds for demonstrations.
The Centre also works with many other groups and facilities to continue to support worldwide field research projects and international conservation programmes. It accepts, treats and rehabilitates injured wild birds of prey. Open all year 10.30am-5.30pm (or dusk if earlier). Closed Christmas and Boxing Day.
Contact: International Birds of Prey Centre, Boulsdon House, Newent, Gloucestershire, GL18 1JJ. 01531 820 286; e-mail: info@icbp.org www.icbp.org

IRISH RARE BIRDS COMMITTEE (1985)
Assesses records of species of rare occurrence in the Republic of Ireland. Details of records accepted and rejected are incorporated in the *Irish Bird Report*, published annually in *Irish Birds*. In the case of rarities trapped for ringing, ringers in the Republic of Ireland are required to send their schedules initially to the National Parks and Wildlife Service, 51 St Stephen's Green, Dublin 2. A copy is then taken before the schedules are sent to the British Trust for Ornithology.
Contact: Secretary: Kieran Fahy, Silveracre, Yoletown, Tacumshin, County Wexford. e-mail: secretary@irbc.ie www.irbc.ie

JOINT NATURE CONSERVATION COMMITTEE (1990)
A committee of the three country agencies (English Nature, Scottish Natural Heritage and the Countryside Council for Wales), together with independent members and representatives from Northern Ireland and the Countryside Agency. Supported by specialist staff, its statutory responsibilities include the establishment of common standards for monitoring; the analysis of information and research; advising Ministers on the development and implementation of policies for or affecting nature conservation; and the undertaking and commissioning of research relevant to these functions. JNCC additionally has the UK responsibility for relevant European and wider international matters. The Species Team, located at the HQ address is responsible for terrestrial bird conservation.
Contact: Joint Nature Conservation Committee, Monkstone House, City Road, Peterborough PE1 1JY. 01733 562 626; e-mail: comment@jncc.gov.uk www.jncc.gov.uk

LINNEAN SOCIETY OF LONDON (1788: 2,000)

Named after Carl Linnaeus, the 18th Century Swedish biologist, who created the modern system of scientific biological nomenclature, the Society promotes all aspects of pure and applied biology. It houses Linnaeus' collection of plants, insects and fishes, library and correspondence. The Society has a major reference library of some 100,000 volumes. Publishes the *Biological, Botanical* and *Zoological* Journals, and the *Synopses of the British Fauna*.
Contact: Linnean Society of London, Burlington House, Piccadilly, London W1J 0BF. 020 7434 4479 (ext.13); e-mail: info@linnean.org www.linnean.org

MAMMAL SOCIETY (1954; 2,500)

The Mammal Society is the only organisation solely dedicated to the study and conservation of all British mammals. It seeks to raise awareness of mammal ecology and conservation needs, to survey British mammals and their habitats to identify the threats they face and to promote mammal studies in the UK and overseas.
Contact: The Mammal Society, 3 The Carronades, New Road, Southampton SO14 0AA. 023 8023 7874 or 023 8001 0981; e-mail: info@themammalsociety.org www.mammal.org.uk

MARINE CONSERVATION SOCIETY (1983)

MCS is the UK charity that campaigns for clean seas and beaches around the British coastline, sustainable fisheries, and protection for all marine life. MCS  is consulted on a wide range of marine issues and provides advice primarily to government, but also to industry, on topics ranging from offshore wind, oil and gas, to marine strategies and fisheries reform. It provides advice to ensure that further action is taken to conserve our seas and reduce the effect of marine activities on marine habitats and species. It has an extensive programme for volunteers, ranging from fund-raising and an annual clean-up of UK beaches, to surveys of species such as basking shark.
Contact: Marine Conservation Society, Over Ross House, Ross Park, Ross-on-Wye HR9 7QQ. 01989 566 017; www.mcsuk.org

NATIONAL TRUST (1895; 3.5 million)

Charity that works for the preservation of places of historic interest or natural beauty in England, Wales and Northern Ireland. It relies on 3.5 million members, 49,000 volunteers, 500,000 school children and millions of visitors, donors and supporters. The Trust protects and opens to the public more than 300 historic houses and gardens, 49 industrial monuments and mills, plus more than 617,500 acres of land and 700 miles of coast. About 10% of SSSIs and ASSIs in England, Wales and Northern Ireland are wholly or partially owned by the Trust, as are 63 NNRs, 33% of Ramsar sites and 45% of SPAs. Central Office: Heelis, Kemble Drive, Swindon, Wiltshire SN2 2NA. Tel: 01793 817 400; (Fax) 01793 817 401.

Contact: The National Trust, PO Box 574, Manvers, Rotherham, S63 3FH. 0844 800 1895; Email: enquiries@nationaltrust.org.uk www.nationaltrust.org.uk

NATIONAL TRUST FOR SCOTLAND (1931; 310,000)

The conservation charity that protects and promotes Scotland's natural and cultural heritage for present and future generations to enjoy. Its 128 properties open to the public are described in its annual *Scotland For You* guide.
Contact: The National Trust for Scotland, Hermiston Quay, 5 Cultins Rd, Edinburgh EH11 4DF. 0844 493 2100; e-mail: information@nts.org.uk www.nts.org.uk

NATURAL ENGLAND

Natural England has been formed by bringing together English Nature, the landscape, access and recreation elements of the Countryside Agency and the environmental land management functions of the Rural Development Service. Natural England is working towards the delivery of four strategic outcomes: 1) A healthy natural environment through conservation and enhancement. 2) Encouraging more people to enjoy, understand and act to improve the natural environment. 3) Ensure the use and management of the natural environment is more sustainable. 4) A secure environmental future.
Contact: Natural England, Head Office – Foundry House, 3 Millsands, Riverside Exchange, Sheffield S3 8NH. 0845 600 3078; e-mail: enquiries@naturalengland.org.uk www.naturalengland.org.uk

NATURAL HISTORY MUSEUM AT TRING (1937)

Founded by Lord Rothschild, the Museum displays British and exotic birds (1,500 species) including many rarities and extinct species. Galleries open all year except Dec 24-26. Adjacent to the Bird Group of the Natural History Museum - with over a million specimens and an extensive ornithological library, an internationally important centre for bird research.
Contact: The Natural History Museum at Tring, Akeman Street, Tring, Herts HP23 6AP. 020 7942 6171; e-mail: tring-enquiries@nhm.ac.uk www.nhm.ac.uk/tring

NATURAL RESOURCES WALES

Natural Resources Wales brings together the work of the Countryside Council for Wales, Environment Agency Wales and Forestry Commission Wales, as well as some functions of Welsh Government. Its purpose is to ensure that the natural resources of Wales are sustainably maintained, enhanced and used, now and in the future.
Contact: Natural Resources Wales, Tŷ Cambria, 29 Newport Road, Cardiff CF24 0TP. 0300 065 3000 (Mon-Fri, 8am - 6pm). Incident hotline: 0800 807 060 (Freephone, 24 hour service). Floodline: 0845 988 1188 (24 hour service); E-mail: enquiries@naturalresourceswales.gov.uk www.naturalresourceswales.gov.uk

NATIONAL ORGANISATIONS

NATURE PHOTOGRAPHERS' PORTFOLIO (1944; 71)
A society for photographers of wildlife, especially birds. Circulates postal portfolios of prints and transparencies, and an on-line folio.
Contact: General Secretary, Geoff White, 38 Village Way, Farndon, Newark NG24 4SX. 01636 658 356; e-mail: kwibble@virginmedia.com
www.nature-photographers-portfolio.co.uk

NORTHERN IRELAND BIRDWATCHERS' ASSOCIATION (1991; 120)
The NIBA Records Committee, established in 1997, has full responsibility for the assessment of records in N Ireland. NIBA also publishes the Northern Ireland Bird Report and is responsible for Flightline, a local rate telephone hotline for rare bird sightings.
Contact: Northern Ireland Birdwatchers' Assoc, 028 9146 7408; e-mail: nibirds@live.co.uk
http://nibirds.blogspot.com

NORTHERN IRELAND ORNITHOLO-GISTS' CLUB (1965; 150)
Formed to focus the interests of active birdwatchers in Northern Ireland, it operates Tree Sparrow and Barn Owl nestbox schemes and a winter feeding programme for Yellowhammers. Has a regular programme of lectures and field trips for members and organises a high quality annual photographic competition. Publishes *The Harrier* quarterly.

Contact: The Honorary Secretary, C Gillespie, Northern Ireland Ornithologists Club, 4 Demesne Gate, Saintfield, Co. Down, BT24 7BE. 02897 519 371; e-mail: carolgillespie@btinternet.com;
www.nioc.co.uk

NORTH SEA BIRD CLUB (1979; 200)
The Club aims to: provide a recreational pursuit for people employed offshore; obtain, collate and analyse observations of all birds seen offshore; produce reports of observations, including an annual report; promote the collection of data on other wildlife offshore. Currently it holds in excess of 100,000 records of birds, cetaceans and insects reported since 1979.
Contact: The North Sea Bird Club, Ocean Laboratory and Culterty Field Station, Newburgh, Aberdeenshire AB41 6AA. 01224 274 428; e-mail: nsbc@abdn.ac.uk
www.abdn.ac.uk/nsbc

PEOPLE'S DISPENSARY FOR SICK ANIMALS (1917)
Provides free veterinary treatment for sick and injured animals whose owners qualify for this charitable service.
Contact: PDSA, Whitechapel Way, Priorslee, Telford, Shropshire TF2 9PQ. 01952 290 999;
www.pdsa.org.uk

POND CONSERVATION
Pond Conservation is dedicated to creating and protecting ponds and the wildlife they support.

It carries out research, surveys and practical conservation, working in partnership with others. It also works to protect the wildlife of other freshwaters. Key projects include: the Million Ponds Project; Garden ponds survey; Pond Habitat Action Plan, in conjunction with the Environment Agency.
Contact: Pond Conservation, 01865 483 249; e-mail: info@freshwaterhabitats.org.uk
www.pondconservation.org.uk

RAPTOR FOUNDATION (1989)
Involved in the care of wild, disabled birds of prey, as well as raptors rescued from breeders. The foundation researches raptor ailments and assists veterinary schools. A full 24 hour rescue service is available for injured raptors and owls and the centre assists in breed-and-release schemes to rebuild populations across Europe. Centre is open to the public (200 birds of 40 different species on display) 10am to 5pm each day apart from Jan 1 and Dec 25/26.
Contact: The Raptor Foundation, The Heath, St Ives Road, Woodhurst, Cambs PE28 3BT. 01487 741 140; e-mail: info@raptorfoundation.org.uk
www.raptorfoundation.org.uk

RAPTOR RESCUE (1978)
Since inauguration, Raptor Rescue has evolved into one of the UK's foremost organisations dedicated to ensuring all sick and injured birds of prey are cared for by suitably qualified people, and wherever possible, released back into the wild. Facilities include secluded aviaries, rehabilitation aviaries/ flights, and foster birds for rearing young to avoid imprinting.
Contact: Raptor Rescue, Bird of Prey Rehabilitation, 0870 241 0609; www.raptorrescue.org.uk
e-mail: secretary@raptorrescue.org.uk

RARE BREEDING BIRDS PANEL (1973; 7)
An independent body funded by the JNCC and RSPB, it collects all information on rare breeding birds in the United Kingdom, so that changes in status can be monitored as an aid to conservation and stored for posterity. Special forms are used (obtainable from the website) and records should be submitted via the county and regional recorders. Since 1996 the Panel also monitors breeding by scarcer non-native species and seeks records of these in the same way. Annual report is published in *British Birds*. For details of species covered by the Panel see Log Charts and the websites.
Contact: The Secretary, Rare Breeding Birds Panel, The Old Orchard, Grange Road, North Berwick, East Lothian EH39 4QT. 01620 894 037; e-mail: secretary@rbbp.org.uk www.rbbp.org.uk

ROYAL AIR FORCE ORNITHOLOGICAL SOCIETY (1965; 250)
RAFOS organises regular field meetings for members, carries out ornithological census work on MoD properties and mounts major expeditions annually to various UK and overseas locations. Publishes a Newsletter twice a year, a Journal annually, and reports on its expeditions and surveys.

Contact: General Secretary;
e-mail: rafos_secretary@hotmail.com
www.rafos.org.uk

ROYAL NAVAL BIRDWATCHING SOCIETY (1946; 250)

Covering all main ocean routes, the Society reports the positions and identity of seabirds and landbirds at sea by means of standard sea report forms. Maintains an extensive worldwide seabird database. Members are encouraged to photograph birds and a library of images is maintained. Publishes a Bulletin and an annual report entitled *The Sea Swallow*. The Simpson Scholarship provides assistance to embryonic ornithologists for studies regarding seabirds and landbirds at sea.
Contact: General Secretary, Cdr Stuart Lawrence; www.rnbws.org.uk

ROYAL PIGEON RACING ASSOCIATION (1897; 39,000)

Exists to promote the sport of pigeon racing and controls pigeon racing within the Association. Organises liberation sites, issues rings, calculates distances between liberation sites and home lofts, and assists in the return of strays. May be able to assist in identifying owners of ringed birds found.
Contact: Royal Pigeon Racing Association, The Reddings, Cheltenham, GL51 6RN. 01452 713 529; www.rpra.org

ROYAL SOCIETY FOR THE PREVENTION OF CRUELTY TO ANIMALS (1824; 43,690)

In addition to its animal centres, the Society also runs a woodland study centre and nature reserve at Mallydams Wood in East Sussex, and specialist wildlife rehabilitation centres at West Hatch, Taunton, Somerset TA3 5RT (0870 0101 847), at Station Road, East Winch, King's Lynn, Norfolk PE32 1NR (0870 9061 420), and London Road, Stapeley, Nantwich, Cheshire CW5 7JW (not open to the public). Inspectors are contacted through their National Communication Centre, which can be reached via the Society's 24-hour national cruelty and advice line: 08705 555 999.
Contact: RSPCA Headquarters, Willberforce Way, Horsham, West Sussex RH13 9RS. 24-hour cruelty line: 0300 1234 999. www.rspca.org.uk

ROYAL SOCIETY FOR THE PROTECTION OF BIRDS (1899 1,000,000+)

UK Partner of BirdLife International, and Europe's largest voluntary wildlife conservation body. The RSPB, a registered charity, is governed by an elected body (see also RSPB Phoenix and RSPB Wildlife Explorers). Its work in the conservation of wild birds and habitats covers the acquisition and management of nature reserves; research and surveys; monitoring and responding to development proposals, land use practices and pollution which threaten wild birds and biodiversity; and the provision of an advisory service on wildlife law enforcement.
The RSPB currently manages

200 nature reserves in the UK, covering almost 130,00 hectares and home to 80% of Britain's rarest or most threatened bird species. The aim is to conserve a countrywide network of reserves with all examples of the main bird communities and with due regard to the conservation of plants and other animals. Current national projects include extensive work on agriculture, and conservation and campaigning for the conservation of the marine environment and to halt the illegal persecution of birds of prey. Increasingly, there is involvement with broader environmental concerns such as climate change and transport.
The RSPB's International Dept works closely with Birdlife International and its partners in other countries and is involved with numerous projects overseas, especially in Europe and Asia.
Contact: RSPB, The Lodge, Potton Road, Sandy, Beds SG19 2DL, 01767 680 551.
Membership enquiries: 01767 693 680.
Wildlife enquiries: 01767 693 690; www.rspb.org.uk
e-mail: (firstname.name)@rspb.org.uk

Regional Offices:
ENGLAND
Eastern England, Stalham House, 65 Thorpe Road, Norwich NR1 1UD. 01603 661 662.
Covers: Beds, Cambs, Essex, Herts, Lincs, Norfolk, Suffolk.

London Office, RSPB London Office, 2nd Floor, 65 Petty France, London, SW1H 9EU. 0207 808 1240.

Midlands, 46 The Green, South Bar, Banbury, Oxfordshire, OX16 9AB. 01295 253 330.
Covers: Bucks, Derbys, Herefordshire, Leicestershire, Northants, Notts, Oxon, Rutland, Shropshire, Staffs, Warwickshire, West Midlands, Worcestershire.

Northern England:
Denby Dale Office, Westleigh Mews, Wakefield Road, Denby Dale, Huddersfield, HD8 8QD. 0300 7772 676.
Covers: Cheshire, Cleveland, County Durham, Cumbria, East Riding of Yorkshire, Greater Manchester, Lancashire, Merseyside, Middlesbrough, North Yorkshire, North East Lincolnshire, North Lincolnshire, Northumberland, South Yorkshire, Tyne and Wear, West Yorkshire.

Newcastle Office, 1 Sirius House, Amethyst Road, Newcastle Business Park, Newcastle-upon-Tyne NE4 7YL. 0300 7772 676.

Lancaster office, 7.3.1 Cameron House, White Cross Estate, Lancaster LA1 4XF. 0300 7772 676.

South East, 1st Floor, Pavilion View, 19 New Road, Brighton BN1 1UF. 01273 775 333.
Covers: East Sussex, Hampshire, Isle of Wight, Kent, Surrey, West Berkshire, West Sussex.

South West, Keble House, Southenhay Gardens, Exeter EX1 1NT. 01392 432 691.
Covers: Bristol, Cornwall, Devon, Dorset, Somerset, Gloucs, Wiltshire.

NORTHERN IRELAND
Northern Ireland Headquarters, Belvoir Park Forest,

NATIONAL ORGANISATIONS

Belfast, BT8 7QT. 028 9049 1547.
Covers: County Antrim,County Armagh, County Down, County Fermanagh, County Londonderry, County Tyrone.

SCOTLAND
Scotland Headquarters, 2 Lochside View, Edinburgh Park, Edinburgh EH12 9DH. 0131 317 4100.
e-mail: rspb.scotland@rspb.org.uk

East Scotland, 10 Albyn Terrace, Aberdeen, Aberdeenshire, AB10 1YP. 01224 624 824.
Covers: Aberdeen, Aberdeenshire, Angus, Moray, Perth and Kinross.

North Scotland, Etive House, Beechwood Park, Inverness, IV2 3BW. 01463 715 000;
e-mail: nsro@rspb.org.uk
Covers: Eilean Siar, Highland.

South and West Scotland, 10 Park Quadrant, Glasgow, G3 6BS. 0141 331 0993;
e-mail: glasgow@rspb.org.uk
Covers: Argyll and Bute, Clackmannanshire, Dumfries and Galloway, East Ayrshire, East Lothian, East Dunbartonshire, East Renfrewshire, Midlothian, North Ayrshire, North Lanarkshire, Renfrewshire, Scottish borders, South Ayrshire, South Lanarkshire, Stirling, West Dunbartonshire, West Lothian.

WALES
Wales Headquarters, Sutherland House, Castlebridge, Cowbridge Road East, Cardiff CF11 9AB. 029 2035 3000; e-mail: cymru@rspb.org.uk
Covers: Blaenau Gwent, Bridgend, Caerphilly, Cardiff, Carmarthenshire, Ceredigion, Merthyr Tydfil, Monmouthshire, Neath Port Talbot, Newport, Pembrokeshire, Powys, Rhondda Cynon Taff, Swansea, Torfaen, Vale of Glamorgan.

North Wales Office, Uned 14, Llys Castan, Ffordd Y Parc, Parc Menai, Bangor, Gwynedd LL57 4FD. 01248 672 850
Covers: Conwy, Denbighshire, Flintshire, Gwynedd, Isle of Anglesey, Wrexham.

RSPB WILDLIFE EXPLORERS and RSPB PHOENIX (formerly YOC) (1965; 168,000)
Junior section of the RSPB. There are more than 100 groups run by 300 volunteers. Activities include projects, holidays, roadshows, competitions, and local events for children, families and teenagers. Phoenix members (13 years and over) receive *BirdLife* magazine every two months, plus *Wingbeat* – the only environmental magazine written by teenagers for teenagers – four times a year.
Contact: The Youth Manager, RSPB Youth and Education Dept, The Lodge, Sandy, Beds SG19 2DL. 01767 680 551; e-mail: explorers@rspb.org.uk and phoenix@rspb.org.uk www.rspb.org.uk/youth

SCOTTISH BIRDS RECORDS COMMITTEE (1984)
Set up by the Scottish Ornithologists' Club to ensure that records of species not deemed rare enough to be considered by the British Birds Rarities Committee, but which are rare in Scotland, are fully assessed;

also maintains the official list of Scottish birds.
Contact: www.the-soc.org.uk

SCOTTISH ORNITHOLOGISTS' CLUB (1936; 2,250)
The Club has 14 branches (see County Directory), each with a programme of winter meetings and field trips throughout the year. The SOC organises an annual weekend conference in the autumn and a joint SOC/BTO one-day birdwatchers' conference in spring. *Scottish Birds* is published quarterly and incorporates the *Scottish Bird News* and the scarce sightings journal *Birding Scotland*. The SOC is based in a large resource centre which offers panoramic views of Aberlady Bay and houses the George Waterston Library.
Contact: The Scottish Birdwatching Resource Centre, The SOC, Waterston House, Aberlady, East Lothian EH32 0PY. 01875 871 330; (Fax) 01875 871 035; e-mail: mail@the-soc.org.uk www.the-soc.org.uk

SCOTTISH NATURAL HERITAGE (1991)
SNH is the Scottish Executive's statutory advisor in respect to the conservation, enhancement, enjoyment, understanding and sustainable use of the natural heritage.
Contact: Scottish Natural Heritage, Great Glen House, Leachkin Road, Inverness IV3 8NW. 01463 725 000; e-mail: enquiries@snh.gov.uk www.snh.org.uk

SCOTTISH SOCIETY FOR THE PREVENTION OF CRUELTY TO ANIMALS (1839; 45,000 supporters)
Represents animal welfare interests to Government, local authorities and others. Educates young people to realise their responsibilities. Maintains an inspectorate to patrol and investigate and to advise owners about the welfare of animals and birds in their care. Maintains welfare centres, two of which include oiled bird cleaning centres. Bird species, including birds of prey, are rehabilitated and where possible released back into the wild.
Contact: Scottish SPCA, Kingseat Road, Halbeath, Dunfermline, Fife KY11 8RY. 03000 999 999; www.scottishspca.org
e-mail: enquiries@scottishspca.org

SCOTTISH WILDLIFE TRUST (1964; 35,000)
The Trust aims to re-establish: 'a network of healthy and resilient ecosystems supporting expanding communities of native species across large areas of Scotland's land, water and seas.' Its main activities focus on managing 123 wildlife reserves and undertaking practical conservation tasks; influencing and campaigning for better wildlife-related policy and action; inspiring people to enjoy and find out more about wildlife. Member of The Wildlife Trusts partnership and organises Scottish Wildlife Week. Publishes *Scottish Wildlife* three times a year.
Contact: Scottish Wildlife Trust, Harbourside House, 110 Commercial Street, Edinburgh EH6 6NF. 0131 312 7765; (Fax) 0131 312 8705; e-mail: enquiries@swt.org.uk www.swt.org.uk

SEABIRD GROUP (1966; 350)

Concerned with conservation issues affecting seabirds. Assists with co-ordination of census and monitoring work on breeding seabirds; has established and maintains the Seabird Colony Register in collaboration with the JNCC; organises regular conferences on seabird biology and conservation topics. Small grants available to assist with research and survey work on seabirds. Publishes the *Seabird Group Newsletter* every four months and the journal Seabird annually.

Contact: Ellie Owen (Secretary), RSPB North Scotland Office, Etive House, Beechwood Park, Inverness. IV2 6AL; e-mail: ellie.owen@rspb.org.uk

SOCIETY FOR CONSERVATION IN AVICULTURE (1993)

The Society aims to promote and develop all species and varieties of birds kept by aviculturists, with special regard to threatened and endangered species both in the wild and in captivity. Officers play an active role in promoting responsible care and ownership of all birds. Members do not have to be bird keepers.

Contact: SCA, PO Box 208, Wirral CH29 9DD. Helpline: 0845 634 2193. www.thesca.org.uk

SOCIETY OF WILDLIFE ARTISTS (1964; 62 Members, 68 Associates)

Registered charity that seeks to generate an appreciation of the natural world through all forms of fine art. Annual exhibition held in Oct/Nov at the Mall Galleries, London. Through bursary schemes, the Society has been able to help young artists with awards of up to £1,000 towards travel, education or the cost of materials.

Contact: The Secretary, Society of Wildlife Artists, Federation of British Artists, 17 Carlton House Terrace, London SW1Y 5BD. 020 7930 6844; e-mail: info@mallgalleries.com www.swla.co.uk

SWAN SANCTUARY (2005)

Founded by Dorothy Beeson BEM, this registered charity operates nationally. Has a fully equipped swan hospital. New site has several nursing ponds and a four acre rehabilitation lake where around 4,000 swans and the same number of other forms of wildlife are treated. 24-hour service operated, with volunteer rescuers on hand to recover victims of oil spills, vandalism etc. **Contact:** The Swan Sanctuary, Felix Lane, Shepperton, Middlesex TW17 8NN. Emergency number: 01932 240 790; www.swanuk.org.uk e-mail: swans@swanuk.org.uk

SWIFT CONSERVATION (2009)

An advice service which aims to reverse the decline in the UK's Swifts. Swift Conservation runs a website providing extensive information on Swifts, and on how to both preserve and set up Swift nest sites. Swift Conservation also runs a lecture and training service, providing guidance for the general public, Planners and Architects. It supplies local advice and help via a network of volunteer helpers, and has links to similar assistance across Europe. Together with the RSPB it conducts an annual cumulative survey of known Swift nest places, from information supplied by the general public and its volunteers. It campaigns for better protection of Swifts and other birds that rely on nest places in or on buildings.

Contact: e-mail: mail@swift-conservation.org www.swift-conservation.org

WADER STUDY GROUP (1970; 600)

An association of wader enthusiasts, both amateur and professional, from all parts of the world, the Group aims to maintain contact between them, help organise co-operative studies, and provide a vehicle for the exchange of information. Publishes the *Wader Study Group Bulletin* three times a year and holds annual meetings throughout Europe.

Contact: The General Secretary, International Wader Study Group, c/o The British Trust for Ornithology, The Nunnery, Thetford, Norfolk IP24 2PU. www.waderstudygroup.org

WELSH KITE TRUST (1996; 1,200)

A registered charity that undertakes the conservation and annual monitoring of Red Kites in Wales. It attempts to locate all the breeding birds, to compile data on population growth, productivity, range expansion etc. The Trust liaises with landowners, acts as consultant on planning issues and with regard to filming and photography, and represents Welsh interests on the UK Kite Steering Group. Provides a limited rescue service for injured kites and eggs or chicks at risk of desertion or starvation. Publishes a newsletter *Boda Wennol* twice a year, sent free to subscribing Friends of the Welsh Kite and to all landowners with nesting kites.

Contact: Welsh Kite Trust, Samaria, Nantmel, Llandrindod Wells, Powys LD1 6EN. 01597 825 981; www.welshkitetrust.org; e-mail: information@welshkitetrust.org

WELSH ORNITHOLOGICAL SOCIETY (1988; 250)

Promotes the study, conservation and enjoyment of birds throughout Wales. Runs the Welsh Records Panel which adjudicates records of scarce species in Wales. Publishes the journal *Birds In Wales* and organises an annual conference.

Contact: Membership details from Welsh Ornithological Society, Alan Williams, Treasurer/Membership Secretary; e-mail: treasurer@birdsinwales.org.uk www.birdsinwales.org.uk

WILDFOWL & WETLANDS TRUST (1946; 130,000 members)

Founded by Sir Peter Scott to conserve wetlands and their biodiversity, WWT has nine centres (see below). The centres are nationally, or internationally, important for wintering wildfowl. Programmes of walks and talks are available for visitors, and resources and programmes are provided for school

NATIONAL ORGANISATIONS

groups. Centres, except Caerlaverock and Welney, have wildfowl from around the world, inc. endangered species. Research Department works on population dynamics, species management plans and wetland ecology. The Wetland Advisory Service (WAS) undertakes contracts, and Wetland Link International promotes the role of wetland centres for education and public awareness.
Contact: Wildfowl and Wetlands Trust, Slimbridge, Glos, GL2 7BT. 01453 891 900; e-mail: enquiries@wwt.org.uk www.wwt.org.uk

CENTRES:
WWT Arundel Wetland Centre, Mill Road, Arundel, Sussex BN18 9PB. 01903 883 355; (Fax) 01903 884834; e-mail: info.arundel@wwt.org.uk

WWT Caerlaverock Wetland Centre, Eastpark Farm, Caerlaverock, Dumfriesshire, Scotland DG1 4RS. 01387 770 200 (Fax) 01387 770 539; e-mail: info.caerlaverock@wwt.org.uk

WWT Castle Espie Wetland Centre, 78 Ballydrain Road, Comber, Co Down, N Ireland BT23 6EA. 028 9187 4146; (Fax) 028 9187 3857; e-mail: info.castleespie@wwt.org.uk

WWT London Wetland Centre, Queen Elizabeth's Walk, Barnes, London SW13 9WT. 020 8409 4400; (Fax) 020 8409 4401; e-mail: info.london@wwt.org.uk

WWT Martin Mere Wetland Centre, Fish Lane, Burscough, Lancashire L40 0TA. 01704 895 181 (Fax) 01704 892 343; e-mail: info.martinmere@wwt.org.uk

WWT National Wetland Centre Wales, Llwynhendy, Llanelli, Carmarthenshire SA14 9SH. 01554 741 087; (Fax) 01554 744 101; e-mail: info.llanelli@wwt.org.uk

WWT Slimbridge Wetland Centre, Slimbridge, Gloucestershire GL2 7BT. 01453 891 900; (Fax) 01453 890 827; e-mail: info.slimbridge@wwt.org.uk

WWT Washington Wetland Centre, Pattinson, Washington, Tyne and Wear NE38 8LE. 0191 416 5454; e-mail: info.washington@wwt.org.uk

WWT Welney Wetland Centre, Hundred Foot Bank, Welney, Nr. Wisbech, PE14 9TN. 01353 860 711; (Fax) 01353 863 524; e-mail: info.welney@wwt.org.uk

WILDLIFE SOUND RECORDING SOCIETY (1968; 327)
Works closely with the Wildlife Section of the National Sound Archive. Members carry out recording work for scientific purposes as well as for pleasure. A field weekend is held each spring, and members organise meetings locally. Four CD sound magazines of members' recordings are produced for members each year, and a journal, *Wildlife Sound*, is published twice a year.
Contact: Hon Membership Secretary, WSRS, Wildlife Sound Recording Society; www.wildlife-sound.org/ e-mail: enquiries@wildlife-sound.org

WILDLIFE TRUSTS (1995; 800,000)
Founded in 1912 and now the largest UK charity exclusively dedicated to conserving all habitats and species, with a membership of more than 800,000 people including 108,000 junior members in 47 individual county trusts. Collectively, they manage more than 2,200 nature reserves spanning over 80,000 hectares. The Wildlife Trusts also lobby for better protection of the UK's natural heritage and are dedicated to protecting wildlife for the future. Members receive *Natural World* magazine three times a year.
Contact: The Wildlife Trusts, The Kiln, Waterside, Mather Road, Newark NG24 1WT. 01636 677 711; (Fax) 01636 670 001; e-mail: enquiry@wildlifetrusts.org www.wildlifetrusts.org

WILDLIFE WATCH (1977; 108.000)
The junior branch of The Wildlife Trusts. It supports 1,500 registered volunteer leaders running Watch groups across the UK. Publishes *Watchword* and *Wildlife Extra* for children, and activity books for adults working with young people.
Contact: Wildlife Watch, The Wildlife Trusts, The Kiln, Waterside, Mather Road, Newark NG24 1WT. 01636 677 711; (Fax) 01636 670 001; e-mail: watch@wildlifetrusts.org www.wildlifewatch.org.uk

WWF-UK (1961)
WWF is the world's largest independent conservation organisation, comprising 27 national organisations. It works to conserve and species, protect endangered spaces, and address global threats to nature by seeking long-term solutions with people in government and industry, education and civil society. Publishes *WWF News* (quarterly magazine)
Contact: WWF-UK, The Living Planet Centre, Rufford House, Brewery Road, Woking, Surrey, GU21 4LL. 01483 426 444; (Fax) 01483 426 409; www.wwf.org.uk

ZOOLOGICAL PHOTOGRAPHIC CLUB (1899)
Circulates black and white and colour prints of zoological interest via a series of postal portfolios.
Contact: Hon. Sec., John Tinning; email: john.tinning@btinternet.com. www.zpc-naturefolio.org.uk

ZOOLOGICAL SOCIETY OF LONDON (1826)
Carries out research, organises symposia and holds scientific meetings. Manages the Zoological Gardens in Regent's Park (first opened in 1828) and Whipsnade Wild Animal Park near Dunstable, Beds, each with extensive collections of birds. The Society's library has a large collection of ornithological books and journals. Publications include the *Journal of Zoology*, *Animal Conservation*, *Conservation Biology* book series, *The Symposia* and *The International Zoo Yearbook*.
Contact: Zoological Society of London, Regent's Park, London, NW1 4RY. 0844 225 1826; www.zsl.org

NATIONAL PROJECTS

National ornithological projects depend for their success on the active participation of amateur birdwatchers. In return they provide birdwatchers with an excellent opportunity to contribute in a positive and worthwhile way to the scientific study of birds and their habitats, which is the vital basis of all conservation programmes. The following entries provide a description of each particular project and a note of whom to contact for further information (full address details of project organisers are in the previous section).

BIG GARDEN BIRDWATCH
An RSPB Survey
The Big Garden Birdwatch has grown into fun for all the family. All you need to do is count the birds in your garden or a local park for one hour over the weekend of 25-26 January 2014 then tell us what you see.
Contact: RSPB, www.rspb.org.uk

BIRD CONSERVATION TARGETING PROJECT
An RSPB survey
The project has been developed to target management and resources towards important sites for scarce and declining farmland and woodland birds. Records are brought together from a wide range of sources, including individual birdwatchers, county bird clubs and national surveys.
The project produces distribution maps which are already being used to guide the spending of hundreds of millions of pounds to benefit birds through agri-environment and woodland grant schemes, and influencing woodland management to benefit birds on publicly owned woodland. The targeting maps help to ensure that government grant schemes are allocated to put the right conservation measures in the right places
Contact: RSPB, www.rspb.org.uk

BIRDTRACK
Organised by BTO on behalf of BTO, RSPB, BirdWatch Ireland and WOS
BirdTrack is a free, online bird recording system for birdwatchers to store and manage bird records from anywhere in Britain and Ireland. The idea is simple. Make a note of the birds seen or heard at each site visited, and then enter your observations on an easy-to-use web page (www. birdtrack.net). There's also a free App for Android and iPhone smartphones through which you can log your sightings whilst you're in the field and upload them at the click of a button. Exciting real-time outputs are generated by BirdTrack, including species reporting-rate graphs and animated maps of sightings, all freely-available online. The data collected are used by researchers to investigate migration movements and the distribution of scarce birds, and to support species conservation at local, national and international scales.
Contact: Nick Moran, BTO.
E-mail: birdtrack@bto.org

BREEDING BIRD SURVEY
Supported by BTO, JNCC and RSPB
Started in 1994, the BBS is designed to keep track of the changes in populations of our common breeding birds. It is dependent on volunteer birdwatchers throughout the country who make two visits, about five hours in total, to survey the breeding birds in a 1x1km square. Survey squares are picked at random by computer to ensure that all habitats and regions are covered.
Since its inception it has been a tremendous success, with more than 3,000 squares covered and more than 200 species recorded each year.
Contact: Kate Risely, e-mail: bbs@bto.org, or your local BTO Regional Representative (see County Directory).

CONSTANT EFFORT SITES (CES) SCHEME
Funded by a partnership between BTO, JNCC, The National Parks & Wildlife Service (Ireland) and ringers themselves
The CES scheme, run since 1983, coordinates standardised summer ringing at over 120 sites across Britain and Ireland. This allows the BTO to monitor trends in the numbers of 25 scrub and woodland species, while simultaneously providing annual estimates of breeding success and survival rates of adult birds.
Information from CES complements demographic information collected by other BTO surveys and feeds into the BTO's Integrated Population Monitoring, highlighting the causes of changes in bird populations. Results are updated annually and published on-line as part of the BirdTrends Report (www.bto.org/BirdTrends).
Contact: Allison Kew, BTO ces@bto.org and www.bto.org/ces

NATIONAL PROJECTS

GARDEN BIRD FEEDING SURVEY

A BTO project
The Garden Bird Feeding Survey is the longest-running study of garden birds in Britain. Each year, approximately 250 householders record the numbers and variety of birds using food supplements and water that they have provided in their garden. Observations are made on a weekly basis from October to March inclusive. Gardens are selected by region and type; from city flats to suburban semis, rural houses to outlying farms.
Contact: Clare Simm, BTO.
E-mail: clare.simm@bto.org

BTO GARDEN BIRDWATCH

A BTO project
Started in January 1995, this project is a year-round survey that monitors the use that birds and other types of wildlife make of gardens. Approximately 15,000 participants from all over the UK and Ireland keep a weekly log of species using their gardens. The data collected are used to monitor regional, seasonal and year-to-year changes in the garden populations of our commoner birds, mammals, butterflies, reptiles and amphibians. To cover running costs there is an annual subscription of £17. Participants receive a quarterly magazine and all new joiners receive a garden bird book. Results and more information are available online: www.bto.org/gbw
Contact: Garden Ecology Team, BTO.
E-mail: gbw@bto.org

GARDEN WILDLIFE HEALTH

A joint scheme of Institute of Zoology, BTO, Froglife & RSPB
This project aims to monitor the health of, and identify disease threats to, British wildlife. The particular focus is on garden birds, amphibians, reptiles and hedgehogs. Members of the public are asked to submit reports of sick or dead wildlife and to submit samples for analysis.
Contact: Garden Wildlife Health line 0207-449-6685; E-mail gwh@zsl.org
www.gardenwildlife.org

GOOSE AND SWAN MONITORING

A WWT project
Geese and swans are a cornerstone of the Wildfowl and Wetland Trust's conservation work. During winter, geese and swans from Canada to central Russia undertake arduous migrations to reach their wintering grounds in the UK. In order to safeguard them WWT tracks how many individuals are in each population, where they are found, and the overall trend of the population

(whether it is increasing, decreasing, or remaining stable). Other demographic measures – most importantly, productivity (how many young are born each year) and survival (or mortality) rates – help to understand the reasons behind any increase or decrease. To get information like this WWT use a number of techniques and tools, including counts and capture and marking. A large amount of this work is carried out by volunteer birdwatchers who give their time to assist with data collection.
Contact: e-mail:enquiries@wwt.org.uk
http://monitoring.wwt.org.uk

HERONRIES CENSUS

A BTO project
This survey, started in 1928, has been carried out under the auspices of the BTO since 1934 and represents the longest continuous series of population data for any European breeding bird (Grey Heron). Counts of apparently occupied nests are made at as many UK heronries as possible each year, to provide an index of current population levels.
Data from Scotland and Wales are relatively scanty, and more contributions from these countries would be especially welcomed. Herons may be hit hard during periods of severe weather and are vulnerable to pesticides and pollution. Currently, population levels are suffering from the recent cold winters. Little Egret and other incoming species of colonial waterbird such as Cattle Egret are now fully included, whether nesting with Grey Herons, or on their own. Counts of Cormorant nests at heronries are also encouraged.
Contact: John Marchant, BTO.
E-mail: herons@bto.org

IRISH WETLAND BIRD SURVEY
(I-WeBS)

A joint project of BirdWatch Ireland, the National Parks & Wildlife Service of the Dept of Arts, Culture & the Gaeltacht, and WWT, and supported by the Heritage Council and WWF-UK.
The Irish Wetland Bird Survey (I-WeBS) is the scheme that monitors wintering waterbirds in Ireland. The survey runs from September to March each winter. Wetlands of all types and sizes are monitored, including estuaries, coastlines, bays, rivers, turloughs, lakes, streams and

flooded fields. Each winter, more than 350 people take part. These counters go out and count waterbirds at over 800 wetlands throughout the country. The counts are done once-monthly by skilled volunteers, as well as by professional staff of the National Parks and Wildlife Service and BirdWatch Ireland.
Contact: Helen, I-WeBS Office, BirdWatch Ireland, 353 (0)1 281 9878; www.birdwatchireland.ie e-mail: hboland@birdwatchireland.ie

NATIONAL BEACHED BIRD SURVEY
An RSPB project
The results of the annual survey are used in conjunction with those from other European countries and aim to contribute to international monitoring efforts to document trends in chronic marine oil pollution and to promote adequate methods of controlling illegal oil discharge to help reduce seabird mortality.
Contact: Sabine Schmitt, Senior Research Assistant; E-mail: sabine.schmitt@rspb.org.uk

NEST BOX CHALLENGE
A BTO project
NBC is an on-line survey which aims to monitor the breeding success of birds in Britain's green spaces. Participants are asked to register one or more nests, or nest boxes, in their garden or local green space, monitoring their progress via regular nest inspections and recording the number of eggs and/or chicks present at each visit. Records of unused boxes are also valuable as they can be used to determine next box occupancy rates. Anyone who has a nest box or nest in their garden or local park can take part.
Contact: Hazel Evans, BTO. E-mail: nbc@bto.org and www.bto.org/nbc

NEST RECORD SCHEME
A BTO Project carried out with funding from the JNCC.
The scheme monitors changes in the nesting success and the timing of breeding of Britain's bird species by gathering information on birds found anywhere in the country, from a Blackbird in a garden to an Oystercatcher on a Scottish loch. Participants locate nests and monitor their progress over several visits, making counts of the number of eggs and/or chicks on each occasion and recording whether they are successful. Information from NRS complements demographic information collected by other BTO surveys and feeds into the BTO's Integrated Population Monitoring, highlighting the causes of changes in bird populations.
More than 40,000 nest records are submitted to

the BTO each year by volunteer surveyors and the results are updated annually and published on-line as part of the BirdTrends Report (www.bto.org/BirdTrends). Guidance on how to become a BTO nest recorder, including best practice guidelines on minimising disturbance while visiting nests, is available online. A free starter pack is available on request.
Contact: Carl Barimore, BTO E-mail: nrs@bto.org and www.bto.org/nrs

RAPTOR AND OWL RESEARCH REGISTER
A BTO project
The Register has helped considerably over the past 30 years in encouraging and guiding research, and in the co-ordination of projects. There is currently almost 500 on-going projects. Barn Owls and Tawny Owls are currently receiving most attention. As to raptors, the most popular subjects are Kestrels, Buzzards, Sparrowhawks, Hobbies and Peregrines, with researchers showing increasing interest in Red Kites, and fewer large in-depth studies of Goshawks, Ospreys and harriers.
Contributing is a simple process and involves all raptor enthusiasts, whether it is to describe an amateur activity or professional study. The nature of research on record varies widely, and includes local pellet analyses, captive breeding and rehabilitation programmes, and national surveys of Peregrines, Buzzards and Golden Eagles. Birdwatchers, both in Britain and abroad, are encouraged to write for photocopies of cards relevant to the species or nature of their work. The effectiveness of the Register depends upon those running projects (however big or small) ensuring that their work is included.
Contact: David Glue, BTO.

RETRAPPING ADULTS FOR SURVIVAL (RAS) SCHEME
Funded by a partnership between BTO, JNCC, The National Parks & Wildlife Service (Ireland) and ringers themselves
The RAS scheme, started in 1998, gathers information on recaptures or re-sightings of adult birds. Ringers choose a target species, typically one that is poorly monitored by CES or general ringing, and aim to catch or re-sight as many of the breeding adults within their study area as possible on an annual basis. These data allow the BTO to monitor survival rates in adult birds, which helps us to understand the causes underlying changes in population sizes as part of the BTO's Integrated Population Monitoring framework. Results are updated annually and published on-

line as part of the BirdTrends Report (www.bto.org/BirdTrends).

Contact: Allison Kew, BTO. E-mail: ras@bto.org and www.bto.org/ras

RINGING SCHEME
Funded by a partnership between BTO, JNCC (on behalf of the Country Agencies), The National Parks & Wildlife Service (Ireland) and ringers themselves

Marking birds with individually numbered metal rings allows us to study survival, productivity and movements of British and Irish birds.

More than 2,700 trained and licensed ringers operate in Britain and Ireland, marking around one million birds annually. Training takes at least a year, but more often two or more years, depending on the aptitude of the trainee and the amount of ringing they do. A restricted permit can usually be obtained more quickly.

Anyone can contribute to the scheme by reporting any ringed or colour-marked birds they see or find. Reports can be submitted online at www.ring.ac or direct to BTO HQ. Anyone finding a ringed bird should note the ring number, species, when and where found and, if possible, what happened to it. If the bird is dead, it may also be possible to remove the ring, which should be kept in case there is a query. Anyone reporting a ringed bird will be sent details of where and when the bird was originally ringed. More info: www.bto.org/ringing/

The 'Demog Blog' for up to date news and stories is at: http://btoringing.blogspot.com

Contact: Jacquie Clark, BTO.
E-mail: Jacquie.clark@bto.org

TOOTH & CLAW
An independent project aimed at improving knowledge about Britain's predators and promoting discussion on the issues that surround them.

Tooth & Claw explores some of the complex issues surrounding our relationship with wild predators and questions how we really feel and why.

Through the web site, Tooth & Claw provides a meeting place between anecdotal input and scientific research and encourages constructive and imaginative dialogue on predator issues. A series of case studies led by powerful imagery will provide insightful interviews and personal accounts of our lives alongside the likes of eagles

and foxes with a glimpse into the future and the return of creatures we have not known for centuries.

Contact: Peter Cairns, Northshots, Ballintean, Glenfeshie, Kingussie, Scotland, PH21 1NX. (44) (0)1540 651 352;
e-mail: peter@wildmedia.org
www.wildmedia.org/our_projects_tooth_and_claw.asp

WATERWAYS BREEDING BIRD SURVEY
A BTO project, supported by the Environment Agency

WBBS uses transect methods like those of the Breeding Bird Survey to record bird populations along randomly chosen stretches of rivers and canals throughout the UK. Just two survey visits are needed during April-June. WBBS began in 1998 and in 2008 took over from the Waterways Bird Survey as the main monitoring scheme for birds in this habitat.

Contact: BTO Regional Representative (see County Directory) to enquire if any local stretches require coverage, otherwise John Marchant at BTO HQ. E-mail: wbbs@bto.org

WETLAND BIRD SURVEY (WeBS)
A joint scheme of BTO, RSPB, JNCC in association with WWT

The Wetland Bird Survey (WeBS) is the monitoring scheme for non-breeding waterbirds in the UK. The principal aims are:

1. To determine the population sizes of waterbirds.
2. To determine trends in numbers and distribution.
3. To identify important sites for waterbirds.

WeBS data are used to designate important waterbird sites and protect them against adverse development, for research into the causes of declines, for establishing conservation priorities and strategies and to formulate management plans for wetland sites and waterbirds.

Monthly, synchronised Core Counts are made at as many wetland sites as possible. Low Tide Counts are made on about 20 estuaries each winter to identify important feeding areas. Counts are relatively straightforward and can take from a few minutes up to a few hours, depending on the size of the site. The 3,000 participants receive an annual newsletter and a comprehensive annual report. New counters are always welcome.

Contact: General Webs Enquiries - Heidi Mellan - WeBS Office, BTO.
E-mail webs@bto.org   www.bto.org/webs

INTERNATIONAL DIRECTORY

David Cromack

Painted Stork is a species found widely throughout India and in parts of SE Asia and China. This one was photographed in the fabled Bharatpur nature reserve in northern India.

International organisations   306

Special interest organisations   312

BirdLife
INTERNATIONAL

The BirdLife Partnership
BirdLife is a Partnership of non-governmental organisations (NGOs) with a special focus on conservation and birds. Each NGO Partner represents a unique geographic territory/country.

The BirdLife Network explained
Partners: Membership-based NGOs who represent BirdLife in their own territory. Vote holders and key implementing bodies for BirdLife's Strategy and Regional Programmes in their own territories.

Partners Designate: Membership-based NGOs who represent BirdLife in their own territory, in a transition stage to becoming full Partners. Non-vote holders.

Affiliates: Usually NGOs, but also individuals, foundations or governmental institutions when appropriate. Act as a BirdLife contact with the aim of developing into, or recruiting, a BirdLife Partner in their territory.

Secretariat: The co-ordinating and servicing body of BirdLife International.

SECRETARIAT ADDRESSES

BirdLife Global Office
BirdLife International
Wellbrook Court, Girton Road
Cambridge CB3 0NA
United Kingdom
Tel. +44 1 223 277 318
Fax +44 1 223 277 200
E-mail: birdlife@birdlife.org.uk
www.birdlife.org

Birdlife Africa Regional Office
c/o ICIPE Campus
Kasarani Road, off Thika Road
Nairobi, Kenya
Postal Address
PO Box 3502
00100 GPO
Nairobi, Kenya
Tel: +254 020 806 8314
Fax: +254 020 806 8315
E-mail: birdlife-africa@birdlife.org
www.birdlife.org

BirdLife Americas Regional Office
Birdlife International
Juan de Dios Martinez N35-76 y
Av Portugal
Quito Ecuador

Postal address
BirdLife International
Casilla 17-17-717
Quito, Equador
Tel. +593 (2) 2464 768
Fax +593 (2) 2469 838
E-mail: americas @birdlife.org
www.birdlife.org/regional/americas/
partnership

BirdLife Asia Regional Office
TM Suidobashi Building
4F, Misaki-cho 2-14-6
Chiyoda-ku
Tokyo 101-0061, Japan
Tel.+81 (3) 5213 0461
Fax.+81 (3) 5213 0422
E-mail: info@birdlife-asia.org
www.birdlife.org/regional/asia/
partnership

BirdLife Europe
Avenue de la Toison d'Or 67
(2nd floor), B-1060 Brussels
Belgium
Tel. +32 2280 08 30
Fax +32 2230 38 02
E-mail: europe@birdlife.org
www.birdlife.org/regional/europe/
partnership

BirdLife Middle East Regional Office
BirdLife International Middle East Division
P. O. Box 2295
Amman 11953
Jordan
Postal address
Amman
Khalda
Salameh El-Ma'aaytah Street
Building No 6. Jordan
Tel: +962 (6) 564-8173
Fax: +962 (6) 564-8172
E-mail: me@birdlife.org
www.birdlife.org/regional/
middle_east/partnership

BirdLife Pacific Regional Office
10 MacGregor Road
Suva, Fuji
Postal address
GPO Box 18332
Suva, Fuji
Tel: +679 331 3492
Fax: +679 331 9658
E-mail: don@birdlifepacific.org.fj

AFRICA

PARTNERS

Burkina Faso
La Fondation NATURAMA 01 B.P. 6133, Ouagadougou 01, Burkina Faso; e-mail: info@naturama.bf www.naturama.bf

Ethiopia
Ethiopian Wildlife and Natural History Society, PO Box 13303, Addis Ababa, Pub: *Agazen; Ethiopian Wildl. and Nat. Hist. News.* (& *Annual Report*); *Ethiopian Wildl.*

and *Nat. Hist. Soc. Quarterly News (WATCH); Walia (WATCH) (Ethiopia);* www.ewnhs.org.ete-mail: ewnhs.ble@ethionet.et

Ghana
Ghana Wildlife Society, PO Box 13252, Accra, Pub: *Bongo News; NKO (The Parrots);* e-mail: ghanawild@4u.co.gh www.ghanawildlifesociety.org

Kenya
Nature Kenya, PO Box 44486, 00100 GPO. Nairobi. Pub: *Bulletin of the EANHS; Journal of East African Natural; Kenya Birds;* e-mail: office@naturekenya.org www.naturekenya.org

INTERNATIONAL ORGANISATIONS

Seychelles
Nature Seychelles, Roche Caiman, Box 1310, Victoria, Mahe, Seychelles. Pub: *Zwazo - a BirdLife Seychelles Newsletter;* e-mail: nature@seychelles.net
www.natureseychelles.org.

Sierra Leone
Conservation Society of Sierra Leone, PO Box 1292, Freetown. Pub: *Rockfowl Link, The.*
e-mail: cssl_03@yahoo.com http://conservationsl.org

South Africa
BirdLife South Africa, PO Box 515, Randburg, Johannesburg 2125, South Africa, Pub: *Newsletter of BirdLife South Africa; Ostrich;*
e-mail: secretary@birdlife.org.za www.birdlife.org.za

Tanzania
Wildlife Conservation Society of Tanzania, PO Box 70919, Dar es Salaam, Pub: *Miombo.*
e-mail: wcst@africaonline.co.tz
www.wcst@arusha.org

Tunisia
Association Les Amis des Oiseaux, Bureau des Projets, Ariana Centre – Bureau C 208/209, 2080 Ariana, Tunis. Pub: *Feuille de Liaison de l'AAO; Houbara, l'.*
e-mail: aao@topnet.tn www.aao.org.tn

Uganda
Nature Uganda, The EANHS, PO Box 27034, Kampala. Pub: *Naturalist - A Newsletter of the East Africa Nat. His. Soc;* e-mail: nature@natureuganda.org
www.natureuganda.org/

Zimbabwe
BirdLife Zimbabwe, P O Box RV 100, Runiville, Harare, Zimbabwe. Pub: *Babbler (WATCH) (Zimbabwe); Honeyguide;* e-mail: birds@zol.co.zw
www.birdlifezimbabwe.co.zw/

PARTNERS DESIGNATE

Botswana
Birdlife Botswana, PO Box 26691, Game City, Gaborone, Botswana; www.birdlifebotswana.org.bw
e-mail: blb@birdlifebotswana.org.bw

Burundi
Association Burundaise pour la Protection des Oiseaux, P O Box 7069, Bujumbura, Burundi;
e-mail: info@aboconservation.org
http://www.aboconservation.org/

Nigeria
Nigerian Conservation Foundation, PO Box 74638, Victoria Island, Lagos. Pub: *NCF Matters/News/ Newsletter; Nigerian Conservation Foundation Annual Report;* e-mail: info@ncf-nigeria

AFFILIATES

Cameroon
Cameroon Biodiversity Conservation Society (CBCS), PO Box 3055, Messa, Yaoundé; e-mail: cbcs_cam@yahoo.fr

Djibouti Nature
Djibouti (DN)
Djibouti Nature is the BirdLife Affiliate in Djibouti. P. O. Box 3088-Djibouti
Djibouti; e-mail: naturedjibouti@gmail.com

Egypt
Nature Conservation Egypt, 10 Managem wa Mahager str, Mohandeseen, Giza.
e-mail: halabarakat2002@yahoo.com
https://sites.google.com/site/natconegy/
E-mail: Natureegypt@gmail.com

Ivory Coast
Cote d'Ivoire (SOS-FORETS), 22 BP 918 Abidjan 22.
E-mail: sosforets@hotmail.com

Liberia
Society for Conservation of Nature in Liberia, SCNL, Monrovia Zoo, Lakpazee, PO Box 2628, Monrovia.
E-mail: scnlliberia@yahoo.com www.scnlib.net

Madagascar
Asity Madagascar, Lot IIN 184 PH Ter Analamahitsy – 101 Antananarivio, Madagascar BP 1074;
e-mail: zicoma@birdlife-mada.org
http://asitymadagascar.org

Malawi
Wildlife & Environmental Socity of Malawi, Private Bag 578, Limbe. E-mail: wesm-hq@africa-online.net
www.wildlifemalawi.org

Rwanda
Association pour la Conservation de la Nature au Rwanda, P O Box 4290, Kigali, www.acnrwanda.org/
e-mail: conserverwanda@yahoo.fr

Zambia
Zambian Ornithological Society, Box 33944, Lusaka 10101, Pub: *Zambian Ornithological Society Newsletter;* e-mail: zos@zamnet.zm www.wattledcrane.com

AMERICAS

PARTNERS

Argentina
Aves Argentina (AOP), Matheu 1246/8, C1249AAB, Buenos Aires. Pub: *Hornero; Naturaleza & Conservacion; Nuestras Aves; Vuelo de Pajaro;*
e-mail: info@avesargentinas.org.ar
www.avesargentinas.org.ar

Belize
The Belize Audubon Society, PO Box 1001, 12 Fort Street, Belize City. Pub: *Belize Audubon Society Newsletter;* e-mail: base@btl.net
www.belizeaudubon.org

Bolivia
Asociacion Armonia, Avenida Lomas de Arena 400, Casilla 3566, Santa Cruz. Pub: *Aves en Bolivia;*
e-mail: armonia@armonia-bo.org www.armonia-bo.org

Canada
Bird Studies Canada, PO Box/160, Port Rowan, Ontario N0E 1M0. Pub: *Bird Studies Canada - Annual Report; Birdwatch Canada;* e-mail: generalinfo@bsc-eoc.org
www.bsc-eoc.org

Canada
Nature Canada, 85 Albert Street,Suite 900, Ottawa, Ontario K1P 6A4. Pub: *Grass 'n Roots; IBA News Canada; Nature Canada; Nature Matters; Nature Watch News (CNF);* e-mail: info@naturecanada.ca
www.naturecanada.ca

INTERNATIONAL ORGANISATIONS

Ecuador
Aves & Conservación (Corporación Ornitológica del Ecuador, Pasaje Joaquin Tinajero E3-05 y Jorge Drom, Casilla 17-17-906, Quito; www.avesconservaccion.org e-mail: aves_direccion@avesconservacion.org

Falkland Islands
Falklands Conservation, PO Box 26, Stanley, Falklands or UK Office, 14 East Hatley, sandy, Bedfordshire SG19 3JA. UK. Pub: *Falklands Conservation.*
e-mail: info@falklandsconservation.com
www.falklandsconservation.com

Panama
Panama Audubon Society, Apartado 0843-03076, Balboa, Ancon. Pub: *Toucan;* e-mail: info@panamaaudubon.org
www.panamaaudubon.org

United States
Audubon Society, 225 Varick Street, 7th Floor New York, NY, 10004. Pub: *American Birds; Audubon (USA); Audubon Field Notes; Audubon Bird Conservation Newsletter;* e-mail: international@audubon.org
www.audubon.org

PARTNER DESIGNATE

Paraguay
Guyra Paraguay, Gaetano Martino 215 esq. Tte. Ross, Asunción. Pub: *Boletin Jara Kuera;*
e-mail: guyra@guyra.org.py www.guyra.org.py/

AFFILIATES

Bahamas
Bahamas National Trust, PO Box 4105, Nassau. Pub: *Bahamas Naturalist; Currents; Grand Bahama Update.*
e-mail: bnt@bnt.bs www.bnt.bs

Brazil
SAVE Brasil
Rua Fernão Dias, 219 conj 2 Pinheiros, São Paulo SP, Brasil 05427-010; http://www.savebrasil.org.br

Chile
Comite Nacional Pro defensa de la Flora y Fauna (CODEFF), Ernesto Reyes 035, Providencia, Santiago 21. Pub: *Boletin Chileno de Ornitologia; Boletin Informativo (WATCH) (Chile).*
e-mail: administra@codeff.cl www.codeff.cl

Cuba
Centro Nacional de Áreas Protegidas (CNAP). Calle 18 a, No 1441, e/ 41 y 47, Playa, Ciudad Habana, Cuba.
e-mail: cnap@snap.cu www.snap.co.cu/

Dominican Republic
Grupo Jaragua (GJI), Calle El Vergel No 33 Ensanche, El Vergel, Santo Domingo. E-mail: jaragua@tricom.net
www.grupojaragua.org.do

El Salvador
SalvaNATURA, 33 Avenida Sur #640, Colonia Flor Blanca, San Salvador. e-mail: info@salvanatura.org
www.salvanatura.org

Mexico
Pronatura, Chiapas, A.C. es: Calle Pedro Moreno # 1 esq. Benito Juárez, Barrio Santa Lucia C.P. 29200, San Cristobal de las Casas, Chiapas, México
e-mail: pronatura@pronatura.org.mx
www.pronatura.org.mx

Puerto Rico (to USA)
Sociedad Ornitológica Puertorriqueña, Inc. (SOPI), SOPI PO Box 195166, San Juan, Puerto Rico, 00919-5166
e-mail: directivasopi@yahoo.com
www.avesdepuertorico.org

Suriname
Foundation for Nature Preservation in Suriname, Cornelis Jongbawstraat 14, PO Box 12252, Paramaribo
e-mail: research@stinasu.sr www.stinasu.sr

Uruguay
Aves Uruguay (GUPECA), Canelones 1164, Montevideo, Uruguay. Pub: *Achara;* www.avesuruguay.org.uy/
e-mail: info@avesuruguay.org.uy

ASIA

PARTNERS

India
Bombay Natural History Society, Hornbill House, Shaheed Bhagat Singh Road, Mumbai-400 023. Pub: *Buceros; Hornbill; Journal of the Bombay Natural History Society;* e-mail: bnhs@bom4.vsnl.net.in www.bnhs.org

Japan
Wild Bird Society of Japan (WBSJ), Maruw Bldg, 3-9-23, Nishi-Gotanda, Shinagawa-ku, Tokyo 141-0031, Japan. Pub: *Strix; Wild Birds; Wing.*
e-mail: hogo@wbsj.org www.wbsj.org

Malaysia
Malaysian Nature Society, PO Box 10750, Kuala Lumpur 50724. Pub: *Enggang; Suara Enggang; Malayan Nature Journal; Malaysian Naturalist.*
e-mail: mns@mns.org.my www.mns.my

Philippines
Haribon Foundation, 2/F, Santos and Sons Building, 973 Aurora Blvd, Cubao, Quezon CIty 1109. Pub: *Haribon Foundation Annual Report; Haring Ibon; Philippine Biodiversity;* e-mail: act@haribon.org.ph
www.haribon.org.ph

Singapore
Nature Society (Singapore), 510 Geylang Road, #02-05, The Sunflower, 398466. Pub: *Nature News; Nature Watch (Singapore);* e-mail: nss@nss.org.sg
www.nss.org.sg

Taiwan
Chinese Wild Bird Federation (CWBF), 1F, No. 3, Lane 36 Jing-Long St., 116 Taipei, Taiwan. Pub: *Yuhina Post;*
e-mail: mail@bird.org.tw www.bird.org.tw

Thailand
Bird Conservation Society of Thailand, 221 Moo 2, Soi Ngamwongwan 2, Tambol Bangkhen, Ampur Meung, Nontaburi 11000. Pub: *Bird Conservation Society of Thailand;* e-mail: bcst@bcst.or.th www.bcst.or.th

PARTNERS DESIGNATE

Hong Kong
The Hong Kong Birdwatching Society, 14/F Ruby Commercial Building, 480 Nathan Road, Kowloon, Hong Kong, People's Republic of China. Pub: *Hong Kong Bird Report;* e-mail: hkbws@hkbws.org.uk
www.hkbws.org.hk

INTERNATIONAL ORGANISATIONS

Nepal
Bird Conservation Nepal, P.O.Box 12465, Kathmandu, Nepal. Pub: *Bird Conservation Nepal (Danphe); Ibisbill;* e-mail: bcn@Mail.com.np www.birdlifenepal.org

AFFILIATES

Indonesia
Burung Indonesia (Perhimpunan Pelestari Burung dan Habitatnya), Jl. Dadali 32, Bogor 16161, PO. Box 310/ Boo, Bogor 16003, Indonesia; e-mail: birdlife@burung.org www.burung.org

Kazakhstan
Association for the Conservation of Biodiversity of Kazakhstan (ACBK), Office 406, 40 Beibitshilik Str, Astana 010000, Kazakhstan. E-mail: office@acbk.kz www.acbk.kz

Kyrgyzstan
NABS Public Association. www.wildlife.kg

Myanmar (Burma)
Biodiversity and Nature Conservation Association (BANCA), 145(B), Thirimingalar Lane, 8th Mile, Ward (4), Mayangone Township, Yangon, Myanmar +951 667 067; e-mail: banca@yangon.net.mm - www.banca-env.org

Sri Lanka
Field Ornithology Group of Sri Lanka, Dept of Zoology, University of Colombo, Colombo 03. Pub: *Malkoha - Newsletter of the Field Ornithology Group of Sri Lanka.* e-mail: fogsl@slt.lk www.fogsl.net

Uzbekistan
Uzbekistan Society for the Protection of Birds (UzSPB), Off.89, Institte of Zoology of Uzkek Academy of sciences, A. Niyazov str.1, Tashkent 100095. E-mail: roman.kashkarov@iba.uz www.uzspb.uz

UNAFFILIATED COUNTRIES

Cambodia
BirdLife International Cambodia Programme, ±9 Street 29, Tonie Basac, Chamkarmon, Phnom Penh. e-mail: admin@birdlifecambodia.org www.birdlifeindochina.org

Laos
BirdLife International in Indochina, No 4 Lane 209, Doi Can, Ba Dinh, Hanoi, Vietnam; e-mail: birdlife@birdlife.netnam.vn www.birdlifeindochina.org

Vietnam
BirdLife International in Indochina, PO Box 89 – 6 Dinh Le, Hanoi, Vietnam. e-mail: birdlife@birdlife.org.vn - www.birdlifeindochina.org

EUROPE

PARTNERS

Austria
BirdLife Austria, Museumplatz 1/10/8, AT-1070 Wien. Pub: *Egretta; Vogelschutz in Osterreich.* e-mail: office@birdlife.at www.birdlife.at/

Belarus
BirdLife Belarus (APB), PO Box 306, Minsk, 220050

Belarus. Pub: *Subbuteo - The Belarusian Ornithological Bulletin;* e-mail: apb@tut.by www.ptushki.org

Belgium
BirdLife Belgium (Natuurpunt-Natagora), Natuurpunt, Michiel Coxiestraat 11N 2800 Mechelen, Belgium. e-mail: wim.vandenbossche@natuurpunt.be www.natuurreservaten.be (Dutch) and Natagora, rue du Wisconsin 3, 5000 Namur, Belgium; e-mail (Natagora): Philippe.funcken@natagora. be - www.natagora.be (French)

Bulgaria
Bulgarian Society for the Protection of Birds (BSPB), PO Box 50, Yavorov Complex, Block 71, vh.4, ap 1, BG-1111, Sofia, Bulgaria. Pub: *Neophron (& UK);* e-mail: bspb_hq@bspb.org www.bspb.org

Czech Republic
Czech Society for Ornithology (CSO), Na Belidle 252/34, 150 00 Prague 5. Pub: *Ptaci Svet; Sylvia; Zpravy Ceske Spolecnosti Ornitologicke.* e-mail: cso@birdlife.cz www.birdlife.cz

Denmark
Dansk Ornitologisk Forening (DOF), Vesterbrogade 138-140, DK-1620, Copenhagen V, Denmark. Pub: *DAFIF - Dafifs Nyhedsbrev; Dansk Ornitologisk Forenings Tidsskrift; Fugle og Natur;* e-mail: dof@dof.dk www.dof.dk

Estonia
Estonian Ornithological Society (EOU), PO Box 227, Vesti Str. 4, EE-50002 Tartu, Estonia. Pub: *Hirundo Eesti Ornitoogiauhing;* e-mail: eoy@eoy.ee www.eoy.ee

Finland
BirdLife FINLAND, Annankatu 29 A 16, FI 00101, Helsinki. Pub: *Linnuston-Suojelu; Linnut; Tiira;* e-mail: office@birdlife.fi www.birdlife.fi

France
(also covers New Caledonia, Wallis & Futuna Islands) Ligue pour la Protection des Oiseaux (LPO), Fonderies Royale, 8-10 rue de Docteur Pujos, B.P. 90263, 17305 Rochefort Cedex. Pub: *Lettre Internationale; Ligue Francaise Pour La Protection des Oiseaux; Oiseau, L' (LPO); Outarde infos;* e-mail: lpo@lpo.fr www.lpo.fr/

Germany
Naturschutzbund Deutschland (NABU), Charitestr. 3, D-10117, Berlin. Pub: *Naturschutz Heute (NABU) Naturschutzbund Deutschland.* e-mail: nabu@nabu.de www.nabu.de

Gibraltar
Gibraltar Ornithological and Nat. History Society, Gibraltar Natural History Field Centre, Jew's Gate, Upper Rock Nature Reserve, PO Box 843, GI. Pub: *Alectoris; Gibraltar Nature News.* e-mail: gohns@gibnet.gi www.gonhs.org

Greece
Hellenic Ornithological Society (HOS), Themistokleous 80, 10861, Athens, Greece. Pub: *HOS Newsletter.* e-mail: info@ornithologiki.gr www.ornithologiki.gr

Hungary
Hungarian Orn. and Nature Cons. Society (MME), Kolto u. 21, 1121 Budapest. Pub: *Madartani Tajekoztato;*

INTERNATIONAL ORGANISATIONS

Madartavlat; Ornis Hungarica; Tuzok.
e-mail: mme@mme.hu www.mme.hu

Ireland
BirdWatch Ireland, Unit 20, Block D, Bullford Business Campus, Kilcoole, Co Wicklow, Eire. Pub: *Irish Birds; Wings (IWC Birdwatch Ireland);* e-mail: info@birdwatchireland.org www.birdwatchireland.ie

Israel
Society for the Protection of Nature in Israel (SPNI), Hanagev 2 St, Tel-Aviv 66186. Pub: *SPNI News.*
e-mail: ioc@netvision.net.il www.birds.org.il

Italy
Lega Italiana Protezione Uccelli (LIPU), Via Trento 49, 43100, Parma. Pub: *Ali Giovani; Ali Notizie.*
e-mail: info@lipu.it www.lipu.it

Latvia
Latvijas Ornitologijas Biedriba (LOB), Kalnciema iela 27-18, Riga LV-1046. Pub: *Putni Daba.*
e-mail: putni@lob.lv www.lob.lv

Luxembourg
Letzebuerger Natur-a Vulleschutzliga (LNVL), Kraizhaff, 5 Route de Luxembourg, L-1899 Kockelscheuer. Pub: *Regulus (WATCH); Regulus Info (& Annual Report) (WATCH); Regulus Wissenschaftliche Berichte;*
e-mail: birgit.jacoby@luxnatur.lu www.lnvl.lu

Malta
BirdLife Malta, 57 /28, Triq Abate Rigord, Ta' Xbiex, XBX 1120, Malta. Pub: *Bird Talk (WATCH) (Malta); Bird's Eye View (WATCH) (Malta); Il-Merill;* e-mail: office@birdlifemalta.org www.birdlifemalta.org

Netherlands
Vogelbescherming Nederland (VBN), Boulevard 12, 3707, BM Zeist. Pub: *Vogelniews; Vogels.*
e-mail: info@vogelbescherming.nl
www.vogelbescherming.nl/

Norway
Norsk Ornitologisk Forening (NOF), Sandgata 30 B, N-7012 Trondheim, Norway. Pub: *Fuglearet; Fuglefauna; Var; Ringmerkaren;*
e-mail: nof@birdlife.no www.birdlife.no

Poland
Ogólnopolskie Towarzystwo Ochrony Ptaków (OTOP), ul.Odrowaza 24, 05-270 Marki k. Warsaw, Poland. Pub: *Ptaki; Ptasie Ostoje;* e-mail: office@otop.most.org.pl
www.otop.org.pl/

Portugal
Sociedade Portuguesa para o Estuda das, Aves (SPEA), Avenida João Crisóstomo, nº 18 – 4º Dir. | 1000-179 Lisboa | Portugal. Pub: *Pardela;* e-mail: spea@spea.pt
www.spea.pt

Romania
Romanian Ornithological Society (SOR), Bd. M Kogalniceanu nr 49, sc. A, ap 8, 0150108 Sector 5, Bucharest. Pub: *Alcedo; Buletin AIA; Buletin de Informare Societatea Ornitologica Romana; Milvus (Romania);* e-mail: office@sor.ro www.sor.ro/

Slovakia
Slovak Ornithological Society (SOS), Mlynske Nivy 41, 821 09 Bratislava, Slovakia. Pub: *Spravodaj SOVS;*

Vtacie Spravy; e-mail: vtaky@vtaky.sk www.birdlife.sk

Slovenia
BirdLife Slovenia (DOPPS), Trzaska 2, PO Box 2990, SI-1000 Ljubljana, Slovenia. Pub: *Acrocephalus; Svet Ptic;*
e-mail: dopps@dopps.si www.ptice.si

Spain
Sociedad Espanola de Ornitologia (SEO), Melquiades Biencinto 34, ES-28053, Madrid. Pub: *Ardeola; Areas Importantes para las Aves.*
e-mail: seo@seo.org www.seo.org

Sweden
Sveriges Ornitologiska Forening (SOF), Stenhusa Gard, SE-380 62 Morbylanga. Pub: *Fagelvarld; var; Ornis Svecica;* e-mail: info@sofnet.org www.sofnet.org

Switzerland
SVS/BirdLife Switzerland, Wiedingstrasse 78, PO Box, CH-8036, Zurich, Switzerland. Pub: *Oiwvos Ornis; Ornis Junior; Ornithologische Beobachter; Der Ornithos; Steinadler;* e-mail: svs@birdlife.ch www.birdlife.ch

Turkey
Doga Dernegi (DD), PK: 640 06445, Yenisehir, Ankara, Turkey. Pub: *Kelaynak; Kuscu Bulteni.*
e-mail: doga@dogadernegi.org www.dogadernegi.org

Ukraine
Ukrainian Union for Bird Conservation (UTOP), PO Box 33, Kiev, 1103, UA. Pub: *Life of Birds.*
e-mail: uspb@birdlife.org.ua www.birdlife.org.ua

United Kingdom
Royal Society for the Protection of Birds, The Lodge, Sandy, Bedfordshire, SG19 2DL;
e-mail: info@rspb.org.uk www.rspb.org.uk

PARTNERS DESIGNATE

Azerbaijan
Azerbaijan Ornithological Society (AOS), Mukhtarov str. 13, apt 16, AZ1001 Baku. e-mail: info@aos.az http://aos.az/eng/index.php

Georgia
Georgian Centre for the Conservation of Wildlife, Nature House (2nd Floor), Didi Digomi, 0131, Tbilisi, Georgia; e-mail: office@gccw.org http://gccw.bunebaprint.ge/

Iceland
Icelandic Society for the Protection of Birds (ISPB), Fuglaverndarfélag Islands, Skulatuni 6, , 105 Reykjavik, Simi 5620477. www.fuglavernd.is
e-mail: fuglavernd@fuglavernd.is

AFFILIATES

Andorra
Associacio per a la Defensa de la Natura (AND), Apartado de Correus Espanyols No 96, Andora La Vella, Principat d'Andorra. Pub: *Aiguerola;*
e-mail: adn@andorra.ad www.adn-andorra.org/

Armenia
Armenian Society for the Protection of Birds (ASPB), Garaegin Njdeh 27/2, 10 Yerevan, 0026, Armenia.
E-mail: armbirds@yahoo.com www.aspbirds.org

Cyprus
BirdLife Cyprus, PO Box 28076, 2090 Lefkosia, Cyprus.

INTERNATIONAL ORGANISATIONS

e-mail: birdlifecyprus@birdlifecyprus.org.cy
www.birdlifecyprus.org

Faroe Islands
Føroya Fuglafrødifelag (Faroese Orginithological Society) (FOS), Postssmoga 1230, FR-110 Torshavn, Faroe Islands; e-mail: doreteb@ngs.fo
www.faroenature.net/foroya-fuglafrodifelag/kunning/blog.html

Liechtenstein
Botanish-Zoologische Gesellschaft (ZG), Im Bretscha 22, FL-9494 Schaan, Liechtenstein;
e-mail: bzg@bzg.li www.bzg.li

Lithuania
Lietuvos Ornitologu Draugija (LOD), Naugarduko St. 47-3, LT-2006, Vilnius, Lithuania. Pub: *Baltasis Gandras;* e-mail: lod@birdlife.lt www.birdlife.lt

Former Yugoslav Republic of Macedonia (FYROM)
Macedonia (MES)Macedonian Ecological Society, Blvd "Kuzman Josifovski - Pitu" 28/3-7, 1000 Skopje Macedonia; e-mail:contact@mes.org.mk - www.mes.org.mk

MIDDLE EAST

PARTNERS

Jordan
Royal Society of the Conservation of Nature, PO Box 6354, Jubeiha-Abu-Nusseir Circle, Amman 11183. Pub: *Al Reem;* e-mail: adminrscn@rscn.org.jo
www.rscn.org.jo

Lebanon
Society for the Protection of Nature in Lebanon, Awad Bldg, 6th Floor, Abdel Aziz Street, P.O.Box: 11-5665, Beirut, Lebanon; e-mail: spnlorg@cyberia.net.lb
www.spnlb.org

Palestinian Authority Territories
Palestine Wildlife Society (PWLS), Beit Sahour, PO Box 89, Palestine. Pub: *Palestine Wildlife Society - Annual Report.*
e-mail: pwls@wildlife-pal.org www.wildlife-pal.org

AFFILIATES

Bahrain
Dr Saeed A. Mohamed, PO Box 1858, Manama, Bahrain.
e-mail: saeed@alreem.com http://bahrainwildlife.com

Iraq
Nature Iraq, House 25, Street 27, Qtr 104 Ashti, Sulaimani, Kurdistan, Iraq. e-mail: info@natureiraq.org
www.natureiraq.org

Kuwait
Kuwait Environment Protection Society, PO Box 1896, Safat 13019, Kuwait; e-mail: rasamhory@hotmail.com
www.keps.org.kw

Qatar
Friends of the Environment Centre, PO Box 1822, Doha, Qatar. E-mail: cefdoha@qatar.net.qa
http:// my qatar.org

Saudi Arabia
Saudi Wildlife Commission (SWC), PO Box 61681, Riyadh 11575. Pub: *Phoenix; The.*
e-mail: ncwcd@zajil.net www.ncwcd.gov.sa/

Syria
Syrian Society ofr the Conservation of Wildlife (SSCW), PO Box 9853, Damascus, Syria;
e-mail: sscw.syria@gmail.com www.sscw-syria.org/ar/

Yemen
Yemen Society for the Protection of Wildlife (YSPW), 29 Alger Street, PO Box 19759, Sana'a, Yemen.
e-mail: wildlife.yemen@y.net.ye

PACIFIC

PARTNER

Australia
(also covers Christmas Island, Cocos Islands, Norfolk Island, Heard & McDonald Islands, Antarctica)
Birds Australia, Suite 2-05, 60 Leicester Street, Carlton, VIC 3053, Australia. Pub: *Australia Garcilla; Birds Australia Annual Report; Eclectus; Emu; Wingspan (WATCH) (Australia); from wingspan@birdsaustralia. com.au;* e-mail: info@birdlife.org.au - www.birdlife.org.au/

French Polynesia
Société d'Ornithologie de Polynésie 'Manu', B.P. 7023, 98719 Taravao, Tahiti, French Polynesia;
e-mail: sop@manu.pf www.manu.pf

New Zealand
(also covers Niue and Tokelau)
Forest & Bird, Level 1, 90 Ghunzee Street, PO Box 631, Wellington 6140. Pub: *Forest & Bird; Forest & Bird Annual Report; Forest & Bird Conservation News.*
e-mail: office@forestandbird.org.nz
www.forestandbird.org.nz/

Palau
Palau Conservation Society, PO Box 1811, Koror, PW96940, Republic of Palau. Pub: *Ngerel a Biib;*
e-mail: pcs@palaunet.com www.palauconservation.org

AFFILIATES

Cook Islands
Te Ipukarea Society (TIS), PO Box 649, Rarotonga, Cook Islands; e-mail: 2tis@oyster.net.ck

New Caledonia (to France)
Société Calédonienne d'Ornithologie (SCO)
BP 13641, 98 803 Nouméa Cedex, New Caledonia
e-mail: president@sco.asso.nc - www.sco.asso.nc

Samoa
O le Si'osi'omaga Society Incorporated (OLSSI), P O Box 2282, Apia, Western Samoa;
e-mail: ngo_siosiomaga@samoa.ws

SPECIAL INTEREST ORGANISATIONS

AFRICAN BIRD CLUB.

 c/o Birdlife International as below. e-mail (general): contact@african-birdclub.org e-mail: (membership and sales): membership@africanbirdclub.org www.africanbirdclub.org
Pub: *Bulletin of the African Bird Club*.

BIRDLIFE INTERNATIONAL.
Wellbrook Court, Girton Road, Cambridge, CB3 0NA, +44 (0)1223 277 318; (Fax) +44 (0)1223 277 200; www.birdlife.org
e-mail: birdlife@birdlife.org
Pub:*World Birdwatch*.

EAST AFRICA NATURAL HISTORY SOCIETY see Kenya in preceding list.

EURING (European Union for Bird Ringing).
Euring Data Bank, c/o BTO, The Nunnery, Thetford, Norfolk IP24 2PU. 01842 750 050. www.euring.org

FAUNA AND FLORA INTERNATIONAL.
Jupiter House, 4th Floor, Station Road, Cambridge, CB1 2JD. Call on +44 (0)1223 571 000; (Fax) +44 (0)1223 461 481. www.fauna-flora.org
e-mail: info@fauna-flora.org
Pub: *Fauna & Flora News; Oryx*.

LIPU-UK
(the Italian League for the Protection of Birds).
 David Lingard, Fernwood, Doddington Road, Whisby, Lincs, LN6 9BX, +44 (0)1522 689 030, e-mail: david@lipu-uk.org www.lipu-uk.org
Pub:*The Hoopoe*, annually, *Ali Notizie*, quarterly.

NEOTROPICAL BIRD CLUB.
 (Central and South America and the Caribbean) c/o The Lodge, Sandy, Bedfordshire, SG19 2DL. Pub:*Cotinga*.
e-mail: secretary@neotropicalbirdclub.org
www.neotropicalbirdclub.org

ORIENTAL BIRD CLUB.
P.O.Box 324, Bedford, MK42 0WG
Pub:*The Forktail; BirdingASIA*.
email: mail@orientalbirdclub.org
www.orientalbirdclub.org

ORNITHOLOGICAL SOCIETY OF THE MIDDLE EAST (OSME).
c/o The Lodge, Sandy, Beds, SG19 2DL.
Pub: *Sandgrouse*. e-mail: secretary@osme.org
www.osme.org

TRAFFIC International (formerly Wildlife Trade Monitoring Unit).
219a Huntingdon Road, Cambridge, CB3 0DL, +44 (0)1223 277 427; (Fax) +44 (0)1223 277 237. Pub:*TRAFFIC Bulletin*.
e-mail: traffic@traffic.org
www.traffic.org

WEST AFRICAN ORNITHOLOGICAL SOCIETY.
R E Sharland, 1 Fisher's Heron, East Mills, Hants, SP6 2JR. Pub: *Malimbus*.
http://malimbus.free.fr

WETLANDS INTERNATIONAL.
PO Box 471, 6700 AL Wageningen, Netherlands, +31 317 485 774; (Fax) +31 317 486 770, Pub:*Wetlands*.
e-mail: post@wetlands.org
www.wetlands.org

WORLD OWL TRUST.
The World Owl Centre, Muncaster Castle, Ravenglass, Cumbria, CA18 1RQ, +44 (0)1229 717393; www.owls.org

WORLD PHEASANT ASSOCIATION.
7-9 Shaftesbury St, Fordingbridge, Hants SP6 1JF. 01425 657 129; (Fax) 01425 658 053. Pub:*WPA News*. e-mail: office@pheasant.org.uk
www.pheasant.org.uk

WORLD WIDE FUND FOR NATURE.
 Panda House, Weyside Park, Godalming United Kingdom. +44 1483 426 444; (Fax) +44 1483 426 409, e-mail: supporterrelations@wwf.org.uk
www.panda.org

QUICK REFERENCE SECTION

David Cromack

Kingfishers may seem relatively common but they are still a Schedule 1 species under the Wildlife & Countryside Act, so you will need a licence to photograph them close to a nest-site. The full list of protected species is on page 323.

Tide tables	314	Birdwatchers and twitchers take note!	323
Sunrise/set times	320		
Sea areas	322	Birdline numbers	325
Schedule 1 species list	323	Index to reserves	326

BRITISH SUMMER TIME

In 2015 BST applies from 01:00 on March 29 to 01:00 on October 25.
Note that all the times in the following tables are GMT.

| Shetland 42, 43 |
| Orkney 44, 45 |

During British Summer Time one hour should be added. Predictions are given for the times of high water at Dover throughout the year.

The times of tides at the locations shown here may be obtained by adding or subtracting their 'tidal difference' as shown opposite (subtractions are indicated by a minus sign).

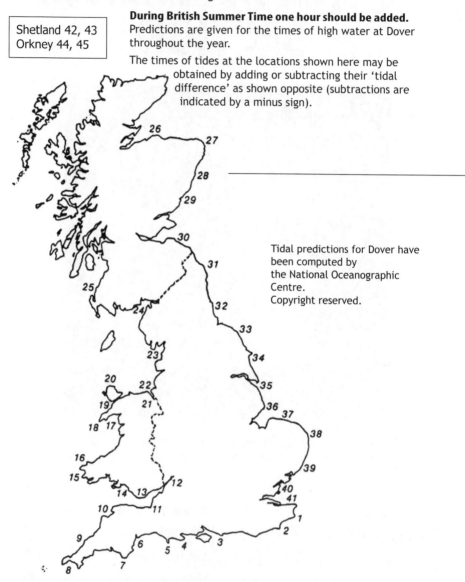

Tidal predictions for Dover have been computed by the National Oceanographic Centre.
Copyright reserved.

Map showing locations for which tidal differences are given on facing page.

TIDE TABLES 2015

Example 1
To calculate the time of first high water at Girvan on February 14
1. Look up the time at Dover (06 01)*
= 06:01 am
2. Add the tidal difference for Girvan
= 0.54
3. Therefore the time of high water at Girvan = 06:55 am

Example 2
To calculate the time of second high water at Blakeney on June 13
1. Look up the time at Dover (20 25)
= 20:25 pm
2. Add 1 hour for British Summer Time
= 21:05 pm
3. Subtract the tidal difference for Blakeney = - 4.07
4. Therefore the time of second high water at Blakeney = 17:18 pm

NB: *All Dover times are shown on the 24-hour clock.
Following the time of each high water, the height of the tide is given in metres. This height only applies to the high water level at Dover and may be different in other areas around the country. (Tide tables beyond April 2016 are not available at the time of going to press.)

TIDAL DIFFERENCES

1	Dover	See pp 316-319		23	Morecambe	0	20
2	Dungeness	-0	12	24	Silloth	0	51
3	Selsey Bill	0	09	25	Girvan	0	54
4	Swanage (lst H.W.Springs)	-2	36	26	Lossiemouth	0	48
5	Portland	-4	23	27	Fraserburgh	1	20
6	Exmouth (Approaches)	-4	48	28	Aberdeen	2	30
7	Salcombe	-5	23	29	Montrose	3	30
8	Newlyn (Penzance)	5	59	30	Dunbar	3	42
9	Padstow	-5	47	31	Holy Island	3	58
10	Bideford	-5	17	32	Sunderland	4	38
11	Bridgwater	-4	23	33	Whitby	5	12
12	Sharpness Dock	-3	19	34	Bridlington	5	53
13	Cardiff (Penarth)	-4	16	35	Grimsby	-5	20
14	Swansea	-4	52	36	Skegness	-5	00
15	Skomer Island	-5	00	37	Blakeney	-4	07
16	Fishguard	-3	48	38	Gorleston	-2	08
17	Barmouth	-2	45	39	Aldeburgh	-0	13
18	Bardsey Island	-3	07	40	Bradwell Waterside	1	11
19	Caernarvon	-1	07	41	Herne Bay	1	28
20	Amlwch	-0	22	42	Sullom Voe	-1	34
21	Connahs Quay	0	20	43	Lerwick	0	01
22	Hilbre Island			44	Kirkwall	-0	26
	(Hoylake/West Kirby)	-0	05	45	Widewall Bay	-1	30

NB. Care should be taken when making calculations at the beginning and end of British Summer Time. See worked examples above.

QUICK REFERENCE

TIDE TABLES 2015

Tidal Predictions : HIGH WATERS 2015

Datum of Predictions = Chart Datum : 3.67 metres below Ordnance Datum (Newlyn)

British Summer Time Dates for 2015 : 29th March to 25th October (data not adjusted)

DOVER — January

Day	Morning time	m	Afternoon time	m
1 Th	07:36	6.0	20:21	5.9
2 F	08:40	6.1	21:16	6.1
3 Sa	09:33	6.2	22:03	6.3
4 Su	10:19	6.4	22:44	6.5
5 M	11:00	6.5	23:22	6.6
6 Tu	11:39	6.5		
7 W	00:00	6.6	12:15	6.5
8 Th	00:36	6.6	12:50	6.4
9 F	01:10	6.6	13:24	6.3
10 Sa	01:44	6.4	13:56	6.1
11 Su	02:17	6.3	14:30	5.9
12 M	02:51	6.0	15:09	5.7
13 Tu	03:33	5.8	16:00	5.5
14 W	04:29	5.6	17:03	5.3
15 Th	05:36	5.5	18:15	5.3
16 F	06:48	5.5	19:26	5.5
17 Sa	07:54	5.8	20:28	5.9
18 Su	08:51	6.1	21:21	6.2
19 M	09:40	6.4	22:09	6.5
20 Tu	10:28	6.7	22:57	6.8
21 W	11:15	6.9	23:44	7.0
22 Th	12:05	7.0		
23 F	00:32	7.1	12:55	6.9
24 Sa	01:20	7.1	13:45	6.8
25 Su	02:06	6.9	14:33	6.6
26 M	02:51	6.7	15:21	6.3
27 Tu	03:42	6.5	16:15	6.0
28 W	04:39	6.1	17:20	5.7
29 Th	05:49	5.8	18:38	5.6
30 F	07:09	5.7	19:57	5.6
31 Sa	08:24	5.8	21:00	5.8

DOVER — February

Day	Morning time	m	Afternoon time	m
1 Su	09:21	6.0	21:48	6.1
2 M	10:08	6.1	22:28	6.3
3 Tu	10:46	6.3	23:05	6.5
4 W	11:22	6.4	23:40	6.6
5 Th	11:56	6.4		
6 F	00:15	6.7	12:28	6.4
7 Sa	00:47	6.6	12:58	6.4
8 Su	01:16	6.5	13:25	6.3
9 M	01:42	6.4	13:52	6.1
10 Tu	02:09	6.2	14:25	6.0
11 W	02:44	6.1	15:07	5.8
12 Th	03:33	5.8	16:06	5.6
13 F	04:40	5.6	17:21	5.4
14 Sa	06:01	5.5	18:46	5.4
15 Su	07:23	5.6	20:03	5.7
16 M	08:30	6.0	21:03	6.1
17 Tu	09:24	6.3	21:54	6.5
18 W	10:14	6.7	22:41	6.9
19 Th	11:01	6.9	23:27	7.1
20 F	11:49	7.0		
21 Sa	00:14	7.2	12:37	7.0
22 Su	00:59	7.2	13:24	6.9
23 M	01:42	7.0	14:08	6.7
24 Tu	02:26	6.8	14:53	6.4
25 W	03:12	6.5	15:43	6.1
26 Th	04:08	6.0	16:45	5.7
27 F	05:18	5.6	18:03	5.4
28 Sa	06:45	5.4	19:30	5.4

DOVER — March

Day	Morning time	m	Afternoon time	m
1 Su	08:06	5.5	20:37	5.7
2 M	09:06	5.8	21:27	6.0
3 Tu	09:52	6.0	22:08	6.2
4 W	10:29	6.2	22:44	6.4
5 Th	11:02	6.3	23:18	6.5
6 F	11:33	6.4	23:50	6.6
7 Sa	12:03	6.4		
8 Su	00:20	6.6	12:30	6.4
9 M	00:45	6.5	12:54	6.4
10 Tu	01:09	6.5	13:21	6.3
11 W	01:36	6.3	13:52	6.2
12 Th	02:09	6.2	14:33	6.0
13 F	02:55	6.0	15:28	5.7
14 Sa	04:02	5.6	16:45	5.5
15 Su	05:30	5.5	18:17	5.4
16 M	07:00	5.6	19:41	5.7
17 Tu	08:12	5.9	20:44	6.1
18 W	09:09	6.3	21:35	6.6
19 Th	09:57	6.7	22:21	6.9
20 F	10:43	6.9	23:06	7.1
21 Sa	11:30	7.0	23:51	7.2
22 Su	12:16	7.0		
23 M	00:36	7.2	13:01	6.9
24 Tu	01:18	7.0	13:43	6.7
25 W	02:00	6.7	14:27	6.4
26 Th	02:46	6.4	15:15	6.1
27 F	03:40	6.1	16:14	5.7
28 Sa	04:48	5.5	17:28	5.4
29 Su	06:15	5.3	18:54	5.3
30 M	07:39	5.4	20:06	5.6
31 Tu	08:41	5.6	20:59	5.9

DOVER — April

Day	Morning time	m	Afternoon time	m
1 W	09:28	5.9	21:42	6.1
2 Th	10:05	6.1	22:18	6.3
3 F	10:36	6.2	22:51	6.4
4 Sa	11:05	6.4	23:21	6.5
5 Su	11:33	6.4	23:49	6.5
6 M	12:00	6.5		
7 Tu	00:15	6.5	12:27	6.4
8 W	00:42	6.5	12:57	6.4
9 Th	01:11	6.4	13:32	6.3
10 F	01:48	6.2	14:14	6.1
11 Sa	02:36	6.0	15:12	5.9
12 Su	03:45	5.7	16:28	5.6
13 M	05:13	5.5	17:56	5.6
14 Tu	06:42	5.6	19:18	5.8
15 W	07:54	6.0	20:21	6.2
16 Th	08:50	6.3	21:12	6.5
17 F	09:38	6.6	21:59	6.8
18 Sa	10:24	6.8	22:44	7.0
19 Su	11:09	6.9	23:29	7.1
20 M	11:55	6.9		
21 Tu	00:13	7.0	12:39	6.8
22 W	00:57	6.8	13:21	6.6
23 Th	01:39	6.6	14:04	6.4
24 F	02:24	6.3	14:51	6.1
25 Sa	03:15	5.9	15:44	5.8
26 Su	04:18	5.5	16:50	5.5
27 M	05:36	5.2	18:09	5.4
28 Tu	06:59	5.3	19:23	5.5
29 W	08:03	5.5	20:21	5.7
30 Th	08:52	5.7	21:06	6.0

National Oceanography Centre (www.noc.ac.uk)

TIDE TABLES 2015

Time Zone: **GMT**
Units: **METRES**

Tidal Predictions : HIGH WATERS 2015

Datum of Predictions = Chart Datum : 3.67 metres below Ordnance Datum (Newlyn)

British Summer Time Dates for 2015 : 29th March to 25th October (data not adjusted)

DOVER — May

Date	Morning time	m	Afternoon time	m
1 F	09:31	6.0	21:45	6.2
2 Sa	10:03	6.1	22:18	6.3
3 Su	10:33	6.3	22:48	6.4
4 M	11:02	6.4	23:18	6.5
5 Tu	11:33	6.5	23:48	6.5
6 W			12:07	6.5
7 Th	00:22	6.5	12:43	6.5
8 F	00:58	6.4	13:24	6.4
9 Sa	01:41	6.2	14:12	6.2
10 Su	02:35	6.0	15:10	6.0
11 M	03:45	5.8	16:19	5.9
12 Tu	05:01	5.7	17:35	5.8
13 W	06:20	5.8	18:50	6.0
14 Th	07:30	6.0	19:54	6.2
15 F	08:27	6.2	20:48	6.5
16 Sa	09:18	6.5	21:37	6.7
17 Su	10:06	6.6	22:24	6.8
18 M	10:52	6.7	23:10	6.8
19 Tu	11:38	6.8	23:55	6.8
20 W			12:21	6.7
21 Th	00:39	6.7	13:03	6.6
22 F	01:20	6.4	13:44	6.4
23 Sa	02:03	6.2	14:27	6.2
24 Su	02:50	5.9	15:15	6.0
25 M	03:44	5.6	16:10	5.7
26 Tu	04:48	5.3	17:16	5.5
27 W	06:03	5.3	18:28	5.4
28 Th	07:11	5.5	19:31	5.6
29 F	08:05	5.5	20:22	5.8
30 Sa	08:49	5.8	21:04	6.0
31 Su	09:26	6.0	21:40	6.1

DOVER — June

Date	Morning time	m	Afternoon time	m
1 M	10:00	6.2	22:15	6.3
2 Tu	10:34	6.4	22:51	6.4
3 W	11:12	6.5	23:28	6.5
4 Th	11:53	6.6		
5 F	00:09	6.6	12:36	6.6
6 Sa	00:54	6.5	13:24	6.5
7 Su	01:45	6.4	14:14	6.4
8 M	02:40	6.2	15:08	6.3
9 Tu	03:40	6.1	16:06	6.2
10 W	04:44	5.9	17:09	6.1
11 Th	05:53	5.9	18:18	6.1
12 F	07:01	5.9	19:25	6.1
13 Sa	08:04	6.1	20:25	6.3
14 Su	09:01	6.2	21:19	6.4
15 M	09:51	6.4	22:09	6.5
16 Tu	10:39	6.5	22:56	6.6
17 W	11:23	6.6	23:40	6.6
18 Th			12:04	6.6
19 F	00:21	6.5	12:44	6.6
20 Sa	01:02	6.4	13:23	6.5
21 Su	01:42	6.2	14:02	6.4
22 M	02:22	6.0	14:44	6.2
23 Tu	03:06	5.8	15:29	5.9
24 W	03:57	5.5	16:21	5.7
25 Th	04:56	5.3	17:21	5.5
26 F	06:02	5.3	18:28	5.4
27 Sa	07:06	5.4	19:28	5.6
28 Su	08:00	5.6	20:05	5.8
29 M	08:48	5.8	21:05	6.0
30 Tu	09:30	6.1	21:47	6.2

DOVER — July

Date	Morning time	m	Afternoon time	m
1 W	10:12	6.4	22:28	6.4
2 Th	10:54	6.6	23:12	6.6
3 F	11:39	6.7	23:57	6.7
4 Sa			12:27	6.8
5 Su	00:47	6.7	13:15	6.8
6 M	01:39	6.6	14:04	6.7
7 Tu	02:33	6.5	14:53	6.6
8 W	03:24	6.3	15:45	6.4
9 Th	04:20	6.1	16:42	6.2
10 F	05:21	5.9	17:47	6.1
11 Sa	06:31	5.8	18:58	6.0
12 Su	07:43	5.9	20:07	6.0
13 M	08:48	6.0	21:07	6.2
14 Tu	09:41	6.2	21:59	6.3
15 W	10:26	6.4	22:43	6.4
16 Th	11:07	6.5	23:24	6.5
17 F	11:45	6.6		
18 Sa	00:03	6.5	12:23	6.6
19 Su	00:40	6.4	13:00	6.6
20 M	01:16	6.3	13:36	6.5
21 Tu	01:51	6.2	14:10	6.3
22 W	02:26	6.0	14:45	6.1
23 Th	03:03	5.8	15:24	5.9
24 F	03:49	5.5	16:14	5.6
25 Sa	04:39	5.4	17:18	5.4
26 Su	05:57	5.3	18:30	5.3
27 M	07:10	5.4	19:38	5.6
28 Tu	08:13	5.7	20:35	5.9
29 W	09:06	6.1	21:24	6.2
30 Th	09:52	6.4	22:09	6.5
31 F	10:36	6.7	22:54	6.7

DOVER — August

Date	Morning time	m	Afternoon time	m
1 Sa	11:22	6.9	23:42	6.9
2 Su			12:09	7.0
3 M	00:31	6.9	12:57	7.1
4 Tu	01:22	6.8	13:44	7.0
5 W	02:12	6.7	14:30	6.8
6 Th	03:00	6.5	15:18	6.6
7 F	03:50	6.3	16:12	6.3
8 Sa	04:50	5.9	17:17	6.0
9 Su	06:03	5.7	18:35	5.8
10 M	07:24	5.7	19:55	5.8
11 Tu	08:35	5.9	21:00	6.0
12 W	09:28	6.1	21:49	6.2
13 Th	10:11	6.4	22:30	6.3
14 F	10:48	6.5	23:07	6.4
15 Sa	11:24	6.7	23:42	6.5
16 Su	00:16	6.5	12:00	6.7
17 M	00:48	6.4	12:34	6.7
18 Tu	01:17	6.3	13:06	6.6
19 W	01:45	6.2	13:33	6.5
20 Th	02:15	6.0	14:00	6.3
21 F	02:52	5.8	14:31	6.1
22 Sa			15:14	5.8
23 Su	03:45	5.6	16:16	5.5
24 M	04:59	5.4	17:38	5.4
25 Tu	06:24	5.4	19:03	5.5
26 W	07:43	5.7	20:11	5.9
27 Th	08:43	6.1	21:05	6.3
28 F	09:33	6.5	21:51	6.6
29 Sa	10:17	6.8	22:36	6.9
30 Su	11:02	7.1	23:22	7.0
31 M	11:47	7.2		

National Oceanography Centre (www.noc.ac.uk)

QUICK REFERENCE

TIDE TABLES 2015

Units: METRES

Tidal Predictions : HIGH WATERS 2015

Datum of Predictions = Chart Datum : 3.67 metres below Ordnance Datum (Newlyn)

British Summer Time Dates for 2015 : 29th March to 25th October (data not adjusted)

DOVER — September

Day	Morning time	m	Afternoon time	m
1 Tu	00:09	7.1	12:33	7.2
2 W	00:57	7.0	13:18	7.1
3 Th	01:45	6.8	14:03	6.9
4 F	02:31	6.5	14:50	6.6
5 Sa	03:21	6.2	15:43	6.2
6 Su	04:19	5.9	16:49	5.8
7 M	05:33	5.6	18:15	5.5
8 Tu	07:03	5.5	19:43	5.6
9 W	08:17	5.8	20:49	5.8
10 Th	09:10	6.1	21:36	6.1
11 F	09:51	6.3	22:14	6.3
12 Sa	10:27	6.5	22:47	6.4
13 Su	11:01	6.7	23:18	6.5
14 M	11:34	6.7	23:48	6.5
15 Tu			12:06	6.7
16 W	00:17	6.5	12:33	6.6
17 Th	00:43	6.4	12:57	6.5
18 F	01:09	6.3	13:21	6.4
19 Sa	01:37	6.2	13:51	6.2
20 Su	02:13	6.0	14:31	6.0
21 M	03:02	5.8	15:30	5.6
22 Tu	04:15	5.5	16:59	5.5
23 W	05:48	5.4	18:34	5.5
24 Th	07:15	5.7	19:49	5.9
25 F	08:20	6.1	20:45	6.3
26 Sa	09:11	6.6	21:32	6.7
27 Su	09:55	6.9	22:16	6.9
28 M	10:39	7.2	23:00	7.1
29 Tu	11:23	7.3	23:46	7.1
30 W			12:07	7.3

DOVER — October

Day	Morning time	m	Afternoon time	m
1 Th	00:33	7.0	12:51	7.1
2 F	01:18	6.9	13:36	6.9
3 Sa	02:03	6.6	14:23	6.5
4 Su	02:52	6.3	15:16	6.1
5 M	03:49	5.9	16:21	5.7
6 Tu	05:00	5.6	17:48	5.4
7 W	06:29	5.5	19:21	5.5
8 Th	07:47	5.7	20:27	5.7
9 F	08:42	6.0	21:14	6.0
10 Sa	09:25	6.3	21:51	6.2
11 Su	10:02	6.5	22:23	6.4
12 M	10:35	6.6	22:52	6.5
13 Tu	11:06	6.7	23:21	6.6
14 W	11:36	6.7	23:48	6.6
15 Th			12:02	6.6
16 F	00:14	6.5	12:27	6.5
17 Sa	00:42	6.5	12:54	6.4
18 Su	01:13	6.4	13:27	6.3
19 M	01:51	6.2	14:08	6.1
20 Tu	02:39	6.0	15:06	5.7
21 W	03:51	5.7	16:34	5.5
22 Th	05:18	5.6	18:07	5.6
23 F	06:45	5.8	19:24	5.9
24 Sa	07:52	6.1	20:23	6.3
25 Su	08:45	6.6	21:11	6.6
26 M	09:32	6.9	21:56	6.9
27 Tu	10:18	7.1	22:41	7.0
28 W	11:00	7.2	23:26	7.1
29 Th	11:45	7.2		
30 F	00:12	7.0	12:30	7.0
31 Sa	00:57	6.8	13:14	6.8

DOVER — November

Day	Morning time	m	Afternoon time	m
1 Su	01:41	6.6	14:00	6.4
2 M	02:27	6.3	14:51	6.1
3 Tu	03:20	6.0	15:51	5.7
4 W	04:23	5.7	17:08	5.4
5 Th	05:42	5.5	18:38	5.4
6 F	07:02	5.6	19:48	5.6
7 Sa	08:03	5.8	20:39	5.8
8 Su	08:51	6.1	21:21	6.1
9 M	09:32	6.3	21:54	6.2
10 Tu	10:06	6.4	22:24	6.4
11 W	10:37	6.5	22:53	6.5
12 Th	11:06	6.6	23:23	6.6
13 F	11:35	6.6	23:53	6.6
14 Sa			12:06	6.5
15 Su	00:25	6.6	12:38	6.5
16 M	01:01	6.5	13:15	6.3
17 Tu	01:42	6.3	14:00	6.1
18 W	02:33	6.1	15:00	5.9
19 Th	03:38	5.9	16:16	5.7
20 F	04:58	5.8	17:37	5.7
21 Sa	06:09	5.9	18:53	5.9
22 Su	07:19	6.1	19:56	6.2
23 M	08:18	6.4	20:49	6.5
24 Tu	09:09	6.7	21:38	6.7
25 W	09:57	6.9	22:25	6.9
26 Th	10:43	7.0	23:12	6.9
27 F	11:29	7.0	23:57	6.9
28 Sa			12:14	7.0
29 Su	00:40	6.8	12:57	6.7
30 M	01:22	6.7	13:41	6.4

DOVER — December

Day	Morning time	m	Afternoon time	m
1 Tu	02:05	6.4	14:27	6.1
2 W	02:52	6.2	15:19	5.8
3 Th	03:45	5.9	16:21	5.5
4 F	04:48	5.6	17:36	5.3
5 Sa	06:03	5.5	18:52	5.3
6 Su	07:13	5.6	19:53	5.5
7 M	08:09	5.8	20:42	5.8
8 Tu	08:56	6.0	21:21	6.0
9 W	09:34	6.3	21:55	6.2
10 Th	10:08	6.4	22:27	6.4
11 F	10:40	6.4	23:00	6.5
12 Sa	11:15	6.5	23:36	6.6
13 Su	11:51	6.6		
14 M	00:15	6.7	12:30	6.6
15 Tu	00:57	6.5	13:13	6.5
16 W	01:41	6.4	14:00	6.3
17 Th	02:29	6.4	14:55	6.1
18 F	03:24	6.2	15:57	6.0
19 Sa	04:25	6.1	17:06	5.9
20 Su	05:33	6.0	18:17	5.9
21 M	06:45	6.1	19:27	6.0
22 Tu	07:51	6.2	20:30	6.2
23 W	08:50	6.4	21:26	6.4
24 Th	09:43	6.6	22:15	6.6
25 F	10:33	6.7	23:02	6.7
26 Sa	11:18	6.7	23:45	6.8
27 Su	00:25	6.8	12:42	6.6
28 M	01:04	6.7	13:21	6.2
29 Tu	01:43	6.6	14:02	6.6
30 W	02:24	6.4	14:45	6.0
31 Th				

National Oceanography Centre (www.noc.ac.uk)

TIDE TABLES 2016

Time Zone: GMT Units: METRES

Tidal Predictions : HIGH WATERS 2016
Datum of Predictions = Chart Datum : 3.67 metres below Ordnance Datum (Newlyn)
British Summer Time Dates for 2016 : 27th March to 30th October (data not adjusted)

DOVER — January

Day	Morning time	m	Afternoon time	m
1 F	03:07	6.1	15:33	5.7
2 Sa	03:57	5.8	16:29	5.4
3 Su	04:56	5.5	17:37	5.2
4 M	06:06	5.4	18:49	5.2
5 Tu	07:15	5.4	19:52	5.4
6 W	08:12	5.6	20:43	5.7
7 Th	09:00	5.9	21:25	6.0
8 F	09:39	6.1	22:03	6.2
9 Sa	10:18	6.3	22:42	6.5
10 Su	10:56	6.5	23:21	6.7
11 M	11:37	6.7		
12 Tu	00:03	6.8	12:21	6.7
13 W	00:47	6.8	13:06	6.7
14 Th	01:32	6.8	13:53	6.6
15 F	02:17	6.7	14:42	6.4
16 Sa	03:06	6.5	15:36	6.2
17 Su	04:00	6.3	16:35	6.0
18 M	05:01	6.1	17:43	5.8
19 Tu	06:13	5.9	19:00	5.7
20 W	07:29	5.9	20:15	5.9
21 Th	08:39	6.1	21:18	6.1
22 F	09:37	6.3	22:07	6.4
23 Sa	10:25	6.4	22:51	6.6
24 Su	11:08	6.5	23:30	6.7
25 M	11:48	6.6		
26 Tu	00:07	6.7	12:24	6.5
27 W	00:44	6.7	13:00	6.5
28 Th	01:20	6.7	13:36	6.3
29 F	01:54	6.5	14:10	6.1
30 Sa	02:29	6.3	14:45	5.9
31 Su	03:06	6.0	15:27	5.6

DOVER — February

Day	Morning time	m	Afternoon time	m
1 M	03:50	5.7	16:19	5.3
2 Tu	04:49	5.4	17:29	5.2
3 W	06:05	5.2	18:49	5.2
4 Th	07:22	5.3	20:00	5.4
5 F	08:24	5.6	20:54	5.8
6 Sa	09:12	5.9	21:39	6.1
7 Su	09:55	6.3	22:21	6.5
8 M	10:37	6.6	23:03	6.7
9 Tu	11:19	6.8	23:45	6.9
10 W	12:04	6.9		
11 Th	00:30	7.0	12:51	6.9
12 F	01:15	7.0	13:37	6.8
13 Sa	01:58	6.9	14:24	6.6
14 Su	02:44	6.7	15:12	6.3
15 M	03:35	6.4	16:08	6.0
16 Tu	04:35	6.1	17:15	5.7
17 W	05:48	5.8	18:37	5.5
18 Th	07:15	5.7	20:02	5.7
19 F	08:33	5.8	21:06	5.9
20 Sa	09:31	6.0	21:54	6.2
21 Su	10:17	6.3	22:35	6.4
22 M	10:54	6.4	23:12	6.6
23 Tu	11:30	6.5	23:47	6.7
24 W	12:04	6.5		
25 Th	00:21	6.7	12:37	6.4
26 F	00:54	6.7	13:08	6.3
27 Sa	01:24	6.5	13:36	6.3
28 Su	01:51	6.3	14:03	6.1
29 M	02:19	6.1	14:36	5.9

DOVER — March

Day	Morning time	m	Afternoon time	m
1 Tu	02:54	5.8	15:21	5.6
2 W	03:47	5.5	16:25	5.3
3 Th	05:03	5.2	17:50	5.1
4 F	06:33	5.2	19:17	5.3
5 Sa	07:49	5.5	20:23	5.7
6 Su	08:45	5.9	21:13	6.1
7 M	09:32	6.3	21:57	6.5
8 Tu	10:15	6.6	22:40	6.8
9 W	10:59	6.9	23:23	7.1
10 Th	11:44	7.0		
11 F	00:08	7.2	12:30	7.0
12 Sa	00:53	7.1	13:17	6.9
13 Su	01:37	7.0	14:03	6.7
14 M	02:23	6.8	14:51	6.4
15 Tu	03:13	6.4	15:45	6.1
16 W	04:12	6.0	16:51	5.7
17 Th	05:28	5.6	18:15	5.5
18 F	07:01	5.5	19:42	5.6
19 Sa	08:21	5.7	20:47	5.8
20 Su	09:18	5.9	21:34	6.1
21 M	10:00	6.1	22:13	6.4
22 Tu	10:36	6.3	22:49	6.5
23 W	11:09	6.4	23:24	6.6
24 Th	11:41	6.5	23:57	6.7
25 F	12:12	6.5		
26 Sa	00:27	6.6	12:39	6.4
27 Su	00:53	6.5	13:04	6.3
28 M	01:16	6.3	13:30	6.2
29 Tu	01:42	6.2	14:01	6.0
30 W	02:16	5.9	14:42	5.8
31 Th	03:05	5.6	15:43	5.5

DOVER — April

Day	Morning time	m	Afternoon time	m
1 F	04:21	5.3	17:07	5.3
2 Sa	05:54	5.3	18:37	5.4
3 Su	07:16	5.5	19:49	5.7
4 M	08:18	5.9	20:44	6.2
5 Tu	09:07	6.3	21:30	6.6
6 W	09:51	6.7	22:15	6.9
7 Th	10:36	6.9	22:59	7.1
8 F	11:21	7.0	23:44	7.2
9 Sa	12:09	7.0		
10 Su	00:30	7.1	12:57	6.9
11 M	01:17	7.0	13:45	6.7
12 Tu	02:04	6.7	14:33	6.4
13 W	02:55	6.3	15:24	6.1
14 Th	03:54	5.9	16:27	5.7
15 F	05:06	5.5	17:45	5.5
16 Sa	06:38	5.4	19:10	5.5
17 Su	07:55	5.6	20:15	5.8
18 M	08:51	5.8	21:05	6.0
19 Tu	09:34	6.0	21:46	6.2
20 W	10:10	6.2	22:23	6.4
21 Th	10:43	6.3	22:57	6.5
22 F	11:15	6.4	23:30	6.5
23 Sa	11:45	6.4		
24 Su	00:00	6.5	12:12	6.4
25 M	00:25	6.4	12:39	6.4
26 Tu	00:50	6.3	13:07	6.3
27 W	01:18	6.2	13:41	6.1
28 Th	01:55	6.0	14:23	5.9
29 F	02:45	5.8	15:22	5.7
30 Sa	03:57	5.5	16:39	5.6

National Oceanography Centre (www.noc.ac.uk)

QUICK REFERENCE

SUNRISE AND SUNSET TIMES
FOR 2015

Predictions are given for the times of sunrise and sunset on every Sunday throughout the year. For places on the same latitude as the following, add 4 minutes for each degree of longitude west (subtract if east).

These times are in GMT, except between 01:00 on Mar 29 and 01:00 on Oct 25, when the times are in BST (1 hour in advance of GMT).

		London Rise	London Set	Manchester Rise	Manchester Set	Edinburgh Rise	Edinburgh Set
January	4	08:06	16:05	08:24	16:03	08:43	15:53
	11	08:03	16:14	08:21	16:13	08:38	16:04
	18	07:57	16:25	08:14	16:25	08:30	16:17
	25	07:49	16:37	08:06	16:38	08:20	16:31
February	1	07:39	16:49	07:55	16:51	08:08	16:46
	8	07:28	17:02	07:42	17:05	07:54	17:01
	15	07:15	17:15	07:28	17:19	07:38	17:16
	22	07:01	17:28	07:13	17:32	07:22	17:32
March	1	06:46	17:40	06:58	17:46	07:05	17:47
	8	06:31	17:52	06:41	17:59	06:47	18:02
	15	06:15	18:04	06:25	18:12	06:29	18:16
	22	06:00	18:16	06:08	18:25	06:10	18:30
	29	06:44	19:28	06:51	19:38	06:49	19:47
April	5	06:28	19:40	06:34	19:51	06:33	19:59
	12	06:12	19:51	06:17	20:04	06:15	20:13
	19	05:57	20:03	06:01	20:17	05:58	20:27
	26	05:43	20:15	05:46	20:29	05:41	20:42
May	3	05:29	20:26	05:31	20:42	05:25	20:56
	10	05:17	20:38	05:18	20:54	05:10	21:10
	17	05:06	20:48	05:06	21:06	04:57	21:23
	24	04:57	20:58	04:56	21:17	04:46	21:35
	31	04:50	21:07	04:48	21:26	04:36	21:45
June	7	04:45	21:14	04:43	21:34	04:30	21:54
	14	04:43	21:19	04:40	21:39	04:27	22:00
	21	04:43	21:21	04:40	21:42	04:26	22:03
	28	04:46	21:22	04:42	21:42	04:29	22:03

SUNRISE AND SUNSET TIMES

		London Rise	London Set	Manchester Rise	Manchester Set	Edinburgh Rise	Edinburgh Set
July	5	04:50	21:19	04:47	21:39	04:35	21:59
	12	04:57	21:14	04:55	21:34	04:44	21:52
	19	05:05	21:07	05:04	21:26	04:54	21:43
	26	05:15	20:58	05:14	21:16	05:06	21:32
August	2	05:25	20:47	05:26	21:04	05:19	21:18
	9	05:36	20:35	05:37	20:51	05:32	21:03
	16	05:47	20:22	05:49	20:36	05:46	20:47
	23	05:58	20:07	06:02	20:21	05:59	20:30
	30	06:09	19:52	06:14	20:04	06:13	20:13
September	6	06:20	19:36	06:26	19:48	05:26	21:10
	13	06:31	19:20	06:38	19:31	05:40	20:54
	20	06:43	19:04	06:51	19:13	05:53	20:38
	27	06:54	18:48	07:03	18:56	06:07	20:20
October	4	07:05	18:32	07:15	18:39	07:21	18:41
	11	07:17	18:17	07:28	18:23	07:35	18:23
	18	07:29	18:02	07:41	18:07	07:50	18:05
	25	06:41	16:47	06:54	16:51	07:07	16:46
November	1	06:53	16:34	07:07	16:37	07:19	16:33
	8	07:06	16:22	07:21	16:24	07:34	16:18
	15	07:18	16:12	07:34	16:13	07:49	16:05
	22	07:30	16:03	07:47	16:03	08:03	15:54
	29	07:40	15:57	07:58	15:56	08:16	15:46
December	6	07:50	15:53	08:08	15:51	08:27	15:40
	13	07:58	15:51	08:17	15:49	08:36	15:38
	20	08:03	15:53	08:22	15:51	08:41	15:39
	27	08:06	15:57	08:25	15:55	08:44	15:44

QUICK REFERENCE

SEA AREAS

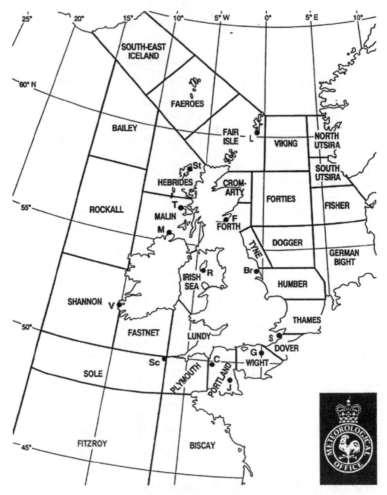

**STATIONS WHOSE LATEST REPORTS ARE BROADCAST IN THE
5-MINUTE FORECASTS**

Br Bridlington; C Channel Light-Vessel Automatic; F Fife Ness; G Greenwich Light-Vessel Automatic;
J Jersey; L Lerwick; M Malin Head; R Ronaldsway; S Sandettie Light-Vessel Automatic; Sc Scilly
Automatic; St Stornoway; T Tiree; V Valentia.

From information kindly supplied by the Meteorological Office

REVISION OF SEA AREAS

On 4 February 2002, the southern boundary of areas Plymouth and Sole, and the northern
boundary of areas Biscay and Finisterre were realigned along the Metarea I/II boundary at 48°27'
North. At the same time, sea area Finisterre was renamed FitzRoy.

Did you know that the FitzRoy shipping area is named after the founder of the Met Office?

SCHEDULE 1 SPECIES

Under the provisions of the Wildlife and Countryside Act 1981 the following bird species (listed in Schedule 1 - Part I of the Act) are protected by special penalties at all times.

Avocet	Fieldfare	Owl, Snowy	Spoonbill
Bee-eater	Firecrest	Peregrine	Stilt, Black-winged
Bittern	Garganey	Petrel, Leach's	Stint, Temminck's
Bittern, Little	Godwit, Black-tailed	Phalarope, Red-necked	Stone-curlew
Bluethroat	Goshawk	Plover, Kentish	Swan, Bewick's
Brambling	Grebe, Black-necked	Plover, Little Ringed	Swan, Whooper
Bunting, Cirl	Grebe, Slavonian	Quail, Common	Tern, Black
Bunting, Lapland	Greenshank	Redstart, Black	Tern, Little
Bunting, Snow	Gull, Little	Redwing	Tern, Roseate
Buzzard, Honey	Gull, Mediterranean	Rosefinch, Scarlet	Tit, Bearded
Chough	Harriers (all species)	Ruff	Tit, Crested
Corncrake	Heron, Purple	Sandpiper, Green	Treecreeper, Short-toed
Crake, Spotted	Hobby	Sandpiper, Purple	Warbler, Cetti's
Crossbills (all species)	Hoopoe	Sandpiper, Wood	Warbler, Dartford
Divers (all species)	Kingfisher	Scaup	Warbler, Marsh
Dotterel	Kite, Red	Scoter, Common	Warbler, Savi's
Duck, Long-tailed	Merlin	Scoter, Velvet	Whimbrel
Eagle, Golden	Oriole, Golden	Serin	Woodlark
Eagle, White-tailed	Osprey	Shorelark	Wryneck
Falcon, Gyr	Owl, Barn	Shrike, Red-backed	

The following birds and their eggs (listed in Schedule 1 - Part II of the Act) are protected by special penalties during the close season, which is Feb 1 to Aug 31 (Feb 21 to Aug 31 below high water mark), but may be killed outside this period - Goldeneye, Greylag Goose (in Outer Hebrides, Caithness, Sutherland, and Wester Ross only), Pintail.

BIRDWATCHERS AND TWITCHERS TAKE NOTE!

Be tick-aware while enjoying the great outdoors

IF YOU'RE a keen birdwatcher, the following situations may be familiar: wandering through bracken to spot nesting locations, walking through long grass to view wetland birds, and waiting in scrubland, watching migratory birds fly overhead. What you might not be so familiar with, however, is checking yourself for ticks afterwards.

Wherever you choose to enjoy birdwatching – be it forest, wetland or coast, UK or abroad – spending prolonged periods outside and in among the bushes increases the chance of being bitten by a tick which, if infected, can lead to the potential problem of Lyme disease.

Says Stella Huyshe-Shires, Chair of the charity Lyme Disease Action: "As a high-risk group, birdwatchers need to be particularly tick-aware. The number of cases of Lyme disease in the UK has risen over the last few years. It's important that awareness of potential problems associated with tick bites increases too."

Ticks, which can be tiny (the size of a full stop on an A4 page) blood-sucking parasites, peak

BIRDWATCHERS AND TWITCHERS TAKE NOTE!

in population from April to October, and are found throughout the UK, North America and across Europe.

Lyme disease causes a range of unpleasant symptoms which may include a circular red rash, headaches, a stiff neck, extreme fatigue, muscle and joint pain, and disturbances of sight, hearing, digestive system and sleep. If left untreated it can progress to the joints, the heart and the nervous system.

To reduce the risk of being bitten by an infected tick, the charity Lyme Disease Action advises birdwatchers to take the following precautions:

- Wear long sleeves and trousers.
- Wear light-coloured clothing so ticks are easier to spot.
- Use an insect repellent effective against ticks (look for those containing the chemical DEET).
- Keep to pathways and try to avoid areas of overgrown vegetation.
- Check for ticks regularly during the day.
- Remove any ticks found attached as soon as possible.
- Pack a tick remover if birdwatching away from home.

Tick removal

Ticks should be removed immediately with a tick removal tool or fine pointed tweezers. Gently pull the tick's body away from your skin directly outwards, without jerking. Do not try to pull the tick out with your fingers, burn the tick or cover it with creams or chemicals. If you don't have a tick removal tool, use a thread of cotton wound round close to the skin and pull upwards or, alternatively, cut a slit in a plastic card and slide that under the tick's body.

Treatment

If you have been bitten by a tick and notice any of the above symptoms, seek medical help straight away. Diagnosed and treated early, Lyme disease can be treated successfully with antibiotics.

DOES AND DON'TS OF REMOVING A TICK

Your main aims are to remove all parts of the tick's body and to prevent it releasing additional saliva or regurgitating its stomach contents into your bite wound.

DO use a proprietary tick removal tool (available from www.lymediseaseaction.org.uk or many vets and pet shops), and follow the instructions provided, or a pair of tweezers.

If no tools are available, rather than delay use a cotton thread. Tie a single loop of cotton around the tick's mouthparts, as close to the skin as possible, then pull gently upwards and outwards.

DO commence by cleansing the tweezers with antiseptic. After tick removal, cleanse the bite site and the tweezers with antiseptic.

DO wash hands thoroughly afterwards.

DO save the tick in a container in case you develop symptoms later (label with date and location). The Health Protection Agency are currently running a scheme to investigate ticks, details available at www.lymediseaseaction.org.uk/information/tick. htm or from the HPA at www.hpa.org.uk.

DO NOT squeeze or twist the body of the tick, as this may cause the head and body to separate, leaving the head embedded in your skin.

DO NOT use your fingernails to remove a tick. Infection can enter via any breaks in your skin, e.g. Close to the fingernail.

DO NOT crush the tick's body, as this may cause it to regurgitate its infected stomach contents into the bite wound.

DO NOT try to burn the tick off, apply petroleum jelly, nail polish or any other chemical. Any of these methods can cause discomfort to the tick, resulting in regurgitation, or saliva release.

A detailed leaflet (free to download) is available from www.lymediseaseaction.org.uk

Leaflets are also available from:
Lyme Disease Action,
PO Box 235, Penryn. TR10 8WZ. UK
Including a donation/sae will help them in their work for people affected by Lyme disease.

Lyme Disease Action (www.lymediseaseaction.org.uk) is a charity striving for greater awareness of Lyme disease and associated tick-borne diseases.

THE COUNTRYSIDE CODE

Launched on 12 July 2004, this Code for England has been produced through a partnership between the Countryside Agency and Countryside Council for Wales. The Countryside Code has been revised and re-launched to reflect the introduction of new open access rights (Countryside & Rights of Way Act 2000) and changes in society over the last 20 years.

● **Be safe – plan ahead**
Follow any signs, even when going out locally, it's best to get the latest information about where and when you can go; for example, your rights to go onto some areas of open land may be restricted while work is carried out, for safety reasons or during breeding seasons. Follow advice and local signs, and be prepared for the unexpected.

● **Leave gates and property as you find them**
Please respect the working life of the countryside, as our actions can affect people's livelihoods, our heritage, and the safety and welfare of animals and ourselves.

● **Protect plants and animals, and take your litter home**
We have a responsibility to protect our countryside now and for future generations, so make sure you don't harm animals, birds, plants, or trees.

● **Keep dogs under close control**
The countryside is a great place to exercise dogs, but it's every owner's duty to make sure their dog is not a danger or nuisance to farm animals, wildlife or other people.

● **Consider other people**
Showing consideration and respect for other people makes the countryside a pleasant Environment for everyone – at home, at work and at leisure.

BIRDLINE NUMBERS - National and Regional

National

Bird Information Service - www.birdingworld.co.uk	09068 700 222
Flightline (Northern Ireland)	028 9146 7408

Regional

	For information	Report sightings
Scotland	09068 700 234	01292 611 994
East Anglia	09068 700 245	07941 333 970
South East	09068 700 240	01845 570 444
www.southeastbirdnews.co.uk		or 08000 377 240

Charges
At the time of compilation, calls to premium line numbers cost 60p per minute.

OTHER BIRD INFORMATION SERVICES

Bird Forum
Free to join, online forum.
www.birdforum.net

BirdGuides
Offers subscription bird news services online and via email, text message and apps for Apple and Android devices.
www.birdguides.com; 020 8826 0934;
e-mail: contact@birdguides.com

Bird Information Ltd
Offers subscription bird news service - available online or pager.
www.birdinformation.co.uk; 0115 871 2888.

Rare Bird Alert
Offers subscription instant bird news service - available online, by pager or phone app.
www.rarebirdalert.co.uk;
newdesk: 01603 456 789.

Rare Bird Network
A free bird sightings service, which covers any bird sighting.
Contact: E-mail: info@rarebirdnetwork.co.uk;
Twitter: @rbnUK; Facebook: www.facebook.com/RareBirdNetwork@rbnUK;
www.rarebirdnetwork.co.uk

INDEX TO RESERVES

A

Abberton Reservoir 117
Abbott's Hall Farm 118
Aberlady Bay LNR 186
Adur Estuary 165
Ailsa Craig 184
Alkborough Flats 96
Amwell Nature Reserve 120
Arne 173
Arundel Wetland Centre 165
Aston Rowant NNR 102
Attenborough Nature Reserve 100
Aylesbeare Common 170

B

Balranald 193
Bardsey Bird Observatory 197
Baron's Haugh 184
Bass Rock/ Scottish Seabird Centre 186
Bawsinch Reserve & Duddingston Loch 186
Beacon Hill/Hawthorn Dene Meadow 131
Bedfont Lakes Country Park 161
Beinn Eighe & Loch Maree Islands NNR 190
Belvide 106
Bemersyde Moss 180
Bempton Cliffs 144
Benacre Broad NNR 126
Berry Head NNR 170
Besthorpe Nature Reserve 101
Blacktoft Sands 144
Blashford Lakes 155
Blithfield Reservoir 106
Blow's Downs 112
Bolton Ings (Dearne Valley) 149
Bough Beech Reservoir 158
Bovey Heathfield 170
Bowling Green Marsh 171
Boyton & Hollesley Marshes 126
Bradwell Bird Observatory 118
Brandon Marsh 107
Brean Down 176
Brechfa Pool 195
Brent (Welsh Harp) Reservoir 161
Bridgwater Bay NNR 176
Broad Ees Dole

(Sale Water Park) 138
Brockholes 136
Brownsea Island Nature Reserve 173
Burnham Beeches NNR 153
Burrator Reservoir 171
Burton Mere Wetlands (Dee Estuary) 130

C

Caerlaverock Wetland Centre 181
Calvert Jubilee 154
Cambus Pools 186
Campfield Marsh 134
Carlton Marshes 127
Carr Vale Nature Reserve 90
Carsington Water 90
Castle Water, Rye Harbour 164
Castle Woods 202
Catcott Complex Nature Reserves 176
Cemlyn 197
Chew Valley Lake 176
Chichester Harbour 165
Chobham Common NNR 162
Church Wood 154
Cleveland Lakes 92
Cley Marshes NNR 123
Cliffe Pools 158
Clunton Coppice 104
Coatham Marsh 147
Coll Reserve 182
College Lake 154
Colwick Country Park 101
Connah's Quay Power Station Reserve 197
Conwy 198
Coombe Country Park 108
Coombes Valley 106
Corrimony 190
Cors Caron NNR 202
Cors Dyfi Nature Reserve 195
Crook Of Baldoon 181
Crowdy Reservoir 168
Croxall Lakes 107
Culbin Sands 187
Culzean Castle Country Park 184
Cwm Clydach 200
Cwm Col-Huw 200

D

Dagenham Chase LNR 161

Dawlish Warren NNR 171
Dearne Valley (Bolton Ings) 149
Dearne Valley (Old Moor) 150
Dee Estuary 140
Dee Estuary (Burton Mere Wetlands) 130
Dee Estuary (Parkgate) 130
Denaby Ings 149
Derwent Walk Country Park 132
Derwenthaugh Park 132
Dingle Marshes 127
Dinton Pastures 151
Ditchford Lakes and Meadows 99
Donna Nook 97
Doxey Marshes 107
Drakelow Nature Reserve 91
Draycote Water 108
Drumburgh Moss NNR 134
Druridge Pools – Cresswell Pond 142
Dungeness Bird Observatory 159
Dungeness NNR 158
Dunkery & Horner Wood NNR 177
Duns Castle Reserve 180
Durlston NNR & Country Park 173
Dyfi NNR 203

E

East Chevington 142
East Dartmoor Woods & Heaths NNR 171
Eden Estuary LNR 185
Elan Valley 195
Elmley Marshes NNR 159
Epworth Turbary 97
Etherow Country Park 139
Ettrick Marshes 180
Exminster & Powderham Marshes 172
Eyebrook Reservoir 94

F

Fair Isle Bird Observatory 194
Fairburn Ings 149
Falls Of Clyde 184
Farlington Marshes 155
Farmoor Reservoir 103
Farne Islands 142
Farnham Heath 162
Fen Drayton Lakes 114
Fenn's Whixall and Bettisfield Mosses NNR 104

INDEX TO RESERVES

Ferry Meadows Country Park 114
Fetlar 194
Filey Brigg Bird Observatory/The Dams 147
Fingringhoe Wick 118
Flamborough Cliffs 144
Fleet Pond LNR 156
Flitwick Moor 112
Forsinard Flows 191
Forvie NNR 188
Fowlmere 115
Fowlsheugh 188
Foxholes Reserve 103
Frampton Marsh 98
Freiston Shore 98
Frensham Common & Country Park 163
Frodsham Marsh 131
Fylingdales Moor Conservation Area 147

G
Garston Wood 174
Gibraltar Point NNR & Bird Observatory 98
Gigrin Farm 195
Gilfach Farm Reserve 195
Goyt Valley 91
Grafham Water 115
Greylake 177
Gunknowe Loch and Park 180
Gwenffrwd-Dinas 203

H
Haddo Country Park 188
Ham Common LNR 174
Ham Wall 177
Hamsterley Forest 132
Handa 191
Hanningfield Reservoir 119
Hardcastle Crags 150
Havergate Island 127
Haweswater 134
Hawthorn Dene Meadow/Beacon Hill 131
Hayle Estuary 168
Helman Tor Nature Reserve 168
Hen Reedbed NNR 128
Hest Bank (Morecambe Bay) 138
Heysham Nr & Bird Observatory 136

Hickling Broad NNR 123
Hicks Lodge 94
Highgate Common 107
Highnam Woods 92
Hilbre Island LNR 140
Hilton Gravel Pits 91
Hobbister 192
Holkham NNR 123
Hollingworth Lake 139
Holme Observatory 124
Hornsea Mere 145
Hungerford Marsh 152

I
Idle Valley (Sutton & Lound Gravel Pits) 102
Ingbirchworth Reservoir 150
Insh Marshes 191
Isle Of May NNR 185

K
Ken-Dee Marshes 181
Kenfig NNR 200
Kielder Water and Forest Park 142
Kingley Vale NNR 166
Kings Mead 121
Kingsbury Water Park 108
Knapp & Papermill 110

L
Lackford Lakes Nature Reserve 128
Ladywalk Reserve 109
Lake Vyrnwy 196
Lakenheath Fen 128
Landguard Bird Obervatory 128
Langford Lake 178
Langford Lowfields 102
Lavell's Lake 152
Lavernock Point 200
Leighton Moss 137
Lemsford Springs 121
Lightwater Country Park 163
Lindisfarne National Nature Reserve 143
Little Marlow Gravel Pits 155
Llyn Cefni 198
Loch Druidibeg NNR 193
Loch Garten-Abernethy Forest 192
Loch Gruinart, Islay 183

Loch Leven (Vane Farm) 189
Loch Of Lintrathen 187
Loch Of Strathbeg 189
Loch Of The Lowes 190
Lochwinnoch 185
Lodmoor Nature Reserve 174
London Wetland Centre 161
Lower Derwent Valley NNR 145
Lower Test Marshes 156
Lullington Heath NNR 164

M
Machrihanish Seabird Observatory 183
Magor Marsh 201
Malvern Hills 110
Maple Lodge 121
Marazion Marsh 168
Marshside 141
Marston Vale Millenium Country Park 113
Martin Down 156
Martin Mere 137
Marwick Head 192
Mawddach Valley 198
Mere Sands Wood 138
Mersehead 181
Middleton Lakes 109
Minsmere 129
Montrose Basin LNR 187
Moor Green Lakes 152
Moore Nature Reserve 131
Moors Valley CP & Ringwood Forest 175
Morecambe Bay (Hest Bank) 138
Mull Eagle Watch 183
Mull Of Galloway 182

N
Nagshead 93
Narborough Bog 95
Nare Head 169
National Wetlands Centre, Wales 203
Nene Washes 116
Newport Wetlands NNR 201
North Cave Wetlands 145
North Hill, Papa Westray 193
North Ronaldsay Bird Observatory 193
North Warren 129
North Wirral Coastal Park 141

QUICK REFERENCE

327

INDEX TO RESERVES

Northward Hill 159
Noss NNR 194
Nosterfield LNR 148
Nunnery Lakes 124

O

Oare Marshes LNR 160
Ogston Reservoir 91
Old Hall Marshes 119
Old Lodge Reserve 164
Old Moor (Dearne Valley) 150
Otmoor Nature Reserve 103
Ouse Fen 116
Ouse Washes 116
Oxwich NNR 201

P

Padley Gorge
(Longshaw Estate) 91
Pagham Harbour 166
Parc Slip Nature Park 201
Parkgate (Dee Estuary) 130
Paxton Pits Nature Reserve 117
Pegsdon Hills Reserve 114
Pennington Flash
Country Park 139
Pilsey and Thorney Islands 166
Pitsford Water 99
Portland Bird Observatory 175
Potteric Carr 151
Prestwick Carr 143
Priorslee Lake 105
Priory Country Park 114
Pulborough Brooks 167
Pwll-Y-Wrach 196

R

Radipole Lake 175
Rainham Marshes 119
Ramsey Island 203
Ravensroost Wood Complex 179
Redgrave & Lopham Fens 129
Ribble Estuary 138
Roadford Lake
Country Park 172
Rough Wood Chase LNR 109
Roundton Hill NNR 196
Rutland Water 95
Rye Harbour 165
Rye Meads 122

S

Saltholme 132

Sandwell Valley
Country Park 109
Sandwell Valley RSPB 110
Sandwich Bay Bird
Observatory 160
Savernake Forest 179
Sculthorpe Moor 124
Seaforth Nature Reserve 141
Sence Valley Forest Park 95
Shapwick Moor 178
Shibdon Pond 133
Shorncote Reedbed 93
Skokholm NNR 203
Skomer 204
Slapton Ley NNR 172
Slimbridge 93
Smardale Gill NNR 135
Snettisham 125
South Stack Cliffs 198
South Walney 135
Spey Bay 188
Spinnies Aber Ogwen 199
Sprotborough Flash/
Don Gorge 151
Spurn NNR 146
St Abbs Head 181
St Bees Head 135
Stanwick Lakes 99
Stithians Reservoir 169
Stodmarsh NNR 160
Strumpshaw Fen 125
Summer Leys LNR 100
Sutton & Lound Gravel Pits
(Idle Valley) 102
Swanwick Lakes Nature
Reserve 157
Swell Wood 178
Swillbrook Lakes 179
Swithland Reservoir 96
Sydenham Hill Wood 162
Symonds Yat 94

T

Taf Fechan 202
Talkin Tarn Country Park 135
Tamar Estuary 169
Tamar Lakes 169
Teesmouth NNR 133
Testwood Lakes 157
The Great Fen 116
The Lodge, Sandy 113
Theale Gravel Pits 153

Therfield Heath LNR 122
Thrapston Gravel Pits &
Titchmarsh LNR 100
Thurrock Thameside
Nature Park 120
Thursley Common NNR 163
Tiddesley Wood Nature
Reserve 111
Timble Ings 148
Titchfield Haven NNR 157
Titchwell Marsh 125
Tollesbury Wick Marshes 120
Top Lodge-Fineshade
Woods 100
Tophill Low Nature Reserve 146
Traeth Lafan LNR 199
Tring Reservoirs 122
Troup Head 189

U

Udale Bay 192
Upton Warren 111

V

Vane Farm (Loch Leven) 189
Venus Pool 105

W

Walney Bird Observatory 136
Warburg Nature Reserve 104
Warnham LNR 167
Washington 133
Watermead Country Park 96
Weeting Heath 125
Welney Wetland Centre 126
Welsh Wildlife Centre 204
Wheldrake Ings 146
Whelford Pools 94
Whitelee Moor 143
Wicken Fen NNR 117
Wigan Flashes 139
Wigtown Bay LNR 182
Wilden Marsh 111
Wildmoor Heath 153
Willington Gravel Pits 92
Wood Lane 105
Woolston Eyes 131
Wrabness Nature
Reserve and Marsh 120
Wyre Forest NNR 112

Y

Ynys-Hir 204